PERSONNEL

The Human Problems of Management

PERSONNEL

The Human

GEORGE STRAUSS

*Professor of Industrial Relations,
School of Business Administration, University of California,
Berkeley, California*

LEONARD R. SAYLES

*Professor of Management,
Graduate School of Business, Columbia University*

Problems of Management

PRENTICE-HALL, INC.

Englewood Cliffs, New Jersey

PERSONNEL: THE HUMAN PROBLEMS OF MANAGEMENT

Strauss and Sayles

Library of Congress Catalogue No. 60-12214

Printed in the United States of America

Seventh printing . . June, 1965

65762-C

To William Foote Whyte

More and more schools of business, recognizing that every manager must cope directly with human problems and not simply pass them along to the staff personnel department, are integrating human-relations/personnel courses into their core curriculum. This book is addressed to the student of business who wants to equip himself to deal effectively with the human problems of the business organization. Although we focus our attention on the business institution, instructors of courses in the closely allied fields of public, educational, and hospital personnel administration will find that much of the content is also relevant to their particular needs.

Traditionally, personnel texts have emphasized description: "This is what companies do or don't do. This is the easy way of handling people." Or else personnel problems have been treated as a series of clinical cases: Each problem is unique and must be solved by a rational analysis of all the facts that are peculiar to it. Personnel problems also have been regarded as falling within the province of one or another of various specialties: industrial sociology, industrial engineering and management, industrial relations, or social psychology.

Preface

We believe that this subject is broader than any of these approaches would suggest. The manager needs analytical techniques that go beyond the transitory practices of specific companies at specific moments in their history. Otherwise he is limited to the rote application of techniques that may be wholly irrelevant to the wide range of problems with which he will be faced in the course of his career. Or, if he limits himself exclusively to clinical procedures, he will fail to develop the managerial scope and flexibility that derive from the ability to fashion valid generalizations.

We have tried to avoid choosing sides among competing approaches. In order to make informed decisions on the human problems of the organization, the manager needs knowledge about individual motivation and behavior in small groups and large organizations, about the impact of technology, about union-management relationships, about the techniques of industrial engineering, and about the skills of face-to-face supervision. He must also have insight into the way in which large organizations function, and into their problems of structure and efficiency. Only then, we believe, can he make a realistic, rational approach to such specific areas of personnel policy as selection, wage and salary administration, and training.

Consequently, what we have tried to say in the chapters ahead does not fit neatly into such categories as "theoretical" or "applied." In one sense this book is "theoretical": we have sought to examine the contributions of the behavioral sciences in the context of management's human-relations problems. But in another sense it is "applied": we have sought, for example, to present specific techniques for evaluating jobs and performance, for conducting time studies, and for establishing safety programs.

The reader will quickly note that the coverage of this book differs from that of the usual personnel text in one important respect: it provides more intensive treatment of certain areas that are often omitted altogether or relegated to supplementary readings. For example, two major sections are devoted to the problems of face-to-face supervision and the structure and functioning of organizations. These have been included because even the most carefully formulated policies are ineffective and useless until they have been implemented by day-to-day practice. Efficient and effective handling of the personnel problems of organizations require analytic tools *and* administrative skills.

We have made frequent cross references to alert the reader to interrelationships among the chapters. And yet each chapter has been written as an independent unit and may be dealt with as such. Instructors will find that they can tailor the sequence and number of chapters assigned to suit the requirements of their specific courses. Thus the instructor of a brief two-credit course emphasizing personnel policies might wish to omit Parts I, II, and III, with the exception of Chapter 4. In a human-relations course, Parts V and VI might be omitted, with the probable exception of Chapters 27 and 28.

At the end of most of the chapters, we have added case problems designed to highlight and dramatize the complex relationships explored in the chapters themselves. We have tried to present representative problems faced by administrators in a variety of organizations. The reader is asked to draw upon both theory and application in solving actual problems taken from our research and teaching files. Each case problem invites the reader to consider the administrative decisions that must be made, the evidence needed as the basis for these decisions, and the analytical framework within which the administrator may act.

Our objective in writing this book has been, not to present a miscellaneous collection of information about research and practice, but rather to suggest a systematic, unified approach to the personnel problems of the business organization. We constantly invite the reader to consider the many ramifications inevitably involved in any personnel problem. We have emphasized concepts and analysis, the questions that must be asked, the data that must be assembled, evaluated, and weighed, and the techniques of administering workable solutions. Finally, we have stressed the criteria that must be exercised in judging the effectiveness of a solution once it has been applied.

The answers we provide are not simple "do this" or "do that" propositions. In fact, in many areas we cannot even suggest answers; we can only try to frame the "good questions." We do, however, try to suggest a rewarding approach and an analytical framework, leaving for the real-life situation the weighing of variables and risks that must inevitably precede any final decision.

We are also aware that many of our generalizations have very serious limitations. Given the incomplete, imperfect state of our present knowledge, the human problems of organization are not easily or certainly solved. The reader should not mistake the seeming finality of the printed word for incontrovertible truth, for there are many contradictory studies and observations in this field. We admit to straddling several fences within the text itself, and we will probably be caught by the reader crossing back and forth, somewhat less candidly, on many other questions. We hope that the student will not permit the semblance of conviction on our part to dull his own critical judgments and his motivation to think through important problems for himself. We may sometimes have oversimplified an exposition for the sake of clarity, and may even have made some topics seem needlessly complex.

We have been fortunate in our opportunities to participate in many empirical social science research projects that bear directly on the contents of this book. For example, we were able to observe directly the work of Douglas McGregor and Mason Haire when both were at M.I.T., to work with R. F. Bales at Harvard, and to follow the work of the Institute for Social Research at the University of Michigan. We have collaborated on field research problems with William Foote Whyte at Cornell, Margaret Chandler at Illinois, and Eliot D. Chapple at Columbia. These studies encompassed field work in perhaps a hundred companies and nearly that many unions. We have interviewed and observed several thousand employees—both managerial and non-managerial—in department stores, utilities, manufacturing companies, and construction and service organizations. We have endeavored to apply the findings derived from this field research in our work with such companies as Ford, Burroughs, I.B.M., General Electric, Sylvania, and the New York Telephone Company.

During the five years that this book has been in preparation, we have been trying in classrooms at Cornell, Buffalo, Michigan, and Columbia, to integrate the problems of theory with the problems of day-to-day administration.

Recent surveys of business education have criticized business courses for their lack of analytical content, for their dullness and "thinness," for their failure to come to grips with essential problems, and for their normative assumptions. In the last chapter of this book we address ourselves directly to some of the criticisms that have been aimed at the "human-relations movement." We sincerely hope that this book as a whole will contribute in some measure to the development of business courses that will excite and challenge the serious student.

Acknowledgments

Like most authors, we have our list of friends and co-workers to whom we are indebted. Mr. Everett M. Sims, our editor, contributed an enormous quantity of energy and skill to the development of the book. Professor Arthur Butler, University of Buffalo; Professor Marten Estey, the Wharton School; Mr. Richard Gordon, Rochester Electrical Contractors' Association; Dr. Walter Gruen, Beth Israel Hospital in Boston; Professor Robert Johnson, Michigan State University; and Mr. James Newman of Westinghouse generously read and criticized many of our chapters. Mr. Chris Kentera of Prentice-Hall provided much encouragement; Miss Nancy O'Donohue lent technical assistance. Our secretaries, Mrs. Carol Botelar and Miss Ann Langenberg, were conscientious and subtle enough to facilitate many improvements in the countless drafts of the manuscript. Successive classes of students found to their delight that criticisms of mimeographed versions of the text and cases could be rewarding, and for their suggestions we are properly appreciative.

George Strauss
Leonard R. Sayles

Contents

3

WORK GROUPS AND INFORMAL ORGANIZATION, 56

Why Groups Are Formed. How Work Groups Are Formed. Internal Organization of Groups. Group Cohesion.

4

THE IMPACT OF THE UNION, 82

The Growth of Unions: Changes in the American Environment. Why Employees Join Unions: Organization Problems. Why Some Workers Don't Join Unions. Internal Organization of the Union. The Union-Management Relationship. Effect of Union Activities on Personnel Administration. Evolution of Sound Union-Management Relations.

PART TWO

Supervision, 103

5

MOTIVATING PEOPLE TO WORK, 105

Authority. Paternalism. Implicit Bargaining. Competition. Providing Opportunities for Need Satisfaction Through Doing the Job.

6

GENERAL SUPERVISION, 124

Elements of Effective Supervision. When Does General Supervision Work Best?

16

THE IMPACT OF SPECIALIZATION ON HUMAN RELATIONS, 353

Advantages of Specialization. Problems Created by Specialization. Organization and Personality.

17

MINIMIZING THE HUMAN PROBLEMS OF LARGE ORGANIZATIONS, 376

Fewer Levels of Supervision. Building Integrated Work Teams. Improving Coordination Between Groups. The Meaning of Decentralization.

18

PERSONNEL AS A STAFF FUNCTION, 395

What Is a Staff Department? Evolution of the Personnel Department. Advising and Counseling Line Managers. The Control Functions of a Staff Department. Staff Service Activities. Appropriate Staff-Line Division of Labor.

PART FIVE

Manpower and Employee Development, 425

19

RECRUITMENT AND SELECTION POLICIES, 427

Whom Should We Look For? Where Should We Look? What Recruitment Methods Should We Use? Selection Methods. Formal Tests.

20

PROMOTION, TRANSFER, SENIORITY POLICY FOR NON-MANAGERIAL EMPLOYEES, 458

PROMOTION POLICY. *Internal Promotion or Outside Recruitment? Selecting Who Is to Be Promoted. Administering the Promotional Program.* HORIZONTAL AND DOWNWARD MOVEMENTS IN THE ORGANIZATION. *Transfer Policy. Downward Movements: Seniority and Layoffs. Regularization of Employment.*

21

TECHNICAL TRAINING, 490

The Nature of Training. Who Should Train? Types of Training Program. Principles and Techniques of Training. Typical Learning Patterns. Job Instruction Training.

22

MANAGEMENT DEVELOPMENT, 509

The Changing Emphasis: An Overview. Planning for Management Development. Providing Experience. Development as a Managerial Responsibility.

23

PERFORMANCE EVALUATION, 527

Performance Rating. Traits or Behavior? The Evaluation Interview. "Also-rans."

24

MANAGEMENT TRAINING, 549

The Goals of Training. Organizational Problems. Ineffective and Effective Training. Conditions for Effective Training. Training Techniques. Who Does the Training? The Role of Staff Personnel in Management Training. Evaluating Training.

Selection Approach: Accident-Proneness. The Staff Approach: The Safety Department. The Line Approach: Safety as a Supervisory Responsibility.

30

SERVICE AND BENEFIT PROGRAMS, 699

What Are Fringe Benefits? Why Fringe Benefits Have Expanded. Company Attitudes Toward Fringe Benefits. Problems of Administration. Unique Financial Problems. Need for Constant Review. Relationship to the Over-all Personnel Program.

PART SEVEN

Management's Responsibilities, 721

31

MANAGEMENT'S RESPONSIBILITIES IN DEALING WITH PEOPLE, 723

Historical Perspective. Satisfaction vs. Profitability. The Contemporary Scene: How Much Human Relations?

COMPONENTS
OF THE PERSONNEL PROBLEM

Personnel administration is the management of people. It is accomplished primarily through direct supervision and the development of official policies. Before we can consider the management of people, however, we need to know more about the people themselves, the raw material to which supervision and policies must be adjusted. And to understand people we need to understand the individual as an individual, his relationship to his job, to the informal groups to which he belongs, and, in many cases, to his union.

John Smith, a brilliant engineer, is appointed laboratory director. After three months of obvious unhappiness, he quits for a much lower-paying job.

Automation is introduced into Department A, making the work easier and cleaner. Still there are numerous petty grievances from the union, and turnover and absenteeism increase rapidly.

In order to help the product development department analyze customer demand, salesmen are asked to submit a brief summary of each of their interviews with customers. Most of the salesmen submit such sketchy reports that they are useless.

Problems like these constantly harass the manager. Why do people behave in such annoying ways?

Let us start with fundamentals. Why do people do anything? In order to satisfy their needs. There are many sorts of need—hunger, pride, lust, desire for advancement. But behind every purposeful human act there is some motivation—either conscious or unconscious—that prompts the individual to try to satisfy some need.

The central problem of personnel administration is to induce a group of people—each with his individual needs and personality—to work together for the objectives of the organization. How can this be done? Only through convincing them that by doing the job they can satisfy their own needs.

These needs vary greatly. The prisoner in a concentration camp may work because of his need for survival; the underprivileged laborer works primarily because of his need for money to exchange for food. Others work because of a desire to get ahead, to derive a sense of satisfaction from accomplishment, or to benefit the community in which they live. In Chapter 1, "The Meaning of Work," we shall talk about the various need satisfactions sought by different groups in the population, with particular emphasis on the desire to get ahead.

Just as individuals differ in the kinds of need satisfaction they desire from work, so various types of work differ in the kinds of satisfaction they offer to workers. In Chapter 2, "Technology and Job Satisfaction," we shall consider the types of satisfaction provided by one of the many forms of work performed in our society: work in mass-production factories. We shall have two purposes in this chapter: (1) to illustrate some key factors that determine whether an individual can derive satisfaction from *the work itself* (as contrasted to pay, social environment, opportunity to get ahead, and so forth), and (2) to emphasize that employee motivation is strongly influenced by the technology of work, and thus to help counteract what may be an excessive emphasis in later chapters on supervision and personnel policies as means of motivation.

Workers obtain satisfaction not only from the work itself, but also from their association with fellow workers on the job. They come together in groups—formal or informal—and their membership in groups affects their behavior. In fact, they may be more influenced by their fellow group members than they are by management. It is as important for the manager to understand and learn to work with groups as it is for him to understand individuals. In Chapter 3, "Work Groups and Informal Organization," we shall explore the influence of the work group upon the individual.

Unions have become so important a force in our society that we must consider them as a separate element impinging on individual motivation and behavior. Though we do not have the space to consider the union movement at length, in Chapter 4, "The Impact of the Union," we will give a brief sketch of the internal dynamics of unions, with particular emphasis on their impact on management.

It's hard to imagine the changes in human life that have come about in western civilization over the past century and a half. For thousands of years the material conditions of our existence (the way food, clothing, and shelter were produced) remained relatively unchanged. And then, after 1800, in an ever-increasing crescendo, we have had steam engines, cotton gins, locomotives, the telegraph, automobiles, aviation, radio, atomic energy, and sputniks. Our way of life has changed unbelievably—but perhaps in no area has the change been greater than in how men earn their living and in the meaning they give to work.

Let us look for a moment at the "industrial relations" of yesteryear—for only by examining the past can we bring into focus the problems of today. Back in 1800, 90 per cent of the American people lived on farms, and the percentage was not much lower in Europe. Although there were large plantations in some sections of the country, most men owned and worked their own farm, receiving help at harvest time when neighbor

[1] We are indebted to Douglas McGregor for many of the concepts discussed in this chapter.

The Meaning
of Work [1]

helped neighbor. The family was the basic economic unit. Father worked in the fields. Mother processed the food (in a way housewives rarely do in this age of supermarkets), cooked the meals, spun the wool, made the clothes, and did the household chores. Brother and sister were assigned simple tasks almost as soon as they could walk. Labor relations and family relations were the same.

Economically, the farm was almost self-sufficient. Of course, with a cash crop the farmer might buy an ax, a flintlock, gunpowder, and such luxuries as dishes, sugar, shoes, and books (though luxuries could be either fashioned at home or done without). If the crop was poor, life was less comfortable, but few people worried about unemployment.

A man was his own boss. No one could tell him when to plant or harvest, or could give him a written warning if he started work three minutes late. True, nature and the weather might prove more tyrannical than any foreman, but what a man produced was his own. His motivation was clear: if he was lazy, his own family suffered.

Furthermore (in contrast to many jobs today) his efforts brought tangible fruit. Looking at his growing fields, he could say with real satisfaction, "Look what *I* have created." He, his family, his life, and his job were all tied together in a rich oneness that many look back on with nostalgia. (Few farmers today, however, would give up the benefits of tractors or electricity, nor would their wives long enjoy dipping candles and spinning wool. There were problems and frustrations in those days, though of a different kind.)

In the city perhaps the farmer had a younger brother, a journeyman wagon-maker. He was a wage-earner, not his own boss. And yet, how different the meaning of his job was to him than to his great-great-grandson who tightens bolts on the final line of Chevy No. 3! In the first place, he knew he would not be a journeyman for long. If he saved his money he might expect to set himself up in business within a few years.

Relations between himself and his boss were simple and easy—at times almost like the relations between father and son. The older man taught the younger what he knew and together they performed the same job. The work was creative and satisfying. Building a wagon required skill, and when the job was finished the worker could see what he had done. He could be proud of his craftsmanship and sure of his place in the world.

Such was the way men earned their living not so many years ago—even though our picture is admittedly somewhat idyllic. (The continuing exodus from farm to city over the last century indicates that for all its disadvantages many prefer our urban civilization to the simple country life.)

The Impact of the Industrial Revolution

The last century and a half has brought a dramatic revolution, not only in what we make, but in how we make it. The industrial revolution has been a revolution not only in technology but also in human relations. As technology grew more and more complex, people became more dependent on one another and the problems of working together become more troublesome. Today the typical American is no longer his own boss; he is not a farmer, but a city dweller—and he works for some one else. Furthermore, the industrial revolution has brought major changes in what it means to be an employee.

SPECIALIZATION

The journeyman wagon-maker did a whole job from beginning to end. But one of the distinguishing marks of the industrial revolution is specialization. Here is Adam Smith's famous description of the changes that were taking place in pin-making 180 years ago, at the dawn of the industrial revolution in England:

> A workman not educated to this business . . . could scarce, perhaps, with utmost industry, make one pin a day, and certainly not make twenty. But in the way in which this business is now carried on, not only the whole work is a peculiar trade, but it is divided into a number of branches, of which the greater part are likewise peculiar trades. One man draws out the wire, another straightens it, a third cuts it, a fourth points it, a fifth grinds it at the top for receiving the head; to make the head requires two or three distinct operations; to put it on is a peculiar business. . . . I have seen a small manufactory of this sort where ten men only were employed and where some of them consequently performed two or three distinct operations. But though they were very poor, and therefore but indifferently accommodated with the necessary machinery, they could, when they exerted themselves, make upwards of forty-eight thousand pins in a day.[2]

Economically, specialization has brought great advantages. But it has brought many disadvantages as well: boredom and the loss of a sense of individual importance, of accomplishment, of pride in work. How much satisfaction can a man obtain from spending his entire day pointing pins?

Further, workers feel that they are shackled to work processes they have had no hand in developing. The Industrial Engineering Department frequently determines every detail of the job, depriving the individual of any chance to show initiative or originality. Specialization has sharpened the dividing line between workers and management.

Specialization has also developed within management. Instead of a single

---

[2] *The Wealth of Nations* (New York: Modern Library, 1937), p. 4.

owner-manager with complete control over the plant, or a foreman with complete control over his department, we have staff departments such as engineering, production scheduling, purchasing, and personnel. No man performs more than a small part of the whole job; no man has significant control over what he does. A dozen staff agencies may be involved in making a simple decision, and the worker is at the very bottom: "Everybody gets consulted but me. I just carry out their orders."

CAPITAL

To make the industrial revolution possible, elaborate machinery was necessary—and machinery requires money. The journeyman craftsman needed little more than his own tools to set himself up in business, but the man on the automobile assembly line cannot hope to compete with General Motors. Unless he wants to operate a small store or a gas station, the modern worker has far less chance to be his own boss than did his great-grandfather.

Even after the average man's chance to become an *independent* industrialist had vanished, the avenue of promotion within the company remained wide open for many years. Fifty years ago an able and ambitious man might conceivably work himself up from sweeper to president. Today, as our technology and business life become more and more complicated, opportunities for the non-college man become increasingly limited. Sociologists call this phenomenon *blocked mobility*. A man can still get ahead through hard work, but unless he is a college graduate it is a much more arduous task than it used to be.

INCREASING SIZE OF BUSINESS ORGANIZATION

The industrial revolution has made business organizations larger and the boss more remote. The journeyman wagon-maker had no trouble talking to his boss; communication was easy. Today, however, a man may spend his lifetime in a steel mill and never talk to the plant manager, let alone the president.

The owner of a wagon shop could easily supervise all phases of manufacture. In a business like AT&T, supervision and coordination require the services of thousands of executives. All this leads to the process of bureaucratization, the making of rules that restrict individual discretion even to the point where top executives find themselves tied down.

CONSTANT CHANGE

In the simple society of the early 1800's, changes were few and far between. Behavior was governed by tradition: there was no need to tell a man what to do—all he had to do was follow the patterns laid down by his ancestors.

Modern industry is subject to constant change. The very fact of change creates two types of problem: (1) Less can be left to routine; careful planning, deliberate orders, and elaborate communications are essential. Since personal experience and tradition are less valued, there is a correspondingly greater need for rules and regulations. (2) People normally resist change, particularly when it is imposed upon them. Consequently the problems of motivating people to work together have grown more complex.

In short, the industrial revolution has done wonders to make life easier for all of us, but at a serious cost in terms of the rewards and enjoyments that individuals derive from their jobs.

Needs Satisfied by Working

In the rest of this chapter we will survey, in a general way, what people want from their work and what happens when their needs are not satisfied. We shall divide these needs into those that are satisfied *off the job* and those that are satisfied *on the job*. Many of the points we shall make about supervision later on revolve around the problems involved in motivating employees who actually *enjoy their work* as distinguished from the problems involved in motivating those who *endure work* only as a means of obtaining other things.

Off-the-job need satisfaction is provided chiefly through the pay check, for pay can be exchanged for food, clothing, and the other physical necessities of life. People are interested not only in the size of their pay check, however; they are also interested in how long their pay will continue—in other words, in *security*. To most people *advancement* means getting more pay. There are some, however, particularly professionals, who feel that they can gain greater prestige in the community or at least among their co-workers through creative accomplishments (such as developing a life-saving drug) even if these accomplishments do not contribute directly to their income.

On-the-job needs fall into two categories: (1) social needs, which are satisfied when the individual is helped or recognized by other people, and (2) egoistic needs, which the individual satisfies by himself. If a man is entirely concerned with social needs, he becomes quite *dependent* on others. If he is interested chiefly in egoistic needs, he will be highly *independent*. We shall discuss in Chapter 7 the importance of securing a balance between dependence and independence.

The table on page 8 summarizes the various needs that we shall investigate in this chapter.

There is nothing hard and fast about these categories (certainly nothing to be memorized). You can easily think of additional needs or suggest how the needs listed here could be profitably combined or further subdivided. We have adopted this particular listing merely because it enables us to organize the discussion according to some sort of outline. Notice too that the amount of space devoted to any one category has no relationship to its relative importance. For instance, we discuss "advancement" at length here only because we shall not be discussing it explicitly elsewhere. On the other hand, the "group" and "supervisory-related" needs are considered at length in later chapters; consequently, they receive little attention here. Finally, notice that many of these needs could be listed in more than one category. For instance, we shall see that getting a pay raise helps satisfy one's off-the-job needs, but it also provides a feeling of accomplishment which helps satisfy an on-the-job need.

Off-the-Job Needs	On-the-Job Needs		
	Egoistic	Social	
Pay	Accomplishment	"Group needs"	Participation
Advancement	important work	friendship	"Supervisory-related needs"
Security	"feeling for whole"	identification	fair treatment
	skill	teamwork	praise
	progress	helping others	acceptance
	completion	being helped	knowledge of where one stands
	Autonomy		attention
	Knowledge		

Our discussion will highlight the fact that the needs that can be satisfied by work vary substantially from one group to another. The executive, for example, is usually more strongly motivated by the opportunity for advancement and the feeling of achievement than is the hourly paid worker.

Off-the-Job Needs Satisfied Through Work

MONEY

Ask a man why he works and in most cases his instinctive answer will be "Money." And yet this isn't the only reason. Men want respect from their fellow workers, enjoyment, a sense of accomplishment, and other forms of non-monetary satisfaction. Both monetary and non-monetary incentives are significant, though their relative importance varies with the circumstances.

First, let's look at what money provides. Naturally, since most people no longer live on self-sufficient farms, their first need is for enough money to "live on"—to provide a "proper" standard of living. But what we accept as a proper standard of living tends to rise over time. Today we consider a house substandard if it lacks running water or central heat; this was not so a hundred years ago. To many people today, an automobile and a TV set are among the essentials of life.

Moreover, our concept of the proper standard of living depends a good bit on what our neighbors have. If the man next door buys a shiny new Buick, our five-year-old Chevy becomes less adequate. In our society money is important not only because it provides a means of being fed, clothed, and housed, but also because it provides a measure of achievement, success, and social position. To be successful means to have a high income, a "good job" is one that is highly paid, to "get ahead" means to make more money.

This tremendous interest in material goods is not a natural characteristic of man but a special trait of our own culture. Many other societies ascribe far less importance to material goods than to holiness, wisdom, and physical and military power. The individual's place in society may be determined purely by who his ancestors were; displays of wealth may be regarded as poor taste. Among certain tribes competitiveness is socially tabu; when the missionaries taught these people how to race, they insisted that every race must end in a dead heat.

Even in our own culture money is ordinarily more important to the salesman than to the teacher or the minister. Some men refuse a promotion with a higher salary simply because it involves "too much responsibility." And there are people without much "get up and go" who are satisfied to live on a minimum level and to spend the rest of their time fishing or building model airplanes.

Although, in the larger community, income may be only a rough measure of status, within the plant it measures very precisely the importance of one's job. Even the difference of a penny in hourly rates may assume great significance. If one job pays $2.62 an hour and another $2.63, it is felt that (a) the $2.63 job is more important, or (b) the $2.62 job should be more highly paid.

Who is more important, the plumber or the electrician? If the plumber gets a 20-cent raise, the electrician wants the same—otherwise he feels he is suffering a cut. The National War Labor Board perhaps only slightly exaggerated when it said: "There is no single factor in the entire field of labor relations which does more to break down morale, create individual dissatisfaction, encourage absenteeism, increase labor turnover, and hamper production than obviously unjust inequalities in the wage rates paid to the same individuals in the same labor group within the same plant." [3]

ADVANCEMENT

The urge to advance, "to get ahead," is particularly strong in America. In many other societies a man is born to a rigidly defined class and follows

[3] Cited in Paul Pigors and Charles A. Myers, *Personnel Administration*, 2nd ed. (New York: McGraw-Hill, 1952), p. 245.

his father's occupation without question; bootblack or king, he fulfills as best he can "the station to which God has called him."

Deep in the heart of every "true" American lies the Horatio Alger dream of unlimited occupational mobility, the belief that every man, no matter how humble his birth, can rise through his own efforts to the highest positions in the land. Children are taught that any virtuous man can work his way to the top. Indeed our fondest stories concern men like Abe Lincoln who through hard work and honesty make their way from log cabin to White House.

To some people, the failure to "get ahead" is almost a moral fault. As a pamphlet of 60 years ago put it, "Business success is due to certain qualities of mind. Anything is yours if you only want it hard enough. Just think of that. *Anything.* Try it. Try it in earnest and you will succeed. It is the operation of a mighty law." [4] A more recent pamphlet prepared by the National Association of Manufacturers agrees: "Your future is strictly up to you. Your opportunities will be limited only by your vision of what your future may become, your abilities and how you use them, your character and your determination." [5]

Historians and sociologists are finding increasing evidence that the "sweeper-to-president" phenomenon has always been something of a myth. Even a century ago opportunities to get ahead were considerably limited. Yet for a long time this myth of unlimited opportunities for "upward mobility" was generally believed and provided hope for millions. As of today this American dream has less substance than it had in the past—even as a dream. True, a child born in the 1960's has a better chance to advance to a higher social status than did his grandfather. But once a man reaches the age of 25 without having gone to college, his chances for advancement are limited. Such men may still want to get ahead, but they must redefine what they mean by getting ahead in terms that are realistically related to their actual opportunities.

A generalization of this sort, however, is much too broad and needs careful qualification. In fact, the importance of advancement as a drive varies substantially among various segments of our population. To be more realistic, let's take several typical groups of workers and examine how they view their possibilities for advancement and how their views affect their behavior and their attitudes toward money. We will talk about five groups: (1) floating, underprivileged workers, (2) factory workers, (3) executives, (4) white-collar workers, and (5) professionals. Each group sees different possibilities of success and each reacts to these possibilities in different ways.

---

[4] Atkinsen, *Thought Force in Business* (Chicago, 1901), as quoted in Reinhard Bendix, *Work and Authority in Industry* (New York: Wiley, 1956), p. 260.

[5] *Your Future and What You Make It.* Fourth "You and Industry Series" (New York: National Association of Manufacturers, 1951), p. 3, as quoted in Ely Chinoy, *The Automobile Worker and the American Dream* (New York: Doubleday, 1955), pp. 9-10.

Floating labor   These are employees who move endlessly from job to job. Lacking education, or handicapped by membership in a minority group, they are disqualified from the better jobs. Experience has "taught" them that they have little chance to get ahead, that there is no point even in trying. Just to hold on to what they have is hard enough. When they find a job they work until they get enough to meet their minimum needs, and when they are out of work their friends support them. Immediate pleasures are their only goal. They show little "drive" or "ambition." Indeed, "only when one knows where his next week's or next month's shelter will come from, can he and his children afford to go in for long-term education and training, the endless search for opportunities, and the tedious apple polishing that the attainment of higher skills and occupational status requires." [6]

Since security and economic advancement mean little for these workers, they look for jobs that provide independence and a feeling of being one's own boss. They may not amount to much, but they retain the freedom of telling off the boss and quitting their job whenever they want to. [7]

Factory workers   The belief that the common worker, through his own efforts, can rise to the position of company president is dying fast. As one study put it:

> The worker learns to set bounds to occupational ambitions. If in his early years he had any illusions about a rapid rise to independence and wealth, these hopes soon wither before the realities of industrial employment. He learns to limit his aspirations to modest and attainable objectives: a change from a second shift, from hourly rated work to incentive work, from a job in labor grade "7" to labor grade "8," or even to another job in the same labor grade which is more desirable for one reason or another. Beyond this most workers have little expectance of going. [8]

Many younger men start to work on an unskilled job expecting that it will be only temporary; they hope to earn a little money and perhaps buy a car, but one day they expect to go to college or start a business of their own. As they get caught up in marriage, family, and mortgages, however, their dreams begin to fade away. [9] Gradually they come to accept their limitations. As one worker told us:

> "I hate the job, but what am I to do? I've got a family to feed and payments on the house. I've got seniority and pension credit. I'm 38 years old. I can't afford to quit and what else could I do? I'm stuck. I made my mistake the day I took this job."

---

[6] Allison Davis, "The Motivation of Underprivileged Workers," in William F. Whyte, ed., *Industry and Society* (New York: McGraw-Hill, 1946), p. 89.

[7] See Richard Centers, "Motivational Aspects of Occupational Stratification," *Journal of Social Psychology*, Vol. 28 (November 1948), pp. 187-217.

[8] Lloyd G. Reynolds and Joseph Shister, *Job Horizons* (New York: Harpers, 1949), p. 89.

[9] For a discussion of these dying hopes, see Chinoy, *op. cit.*

In theory, most companies give outstanding workers an opportunity to rise to the top. Yet the technical requirements of modern industry mean that many supervisory jobs can be handled only by men who have had scientific training in college. And since it now is much easier to go to college than it was 50 years ago, management can easily satisfy its supervisory requirements by drawing exclusively on college graduates, thus leaving the mere high-school graduate with little chance for promotion. Moreover, management frequently reserves supervisory jobs as a training ground for those who are being tested for more responsible positions. Increasingly the highest job to which a production worker can aspire is a "factory clerical" position such as expediter or clerk, a position that carries with it slightly higher pay and status, and slightly more freedom from supervision.

It is hard for management today to determine who among the rank and file does have promise and ability, for many jobs offer the worker little chance to display initiative. The docile, submissive worker may be regarded as the good worker. The man with ideas is restless and the union is often more likely than management to give him a chance to express himself. (There is some tendency for management to consider active union members as potential foremen.)

At the same time the unions have done much to reduce the chances of a man to forge ahead on the basis of individual ability. They have emphasized seniority rather than merit, and management has tended to go along with their emphasis. In addition, pay grades have been compressed in many companies so that the range of pay between the top- and bottom-paid jobs among unskilled and semi-skilled workers is quite narrow. Skilled jobs, such as that of tool and die maker, are filled through an apprenticeship program, and few men are accepted for such training after 30. Once a man reaches this age, his chances of rising out of the semi-skilled class are slight.

Some opportunities for upward mobility are, of course, still open to the average worker, but these are somewhat limited:

1. He can establish a small business, such as a bar, a store, a gas station, or a TV repair service. In every plant a substantial minority have made this attempt and failed—though not all fail [10]—and many more dream, with various degrees of seriousness, of going into business for themselves. A high proportion of workers carry on small business ventures after work as a side line which gives them extra income and a chance to express themselves in a manner they cannot enjoy on the regular job.

2. If he is still young, he can go to college or school at night, in the hope of being able to move ahead after graduation.

---

[10] Seymour Lipset and Reinhard Bendix, "Social Mobility and Occupational Career Patterns, II, Social Mobility," *The American Journal of Sociology*, Vol. 57, No. 5 (March 1952), pp. 494-504.

3. If he realizes that he cannot advance on his own, he may transfer his aspirations to his children. Many factory workers make great financial sacrifices in order to send their children through college.

4. Over the years he may come to regard seniority as a way of getting ahead. After all, unions emphasize seniority as a determinant in layoffs and promotions, and management plays up such symbols as long-service pins. Thus both union and management work together to translate seniority into a substitute for promotion.

5. For some workers, the union provides a chance to "get ahead." Although there are few full-time union jobs with regular salaries, there are many part-time posts, such as steward or executive board member. Negotiating with management, handling grievances, and dealing with day-to-day union business offer many opportunities for creative expression and personal satisfaction. In a sense, union activity provides advancement in terms of status, though not in terms of money.

6. Many workers feel they are advancing when they move to a job that may not be better-paying but that seems "better" in the sense that the work is cleaner, the pace is slower, or it is away from the assembly line.

7. Finally, if the individual cannot advance by himself, the group to which he belongs may be able to advance the interests of its members. So long as his union can win him a 10-cent hourly wage increase each year, he feels that he has tangible evidence of progress. This helps explain why many unions insist on some gain each year no matter how slight, even when the cost of living remains constant.

8. Many workers interpret "getting ahead" in terms of security and material possessions. As one man put it, "If you've got security, if you've got something to fall back on, you're getting ahead." [11] They measure success not in terms of what they do, but in terms of what they own—a bigger car or a new TV set. "We are all working for one purpose, to get ahead. I don't think a person should be satisfied. My next step is a nice little modern house of my own. That's what I mean by bettering yourself—or getting ahead." [12]

Some workers, however, seem to reject the idea of getting ahead completely—no matter how it is defined. A study of a gypsum mill compared the motivation of "surfacemen" with that of miners:

> It was, for example, frequently possible to predict which houses . . . belonged to miners simply by noting their unpainted and unrepaired exteriors; this, despite the fact that miners' take-home pay always averaged higher than surfacemen. Miners' work habits were more likely to be directed to the satisfaction of their immediate needs. Surfacemen, however, believed in "steady" work practices and they insisted money should be saved, "not burned up.". . . To the miner, however, money was a source

---

[11] Chinoy, *op. cit.*, p. 126.
[12] *Ibid.*

of "independence," and an instrument for satisfying desires often *forbidden* by middle class values. If the surfaceman wanted to compete with and impress his neighbors by buying a new car, the miner preferred to "set one up for the boys." He wanted to be a good fellow, not a better one.[13]

Particularly when the job itself offers little satisfaction or prospect of advancement, workers tend to turn to recreational activities to provide satisfaction and meaning to life. Indeed, as working hours become shorter and work becomes less satisfying, leisure-time activities will become increasingly important in workers' lives. As workers become less concerned with "getting ahead," they become more concerned with enjoying life as it is.

Executives   Across the vast spectrum of white-collar workers (from office boy to president) the desire for advancement is strong. It is, particularly strong among executives, for whom advancement is a primary goal and one that profoundly affects their personal life. For them, getting ahead is not a *means* to happiness, it is the supreme form of happiness—well worth all the ulcers involved.

It seems, however, that executives desire advancement as much for the status and power it brings as for the extra money it provides. High tax rates in the upper-income brackets mean that the government gets the lion's share of any salary increase. But in our society salary is an index of success, a measure of a man's accomplishments. "The part of the pay stub that shows income before taxes may be cause for hollow laughter, but it is still the part that is critical, and the man who makes $35,000 a year finds little consolation in the thought that his $37,000 a year rival nets only $892 more than he does." [14] Salary is the score card that measures how far and how fast the executive has moved ahead. What he does with the money he makes may be less important to him than the mere fact of earning it.

The manner in which the executive wins his advancement seems to be undergoing significant change.[15] There is some evidence that the "inner-directed man," the disciple of rugged individualism who pushed ahead on his own abilities, is being replaced by the "other-directed man," the good team worker who gets along with others and is skilled in committee work and human relations.[16]

---

[13] Alvin Gouldner, *Patterns of Industrial Bureaucracy* (Glencoe, Ill.: Free Press, 1954), p. 125.

[14] Editors of *Fortune, The Executive Life* (New York: Doubleday, 1956), p. 66.

[15] The distinction we are making here may, however, be simply a distinction between men *on the top* and those still *working up.*

[16] The terms "inner-directed" and "other-directed" come from David Riesman, *The Lonely Crowd* (New Haven: Yale University Press, 1950), especially pp. 166-174. Similar points of view are expressed by W. H. Whyte, Jr., *op. cit.,* and Reinhard Bendix, *Work and Authority in Industry* (New York: Wiley, 1956), Pt. IV. We shall discuss their criticisms of "human relations" later.

Top executives in the past were likely to be self-made men whose personal history was intertwined with the companies they themselves had created. Rough and ruthless, rarely conformists, they were firm believers in the "Protestant Ethic" of self-reliance. Today an executive is more likely to be an "organization man." [17] Changing economic conditions have made it much harder to duplicate the feats of a Rockefeller or a Ford, and the average college graduate today thinks of success in terms of working his way up through a company rather than starting a business of his own.

The good organization man is under strong pressure not to be too different—not to be an "odd ball" or too openly ambitious. Instead, in his behavior, his leisure and social activities, his politics, his opinions, and even in his private values, he tries to conform to accepted middle-class standards. His spouse, too, must be a good company wife if she is not to jeopardize her husband's success. The ability to get along with others is often rewarded more than personal drive: back-slapping is more encouraged than initiative.

This picture of the organization man, as painted by fiction writers, magazine editors, and sociologists, may be somewhat exaggerated. But there can be little doubt that the meaning of getting ahead on the executive level has changed greatly since 1900. As with hourly-paid employees, teamwork is becoming increasingly important. Yet the conflict between teamwork and personal ambition continues and has provided the theme for some of our most provocative novels and essays.[18]

White-collar workers   The lower ranks of white-collar workers fit in somewhere between executives and production workers. They have a strong desire for advancement, but only limited opportunity to achieve it.[19] For some workers, just getting a white-collar job is a form of advancement, and factory workers will often accept a white-collar job that pays less than they have been earning. Office work is regarded as cleaner, more pleasant, and of higher status than factory work, and many employees feel that it is more challenging.

In general, white-collar workers still pay lip service to the Horatio Alger ethic that anyone can advance as far as he wishes, provided he works hard enough. Actually, however, opportunities for advancement are limited. The old middle class of independent businessmen is giving way to a new middle

---

[17] See W. H. Whyte, Jr., *The Organization Man* (New York: Simon and Schuster, 1956).

[18] See the works of D. Riesman, W. H. Whyte, J. P. Marquand, S. Wilson. Should (or do) young executives look upon teamwork as an end in itself or only as a means toward personal advancement (and isn't the latter pure hypocrisy)? Is the overemphasis on teamwork merely an effort to brainwash the man with the new idea into conforming? At what point should a man think of his own personal off-the-job satisfactions and tell the company and its demands to go hang? According to the novelists, these seem to be among the central dilemmas of our society.

[19] See Nancy Morse, *Satisfactions with White Collar Jobs* (Ann Arbor: Institute for Social Research, University of Michigan, 1953).

class of managerial employees who have greater security but less chance of hitting the jackpot of success on their own.[20] As a consequence, many white-collar workers substitute the goals of security and prestige for personal advancement.[21]

The white-collar worker's chances of advancement depend to a large extent on his education, for most white-collar jobs require at least a high-school diploma, and many call for a college degree. Thus education is of tremendous importance; it is the best and surest way of getting ahead.

White-collar "psychology can be understood as the psychology of prestige striving." [22] The symbols of status, aside from monetary considerations, are especially important. In the matter of job titles, for example, higher-paid workers like to be called *director* or *manager*. And for lower-paid employees, promotion from *typist* to *stenographer* to *secretary* may be worth more than a pay increase. If the job title itself means nothing, then the firm one works for may be used as a symbol of personal success. "The typist or salesgirl does not think in terms of what she does, but as being 'with Saks' or 'working at *Time*.'" [23]

In recent years white-collar work has become increasingly routine (the widespread use of office machinery makes it seem almost like factory work), opportunities for promotion have declined, and in many cases wages have dropped below the factory level. As a consequence, the distinction of being a white-collar worker is becoming less important. Some white-collar workers have turned to unions, but, since their middle-class dreams have not been completely dissipated, these unions have a character of their own: they emphasize professional development and fair opportunities for advancement more than general wage increases.[24]

In short, the desire for advancement is stronger among white-collar than among production workers. However, particularly for those who lack a college degree, the opportunities for advancement are declining. As a result many white-collar workers scale down their ambitions and accept the goals of security and prestige, others join unions, and still others—these who have failed to make an adjustment—are unhappy and frustrated about their place in life.

Professionals Professionals are doctors, lawyers, economists, and other specialists who identify themselves with some outside group that maintains

---

[20] See C. Wright Mills, *White Collar* (New York: Oxford University Press, 1953), Ch. 4.

[21] Roland J. Pellagrini and Charles H. Coates, "Executives and Supervisors: Contrasting Definitions of Career Success," *Administrative Science Quarterly*, Vol. 1, No. 4 (March, 1957), pp. 506-512.

[22] Mills, *op. cit.*, p. 240.

[23] *Ibid.*, p. 241.

[24] See George Strauss, "White Collar Unions Are Different!" *Harvard Business Review*, Vol. 32, No. 5 (September 1954), p. 73.

high standards of performance and behavior and insists on a lengthy training period as a prerequisite to membership. Many groups are striving to professionalize themselves and thus join the ranks of the older established professions. For example, social workers, hospital administrators, purchasing agents, and time-study engineers are attempting to establish standards that will set them apart—and, hopefully, above—individuals who claim some competence in these fields but who lack formal preparation or adequate experience.

Professionals have their own standards as to what constitutes advancement. To be sure, they are interested in higher incomes and status titles (though they sometimes deny this).[25] But they also seek recognition from their fellow professionals. Thus they are tied to a criterion of excellence that exists outside the organization for which they work. In a way they have a dual loyalty.[26]

This dual loyalty may both help and hinder the administrator. A man's feeling of professional pride may motivate him to work harder and to maintain higher standards than he would otherwise. A recent study of hospitals found that this motivation was an important element in explaining the doctor's high level of voluntary cooperation in accepting many unpleasant administrative procedures:

> The individual's own understanding of what is proper behavior, a "professional conscience," tends to insure that the individual will act ethically. Though the degree of external self-control varies from one doctor to another, the stability of medical and hospital systems depends on the fact that most doctors censor themselves fairly severely.[27]

On the other hand, severe conflict arises when a man is more interested in winning recognition from his professional colleagues than from the organization for which he works. For example, the medical profession has a tendency to look down on physicians who take administrative jobs in hospitals, and for this reason highly qualified men may refuse such assignments. Similarly, engineers, scientists, and professors sometimes turn down promotions that require administrative work which may interfere with their research.

One author has put it this way: Management believes "that an individual's success is primarily a product of his position on the management ladder.... [Yet] many technicians in this environment, though not all, still cling to their belief that success for an individual should be as a result of his technical achievements. They are more interested in approbation by their colleagues than in the promotions offered by management. Such a radically completely different way of thinking is often completely foreign to the manager; his

---

[25] See Robert Weiss, *Process of Organization* (Ann Arbor, Mich.: Survey Research Center, Institute for Social Research, 1956), p. 48.

[26] See Leonard Reisman, "A Study of Role Conceptions in Bureaucracy," *Social Forces*, Vol. 27, No. 3 (March 1949), pp. 305-310.

[27] Temple Burling, Edith Lentz, and Robert Wilson, *The Give and Take in Hospitals* (New York: Putnam, 1956), p. 86.

values are too different, and he finds it difficult to understand what makes professionals in technical fields behave 'so queerly.' " [28]

The meaning of advancement to different groups   In a very general and oversimplified way, we have been talking about what advancement means to five groups of workers. (Other important groups, such as salesmen, have not been mentioned at all.) These groups measure advancement in different terms—more security, more responsible jobs, higher incomes, greater status, or recognition from one's colleagues. There is, of course, a good deal of over-lapping among these groups, and there is a limited but real opportunity for people to move from one group to another.

In addition, the individual's level of aspiration depends to a great extent on his family background. The son of underprivileged parents who have never known security is content with far less than someone from a middle-class background. An ex-farmer is more likely to try to get ahead on his own than is a worker with a city upbringing. Similarly, a girl from a middle-class background may regard waiting on table as a defeat, while, for a girl from a farm, "The restaurant becomes . . . a foothold in the life of the city, and it may also make it possible for [her] to rise in the world." [29] These differences in background condition the worker's concept of what constitutes acceptable advancement.

Management must recognize the existence of these differences in dealing with individual employees. A rising member of middle management, for ex-ample, who is very anxious to get ahead must understand why piece-workers are more likely to engage in production restrictions than to earn all they possibly can and try constantly to win a promotion. Certainly competition is much less effective in motivating production workers than it is in motivating white-collar employees or executives. Indeed, many of the difficulties among these groups arise from the failure to understand each other's motivation.

JOB SECURITY

Job security is one of the most important of human needs; for many people it is more important than either pay or advancement. The major impetus for unionization, the most serious problems of superior-subordinate relations, the fears surrounding changing technology—all revolve around the need for security.

It is not enough for a man to have his physical needs satisfied from day to day; he wants to make sure that they will continue to be satisfied in the future. As we have seen, the average hourly-paid worker has given up his

---

[28] Charles D. Orth, 3rd, "More Productivity for Engineers," *Harvard Business Review*, Vol. 35, No. 2 (March 1957), pp. 54-55.

[29] William F. Whyte, *Human Relations in the Restaurant Industry* (New York: McGraw-Hill, 1948), p. 153.

dreams of advancement, except in a very limited sphere. But as a consequence he has become even more anxious to hold on to what he has. In the days when a man could go back to the farm, it didn't matter too much if he lost his job; but today it is a catastrophe, both physically and psychologically, particularly for older workers. Numerous studies indicate that even two decades after the Great Depression of the 1930's, the major fear of many workers was that they might lose their job. Automation and the seasonal nature of many industries serve to heighten this fear.[30] As a result, hourly-paid workers put great emphasis on seniority, on their property right in a job. For the unskilled worker, seniority offers a feeling of security akin to that enjoyed by the farmer who owns his own property, or by the craftsman who possesses special skills. Seniority also makes it harder for an unemployed worker to find a new job and thus encourages him to hold on to his present job.

Primarily Egoistic Needs

The need for money, for advancement, and for security are what we have called off-the-job needs, in the sense that money is spent and status and seniority are enjoyed primarily off the job. The needs that we are about to discuss can be satisfied for the most part on the job itself. These on-the-job needs can be roughly subdivided into two categories: egoistic and social. We shall start with egoistic needs.

ACCOMPLISHMENT

"The trouble with this work is that I don't have any feeling of accomplishment. I'm just nobody, doing nothing, getting nowhere. I'm just a cog, so small I'd never be missed." So one worker explained his dislike for his job, even though it was one of the highest-paying jobs in the plant.

One of man's strongest needs is the need for a sense of accomplishment, for the feeling that one is getting something done, that one's work is of importance. The word "accomplishment" is rather nebulous, however, for it means many things to different people. Let us examine some of the dimensions of this term.

Importance of the work   Work that seems pointless is bound to lead to frustration. One of the most unpleasant forms of punishment used by the military is to have men dig holes and then fill them in again. Compare this with the rich reward that people who perform even menial tasks in a hospital get from "helping people."

---

[30] Fred H. Blum, *Toward a Democratic Work Process* (New York: Harpers, 1953); Charles R. Walker, *Toward the Automatic Factory* (New York: Harpers, 1957), pp. 175-188.

Two English researchers, in a study of a candy factory, once found that the greatest dissatisfaction centered in a small work group whose job consisted of unwrapping defective chocolates as part of a salvage operation.[31] The workers felt that their job was far less constructive than that of the other operators.

Telephone supervisors report that production and morale are always higher during an emergency. As one said, "It's amazing. An operator may be a low producer and a disciplinary problem, often tardy and absent, but come a blizzard when the highways are closed, she will walk long distances to come to work."

The satisfied worker takes pride in the product he makes: "I get a big kick every time I see it in the store," or "Our widgets are made to the finest tolerance in the industry." The various forms that this sense of accomplishment may take are suggested by the following quotations: [32]

> *Responsibility for the welfare of others:* "I am very proud of my job because I examine the mine to make sure it is safe. I save a lot of lives by taking chances for them."—*Miner.*
>
> *Service to others:* "There is a lot of satisfaction out of putting something on a man you know looks well on him, and that he is going to get a lot of compliments and he's going to be pleased and all that."—*Salesclerk.*
>
> *Satisfaction in product:* "When you are selling sterling silver, you've got something to talk about and you talk about it truthfully. It's something that turns into an heirloom—never wears out."—*Salesclerk.*

The elevator operator, the janitor, and the groundskeeper—all *want* to feel that their job is important, and good supervision can do much to enhance their sense of accomplishment and their feeling of self-respect, as we shall see in later chapters.

How the work fits into the whole   During World War II, the morale in a small plant was very low and turnover was high. Most of the employees were women who spent their days producing a small metal part that had no obvious importance. The women had no idea what it was used for, nor would management tell them. Then one day they were taken by bus to a nearby aircraft plant where they were shown that the part was a very important component of the tail assembly of a very important plane, the B-29. For a while at least, production and morale soared.

For a soldier, one of the most important causes of low morale is the feeling that he, as an individual, is unimportant. Since secrecy must be maintained during a military campaign, the soldier, ignorant of the significance of his activities, concludes that they are pointless. Officers may claim that "there

---

[31] S. Wyatt and J. N. Langdon, *Fatigue and Boredom in Repetitive Work,* Industrial Health Research Council, Report No. 77 (London: H. M. Stationery Office, 1938).

[32] Eugene A. Friedmann and Robert J. Havighurst, *The Meaning of Work and Retirement* (Chicago: University of Chicago Press, 1954), pp. 77, 110, 119.

is a reason for everything you do in the Army," but enlisted men can't help but be skeptical.

Similarly, in modern industry it is often extremely difficult for the worker "to see his place in the scheme of things, to appreciate his contribution to the total process. Too often the individual job is like the isolated pieces of a jigsaw puzzle. And because there are so many 'pieces,' those at the work level generally have only the haziest notion of the total pattern. . . . In a real sense, therefore, the job loses its meaning for the worker—the meaning that is in all terms except the pay envelope." [33] To counteract this sense of isolation, many companies take new employees on orientation trips through the plant. Articles in company periodicals that explain the uses of products and how they are made also contribute to a feeling for the whole and a sense of teamwork.

Skill   All of us enjoy the sense of creativity that springs from doing something well, from being "on top" of our job. The housewife is proud of her cleanliness or her shortbread, the safe-cracker of his sensitive fingers, the professor of his brilliant lecture or his searching questions.

We also like to imagine that our job requires unusual skill, and as a consequence we tend to exaggerate its importance. When describing their job, workers often stress its difficulty, complexity, and the length of time required to learn it. Every machine seems to have special quirks in the eyes of its operator.[34] Every trade has its tricks which require skill, ingenuity, and expertise. Even the janitor feels he has developed a number of special techniques (knowing that Executive A likes his desk dusted, but that Executive B never wants his desk touched) that raise him above the level of unskilled labor.

Thus employees resent any implication that they can be easily replaced by untrained workers. Partly, of course, such an implication threatens their job security. But there is more to it than that: If anybody can do your job, what can you say that you have accomplished in your working life? What more significant sign of utter failure? True, many workers feel that they contribute nothing to their job that a completely untrained man could not contribute, but they are dismally discouraged by this realization. As individuals, they feel they are accomplishing nothing.

This sense of frustration helps explain the popularity of do-it-yourself projects, many of which involve no economic saving for the home craftsman but do provide a sense of skill and creativity. A worker may come home tired from the factory or office and "rest" by working hard in his basement or garden.

---

[33] James C. Worthy, *Some Observations on Frederick W. Taylor and the Scientific Management Movement,* paper delivered before the Society for Applied Anthropology, Columbia University, New York City, April 9, 1954.

[34] See Morse, *op. cit.,* p. 65.

For the skilled craftsman the feeling of skill is particularly important; he resents anything that threatens it. Many companies have discovered that it is harder to get employees to lower their standards of quality than to raise them. When management decides that customers will accept lower quality, and that looser tolerances can be maintained, skilled workers stubbornly resist the consequent reduction in the skill content of their jobs. They take real pride in their job and have no desire to make it less difficult. Looser standards mean less sense of accomplishment.

It is for this reason that many companies are plagued by running battles between engineers and top management. The engineers insist on close tolerances and top quality; they try to delay a new model from being put into production until all the "bugs" have been eliminated. Top management regards this desire for perfection as financially ruinous.

Progress and completion   If an employee is to have a feeling of achievement, he must have some way of measuring his progress. Everyone wants to know "How am I doing?" People like "feedback" even when there is no reward or penalty attached to failure or success. Thus when a man idly throws a piece of paper at a wastepaper basket he is interested in whether it goes in (even if he doesn't have to clean up afterward). Only if he can set up some goal and know that he has reached it can he feel this sense of achievement. Many routine jobs are considered boring and monotonous precisely because they give the worker no way to check his progress.

Productiveness   Perhaps all that we have been saying adds up to one point: most people have a genuine desire to be productive, to keep busy.[35] Certainly our observations cast doubt on the common assumption that most workers prefer to "goldbrick" than to work. In fact, it is harder to look busy than to work. Time passes more quickly when a worker is absorbed in what he is doing than when he is trying to avoid work. In our society, a healthy individual feels lost without some sort of job or hobby. Normally, expending mental and physical energy is a pleasant not a painful experience.

But if all this is true, how can we explain the fact that people often do loaf on the job and go to extraordinary extremes to avoid work? Usually such behavior is a sign of dissatisfaction with the job, with supervision, or with the company as a whole. Workers who feel that they have been treated unfairly direct their energies toward beating the system and show high skill in doing as little work as possible. This response, however, is a sure sign that the organization is beset by severe problems.

The sense of productivity and accomplishment is particularly important

---

[35] One astute student suggests that once people have started to work they have almost a compulsion to keep on going, an urge that he calls "traction." W. Baldamus, "Types of Work and Motivation," *British Journal of Sociology*, Vol. 2, No. 1 (March 1951), p. 47.

to executives. One study, which made extensive use of psychological tests, reported:

> They conceive themselves as hard working and achieving people who must accomplish in order to be happy. . . . They obtain continual stimulation from the pleasure of immediate accomplishment. They feel the necessity to move continually upwards and to accumulate the rewards from increasing accomplishments.[36]

For executives, work comes first; families, community activities, and leisure come second. The executive's typical work-week includes "45 to 48 hours of daytime work; one night working late in the office, two nights working at home, one night entertaining." [37] This endless drive to produce affects their whole life.

> Executives are well aware that this absorption means less time with their wives and children. Younger executives, in particular, accuse themselves; they often mention some long planned project to do something with the little boy, like building a boat. But they add ruefully, they probably never will. "I sort of look forward to the day my kids are grown up" says one sales manager. "Then I won't have a guilty conscience." [38]

AUTONOMY

> "You know, it's a funny thing. I work all day at the plant and then I come home and what do I do? I work some more—I mean in the shop in the basement. I love to do things with my hands. Funny, that's what I do at work—only it's different.
> "You see at work I don't have any freedom. That's the difference. The company tells me when to start working, when I get time to go to the john, when I get my lunch and how long (I get .7 hours—that's 42 minutes for anyone who isn't an engineer). They tell me how fast to work and exactly what motions to make. About the only thing I'm free to do is to think how damn lousy the job is.
> "Now, at home I'm my own boss—and believe me, that's a wonderful feeling."
>
> *—Autoworker*

Most people like being their own boss. Yet in modern industry only a few employees really have this feeling. The process of specialization has deprived the individual worker of his freedom to plan and organize his own job and has transferred initiative and responsibility to management. As Frederick Taylor, father of the scientific management movement, once put it, "Each man must learn how to give up his own particular way of doing things, adapt his methods to the many new standards, and grow accustomed to receiving and obeying directions covering details, large and small, which in

---

[36] William E. Henry, "The Business Executive: A Study in the Psychodynamics of a Social Role," *The American Journal of Sociology*, Vol. 54, No. 4 (January 1949), p. 287.
[37] Editors of *Fortune, op. cit.,* p. 65.
[38] *Ibid.,* p. 70.

the past have been left to his individual judgment." [39] The effect of this approach has been to strip many jobs of every opportunity for spontaneity and creativity.

Sometimes the tall stories told by workers are indicative of their hidden desires. For instance, there is the tale of the assembly-line workers who fixed their cars so that when you stepped on the accelerator the windshield wiper started flapping and the horn blew "honk-honk." Then there is the story about the skilled glass blower who for years had been making glass rabbits with straight ears. One day he decided to let the ears droop. "I thought it might be a nice change," he told an amazed management. Bakers speak in awe of the man who filled a Vienna twist with eclair mix. These stories reveal men's dreams of doing things in their own way.

Initiative and imagination are essential to any sense of autonomy; yet too often management fails to use the creative abilities of employees. As a consequence, they display their initiative and imagination in forms of which management disapproves, such as sabotage, union activity, and horseplay. Often the creative individual is considered a troublemaker.[40]

We must not paint too black a picture, however, for on many jobs workers do have a good deal of freedom. We have all seen janitors who really felt they were kings of all they surveyed—and behaved accordingly. Skilled workers, guards, inspectors, and many production workers frequently have this same feeling of independence.

How a man feels depends on both the type of work he does and how he is supervised. Of course, no one can be boss of everything, but within limits an employee can feel that he is his own boss. This is particularly true if he can feel that what he does is determined by the objective requirements of the situation rather than by human orders. (From an objective point of view, the substation operator in a public utility has almost no freedom; he must constantly make adjustments to meet the changing demands for power. Yet he feels quite independent, since he gets his orders from dials rather than from people.)

Many jobs demand such a high degree of teamwork that the individual worker is deprived of all opportunity to make decisions by himself. But in a situation like this it is often practicable to have the decisions made by the group as a whole. *Participation* in decision-making by the group is the equivalent of autonomy for the individual.

KNOWLEDGE

The desire for knowledge is a basic impulse in human beings. People like to know not only "what" is happening to them but "why." They want

---

[39] Frederick W. Taylor, *Shop Management* (New York: Harpers, 1919), p. 113.

[40] Some observers report that the trend toward conformity is causing the same thing to happen on the management level. W. H. Whyte, Jr., *op. cit.*

both to understand the present and to predict the future. Arbitrariness, caprice, and unexpected events all make it hard for us to fashion an orderly, reasonable explanation of the events that shape our lives. To be at the mercy of people and forces that we can neither understand nor control is a serious threat to our sense of security. Take, for example, the unrest that prevails in a shop after a familiar, well-known supervisor is replaced by a new man with unknown preferences, attitudes, and idiosyncrasies.

People want to know about things that are directly important to them, and also about those that are not. Satisfying idle curiosity is a way of spending one's time. The village busybody and the bored mechanic have nothing better to do than to pry into other people's business. The desire for information is so strong that if the truth is not available appropriate substitutes will be fashioned. As might be expected, rumors flow most readily when people are bored, insecure, and uninformed.

The quest for knowledge has more constructive elements as well. Many people find that learning gives them a sense of achievement. Being an expert on something—whether it is baseball, trout flies, the fine points of one's job, or the ramifications of union politics—gives the individual a sense of uniqueness and progress.

Primarily Social Needs

We shall say relatively little about social needs at this point, since we shall discuss them at length in future chapters.

"GROUP NEEDS"

Man is a social animal. He craves *friendship,* is unhappy when left alone for too long, and often associates with his fellows just because he is hungry for companionship. Particularly for employees who have an unsatisfactory home life, the job provides a large part of their social need satisfaction.

It is social banter that makes many jobs bearable. If there is nothing more constructive to talk about, small issues can be magnified, and boredom can be relieved through circulating rumors. In the informal social life of the plant the worker has a chance to demonstrate skill and initiative. Some employees, such as telephone operators and salesclerks, gain great satisfaction from talking to customers.

The job frequently satisfies other social needs besides the need for companionship. Belonging to a clique provides employees with a sense of *identification* and belonging, and they insist on forming "informal groups" even in the face of management opposition. When they are unable to achieve such social satisfactions, the job becomes less desirable.

Merely working together, *teamwork, helps to build morale*. Most people like *helping others* (this may well be a variation on the maternal and paternal instincts common to all higher animals). Also, when we need it, we like to be *helped* by others.

NEEDS DIRECTLY RELATED TO SUPERVISION

Another set of needs develops out of the subordinate's relationship to his supervisor. Naturally the subordinate wants *to be treated fairly:* he wants a fair hearing when he thinks his supervisor has made a wrong decision, and he wants the right to appeal over the supervisor's head. Most people like *praise* when they do something well (though sometimes praise from a fellow worker is more meaningful than praise from management). The average worker also expects acceptance from his supervisor—that is, understanding and consideration when he makes a mistake. Finally, he wants to *know where he stands*.

Regardless of whether he is doing badly or well, the typical worker wants some *attention* from his boss. Individuals differ in the amount of attention they desire, however, for some want to be left strictly alone and others constantly run to the boss for reassurance. The supervisor must adjust his supervisory practices accordingly (and yet avoid charges of favoritism). But we shall have more to say about this later on.

Relative Importance of Various Needs

We have listed various needs in what is clearly an arbitrary fashion. Many more needs could be mentioned and many of those that we have mentioned could be combined or subdivided. Our purpose has been merely to illustrate the range of needs that people would like to have satisfied on the job.

Which of these needs do employees feel the most important? This question has been the subject of extensive research.[41] The answer has been found to vary with the individual concerned, his job, the general economic climate, and a host of other factors. (In fact, in our discussion we have sought to highlight the differences in relative importance attached to different need satisfactions by discussing various groups—for example: professional workers and executives.) Several generalizations seem valid, however:

1. There seems to be a hierarchy of needs. Without air we would suffocate in a few minutes; without water we would die of thirst in a few days. Yet few of us think of these needs as all-important, since we can satisfy them

---

[41] For comprehensive surveys, see Robert Hoppock, *Job Satisfaction* (New York: Harpers, 1935), and his bibliographies which appeared in *Occupations* until 1952. H. Alan Robinson has continued the series in the *Personnel and Guidance Journal.*

with a minimum of effort. Our basic needs are for food, housing, and clothing. Only when these are reasonably well met do other needs, such as respect and achievement, move to the front.

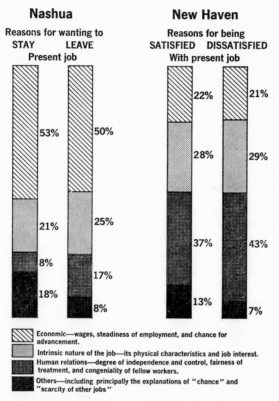

Nashua

Reasons for wanting to
STAY   LEAVE
Present job

New Haven

Reasons for being
SATISFIED   DISSATISFIED
With present job

Economic—wages, steadiness of employment, and chance for advancement.

Intrinsic nature of the job—its physical characteristics and job interest.

Human relations—degree of independence and control, fairness of treatment, and congeniality of fellow workers.

Others—including principally the explanations of "chance" and "scarcity of other jobs"

This point is nicely illustrated by two studies that have been made of job satisfaction. In a study in Nashua, New Hampshire, workers were asked why they wanted to stay on their present job and were requested to list any reasons why they might like to leave it.[42] In a similar study in New Haven, Connecticut, workers were asked to give the reasons why they were satisfied or dissatisfied with their present work.[43] Notice that the relative importance of the various needs was the same whether the workers were responding in terms of staying on or quitting the job, or in terms of being satisfied or dissatisfied. But between the groups there was a significant difference. In Nashua, half emphasized economic reasons; in New Haven, only about one-quarter. Why such a difference?

The answer can be found in the economic conditions existing in the two

[42] Charles A. Myers and George P. Shultz, *The Dynamics of a Labor Market* (Englewood Cliffs, N.J.: Prentice-Hall, 1951), pp. 130-131.
[43] Reynolds and Shister, *op. cit.*

communities when the study was made. New Haven was enjoying a period of full employment when jobs were plentiful and minimum economic needs were being met. Consequently, social and psychological factors were more important. In Nashua there was substantial unemployment, created by the closing of a large textile plant. In effect, the men here were saying, "Better a bad job than no job at all."

> The attractiveness of any one job factor (such as wages), in other words, is a consequence of the extent to which other job satisfactions or expectations are being fulfilled at the time. When a worker enjoys a steady job paying good wages, he is understandably more concerned about the treatment he gets from his supervisors, the degree of independence and control he has on the job, and whether the job is interesting. But when he loses his high paid job he is more concerned about regaining steady, well-paid employment.[44]

2. People strive to satisfy needs only to the extent that there is a reasonable chance of success. Needs that are already being satisfied or that there is no hope of satisfying do not seem important. For example, when a group of hospital doctors were asked what they wanted most from their jobs, they mentioned prestige and advancement.[45] What about their sense of accomplishment in curing the sick? That was taken for granted. In general, the motivations reported were more self-centered than idealistic. Hospital maids, on the other hand, emphasized the satisfactions they derived from helping people. Why? The maid's job in itself has little prestige—but she does work for the hospital and that does have prestige. Cleaning rooms requires little skill, but the maid derives a feeling of accomplishment from her work because it obviously helps the patients. The important question is what needs workers feel they can satisfy in the present situation, not what they might want in a totally different situation.

3. To some extent, people will give up one source of need satisfaction in return for another. Once job security is obtained, workers will accept loss of social and egoistic need satisfactions only in return for a significant increase in pay.[46] Conversely, many will accept lower wages in return for a more desirable job. As one worker put it:

> "Sure this job doesn't pay much. But nobody pushes you and you are your own boss. I could get more in the mills, but I would hate myself for doing it: push, push, and bosses. Life is too short. I like the guys here."

[44] Myers and Shultz, *op. cit.*, pp. 132-133. This same concept of a hierarchy of needs has been developed at length by A. H. Maslow, *Motivation and Personality* (New York: Harpers, 1954), Chapters 6-8.

[45] We are indebted to Temple Burling, Edith Lentz, and Robert Wilson. who permitted us to read the interview notes collected in a study published as *The Give and Take in Hospitals* (New York: Putnam, 1956).

[46] The overwhelming majority of employees in an automotive assembly plant indicated that they liked their pay but disliked the job as such. They took the job only for the extra income. Charles R. Walker and Robert Guest, *The Man on the Assembly Line* (Cambridge: Harvard University Press, 1952), p. 143.

4. Management is sometimes deceived by worker demands for money, for money has many meanings in terms of need satisfaction. If one looked solely at union demands on management and at the overt causes of strikes, one might well conclude that workers were interested in money alone. Yet, as we have seen, this is not the whole picture.

There are two reasons for this overemphasis on the monetary factor. In the first place, workers may regard higher earnings as a partial compensation for the lack of other forms of need satisfaction. Second, money has a symbolic value. Money earnings are tangible; psychic earnings are not. If you are going to gripe, you seize on something tangible to gripe about. Dissatisfaction with the job in general is only semiconscious and hard to put into words. If workers went to the boss with a demand that he provide them with more interesting work, they would feel pretty foolish; but a demand for an increase of 10 cents an hour is something that can be put in writing.

From the union point of view, of course, the size of the pay check is a measure of the union's strength and the officers' bargaining skill. Wage improvements can be obtained for everyone at one fell swoop around the bargaining table, but the union can improve human relations only piece-meal through the grievance procedure.

Conclusion

If the manager is to understand the reactions of subordinates to their job and to changes in their job, he must understand what they want from work. An understanding of the satisfactions they seek—and how they seek them—will help the manager in making countless day-to-day decisions covering the whole range of personnel administration—selection, compensation, discipline, and all the rest. This understanding is one of the keys to effective supervision.

"A man's work is a good clue to the course of his life, and to his social being and identity." [47] In centuries past, particularly when civilization was flourishing in Greece and Rome before the birth of Christ, work as such did not occupy such an exalted position as it does in the United States today. In fact, those of higher social status did not expect to work, for work was primarily restricted to slaves and to free citizens who lacked independent resources. The citizen of Greece felt no need to apologize to his contemporaries for not working, as do many people today who can easily afford not to work.

In the Middle Ages work took on many religious connotations. Work was clearly a duty—to fulfill one's predestined "calling." It was also regarded as an ordained punishment for the sins of man. To fail to work was immoral.

---

[47] Everett C. Hughes, *Men and Their Work* (Glencoe, Ill.: Free Press, 1959), p. 7.

Our present feelings about the idle—that they are somehow not behaving very morally—is a reflection of this religious emphasis.

Today we accept work as a part of a healthy, normal life. All the psychological, economic, and social rewards stemming from active employment cause people to feel they are being deprived if they do not have an opportunity to work at jobs that will give them these rewards.

At the same time, there are certain contrary trends in contemporary life. The shortened work-week, with the predicted four-day week, is likely to reduce the importance of work over the next few generations. Leisure-time pursuits are constantly increasing in significance as sources of satisfaction. More vacations, longer weekends, earlier retirement, more general cultural emphasis on leisure and its pursuit—all these influences are eroding the key position held by work in our daily lives. It is impossible to predict, of course, whether the satisfactions derived from do-it-yourself projects, membership in clubs, and increased awareness of the world at large will take the place of work-centered satisfactions. Nevertheless such trends must be considered in any realistic evaluation of the importance of the job in the life of the employee.

Even though work itself eventually becomes less important as a source of satisfaction, today most people still want more from their work than such "off-the-job" satisfactions as pay, security, and advancement. It is easy to forget that the very act of working satisfies basic human needs in modern society. Freud listed work along with sex as man's two most basic drives. The importance of work in modern life is suggested by the impact of unemployment and retirement on workers who have been active and productive for decades.[48] Unless the retired employee can find some other form of work (a hobby, for instance), the psychological effect of idleness may be extremely demoralizing. All of us have heard comments of this sort: "After Dad was pensioned off he just fell apart. He didn't know what to do with himself and just lost the will to live." Unemployment can be even more demoralizing.

The average man spends nearly a third of his waking hours on the job. If that job is not satisfying, he may suffer real frustration with results that are costly both to himself and his employer. An unhappy employee carries his unhappiness to his family and the community. Low morale leads to inefficiency, slow-downs, and discontent. In short, everyone loses.

But if a man doesn't like his job, why doesn't he quit it? If he has a family to support, quitting a job is a serious matter. With seniority becoming increasingly important, most employees in blue-collar work and lower-ranking white-collar jobs expect to spend the rest of their lives on their present job. Further, union agreements make it increasingly difficult for management to

---

[48] E. Wight Bakke, *Citizens Without Work* (New Haven: Yale University Press, 1940); Eugene A. Friedmann and Robert J. Havighurst, *The Meaning of Work and Retirement* (Chicago: University of Chicago Press, 1954).

discharge misfits. Since employee and employer are wedded to one another, the only answer is mutual adjustment. How can this be achieved? This is the question that we shall try to answer in the chapters ahead.

Problem I

The Engineering Company designs and supervises the erection of chemical and petroleum processing plants. It employs a large number of engineers with college degrees, most of whom work in the Field Division or the Drafting Room.

The approximately 1000 engineers in the Field Division supervise the erection of plants throughout the world. As of 1956 (the date of this case), new college graduates received $425 a month. After five years they might reasonably expect $800 a month; after 20 years, $1500. However, many do not reach these higher salaries. By the end of two years over half either quit or have been discharged. Top management engages in frequent purges, weeding out those it thinks are incompetent. Fierce competition is encouraged for the top jobs. Men are often transferred from one part of the country to another with as little as one week's notice. This creates particular hardships for children who must be constantly uprooted from school. Working conditions on the job are usually poor, with wind, rain, heat, and cold being common.

The Drafting Room contains approximately 500 graduate engineers. Prior to 1935, when the company was much smaller, high-school graduates were hired to do drafting, but during the depression men with college diplomas could be obtained for very little money and the policy of hiring them was started. It is continued to this day. Pay starts at $2.90 an hour and reaches $3.85 after two years— the highest drafting pay in the city. No one has been laid off for lack of work since the early depression days, and discharges for incompetence are rare. There is one section head for every 20 men (salary $8,500). Promotions to this job are normally by seniority.

The drafting work on a single project may take as long as two years to complete, and prior to 1950 each project was given to a small group of men who would work on it from beginning to end. Beginning in 1950, substantial changes were made in organization. Individual offices were eliminated and all operations were placed in one large well-lighted air-conditioned room. Each man was given a specialty such as heating or wiring, and work proceeds from one department to another on an assembly-line basis.

In both divisions liberal vacations, sick leave, and a retirement plan are provided. As yet none of the engineers are unionized.

1. List separately for each division the needs which are and are not satisfied.

2. A union organized the engineers in one of these divisions. Which division is most susceptible to unionization? Why? (Note: The description refers to the period before unionization.)

The mass-production factory is a triumph of American ingenuity, a key to our high standard of living, and, in a way, a symbol of American life. How do people react to mass-production work? What can management do to make this type of work less boring? In this chapter our strongest emphasis will be on the assembly line.[1] This is not because the asembly line is especially typical of American industry but because it represents an extreme—an extreme of specialization and subordination of man to machine. As Daniel Bell, formerly Associate Editor of *Fortune,* has commented:

> Its rhythms in a subtle fashion affect the character of work the way a dye suffuses into cloth. And its rhythms are spreading. Coal mining, once a highly individualistic occupation . . . now with mechanization of the cutting and conveying of coal, takes on the aspect of routinized factory work. The in-

[1] In this chapter we shall rely considerably on unpublished research of our own, as well as on Georges Friedmann, *Industrial Society* (Glencoe, Ill.: Free Press, 1955), and Charles R. Walker and Robert Guest, *The Man on the Assembly Line* (Cambridge: Harvard University Press, 1952).

Technology
and Job Satisfaction

stallation of high speed calculators and tabulating machines in the company office has made of the white collar worker a serrated row of bobbing and mechanically paced drones. The introduction of mechanized materials handling instills into the distributive sector of economy its own mechanical rhythms.[2]

Although we shall be concerned chiefly with the factory, we must remember that at least some of the work in large department stores, modern mechanized offices, and other service organizations also involves mass-production characteristics. Even though automation has altered the nature of many jobs, supervisors in the foreseeable future will still be dealing with employee reactions to "mass-production work" in a wide variety of occupations.

In the preceding chapter we reviewed what employees are *seeking* from work. Here we shall look at the other side of the picture: what their work *offers* them in terms of interest and satisfaction. We shall consider three problems:

1. Psychological reactions to mass-production work.
2. Employees' attempts to reduce boredom.
3. What management can do to make work more satisfying.

Psychological Reactions to Mass-production Work

FATIGUE AND BOREDOM

Fatigue is the product of chemical, physical changes in the nerves and muscles of the body that make it difficult to continue work. Factory work is far less fatiguing today than it once was. Gross physical movements, such as lifting heavy weights, are more and more being performed by machinery. True, certain "finger" jobs still require incessant, repetitive use of a small number of muscles, and this activity may be more fatiguing than broader movements involving the whole body or more of the body muscles. Still, fatigue created by excessive physical effort is no longer a major problem in most modern factories.

Boredom is a more serious problem today. Boredom sets in when the worker loses interest in his job and time hangs heavy on his hands. With little motivation to do the job, his morale falls and his productivity may decline— unless there is some standard of output set either by custom or the pace of the assembly line. (Extreme boredom may make it impossible for the worker to meet this standard.)

Boredom and fatigue are closely related, though one may occur without the other. There is no question that the "nervous strain" of boredom actually makes one physically more tired. When boredom is minimized, the body may

---

[2] "Work in the Life of an American," *Manpower in the United States,* William Haber, et al., eds. (New York: Harpers, 1948), p. 15.

release additional stores of energy and actually make the job easier. We all know of instances in which people have performed feats of strength and endurance in time of danger that they could never duplicate under ordinary circumstances.

It is possible to compare the effects of boredom and fatigue by plotting production curves for the various hours of the day. A typical fatigue chart looks like this:

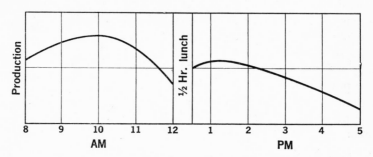

This fatigue curve shows the performance of highly motivated workers doing very hard work. Notice that after the warm-up period, production drops steadily till lunch. After lunch it rises for a short period and then drops steadily again until the end of the day. (The curve would be more complex if there were rest periods in the morning or afternoon.)

Naturally a chart of this sort applies only to jobs that are paced by the worker himself. On *machine-paced* jobs the worker has no control over his pace. Additional fatigue, however, may be caused when the machine's pace is different from the worker's natural pace. It is especially tiring for a worker who wants to slow down at the end of the day to be driven relentlessly on by the machine. This increased fatigue is reflected in lower quality and more frequent accidents near the end of the day.[3]

A typical boredom curve gives us a different picture. Notice the dips that show up in the middle of the morning and the afternoon, and the substantial upswings at the end of these periods. The curve illustrated on page 35 applies to relatively simple but highly repetitive jobs which arouse considerable boredom.[4]

Fatigue is caused by the excessive use of the nerves and muscles of the

---

[3] Norman R. F. Maier, however, objects to the practice of running machinery faster in the earlier part of the day and then letting it slow down later on. "This procedure is definitely contrary to the principles of fatigue. It is based upon the mistaken belief that men should spend their energy when they have it available. Actually, it requires men to spend most of their working day in a fatigued condition." *Psychology in Industry,* 2nd ed. (Boston: Houghton Mifflin, 1955), p. 429.

[4] See P. C. Smith, "The Curve of Output as a Criterion of Boredom," *Journal of Applied Psychology,* Vol. 37, No. 2 (April 1953), pp. 69-74.

body. But what causes boredom? Boredom springs from many factors, but we shall limit ourselves to five common factors that are directly related to mass-production work: (1) lack of variety, (2) lack of opportunity to exercise skill or autonomy, (3) inadequate sense of accomplishment or progress, (4) inability to control one's work pace, and (5) the need for only surface attention or none at all.

Not all workers find mass-production work boring. Some welcome it as a

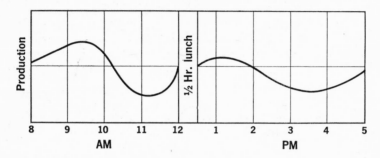

pleasant opportunity to daydream, and others, of low intelligence, actually find it challenging. We shall discuss these responses at the end of the section.

LACK OF VARIETY

An important determinant of job satisfaction is the length of the *job cycle:* how long it takes to perform a job operation before having to start it all over again. For a college professor the work cycle may be a semester; for a skilled craftsman, it may be several days or weeks. But for the man on the assembly line the work cycle may last less than a minute. Then he has to repeat the same cycle over and over again, with a deadening lack of variety.

This lack of variety is largely a result of the application of the principles of specialization. Throughout the industrial revolution there has been a constant tendency to keep dividing up the work in order to increase output. In accordance with the principles of Frederick W. Taylor, each man's job is made as simple as possible. The number of separate operations he performs is kept at a minimum. As the job is broken into smaller and simpler parts, the worker finds the job cycle becoming shorter, the work more repetitious. At the extreme, he may be simply tightening one or two bolts. It is hardly surprising that workers on the assembly line often complain about the lack of variety.

> "The job gets so sickening—day in and day out plugging in ignition wires. I get through with one motor, turn around, and there's another staring me in the face. It is sickening." [5]

---

[5] Walker and Guest, *op. cit.,* p. 55.

On jobs of this sort all mental challenge has been eliminated, and in most cases only a few muscles are involved. Life seems one endless procession of bolts to tighten. In a study of the automobile assembly line, Walker and Guest found a high correlation between the number of operations a worker's job called for and his level of interest in his job.[6]

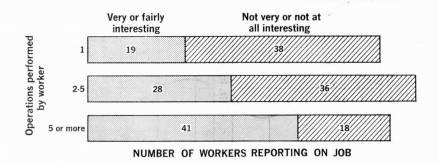

NUMBER OF WORKERS REPORTING ON JOB

In this same study, employees who worked off the assembly line remarked frequently about how much better their jobs were. For example: [7]

> "I move a few cars around. I perform quite a few things actually. That's enough variety to satisfy me. It's not like turning a screw all day on the production line."

LACK OF OPPORTUNITY TO EXERCISE SKILL OR AUTONOMY

Excessive specialization deprives the worker of any real sense of skill. Work that has been so subdivided and simplified that it takes almost no time to learn provides little challenge or interest. The worker has no sense of doing a whole job—he sees only part of the total process—and thus his contribution seems negligible and unimportant. Workers who exercise skill take pride in their achievement, but a man who has learned his job in a few hours knows that he can be replaced by almost anyone who happens along. This is one explanation of the tendency of mass-production workers to exaggerate the complexity of their jobs: it is just too humiliating for them to admit how simple their work actually is.

Walker and Guest found a great deal of dissatisfaction among workers who had a genuine desire to do "quality" work but who were prevented from doing so.[8]

> "I try to do quality work, but I'm too rushed. This keeps me from getting pleasure from the work. They say 'haste makes waste,' and they're getting plenty of both."

[6] *Ibid.*, p. 54.
[7] *Ibid.*, p. 56.
[8] *Ibid.*, pp. 59-60.

By contrast, workers who could fulfill their desire for "quality" expressed considerable satisfaction with their work:

> "You can take time to get quality. It's not like on the line when you have to rush so much. And I get work satisfaction. It makes me feel good when I put in a good day's work and get no kickbacks."

Mass-production workers have little sense of autonomy. We have already spoken of the desire of most employees to be their own boss, to exercise some control over the work situation. Yet opportunities for discretion and judgment, or even for determining one's work methods, are at a minimum in mass-production work. All the decisions are made by the Industrial Engineering Department.

There is an implicit assumption in specialization that some people will do the thinking and others the work. As Henry Ford put it, "The average worker, I am sorry to say, wants a job in which he does not have to put forth much physical energy on—above all, he wants a job on which he does not have to think." [9] But this approach to what the "average worker" wants has been criticized as destructive of morale and wasteful of human abilities:

> Scientific management has failed to utilize properly the greatest resource at its command: the complex and multiple capacities of people. On the contrary . . . it has deliberately sought to utilize as narrow a band of personality and as narrow a range of ability as ingenuity could devise. The process has been fantastically wasteful for industry and society.[10]

Workers put the point more bluntly: "They tell you that you are paid to work, not to think. Who are those bosses to think they are so good?" Frederick Taylor himself was aware that specialization might eventually eliminate all chance for the worker to show ingenuity or creativity. "One of the very first requirements for a man who is to handle pig iron as a regular occupation is that he shall be so stupid and so phlegmatic that he more nearly resembles an ox than any other type." [11]

It should be noted—and we shall return to this point later—that workers differ in their desire to exercise skill and autonomy. Some have no desire for creative challenge on the job—they are happy enough to daydream. Others are deeply disturbed because their work provides so little interest and meaning.

---

[9] *My Life and Work* (New York: Doubleday, 1922), p. 22.

[10] James C. Worthy, *Some Observations on Frederick W. Taylor and the Scientific Management Movement*, Address given to the Society for Applied Anthropology, New York, April 19, 1954.

[11] Frederick W. Taylor, *The Principles of Scientific Management* (New York: Harpers, 1947), p. 40.

INADEQUATE SENSE OF ACCOMPLISHMENT

"This job is endless. It just goes on and on. You don't feel that you are getting anywhere."

All the factors that we have mentioned so far contribute to the mass-production worker's inadequate sense of accomplishment. In addition, certain psychological laws seem to be at work here: (1) People like to have *significant* goals to work for—goals that seem important and meaningful. (2) They feel satisfied when they attain these goals and dissatisfied when they do not. (3) They like to know how much progress they are making toward their goals.

We all feel that we are accomplishing something when we can break our work down into units that can be completed successively. If we have two assignments to complete, we breathe a sigh of relief as soon as we finish one. When we are driving a long distance, we break the trip down into sections and feel great satisfaction as we pass by each check point.

Mass-production work characteristically fails to provide this sense of completion, or even a feeling of progress toward a goal. Each employee does only a small, specialized part of the total job. Rarely does he have a chance to look at the finished product and say, "Mine, all mine."

In their study of the automobile assembly line, Walker and Guest talked to many workers who said they would like to do the whole job from beginning to end.[12] Walker compared work on the assembly line with work in a steel tube mill:

> On the assembly line, only a small fraction of the "product" is ever seen or handled by most workers. In the tube mill, the whole product, from billet to finished product, as it moves through a series of machines, is worked on by everyone and can be followed by the eye of the members of the crew. Workers frequently go to the cooling and inspection tables to look over for their own satisfaction, the job which they have just done.[13]

INABILITY TO CONTROL WORK PACE

A shoemaker can decide how rapidly he wants to cut and sew, and a worker who runs a treadle-operated sewing machine can determine how fast the machine will work. But on the assembly line the machine determines how fast the man will work.[14] The inability to control one's work pace has significant implications.

---

[12] Walker and Guest, *op. cit.*, pp. 154-155.

[13] Charles R. Walker, "Work Methods, Working Conditions, and Morale," Arthur Kornhauser, Robert Dubin, and Arthur Ross, eds., *Industrial Conflict* (New York: McGraw-Hill, 1954), pp. 353-354.

[14] True automation, as we shall see, goes one step further. Here men *watch the machine* and step in only when it needs repair.

In the first place, machine-paced work demands that everyone work at the same pace. Yet research indicates that workers grow less fatigued and enjoy their work more when they can work at their own rhythm,[15] avoiding abrupt movements and jerky stops and starts. Everyone has a natural tempo at which he works best. Some will be quite happy on a job on which they work relatively fast; others find it impossible to maintain a fast pace.

Before the industrial revolution, work songs were a popular device for establishing a recurrent, rhythmic work pace. In the medieval world, for instance, weavers "were well known by the name of *Lollards,* because, in fact, while working they 'lolled' (mumbled), singing some cradle song in a low voice, or, at least mentally. The rhythm of the shuttle, thrown and drawn back, became associated with the heart's rhythm; in the evening it often happened that a hymn or a lament was woven with the cloth." [16] Sea shanties and marching songs are still part of our folk lore, though they are seldom used for their original purpose. These rhythms have an effect similar to that of a "pacer" in racing. Here and there we still find work chants, even in modern industry. In mass-production work, however, the relentless rhythm of the assembly makes such natural pacing difficult or impossible.

Most people also like to vary their work rhythm during the course of the day. They may work fast for a while, and then slow down gradually as the day wears on. This variety in pace helps to reduce both fatigue and boredom on the job. The assembly line, however, makes no provision for the preference of individual workers. It sets the pace for him and never lets him change it. Thus the machine may be a worse autocrat than any foreman.

Fortunately, on most mass-production jobs workers do have a slight opportunity to vary their pace through "building a bank" or "getting into a hole." On some jobs a worker can hurry up a bit and build up a reserve or "bank" of completed work and then take a break for a few seconds while the work slides by. By pushing 15 seconds ahead and then falling 15 seconds "in a hole," an energetic worker can earn himself a 30-second break. This gives him a chance to loosen his collar, stretch and yawn a bit, and perhaps talk to his neighbor. (Unfortunately, some managers may regard even this hard-earned breathing spell as evidence that the worker is loafing.) On other jobs, however, chances to build a bank or get into a hole are very limited, and it is on these jobs that worker dissatisfaction seems highest.

Finally, machine-pacing creates a feeling of tension, a fear that if you relax even for a split-second things may get out of hand.

> "The bad thing about assembly lines is that the lines keep moving. If you have a little trouble with a job, you can't take the time to do it right."

---

[15] Friedmann, *op. cit.,* p. 159.

[16] Michelet, *Le Peuple,* 2nd ed. (Paris: 1846), pp. 84-85; cited in Friedmann, *op. cit.,* pp. 158-159.

"The work isn't bad, it's the never-ending pace. . . . The guys yell 'hurrah' whenever the line breaks down. . . . You can hear it all over the plant." [17]

Not everyone objects to machine pacing. Some workers prefer the assembly line because it tells them exactly how much to do. At least the "line" controls them impersonally; it keeps the foreman from breathing down their neck.[18] Further, it eliminates the need to pay attention to how fast they are working and thus makes it possible for them to daydream. In effect, the machine sets a rhythm which their body seems to accept. As we shall see, if there were enough employees of this type, there would be few complaints of being "tied to the line."

THE NEED FOR ONLY SURFACE ATTENTION OR NONE

Another factor affecting the degree of satisfaction a worker derives from his work is the amount of attention it requires. A doctor enjoys his work because his job is constantly new and challenging and absorbs all his attention. Jobs like this are said to require *depth attention*. At the other extreme are the so-called *no-attention jobs*, which are so routine that the worker's mind is free to wander at will. Dishwashing is an example of such work; so, too, is driving over a straight highway with little traffic. Our mind is a thousand miles away, although unconsciously we are still watching the road.

The least-satisfying of all are jobs that require *surface attention.* Here the worker is obliged to perform a routine, unchallenging chore but at the same time to remain relatively alert. ". . . The mind, though not wholly absorbed by work, cannot free itself entirely from it." [19] Examples of this sort of work are driving in heavy traffic, grading exam papers, or adding up columns of figures. These jobs do not provide the challenge, interest, and sense of autonomy provided by depth-attention jobs; nor do they permit the employee to daydream as he can on a no-attention job.

These classifications, of course, are simply points on a continuum, for there are relatively few cases of, say, a purely no-attention job. Further, the attention demanded by a particular job depends largely on the abilities of the individual employee. A very bright employee may find that a job requires only surface attention, while a less able employee may find that the same job requires depth attention. (The implications for employee selection are obvious.)

Similarly, the amount of attention required varies with the worker's ex-

---

[17] Walker and Guest, *op. cit.*, p. 51.

[18] For an insightful discussion of the point, see Frank B. Miller, " 'Situational' Inter-actions—A Worthwhile Concept?" *Human Organization*, Vol. 17, No. 4 (Winter, 1958-59), p. 46.

[19] Friedmann, *op. cit.*, p. 146.

perience. Learning a new job always requires depth attention; then for a while only surface attention is needed; and finally, almost none at all. When we first learn to drive a car, driving demands depth attention. Later we show surface attention. Only when the routine aspects of driving are purely automatic can we be called a good driver. Yet, even for a good driver, maneuvering into a tight parking space calls for depth attention.

As a worker gains experience on a job, a semiconscious monitor seems to take over to sound the alarm when trouble develops. As one girl described her job: "I used to give full attention to the machine. However, now I can tell what is wrong by the sound. The job's sort of automatic—like driving a car." The sudden need to devote depth attention to what is ordinarily a no-attention job is a very disturbing experience to some operators. In one factory we observed a girl who was assigned to flip a switch every 45 seconds whenever the automatic controls on a certain machine broke down. This would seem an easy enough job, but here is how she described it:

> "This is the worst job I've ever had. I always find myself asleep. I've been having a lot of close calls. If I had to flip it every 5 or 10 seconds it would be a lot easier, but in 45 seconds your mind starts wandering."

DAYDREAMING

Daydreaming is one means of escaping from the boredom of a no-attention job. As Bell puts it, "The revolt against work is widespread and takes manifold forms in the United States. First and foremost it appears in the constant evasion of thought about work, the obsessive reveries while on the job." [20] Here are some typical comments made by workers who spend their days on routine, boring jobs:

> "If I thought about the job all the time I'd go nuts. I think about vacation and going hunting. You don't even know you are working."

> "I think about all kinds of things, particularly about home. The job gets sort of automatic, like driving a car.... Of course, there is terrific responsibility and you have to make sure that the machine keeps on running and the parts are right. Somehow you do this without thinking."

The sort of daydream in which workers indulge varies with the individual and the situation. [21] The man who is unhappy with his job and bitter over life in general is likely to brood over his miserable lot. If the work group as a whole is dissatisfied with the job and with the group's relationship with management, the workers tend to dream up grievances and engage in what Mayo calls "obsessive thinking." "Day-dreaming emphasizes the worker's

---

[20] Bell, op. cit., p. 11.
[21] See S. Wyatt and J. N. Langdon, Fatigue and Boredom in Repetitive Industrial Work, Industrial Health Research Board, Report 77 (London: H. M. Stationery Office, 1937), p. 10.

grievances and, especially if he is already depressed, crystallizes around them all his irritation with the conditions of his life." [22] These feelings may be expressed aggressively through what Roethlisberger calls "compulsive complaints," endless grumblings about unimportant matters that serve as symbols for bigger ones.

In one study made by the authors, casual observation suggested that workers who daydreamed worked at a more constant pace than those who did not. [23] Daydreamers who were removing parts from the production machines rarely fell behind, and those who fed parts into the machines maintained a maximum bank. With this margin of freedom the workers were able to think of other things. Most of the complaints about being machine-paced and "tied to the line" came from those who reported they did not daydream on the job.

Whether daydreaming is a practice that should be encouraged seems to depend on the nature of the job. "If day-dreaming does not interfere with good work it is probably a desirable adjustment, but if constant alertness is imperative, it may cause errors and accidents." [24]

WHO ADJUSTS TO MONOTONOUS WORK?

Almost all workers regard a job that requires surface attention *from them* as boring, mentally exhausting, and undesirable. [25] (This is true even if the same work might require depth attention or no attention from someone else.) But there are some workers who can adjust moderately well to monotonous, no-attention jobs. These workers seem to have little need to derive satisfaction from the job itself and spend their working days in daydreaming.

Others are unable to daydream on the job, either because the nature of their work does not permit them to withdraw their attention or because their personality is such that they want greater challenge from their jobs. These people experience boredom on no-attention jobs.

Whether or not a worker succeeds in adjusting to monotonous work depends in part on his level of aspiration and the importance of the job to his over-all goals. In our own studies, we have found that men as a whole seem less satisfied with monotonous work than women. Single women seem less satisfied than married women, who often speed their work hours thinking about family activities. Among men, the most contented are oldsters approaching retirement, boys awaiting induction into the armed services, and

---

[22] Friedmann, *op. cit.*, p. 146.

[23] See also Wyatt and Langdon, *op. cit.*, p. 35.

[24] Maier, *op. cit.*, p. 470. Dale Yoder, on the other hand, seems to imply that day-dreaming is generally undesirable. *Personnel Management and Industrial Relations*, 4th ed. (Englewood Cliffs, N. J.: Prentice-Hall, 1956), pp. 735-736.

[25] Possibly some workers with serious emotional problems may prefer surface-attention work which keeps them from thinking about these problems.

farmers who take a job to supplement their income. Among both sexes, those with high ambitions are the first to quit monotonous jobs.

One study makes this conclusion: "The groups satisfied with relatively routine work appear to be deriving satisfaction from other aspects of the work situation, rather than the work content itself." [26] There is evidence that the "monotony susceptible worker tends to be less contented with life in general than the worker who is non-susceptible [and] . . . more poorly adjusted in her relations to family and home. The non-susceptible liked better the routine kinds of housework, and preferred the quieter forms of recreation." [27] Other studies suggest that extroverts and those with higher intelligence are likely to be bored with monotonous jobs. [28]

For many people the desire to do an interesting, worth-while job, and to have a voice in determining how they do their work, is so compelling that they experience acute frustration when that desire is blocked. And with frustration comes aggression.

Employees' Attempts to Relieve Boredom

Employees resort to numerous diversions in their efforts to relieve boredom. They may try to make a game out of their work, for example, or turn to social, union, or anti-company activities. And all these activities may be used as a means of working off aggression.

MAKING A GAME OUT OF WORK

In spite of the obvious inefficiency of the practice, some people like to mow their lawns in fancy figure eights. Making a game out of work provides variety, gives the worker a chance to show his creativity, and supplies goals to work toward.

On jobs that are not tightly machine-paced, the worker may experiment with various speeds and set himself various output goals. Workers on piecework are particularly likely to set goals for themselves (sometimes called "bogies") and to engage in elaborate calculations to make sure that they produce neither more nor less than the bogey. [29] (This practice is called

---

[26] Nancy Morse, *Satisfactions in White Collar Jobs,* (Ann Arbor, Mich.: Institute of Social Research, University of Michigan, 1953), p. 65.

[27] Reported in Thomas A. Ryan, *Work and Effort* (New York: Ronald, 1947), p. 205.

[28] Wyatt and Langdon, *op. cit.,* pp. 19-20. There is also evidence that those with higher intelligence are more likely to quit monotonous jobs than those with lower intelligence. But this may be due only to the fact that those with higher intelligence have greater opportunity elsewhere. A. G. Brills, "Fatigue in Mental Work," *Psychological Review,* Vol. 17 (1937), pp. 436-453.

[29] For an excellent discussion of this practice, see Donald Roy, "Work Satisfactions and Social Rewards in Quota Achievement," *American Sociological Review,* Vol. 18, No. 5 (October 1953).

"making out.") Although the primary purpose of these calculations is to avoid overproduction that might lead to a cut in the piece rate, they also provide a satisfying diversion from the monotony of work.

Fantasy is another form of game-playing. A female assembly-line worker who had wanted to be a nurse said, "These (pieces) are always getting in trouble. They are sort of helpless, like sick people." Another woman commented, "This job is like cooking. It's something to do with your hands. It keeps you busy."

SOCIAL ACTIVITY

A man who is completely absorbed in his job feels little need to talk to others, but one who is bored may want to converse to break the monotony. Understandably, social activities are extremely important in mass-production work where other forms of satisfaction are largely absent. Chit-chat and interest in what the other fellow has to say relieve tension and make the time pass much faster. Thus a rich social life develops on the job, with a great deal of group feeling. In itself, this is a healthy development, though it may lead to group activities, such as work restriction, of which management does not approve.

At times working conditions make conversation difficult or impossible. There may be a high noise level, or a man may be tied down to his workplace and unable to talk to anyone but the fellow on his left or right. Under such circumstances morale is likely to be low, and workers often take long breaks in the washroom just to talk to each other. The coffee break provides an opportunity for social contact. Long a tradition in the American office, it has spread to the factory in recent years.

Social games also provide an important form of diversion. Gambling of various sorts is common in many offices and factories, from flipping coins to see who pays for coffee, to World Series pools, to bookmaking and numbers games. Horseplay (mock fighting, high jinks, and brawling) combines both social activity and a chance to release aggression. It is quite common in monotonous work and unless it is curbed it may lead to serious accidents.

These on-the-job social activities have become extremely important to workers in mass-production industries. Two astute observers have remarked, "Workers seem to want to buy leisure inside rather than outside the plant. ... They may, like many of us in business and professional strata, prefer to complain at home of their hard day's work while secretly profiting from its trivialities." [30]

---

[30] David Riesman and Warner Bloomberg, Jr., "Work and Leisure: Fusion or Polarity," in Conrad Arensberg, et al., Research in Industrial Human Relations (New York: Harpers, 1957), pp. 72-73,

CHANGING JOB REQUIREMENTS

Workers sometimes reduce the monotony of their jobs by introducing variations in their work that are unplanned by management. They may exchange work, modify parts of the job, and avoid others altogether. They drag out set-ups, find excuses to pick up parts more frequently than necessary, and perhaps let the machine break down in order to create a slight change in pace.

ABSENTEEISM AND TURNOVER

Another means of adjusting to unpleasant work is to avoid it as much as possible. In practice this leads to absenteeism, frequent visits to the dispensary, excessive time spent in the washroom, feigned illness, and even quitting.

Walker and Guest found correlations between short absences and the "mass-production characteristics" of jobs on the assembly line. Absenteeism was highest on the jobs that required the least skill, were most repetitive, gave workers the least chance to express themselves, and so forth.

Extent of mass-production characteristics

	High	Low
Few absences	35	54
Many absences	54	32

Absenteeism related to mass-production characteristics of job (175 workers). High and low mass-production characteristics are measured in terms of the job's (1) degree of repetitiveness, (2) degree of mechanical pacing, (3) skill, as measured by learning time, (4) frequency as to break in job routine, (5) frequency of social interaction, and (6) size of interacting group. Charles R. Walker and Robert Guest, *The Man on the Assembly Line* (Cambridge: Harvard University Press, 1952), p. 120.

ANTI-MANAGEMENT ACTIVITIES

In a sense, anti-management activities are an overt reaction to the frustration of mass-production work. Active union participation, for example, provides an opportunity to release aggression and to enjoy a sense of skill and accomplishment that is denied on the job. Similarly, sabotage and wildcat strikes enable a demoralized work group to let off steam.[31]

[31] Leonard R. Sayles, "Wildcat Strikes," *Harvard Business Review,* Vol. 32, No. 6 (November 1954), pp. 42-52.

Workers sometimes make a game out of causing the boss trouble. The incentive system may easily degenerate into a contest between workers and management, with the workers engaging in output restrictions and ingenious attempts to fool the time-study man through clever acting. Since there is a lack of other outlets, the motivation and creative energy which might have been used for genuinely productive activities is used instead to disrupt the organization.

What Management Can Do
to Increase Job Satisfaction

Factories are engineered primarily in terms of mechanical efficiency, with, perhaps, some effort to minimize the muscular strain on workers. That factory work also creates psychological and social strain has been little considered by most engineers. And yet, if our goal is to increase the satisfaction obtained from the job itself, it would seem that one of the first places to make changes is in the technology of work. There are other factors, of course, that must be considered, such as supervision, the relationship between individual workers and between groups of workers, and personnel policy. But we cannot ignore opportunities to make the work itself more meaningful, or at least more tolerable. What, specifically, can management do?

JOB ENLARGEMENT

Specialization has been pushed to the point where the smallest possible band of a worker's ability is being utilized. Already efforts are being made to reverse this process, and with some success.[32] To accomplish this reversal, the engineering factors involved in each individual job must be carefully analyzed. Perhaps the assembly lines can be shortened so that there will be more lines and fewer workers on each line. Perhaps, instead of assigning one man to each job, a group of men can be assigned to a group of jobs and then allowed to decide for themselves how to organize the work. Such changes permit more social contacts and greater control over the work process.

JOB ROTATION

Many companies are seeking a solution to on-the-job boredom through systematically moving workers from one job to another. This practice provides more variety and gives workers a chance to learn additional skills. The company also benefits, since the workers are qualified to perform a number of different jobs in the event of an emergency.

---

[32] For a résumé of the literature in this area, see Chris Argyris, *Personality and Organization* (New York: Harpers, 1957), pp. 177-181.

On the automobile assembly line, for example, the utility man (sometimes called a "floater") is qualified to handle a number of jobs and takes over for workers who are absent or taking a break. In Walker and Guest's study, none of these men complained of monotony or lack of job interest.[33] At least four reasons can be given for their satisfactory work adjustment: (1) they are constantly changing their job, (2) they make use of a wide range of skills, (3) they get to know every operation and feel more involved in the final product, and (4) they get to know all the workers on the line.

Yet in one situation studied by the authors, some of the workers objected to being rotated from job to job and jolted out of their routine. They looked upon their job almost as a piece of personal property; being an "expert" on one particular type of work gave them a feeling of status and importance that they lost when they were moved around.

In general, those who opposed job rotation worked on no-attention jobs and enjoyed daydreaming. Being shifted from spot to spot converted these no-attention jobs to surface-attention jobs and made reverie more difficult. On the other hand, workers whose regular job prevented them from daydreaming endorsed rotation as a relief from monotony.

Thus the choice between job rotation and permanent assignment depends on the nature of the job and on the people who work on it. In many cases the decision can be made by the workers themselves. Having made the decision themselves, they will be more likely to accept it.

CHANGE OF PACE

Anything that will give the worker a chance to change his pace when he wishes will make him feel less like a robot and more like a human being —and will lend variety to his work.[34] Further, if workers are permitted to change their pace they can build "banks" and thus obtain visible evidence of accomplishment.

SCHEDULED REST PERIODS

Extensive research on the impact of rest periods indicates that they may increase both morale and productivity. Scheduled rest periods bring many advantages:

---

[33] *Op. cit.*, p. 58.

[34] One of the most insistent demands of the United Automobile Workers has been for the right to control the speed of the assembly line. This and safety are the two areas about which the union has the right to strike at any time. For two experiments in which workers substantially increased their output when given control over their work pace, see John R. P. French, "Field Experiments: Changing Group Productivity," in *Experiments in Social Psychology*, James G. Miller, ed. (New York: McGraw-Hill, 1950), p. 86; and William F. Whyte and others, *Money and Motivation* (New York: Harpers, 1955), Chapter 10.

1. They counteract physical fatigue.
2. They provide variety and relieve monotony.
3. They are something to look forward to—getting a break gives a sense of achievement.
4. They provide opportunities for social contacts.

Research also suggests that the most beneficial rest periods are those that come just after the rate of output starts to decline—that is, relatively near the peak of the output curve. Needless to say, unduly frequent rest periods lead to an inefficient number of stops and starts.

Even where there are no formal rest periods, technology permitting, every worker takes a break once in a while, perhaps just by slowing down a bit, or going to the washroom or the coffee machine. If management tries to forbid this practice, workers will still "bootleg" breaks into the work schedule, although the value of the breaks in reducing fatigue will be impaired. Management must recognize that many of the rest periods workers take are minor goals that they set for themselves and rewards they give themselves for making certain quotas, rather than just the result of a desire to get away from work.

But if workers are going to take breaks anyway, why must everyone be required to stop work at the same time? On an assembly line, obviously, individual workers cannot be permitted to stop for a smoke whenever they feel like it. And on other types of work they might abuse the privilege of being able to take a break at their own pleasure, or, at least, they might distribute their breaks inefficiently. Scheduled rest periods seem to reduce the incidence of unscheduled ones.

On the other hand, as we have seen, many jobs fall into natural work units, and the natural time to take a break is at the end of a unit. Indeed, a few moments of relaxation at this point accentuate the feeling of accomplishment. Rest pauses scheduled for the whole department may tend to destroy these natural units, interrupt the work, and reduce the pulling power of the job. Further, when management *tells* workers when to rest, they have less feeling of autonomy than if they were to make the decision for themselves.

Obviously no simple answer is possible. If management is sensitive to the problem, however, it can decide, for any given situation, whether the department as a whole, or certain groups within the department, should take rest periods together, or whether individual decisions are more desirable.

SHORTER HOURS

How long should the work-day be? During World War II the British discovered that a shorter work-day sometimes leads to higher production. After the shock of the Dunkirk disaster, the work-week of British factory workers was increased from an average of 56 hours to 69.5 hours. After an initial spurt, production started to fall off until at last it was 12 per cent lower than it had been before the change in hours. Then, when the shorter work-week was restored, production increased to a higher point than ever before. In one case when the work-day was reduced from 12 to 10 hours shop accidents dropped 70 per cent—indicating that fatigue may also create serious safety problems.

MUSIC

In recent years many companies have begun to play recorded music during work hours. Brisk marches are recommended for certain times of the day, more soothing melodies for others. Claims have been made that music leads to higher production and that some types of music (marches, for instance) have a more beneficial effect than others. Other studies show that although the effects on production are negligible, workers generally enjoy listening to the music, provided it isn't too loud or incessant. Obviously the effect of music varies from one industrial situation to another.

Where the work pace is actually set by the asembly line, of course, music might increase morale and reduce scrappage, but it could have no effect on the production rate itself. And in situations where a "good day's work" is set by custom or group pressure, music may speed things up during part of the day, but more time will be spent in loafing during the rest of the day.

Though the effect of music on output may be questioned, it does give workers something to occupy their minds, reduces boredom, and provides an added sense of rhythm. Further, if employees are consulted on what they would like to have played they may gain some sense of participation. By making the factory a more pleasant place in which to work, music may reduce absenteeism and turnover. If management expects employees to work harder out of sheer gratitude for the pretty music, however, it is in for a real disappointment.

GIVING A FEELING OF ACCOMPLISHMENT

There are many ways in which management can give employees a feeling of accomplishment, though few are appropriate to every situation.

Setting goals   In order to satisfy the natural desire for specific assignments, and in order to provide definite goals toward which to work, some companies permit workers to leave early (without loss of income) when they have finished their job. Other plants set daily production quotas which are announced to the entire work force. When these quotas are "accepted" as being "fair" (see p. 165), they may well provide motivation for higher production. In a sense, working to achieve a quota makes a game out of the work. On the other hand, employees may regard quotas as a form of management pressure. They will work hard for goals that they have set for themselves, but strongly oppose "unfair" goals set by management.

In any case, psychologists tell us that goals are much more effective (1) if they are realistic, if there is a reasonable chance of attaining them, and (2) if they can be achieved in the relatively near future. Finishing a chapter in an hour is a far more compelling goal than reading a library in a lifetime, or reading a whole book in an hour.

Breaking the work down into meaningful units   Earlier we pointed out that most people get a sense of accomplishment from completing a whole job. But just what constitutes a "whole job" and precisely what is meant by "completion" are matters that can be manipulated by management. By breaking the work down into units or batches, management can give the employee a feeling of completion every time he finishes one batch. The desire to finish a unit has a strong "pulling power" and also enhances the worker's efficiency.

If the natural work unit is too big, the goal of completion seems too remote to elicit a strong desire to achieve it. On the other hand, the natural unit may be too small to entice the worker into additional effort. The man who tightens bolts on an assembly line gets little satisfaction from having completed the tightening of an individual bolt; there are just too many to tighten in a day.

Work units that are too large should be broken down and those that are too small should be lumped together. How large is the optimal unit? One study suggests that it should last for an hour or an hour and a half, depending on the situation.[35]

Maier reports an ingenious example of how the boring work of telephone maintenance in the central office was broken down into smaller units:[35a]

> There is no challenge of diagnosing trouble, and the job is very confining since a man can work for hours within the space of a few feet. There is never a real experience of progress. When the job is finished the worker starts all over again.
>
> In one office the frames on which the men worked were subdivided by means of chalk lines. . . . Each block required between one and a half and two hours to complete. The worker made his choice of . . . unit. . . . The benefits of this pattern of work were immediately apparent. . . . Once a man selected a block he worked until it was finished.
>
> Every time a man completed a unit he took a smoke or a stretch. Even lunch and quitting time found no untagged units. The men liked the plan and the supervisors reported that complaining decreased and the trouble with meeting work schedules was eliminated.

You can probably think of dozens of instances in which you have set up sub-goals to make a large job easier—for example, dividing the lawn up into small sections when you mow the grass.

---

[35] D. Cox and K. M. D. Sharpe, "Research on the Unit of Work," *Occupational Psychology*, Vol. 25, No. 2 (April 1951), pp. 90-108.

[35a] *Op. cit.*, p. 489.

Similarly, smaller jobs can be grouped together. In one plant, parts used to be sent on to the wrapper by means of a conveyor belt. Now that they are delivered in trays of a hundred, production has increased substantially. Completing a unit has even more significance if it is marked by a rest pause or by some special sign of recognition (a notation is made on a board), or even by a momentary change in activity (the worker wraps up a package).

Other forms of goals   On some jobs—for instance, in continuous-flow processes in chemical plants—there are no natural units at all. Here management may be able to provide other forms of goals, such as producing x amount per shift, reducing the time required for repairs by a given percentage, or avoiding breakdowns for an entire shift. Or management may change the form of goal altogether.

> One of the most interesting human relations studies arising out of World War II related to the Royal Air Force. Fighter pilots at a certain air base were growing discouraged because an almost perpetual fog kept them from contacting enemy bombers. Their discouragement was reflected in careless flying and high accident rates. When the pilots accepted as a goal the conquering of the weather, which became their new enemy, morale was substantially raised and accidents declined. Thus their need for accomplishment was no longer frustrated.[36]

Providing information on progress   Even where production has nothing to do with incentive earnings or opportunities for promotion, employees like to know how they are doing. When we drive along a turnpike on a foggy night, we feel anxiety because we don't know how far we are from our destination.

> In a plant that manufactured a large number of small items at high speed, management installed computers on each of the lines, just for supervisory purposes. Soon the employees were spending so much time sneaking a look that additional counters were installed at each work place. Informal competition developed both between lines and between shifts on the same line. Then the foreman brought in a blackboard and chalk and the men began posting their records. (*Question:* What might have happened had management deliberately tried to foster competition?)

An aircraft manufacturer posts bar graphs showing the length of time actually taken to complete various components of the plane as compared to the time planned.[37] A telephone company uses indices of efficiency, particularly among its white-collar employees.[38]

---

[36] See T. T. Patterson, *Morale in War and Work* (London: Max Parish, 1955).

[37] John Walsh and Max Shousen, "Scoreboards Boost Production," *Supervisory Management* (May 1956), p. 4.

[38] Of course, such indices may be regarded as a method of exerting pressure. Or they may encourage quantity at the expense of quality. We shall discuss some of these factors later. See Peter M. Blau, *The Dynamics of Industrial Bureaucracy* (Chicago: University of Chicago Press, 1955), Chapter 3.

Avoiding interruption of natural units   A man who is engrossed in his work resents being disturbed and wastes a good bit of time trying to pick up his work again. Secretaries object to being asked to do something else when they are in the middle of a letter. It is almost a matter of simple courtesy to say, "When you get a break for a minute, could you do this?"

Similarly, workers object to starting a new job just before quitting time, although if they are behind schedule on an existing job they will spurt to finish it up. There is often trouble between shifts when one shift leaves unfinished work for the next shift to complete.

Stressing the importance of the job   If the job becomes too specialized, the worker loses his feeling for the relationship between his work and the over-all process. He would like to feel both (1) that he plays a significant part in the work process as a whole, and (2) that the process itself is important.

Many companies take new employees on a trip through the plant to show them how the work they will be doing fits into the total picture. During World War II war heroes were invited to visit war plants, and demonstrations were staged to dramatize what happened when a part misfunctioned. In indoctrinating new employees the telephone company impresses on them the importance of their jobs in saving lives and in helping people in trouble.

Secretaries often comment that what makes their work interesting is that when they type important letters they get the feeling that they are at the center of things. Naturally, their interest, as well as the efficiency and intelligence with which they do their work, increases if the boss fills them in on the background of each letter (for an exceptional case, see p. 148).

GREATER AUTONOMY

Possibly the single most effective way of increasing job satisfaction is to give workers more freedom to do their work in their own way—or, if that is impossible, to let the work group as a whole make this decision or at least be consulted when decisions are made. Since this whole area is closely related to the supervisor-worker relationship, however, we shall postpone detailed discussion of it to a later chapter.

Automation

How will automation affect the attitude of employees toward their work? [39] Before we try to answer this question, we must first be careful to define what we mean by the term "automation." In recent years, it has come to be used very loosely—it has even been applied to mechanical dishwashers!

---

[39] For an excellent discussion, see Bernard Karsh, "The Meaning of Work in an Age of Automation," *Current Economic Comment,* Vol. 11, No. 3 (August 1957), pp. 3-13.

Those who are aware of its more technical meaning try to limit its use to three kinds of techniques.[40]

1. The use of electronic data-processing machines (electronic brains like UNIVAC) for office work and decision-making.

2. Tying together two or more automatic machines to reduce material handling and the need for human beings to feed machines.

3. Feedback control mechanisms to make machine adjustments, thus reducing the need for operators and set-up men. (A typical feedback control is the house thermostat, which, on the basis of its reading of room temperature, *feeds back* to the oil burner information on whether it should provide more or less heat.)

The effect of automation on job satisfaction depends largely on the degree of automation that is introduced. With complete automation the operator is entirely eliminated. The machine feeds itself, inspects its own work, adjusts itself when it is operating imperfectly, and makes minor repairs. Electronic "brains" give it instructions on what to do and coordinate its activities with the activities of other machines. All that is left for man to do is to design the machine (with the aid of computers) and to make major repairs. As yet, there are few instances of *complete* automation.

In partially automated situations, the operator must still watch and control the equipment. Yet the job requirements are substantially different from the requirements in non-automated processes. The work is physically easier, safer, and less subject to discomfort from heat, dampness, and so forth. The manipulative skills are almost completely eliminated, except among repairmen. On the other hand the job requires responsibility and alertness (surface attention). Walker describes the job requirements of a worker in a rather highly automated steel mill: "A basic skill . . . is the ability to remain continually on the alert, to deduce quickly what needs to be done, and to act with split-second speed and accuracy when the need arises. . . . How different it is from the skill of a craftsman's job on the one hand or of an ordinary machine operator on the other." [41]

We have evidence from early studies in this area that workers who are transferred to automated jobs have rather mixed feelings at first.[42] They find the work much more interesting but more demanding. Although they spend

---

[40] See George B. Baldwin and George Shultz, "Automation: A New Dimension to Old Problems," *Proceedings of the Seventh Annual Meeting Industrial Relations Association,* 1955, p. 114; see also *Automation and Technological Change,* Hearings before the Subcommittee on Economic Stabilization to the Joint Committee on the Economic Report, 84th Congress, First Session (1955).

[41] Charles R. Walker, *Toward the Automatic Factory* (New Haven: Yale University Press, 1957), p. 195.

[42] Walker, *op. cit.;* Floyd C. Mann and L. Richard Hoffman, "Case History in Two Power Plants," *Man and Automation* (New Haven: Yale University, The Technology Project, 1956).

less physical energy, many find themselves exhausted at the end of the day by nervous strain. In addition, they complain that (1) social activity is restricted because they have to stick close to their job, (2) since there are fewer workers, they work too far apart to be able to converse easily over the noise, and (3) they find it difficult to feel identification with their work, since clearly it is the machine that does the work, not the man.[43] As the workers gain experience, however, they report that they regard the new jobs as vastly improved over the old.

At higher levels of automation, the machine takes over more and more of the responsibilities of the operator. At times the job is reduced to the routine chores of feeding and watching the machine.[44] One study concludes that automation "often tends to reduce the skill and training required of the work force." [45] Finally, with complete automation, the operator is almost entirely eliminated. The repair jobs that remain require depth attention, high skill, and naturally are man-paced rather machine-paced.

There is an important difference in worker motivation between a non-automated job and an automated job. On the assembly line there is no real incentive for workers to keep the equipment running smoothly. The more uninterruptedly the line runs the more work the operator must do. But with automation the operator has almost nothing to do as long as the equipment is operating smoothly, the only time he really has to work is when it breaks down. Consequently, he is strongly motivated to keep things in good running order. And, since good work is self-rewarding, such jobs are more likely to be satisfying. (If the job involves feeding or watching the machine, however, this generalization does not hold true.)

Clearly, automation means different things in different situations, and it is impossible to state firmly that it either decreases or increases job satisfaction. On the whole, there is reason for guarded optimism that automation may restore much of the skill and feeling of being one's own boss that individual craftsmen experienced in an earlier day. Automation is still in its early stages, however, and it has far from eliminated all the routine, boring jobs—in some instances, it has even created more.

Conclusion

In this chapter we have tried to explore the implications of mass-production, assembly-line jobs for intrinsic job satisfaction. We have used this single type of work, not because it is perfectly representative of all or

---

[43] William Faunce, "Automation and the Automobile Worker," *Social Problems,* Vol 6, No. 1 (Summer 1958), pp. 68-78.

[44] See Harlow F. Craig, *Administering a Conversion to Electronic Accounting* (Boston: Graduate School of Business Administration, Harvard University, 1955).

[45] James R. Bright, "Does Automation Raise Skill Requirements?" *Harvard Business Review,* Vol. 36, No. 4 (July 1958), p. 97.

even most of the jobs performed by American workers, but because abundant research materials are available and because the analysis suggests methods for dealing with other types of work. In fact, some of our conclusions are equally relevant to more skilled, even professional jobs. The problems of pacing, monotony, goals, and interruptions are common to any work environment. Indeed there have been boring, non-satisfying jobs all through history—long before the industrial revolution.

More specifically, we have tried to focus attention on the nature of the work process itself and on the importance of work in shaping employee attitudes and behavior. This examination of the day-to-day reactions of mass-production workers will also be useful as a bench mark in comparing other types of work. We must emphasize again, however, that the effect of various techniques for reducing boredom and fatigue cannot be considered in isolation from such factors as styles of supervision, union-management relations, the stage of business cycle, and so forth. The very fact that it is more difficult for individuals to obtain satisfaction from the work itself greatly increases the importance of the social satisfactions provided by fellow workers (as we shall see in the next chapter) and the need for good supervision (to be considered in the chapters to come).

Problem I

The Schlerpinsuds Brewing Company has been plagued with trouble among its *bottle inspectors,* whose job is to check each bottle carefully to make sure that it is absolutely clean as it leaves the bottle-washing machine. Though there have been many attempts to develop mechanical inspecting devices, none of these has worked with 100 per cent accuracy. As a consequence, each bottle must be visually inspected as it passes by the inspector on a conveyor belt. Although this job is highly paid, it is hard to find men to take it and many quit after working only a few months.

1. What seems to be the basic problem here?
2. What suggestions can you make for solving it?

Problem II

All candy made by the Quality Candy Company is wrapped by hand. Candy is brought to each wrapper by chute. She wraps each piece and then drops it into another chute which leads to packers in another room.

Each girl handles a different kind of candy and their work locations are isolated from each other.

1. How will the girls react to this sort of work?
2. What can be done to increase their morale and output?

We have seen that social needs are among the most powerful and compelling on-the-job motivations. The people who make up organizations behave as members of groups, and their membership in these groups helps shape their work behavior and their attitudes toward the organization and the job. Groups exist at every level in the organization —from janitors to vice-presidents. They are in fact a basic building block of the organization. Since management can achieve its ends only through working with people, it must work through groups. But before we can consider the problems involved in supervising groups, we must first understand why groups develop and how they function.

Why Groups Are Formed

COMPANIONSHIP

Man is a social animal. Psychologists may argue about whether man is born with the need for society or acquires it early in life; yet the need for relationships with other people is one of the strongest and most constant of human drives.

3

Work Groups
and Informal Organization

Hermits, motivated by peculiar needs, may shun their fellows, but most people eagerly seek companionship.

As we have discovered, many jobs call forth only a small fraction of a person's total abilities. To management we may be just another unit of labor or a time-clock number; to our friends on the job we are individuals. From day to day the job is very much the same, but the group provides the diversity and change that are lacking in the work itself.

All of us have had the experience of arriving in a new situation and feeling completely lost and lonely until someone said a friendly word and recognized us as a person. What a difference it makes! Perhaps the job isn't interesting—but you do like to talk about the latest fishing trip or the Yankees' five-game winning streak.

Research indicates that employees who have no opportunity for close social contact find their work less satisfying, and this lack of satisfaction often reflects itself in lower production and higher turnover and absenteeism. Many years ago Elton Mayo observed that employees in a textile plant who worked at isolated jobs were highly dissatisfied and consistently failed to meet production standards. Staggered rest periods helped a little. But when the company permitted these workers to take rest periods *as a group*, production and satisfaction both increased.[1] Another company, where the girls worked in small, isolated booths, had the same experience. When management put glass partitions between the booths, the rate of turnover and the number of grievances both dropped sharply. Similarly, researchers in hospitals have discovered that maids feel uncomfortable when they work only in the company of high-status personnel (doctors, nurses, etc.) with whom they cannot associate with ease. Several hospitals have found that when three or four maids are grouped together as a team, turnover falls and a much better job is done.[2]

IDENTIFICATION

The difference may be subtle—but people want more than just friends, they want to *belong*. One can sense that he is part of a larger organization only by indirection, but the shared experiences of one's immediate colleagues are among the most meaningful and potent sources of job satisfaction.

Extensive studies during World War II indicated that soldiers' willingness to show bravery and make sacrifices was correlated not with loyalty

---

[1] Elton Mayo, *The Human Problems of an Industrial Civilization* (Boston: Graduate School of Business Administration, Harvard University, 1946), pp. 42-52. It should be noted that other factors were introduced that contributed to the improved morale and productivity. The work was broken up into self-contained tasks, and the rest periods themselves helped combat fatigue and monotony.

[2] Temple Burling, Edith Lentz, and Robert Wilson, *The Give and Take in Hospitals* (New York: Putnam, 1956), pp. 181-192.

to country or understanding of the war issues, but with loyalty to the immediate group. In other words, men committed acts of heroism that were motivated largely by the desire not to let their buddies down.[3]

Having learned this lesson, the army abandoned its system of bringing individual replacements into combat units and instead began rotating units as a whole.

During the same war the rapidly growing West Coast aircraft industry was troubled by extremely high turnover. No sooner was a worker partially trained than he quit. Research indicates that this pattern was associated with the absence of stable work groups. Since new employees never became part of a stable group, they developed no loyalty to the group and either quit or asked for a transfer at the slightest dissatisfaction.[4]

Other studies indicate that smaller groups tend to enjoy higher morale.[5] Employees working in large departments where everybody does the same job find it hard to form stable social groupings and often have low morale. Many companies with large secretarial pools are putting up waist-high barriers on the office floor to encourage the development of social groups and team spirit.

Even where there is no obvious reason for special groupings, people try to form them. One of the authors remembers his wartime experience in the army. On several occasions he found himself in a barracks with a new outfit where everyone was a stranger to everyone else. At first people wandered around the bunks aimlessly. But very soon they began to discover bonds of common experience and background (for example, athletic or educational interests). By the end of the first day there were already well-established cliques which determined with whom you sat at meals, spent your leisure time, or went out with on passes. Indeed loyalty to this intimate group seemed to develop long before loyalty to the outfit as a whole.

UNDERSTANDING FROM FRIENDS

The daily work routine is rich in opportunities for frustrations and tension. Whether we are harassed by an overbearing customer, an obstreperous typewriter, or a picayune inspector, we all seek a sympathetic ear, preferably from someone who has had similar experiences and can thus share and understand our troubles. Lacking this outlet, organizations have to rely on the clumsy and expensive system of employee counseling, in which outsiders "hear out" employee troubles.

---

[3] E. A. Shils, "Primary Groups in the American Army," in R. K. Merton and P. F. Lazarsfeld, eds., *Continuities in Social Research: Studies in the Scope and Method of the American Soldier* (Glencoe, Ill.: Free Press, 1950), pp. 16-39.

[4] Elton Mayo and George F. F. Lombard, *Teamwork and Labor Turnover in Aircraft Industry of Southern California* (Boston: Graduate School of Business Administration, Harvard University, 1944).

[5] A. P. Hare, "Interaction and Consensus in Different Sized Groups," *American Sociological Review*, Vol. 17 (1952), pp. 261-267.

PROVIDING ANSWERS

Whenever we are thrown into a new social situation, we are uncertain about how we are expected to behave. How much time should I take for a coffee break? Is it all right to talk to fellow employees while the boss is in the room? Must all copy be shown to the advertising manager? Our work days are filled with ambiguous situations. Even where there are established rules, one question remains: Is everybody expected to live by the letter of the law? Most employees don't want to violate the generally accepted "rules of the game"; at the same time they don't want to conform to restrictive rules that everyone else ignores. They want to know the "right" thing to do. The group fills an important need by providing all its members with a kind of "guide to correct behavior"—correct not in terms of any written policies, but in terms of what is actually acceptable.

HELPING SOLVE WORK PROBLEMS

A new sales clerk may not be sure about how to handle a complicated problem of returning some merchandise. A lab technician may be hesitant about asking his boss to repeat instructions, yet he is afraid that he may ruin the experiment unless he receives additional information. In each case the employee turns to his fellow workers for assistance.

The group's solution to a problem may differ from what management expects, and it may even be more efficient. Red tape is eliminated; shortcuts are evolved; informal channels of communication are established to cut across department boundaries; workers swap parts of their jobs to make them easier or more enjoyable. By the same token, work groups may also engage in feather-bedding and work-restriction.

Most people find their work easier and more interesting when they can work together with someone else. In fact, some workers, such as steel-construction crews, moving-van men, and baseball players, must coordinate their efforts if they are to do their job. Certain jobs can be done by isolated workers, but working as a group often results in higher individual motivation and a faster work pace. Some groups observe regular rituals (such as a coffee break when a given task is done) which serve to emphasize the group nature of the task.[6] Even schools are experimenting successfully with teaming students together rather than allowing each pupil to work alone or wait his turn to recite. Team members provide mutual help which increases the rate of learning.

---

[6] For example, see Donald F. Roy, " 'Banana Time': Job Satisfaction and Informal Interaction," *Human Organization,* Vol. 18, No. 4 (Winter 1959-1960), pp. 158-168.

PROTECTION FOR THE MEMBERSHIP

So far, we have been speaking about the psychological security and social satisfaction enjoyed by the individual members of the group. The solidarity of the group also provides other personal benefits and protection.

The most obvious protection provided by the group springs from its ability to resist management's demands for additional output, longer work hours, and higher quality. The group may even seek to discourage changes in plant layout that would destroy established social relations. Most dynamic organizations have a tendency to introduce changes in work methods and routines at a faster rate than the individual can adjust to them.[7] The pace at which these changes are introduced can be materially altered by a determined work group.

Without a sense of group allegiance, individual workers may also behave in ways that will injure their fellow workers. The work group often disciplines members who try to earn the supervisor's favor by "squealing" on fellow employees or by turning out too much work, or who fail to help their fellow workers on the job.

> A market-analysis office was required to prepare reports for top management. As time passed, the men made these reports increasingly elaborate, using colored graphs, photographic reproductions, and ever-more detailed data. Some of this window-dressing had real value, but most of it was designed to catch the boss' attention. At last, the men realized that they were spending tremendous amounts of uncompensated overtime in their efforts to outdo one another. Finally, they got together and agreed on standards to limit their competitive efforts.

In some groups the members actually agree on the level of output each will put forth so that no one member will out-perform the others.

The most common target of group power is the immediate supervisor. Most supervisors are quick to recognize that although they have the authority to make a wide range of decisions, to make certain decisions would be downright foolhardy. The members of the group can express their displeasure by cutting down their work pace, sabotaging the work (discreetly, of course, so that blame will be hard to place), or making their boss look inept to his own supervisors. This is probably the most potent form of protection that the group can offer its members.

How Work Groups Are Formed

When an engineer designs the plans and technology for a new factory, and when an architect designs the office layout, they are also designing the

---

[7] See F. J. Roethlisberger and W. J. Dickson, *Management and the Worker* (Cambridge: Harvard University Press, 1939).

social relations that will prevail within the organization. Management determines where men will work and what opportunities they will have to contact each other during the day. It also determines rates of pay, conditions of work, and the various symbols that are associated with each job. Given these basic elements, a sophisticated observer can predict the social relations that will exist within the organization long before the first employee enters the building.[8]

In telling men where and how they are to work, management is also telling them with whom they will come into contact. Normally, individuals develop friendships with the people they see most often. In fact, employees who have the greatest opportunities to make contacts on the job make the largest number of friends and are in the best position to become leaders of the group.

> A study of a housing project for married students indicated that friendship patterns were determined by apartment locations. Most families made a majority of their friends within their own building and especially on their own floor. Furthermore, those whose apartments were located on the ground floor nearest the building entrance had the best chance of becoming social leaders. Those who were physically isolated in end units were also most socially isolated and least liked.[9]

MULTIPLE-GROUP MEMBERSHIP

Most people belong to a number of informal groups. Take, for instance, Bill Jones, a college student. He has one group of friends in his dorm, another who take the same classes with him, a third who participate in the same sports, a fourth with whom he engages in an extra-curricular club. His girl friend may introduce him to several other groups. When he goes home on vacation he exercises his membership in still other groups (though his identification with them will be less strong than before he left). And if he is a Methodist, a Republican, and a sophomore, he may feel a certain affinity to other Methodists, Republicans, and sophomores.

The same patterns prevail in the factory or office. Adam Pepel is a tool clerk. He has many friends among the men he serves, and he has other contacts and common interests with his fellow tool clerks. He eats lunch with another group and goes bowling with still another. Moreover, he is an officer in his union and shares common attitudes with other officers. In short, Adam belongs to five or six "informal groups."

Now each of these groups has a different membership, although there may

---

[8] For two such predictive studies, see A. Zaleznik, C. R. Christensen, and F. J. Roethlisberger, *The Motivation, Productivity and Satisfaction of Workers: A Prediction Study* (Boston: Graduate School of Business Administration, Harvard University, 1958); and L. R. Sayles, *Behavior of Industrial Work Groups* (New York: Wiley, 1958).

[9] See Leon Festinger, Stanley Schachter, and Kurt Back, *Social Pressures in Informal Groups* (New York: Harpers, 1950).

be a great deal of overlapping. For some purposes one group is the most important to Adam; for others, another. The mere fact that he belongs to several groups, however, may subject him to considerable stress when their respective interests come into conflict.

Suppose, for instance, that the tool clerks decide as a group that the men are making the record-keeping task harder by failing to fill out tool requisition cards carefully. The tool clerks agree, with their boss' approval, that in the future none of them will give out tools unless the cards are properly prepared. As long as he is in the company of his fellow tool clerks, Adam feels that this is a fine decision. But once he is back among his friends on the job, he finds he just can't refuse fellow workers who have failed to fill out the cards. So he backs down and is unhappy when his fellow clerks accuse him of breaking his word.

THE GROUP BECOMES AN ORGANIZATION

Workers form friendship groups based on their contacts and common interests—and these groups arise out of the life of the organization. Once these groups have been established, however, they develop a life of their own that is almost completely separate from the work process from which they arose. Completely new activities and customs grow up, ranging from sharing coffee breaks and lunches to participating in small lotteries (for example, whose paycheck serial number makes the best poker hand?) and off-the-job parties and sports activities. Soon a rich social life develops, full of small incidents and seemingly trivial details, which relieves the boredom of the job.

Gradually the members gain a sense of pride in their group. When a common problem arises (such as what to do about an increase in work load), they have a natural tendency to discuss it with one another and formulate some mutually acceptable plan of action. Over a period of time, informal modifications are introduced into the formal job procedures.

The bonds that hold the members together continue to increase in strength until at last the group becomes an entity that is something more than a mere collection of people. It develops a customary way of doing things—a set of stable characteristics that are hard to change. It becomes an *organization*.

Internal Organization of Groups

Even after a group has become well established, management may ignore its existence or show open hostility to it. How, then, does the group accomplish its objectives and perpetuate itself? Simply by developing a set of unique characteristics that determine the members' relationships to one another and to supervision, the standards of conduct that are approved and enforced by the group, its system of rewards and punishments, and its system of communication.

All these aspects of group life are in balance with one another, or, as the social scientist would say, they are in equilibrium: (1) they are all interrelated, (2) a change in any one of them has an immediate effect on all the others, and (3) the members strongly resist changes in any part of this interrelated system. What, specifically, are these characteristics that dictate the internal organization of the group?

LEADERSHIP

Every group has informal leaders—individuals who have a special sort of status which results in their being followed by other members of the group. The informal leader is a very different sort of leader from the supervisor appointed by management. The formally appointed leader is followed because directly or indirectly he has the power to discharge those who refuse to obey his orders. The informal leader has no such power. Why, then, is he followed?

He is followed because the members learn that the group will not provide them with the benefits they seek unless they have some established leadership. Someone has to take the initiative in getting people to recognize that there is a common problem to be solved. The leader circulates through the group to urge a united front against a new threat from management, or to devise punishment for an uncooperative fellow member. In the process of developing consensus on what needs to be done, a successful leader is careful to sound out the members and to smooth over internal differences of opinion by personal persuasion and suggested compromises. He also serves as the group's representative in contacting the supervisor, or the union, or other work groups.

In summary, the leader performs vital functions that contribute to the group's ability to survive in its environment:

1. He initiates action.
2. He facilitates a consensus.
3. He provides a link or liaison with the outside world: managers, other work groups, the union.

Most observers have a tendency to refer to *the* informal leader, as though a single leader could be identified in every group. Actually, unless the group is very small, the functions we have described are usually shared by several active individuals who together comprise the leadership of the group. While the supervisor is most aware of the employee who contacts him as the group's representative, he must recognize that within the group, in less obvious positions, there may be other equally influential leaders adept in the use of human-relations skills.

Many studies have been conducted to determine the personality traits that characterize the effective group leader, but none of these studies has been altogether successful. It appears that each group requires a type of leadership suited to its own particular needs. These studies do suggest one important generalization, however: The group leader must live up to the group's idealized conception of what a group member should be. In the study of the bank-wiring room at the Western Electric Company, the informal leader of the group was described as follows:

> He was a key member of the superior clique and . . . one of the two men whose output conformed most closely and consistently to the accepted idea of a proper day's work. . . . In every way, indeed, he embodied the norms the group had adopted as its own. He never broke a rate, "chiseled," "squealed," or took a superior tone. . . .[10]

Some members of a group may aspire to a position of leadership without ever winning group acceptance. Outsiders may assume that these men are more influential than they actually are, for they are particularly active in contacting others. It is important to distinguish between the two types of leader, since the false leader rarely represents the true feelings of the group he pretends to lead.

GROUP STANDARDS

The urge to conform to group standards pervades most social life. Teen-age boys must be careful not to act too differently if they want to be accepted by the gang. Adolescent girls must dress like the other girls in their crowd, even if their parents object. There are group standards in industry as well. Some of these standards exist for the sole purpose of making life more enjoyable for the group members: The accounts receivable department always goes out together for lunch; the maintenance gang spends its breaks playing gin rummy; a new father is expected to pass out cigars when the child is born. If you don't do these things—you don't *belong*.

Other customs serve to make the job easier or to heighten the quality of workmanship. Waiters agree among themselves to share all tips equally and to help one another serve and clear tables during rush hours; clerks in department stores develop procedures for drawing merchandise from stock; if a college professor has to miss a class, his colleagues will try to stand in for him; retail clerks "spell" one another so that all the counters will be covered while one clerk is taking a break. All these customs reflect the expectations of group members with respect to one another's behavior.

Probably the most important group standards are those that protect the members of the group against real or imagined outside dangers, particu-

---

[10] George Homans, *The Human Group* (New York: Harcourt, Brace, 1950), pp. 147-149.

larly from management. As we have observed, production workers may agree on a level of output and exert pressure on those who deviate from it—especially on those who produce more than the accepted "bogey." "Eager beavers" in the classroom are frequently reminded that "C" is the "gentleman's grade." Group standards of good workmanship and high quality often make management's task easier; for the group, by taking "troublemakers" in hand, reduces the need for management to impose discipline.

Thus from management's point of view, the pressure to conform to group standards may be most desirable. A standard that a worker can be five minutes late also means that the group will prevent him from abusing this privilege.

A group of white-collar employees was frequently given the afternoon off when the ball team played a home game. Without any prompting from management, the employees agreed among themselves to come in an hour early to compensate for the short days. Employees who were unenthusiastic about this informal change in the schedule were pressured into conforming, and management gained the extra work time.

Larger groups, particularly in professional pursuits, often maintain ethical standards designed to further the goals of the over-all membership. A recent study of hospitals, for example, noted that the high level of teaching competence maintained by the senior medical staff, and the high quality of patient care maintained by the junior staff members, could be largely explained in terms of the allegiance felt by both groups to standards of professional conduct.[11] Many a professional, whether he is an attorney, an accountant, or a scientist, undoubtedly is tempted to take short cuts that would save him time and money, and he may be absolutely certain that these short cuts would go undetected. And yet the standards that he has "internalized" during years of training and association with a professional group hold him to certain fixed patterns of behavior.

GROUP NORMS

In addition to group standards of behavior there are also group standards of attitude—or *norms*. People who work closely together naturally adopt common points of view that everyone is expected to share: "Ours is a good job (or a bad one)." "Most people don't realize how difficult our job really is." "Inspection is trying to make our job rough." "You've got to be a college man to make supervisor."

Many of these standards of attitude are without factual basis, of course. They are simply myths that have risen from the group's fears or wishes. Yet the group's acceptance of them *is* a fact—a fact that management must take into account.

---

[11] Burling, Lentz, and Wilson, *op. cit.*, pp. 79-80.

Some years ago, the job of heater in a steel crew was dangerous and difficult. Primarily a hand operation, it required great skill to lift large bars of metal into the furnace via a pulley system. The intense heat made the job even more unpleasant. Now the worst part of the job is handled by automatic equipment, and the operator works some distance away from the furnace. But heaters still feel that their job deserves special financial consideration. Fellow workers support them in this claim, even though it means that more difficult jobs are paid less.

As we have said, the individual becomes wedded to the group as a result of constant association and socializing. Members begin to think and act alike, not only in order to enjoy the fruits of group membership, but because the very process of living together reinforces certain feelings and attitudes in the mind of each member. These attitudes may have existed only weakly before, if at all. Before going to work in XYZ Company, a recently graduated chemical engineer considered himself moderately well-trained and useful. After working in a research group composed entirely of chemical engineers, however, he decides that chemical engineers are the most skilled and valuable group in the laboratory. Through constant interaction with a group, certain predispositions are reinforced, or even distorted, in the minds of the members.[12] Further, the goals of the group gradually become as important to each member's feeling of accomplishment as his own individual needs. Once the group has become truly established, the individual members come to identify themselves with its successes and failures.

PRESSURES TO CONFORM

Why is it that most people are so anxious to conform to group standards? In the first place, as members of the group, they look at things from the group point of view; they tend to identify with the group and, since it helps meet their needs, they accept its goals. Even those who have misgivings about the validity of the standards go along anyway, because they want to be well regarded by their fellows. Finally, the group has effective means of punishing those who insist on doing things their own way.

Ostracism is one of the most effective forms of group punishment. A member who overproduces, who fails to share important information, or who is officious may find himself isolated from his fellow workers. In extreme cases, no one will talk to him or even acknowledge his presence. In less extreme cases, the deviate may be excluded from ordinary social activities, such as getting the morning coffee, or may be greeted coldly when he reports for work. When he has trouble, no one will come to his aid. Or his connection with the "grapevine" may be rudely cut off. Over a period of time the work situation can become intolerable for the victim.

Sometimes the group resorts to more direct techniques. Someone may

---

[12] Ross Stagner, *Psychology of Industrial Conflict* (New York: Wiley, 1956), p. 9.

"accidentally" let management know about some of the deviate's mistakes. Fellow workers may be slow in giving him the parts or the information he needs. His equipment or desk may be "adjusted" while he is away. In the bank-wiring-room study, one of the inspectors failed to live up to certain group norms. The other workers flooded his inspection station with work so that he could not possibly keep up with it, and they "adjusted" his testing equipment so that it failed to work properly.[13]

The punishments devised to enforce group standards are sometimes highly ingenious. In one office, supervision was lenient in permitting employees to arrive late for work. When one man began to abuse this privilege by arriving very late every day, the group was afraid that management would start to crack down on tardiness. Whenever this employee came in late, his fellow workers applauded him warmly. This gesture served to emphasize their displeasure, and, it was hoped, would encourage management to deal with him on an individual basis.

FRIENDSHIP PATTERNS

Some observers have referred to these informal work groups as though they were internally homogeneous or uniform. Nothing could be less accurate; in fact, understanding the variety of relationships between members is as important as noting the uniformities surrounding the common core of leadership and group standards. Even when a number of employees share a common allegiance to the same group, their feelings toward one another may vary widely.

Sociometry is a field of inquiry designed to explore these diversified relationships within the group.[14] It is largely concerned with "social choices." One of the most valuable tools developed by this approach is the *sociometric map* or sociogram, which is simply a means of picturing the "social choices" within a group. For example, each worker in a given department is asked to list the other individuals in the department he likes best. Then a map is drawn with a circle representing each individual and an arrow from the chooser to the person he chooses.

The sociometric map below was drawn on the basis of answers to the question: Whom do you like best? But other questions might be used equally well, such as: With whom would you most like to work? Who is the most productive member of the group? With whom do you talk most often? With whom do you spend most of your time? Each question might lead to a somewhat different sociometric map, but each would provide valuable insight into the informal structure of the group.

---

[13] Roethlisberger and Dickson, *op. cit.*, p. 487.

[14] Sociometry was the brain child of J. L. Moreno. See his *Who Shall Survive?* (Beacon, N.Y.: Beacon House, 1953); see also Helen Hall Jennings, *Leadership and Isolation* (New York; Longmans, Green, 1950); and the various issues of the journal *Sociometry*.

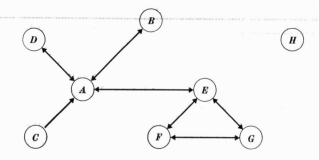

Sociometric map. A and B have chosen each other. C has chosen A, but A has not chosen C. EFG represent a clique, since each member has chosen the other two. The relationship among E, F, and G is tighter than that between A, B, C, and D, for in the first case each person chose all the rest, while in the second their relationship depends on their common relationship with A. H is an *isolate:* he has chosen no one, no one has chosen him. B is only slightly more popular. A is obviously a leader, for he has been chosen more often than anyone else and also is the only connecting link between cliques BCD and EFG.

STATUS SYSTEMS

Just as soon as a loose aggregation of individuals develops into a genuine group, subtle status differences begin to arise. Roughly defined, status is a measure of a person's prestige within the group. It is an index to how important he is, to his position in the "pecking order."

Status provides a sense of security, and failure to have one's status recognized generates insecurity. Think of the senior who is mistaken for a sophomore, or the professor who is introduced as a student. Moreover, status provides a reassuring guide to the members of the group in their contacts with one another. A man with high status expects and receives greater deference than a man with lower status.

How is status determined? What criteria do people use in assigning higher standing to Mr. A than to Mr. B? Some status decisions are based on the attitudes and behavior of management; others are entirely the product of the informal organization of the group.

Status often depends on *job title.* Obviously a superintendent is more important than a general foreman and a general foreman outranks a foreman. Engineers outrank technicians, secretaries are "above" stenographers. In almost every organization the job titles are subtly graded according to levels of status, and the status of each individual depends in part on the job he holds.

Pay, of course, is one of the most important determinants of the status accorded to each job. Higher pay means higher status, and even a difference of a few cents per hour may have a significant effect on a job's status. The new manager may find this bewildering and unreasonable.

Take the case of the checkers and the loaders in one newly unionized plant. The checkers received $1.70 an hour, the loaders $1.60. The checkers insisted that since keeping records involved great responsibility and required a high-school education, they should receive a pay increase of at least 30 cents. The loaders felt that since their job required considerable skill and physical effort, they should be paid as much as the checkers. The union succeeded in getting 20 cents for the checkers, but won 30 cents for the loaders—and the checkers were more unhappy than ever.

Understandably, many companies encourage their employees to keep their pay scale secret.

How one is paid also helps to determine status. Some companies have monthly, semi-monthly, and weekly payrolls. Being a salaried man on the monthly payroll may be less convenient, but it carries much more prestige than getting a weekly *wage* (which may be computed on an hourly rather than an annual basis). Sometimes unskilled casual workers receive their pay by the day.

Work schedules are also a useful index. The hourly-paid man comes in at 7:30, the office clerks at 8:30, and the executives dribble in from 9:00 on—but the executives often work late at night. The freedom to choose one's hours, or being excused from punching the time-clock, is a mark of distinction. (Henry Ford once made all his executives punch the time-clock—thus lowering even further what was already rock-bottom morale.)

In which company lunchroom can you eat? Are tables reserved for you? Can you leave the building for morning coffee? Do you receive a daily copy of the *Wall Street Journal?* The allocation of these *special privileges* follows status lines.

Then there's the question of *where one works.* In the field or in the home office? In the new building where the important operations occur—or over in the "boneyard"? In some offices, the closer a man works to the big boss the more status he enjoys. To be able to say "I work on the fourteenth floor" may be the pinnacle of prestige.

We once interviewed a girl whose eyes were still red from crying. Her problem: She had worked her way up till her desk was right next to the office manager, and she thought she was next in line when the office manager retired. Now the boss had shifted her to the back of the room. What were her future possibilities? What would the other girls think of her?

In factories, higher status is often accorded to the man who works near the focal points of employee interaction than to the man who works in an isolated position. Working near the end of the production line carries more status than working near the beginning—for the finished product is more valuable and the job more responsible.

Among the job factors that affect status are: cleanliness, freedom from supervision, amount of training and skill required, and opportunity for promotion. A study of the restaurant industry revealed substantial differences in the status enjoyed by employees who worked with various vegetables:

> At the top were luxury or decorative items such as parsley, chives and celery. At the top of the regular vegetables were green beans. Next comes spinach and carrots. Next to the bottom were sweet and white potatoes, and onions were considered the most undesirable of all. . . .
>
> Comments of the workers showed that they valued lack of odor, crispness, and cleanness in handling most high in vegetables, whereas the vegetable that had an odor and that stained the hands or was sloppy to handle was held in low esteem. The low standing of potato peeling is too well known to require comment, but here at least the workers said they preferred potatoes to onions because they did not smell or stain the hands. . . .[15]

Most jobs carry with them certain *symbols* that bestow varying degrees of status. In the army, shoulder insignia denotes officer rank. Paratroop boots or wings indicate that enlisted men belong to elite outfits (and for this reason, during World War II, many men wore them without authorization).

In industry, too, there are countless widely recognized symbols. Take clothing, for example. Executives (and often office people) wear coats. Foremen wear white shirts. Hourly-paid workers wear work clothes. The chef's hat and the machinist's apron or shop coat are more specialized symbols of prestige.

> Even though there was no plant rule, in one situation only the higher paid machinists wore white coats, the rest had white aprons. One lower paid man wore a coat for a week—but social pressure forced him to discard it.[16]
>
> Some time ago, one of the authors conducted a series of interviews in a plant. Wanting to make it clear that he was primarily interested in studying the union and the work force—and that he was not connected with management—he was careful to wear T-shirts whenever he was in the plant. One day he made the mistake of coming in with a regular shirt and tie. Several workers asked, "What's wrong—sold out to management?"

Among executives, the *type of office* a man has bears strongly on the amount of status he enjoys. Does he have his own office? How large is it? Does he have his own secretary? Does she have a separate office? What type of desk does he have? Does he have a phone? Or, even better, *two* phones? As one carpet company puts it, "A title on the door rates a Bigelow on the floor." [17]

---

[15] William F. Whyte, *Human Relations in the Restaurant Industry* (New York: McGraw-Hill, 1948), p. 36.

[16] Abraham Zaleznik, *Worker Satisfaction and Development* (Boston: Graduate School of Business Administration, Division of Research, Harvard University, 1956), p. 21.

[17] For a sensitive discussion of executive status problems, see J. P. Marquand's novel, *Point of No Return* (New York: Little, Brown, 1949).

The story is told of a vice-president who suffered a nervous break-down after his company moved into new office quarters. The accommodations were fine, but his desk was smaller than those of the other VP's, so obviously he was going to be eased out—or so he thought.

Status depends on *who one is* as well as what one does—that is, on the attributes or characteristics that the employee brings with him from his community and home. The boss' son has status in the plant regardless of what he does—and so does the captain of the plant baseball team. Among the qualities that confer status are education, age, seniority, sex, and ethnic background. Typically in business women are ranked below men. Unfortunately, in our society Negroes are often accorded lower status just because of the color of their skin. The same holds true in some places of Mexicans, Indians, and Asiatics. Other ethnic groups are also arranged according to a regular status hierarchy, with Anglo-Saxons usually at the top and people of southern European background near the bottom. The relative positions on this status ladder may vary from one community to another (for instance: in some places Poles may rank higher than Italians; in other places the reverse may be true), but in every case there is some kind of ranking, together with a struggle between groups to pull themselves up the ladder and others down.

Individual behavior also seems to have some influence on status. People with pleasant personalities, specialized skills, or leadership traits ordinarily enjoy high status, as do individuals who conform closely to the behavioral standards of the group. The man who just doesn't know "how to behave" is likely to lose status—either in an exclusive club or on the factory floor.

STATUS INCONSISTENCY

Thus there are several different indicators of status—title, pay, type of work performed, symbols, and others. In a sense, each of these is a thermometer which measures a different aspect of status. So long as all these status "thermometers" give approximately the same readings, status is not likely to cause trouble in the organization. But when they read differently, when the various indicators of status give inconsistent or ambiguous measures of status, personnel unrest and dissatisfaction occur. Let us look at some examples.

One typical group standard requires that the more prestigeful group members occupy the more prestigeful jobs. The longer-service, better-educated employee in a restaurant kitchen would resent being assigned to onion-peeling, particularly if junior employees were chopping greens and celery. This violation of a group standard would produce a disturbing status inconsistency. The same problem prevails when an employee is promoted to a department manager's job but is not given the type of office usually assigned to men of that rank. The university is not immune to these problems. In university towns, the assistant professor who moves into a section of the community normally regarded as the preserve of full professors is considered "strange" or aggressive.

Often the supervisor is unaware of the subtle distinctions drawn by the group among various jobs, work locations, and types of equipment. Seemingly innocent changes in job assignment or work location may precipitate ill feeling and resentment.[18]

> The metal drawing department had four kinds of machines. Though work on each machine paid the same wages, there were noticeable differences in ease of operation. From the group point of view, it was a promotion to move to a Z machine and a demotion to move to an X machine. This attitude made it much harder for management to transfer men as production needs dictated and led to many grievances, particularly when management tried to move informal leaders to "lower-ranking" jobs.

Thus, the group's conception of what is right and fair is of critical importance in understanding employee reactions to the work situation.

Group Cohesion

Just as the work group is internally differentiated, there are also significant differences *among* groups. One of the most important is the degree of unity or cohesion within the group. All the elements of group behavior that we have mentioned are influenced by this factor.[19] The more united the group, the greater the likelihood that all members will conform strictly to group standards (in part as a result of heightened pressures to conform) and the greater the likelihood that a small leadership core will represent without challenge the feelings of all members. By definition, cohesive groups are

---

[18] Professor George Homans of Harvard University has developed what he calls a "theory of distributive justice": First, there are certain elements that a member brings to his job from his past or puts into his work on the job. Examples are age, seniority, sex, ethnicity, responsibility, and education. Homans calls these "investments." Second, there are other status factors the worker expects to get out of his job. Examples are the material rewards (pay, etc.), the interest of the job, and status itself, the prestige accorded him by his fellows. These Homans called "rewards" or "returns."

According to Homans, when the "investments" of an individual member or of one subgroup are higher than those of another, *distributive justice* requires that their "rewards" should be higher, too. When "distributive justice" does not prevail—*i.e.*, when investment is not equal to reward—Homans predicts there will be trouble on the job. (Zaleznik, Christensen, and Roethlisberger, *op. cit.*), p. 53.

[19] For two excellent discussions of cohesion, see Dorwin Cartwright and Alvin Zander, eds., *Group Dynamics: Research and Theory* (Evanston, Ill.: Row, Peterson, 1953), pp. 73-91; and Stanley Seashore, *Group Cohesiveness in the Industrial Work Group* (Ann Arbor: Survey Research Center, University of Michigan, 1954). Not only is cohesion related to morale, but the two have actually been equated. See David Krech and Richard S. Crutchfield, *Theory and Problems of Social Psychology* (New York: McGraw-Hill, 1948).

internally consistent in their measures of status and are more likely to act in unison when their expectations are violated, either by management, by one of their own members, or even by another group.

In personnel administration, it isn't enough simply to recognize that such differences among groups exist. We also want to be able to predict the conditions that will produce either united or disunited groups. From our own research and that of others, the following factors emerge as some of the determinants of group cohesion.

STATUS OF THE GROUP

Other things equal, people are more likely to feel loyalty toward a high-status group than toward a low-status group. Social climbers, for example, are more careful to conform to the norms of the group to which they aspire than to the norms of a group from which they want to escape. Indeed, there is a kind of circular process at work here: a high-status group elicits greater loyalty from its members, which in turn makes the group even stronger and more likely to gain increased status.

What determines the status of a group? All the factors noted above as determining individual status contribute, though interrelations between these factors become quite complex at the group level. For example, when we asked utility employees to compare their importance relative to that of other groups in the organization, among the factors they mentioned were:

1. The company has recognized the difficulty and responsibility associated with our jobs by establishing a special test which new employees must pass before they can do our type of work.

2. Because of the difficulty and dangerous nature of our jobs, no one else can touch our work—although in an emergency we can fill in on other jobs.

3. Our job is a good training ground for high responsibility. Over the years a number of our men have gone on to top management posts.

4. Our office used to be located in company headquarters. Now we are in an isolated building where no one goes unless he has to.

5. Before the company made any major decision our old boss used to be consulted. He was a very important man. Our present boss isn't thought of too highly and doesn't carry much weight in company affairs.

In effect, these employees were listing a number of status criteria: the intrinsic nature of the work, their level of responsibility, their opportunities for promotion, the boss' standing, and even their physical location. Several organization changes (noted in factors 4 and 5) had recently led to a substantial reduction in the status of this group. As a result, the members took less interest in informal company activities and even in the union, and they showed less satisfaction in being identified with the department. Similarly, employees working at the very bottom of the organization's promotional ladder seldom develop a strong attachment to their work groups. In fact, they sometimes regard themselves as only temporary members of their group.

SIZE

Small departments are more closely knit than large ones. Loyalty, as we have seen, is a product of constant, face-to-face contacts. Naturally it is easier to have close relationships with all the members of a small group than with all the members of a large one.

HOMOGENEITY

Groups whose members have different interests and backgrounds are often less effective in promoting their own interests than groups whose members are more homogeneous. When people with sharp differences in rates of pay and job duties, for example, work near one another, the resulting informal group is seldom cohesive. This lack of homogeneity may reflect itself in the formation of competing subgroups or cliques, and conflict between these cliques may become so intense that any area of common interest is almost obliterated.

COMMUNICATIONS

Groups in which the members can communicate easily with one another are more likely to be cohesive. Internal group unity can be thwarted in noisy steel mills or along assembly lines.[20] Even scattered groups, like maintenance crews, may become tightly knit if the technology of work requires or permits them to interact frequently with each other. We have observed one highly cohesive group whose members never saw each other on the job and yet was sufficiently cohesive to dominate the union and win substantial wage increases: these were electrical utility sub-station operators whose jobs required them to communicate by phone. Indeed one of the determinants of group cohesion is the speed with which rumors or other messages can be transmitted through the group,[21] for rumors contribute to the feeling of common identity.

ISOLATION FROM OTHER GROUPS

Physical isolation from other groups of workers tends to build cohesiveness. Miners, for example, have demonstrated in countless lengthy strikes that they will stick together more stubbornly than workers who are

---

[20] Charles R. Walker, Robert Guest, and Arthur N. Turner, *Foreman on the Assembly Line* (Cambridge: Harvard University Press, 1956), pp. 131 ff.

[21] See Alex Bavelas, "Communications Patterns in Task-Oriented Groups," in Cartwright and Zander, *op. cit.*, pp. 493-506.

more socially integrated with the rest of the community.[22] Similarly, a study of a *kibbutz* (cooperative farm settlement in Israel) shows that isolated settlements are more likely to solve their problems harmoniously than are those located in more populous sections of the country.[23]

Where there is no sharp line between one group and another, cohesion is difficult to achieve. For example, on the assembly line *B* may interact with *A* on his left and *C* on his right, while *D* may interact with *C* on his left and with *E* on his right. Thus a chain of interactions develops but little group solidarity.[24]

SUPERVISORY PRACTICES

The customary behavior of the supervisor has a direct influence on the degree of cohesion that exists within a group. By fostering competition, and by constantly comparing one worker with another, he may make close relations impossible. On the other hand, he can build solidarity by rewarding cooperative behavior. Among members of management, where there is often sharp competition for promotion and recognition, there is less cohesion than among hourly-paid employees who look to the union for protection against supervision and have much less expectation of promotion.

OUTSIDE PRESSURE

Group members draw together when they are threatened by a common danger. A group of employees may forget their personal differences and close ranks against a new supervisor who is regarded as a threat to the group. The speed with which long-standing feuds are healed under pressure from a common enemy is sometimes wondrous to behold.

What happens when the pressure is removed? Group solidarity may diminish somewhat, but the cooperative patterns that arose during the time of crisis may well persist. Thus the supervisor who inadvertently produces a strong anti-company clique may find that it survives long after the original grievances have been eliminated.

> In order to introduce a new incentive program, a large manufacturing company hired several new time-study men. As the program got under way, the men met intense opposition from the older industrial engineers, who felt the new program would endanger their relationships with their subordinates, and among the employees themselves who feared that the new program would mean "tighter" work standards. As the hostility

[22] Clark Kerr and Abraham Siegel, "The Interindustry Propensity to Strike—An International Comparison," Arthur Kornhauger, Robert Dubin, and Arthur Ross, eds., *Industrial Conflict* (New York: McGraw-Hill, 1954), pp. 191-193.

[23] Amitai Etzioni, "Solidaric Work-Groups in Collective Settlements," *Human Organization*, Vol. 16, No. 3 (Fall 1957), pp. 2-6.

[24] Zaleznik, *op. cit.*, pp. 120-121.

mounted, the time-study men drew closer together. Then management capitulated to a strike called to protest the new standards, and the whole program suddenly collapsed. Some of the men in the defunct time-study department were offered other jobs in the organization; still others were helped to find jobs in the adjacent area. Even though the members now work in widely scattered locations, the group continues to meet regularly for dinner and a "chat about old times." Welded together by the pressure they shared, they became a closely knit group.

Changes in accustomed ways of doing things, and sudden cancellations of prerogatives, may also draw employees together. Management opposition to their new solidarity may serve only to strengthen the group.

SUCCESS

A group is likely to be stronger and more cohesive if it has engaged successfully in cooperative action in the past. This is the familiar circular pattern: cohesive groups are more successful and successful groups are more cohesive. Success, however, is largely a matter of luck and depends on many other factors; for example, whether the group occupies a strategic position in the flow of work.

If a small group discovers that it can cripple a plant by refusing to work, it can use this leverage to win special concessions in the future. Once the group loses this strategic advantage, however, it may fall apart.

The machine polishers had a reputation for winning grievances and exercising control over the union. A new invention caused the company to cut down on the number of machine polishers employed. The company also failed to loosen up what the polishers felt was an outmoded incentive plan.

Members of the group began to blame their informal leaders for what had happened. With the recognition of failure came an unwillingness to stick together any longer. Workers began to squabble with one another, particularly over who should have priority to certain jobs. Personal recriminations followed and gradually the men began to request transfers to other departments.

Naturally, when members find that their own group is not successful in protecting them or winning benefits for them, they are unlikely to abide consistently by group standards. In fact, members may begin to seek other affiliations that offer more security and status. This defection further weakens the group, and it becomes less and less successful.

Conclusion

In this chapter we have sought to analyze one important component of every organization: the aggregations of employees we have called groups. Although the boundary lines that determine group membership are affected by management's job assignments and supervisory practices, each group develops a momentum of its own. As a result, there is a constant elaboration of informal organization which does not appear on any chart or plan of the company's operations.

People seek membership in existing groups and form new groups for a wide variety of reasons. But at the bottom there always seems to be a search for satisfactions that are not provided directly by the job or by the supervisor —satisfactions such as companionship and protection.

Informal groups have a life of their own; they have customary ways of doing things and of looking at things; they have their own leaders and a minutely defined status hierarchy. These are the stable, enduring components of group life. In other words, informal organization is a *reality* that management can ignore only at its own peril.

Management sometimes tries to evade this reality by emphasizing the organization as a whole, even to the point of trying to break up what it regards as destructive cliques. Yet loyalty to the face-to-face group, to one's fellow workers, is much stronger than loyalty to the larger entity. Indeed, management can develop over-all loyalty only by encouraging teamwork and informal relations. The group may exercise far stronger control over its members than does management itself.

Other managements seek to by-pass the group by telling supervisors they should concentrate on dealing with each employee as an individual. It is certainly true that the supervisor must spend much of his time dealing with the personal needs and idiosyncrasies of his subordinates, yet he is completely missing the realities of the situation if he fails to see that the group is something more than the sum of the individuals concerned.

A good supervisor must understand the social organization with which he works, just as he must be familiar with tools, materials, and technological processes. If he is to avoid making unwitting mistakes, he must know the status structure of the group, its informal leaders, its standards and norms. This knowledge will strengthen his tools of leadership immeasurably.

Does this mean that management must *accept* group standards as they are—for example, that it should do nothing to overcome a thoroughly unacceptable "bogey"? No, we think not. In later chapters we shall discuss ways in which management can work through the informal organization instead of fighting it.

First, however, we shall examine an organization that often grows out of the informal organization and exercises strong influence over it: the union.

Problem I*

Over the years, salesmen in the ABC Company had developed the habit of perusing office records. Management was anxious to discourage this practice for

---

* We are grateful to a former student, J. J. Nerenberg, for the outline of this case.

fear that a salesman who had become intimately familiar with company costs and customers might go over to a competitor. The problem was intensified when new offices were constructed separating the salesmen's quarters from those occupied by the office staff. The salesmen were now expected to request necessary information from the office staff over a four-foot counter, and were never to enter the new premises. Here is the way one observer described the salesmen's determination to preserve the practice of looking at the records:

> "At first the salesmen would try to think of every conceivable way to 'break the barrier.' It became a matter of pride to see if they could enter the office and walk around. They said they had to speak to the accountant, to consult with the president, to check an order with a clerk, to pick up some clean towels—almost any excuse."

Management reacted by making the rules against infiltration even more rigid. All salesmen were absolutely forbidden to enter the office except for exceptional reasons. This time the reaction was even more severe. The salesmen began to complain about every sort of petty detail in the office. Their favorite complaint was that the switchboard operator was not giving them all their messages. Next they began to find all sorts of fault with their new quarters. The ceiling tile was laid improperly, the phones were on the wrong side of the desk, the lighting was inadequate, the floor was not cleaned regularly. Fights broke out between the salesmen and the sales manager, and the salesmen began to make aggressive remarks about the office force. They became more clannish and self-conscious.

1. Basically, the changes management introduced were modest ones, and they did not "hurt" the salesmen. Why, then, were they exhibiting such aggressive behavior?

2. What group factors were affected by the change?

3. To what extent were these predictable reactions and of what value would such predictions be to supervision?

Problem II*

Every summer, the Children's and Infants' Department of Hackett's Department Store had been plagued by friction between the regular full-time clerks and the temporary summer replacements.

The regular clerks had developed close social ties in the years they had spent together. They had a common ethnic background and all but two were unmarried or widowed. Whenever possible, they took their coffee and lunch breaks together and often saw each other after work. Further, the department had frequent slack periods when the clerks could sit around and talk together.

These replacements were drawn either from a "flying squad" of full-time employees who were assigned to different departments as need dictated, or from young high-school girls who took the jobs for the summer. Both groups were extremely unhappy at being sent to the Children's Department, and two of the high-schoolers asked for transfers after a short stay. The reasons became quickly evident. The independent work-structure evolved by the regulars had resulted in a department pattern which violated the store rulebook. There was, for example, a definite "pecking order" governing who could take coffee breaks when, and there were frequent unexplained disappearances and early preparations for departure at

---

* We are indebted to a former student, Eben W. Keyes, II, for this case.

closing time. The regulars made little effort to assist or advise the newcomers, and criticized them constantly behind their backs. There were seldom more than two part-time girls in the department at any one time, and since they were unlikely to have known each other before there was little opportunity for them to develop any relationship.

The major difficulties occurred in the area of commission sales. Although the full-timers had an unspoken agreement not to "push hard" for sales achievements, they bitterly resented any commission earned by replacements. They argued that as senior workers they deserved the lion's share of the commission income. The part-timers didn't need it as much as they did, nor had they worked to build up the department. Furthermore, the full-timers thought of themselves as embodying all the sales know-how in the department; the part-timers "didn't know how to sell." Catastrophe occurred when one of the part-timers made a substantial sale and "sabotaged" the commission of one of the regulars. The high-school girl came to the assistant buyer in tears; she had sold a crib when the full-timer in her area was absent from the department, and had been roundly berated for making the sale! She was told that she did not understand the merchandise, and that the other clerk could have made a larger, more profitable sale.

The part-timers were naturally anxious to build up a good sales record. They were motivated to do a good, capable job—either with a view to winning perma-nent employment, or, in the case of the "flying squad," to convince management that they were worthy of promotion.

As a result, the "old girls" gave either misleading or incorrect information about merchandise or department policies to the part-timers, in order to slow them down and make their job performance less impressive. When a replacement turned to a full-timer for help while serving a customer, the full-timer would frequently take over and consummate the sale. Part-timers were often sent to the stockroom for more goods or were asked to rearrange displays. The full-timers were directing their energies into undermining the part-timers instead of into trying to improve their own sales records.

1. How do you explain the behavior of the full-time clerks in this department?

2. Was management gaining any compensating advantages from the increased co-hesiveness of the full-timers?

3. Is it realistic or typical to find employees doing average or below-average work and still viewing themselves as top-notch salesmen, as in this case?

4. What would you do if you were the buyer (department head) in this case?

Problem III*

The old "standard" spinning machines in a large manufacturing plant were operated chiefly by high-seniority men paid on an hourly rate. For nine years the company had been experimenting with new machines that were faster and easier to run. During the experimental period, the machines had been operated by younger men with low seniority. After a two-year tryout, these operators had been put on incentive rates.

To obtain the union's approval, management granted a "loose" rate (one on which it is easy to obtain high earnings). The union readily accepted, believing

---

* This case is adapted from the authors' earlier book, *The Local Union* (New York: Harpers, 1953), pp. 43-58.

that unless the long-run productivity of this particular department was improved, the company would move its operation to another plant.

The old spinners, however, who were politically powerful in the union, resented the incentive system. They feared that it would set a precedent for working too fast and perhaps even reduce the amount of work available to them. Eventually this could mean fewer jobs.

Even before the incentive plan was accepted, the men on the old spinners derided the younger men as "damn fools for working themselves to death." In turn, the younger men were resentful of the old spinners' "creamy jobs" and were upset that the seniority system forced them to take what was then less desirable work, with little chance of obtaining jobs on the old machines.

After the incentive plan was put into effect, the men began to compare their paychecks in neighborhood bars. It became obvious that the younger men, on incentive, were earning a great deal more than the older spinners on their hourly rate. Since the two types of machine were located right next to each other, the old spinners were able to watch the ever-increasing production on the other line. With growing anxiety, they saw the differential in earnings grow larger and larger.

The two lines had never been friendly, but now they began to exchange angry threats. Several top-seniority spinners told the "youngsters":

> "You guys better save what you are earning because you're not going to be on these jobs very long. We're coming over to take them. They're ours because we're the oldest men in the department."

To be sure, some of this was in jest, but the serious undertone prompted a group of the youngest, who had nothing to lose, to tell off their adversaries:

> "Don't start anything because if you try to bump us [use the seniority provisions of the contract to take their jobs] we're going to fix those jobs so no one wants them."

In reply, the hourly-rate spinners emphasized their right to the job as older, senior employees in the department:

> "Why should some young guy that has been in the plant less than a year be taking home thirty dollars more a week than guys like us that have been here more than fifteen years? We'll be the laughing stock of the plant."

The new spinners were just as self-righteous:

> "We took these jobs when no one else wanted them. We stuck to them through a two-year trial period when everyone else was laughing at us, and you fellows have no right to come over and bump us off."

The old spinners first tried to pressure their stewards and grievancemen into taking action. Some of them informally contacted the local president and the international representative to get their opinion on whether or not it would be legal for them to bump onto the new machines. When they received no reply, three of the more vocal old-timers submitted a formal grievance to their steward outlining their right to the new job and demanding that the union do something about the threat of the youngsters to use production increases to "ruin the new job."

In the meantime, the incentive workers made good their threat to accelerate production, hoping thereby to discourage the older men from any further interest in the job. Their logic was this: if they worked very hard, management would expect much more production than the older men, who had been "spoiled" by their hourly rates, would be willing to put out.

The older men responded by calling a departmental meeting, as authorized by the union constitution. The younger men boycotted the meeting but learned of the results the next day. They, too, submitted a formal grievance in writing, enunciating their claims to the incentive jobs.

1. Analyze the sources of this conflict in terms of the type of group factors involved.

2. Assess the likelihood that struggles *between* employee groups will be an important personnel problem in most organizations.

3. Where these inter-group problems exist, to what extent is management also a participant? Why?

Over 17,000,000 Americans belong to unions. This simple fact of industrial life has profound implications for management and personnel administration. Although we can treat the subject of labor-management relations only sparsely in this chapter, we will consider why workers join unions, how unions behave, how their behavior affects management, and what management can do to improve its relationship with unions.

The Growth of Unions: Changes in the American Environment

Unions are not a new phenomenon in American life. There were scattered efforts to form trade unions early in the nineteenth century and, by the close of the century, the American Federation of Labor was well established in a number of skilled crafts. Yet until the 1930's union membership outside these crafts was highly unstable. Though unskilled workers sometimes joined unions in time of prosperity, they abandoned them when hard times returned. This pattern began to change drastically during the great

4

The Impact of the Union

depression of the 1930's, when a relatively large, permanent trade-union membership emerged not only in the traditional crafts where workers had found it easier to organize, but also in mass-production industry.

Certain changes in the American economic and political environment coincided with this growth:

1. The depression cost American business a great deal in terms of prestige and employee confidence. The unions, on the other hand, gained in prestige. Many observers regarded them as a healthy check on business power (a check that might help to moderate the business cycle). Gradually unions began to escape the un-American stigma they had borne for decades.

2. Government at both the state and federal levels, which had traditionally handicapped union organization (e.g., by unfavorable court decisions and the use of injunctions), became more favorably disposed to labor. In fact, new legislation like the Wagner Act (1935) actively encouraged union organization.

3. A substantial segment of the working population began to accept as permanent the role of wage-earner, realizing that it was not just a temporary stop on the road to owning one's own business. As we observed in Chapter 1, the American dream of moving constantly along to better jobs had lost its luster for some and had been replaced by a desire to protect the present situation. With this acceptance came an interest in improving one's lot as an employee through union membership.

4. The decline in immigration and the rise in educational standards have tended to make our population more homogeneous. Frictions among minority groups that once made union organization difficult are disappearing. Relatively high standards of education have raised the level of employee aspiration. No longer satisfied with just having a job, they are demanding more and more from their jobs. And they regard the union as a valuable ally in getting what they want.

5. The unions' growth provides some of its own impetus. Greater acceptance of unions by the community, and increased union prestige as a result of participation in civic and governmental affairs, increase the attractiveness of membership, as does identification of the steadily rising wage level since 1940 with the increasing strength of unions.

Why Employees Join Unions: Organization Problems

Almost every union member is also an employee and has joined his union because he hopes it will better his relationship with his employer. Why does he feel this is necessary? Many managers have two oversimplified explanations of why workers join unions: The first is that the company has been foolish or selfish, or both. By providing unsatisfactory working conditions and wages, by permitting supervisors to play favorites, management has actually encouraged its employees to seek out a union. Such conditions undoubtedly stimulate the growth of unions. But what about the many well-managed organizations that have been unionized? What has motivated the workers of these companies to join unions?

Here is where the other explanation comes into play. Unionization, it says, must be the result of outside agitators, rabble-rousers, and radicals who by lies and deceit stir up an otherwise satisfied work force. This reason also is an oversimplification. To be sure, professional organizers from the outside have a great deal to do with bringing workers into the union fold. And they often make use of a small number of strategically located insiders who are willing to take on the task of agitating for the new union. But this is only a small part of the total explanation.

Below we have summarized the opinions of many careful observers of union organization.

DESIRE TO CONTROL BENEFITS RECEIVED

In our society, many employees are unhappy when they are completely dependent on someone else for the satisfaction of their needs. Even when that "someone else" is very good, as many managements have been, and provides good wages, steady employment, and desirable working conditions, workers tend to be uneasy when they have no power to control the benefits received. In fact, management makes matters worse by emphasizing how much it has "given" its employees (that is, benefits provided at the discretion of the company, not given because they *had to* be given). In telling people that they should be thankful for what has been voluntarily given them, the company is also saying that what it has given can also be taken away. Employees also wonder what they are going to have to give in return for these gifts—how much extra effort, what display of loyalty. Also, being the recipient of another's generosity generates a feeling of insecurity, for it implies that the recipient is somewhat child-like and must be "taken care of" by a "father who knows best."

Even in organizations where employees have always been treated with complete fairness and justice, stories circulate that John Jones over in Department 16 has been severely penalized for something he didn't do because a supervisor "had it in for him." In any situation where we lack the power to control what happens to us, we are more than ready to believe these "atrocity" stories and think, "Next time that could happen to us." The truth or falsity of the rumor may be unimportant.

Furthermore, in a large company where top management is many levels removed from the individual employee, the individual's sense of dependency and lack of control over what happens to him is magnified.

DESIRE FOR SELF-EXPRESSION AND MEANS
OF COMMUNICATING TO HIGHER MANAGEMENT

Many an employee feels that as far as his company is concerned he is nothing more than a time-clock number. Though few workers would want the responsibility of management, they would like greater opportunity to express themselves. In part, this is just the desire to complain when hurt. More important, as individuals we all have a need to express our point of view, not just to "get more" for ourselves, but to enjoy the feeling of being a whole person instead of a pair of hired hands.

The single employee is reluctant to express his opinions to his boss, but the union promises him an opportunity to protest inequities, to believe that if something goes wrong he will have a chance to be heard. The union offers a direct road to participation, for its leaders have access to the top decision-making levels of the organization.

Without a union, most employees feel they have no means of "safely" going over the head of their boss with a problem. This feeling of helplessness is particularly acute when the immediate supervisor is unsympathetic to their demands either because he has no decision-making authority of his own (a point that will become clearer when we discuss organizational problems in Chapter 15), or because he has a natural unwillingness to reverse his own decisions. If only they can gain access to higher levels in the organization, employees reason, they may find someone with the authority to satisfy their requests. The union seems a good means of gaining that access.

Without a representative to speak for them, workers are naturally reluctant to bypass their supervisor and state openly that they are dissatisfied with his decisions. After all, they must rely on this man to do many things for them. There are a hundred and one ways in which a supervisor can make their working life unpleasant and unrewarding. Discretion is frequently the better part of valor; when the supervisor says "No," most employees accept it as the final word.

Full-time union leaders, who do not depend on management for their livelihood, have no fear whatsoever of management retaliation and are more than eager to speak up vigorously. By making the worker part of a united group, the union provides him with a mechanism for making his demands heard.

DESIRE FOR ACCEPTANCE IN THE GROUP

Once the union has established itself in the organization, it begins to fill other needs as well. One of the most important of these needs is the desire to be an accepted member of the group. Few of us want to be left out of something that those with whom we live and work are sharing. The union gives a sense of belonging, of being accepted as "one of the boys." And it also exerts social pressure on those who aren't members:

> "No, I don't like unions. I never had anything to do with them before. But in a company like this, you've got to join—it's the thing to do, just like getting all dressed up to go to church."

IMPROVEMENT OF ECONOMIC CONDITIONS

Most people want *more* than they are getting—even in top-paying companies. Seldom do we find a man who is convinced that the economic returns and physical satisfactions provided by his job are perfect and quite beyond improvement. In the United States, the greatest growth period of unions has coincided with a rapidly rising income level for workers. Whether the unions have really obtained higher wages, better pension, insurance, and other benefits for their members, or whether these would have come anyway through normal economic and social processes, is not the point; the point is that an impressive number of employees *believe* that unions are responsible for improving their economic lot.

CONTRACT COERCION

Even stronger pressures to join a union are provided by the *union security* agreements negotiated in labor contracts. The most typical of these, the "union-shop" clause, requires all new employees in a particular firm (after some brief probationary period) to join and pay dues to the union that has won bargaining rights. If they fail to join, they must forfeit their job. A government survey in 1954 found that two-thirds of all labor contracts sampled provided for such a condition of employment, thus insuring that unions in these companies will automatically obtain all new employees as members.[1]

These explanations of the growth of unions are summarized in the following statement by one noted observer of the union movement:

> ... The worker's job is more than a means of earning an income. It is also a way of life. A union develops when enough workers in a plant conclude that the union will make their life in the plant more satisfying than it has been in the past. [We would add: and when they conclude that the union will help them hold on to things they have found satisfying in the past but are fearful of losing.] The decision to join is by no means strictly a rational decision. It is probably more like religious conversion than like deciding to buy a pair of shoes. The worker does not estimate whether the results he will get from the union will be worth the dues he

---

[1] Theodore Rose, "Union Security Provisions in Agreements, 1954," *Monthly Labor Review*, Vol. 78 (1955), pp. 649-658. Union-management agreements which require union membership as a condition of employment are not legal in those states that have passed so-called "right-to-work" laws, however.

pays. He is confronted with an emotional appeal, an urge to take part in a social and political crusade, and he finally decides to accept. Moreover, the decision to join is usually not an individualistic decison. The first few workers in a plant who join the union have to make up their own minds. After a nucleus has been secured, however, the growth of the union develops into a mass movement. Most of the workers join because others have done so, and holdouts are gradually brought into line by the pressure of social ostracism in the plant.[2]

PRECIPITATING CAUSES

We have been describing some of the underlying reasons for the growth of unions. But how can we explain why a union is organized in a particular company at a specific time? Here are some typical precipitating causes:

1. A change in the top management of the plant. Employees fear that the new management will be less friendly and will not preserve the favorable conditions they are used to.

2. Specific problems arising from incentive payment systems, particularly new standards.

3. The cutting off of promotional ladders—for example, requiring that all new supervisors have college degrees.

4. Sudden cutbacks and layoffs.

Why Some Workers Don't Join Unions

Not every employee, of course, belongs to a union, although federal and many state laws protect the right of workers to join if they want to.[3] Approximately 17.5 million Americans are members of trade unions; but this membership is not equally distributed geographically or industrially, nor has total union membership expanded recently in the United States. Unions have been more successful in the older and more heavily populated industrial centers of the East and Midwest. They have been less successful in the South. Manufacturing, mining, transportation, and public utilities have been relatively well organized. It has been estimated recently, for example, that approximately 80 to 90 per cent of the eligible employees in manufacturing and public utility plants in the more heavily industrialized sections of the country are union members.[4] On the other hand, office workers and those

---

[2] Lloyd Reynolds, *Labor Economics and Labor Relations* (Englewood Cliffs, N. J.: Prentice-Hall, 1954), p. 60.

[3] The basic federal statute protecting the right of workers to join unions and prohibiting employers from interfering with the organization of unions is the National Labor Relations Act of 1935 (the Wagner Act) as amended by the Labor-Management Relations Act of 1947 (the Taft-Hartley Act) and the Labor-Management Reporting and Disclosure Act of 1959 (the Landrum-Griffin Act).

[4] Neil W. Chamberlain, *Labor* (New York: McGraw-Hill, 1958), pp. 10-12.

in the service industries and in wholesale and retail trade have not been receptive to union organization. Except in the largest cities, the proportion of employees unionized in these industries hovers around 10 per cent.[5] Women and professional workers have tended to shy away from union membership.

Since union membership is associated with "blue-collar work," many white-collar employees fear that joining a union would lower their social status. Many of these employees work in close proximity to management and hope to move into management positions themselves.[6] Further, the fact that they are broken down into small, uncohesive groups makes it difficult for them to develop the kind of consensus necessary for union organization.[7] Professional and technical employees tend to believe that they can get along "on their own" and that their individual chances for advancement should not be tied to the status of the whole group.

As we suggested earlier, some communities—for example, small towns in the South—have been hostile to unions for a variety of historical and social reasons. Understandably, employees in these communities shy away from union membership.

The recent failure of unions to expand may also be attributed to a series of blows to their status in American life. One of the most important of these was the evidence of corruption turned up by Senator McClellan's Senate Committee (The Select Committee on Improper Activities in the Labor and Management Field). Although the majority of American unions were not involved in this corruption, a significant number of instances were disclosed in which union leaders committed illegal acts. Essentially two types of crimes were involved, and both were more concentrated in unions bargaining with small, widely scattered employers. Corrupt leaders threatened strikes and boycotts if company officials refused to hand over sums of money for their personal use. This small number of unscrupulous leaders also tapped accumulated dues and premiums paid to health and welfare funds by employees and employers.[8] Both types of crime indicated that part of the union movement had been infiltrated by men who were interested in their personal aggrandizement at the expense of the welfare of the organization. As a result of these disclosures, the union movement lost some of its reputation for crusading for improvements in the status of the common man.

There has been growing management resistance to union demands for

---

[5] *Ibid.*, p. 12.

[6] George Strauss, "White Collar Workers are Different!" *Harvard Business Review*, Vol. 32, No. 5 (October 1954), pp. 73-82.

[7] Interestingly, engineers join unions when they work closely together in large undifferentiated groups, as in some of the huge aircraft and electronics plants.

[8] Since many of the funds were supposed to be jointly administered by the company and the union, management bears some responsibility in not exercising closer surveillance. Some employers also sought to bribe union leaders as a means of obtaining easier contract terms ("sweetheart agreements," as they are called).

improved economic benefits. The union's ability to participate in day-to-day decision-making affecting employee work loads and standards has come under sharp scrutiny. Management opposition to union gains, emanating in part from increased competitiveness in product markets and decreased shortages in labor markets, has also served to detract from the union's momentum and prestige.

Internal Organization of the Union

THE LOCAL UNION

Now let us look at the rather complex structure of the unions themselves. Some employees are organized on the basis of the company or plant in which they work—for example, all the employees of the Carter Chemical Company's Atlanta plant are eligible to join an *industrial* local union whose membership is restricted to these employees. Frequently the white-collar clerical employees of such a company, or its most highly skilled maintenance employees, may belong to separate local unions. Industries that employ several clearly defined trades are usually not organized by unions on a plant or company basis. Rather, all employees in a given geographic area, usually a community, who have the qualifications to practice the trade, are eligible for membership in a *craft* local union—for example, all unionized bricklayers in Rochester, New York, belong to the same local, regardless of which employer they work for. Community-wide locals are also found where the employer unit is relatively small (for example, all the dry-cleaning plant employees in town might belong to a single local of the Teamsters), or where employees are likely to shift from one employer to another (for example in the needle trades).

Why do we emphasize this difference between unions that are organized on the basis of an employer unit, and unions that are organized on the basis of a geographic area? Because the governments of these two types of local union are quite different. Where the membership is derived from many different companies in a clearly defined geographical area, the union is likely to vest a great deal of authority in an elected *business agent,* who works full time on the negotiation of contracts, grievance problems, and the protection of the union's job jurisdiction.[9] Since these agents service many widely dispersed members who work for a variety of employers, they are very powerful and management must be willing to deal regularly with them. Unfortunately, most of the corruption mentioned above has arisen in this

---

[9] Chapter 19 discusses the role of this type of union in obtaining jobs for members. Unions organized on the basis of an employer unit are usually not active in getting jobs for members, nor are they concerned with making sure that no job in the community for which one of their members is qualified is filled by a non-member. For a detailed description and analysis of "business agent" type unions, see George Strauss, *Unions in the Building Trades* (Buffalo: University of Buffalo, 1958).

type of union, and, because of the growth of so-called service industries in the United States, this type is expanding at the expense of unions organized by employer units.

By contrast, in unions organized on a company or plant basis authority usually is dispersed among a number of leaders, many of whom continue to work at their regular jobs.

THE LOCAL LEADERSHIP

The local union has two types of officer: *Executive-board members* handle the union's internal business—finances, administration of election procedures, appointment of committee members, social functions, and so forth.[10] *Grievance officials* handle relationships with management—the union's collective bargaining business. These latter officials have a variety of titles, depending on the union and their rank—business agents, committeemen, stewards, grievancemen, chief stewards, and so forth. Most of these officials continue to work for the company in their regular jobs while they are serving in their union capacity, and the company often pays for the time they spend handling employee grievances. Larger and wealthier locals, however, may engage full-time elected officials to handle their grievances and negotiations.

THE MEMBERSHIP

The most active union members—the elected officers—are employees who have more energy and ambition than they can expend on their jobs. Essentially discontented and anxious to get ahead, they often turn to the union when their drives are frustrated elsewhere.[11] Many of these men may be excellent workers, and management frequently finds that leadership in the union may provide a clue to supervisory ability.

This active group, together with members who do not hold office but who attend union meetings and participate in the local's political life, is likely to include no more than 5 per cent of the membership, and frequently a good bit less. Most of the members prefer to "let George do it" when it comes to taking an active role. They pay their dues as they would pay premiums on an insurance policy, and they have little to do with the organization except when a grievance arises or when a strike takes place.

Few members seem to feel that union membership conflicts with their loyalty to the company that provides them with job and wages. For many, the union is a way of "making the company better." Of course, unions also attract

---

[10] In some unions, the executive board is involved at some stage of the grievance procedure as well.

[11] Leonard Sayles and George Strauss, *The Local Union* (New York: Harpers, 1953), pp. 99-132.

members with deep-seated hostility toward management who seek to embarrass their supervisors through union activity.

THE INTERNATIONAL UNION [12]

Most local unions are affiliated with an international union that provides them with certain services. You are probably familiar with the names of many of these organizations: The Steelworkers, the Autoworkers, the Teamsters, the Carpenters.[13] Primarily, the internationals deal with union problems that are out of reach of the local, such as industry-wide bargaining problems, government relations, and organizing the unorganized.

The international union usually hires "international representatives" to help the local union get established and to present local bargaining problems directly to management. These officials often participate in the later stages of the grievance procedure, which is described in the next section. Their most important job, however, is usually the handling of contract negotiations. The decision-making body for the international union is the *convention*, which is held once every year or two, or even more infrequently.

A large number of American international unions have joined together in the AFL-CIO, which serves as a general trade union organization.[14] It has almost no direct power over collective bargaining matters, for most of its activities concern internal union problems and relationships with the government. There are also other units in the union movement, such as city councils and state federations, organized to deal primarily with various levels of local and state government.

THE UNION AS A POLITICAL BODY

If management is to deal with the union successfully, it must recognize that the union is a political body. Nearly all union officials—at both the local and international levels—are elected, and many union decisions, particularly at the local level, are made by direct membership vote. Thus, most decisions do not flow from top down as they do in management; officers cannot guarantee that the members will do as they are told, particularly in democratic unions, and members can always engage in wild-cat strikes. Consequently, in order to win elections, officers must always win something in their negotiations with management. They frequently go through the motions of pressing grievances in which they do not believe.

There is widespread apathy among union members—for example, the local

---

[12] The national organization is usually referred to as the "international" union in recognition of the fact that it may have members in Canada.

[13] These are not the formal names of these international unions, but they are commonly referred to in this fashion.

[14] A number of large, important international unions are not included in the AFL-CIO, such as the railroad brotherhoods, the Teamsters, and the Mineworkers.

union meeting, which is the major decision-making forum for the local, is usually very poorly attended. And yet, in spite of this apathy, management must recognize that what the union leaders do must at least *appear* to the members as satisfying their needs. Failure to recognize this fact may lead to a serious miscalculation of the behavior of union leaders. While a top-management official in a negotiation may be able to make firm decisions on his own, the union negotiator may have to get membership approval before he can make a binding commitment. Unions are certainly not models of pure democracy, but in most unions an aroused membership can turn out its leadership in favor of another group.

The Union-Management Relationship

How does the existence of a union affect company personnel adminis-tration? It is not enough for management to say, "Sure, we have a union. It's out to protect its members and get as much for them as it can." Typical union-management problems involve a number of different people in both organizations, with distinctive points of view and interests. As a result, most labor-management problems are quite complex.

Union-management relations are seen most dramatically during *contract negotiations,* when the parties meet together to determine the wages, fringe benefits, and working rules that will prevail until a new contract is nego-tiated one, two, or more years from now. But the negotiation of labor agree-ments takes much less time than the handling of *grievances.*

Even when a union exists, management continues to make most of the personnel decisions: who shall be hired, disciplined, promoted, given an increase in pay, have his working conditions or hours of work changed, and so on. Very few such decisions are ever made jointly, although the contract is designed to establish certain limits or checks on the decisions that man-agement can make in these areas. *After* a supervisor takes action, however, the union can challenge the decision and file a grievance claiming that man-agement is acting in violation of either the contract or of past practice (which becomes the equivalent of the contract).

JOHN JONES HAS A GRIEVANCE

Let us examine a hypothetical case to illustrate the ramifications of what may appear to be a simple grievance involving a typical management personnel decision. Notice especially the number of people who are involved and their diverse points of view and strategies, and the many decisions that must be made by the participants.[15]

---

[15] This case does not describe the exact procedure by which every employee com-plaint would be handled. The number of steps and the union and management personnel

The employee's problem   John Jones works as a laboratory assistant in the animal experimentation station of a large drug company. His work involves feeding, washing, and weighing animals, building cages, and occasionally cleaning them. Recently, Jones has noticed that he is required to spend much more time cleaning cages than do the other assistants. Since this is the least pleasant and lowest-status of all his tasks, he thinks it is unfair that he should have to do so much of it.

The supervisor's reaction   When Jones discusses his problem with the supervisor, Brown, he is told that job assignments are arranged in order to use the work force most efficiently. All assistants are hired with the understanding that they will be doing one or all of the tasks noted above. Brown feels that some of the other men are more skilled in handling the animals and doing minor construction work. So it seems a better use of manpower to have Jones spend more of his time cleaning cages.

Enter the union   Unsatisfied by Brown's answer, Jones considers calling in the union for help. He hesitates for a while, for fear that such a step may antagonize his supervisor and win him the reputation of troublemaker. Then he decides that after all this is what he pays dues for. So Jones contacts the union steward for the laboratory, who happens to work in an adjacent building, and the steward discusses the problem with Brown. The steward reports back to Jones the next day:

> "Brown refuses to do anything. He says it's his job to make decisions like this one, and he is not trying to discriminate against you. I'm not satisfied with his answer. I'll see the chief steward tonight at the union meeting and see what he says."

Note what has happened: The steward has tried unsuccessfully to represent the worker and now has turned the case over to a higher level in the union which can contact higher management.

The union's reaction   The steward goes to the chief steward and describes the case. Here is the chief steward's reaction:

> "This is not a simple case; we have to be careful. In the first place we have to consider the reaction of the other men in the department. Jones is the newest employee; they may get pretty sore if more of this cleaning work is thrown at them. Secondly, the whole thing may backfire. Our present contract is weak on this point. There is actually nothing to prevent the company from changing a man's work, and if they start giving him a lot of the dirty jobs if they want to be mean about it, they might be able to justify paying him less money since his work may now be less skilled

---

who become involved at each step vary greatly from one labor contract to another. But this case is not atypical. Many "grievances" do not get written down and processed through a formal procedure; they are handled verbally in the regular, day-to-day contacts of union and management officials.

than before. Our only chance to win would be if we could show that the supervisor was doing this to Jones because he didn't like him. That would be covered by Clause 14. Discuss it with Jones and, if he has some evidence on this, get him to sign a grievance."

Note the implication behind this reaction: The union is not just the representative of the individual worker. It also has to think of its total membership. Actually, many grievances and worker demands are directed against other employees, not against management. One employee wants the "dirty work" to be given to another; younger workers want a big wage increase; older workers would prefer greater pension benefits. Several departments struggle among themselves for seniority rights or a new job that has just been created. The union depends on the support of its total membership; dissatisfied members may succeed in ejecting officers from office or in overthrowing the union itself. Clearly, the union must consider the over-all implications of each grievance and demand.

Moreover, the union has to consider its strategic position vis-à-vis management. The union has certain institutional objectives. For example, it is seeking to strengthen its own position in the company somewhat independently of particular employee or group needs. Creating a fuss about Jones' complaint might lead management to insist on its contractual right to change jobs as it sees fit. Of course, the union might be aroused to seek a stronger contract at the next negotiations.

The middle steps of the grievance procedure   Jones agrees to sign the formal grievance papers charging Brown with discrimination. He notes on the printed form that his assignment to excessive cleaning duties followed an argument with Brown over new coveralls. "When I complained that my coveralls [supplied by the company] were too torn, Brown said I was always complaining and ought to have something to really complain about for a change." The grievance is also signed by the steward; the supervisor himself signs it, but only after adding this note: "Grievance refused—employee has not been discriminated against." Then the chief steward sends the grievance to the laboratory manager, asking for an appointment to talk the matter over.

Management's reaction   When the manager receives the grievance, he calls in the supervisor, Brown, to get his version of the case; he also checks with the personnel director to see whether similar cases have established precedents in this area that would affect the settlement.

The manager is at first concerned that this might be a case of discrimination. The company has a firm policy that no supervisor is to allow personal feelings to enter into personnel decisions. Having satisfied himself that Brown was right, the manager feels that he cannot grant the grievance. To do so would be to open the door to a stream of union challenges of work assignments. The manager tells the chief steward that, even though a man may feel he is getting more than his share of the unpleasant jobs, it is up to the supervisor to make such decisions in accordance with his own work requirements and the available manpower. So, while he will caution Brown to make sure such assignments are dictated by work needs and not by his personal feelings toward particular employees, the grievance will have to be refused. He writes: "No contract violation, supervisor was acting within normal management prerogatives."

Higher levels of the grievance procedure   The next move is clearly up to the union. The chief steward and the steward explain to Jones that he has a weak case. No one has heard the supervisor threaten Jones and, even if the supervisor admitted using threats, that would not prove he was discriminating. Well, yes, there are some other steps that might be taken. The union's business agent could take the case up with the division superintendent of the drug company. If the company still refused to agree to divide the work up more equitably, the case could then be taken to arbitration.[16]

The chances of winning, however, are not good, Jones is told. The chief steward advises Jones to be alert for other evidence of discrimination that would enable the union to reopen the case. He promises that the union will also try to obtain a contract clause next year to prohibit, without specific union approval, changes in work assignments that are equivalent to job transfers.

Even though the chances of success were very slight, the chief steward might have decided to push the case anyway. Grievances provide interesting, challenging work and relieve the monotony of his highly routine job in the company. And yet most union leaders are not anxious to build up a reputation for pressing "poor cases" too vigorously. They want their opposite numbers in management to believe that they are sensible men who can tell the difference between just and unjust claims—but that they are also tough, of course.

Effect of Union Activities on Personnel Administration

What over-all effect does the existence of a union have on the organization as a whole and on the management of personnel? The following discussion, which goes beyond the specific grievance problems we have described, will also suggest some of the reasons why many companies have resisted unionization.

---

[16] Most union-management agreements provide for the introduction of a third party, an impartial outsider, to decide grievance issues that have not been resolved through the normal grievance procedure. Arbitration is designed to preclude the use of strikes or lock-outs in the grievance procedure, although these economic pressure weapons are retained for use during disputes over new contracts.

CHALLENGES MANAGEMENT DECISIONS

The existence of a union means that all personnel decisions are subject to close scrutiny and, perhaps, active challenge. In a non-union situation, employees may grow dissatisfied and harbor a sense of injustice or injury, but they are not necessarily willing to express their attitudes. The union gives them a means of taking action, not only by approaching the immediate supervisor, but also by reaching higher in the management structure with their demands. For the manager who relishes unchecked authority, this is an unpleasant experience, and almost any supervisor would prefer to have his orders and decisions go unchallenged.

Furthermore, the union is in a strategic position to compete with management for the loyalty of employees. For example, it may try to claim credit for any improvement in wages or vacations—even implying that these benefits had to be wrung from an unwilling management. Particularly in the organizational stage, when the union is trying to establish itself, it may caricature company executives and their "desire to sweat labor." Such charges of dishonesty and high-handed tyranny come as a rude shock to executives, particularly to those who think of themselves as benevolent, thoughtful employers. These managers are likely to fear that the union will deprive them of the opportunity to serve as protectors of their employees.

FORCES BETTER PERSONNEL POLICIES

The awareness that the union is ready to challenge supervisory actions stimulates management to exercise more care in shaping personnel policies. Mistakes can be costly, not only in terms of the time and goodwill lost through grievance-processing, but also in terms of the new contractual demands that are likely to spring from employee dissatisfaction. For example, in one company the supervisors made a habit of asking workers just before quitting time to work overtime and pressured those who had other commitments either to stay or face the consequences. Here the union demanded and won a clear-cut contractual prohibition against mandatory overtime work.

Thus, in all the areas that we shall discuss later on—for example, selection, promotion, wage administration, assessment, supervision, and discipline— the growth of unions has been an impetus to the development of better personnel policies.

THREATENS EFFICIENCY

Management resists the union not just because of the union's effect on the decision-making process, but also because of its possible effect on costs and efficiency. The union usually wants to introduce rigid rules preventing one man from doing another man's work. If a supervisor is prevented from assigning work in a way that will take advantage of the employees' aptitudes and experience, management reasons that labor costs are bound to go up. So, too, management fears that the union may want to introduce barriers to efficient work methods, reduce work loads, and, in general, hold back productivity.

TENDS TO LIFT PERSONNEL DECISION-MAKING
TO HIGHER LEVELS OF MANAGEMENT

A supervisor who fails to understand the contract may inadvertently prompt an embarrassing grievance and strengthen the union's argument that the company is "unfair." A thoughtless decision in one department may set a precedent that will be very costly to the company for a long period of time in other departments as well. For example, in our hypothetical case above, the laboratory manager was anxious to avoid establishing the precedent that work assignments were not a management prerogative. Fearing such contingencies, many companies have withdrawn from lower-level supervisors the authority to make certain personnel decisions.[17] This authority has been delegated to higher levels of management and, in many cases, newly formed or enlarged staff departments with specialists trained in labor relations have been given a more important role in personnel.[18]

INTRODUCES "OUTSIDERS" INTO THE FIRM'S LABOR RELATIONS

As we have seen, the membership of a union usually embraces people outside the firm as well as inside.[19] Not only does the union have institutional goals distinct from those of the company (it wants to grow and prosper and its officers want to be re-elected), but it is also concerned with more than one employer. The union seeks wage increases in one company to set a precedent that will make it easier to negotiate a favorable contract elsewhere. Frequently arbitration decisions set precedents affecting labor relations in many companies. As a result, many company officials feel that the problems to which union officers force them to devote time are not restricted to the interests of the particular organization and its employees.

As we observed above, some local unions are headed by full-time business agents who have no formal association with the firms with which they negotiate. International representatives, of course, may be even further removed

---

[17] The changing organizational position of the supervisor is explained in greater detail in Chapter 15.

[18] The problems created by the growing importance of staff personnel departments are analyzed in Chapter 18.

[19] Many independent unions, however, which are not affiliated with international unions, have no organizational relationships beyond the company in which they are organized.

from the scene, although they may have a direct influence on the actions of the local union.

In principle, many managers resent the fact that the union brings "outsiders" onto the scene; in practice, however, they often find that the outsiders are more dispassionate and better able to understand the company's side of a grievance than their own employees would be.[20]

Evolution of Sound Union-Management Relations

There is little question that the introduction of a union may prove a traumatic experience for management. At the outset, the union may try to dramatize every company mistake, and the early days may be spent in destructive warfare rather than in the constructive solution of problems. In many firms this period may drag on for years in a kind of armed truce, with both sides trying to capitalize on the mistakes of the other. Gradually, however, most managers learn to live with the union and may even come to admit that the union has had a beneficial effect on the organization.

OPPORTUNITIES FOR IMPROVED PERSONNEL RELATIONS

To the management that is willing to explore new techniques, the introduction of a union into the organization need not be a catastrophe. The union can actually help management improve employee relationships.

Labor relations involve a problem that every company must face, whether or not its workers are unionized: this is the problem of adjusting the needs of the individual to the needs of the organization. Without a union, employees may find other means of protesting what they think is unfair: slowdowns, sabotage, or quitting. The union provides a peaceful means of resolving such disputes or differences in a way that will maintain productivity and preserve the work force intact.

Increasingly, managers are recognizing the merits of informal discussion of common problems. Even on subjects solely within the area of management prerogatives, they are learning that the union can serve as a channel of communication with the work force and can provide an aid in discovering and correcting weak spots in the plant.

Supervisors who are sensitive to human relations prefer to obtain group agreement before initiating changes in work procedure. Rather than deal

---

[20] Managers even find themselves facing this dilemma: Some unions which are not democratic, where the officers are not directly responsive to the demands of the membership, are easier to negotiate with than more democratic unions. Because the leadership in the latter group must face constant political criticism, they must be more careful of the agreements when the political pressure becomes great—e.g., when a wildcat strike seems to be gaining widespread membership support.

with a large number of individuals with diverse points of view, they realize that it is far more efficient to sit down with a responsible union leader. He is the single spokesman, who presumably represents the unified opinion of the entire work group and can subsequently sell his opinion to the group. In a sense, strong local unions are a guarantee that agreements will be honored.

Management learns that it can introduce changes in working conditions with much less friction if it consults with the union beforehand. Rather than sitting back and waiting for the union to raise problems, the company can make the first move and involve union officials in clearing up potential trouble areas.

> "We knew we were going to have a lot of squawks over new job assignments when we brought automation into the department. This could have meant a hundred grievances and months of wasteful talk. Instead we went to the union and told them what our plans were, how many of what kinds of jobs there would be after the change. We got them to work with us in deciding who was going to stay in the department and how transfers would be arranged. We also negotiated the rates on the new jobs."

Consulting with the union prior to the development of grievances often produces a valuable by-product. As we have seen, union officials are typically active men who want to keep busy. If they can be involved in handling constructive questions, they are less likely to seek out problems and grievances.

THE SUPERVISOR'S ROLE

The chances of converting hostility-ridden, destructive labor relations into a constructive pattern depend largely on the ability of the supervisor to adapt to the existence of the union. When a union is first established, the supervisor may have difficulty dealing with subordinates who are also active union organizers. At the outset, he needs to distinguish between the outspoken rabble-rouser and the genuine informal leader. The free-wheeling organizer may be motivated by deep-seated personality problems or personal grievances. Often he does not have the confidence of the group as a whole.

Instead of assuming that aggressive talk and behavior are in themselves evidence of valid leadership, the supervisor should give the members of the group an opportunity to decide whether the man who tries to usurp leadership is in fact the man they want as a leader. If they perceive that he is prompted by selfish motives and is overbearing and clumsy in his approach, they may reject him voluntarily. On the other hand, if the supervisor attempts to punish him, he may become a martyr and actually gain the group's support.

In short, the supervisor should recognize that most employees experience no serious conflict between loyalty to the union (which they see as a sort of insurance program to protect them against future contingencies) and loyalty to management (to whom they owe appreciation for their jobs and economic well-being). So, if the supervisor rejects or becomes suspicious of everyone who expresses pro-union sentiments, he may alienate a number of very capable employees who, were they accorded responsibility and trust, might have identified themselves strongly with the company.

The manager also should be alert to the special problems affecting the union leader's behavior: he may be under conflicting pressures, one group wanting him to do one thing, another group insisting on something else. The manager should recognize the political position of the union leader and learn how to cope with him intelligently rather than bemoaning the fact that unions are political institutions.

> Management representatives quickly learn to differentiate between the grievances on which the union leaders face strong political pressures and those which they are merely "going through motions" of pressing. . . . A shrewd management learns not to embarrass union officials before a close election. . . .
>
> We have observed many episodes such as the following telephone call by a union leader to a personnel director:
>
> "Look, Bill, we'll admit that Charlie Jones was drunk last week. Frankly we don't have a leg to stand on. If you'll take it easy on him—after all this is his first offense—we'll waive the formal hearing. And that'll save you a lot of time and money. . . ."
>
> These are not collusive dealings but rather part of the flexible process by which both sides adjust to new problem situations which could not have been foreseen when the contract was written.[21]

Thus, as time passes, the union abandons its role as a *competitor* for the loyalty of the worker. It takes on the role of a *policeman* who calls "halt" when a company representative makes a mistake, but who also keeps the member-employee within the bounds of legal decisions and practices. In some companies, this evolutionary process advances to the point where the union becomes a genuine *collaborator,* sharing with management the problems of improving efficiency and productivity. This is a subject we shall return to in Chapter 28.

Conclusion

Although the union cannot eliminate management's responsibility for the conduct of personnel administration, it can become an integral part of the personnel program. Even though its roots lie outside the organization, its existence is a reflection of employee needs and dissatisfactions. Some personnel problems, particularly in larger organizations, may be almost beyond the ability of management to solve, and the manager need not feel

---

[21] Sayles and Strauss, *op. cit.,* pp. 18-19.

that the establishment of a union is evidence of his own failure. Thus, it is unrealistic to think of personnel administration as an *alternative* to unionization.

Union-management relations provide another challenge for management. In many companies, the necessity of working through these problems is just as much a part of the managerial job as developing budgets and work schedules, and issuing orders. While negotiation and consultation are time-consuming, frequently frustrating, and certainly threatening, they require some of the same supervisory skills and persistence that are necessary to carry out other management functions. These responsibilities cannot be avoided, nor would it be healthful for the organization if they could.

This chapter has hardly scratched the surface of the role of the union in organizations. Readers who are interested in further information on union organization, union policies, and collective bargaining may find excellent summaries of current research in the following publications:

E. Wight Bakke, *Mutual Survival: The Goal of Unions and Management* (New York: Harpers, 1947).

Jack Barbash, *The Practice of Unionism* (New York: Harpers, 1956). An "insider's" account of how unions operate.

Neil W. Chamberlain, *Labor* (New York: McGraw-Hill, 1958). A scholarly textbook that carefully surveys the entire field.

N. W. Chamberlain, F. C. Pierson, and T. Wolfson, eds., *A Decade of Industrial Relations Research* (New York: Harpers, 1959). A good review of most of the research that has been carried on in the academic world during the preceding ten years, as summarized by seven respected authorities.

Frederick H. Harbison and John R. Coleman, *Goals and Strategy in Collective Bargaining* (New York: Harpers, 1951). A short but highly important book that describes the varying degrees of harmony in union-management relationships.

A. Kornhauser, R. Dubin, and A. M. Ross, eds., *Industrial Conflict* (New York: McGraw-Hill, 1954). A collection of essays by outstanding authorities who view labor relations from the psychological, sociological, and economic points of view, respectively.

Lloyd G. Reynolds, *Labor Economics and Labor Relations*, 3rd ed. (Englewood Cliffs, N. J.: Prentice-Hall, 1959). One of the most widely used textbooks, covering the entire field of labor economics and labor relations.

Leonard R. Sayles and George Strauss, *The Local Union* (New York: Harpers, 1953). The results of several years of field study in the organization and day-to-day problems of a variety of local unions.

Benjamin M. Selekman, *Labor Relations and Human Relations* (New York: McGraw-Hill, 1947). An older but highly respected analysis of the intimacies of plant-level industrial relations.

Joseph Shister, *Economics of the Labor Market*, 2nd ed. (Chicago: Lippincott, 1956). A dispassionate, scholarly text.

Problem I

Harold Keller has worked twenty years for the James Company. During that period, he has risen to the top of his promotion ladder: a machinist first-class and one of the highest-paid nonsupervisory employees in the company. About five years ago, the workers in the company were organized by a union; Keller played no active part in the organizing campaign. About a year ago, Keller developed an illness that was difficult to diagnose; although he lost strength and energy, he was able to continue at work. Because of his good record and long service, the company found a number of special assignments for him and maintained his wages until he regained his health.

Just recently, the men in the machine shop in which Keller worked staged a wildcat one-day walk-out that did not have the formal authorization of the local union. Employees in other departments were not involved. The men in the machine shop claimed that their wages had declined relative to wages in many other departments because they had had no opportunity to work more than 40 hours a week. Men in many of the other departments were working 45 hours and 50 hours a week.

Much to the surprise and disappointment of the machine-shop supervisor, Keller not only participated in this protest demonstration, but actually appeared to be one of the leaders.

1. Does Keller's action seem reasonable in light of the consideration management accorded him during his illness?
2. What should the supervisor do with Keller now?
3. How typical do you think this case is?
4. What is your reaction to the complaint of the men in the machine shop?

Problem II

The company guards at the Rembrandt Company were among the last groups to join a union, but they had always expressed a great deal of dissatisfaction over their work schedules. For many years there had been charges of favoritism in the assignment of work hours. Guard work had to be carried on around the clock, and employees who were assigned to the less desirable shifts or to week-end duty complained that they should have better working hours.

The issue of "fair working schedules" was plugged hard by the new union in signing up new members, and it was one of the first questions raised by the union leaders when they met with management to negotiate their first labor contract. In fact, this issue took up the first two weeks of negotiation.

When the issue was finally settled, management discovered that the agreement with the new guard union specified a work schedule that was almost identical with the one that had existed prior to unionization. Nevertheless, the union and the membership seemed satisfied with the agreement, and there was no longer the heavy stream of complaints about work assignments.

1. How do you explain this strange development? Were the employees dissatisfied before and, if so, why did they appear satisfied after the agreement was made?
2. What scheduling difficulties may the union leaders have become aware of during their two-week discussion with company representatives?

SUPERVISION

Up to this point we have been dealing with the "ingredients" of the business organization: people and their needs, technology and its impact, groups, and unions. In the following chapters we shall talk about the *supervisor,* whose job it is to blend all these ingredients in such a way as to enable the organization to satisfy its basic needs for production and profit.

What is a supervisor? A supervisor is one who is responsible for getting a job done that is too big to do by himself— a job that he can accomplish only through other people. True, he must have some technical ability. But it is the fact that *he must get his work done through others* that sets him apart as a supervisor and that creates the problems that we shall discuss in this section.

Clearly, supervision is not just a matter of giving orders or overseeing subordinates to make sure they follow rules. Supervision means building an effective work force and motivating each member of it to turn in his best performance. This is the job of every

supervisor, whether he is president of the company, a regional sales manager, or a foreman on the line.

To be sure, supervisors have other functions besides dealing with subordinates. Depending on their level in the hierarchy, they may have to make decisions relating to finance, marketing, production, research, advertising, scheduling, quality control, public relations. Technical, analytical, and imaginative skills may be as essential as human-relations skills. The supervisor may have to deal with customers, suppliers, government agents, superiors, staff representatives, and other supervisors on his own level. Yet one of the most critically important skills of any supervisor is skill in *leadership,* and in this section we shall emphasize the supervisor as leader.

What is the difference between a good leader and a bad one? Styles of leadership vary greatly from one situation to another. The techniques used by "a maid to control her man" are very different from those used by a drill sergeant. The political demagogue, the parish priest, the president of the senior class, the father of a family—all are leaders. And so are the unofficial, informal leaders we met in an earlier chapter. Each uses a style of leadership appropriate to his own situation. As we shall see, in business, too, there is a wide range of leadership behavior.

Every supervisor, however, faces the problem of motivation. When a man works for himself, either at his job or at a hobby, he works with enthusiasm and energy. How can we get him to work in the same way in our complex mass-production society, where men work not for themselves, but for others, and where the satisfaction derived from the work itself is often meager? As we shall see in Chapter 5, there are various means of "Motivating People to Work," some appropriate to one situation, others to another. Nevertheless, in our opinion the most generally appropriate form of supervision (with exceptions that we shall note) is what has been called "general supervision."

The supervisor who engages in general supervision tries to set up a situation in which subordinates obtain need-satisfaction through doing their job. He has three tasks:

1. He must try to create a work situation that provides subordinates with the maximum opportunity for accomplishment, self-expression, and individual development consistent with the needs of the organization. This means, for instance, that he will delegate authority, provide goals to work for, and supervise by results. Instead of issuing detailed instructions, he will train people to make decisions by themselves. His aim is to give people the feeling that they are their own boss; his hope is that subordinates will work hard because doing so will give them increased satis-

faction. All this is involved in "General Supervision" (Chapter 6).

2. If the organization is to achieve its fundamental objectives, however, the supervisor must place limits on the freedom granted to subordinates. Furthermore, many people have little desire for independence, and there are many situations that afford little opportunity for autonomy, even if it is desired. All this means that the supervisor must frequently exercise authority and order people to do things that are distasteful to them. The problem is for the supervisor to exercise authority in a manner that will make it most palatable to subordinates (Chapter 7, "The Supervisor's Use of Authority").

3. Both the supervisor and his subordinates are members of the same work group, and the group has certain standards and norms of behavior. The supervisor's job is to avoid head-on clashes with these norms and, if possible, to modify them in management's interest. In Chapter 3 we spoke of the informal leader who wins group acceptance by helping the group reach its objectives. To some extent, the general supervisor acts like an informal leader (Chapter 8, "The Supervisor and the Group").

Before we go on to discuss these three aspects of general supervision, we must point out that no one form of supervision is equally good in all situations. What form is best suited to a given situation depends on many factors: the type of work, the cohesiveness of the group, the group's attitude toward management, the individual needs and personality of the subordinate, and the personality, experience, and technical ability of the supervisor. The best supervisor is the one who is sensitive to the needs of each situation and adjusts his style of supervision accordingly.

One of the basic problems in any society is how to motivate people to work. In a mass-production society this is not an easy task, since many people derive only slight personal satisfaction from their jobs, and enjoy little sense of accomplishment or creativity. In large organizations people must work together, follow orders they may neither understand nor approve, and obey instructions from superiors whom they had no part in selecting and may never see. Few have the opportunity for self-expression or the freedom from control enjoyed by the farmer or the independent businessman or the professional man. How can one motivate people who have boring jobs, little freedom to make decisions on their own, and the normal human quota of laziness and stubbornness?

The basic problem of motivation is how to create a situation in which employees can satisfy their individual needs while at the same time working towards the goals of the organization. This day-to-day burden of providing motivation necessarily falls on the supervisor's shoulders.

In this chapter we shall consider five alternative methods used by supervisors to motivate

5

Motivating People
to Work

people: (1) authority, (2) paternalism, (3) implicit bargaining, (4) competition, and (5) providing opportunities for need satisfaction through doing the job. (We can make no claim to having exhausted the list of possible forms of motivation.)

Our thesis is that each of these methods has its advantages and limitations, but that the first four methods have such undesirable side-effects in terms of employee behavior that in *many* situations and *in the long run* (note our qualifications) the fifth may be preferable.

Let us now consider each of these methods and its impact on employee behavior.[1]

Authority

The traditional form of motivation in industry (and the one that seems to come easiest to most supervisors) emphasizes authority. At its crudest, this method consists of forcing people to work by threatening to fire them if they don't. The assumption behind this approach, of course, is that the only reason people work is to earn money, and that they will work only if driven to it by fear of losing their jobs. It ignores the fact, mentioned in Chapter 1, that people also want intrinsic, on-the-job satisfactions from their work.

This approach further assumes that since no one likes work, people will try to get away with doing just as little as they can. To prevent them from doing so, there must be close supervision. Management must tell every worker exactly what he is to do every minute of the day; it must spell out every rule and give the worker the narrowest possible range for discretion. Often rules are promulgated just to "show who's boss." Individuals are kept busy "to keep them out of trouble."

This thinking is inherent in some of the less sophisticated versions of scientific management: men are hired to work rather than think, and the smallest possible segment of human ability should be used on the job. It is also related to what has been called the "commodity" or "contractual" theory of labor, which holds that labor can be bought and sold just like material supplies—and can be treated in the same way.[2]

The philosophy behind such tactics is essentially this: "Be strong. Be tough. Get the job done by breaking down resistance and antagonism." This approach paid off fairly well in the early days of the Industrial Revolution when workers and their families were so close to starvation that the material, off-the-job needs for food, clothing, and shelter were paramount. In

---

[1] Our thinking in this chapter has been greatly influenced by Douglas McGregor.

[2] For an analysis similar to ours, see F. J. Roethlisberger, "The Human Equation in Employee Productivity," *Readings in Personnel Administration,* Paul Pigors and Charles A. Myers, eds. (New York: McGraw-Hill, 1952), pp. 114-120.

recent years, however, people have begun to expect more from their jobs than sheer punishment. As a consequence, the policy of "be strong" has become less effective as a motivating device.

1. In the first place, as we discovered in Chapter 1, as our standard of living has gone up, people have begun to look for social and egoistic satisfactions as well as for economic ones. This is particularly true in times of full employment.

2. Fifty years ago children were taught, both at home and at school, to show strict obedience to their elders. And so the child-grown-man found little difficulty adjusting to stern discipline in the office or factory. Recent years have seen a revolution in the way children are brought up. Freedom and self-expression are encouraged in the home; schools emphasize spontaneous discussion and individual expression. As a consequence, the young worker of today finds it hard to accept autocratic leadership on the job.

3. Basic to the philosophy of "be strong" is the expectation that if a man doesn't do what the boss tells him to do, he will be fired. Unions, however, have made it more difficult to fire a man; in effect, they have lowered the minimum with which a worker can get by.

APPLICATION TO WHITE-COLLAR WORKERS

Today the policy of "be strong" is applied less commonly to hourly-wage employees than to executives, supervisors, and white-collar workers. With no union to protect them and with a keen interest in advancement, the fear of punishment (either through discharge or denial of promotion) is more effective in motivating these individuals. This is one reason we hear so much about "pressure" in many business offices. A top executive described his use of the "be strong" approach this way:

> As soon as we examine the budget results and see a fellow is slipping, we *immediately* call the factory manager and point out, "Look Joe, you're behind on the budget. What do you expect to do about it?" True, he may be batting his brains out already on the problem but our phone call adds a little more pressure.[3]

The consequent feeling of frustration is intensified because the white-collar employee typically does not have the channels of redress or the opportunities to express aggression that are available to his blue-collar brother. Top management insists on "loyalty," obedience in spirit as well as in form. Here is how a plant manager put it in asking one of the authors to teach a course on human relations:

> "I want you to teach them loyalty. We need the same enthusiasm down the line in putting orders into effect which we have in drawing

[3] Chris Argyris, *The Impact of Budgets on People* (New York: Controllership Foundation, 1952), p. 5.

them up—even if they don't understand or agree with what we want. The trouble is that our policies on cost reduction and so forth are carried out in a half-hearted sort of way." [4]

It is common practice for top management to set goals (increased sales, lowered costs, and so forth) for their executives, and then to exert constant pressure to insure that these goals are met. The penalty for not doing so is usually the withholding of promotions or salary increases, if not outright discharge.

Some companies deliberately set their goals too high. Every time a goal comes close to being met, management raises it even higher, hoping as a consequence to stir employees to work harder and harder. As one supervisor remarked, "My philosophy is always give a man more than he can finish. That way you can be sure you are getting the most out of him."

IMPACT ON PEOPLE

The trouble with "be strong" as a form of motivation is this: It ignores the fact that people are not passive, inert machines and that they often react in ways not intended by management.

1. This policy normally provides no incentive to work harder than the minimum required to avoid punishment. The minimum may be fairly low in the case of unionized workers who are promoted on the basis of seniority and who have a union to protect them if they are fired. In the case of white-collar workers and executives, however, the minimum may be considerably higher, particularly if they are anxious for promotion.

2. The essence of "be strong" is the application of pressure. But when subjected to *too much* pressure, employees fight back. When they can, they fight through their union. If they have no union, they engage in slowdowns, sabotage, and spoilage. [5] As one worker commented, "In my shop there is an undeclared war of nerves. If management won't treat us like men, we aren't going to show much respect for them."

Part of this "war of nerves" consists of workers' efforts to get away with doing as little as possible; there is no incentive for doing more than the minimum, but there is a great deal of satisfaction in making management look silly. Naturally, management reacts by deciding, "We have to watch these men like hawks if we are to get anything done at all." Both sides spend a tremendous amount of energy trying to outsmart the other. Production is lower than it might otherwise be, and management, in frustration, often strikes back irrationally, perhaps by imposing needless restrictions or by firing

---

[4] Incidentally, at the time the course was offered the supervisors knew that a third of them would be laid off in three months.

[5] See Stanley B. Mathewson, *Restriction of Output Among Unorganized Workers* (New York: Viking, 1931).

alleged ringleaders. Thus a vicious cycle is set in motion, a cycle of restraints and evasions, more restraints and more evasions.

As J. S. Mill said a century ago, "Nor are the greatest precautions more than very imperfectly efficacious, where, as is now almost invariably the case with hired laborers, the slightest relaxation of vigilance is an opportunity eagerly seized for eluding performance of their contract." [6]

3. To protect themselves from pressure, employees organize groups and cliques, as we saw in Chapter 3. And already-existing groups may be drawn closer together and take on a new purpose, that of protecting themselves against management pressure. As we have seen, work groups frequently establish "bogeys" or standards of output that no member is expected to exceed—in spite of what management wants. Group members may even conspire to "cover" each other's mistakes and to punish "squealers." As a result, higher management is kept ignorant of what is happening on subordinate levels and therefore cannot inflict the discipline that is necessary if "be strong" is to succeed.

This policy of self-protection is openly practiced by hourly-paid workers; even executives, however, often band together in an implicit alliance to protect themselves against their own superiors. Such an alliance may be highly effective even though it is never actually talked about.

4. Probably the most serious trouble with "be strong" is that it ignores a basic factor in human behavior: when people are put under too much pressure they become *frustrated*. (Note: we say *too much* pressure. Most of us respond well to some pressure, but all of us have a critical point—which differs from one person to another—beyond which frustration sets in.)

When people become frustrated they react in strange ways that tend to reduce the effectiveness of the organization in its main task of getting out production. Often their behavior seems quite irrational, in the sense that it cannot be understood in terms of the apparent stimulus.

> Superintendent Jones' secretary usually does a fine, conscientious job. Today she forgot to type an important letter. Jones bawled her out unmercifully.

Jones is normally a kind man. Why did he act this way today? Certainly his behavior was not designed to get the letter out more quickly, or even to prevent his secretary from making mistakes in the future. The fact is that he had been trying to meet an important deadline with an inadequate staff of men, and his boss had just called him up to spur him on.[7]

Another response to frustration is *aggressiveness,* which expresses itself in

---

[6] J. S. Mill, *Principles of Political Economy,* People's Edition (London: Longmans, Green, 1891), p. 68.

[7] Of course, the stimulus may have been provided by home problems (his baby may have cried all night) or by other forms of pressure (he may have had a fight with the union steward).

many ways. Instead of bawling out his secretary, Jones might have picked a fight with another supervisor, had a hassle with his wife, or whammed a small, defenseless white ball around the country-club park. If his frustration became too intense, it might have led to psychosomatic illnesses, such as high blood pressure or ulcers:

> Once we observed a group of working supervisors who had been strongly pressured to increase production under difficult circumstances with no backing from management. There were nine men regularly assigned to the day shift. One had a nervous breakdown, another had a fatal heart attack that was generally attributed to overwork and fatigue. Of the remaining seven, five had serious illnesses and in most cases no organic cause could be determined. All this happened during a period of twelve months. Meanwhile, the men on the night shift, where pressure was much less, had an almost perfect health record.

There are many other reactions to frustration. Some people *repress* their feelings for a long time and then suddenly blow up without notice. Others *regress* to less mature levels of behavior. Everyone is familiar with the three-year-old who reverts to thumb-sucking when a baby brother arrives on the scene. Similarly, adults who are frustrated by excessive pressure may find it difficult to make decisions or react intelligently and may engage in juvenile (and aggressive) activities such as horseplay. Under extreme frustration, they may simply fall into *resignation* and give up trying altogether. Possibly the underprivileged, floating employees mentioned on page 11, who despaired of trying to improve themselves economically, had reached a state of resignation.

Frustration may also lead to *scapegoating*—that is, picking on those who are weak and defenseless. It is not accidental, for instance, that racial tensions in plants are higher when times are bad and layoffs are pending. Another response is *fixation*, in which the individual persists in some fruitless activity, such as Lady Macbeth's handwashing, even though it obviously accomplishes nothing. When assigned a difficult problem, some supervisors spend their time shuffling papers rather than trying to work out a realistic solution.

Finally there is *sublimation*, in which the individual turns away from the source of his frustration. The supervisor who has been under excessive pressure may lose all interest in his work and throw himself into hunting or gardening (just as a girl who has been jilted may "drown her sorrows" in music or school work).

The collective reaction of a group of workers to frustration may have a devastating effect on the entire organization. It may disrupt group solidarity and cooperation, turning departments, groups, and individuals against one another. It may lead to rumor, mistrust, and suspicion. It may result in unexplained wildcat strikes or a general state of snarling irritability. In every case, the basic objective of the organization—*production*—is bound to suffer.

THE VALUE OF AUTHORITY

To put this whole problem another way, when a rider whips his horse he must remember that the horse may dash off in any direction. A high degree of control is required to make sure it goes where the rider wants. If the only form of incentive operating is the employee's desire to escape punishment, there is no guarantee that he will perform his job in the way management desires *unless* all alternative courses of action are blocked.

Thus the effectiveness of the "be strong" technique of motivation is subject to significant limitations: (1) it motivates employees to do only enough work to keep from being fired; (2) it motivates them to "get away" with as much as possible (often making a game of it), thus leading to a vicious cycle of further management restrictions and employee evasions; (3) it motivates them to band together in self-protection, and (4) it leads to frustration and in turn to a whole series of deleterious side-reactions that jeopardize production.

"Be strong" works better in the short run than in the long run. It is most effective during depressions when men are desperate for work, in non-unionized situations, and among white-collar workers anxious for promotion. (Yet even in these situations it gives rise to undesirable side-reactions.)

As we shall see, there are times when a supervisor, because of his position, must use threats, either implicitly or explicitly. But a supervisor who relies solely on threats as a means of motivation is likely to develop a group of subordinates who at best are cowed into fearful rigidity and at worst are openly rebellious.

Paternalism

As a substitute for "be strong," many managements have adopted the philosophy of "be good." They have sought to raise employee morale by providing good working conditions, fringe benefits, employee services, and often (but not always) high wages. This is the philosophy of paternalism.

The arguments for paternalism have been stated in two forms, which we shall call the naive and the subtle. The naive argument holds that if management is good to employees they will work harder out of loyalty and gratitude. The more subtle argument ignores the question of gratitude; it holds that liberal benefits and good working conditions make for happy employees, and that happy employees work harder.

"NAIVE" PATERNALISM

Naive paternalism is pretty much outdated, having had its heyday in the 1920's. In part, its wide adoption at that time was the result of genuine interest by employers in their employees, as well as the belief that "be good" was a superior form of motivation to "be strong." In part, too, its popularity was a reaction to the rise of unionism during and immediately after World War I. In any case, under the banner of the "New Industrial Relations," management became interested in a wide variety of projects, varying from cafeterias and recreation programs for employees to cooking classes for their wives. Some of these programs were designed to change the employees' personal lives as well as their on-the-job performance. The Sociology Department of the Ford Motor Company of an earlier day went further than most programs. Headed by a Protestant minister, this department was manned by thirty investigators.

> In what amounted to a brief reign of benevolent paternalism, these gentlemen and their house-to-house canvassers imposed . . . a set of rules which blended good sense with Ford whims and Puritan virtues.
> On the positive side, the men . . . behaved like the home visitor of the modern public welfare agency. They doubtless helped to "Americanize" Ford's vast body of immigrant workmen. Their charges were encouraged to start savings accounts and to budget their incomes. They were given elementary lessons in hygiene and home management. . . .
> At worst . . . its agents became, to some extent, collectors of tales and suspicions. . . . Hearsay as well as fact found its way into a card catalogue where a record was kept of every worker's deviations. . . . Frittering away one's evenings "unwisely," taking in male boarders, sending funds to the "old country"—these things came to be regarded as earmarks of "unwholesome living." The use of liquor was forbidden . . . as was marital discord that resulted in a separation or divorce action.[8]

Ford's program was shortlived, but similar patterns of paternalism were developed in other companies. There is little evidence that any of them were particularly successful in eliciting gratitude, in motivating workers to do a better job, or even in staving off the development of unions. In fact, some of the companies with the best-known histories of paternalism later became scenes of bitter labor-management strife.

There are good psychological reasons for believing that if management expects employees to work harder out of gratitude for benefits, then paternalism will fail to accomplish its purpose. What actually happens may be this:

1. Paternalism may engender resentment rather than gratitude. People don't like to feel dependent on someone else. They prefer to decide for themselves what they want. Letting others decide what is good for them makes them feel infantile and lowers their sense of importance. In spite of stories to the contrary, most people prefer to earn things for themselves rather than having everything handed to them by others. Unearned rewards given out of the kindness of the employer's heart often are regarded as

---

[8] Keith Sward, *The Legend of Henry Ford* (New York: Rinehart, 1948), p. 59.

slights to the employee's sense of self-esteem. Instances of "biting the hand that feeds one" are quite common.

A dramatic example of "ingratitude" was shown in a branch factory of a nation-wide company located in a small hill town in the South. As was typical of the area, most of the houses in town were owned by the company.

Some years back, the company president's wife, Mrs. X, passed through and was shocked by the poverty of the town and the ugliness of the factory. A religious woman, she convinced her husband that something should be done—and she was given a free hand to do her best.

Her first step was to attack the diet problem. A dietician was imported from the North. When no one showed up for her classes, Mrs. X complained to the factory manager. Next session an impressive number of women "voluntarily" signed up for the program.

Heartened by this victory, she made similar efforts in other directions. A model home was set up, and attractive (by big-city standards) modern furniture was offered for sale at wholesale prices. Mrs. X had little success as an order-taker until the factory manager accompanied her on her visits through the town.

The next step was to paint the factory equipment in bright cheerful colors. Then one day potted geraniums appeared at the factory windows. This was the last straw. The men went on strike, threw the geraniums out the windows, and joined the union.

2. Paternalism incorporates some of the basic assumptions of "be strong." People are expected to be docile in return for their gifts, and work is still regarded as a form of punishment that people undergo only in return for a reward. Moreover, many of the rewards must be enjoyed *off* the job. Little effort is spent on making the job itself more rewarding.

Although paternalism emphasizes the positive nature of the gift, it also carries with it a negative threat: "If you don't do your job as ordered, your gifts will be taken away." In most instances, since the rewards are distributed without discrimination to everyone on the payroll, there is little incentive for the individual worker to do more than the minimum required to keep from being fired.

3. As time passes, the novelty of being given free "hand-outs" wears off, and employees begin to take their benefits for granted. Once they come to regard benefits as part of their regular compensation, management is obliged to provide increasingly impressive gifts. Otherwise the workers will turn resentful, and management will get no credit at all.

"SUBTLE" PATERNALISM

Today the more naive version of paternalism is seldom resorted to, except by smaller companies. The more subtle version of paternalism is quite common, however. Management showers workers with high wages, fringe benefits, good working conditions, and all the rest, in the hope that they will have higher morale and *therefore* work harder. The only trouble with this assumption is the *therefore*. Since everyone shares equally in these benefits, there is no reward for good work and no incentive to increase output.

The term *morale* has been used in many different ways; but if morale means the employees' attitude toward the company as a whole, there is little evidence that high morale is necessarily associated with high productivity.[9] Just the reverse may be true. Morale may be very low in a concentration camp, yet production very high. Similarly, workers may be well satisfied to "goof off" in a department where the work pace is extremely slow. A recent confidential study of a nation-wide manufacturing company showed that the plant with the highest production rate had the highest morale, while the plant with the next-highest production rate had the lowest morale. Apparently efforts by management to raise morale do not necessarily raise productivity.

THE VALUE OF PATERNALISM

We have applied the term paternalism to the philosophy which holds that high wages, good treatment, and so forth will automatically motivate employees to work harder. And we have suggested that this is an oversimplified theory of human behavior. Does this mean that it is a complete waste of money to try to make the company a better place in which to work? Of course not. Properly presented, fringe benefits and employee services are an important part of any personnel program. (See Chapter 30.) Such benefits bolster the company's reputation in the community and attract better workers. They also help to reduce turnover, for good workers are less likely to leave the company's employ. Further, a feeling of security serves to reduce tension among employees and this, to some extent, may contribute to higher productivity.

Without question, efforts to make the company a better place in which to work do pay off in terms of better workers and more harmonious relations on the job. But they provide little *direct* motivation for workers to contribute more than a minimum effort. Thus they provide only a partial answer to the problem of how to motivate workers most effectively.

---

[9] There is some slight evidence that groups which *as a whole* have favorable attitudes toward the company may be slightly more productive. In spite of a great deal of research, however, there is no convincing evidence that *individuals*, within any group, who have more favorable attitudes toward the company do a better job. See Arthur H. Brayfield and Walter H. Crockett, "Employee Attitudes and Employee Performance," *Psychological Bulletin*, Vol. 52, No. 5 (September 1951), pp. 396-424.

Implicit Bargaining

One of the most common forms of motivation today (though some supervisors may hate to admit it) is bargaining. In this approach, management encourages workers to put out a "reasonable" volume of work by making an agreement to provide, in return, "reasonable" supervision (though the bargain is usually a matter of implicit "understanding" rather than any explicit agreement on terms).[10] In a sense, management agrees not to use force if the employees will agree not to restrict output unduly. The chief difference between this approach and the two forms of motivation already discussed is that the terms of the bargain (namely, what constitutes *reasonable* supervision, and what constitutes *reasonable* output) are agreed upon more or less voluntarily by both parties.

Thus in practice the level of output and the conditions under which men work are not determined unilaterally by the supervisor, but through unwritten agreement between supervisor and subordinate. Just how favorable the final agreement is to each of the parties is determined by their respective bargaining power. Let us look for a moment at the weapons in the possession of each party.

The workers' major weapon is this: either they can display cheerful cooperation and maintain high production or else they can indulge in excessive clumsiness, misunderstanding, or overt slowdowns or strikes.

The supervisor's most obvious weapon is his power to discipline workers who fail to produce. In practice, in the typical unionized situation, formal discipline is difficult to impose unless the worker's production is completely out of line. Still the supervisor has at his disposal a whole arsenal of minor weapons: small but highly prized "plums," minor concessions, and petty but very real punishments. He can assign easy jobs or hard ones. He can make concessions in terms of time off and accept obviously false excuses for absenteeism or tardiness—or he can nag employees for minor offenses. He can provide the help that makes a job easier—or he can make work almost impossible (this is a particularly telling weapon where piece-work is involved).

Sometimes the immediate supervisor permits minor violations of rules as part of the bargain. Superintendents in one gypsum mill allowed workers to punch the clock a little early so they could make more overtime, and to take limited amounts of material home with them for their own repair work.[11] In other situations, employees are permitted to take coffee breaks, make personal calls on the company phone, or take home company pencils. In return for this "indulgency pattern," [12] they implicitly agree to work

---

[10] At times, of course, management does engage in explicit bargaining with the union over the level of production.

[11] Alvin Gouldner, *Wildcat Strike* (Yellow Springs, Ohio: The Antioch Press, 1954), pp. 19-20.

[12] *Ibid.*

harder. Although such agreements are never put into words, they are tacitly understood by everybody concerned. As one worker put it:

> Our policy is to live and let live. We give the foreman reasonable production. He protects us from the time-study man who tries to jack up the output rate and looks the other way if we take a smoke. We look out for each other.

These privileges are extended only so long as the supervisor feels that the subordinates are doing a satisfactory job. Otherwise they are withdrawn.

> A case in point was the "no-floating around rule" which specified that workers must stay at their workplace, except to go to the washroom or eat. When foremen felt that things were going smoothly in their group, that their men were "doing a day's work" and were friendly and "co-operative," they would allow their workers to "sneak off" for a smoke, and they would make no caustic remarks if they wandered over to talk to a friend. If, however, a man or a group was felt to be "goofing off," or was being "snotty," foremen were more likely to invoke the "no floating" rule.[13]

An analogy may be drawn between the indulgency pattern and bank deposits. Both subordinates and supervisors build up credits by doing favors for the other party, and both expect to draw on their account when they need a favor for themselves.

Perhaps this bargaining approach can best be understood in negative terms: The supervisor agrees not to push the men if they will agree not to restrict production. The fear that the other side will break the bargain provides motivation for living up to it. Just as a supervisor can withdraw his indulgency if he fails to get cooperation from his subordinates, so they can withdraw their cooperation if the supervisor fails to be indulgent.

In many situations this policy of "live and let live" is the most realistic approach available to the supervisor. For all its disadvantages, it does make possible a reasonably satisfactory level of production and reasonably harmonious worker-supervisor and labor-management relations. Employees enjoy a sense of independence that they are denied under "be good" and "be strong." To be sure, they are motivated in part by the fear that if they fail to produce the supervisor will withdraw their petty benefits. Probably equally important is the feeling that since the supervisor is "fair" to them, it is only proper that they put out a "fair day's work."[14]

Yet unless bargaining is coupled with more positive forms of motivation, it suffers from many of the disadvantages of "be good" and "be strong." Work is still considered a punishment that one endures only for the sake

---

[13] Alvin Gouldner, *Patterns of Industrial Bureaucracy* (Glencoe, Ill.: Free Press, 1954), p. 173.

[14] The reader may ask, "What is the difference between this and paternalism; aren't they both based on a sense of mutual obligation?" The difference is hard to explain, but can easily be felt in practice. It is due chiefly to the fact that (1) the bargain is between *equals,* and (2) the relationship is usually highly *personal.*

of receiving the benefits that may accrue from living up to the agreement. Each side does something unpleasant in return for something pleasant. From management's point of view, bargaining offers little opportunity to raise production. Indeed, production is often stabilized at a fairly low level.

Competition

Another form of motivation is competition for the pay increases and promotions that go to the men who do outstanding jobs. Competition furnishes several forms of need satisfaction. The prospect of winning a promotion or a pay increase provides a meaningful goal to work toward. And actually attaining the goal means that the employee enjoys an economic reward, as well as a sense of accomplishment and completion, a sense of progress, and added social prestige. Less supervision is required on jobs where competition provides a reasonably satisfactory source of motivation, since each man is on his own to do the best job he can. There is no need to push him.

Competition is not particularly successful as a motivating device among factory workers, however. In union plants the principle of seniority substantially decreases the possibility of winning a promotion on the basis of hard work alone.[15] The trend to reserve foremen's jobs for college-trained men has reduced the factory worker's chance of rising into management. In addition, there is growing recognition that promotion to supervisory jobs should be made on the basis of potential supervisory ability, rather than as a reward for outstanding production. In theory, the incentive (piece-work) system does provide an opportunity for workers to compete with one another. In practice, however, they usually cooperate to restrict output and prevent competition.

Among blue-collar workers, competition among *groups* is often more effective than it is among *individuals*. We have observed numerous incidents where competition has arisen almost spontaneously between groups to see who will put out the most work, make the biggest reductions in scrap losses. and so forth. Workers seem to enjoy the increased sense of group belongingness, the excitement of the game, and the thrill of winning.

Competition among individuals is much more widely accepted on the white-collar and managerial levels. Indeed, among salesmen, it is the traditional form of motivation. Yet even among non-factory employees competition as a means of motivation suffers certain limitations and undesirable side-effects:

1. Not everybody is equally interested in advancement. Some people are highly ambitious, but others—who may be just as competent and hard-

---

[15] In fact, one of the purposes of the union as an institution is to reduce or eliminate competition among its members.

working—seek to avoid situations where they have to "cut the other man's throat" to get ahead. And many people, reasonably satisfied with their present job and earnings, do not want to expend the extra effort necessary to win a promotion.

Many engineers and scientists are more interested in professional advancement than in promotions, particularly if the higher-rated job takes them from their laboratory and saddles them with administrative chores. In a sense, these men are competing, but they are competing for professional recognition rather than for the goals management has set for them.

2. Excessive competition has been known to disrupt an entire organization. "A football team may compete successfully with other teams, but it does not follow that it will compete best if its members are in competition with one another." [16]

As we shall see in Chapter 16, the modern industrial organization is being broken down more and more into specialized activities, such as credit, sales, advertising, engineering, product development, and so forth, none of which can be carried on without continuous cooperation from people who are performing other activities. There are fewer and fewer one-man operations, particularly at the higher levels of management. As a consequence, cooperation is vital to sustained productivity.

3. On many jobs it is difficult to measure who has been most successful, since it is impossible to identify the output of each employee. Even when objective measures are appropriate they are hard to formulate, and using them as the primary basis for distributing rewards may itself lead to a distortion of effort through an overemphasis on the factors being measured. (See Chapter 14.) Yet unless there is some purely objective way of determining who should receive promotions and rewards, competition may make subordinates overly dependent on their boss.

Overdependence tends to transform the subordinate into a "yes man" who is so fearful of making mistakes that he never has a chance to learn from them. The supervisor who is constantly looking upward toward his boss rather than downward toward his subordinates is likely to do a poorer job of supervision, and he is certain to inhibit upward communication. But more of this in Chapter 15.

4. Efforts to encourage competition are often regarded as pressure, and, as we have seen, excessive pressure is frustrating. Aggression and regression are common by-products of the contests conducted by sales organizations. *Time* magazine writes that:

> Many firms have ... enlisted salesmen's families in ulcer-building campaigns to spur the breadwinner on. One company regularly sends cards to the home showing the salesman's standing in the current company contest, gives wives tags to hang on furniture around the house to remind

---

[16] Harold Leavitt, *Managerial Psychology* (Chicago: University of Chicago Press, 1958), pp. 258-259.

their husbands of the furnishings they can earn. Some firms have even sent buzzers and shrill whistles to salesmen's children; when dad asks what the noise is all about, the kids are instructed to tell him it's only a reminder to straighten up and sell harder.[17]

Salesmen, perhaps, are able to stand a higher level of pressure than most people. However, as *Time* remarks:

> Such constant pressure from home and office is bound to take its toll on even the strongest salesman. . . . "You can carry this business of pounding away at a salesman too far," says Republic Steel's General Sales Manager L. S. Hamaker. "It can be too demoralizing." [18]

Excessive emphasis on competition is particularly frustrating to the loser. Since most promotional hierarchies are shaped like a pyramid, with fewer jobs at the top than at the bottom, there are always more losers than winners.

Many work groups actually band together to protect themselves from attempts to encourage competition, either by formulating group standards of "fair competition" or by banning competitive practices altogether. (For an example, see Chapter 3.) This response is most common among hourly-paid workers, but employees at all levels apply pressure on the "eager beaver."

In conclusion, excessive competition may do more harm than good. In its pure form, the philosophy of competition as a motivating device seems to assume that work is itself uninteresting. When used in moderation, however, and in conjunction with other forms of motivation, competition between individuals may be useful, particularly with certain groups (salesmen, for example), and in situations where teamwork is not essential.

Providing Opportunities for Need Satisfaction Through Doing the Job

A fifth approach to the problem of motivation (and one that we feel is preferable in many situations) is to provide opportunities for need satisfaction through doing the job itself, so that people will enjoy doing good work. Here, the better job an employe does, the higher his level of job satisfaction will be. This approach requires management to discard the assumption that work must be *objectionable*. It also de-emphasizes economic motivation and off-the-job need satisfactions.

The economic factor, of course, will continue to be very important. In our society, pay is a means of obtaining status and material well-being, and many men (though not all) will work hard on a distasteful job if there is opportunity for advancement. The hourly-paid worker, however, to a large

---

[17] *Time*, Vol. 72, No. 2 (July 14, 1958), pp. 75-76.
[18] *Ibid.*

extent expects to get his increased economic returns from union-initiated wage increases or from promotions based on seniority rather than on outstanding work. Incentive (piece-work) systems may provide some economic motivation for such workers, but here too, as we shall see, the fact that workers establish quotas indicates that they do not respond to economic motivation as readily as management expects.

We have seen that in informal groups people work together and accept the orders of their leaders in order to achieve group objectives. In the same way, it is management's task to create conditions under which people "will willingly and voluntarily work toward organizational objectives" [19]—because they enjoy their work and feel it important to do a good job. This desirable attitude has been called by various authors "spontaneous cooperation" [20] and "internalized motivation." [21] As J. S. Mill put it, "Nor are the greatest outward precautions comparable in efficacy to the monitor within." [22]

To repeat, employees are motivated to make their best efforts when they enjoy opportunities for need satisfaction through working. Notice how this approach differs from paternalism. In paternalism the employee is *given* need satisfaction; here he *obtains* the need satisfaction *through his own work* —work that he enjoys and work that helps management.

The preceding chapters have already given some hints about how these opportunities can be provided. While later chapters will make other suggestions, we shall list the major themes here.

1. We have already seen how intrinsic job satisfaction can be increased through redesigning the job—through job enlargement, job rotation, greater understanding of how the work is coming along, feeling of the whole, and so forth.

2. We have also considered the importance of social satisfactions on the job. Opportunities can be provided to develop friendships and to work together as a team. When members of the group can participate in solving work problems, they become more involved in the job itself and their productivity rises.

3. Equally, if not more, important is the style of leadership shown by management. In the next chapter we shall suggest ways in which the supervisor may engage in "general supervision." Workers may be given an opportunity to enjoy a feeling of accomplishment in their work and, in so far as possible, to be their own boss. Under such circumstances supervisors con-

---

[19] Douglas McGregor, *The Supervisor's Job.* Mimeographed; undated.

[20] See Elton Mayo, *The Social Problems of an Industrial Civilization* (Boston: Graduate School of Business Administration, Harvard University, 1945).

[21] Rensis Likert and Daniel Katz, "Supervisory Practices and Organizational Structure as They Affect Employee Productivity and Morale," *Human Factors in Management,* Schuyler Dean Hoslett, ed. (New York: Harpers, 1951), 2nd ed., p. 100.

[22] Mill, *op. cit.,* p. 111.

ceive of their job as a way of helping their subordinates rather than as a means of pushing them.

Glance back for a moment at Chapter 1 and notice some of the needs we listed there:

skill	praise
autonomy (being one's own boss)	acceptance
achievement	attention
understanding	self-confidence
knowledge of where one stands	

These are the needs that general supervision helps to satisfy.

Does this approach seem somewhat visionary? Perhaps. But there is considerable evidence that an increasing part of American management is coming around to the position that, theoretically at least, general supervision does provide a realistic approach to the problem of motivation. (One may still be skeptical, however, about the extent to which this philosophy is actually being implemented.)

A DIFFERENT ANALYTIC FRAMEWORK

Let us examine the problem of motivation in a different framework, and, in the process, summarize some of the points we have been discussing. Take a situation in which workers are producing at 70 per cent of the efficiency that might be expected on the basis of purely technical considerations. Obviously certain forces are operating to prevent this rate from being higher. For instance:

1. Dislike of the work.
2. Fear of working oneself out of a job.
3. An informally set "bogey."
4. Dislike of the foreman.

Yet another set of forces must also be operating to keep the rate *as high as* 70 per cent. These may be:

1. Fear of losing one's job if less is produced—or at least fear of losing special privileges.
2. Pressure exerted by the foreman.
3. Financial incentives (if there is piece-work).
4. Fear of being caught idle.

Presumably, if 70 per cent is the rate of production, two sets of forces have reached a balance at what has been called "quasi-stable equilibrium." [23] A system has been established in which one need is balanced against another:

---

[23] This concept of "quasi-stable equilibrium" was developed by Kurt Lewin. See his "Frontiers in Group Dynamics," *Human Relations*, Vol. 1, No. 1 (1947), pp. 5-42.

pay vs. physical fatigue, fear of the foreman vs. fear of the informal group, and so forth. (See *A* in diagram below.)

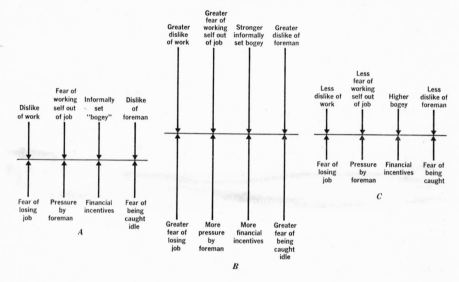

A shows quasi-stable equilibrium; *B* shows higher equilibrium with strengthened upward forces; *C* shows higher equilibrium with weakened downward forces.

Now if management wants to increase production, the typical approach is to strengthen the upward forces (*B* in diagram), perhaps by having the foreman apply even more pressure or by installing a piece-rate. Of course, the higher production climbs, the more the workers' resistance is raised—until, finally, a new equilibrium is reached where the two sets of pressures are once more in balance. However—and this is a crucial point—at the new equilibrium stronger forces are operating on each side and tension is at a higher level.[24] Frustration is greater and workers are more likely to devise techniques to insulate themselves from the pressures acting on them. From management's point of view, this is not a very efficient way of doing things. It is like driving a car with the brakes on.[25]

Fortunately, there is a more efficient way of accomplishing the same objective. Instead of strengthening the upward forces, management can weaken the downward forces (*C* in diagram), perhaps by making the work less disagreeable, or by inducing workers to change their bogey, or by reducing their dislike for the foreman. Here, too, a new equilibrium will be reached, at a higher rate of production but at a lower level of tension.

In brief, this is the approach to motivation that we refer to as general

[24] *Ibid.*
[25] See Mason Haire, *Psychology in Management* (New York: McGraw-Hill, 1956), Chapter 6.

supervision. Essentially, it consists of making a determined effort to reduce the undesirable characteristics of the job and to create a situation in which people derive genuine need satisfaction from the work they do day by day.

Conclusion

One of the central problems of any organization is to motivate its members to work for the organization's over-all objectives. In the family, the primitive society, or the voluntary social club, this may be a relatively easy matter. But in the larger organizations of our society, motivating employees is a difficult problem.

Traditionally, management has resorted to the policy of authority or punishment. With the growth of unions, a rising standard of living, and changing patterns of discipline in home and school, this approach is becoming less and less effective. It motivates people only to produce the minimum necessary to keep from getting fired. Moreover, we are beginning to realize that this policy creates frustration and undesirable side-effects.

The "be good" approach, it has been discovered, is not much more useful. Perhaps it will help recruit employees, but it does little to motivate them once they are on the job. People rarely work harder out of gratitude. Again, this approach provides little incentive to produce more than the minimum output required to avoid discharge.

Bargaining seems a somewhat more realistic approach, particularly in unionized situations. It provides an atmosphere of live and let live, but it rarely furnishes any motivation to *increase* production.

Competition has only limited effectiveness as a motivating device on jobs where there is little opportunity for promotion or where seniority prevails. Excessive competition may actually disrupt teamwork and lead to frustration and a host of undesirable side-effects. It, too, emphasizes off-the-job satisfactions.

We have suggested that the most promising approach to motivation is general supervision, in which management tries to provide opportunities for need satisfaction on the job.

(*Since all chapters in this supervisory section are closely related, we have grouped all the relevant problems together on pp. 186-192.*)

General supervision (as contrasted to close supervision) gives subordinates an opportunity to make decisions for themselves and enables supervisors to concentrate on training them to do a better job. General supervision is really a form of job enlargement, for it gives each subordinate a sense of being his own boss and of exercising control over his work environment. It relies on the satisfactions that people derive from deciding how to do a good job more or less in their own way. It tends to offset the monotony and lack of autonomy that technology has built into certain jobs.

RESEARCH FINDINGS

Research into the characteristics of effective supervision is still in its preliminary stages. Some of the most important investigations have been conducted by the Survey Research Center of the University of Michigan, the General Electric Company, and the Yale Technology Project. These studies have used a number of different research techniques and have defined "effective supervision" in several different ways—in terms of

General Supervision

objective measures of productivity, the morale of the supervisors' subordinates, and evaluation by the supervisors' superiors.

The Michigan studies investigated a series of departments of approximately the same size, one group of which had high productivity, the other of which had low.[1] The departments did roughly the same sort of work and had personnel more or less similar in age, training, and aptitude. Two of these groups, in the Prudential Insurance Company, consisted of girls who did the routine clerical work required to keep insurance records up to date. The only difference between these divisions (other than that half had high productivity and half low) was that they dealt with different geographical areas (although all departments were located in the home office). Similar studies were made in railroad section gangs, in an automobile assembly plant, in a tractor plant, and in two governmental agencies.

The Michigan studies were based on interviews with supervisors, their superiors, and their subordinates. In the General Electric study, foremen were observed on the job, and the findings were based on what the observer actually saw.[2] The Yale study combined the observational and the interview approaches.[3] These studies all came roughly to the same conclusion—namely, that general supervision is more effective than close supervision.[4]

Elements of Effective Supervision

Let us start with the bald statement, which has been only partly proved by research, that *in many situations* the most effective supervisor is the one who (1) delegates authority, (2) makes definite assignments and supervises by results, (3) minimizes detailed orders, (4) uses low pressure, (5) trains subordinates, (6) does different work from that done by his subordinates, and (7) spends his time on long-range rather than short-range problems. This is the pattern of what we call general supervision. Notice the phrase that we have italicized: *in many situations.*

General supervision is not a cure-all for all supervisory problems; good

[1] These studies have been summarized in Robert L. Kahn and Daniel Katz, "Leadership Practices in Relationship to Productivity and Morale," *Group Dynamics,* Dorwin Cartwright and Alvin Zander, eds. (Evanston, Ill.: Row, Peterson, 1953), pp. 612-628. See also Nancy C. Morse, *Satisfactions in White Collar Jobs* (Ann Arbor: Survey Research Center, University of Michigan, 1953).

[2] Quentin D. Ponder, "The Effective Manufacturing Foreman," in *Proceedings of the Tenth Annual Meeting* (Madison, Wisc.: Industrial Relations Research Association, 1957), pp. 51-54; General Electric Company, Public and Employee Relations Research Service, *The Effective Manufacturing Foreman* (processed, 1957).

[3] Charles R. Walker, Robert H. Guest, and Arthur N. Turner, *The Foreman on the Assembly Line* (Cambridge: Harvard University Press, 1956).

[4] For a critical approach to this type of research, see Michael Argyl, Godfrey Gardner, and Frank Cioffi, "The Measurement of Supervisory Methods," *Human Relations.* Vol. X. No. 4 (Fall 1957), pp. 295-314.

first-line supervision alone cannot elicit high productivity; the quality of worker-supervisor relations is not determined solely by the supervisor's personal skills. There are many other factors involved. And general supervision itself may be frustrated by such factors as poor union-management relations, internal conflicts within the work group, and poor personnel practices on other levels of management.

The general supervisor assumes that, given the chance, the average employee wants to do a good job. This isn't always true, of course. Many jobs are inherently distasteful and boring, and there are many employees who, for reasons of personality or previous experience, react poorly to the freedoms permitted by general supervision. But we shall discuss these reservations at length later on.

DELEGATION OF AUTHORITY

As we said in Chapter 1, most people like being their own boss. They like the freedom of making their own decisions. Yet can this freedom be permitted when a man works for someone else? To a considerable extent it can, provided the supervisor delegates authority and gives his orders in broad, general terms. A successful plant manager exaggerated only a bit when he said:

> "I never make a decision by myself. Oh, I guess I've made two or three since I have been here. If people know their job, I believe in letting them make their own decisions. Of course, if there is anything which affects the entire plant, the two assistant managers, the three staff chiefs and sometimes the assistant staff chiefs come in here and we discuss it. But I don't believe in saying 'This is the way it is going to be.' "

Low-production supervisors in the studies cited were unable to take this approach. They "were found to check up on their employees more frequently, to give them more detailed and more frequent instructions, and in general to limit their freedom to do their work in their own way." [5]

The general supervisor, by contrast, is primarily interested in results, and he permits his subordinates to decide how to achieve these results. He sets goals, tells his subordinates what he wants accomplished, fixes the limits within which they can work, and (in cases where the subordinates are adequately trained) lets them decide how to achieve these goals. In other words, he gives each subordinate the maximum freedom he can handle consistent with the aims of the organization.

What are the advantages of this approach to supervision?

1. Few superiors have the time to handle both their own job and the jobs of their subordinates. The close supervisor who tries to make every

---

[5] Daniel Katz and Robert L. Kahn, "Human Organization and Worker Motivation," *Industrial Productivity,* L. Reed Tripp, ed. (Madison, Wisc.: Industrial Research Association, 1951), p. 157.

decision by himself frequently exhausts himself physically and mentally. Furthermore, his decisions may be not as good as those of his subordinates. since the man who is closest to the problem usually understands it better than anyone else.

2. As superiors intrude on matters that rightfully should be handled by their subordinates, problems have a tendency to snowball. One subordinate described the situation this way:

> "As long as the boss gives us the right to make our own decisions, we cooperate with him. We report to him all the information he needs to answer to his boss, but the little things we don't bother him with. But if he doesn't give us any freedom we can make his life miserable. We can bombard his office with reports on everything we do. We can refuse to make a decision till we talk to him about it. We can stop saving his time by sifting the important from the unimportant and can keep him on the run."

3. A subordinate can take pride in results that are directly attributable to his own decisions. He cannot do so when someone else makes all the critical decisions.

4. Delegation helps to develop the talents and abilities of subordinates. It is hard to train people to take the risks of decision-making without putting them in a position where they have to make these decisions on their own. The exercise of authority cannot be learned through reading or listening to lectures; it can be learned only through practice.

Naturally the greater the area of freedom given the subordinate, the greater the feeling of autonomy he will enjoy. But limits must always be set on the subordinate's freedom, and it is essential that he recognize these limits. Obviously the subordinate cannot be given authority to do *everything* he wants: well-understood limits makes it possible for him to exercise genuine freedom within the prescribed limits. Sometimes these limits are implicit and need not be spelled out in detail:

> Suppose you are the office manager and the Big Boss tells you: "Go ahead, use your own discretion in redecorating the office. Anything you say, goes!" Beware! He doesn't really mean that. There are certain clearly understood limits within which you must work. You must abide by the city building codes and the union contract. You cannot exceed the budget. Further, you must go through the purchasing department, fill out the proper forms, and so forth.
>
> Also there are implicit limitations. If you are at all smart you know that the redecorating had better play second fiddle to keeping production going. Unless you are on Madison Avenue, the office had better wind up looking like an office, not like a ladies' lounge or a Japanese garden.

Where there is room for questions, it is important for the supervisor to state the limitations clearly. Often it seems that people are objecting to responsibility when what they are really objecting to is the uncertainty of what their responsibility is. To feel secure on the job, every subordinate must know what is expected of him.

Many supervisors are temperamentally incapable of letting others do things their own way; they are afraid to let subordinates make mistakes that may ultimately injure their own position. Mason Haire describes the attitude toward delegation displayed by two new species observed by the Indoor Bird Watcher's Society:

> The White-Shirted Hoverer [specializes in] assigning a task and then standing over it to see that it is done. His effect is probably not as devastating, however, as that of the Pin Striped Oopster, the bird which, as soon as the task has been delegated, feels he must follow every step of the operation crying, "Oops! Oops!" at regular intervals.[6]

The subordinate himself may frustrate attempts by his supervisor to delegate authority. In spite of assurances that he is really expected to exercise his own judgment, he may decide that it would be safer to check with his boss before making a difficult decision. If the boss capitulates to this adulation and delivers an opinion on every question that comes up, the subordinate gradually assumes that he would be foolish to make any decision on his own. This way he can't lose. If things go well, he will get the credit anyway. If the decision proves unwise, the subordinate was just following the boss' guidance.

DEFINITE ASSIGNMENTS AND SUPERVISION BY RESULTS

Implicit in the delegation of authority are the making of definite assignments and supervision by results. (The two can hardly be considered separately.) Management says in effect, "This is your job. You are in charge. As long as you get the job done, we don't care *how* you do it." This approach, which is in sharp contrast to detailed, minute-by-minute supervision, is often called "supervision by exception."

Definite assignments   The manager who practices close supervision gives detailed orders but sets no over-all goals toward which to work. As soon as the subordinate finishes one task, the manager gives him another. The manager's only goal seems to be to "keep the men busy." Few practices can be so destructive to morale.

> The engineers studying a factory operation insisted that the men could produce 500 units a day. The men said this was impossible. But one day, under the plant manager's urging, they really made an effort and reached the quota thirty minutes before the end of the shift. While they were congratulating themselves on their accomplishment, the plant manager

---

[6] Mason Haire, *Psychology in Management* (New York: McGraw-Hill, 1956), p. 57. Haire gives credit for this ornithological discovery to Dr. Myles Mace of the Harvard Business School.

saw them "loafing" and sent them back to work, saying that if they could finish 500 units in seven and a half hours, they ought to be able to get up to 550 or 600 tomorrow. And that is what he was expecting! Next day production went down to 350.

When workers have experiences of this sort day after day, they develop attitudes that have a disastrous effect on output. "Work hard and what rewards do I get? More work. I might as well just look busy."

General supervision requires that employees be given *definite assignments*, in terms of *results expected*, rather than *specific instructions*, which tell them how the results are to be obtained. If a worker has a definite assignment and knows that that is all he is expected to do, he has a goal to work for. He knows that if he works harder now he will have the reward of an easier time later on. He won't have to look busy to keep out of trouble. (Once a worker told us, "I'm always in trouble because I work hard and finish up and the boss sees me doing nothing. The man next to me has no trouble with the boss; he's slow and it looks like he is always working.")

Some organizations allow employees who have finished their day's work to go home and still collect eight hours' pay. In England this practice is known as "job and finish." [7] In America, utility company meter readers, postmen, and garbage men often work on this basis. In all these occupations close supervision is almost impossible. (Of course, if a man finishes much too soon, the supervisor has an indication that the work has been assigned inequitably. Still, management must be careful not to kill incentive by using the fact that a man has a few free minutes as an excuse to give him extra work.)

Naturally, many assignments cannot be as specific as "Process 150 forms a day." Some must be more general, such as "Wait on all the customers who come to your counter." The latter sort of assignment does not in itself constitute a definite goal to work toward (unless it is put this way: "Take care of all these customers and you will have a few minutes break till the next group comes"). Still a general assignment (such as "take care of all customers") provides more autonomy than a host of specific instructions. There is real satisfaction in knowing, "This is my job. Here I am in charge. As long as I do it adequately, no one will interfere with me. I will be judged on how well I do."

Along with setting goals, the supervisor should provide all relevant explanations and information. Moreover, the goals he sets must be realistic. Otherwise the subordinate may feel that he is caught on a treadmill, in a constantly frustrating attempt to achieve the impossible. There is a good deal of psychological evidence indicating that goals are more effective if a definite time limit is established for reaching them.

---

[7] Stephen A. Richardson, *The Social Organization of British and American Merchant Ships* (mimeographed; New York State School of Industrial and Labor Relations, 1954), p. 22.

Supervision by results   Typically, when supervision by results is practiced, higher management sets down, either implicitly or explicitly, certain performance standards or goals that the subordinate is expected to meet. So long as these standards are met, management interferes very little, except perhaps to give the subordinate praise, promotion, or some financial reward. Only when serious trouble develops does higher management step in. The establishment of standards has advantages from the point of view of both management and the individual employee.

1. The very fact that employees know their efforts are being measured may stir them to work harder. Statistical measures are sometimes more effective in insuring high output than are specific rules. To require each supervisor to make a monthly report on scrap loss may be more effective than a whole series of regulations or exhortations on avoiding waste. Such controls may also provide a swift means of altering the behavior of subordinates. Notice how this approach worked with interviewers in a public employment agency:

> Formerly, statistics were kept only on the *total* number of interviews carried on per month by each interviewer. This system motivated the interviewers to make a large number of *interviews,* but it gave them no incentive to find *jobs* for applicants. There was an immediate change in their behavior when statistics were also kept on the percentage of applicants who actually got jobs. In a two-month period the percentage of jobs filled jumped from 55 to 67. As one interviewer put it: "There is no tendency to get rid of an applicant as there was before.... Since they are measured by placements, everybody tried to get a job for every applicant." [8]

2. Supervision by results makes each man feel that he is his own boss. He understands what is expected of him and is encouraged to show initiative and develop his potentialities. He has a goal to work for and a feeling of completion when he reaches it. This approach encourages competition between individuals and groups—though excessive competition has certain disadvantages, as we have seen.

3. The existence of a clear-cut set of performance standards makes it easier for superiors to criticize the shortcomings of their subordinates. Employees are often resentful when their boss talks about their personal failings: it is quite another matter when the criticism is couched in terms of helping them improve their record. In fact, the mere existence of such records tends to reduce the need for the supervisor to prod employees; they know automatically when they have fallen down on the job. [9]

4. This approach to supervision makes it possible for higher management to discover which departments are having trouble and to take remedial

---

[8] Peter M. Blau, *The Dynamics of Bureaucracy* (Chicago: University of Chicago Press, 1955), p. 37.

[9] For further discussion of this point, see *ibid.,* p. 40.

measures quickly. As we shall discover in Chapter 14, this is a form of feedback or upward communication.

5. Similarly, supervision by results makes it possible to evaluate employee and supervisory effectiveness and to decide who should get promotions or pay increases.

Excessive use of statistical controls leads to many problems, but we shall defer our discussion of them to Chapter 14.

KEEPING DETAILED INSTRUCTIONS AT A MINIMUM

Close supervisors are inclined to give detailed instructions telling subordinates exactly how and in what sequence they want things done. Detailed instructions tend to make a man feel like an automaton, for they curtail his area of freedom and make it difficult for him to learn, even by making mistakes. He experiences little involvement in his work and can justly conclude, "I'm not expected to do any thinking around here."

General supervisors, by contrast, try to let their subordinates work out details for themselves and thus satisfy their needs for autonomy and self-expression. Instead of rattling off a list of orders, general supervisors are more likely to communicate helpful information or make suggestions. They explain *why* they want things done and point out how the subordinate's contribution fits into the over-all plan.

Compare, for example, the difference in approach used by two office managers as they handed out the same assignment:

> *Office Manager A.* "Call Jones Office Equipment and the Wilson Supply store. Get them to quote you prices on all the office dictation equipment they sell. Ask them to give you a demonstration. Invite two managers to the demonstration, Ellis and Conrad, and let them try it out. Get them to put their reactions on paper. Then prepare me a report with the costs and specifications of all the equipment. Oh, yes, be sure to ask for information on repair costs, how often each is likely to break down, who has to be called for repairs. And don't forget to find out if we can get a system that will also provide permanent records. . . ." (And so on.)

> *Office Manager B.* "I'd like to do something about our stenographic system. A lot of the executives who don't have secretaries of their own are complaining that it takes them too long to get a girl who can handle their dictation. Could you check up on some of the various kinds of dictating machines, find out their prices, advantages and disadvantages, and give me a recommendation as to what we should do? I think we can spend $2000. Possibly you could talk to some of the executives to get their ideas."

Office Manager A tried to think of all the contingencies, and in doing so gave his subordinate the feeling he was little more than an errand girl. However, he took so much trouble trying to think of all the possibilities that he might as well have done the work himself. Office Manager B communicated the over-all purpose of the assignment but let his subordinate carry out the details.

It has been said that the best supervisor is the one who gives the fewest orders. How can the supervisor get what he wants without giving orders? We will mention only a few points, some of which will be developed at greater length elsewhere.

1. Fewer orders are required if the supervisor sets general goals and delegates the authority for reaching them. As we shall explain in Chapter 8, such delegation can be made to groups as well as to individuals.

2. When a subordinate is uncertain about what to do, the superior may listen to him and help him work out his solution rather than impose one on him. Training of this sort makes it possible for a man to learn to make decisions for himself without the need for being constantly checked by his supervisor.

3. Establishing a routine for the job reduces the number of orders that have to be given (though possibly at the cost of boredom). Many a janitor feels he is king of his building; he rarely receives orders; he knows exactly what he should do. Similarly, a telephone operator may have little freedom to show discretion, but once she knows her job no one need tell her what to do. As a chief operator put it:

> "A telephone operator doesn't have much leeway. But if they know their job I don't check up on them often. This gives them the feeling of being their own boss."

Usually it is a situation characterized by constant change that requires the most direction:

> In their drive for change and progress many executives overlook the stabilizing nature of work routines that can be built up and carried on by workers without constant attention from their supervisors. They fail to see that frequently imposed changes not only upset work habits of individuals, but also have a seriously disturbing effect on the pattern of human relations that ties workers to each other and their supervisors.[10]

4. When a man knows his job well, the mere giving of information serves as a substitute for an order. Note the difference between these two statements: "Bill, bring some parts over to Machine 16," and "Bill, Machine 16 is down to six parts." The second provides Bill with the information he needs to make his own decision—and it assumes that he will make the correct one. It makes it possible for him to serve Machine 3 first if it has fewer parts than Machine 16. In addition, providing a man with abundant information has a positive effect on his morale, even if he doesn't need all the information in order to do a good job.

---

[10] William F. Whyte, *Human Relations in the Restaurant Industry* (New York: McGraw-Hill, 1948), p. 263.

5. Many jobs are set up so that the *situation* rather than the person provides the orders. In a way this is true in a hospital operating room:

> Although innumerable orders have been precisely responded to, most of them have flowed from the dictates of the patient's presence and condition. In a very real sense, few of the directives during surgery are arbitrary decisions on the surgeon's part. Rather, in the last analysis, the patient's needs have been the controlling element in the entire situation. Thus the person who seems to be the least capable of exerting authority—the supine, unconscious "object"—has in fact assumed the star role and the preponderant influence in the course of the drama.[11]

Electric utility sub-station operators, who often work completely by themselves, report feeling that they are completely their own bosses, when in fact they constantly have to respond to "orders" issued by dials and meters.

Jobs can be rearranged so as to reduce the number of "human orders." We once observed a factory in which there was constant friction between operators and inspectors; the main trouble was the operators' resentment of what they felt was the inspectors' constant badgering to keep up quality. Only one inspector was able to maintain good relations. The secret of his success was that he rarely told a man that he had made a mistake; instead he showed the operator the offending part, with the proper dimensions marked in chalk.

In spite of the many unpleasant aspects of assembly-line work, at least the work pace is dictated by an impersonal mechanism, rather than by a flesh-and-blood foreman. "We are more likely to be frustrated by an interference caused by another person than by one caused by a physical object, because we are more likely to experience people as interferences rather than problems." [12]

LOW PRESSURE

Research studies suggest that the most striking difference between low-productivity and high-productivity supervisors is in their use of "pressure." Notice how these supervisors "push" their men:

> I handle the amount of work given each clerk. Watch the dates and time the work so that everything gets out on schedule. If a letter comes in late, we have to speed up handling it—give it special attention. It has to be rushed along—handled in a different fashion than the usual run. I have to watch this to see that we make up time lost in other departments.[13]

---

[11] Temple Burling, Edith Lentz, and Robert Wilson, *The Give and Take in Hospitals* (New York: Putnam, 1956), p. 262.

[12] Norman R. F. Maier, *Psychology in Industry*, 2nd ed. (Boston: Houghton Mifflin, 1955), pp. 80-81.

[13] Katz, Maccoby, and Morse, *Productivity, Supervision, and Morale in an Office Situation*, p. 18.

> I know what is supposed to be done in this section—hit the work in and out—and hit it right, not slipshod.[14]

> A factory is a kindergarten. We've got schedules to meet and my job is to make sure that we meet them. . . . If you start babying the men, they will take advantage of you. They expect you to be tough.

Apparently the supervisors quoted here have little trust in their subordinate's initiative or judgment and feel that they have to check up on them constantly to make sure they carry out instructions.

Notice the difference in attitude reflected in this comment:

> We use the honor system. There are so many men and so much work comes in. We leave it to each man to take his share and get it done.[15]

The following remark was made by a supervisor who did exactly the same job as the first two supervisors quoted above.

> If you keep your employees from feeling hounded they are more likely to put out the necessary effort to get the work done on time. . . . I tell them "if you feel the job is getting you down, get away from it for a few minutes."[16]

Implicit in these different attitudes toward subordinates are distinct assumptions about human motivation. The close supervisor practices the philosophy of "be strong," saying, in effect, "Work is punishment. The only way to get people to work is to make them scared of losing their jobs. If I were to leave the shop, everyone would stop work." (And, no doubt, in his case, this is exactly what would happen.)

But the general supervisor seems to be saying, "As far as I am concerned, the average man wants to do a good job—at least until proven otherwise. If I walk away, production will continue as usual." (And in his case, this too would probably happen.) One study comments as follows on foremen who display this attitude: "These foremen clearly believed in the willingness and capacity of their men to do a good job, and accordingly acted toward them with this basic assumption in mind. The men, therefore, tended to react in ways which justified the expectation held of them."[17]

Does the absence of pressure mean that subordinates should have complete freedom to set their own standards? Quite the contrary. High standards are essential if the company is to be profitable. They are also important from the standpoint of morale: most people derive satisfaction from completing a difficult task; an easy task presents too little challenge. Throughout history effective leaders have inspired their followers to strive for almost impossible goals.

---

[14] Rensis Likert and Daniel Katz, "Supervisory Practices and Organizational Structure as They Affect Employee Productivity and Morale," *Human Factors in Management*, 2nd ed., Schuyler Hoslett, ed. (New York: Harpers, 1951), p. 92.

[15] Katz, Maccoby, and Morse, *op. cit.*, p. 18.

[16] Likert and Katz, *op. cit.*, p. 93.

[17] Walker, Guest, and Turner, *op. cit.*, p. 16.

In one sense the general supervisor does apply pressure when he sets the goals that he expects his subordinates to achieve. This is a very different kind of pressure, however, from the nagging, "breathing down a man's neck" type of pressure exerted by close supervisors. If subordinates accept the goals of the organization as valid, they tend to feel that the pressure to do a good job originates from the goals themselves rather than from the supervisor.

Even the best supervisor, of course, sometimes experiences the temptation to bear down on his subordinates. This is particularly true when the supervisor himself is being subjected to pressure from above. And yet, as one general foreman put it:

> If the foreman is in trouble, it doesn't do any good to tell him he is in trouble—he already knows it. But the thing to do is to see if you can help him. Sometimes I say to a foreman "You solve it. I don't care what the difficulty is." But when I do that, I think it has a bad effect. I try not to push the foremen. I try to be as much help as I can.[18]

In other words, this general foreman is interested in training subordinates.

TRAINING SUBORDINATES

General supervision is not the same as no supervision at all. In fact, general supervision may be more time-consuming than close supervision, for the supervisor must devote a great deal of energy to training others to make decisions.

The close supervisor tends to equate training with the never-ending issuance of specific instructions; to him, training and detailed supervision are identical. He has no interest in helping his subordinates learn so that they can do without close supervision.

Well-trained men have no need for detailed instructions. It has been said that the test of a good supervisor is what happens when he is away from his department. If he is effective, everything runs so smoothly that he is hardly missed. In a sense, the supervisor's goal should be to work himself out of a job. (Fortunately for him, he will never be completely successful in doing so.)

Training by general supervision is usually more effective than ordinary lecturing or demonstration. Also, through its emphasis on individual dignity and self-development, it lifts worker morale and helps create an atmosphere in which further general supervision is possible.

The general supervisor explains the *why* of his instructions; he gives his subordinates the theory, the over-all framework within which this particular instruction fits. Provided with this framework, subordinates can cope with unusual problems without having to run to their boss for new instructions

---

[18] *Ibid.*, p. 47

every time a problem arises. Patient explanation and demonstration by the supervisor is frequently an essential first step. But in many areas of learning it is more effective if the trainee is given an opportunity to think out his problems by himself—under guidance.

Later on (in Chapter 21) we will talk about specific training techniques. Here we will mention only the difference in training philosophy between high-productivity and low-productivity supervisors. Even where there is a formal training department in the organization, the most valuable training still comes from one's immediate boss, for he is the one who provides the on-the-spot clues as to what should or should not be done.

The effective general supervisor tries to introduce elements of training into all his contacts with subordinates. For instance, when giving a new assignment he tries to avoid saying, "I want you to do it this way." Instead, he asks, "Do you have any ideas how this should be done?" and then encourages the subordinate to work out the problems involved. Possibly the supervisor can listen to the subordinate as he thinks through the problems out loud. If the subordinate cannot arrive at a satisfactory solution on his own, of course, the supervisor offers suggestions. But he is careful to give the subordinate maximum opportunity (consistent with his ability) to figure things out by himself.

This approach to training is substantiated by two psychological laws: (1) Active learning is more effective than passive learning in bringing about a change in attitude or behavior. People learn more easily when they work out solutions for themselves than when they are provided with ready-made answers. (2) Learning is more effective when people can see the results of their actions and can correct their own mistakes. In other words, "feedback" is an important element in learning.

DOES WORK DIFFERENT FROM THAT DONE BY SUBORDINATES

There is an old tradition that the good supervisor is the one who rolls up his sleeves and works alongside his subordinates, often setting an example by his efforts. The evidence suggests that this is a myth. Of course, in an emergency the good supervisor will always pitch in to help. And there are certain supervisory jobs that require close technical coordination, jobs such as that of orchestra conductor or aircraft pilot. With these exceptions, however, research indicates that the high-productivity supervisor devotes his time to activities that pay off only in the long run, such as planning, improving human relations, and coordinating activities with other departments. The low-productivity supervisor is more likely to do the same sort of work as his men, and to concentrate on paper-work and short-term activities such as checking up on his subordinates or arranging for materials.

How can we explain these differences? In the first place, the close supervisor may seek to avoid the personal contacts inherent in effective leadership.

He may feel more secure working with his hands than trying to cope with human-relations problems. This is particularly true of the man who has come up through the ranks and to whom the supervisory position has been given as a reward for hard work, technical competence, and seniority rather than as a recognition of leadership abilities. Faced with an entirely new and confusing set of problems that he is ill-equipped to handle, he retreats to a behavior pattern in which he feels secure. The following account describes what happened to head nurses in a hospital—but it applies equally well to business situations:

> In some hospitals women were raised to positions of authority over nursing floors because they had worked there the longest and had proved to be excellent craftsmen. Sometimes they had no experience whatsoever in organizing the work of others. Such a person, since her field of competence lay in the art of nursing rather than in supervision, tended to do what she was best at, which was to give direct bedside care. She put off the other parts of her job, resenting the time spent on paper-work, supervision and teaching. Sometimes a head nurse would have so much pride in her command of nursing skills that she found great difficulty in accepting the less perfect work of subordinates. She would follow each student or auxiliary around, picking up where they left off and finishing the job for them. . . .
>
> Another type of retreat was that taken by the head nurse who centered all her attention on paper work. Sometimes this was an older woman who looked upon her promotion to this post as a graduation from hard labor, a kind of semi-retirement from the strains of bedside nursing.[19]

The very fact that the supervisor works alongside his men means that he must engage in close supervision. His presence provides a form of "pace-setting," and his men cannot help but feel that his directions and example are a reflection of his belief that they cannot be left to do the job on their own.

True, it is difficult for a manager to avoid close supervision of this sort. Every supervisor feels a strong temptation to fix up a subordinate's mistakes himself rather than explain what should have been done. Doing something oneself is usually easier than teaching. As a supervisor in an engineering laboratory put it:

> "Frankly, I've had a lot more experience than anyone in my section. Most of the time when I hand out a problem I know the solution. It requires super-human control to let those guys take three times as long as I would to get the answer. But how else can they learn?"

The close supervisor either keeps nagging his subordinates, feeling that constant pressure is the best way to get results—or does the work himself and thus avoids personal contacts altogether.[20] The general supervisor, how-

---

[19] Burling, Lentz, and Wilson, *op. cit.*, pp. 113-114.

[20] We admit that the term "close supervision" hardly applies to the man who avoids all personal contacts and fails to supervise at all. Yet when this individual does supervise, he is bound to supervise in detail.

ever, tries to provide explanations and motivate his employees to improve their performance. Instead of rushing in and taking the job into his own hands, he is patient enough to help a subordinate who has failed.

CONCENTRATION ON LONG-RANGE PROBLEMS

There is a significant difference between the way the general supervisor and the close supervisor spend their time on their job. This difference illustrates many of the points previously made and in a sense helps summarize the chapter.

Various research studies, and our own observations as well, suggest that the close supervisor is a man who runs from crisis to crisis "putting out fires." He is concerned exclusively with the here and now (or perhaps checking on the past). He has no time for anything but short, specific instructions. Often he dispenses even with these, and pitches in to do the job himself.

The general supervisor, on the other hand, looks to the future. He spends more time on planning, working to improve relations with other departments, setting goals, and training subordinates so they can meet emergencies without coming to him.

When employees are well trained and when work is delegated, the supervisor has time to concentrate on the over-all problems of his department and to develop new, more permanent solutions rather than just coping with each problem as it comes along. For instance, how does the supervisor react when a severe problem suddenly arises that calls for several men to work overtime? Does he go to each man in the department to ask him whether he is willing to stay late? Or does he develop a method of getting people to indicate in advance when they want extra work? The time the supervisor saves by adopting the second approach can be used for many useful purposes, including—as we shall discover in Chapter 15—the improvement of relations with his boss, staff sections, and other departments with which his own department has to cooperate.

The General Electric study reported this observation:

> The least effective foremen spent the greatest percentage of their time finding immediate solutions to short-range production problems, while the most effective foremen spent the greatest percentage of their time on activities which involved planning and organizing the longer range aspects of the job. The less effective foremen spent more time checking on work progress or status, securing materials, supervising materials or production movement, and similar activities which successful managers apparently delegate. Probably because of their greater emphasis on training employees, their belief in the abilities to carry out their assigned tasks without checking, and greater success in organizing the work of their groups, better foremen did not find it necessary to continuously check the conditions in their area.[21]

---

[21] Ponder, "The Effective Manufacturing Foreman," *op. cit.*, p. 47.

Here is a summary of the findings on how the two groups of GE foremen spent their time: [22]

| | Foremen | |
	Effective	Ineffective
Production	20%	40%
Personnel administration	23	12
Equipment and methods	14	8
Quality	6	6

There were similar differences in the pattern of communication between supervisors and their work groups: [23]

| | Foremen | |
	Effective	Ineffective
Giving *specific* work orders	3%	15%
Giving *general* work orders	5	1
Passing information to the group or engaging in two-way discussions with members of the work group	67	47
Receiving information from workers	25	37

Ponder comes to this conclusion:

> When the more-effective foremen found it necessary to give direction to the work of their employees, they would do so in a general way, giving explanations and suggestions, but leaving details of method and sequence up to the worker. The less effective foreman, on the other hand, gave a far greater number of direct work orders, without explaining why a job should be done, or how the specific order related to the overall work pattern.[24]

The General Electric study revealed that there was little difference in the *total* amount of time spent by the two types of supervisor with their subordinates, but that the effective supervisors had fewer and therefore longer contacts than ineffective supervisors. The short contact is sufficient for an abrupt order or a question; more time is required if there is to be a meaningful explanation or a two-way discussion. The very fact that the general supervisor permits his subordinates greater freedom means that fewer contacts are required.[25]

General supervisors seek to develop an atmosphere in which workers feel

---

[22] *Ibid.*, p. 47. The percentages do not add up to 100 because a number of miscellaneous activities are omitted.

[23] *Ibid.*, p. 52.

[24] *Ibid.*, p. 52.

[25] The average length of the supervisor's contacts depends in part on the technology of the work he is supervising. Supervisors on the assembly line, for example, may well have shorter average contacts than maintenance supervisors. See Walker, Guest, and Turner, *op. cit.* We would hypothesize, however, that if technology is held constant, high-production supervisors in most cases will have fewer and longer contacts.

free to bring their problems to them. In this atmosphere subordinates ask for help and information when it is needed, thus reducing the supervisor's need to give instructions. As one foreman told us:

> "As far as getting action is concerned, it doesn't make much difference whether you *tell* a man what to do or he *asks* you. But it makes all the difference in the world in how he feels. So I try to be available for questions instead of telling people."

The G.E. study found that effective foremen were aware of this difference: "The lower-rated foremen spent more time seeking information from others, while the higher-rated foremen spent more time answering requests for information." [26]

What picture of the general supervisor emerges from all these observations? The picture of a man who is abreast of his job, who gives his subordinates a broad range of freedom, and who is regarded by them as a source of help rather than a source of pressure. In the studies cited, the supervisors who exhibited these characteristics were also the ones who had the most effective, productive subordinates.

When Does General Supervision Work Best?

Earlier in this chapter we pointed out that general supervision is not a cure-all, that in many circumstances it must be supplemented by other forms of motivation, such as authority and bargaining. When does general supervision work best? The research data here are very scanty and the best we can do is offer hypotheses largely unsupported by evidence.

WHERE THE WORK OFFERS INTRINSIC JOB SATISFACTION

There is some evidence that general supervision is most effective where the job is challenging, where the work cycle is long, and where there is opportunity for intrinsic job satisfaction. In contrast, where there is little opportunity for creativity and internalized motivation, the policies of bargaining or "be strong" may be the only ones possible. [27] One study showed less positive relationship between general supervision and productivity on jobs where the work was machine-paced than on jobs where the men paced themselves. [28]

---

[26] *Ibid.*, p. 51.

[27] Nancy Morse, *Satisfactions in White Collar Jobs* (Ann Arbor: Survey Research Center, University of Michigan, 1953), p. 46.

[28] Michael Argyl, Godfrey Gardner, and Frank Cioffi, "Supervisory Methods Related to Productivity and Labor Turnover," *Human Relations*, Vol. XI, No. 1 (1958), p. 38.

IN THE LONG RUN RATHER THAN THE SHORT RUN

Even under close supervision a work group may be highly productive, particularly in times of widespread unemployment when men are fearful of losing their jobs. In fact, management has often found that the best way to get an immediate increase in production is to increase pressure and to impose close supervision. In the long run, however, close supervision may well lead to a deterioration of morale and productivity and to what one author calls "a liquidation of human assets." [29]

> One experiment involved four divisions of a large company, each of which had about 100 clerical employees.[30] In two of these divisions managers and supervisors were trained in the principles of general supervision. In the other two divisions management cut the number of employees by 25 per cent without reducing the work load and systematically intensified the pressure and closeness of supervision. By the end of twelve months both groups had increased productivity. But the closely supervised group had increased theirs by 25 per cent compared with a 20 per cent increase for the group under general supervision. The employees under general supervision, however, showed significant improvements in measures showing loyalty, feeling of responsibility, and involvement in work. In the other group these same indices declined dramatically.

Of course, lowered morale need not lead to a decline in production. But increased pressure may well result in resistance on the part of individuals, informal work groups, and the union, in restriction of output, and in all the familiar symptoms of aggression that we discussed earlier. Under these circumstances management is often tempted to enter into the vicious cycle of closer and closer supervision, to which the employees reply by sabotage, wild-cat strikes, and ever-tightening output restrictions.

On the other hand, the sudden introduction of general supervision is unlikely to lead to an immediate increase in production where the individuals involved have become accustomed to close supervision. If, because of their previous experience, workers expect to be pushed into work, chances are that they will abuse any relaxation of pressure unless the process is handled with great skill. They may look upon the supervisor who tries to apply general supervision as weak and flabby.[31] At times the supervisor who is being trained to use general supervision is regarded by his subordinates as more threatening because his behavior is less predictable. Employees sometimes find it easier to work for a hard-bitten so-and-so whose behavior is more predictable than one who seems to be changing his behavior every day.

---

[29] Rensis Likert, "Measuring Organizational Performance," *Harvard Business Review,* Vol. 16, No. 2 (March-April 1958), pp. 41-50.

[30] *Ibid.*

[31] For an excellent discussion of some of the problems involved in introducing general supervision into an organization, see Paul R. Lawrence, *The Changing of Organizational Behavior Patterns* (Boston: Harvard University, Graduate School of Business Administration, 1958). The point made above is discussed on pp. 196-197.

WHERE THE PATTERN OF SUPERVISION
IS CONSISTENT THROUGHOUT THE ORGANIZATION

The *over-all* pattern of supervision is more important than any one aspect of it. There is a danger that supervisors may adopt certain features of general supervision and disregard others. A supervisor who delegates authority but neglects to train his subordinates to exercise authority intelligently may well have worse results than the supervisor who retains all authority for himself.

More important than any particular supervisor's style of leadership is the general pattern of human relations that prevails in the organization. It is very difficult for a supervisor to practice general supervision if his boss and his fellow supervisors all practice and expect close supervision, particularly if the boss fails to back him up and show tolerance for his mistakes.

WHERE WORKER AND UNION-
MANAGEMENT RELATIONS ARE HARMONIOUS

Obviously, general supervision is more difficult to practice in the face of a militantly anti-management union or where subordinates are bitterly divided on ethnic or other grounds. Similarly, it is hard to elicit cooperation in communities where there is a long tradition of hostility to management and where everything a "boss" does is automatically looked upon with suspicion. On the other hand, where management works toward general supervision with patience and insight such attitudes may slowly change.

WITH CERTAIN TYPES OF PEOPLE

In the next chapter we shall discuss how people differ in the amount of responsibility they are willing to accept. There are some workers with a low level of ambition or imagination who live their life away from work and ask only to be allowed to daydream on the job. There are others who have become so accustomed to the authoritarian approach in their family and previous work experience that they regard general supervision as no supervision at all. They abuse the privileges it bestows on them, and they refuse to accept the responsibility it demands.

Conclusion

General supervision is an approach to supervision which assumes that people will work harder if they are given the freedom to make their own decisions. It relies on internalized motivation, the satisfaction people derive from being free to do a good job more or less in their own way.

The general supervisor gives his subordinates definite assignments and then delegates authority to them (within clear limits) so that they can decide by themselves how to carry these assignments out. Rather than giving specific instructions or constantly pressuring his subordinates to work harder, he is concerned with training and long-term planning, with trying to make it easier for them to get good results. (It should be emphasized that the general supervisor is as interested in results as any other supervisor; it is the *method* by which he seeks to obtain these results that makes him different.)

Much of the research suggests that general supervision results in higher productivity. As we have suggested, however, this is not always true. As we see it, the effectiveness of general supervision depends on such factors as the personality, background, or type of work done by the people being supervised as well as on the organizational structure, consistency of supervision, and general human-relations atmosphere of the organization.

Only in rare instances is general supervision enough in itself. Even the general supervisor must frequently call foul and exercise his authority as *boss*. "It seems desirable to dispel a certain tendency to believe that the human problems of management can be solved by a Pollyanna approach, that all one has to do is smile, be amiable, and dispense enormous amounts of praise. This is not true, because human beings are imperfect, and management leadership still requires a certain mixture of firmness, fortitude, objectivity, and decisiveness in dealing with the human factor." [32] But there are ways of making it easier for the subordinate to live with this threat over his head. These we shall discuss in the next chapter.

---

[32] John M. Pfiffner, *The Supervision of Personnel*, 2nd ed. (Englewood Cliffs, N. J.: Prentice-Hall, 1958), p. 220.

In the preceding chapter we pointed out that general supervision, in spite of its many merits, may not always be sufficient in itself to motivate people to work with maximum efficiency. There are times when the supervisor has no choice but to resort to the use of "authority" or "bargaining," for example. The fact is that there is no black-and-white contrast between general supervision and other forms of motivation. Inherent in the effective use of general supervision is the supervisor's ability to exercise authority when the situation demands.

Some readers may have decided that the general supervisor is a manager who doesn't supervise at all, or who supervises hardly at all. But this is not the case. It is not easy to develop teamwork and to motivate a group to work for management's objectives. Sometimes people have to be pushed. Even the supervisor who spends most of his time formulating long-range projects, and in training his subordinates so that they can satisfy their needs through doing a good job, must sometimes take actions that are restrictive and even unpleasant.

The Supervisor's Use of Authority

We have spoken, for example, of delegating authority with clear *limits*, and of supervision *by results*. It is the supervisor, not the subordinates, who sets the limits. And if the limits are exceeded, or if the results are unsatisfactory, it is the supervisor who must somehow restrain or reprimand the subordinates responsible.

Subordinates can hardly be expected to forget that their boss (or someone at a higher level of management) has the power to discharge them and to withhold benefits and promotions. Regardless of how effectively the relationship between subordinates and superior is cloaked in democratic procedure, no one forgets for a moment that there are very real differences in power between them.

Thus it is impossible to escape completely from the authoritarian aspects of the boss-worker relationship. No matter how hard the supervisor tries to avoid close supervision, there are times when he has no other choice. In every work situation problems of reward and discipline inevitably arise, and these problems often lead to frustration and bad feeling.

In the ideal situation, of course, the supervisor would be obeyed and respected even if he never resorted to formal authority. Certainly the supervisor should try to maximize the amount of satisfaction subordinates derive from their work. In practice, it may be more realistic to try also to create conditions in which people will *accept* formal authority with as much enthusiasm and with as little resentment as possible. One of the supervisor's goals should be to minimize the amount of frustration that inevitably arises when he acts as boss, and to make his exercise of authority as palatable as possible.[1]

Ambivalence Toward Authority

The supervisor's job is complicated by the fact that people feel a certain ambivalence toward authority. In Chapter 1 we talked about independent and dependent needs, which we also called egoistic and social needs. Among the many independent needs we listed were the need for a sense of accomplishment, autonomy, and skill. To illustrate dependent needs we mentioned the need for praise, fair treatment, and approval.

Most of us have complicated, mixed feelings toward independence and dependence. We value freedom but sometimes feel lost and anchorless when we have too much. We like protection but we don't like interference.

If management fails to provide enough independence on the job, employees will exercise independence on their own by resorting to absenteeism, union activity, slowdowns, and the like. On the other hand, employees find it

---

[1] Our discussion in this chapter is influenced by Douglas McGregor, "Conditions of Effective Leadership in an Industrial Organization," *Journal of Consulting Psychology,* Vol. 8, No. 2 (March 1944), pp. 55-63.

difficult to adjust to too much independence, for no one can stand completely by himself. Most of us like to be assured that we are doing the right thing and that we will receive help when we are in trouble. On occasion we even like to have other people make tough decisions for us. Clearly, then, we exhibit an ambivalent attitude toward authority: we resent being made to feel overly dependent, and we become uneasy when we are given complete independence.

The policy of "be strong," under which employees know that they are expected to do exactly what they are told, minimizes the sense of independence. The policy of "be good" fosters dependence, for it regards the ideal employee as the "loyal worker" who follows instructions to the letter without a thought of his own. General supervision, on the other hand, helps satisfy the need for independence that is present to some extent in everyone. Even so, some accommodation must be made to the people who require the security and assurance of knowing that someone is interested in them, and to others who must be restrained lest they abuse their freedom.

Working in a large-scale organization requires that every subordinate be to some degree dependent on the organization generally and on his supervisor in particular; individual independence inevitably must be sharply restricted. But his dependence should not stifle the individual or impair his chances for self-development. In this chapter we shall consider how the supervisor can handle this problem of dependence without being unduly restrictive and authoritarian.

DIFFERENCES AMONG PEOPLE

First we must note that there are substantial differences in the amount of freedom people can tolerate. One person may flourish under supervision that another might find extremely restrictive.

Consider the case of two hospital floors supervised by very different head nurses.[2] The first head nurse (Miss Smith), though extremely courteous, was strict and uncompromising with nurses who violated regulations. She insisted that conversation be kept to a minimum and handed out clear, unambiguous work assignments to her nurses.

The second head nurse (Miss Rogers) had a much more informal, almost kidding, relationship with her subordinates and patients. She consulted with her nurses about problems and changes and succeeded in developing a strong feeling of camaraderie on the floor.

Now you might assume that all the nurses would have preferred Miss Rogers' floor to Miss Smith's—but they didn't. The hospital let nurses choose which floor they wanted to work on; both floors were quite popular, but with different groups of nurses. In general, the older women liked the security of

---

[2] This case is based on research by Dr. Edith Lentz, School of Public Health, University of Minnesota.

Miss Smith's floor, where everything went according to predetermined routine. As one older nurse put it:

> "I honestly feel I need a responsible person nearby to supervise me. I need guidance and therefore I prefer to work where there is fairly close supervision. . . . I like things in an orderly fashion. . . . [On Miss Rogers' floor] things are done too sloppily."

Most of the younger girls preferred the independence allowed them by Miss Rogers, although a few younger girls with a farm background preferred to be under Miss Smith.

Why these differences? For one thing, nurse training in recent years has become less strict than it once was, and the younger nurses have never experienced close supervision. More important, these differences may reflect an attitude toward authority that the younger girls developed in their formative years at home and at school, an attitude influenced by the wide range of freedom permitted to modern children.

For many young people who have never had the experience of taking orders, the strict discipline required on the typical starting job (in industry or hospital) comes as a genuine shock. Those brought up on the farm, on the other hand, are introduced to chores (now a rarity in many city families) at an early age. For them, work and discipline are more easily taken in stride. Indeed, subordinates' feelings toward their boss are often colored by the relations they had with their parents and the emotional maturity and security they developed as children.

Moreover, the expectations of various groups in the population differ profoundly. College graduates, for instance, expect a great deal of responsibility and freedom. Certain ethnic groups, on the other hand, have trouble accepting the concept that people should make decisions for themselves, particularly decisions concerning work. For example, peasants from Latin countries who have worked for years under the control of *patrons* may find a sudden dose of independence extremely unsettling.[3]

Finally, certain types of work permit greater independence than others. Teachers, for instance, expect and are given more freedom than soldiers. Many jobs are so boring and routine that there is only slight opportunity for independent discretion.

Clearly, then, general supervision is not equally effective for all groups. Some people need to be pushed to work. Others resent being pushed. It is extremely important that these differences be understood by personnel directors, guidance counselors, and all others who help channel people into jobs. To take one example: people who demand a high degree of independence will usually be happier working as traveling salesmen than as bank clerks.

---

[3] Americans have often run into trouble trying to apply general supervision abroad. Since the employees are not prepared for this kind of treatment, they think something is wrong with a boss who doesn't act like a boss.

It is also important for supervisors to develop an awareness of the different attitudes toward freedom held by their subordinates.[4] One of the authors learned this lesson the hard way when he was working in a government office some years ago and was assigned an elderly secretary. Imbued with the principles of good human relations, he explained in detail the background of every letter he dictated, asked for her comments on style, and even suggested that, if she wished, she could draft some of the letters herself. At last she burst out, "I'm not paid to do that kind of work! That's your job."

To summarize: (1) modern industry requires that subordinates be in part dependent on their superiors for need satisfactions; (2) most people exhibit an ambivalent attitude toward dependence, wanting both the comfort and assurance it provides and also the freedom and autonomy it denies; and (3) attitudes toward independence differ widely from group to group and from individual to individual.

Exercising Authority

In the rest of this chapter we shall consider some of the ways in which the supervisor can make his exercise of authority more palatable to subordinates. The way in which he goes about giving orders, pointing out mistakes, and imposing discipline has a significant effect on how these actions are received. Further, the supervisor may develop loyalty among his subordinates by acting in the way *they* think a good boss should. To a considerable extent, this is a matter of getting to know them as individuals, being fair in handing out both assignments and favors, providing all the information necessary to do a good job and to satisfy curiosity, and giving subordinates a "break" when they are in trouble.

CONSULTING WITH SUBORDINATES

The way in which a supervisor issues an order influences the way in which it is received. With routine orders there usually is little trouble. But before a supervisor issues an order that will have a major impact on his subordinates, or an order that they are likely to resist, it is better for him to discuss it with them than to impose it unilaterally with no opportunity for questions or objections.

The wise supervisor explains such "critical" orders orally at first, though later he may put them in writing for permanent reference. To be sure, it may take more time to issue instructions orally rather than in writing. Yet, as we will see in Chapter 9, voice communication is often more effective than the written word. It permits the supervisor, if necessary, to present a de-

---

[4] See Theodore V. Purcell, "Observing People," *Harvard Business Review*, Vol. 33, No. 2 (March 1955), pp. 90-100.

tailed explanation of what he wants and why he wants it—and in a way that is tailor-made to the needs of the individual subordinate.

The effective supervisor also permits the subordinate to comment and to ask questions (at least within the limits set by other demands on the supervisor's time). This gives him a chance to judge how the subordinate is reacting to the proposed order and enables him to answer objections, explain points that are not clearly understood, or make arrangements for exceptional circumstances that may require special procedures. Moreover, the subordinate may come up with suggestions that will make the proposed order more workable—or he may object so strenuously that the supervisor will decide to withdraw the order altogether.

Doesn't the supervisor lose respect when he modifies or withdraws an order in face of his subordinate's objections? Yes—if his original instructions were stated in terms of "this is what I order you to do." No—if he has said, "I have been thinking about this and would like your reaction." There is a gain even if the supervisor eventually decides that he must impose an order over his subordinate's objections, for at least the subordinate has had a chance to be heard and to let off steam." [5]

Finally, a subordinate is more likely to carry out an order if he has specifically agreed to do so, for he is then committed to take some action. If the supervisor closes the discussion with the question, "Are you willing to give it a try?" he is likely to get assent. Even though this assent may be enforced, there has been an explicit agreement to go along. Suppose the subordinate refuses to assent? In most instances it is better to bring the resistance out in the open at the outset than to assume that the order will be carried out when in fact it will be sabotaged.

LISTENING TO SUGGESTIONS

Even when the supervisor cannot give his subordinates freedom to make decisions by themselves, he can encourage them to make suggestions. This practice provides the supervisor with a host of useful ideas and a more accurate feeling for what his subordinates are thinking. It provides subordinates with an opportunity to express themselves and to feel that they have made a valuable contribution to the operation of their organization.

The supervisor should not only listen to the suggestions that are brought to him; he should actively seek them out. There are many areas in which the supervisor doesn't have all the facts that he needs to make important

---

[5] To prevent misunderstanding, let us make clear what we are *not* saying: First, we are not saying that a supervisor should never issue an order. On the contrary. But *how* he issues the order *is* important. Second, we are not saying that the supervisor should *always* consult with subordinates before issuing orders or always propose them first in a tentative form ("I am thinking of...."). Obviously such an approach is not always required—and even where consultation might be useful in itself, the supervisor may not have time to do so.

decisions. Or perhaps he feels perfectly confident that he can make a good decision, but has some doubts about whether his subordinates will accept it. Under such circumstances it may pay for him to ask for suggestions. This approach will certainly result in better acceptance of the decision, and it may improve its quality as well. There is no obligation for the supervisor to accept all the ideas presented, so long as he considers them seriously. If he rejects all suggestions out of hand, however, his subordinates will soon see through his pretense.

Many of the suggestions made by subordinates are remarkably valuable. Understandably, the man who works close to a job day after day often knows more about it than his boss.

> Management in a small steel plant was facing an unusually stubborn problem. Product quality had fallen off and none of the engineering staff was able to come up with a solution. Expensive consultants also failed to stem the increasing flow of scrap. Finally, the plant manager called some of the old-timers together, explained the problem, and told them the firm would face bankruptcy if the problem wasn't solved. After a few minutes' discussion, one of these workers suggested the cause of the trouble and how to solve it. When asked why he hadn't produced this important information before, he answered, "I wasn't asked." [6]

People derive great satisfaction from knowing that their suggestions are being considered and even more if they are actually put into use. Everyone is enthusiastic about implementing his own ideas.

But what happens when management is obliged to reject a suggestion? Even here the suggestion has served a purpose. First, the subordinate did have a chance to express himself and to be heard. Second, by explaining why the suggestion was rejected, the supervisor can improve the subordinate's understanding of the problem and perhaps stimulate him to produce better suggestions in the future.

PROVIDING INFORMATION

The research studies cited on p. 125 indicate that high-production supervisors tend to give their subordinates as much information as they can about job performance and the job itself. This information helps the subordinate do better work by enabling him to make wiser decisions; moreover, it heightens his sense of security.

Few of us are content to be at the mercy of forces we do not understand. "Knowledge is power, primarily because it decreases dependence on the unknown and unpredictable." [7] Though the organization may be scrupulously fair, the subordinate will feel insecure unless he knows what he is expected to do and what is likely to happen to him in the future.

---

[3] From the experience of Joseph Scanlon, as told to the authors.
[7] McGregor, *op. cit.*, p. 59.

Understandably, employees are keenly interested in knowing what is expected of them on the job. For some this need is satisfied only when they receive explicit direction in every aspect of their work. You will remember the nurse who said, "I need guidance and therefore I prefer to work with a fairly strict supervisor."

> The older girls on Miss Rogers' floor complained because they did not receive enough detailed instructions; the younger girls on Miss Smith's floor felt insecure because Miss Smith failed to provide enough information for them to make decisions on their own, and had a habit of issuing unexpected and seemingly arbitrary orders.

Even those who value the freedom to make decisions themselves feel more self-confident in a well-structured situation. When they are given an order, they want some explanation of what is to be done, why it is to be done, and what limits will be set on their freedom—as well as any background information necessarly to help them do a better job or to satisfy their natural curiosity.

The subordinate is especially curious to know *where he stands with his boss.* For white-collar workers in particular, "getting ahead" is of paramount importance. The subordinate constantly asks himself "How am I doing?" and tries to divine from the boss' tone of voice or facial expression whether his performance is finding favor. The subordinate is directly dependent on his boss, he wants to please him, and he wants some sort of feedback or evaluation to indicate how his efforts are being received.

Finally, employees are keenly interested in knowing about anything that will have an effect on their future prospects or their work. What's the production level likely to be next week? Has the shipping department received the parts I need? Are the rumors true that this department will be automated? How will this affect me? How bad are the squawks down the line about the bum job I did yesterday? To the worker who is deprived of this sort of information, the future seems uncertain and sinister. Relegated to unrelieved ignorance, he develops what psychologists call a short-term perspective and loses all sense of involvement in his work.

CREATING A FEELING OF APPROVAL

Since employees are dependent on their boss, it is all-important for them to feel *accepted* by him, to feel that he appreciates both their work and themselves as individuals. Note, though, that acceptance means different things to different people.

> We once interviewed two lacquer-mixers who worked pretty much by themselves at opposite ends of a long factory floor. They did the same job and were under the same foreman (who said both did a good job). The first mixer said: "I've got a good boss. He knows I know the job so he leaves me alone, he never bothers me." The second mixer said: "My fore-

man doesn't care whether I'm dead or alive. He's a bum foreman who doesn't show any interest in his men or how they are doing."

Obviously these two men looked upon supervision very differently. The first saw supervision as something restricting, to be avoided if possible. The second expected help and reassurance from his boss. The important point is that both men were anxious to win approval and acceptance, but what came through clearly as acceptance to one man seemed outright rejection to the other. The supervisor must be alert to these subtle differences in the manner in which his behavior—however well intentioned—is interpreted.

A feeling of approval is a guarantee that each person is accepted as a person. It is an adult version of the child's feeling that his parents love him. It is the assurance that though the supervisor may chastise me for my mistakes, he values me as an individual. He is not out to get me. He is out to help me.

The supervisor can foster a feeling of approval in many different ways: taking an active interest in subordinates, listening to their problems, giving praise when justified, showing tolerance when mistakes are made, and so forth. Notice that we say *feeling* of approval. We are talking about the resultant of the over-all supervisory pattern rather than about any one specific act. In fact, the existence of such a feeling helps determine how individual acts are interpreted. *If* such a feeling exists, employees may tend to excuse their boss' mistakes; if it does *not* exist, they may exaggerate his mistakes out of all proportion. For instance, in the absence of a feeling of approval, a boss' attempt to show interest in his employees may be seen as meddling.

Thus the over-all pattern of the supervisor's behavior is infinitely more important than any specific gesture. Take kindness and courtesy as an example. Obviously saying "please" and "do you mind" is important, but employees soon see through superficial gestures if they conflict with the rest of the supervisor's behavior. In some situations cusswords are better evidence than icy courtesy that the boss likes you. Although most human beings like praise, they are suspicious of indiscriminate praise.[8] Further, it is not enough to praise good work. People have bad days as well as good; a real feeling of approval assures the individual that he can make mistakes once in a while without being punished.

In short, the existence of a feeling of approval means that the supervisor has demonstrated a personal loyalty to his subordinates. Until he has done so, he cannot expect loyalty to flow the other way.

HANDLING MISTAKES

In the preceding chapter we suggested that supervisors should set realistic goals for their subordinates, train them to do the best job they

---

[8] Praise given in public may give rise to charges of favoritism—and those who are not praised may feel that the supervisor is resorting to an undercover form of criticism against which they cannot defend themselves.

are capable of doing, and then give them a wide margin of freedom. But this does not mean that management should sit idly by when employees violate rules, turn out sloppy work, or fail to do their job. Quite the contrary. Not only is such laxity bad for production (and the company exists to make a profit); it is also unfair to the conscientious worker who carries out his assignments effectively, and it even serves to encourage the "culprit" in his bad work habits.

The supervisor cannot ignore mistakes. But the manner in which he handles them may determine whether his subordinates will resent his use of authority or will come to look upon him as a source of help.

Blame or help?   Research studies reveal that the difference between high-production and low-production supervisors lies not in their interest in eliminating mistakes, but in their manner of *handling* mistakes. Note the difference between these two comments: [9]

> "My boss thinks that whenever anything goes wrong it's always [my] fault. . . . He never says what he can do to help you, but he always picks your job apart. He tries hard, but he is too ready to condemn rather than help."

> "My boss is the best man I have ever worked for. He finds out what's troubling you before he tells you what to do, and he'll ask why. . . . Other supervisors come down here and start yelling at you before they find out what's wrong. But not him."

When something goes wrong, the low-production supervisor is interested above all in fixing blame and bawling out the person responsible ("Well, what sort of excuse do you have?"). He has a tendency to look to the past, to "cry over spilt milk," and to assume that all negligence is deliberate. What is the effect of such an approach? The subordinate denies responsibility, tries to pass the buck to someone else, or at least to find some sort of excuse to show that he really wasn't at fault. This approach encourages the "stool pigeon" and tends to make the development of harmonious groups almost impossible. If the group *does* succeed in working together in such an atmosphere, it directs its efforts *against* the supervisor.

The policy of blame-placing often defeats its own purpose: it makes employees so tense and insecure that they make even more mistakes. And it motivates them to cover up errors and spend their time trying to avoid *looking* wrong. As a result, upward communications is impaired and higher management can never get a clear picture of what is really happening below. A kind of game develops: in an effort to uncover the deceptions of subordinates, higher management sets up inspection systems and elaborate control reports, while the subordinates become increasingly adept at hiding mistakes.

In contrast, high-production supervisors tend to look forward, rather than

---

[9] Charles R. Walker, Robert H. Guest, and Arthur N. Turner, *The Foreman on the Assembly Line* (Cambridge: Harvard University Press, 1956), p. 45.

backward. They are interested in discovering what happened, why it happened, and what can be learned from it rather than in fixing responsibility. They look upon mistakes as an opportunity to provide training.[10]

Mistakes as a means of learning   If the supervisor insists that subordinates must never make a mistake, he is also insuring that they will never assume any real responsibility. Not that the subordinate should be encouraged to make mistakes. Far from it. But if he feels that one mistake is disastrous, he will be completely inhibited from taking any responsibility or initiative. The boss who feels that every mistake is a calamity must abandon all hope of improving the performance of his subordinates.

Actually, doing something wrong is often the most effective way of learning to do it right. Getting "burned" a few times may be the only way for us to learn that some of our pet ideas really won't work. A superior should weigh very carefully the cost of a mistake against the value of having the subordinate learn both (1) that he has the freedom to act on his own, even to make mistakes, and (2) that the particular way he has chosen was wrong. Overprotection by the superior means underdevelopment by the subordinate.

In effect, when mistakes are overpunished by severe criticism, people learn not just to avoid *specific* behavior, but to avoid *any* situation where a mistake is possible. When a subordinate has taken the initiative and his action has turned out badly, the supervisor can buttress his sense of independence by saying, "You made some mistakes in handling this, but I am glad you were willing to experiment and to take responsibility on your own." Of course, if the subordinate continues to make mistakes or exceeds his authority, then it may be necessary to take disciplinary action.

Calling mistakes to subordinates' attention   When the supervisor should call a mistake to a subordinate's attention is a matter of judgment that depends both on the situation and on the subordinate's personality. "Many times workers recognize their own mistakes and take steps to remedy them before the supervisor steps in. If, then, the supervisor pushes his criticism anyway, the worker becomes resentful. It is only when workers are unaware of their mistakes or seem not to be profiting from them that the supervisor should step in." [11]

On the other hand, it is clearly foolish to let a subordinate continue to make mistakes when he is obviously making no progress in solving them or when

---

[10] For two studies which show that supervisors who engage in non-punitive handling of mistakes have higher production, see Michael Argyl, Godfrey Gardner, and Frank Cioffi, "Supervisory Methods Related to Productivity, Absenteeism and Turnover," *Human Relations,* Vol. XI, No. 1 (1958), p. 38; and Robert L. Kahn and Daniel Katz, "Leadership Practices in Relation to Productivity and Morale," *Group Dynamics,* Dorwin Cartwright and Alvin Zander, eds. (Evanston, Ill.: Row, Peterson, 1953), p. 621.

[11] William F. Whyte, *Human Relations in the Restaurant Industry* (New York: McGraw-Hill, 1948), p. 270.

they are causing great harm to the organization. Leaving a subordinate in the dark when he is doing a poor job is unfair both to him and to the organization as a whole.

Most people say they prefer to have their mistakes pointed out so that they can take steps to correct them. Yet constructive criticism is always difficult to present, and if it is badly presented it leads to resentment.

Some supervisors find it temperamentally difficult to correct their subordinates. They are unsure of the soundness of their own judgment; or they resist accepting the responsibility of "playing God" and judging other men; or they are reluctant to risk injuring the personal relations they have established with their men. As a consequence, one often hears supervisors defending their failure to offer constructive criticism: "You shouldn't correct anyone until you are 100 per cent sure you are right. You have got to get all the facts." But this is an exaggeration of the problem. There is no need to prove the other man *wrong*. The question of guilt is irrelevant. What *is* relevant is to discuss the trouble in terms of "What happened? What can be done about it?"

Investigating mistakes   Some observers say that a supervisor should never try to correct a subordinate unless he can offer a better alternative. The cautiousness implied in this approach is commendable, and yet little harm is done when the supervisor says, "There seems to be something wrong here. Frankly, I don't know the answer, but perhaps we can work it out together." Certainly this is better than letting anger and suspicion mount until one has "all the facts." Lack of frankness between superior and subordinate cannot help but generate tension and misunderstanding.

> When a mistake is made, ask the worker how it happened. *Let him tell you.* If his explanation is weak, he'll recognize it in telling the story, and so will you. You won't have to rub it in, in most cases, because he knows what is expected of him and is willing to recognize his own failings—when he isn't pushed and prodded with them.
>
> Then ask him to *tell you* how the mistake can be avoided in the future. You don't have to accept his solution but, with this approach you are more likely to get him to accept responsibility for his actions and to try to do something constructive.[12]

Letting the subordinate explain what went wrong and then work out his own solution has a definite educational value. As one supervisor put it, "When you go to them that way and let them explain, they feel a lot better. Sometimes they will come to you and tell you when they make a mistake, and you can really talk it over. That's very important."[13]

Often the problem involves the entire group and can best be handled by group discussion. But here, too, the supervisor can refrain from trying to pin

---

[12] Whyte, *op. cit.*, p. 269.
[13] *Ibid.*, p. 268.

the blame on one or two individuals and concentrate instead on working out a solution for future activities that is satisfactory to everyone.

Criticism   Most mistakes are due to ignorance or lack of skill, and can be handled through training without resort to overt criticism. Some mistakes, however, are clearly due to negligence; here the supervisor has no choice but to let the subordinate know that he is dissatisfied with the subordinate's level of performance. But unless the supervisor is tactful in making his criticism, he will jeopardize his relationship not only with the subordinate but with the whole work group as well. Whyte suggests some useful rules:

> **1.** The criticism should be voiced in a matter-of-fact manner. Emotional heat on the part of the critic seems to beget a defensive reaction on the part of the surbordinate. Only when the subordinate refuses to act on the criticism does it seem advisable to apply the heat.
> **2.** The criticism should be focused on the job operation and should, as much as possible, avoid placing of personal blame.
> **3.** After it has been stated, the criticism should be dropped—unless the mistake has not been corrected. Men speak of the emotional tensions they have been under when working for a [supervisor] who would not only criticize you but would then seem to be "down" on you for a long time thereafter. One man described the more effective approach in this way:
>
> > "Ed will tell you right to your face how he wants it done. Oh, sometimes we might have a little argument about it, but when the argument is over, it is really over and forgotten. He never gets down on you. You like to work for a fellow like that."
>
> **4.** Criticism should be balanced by giving credit for good work. No matter how skillfully a man makes his criticism, if he has only critical remarks to make, he destroys cooperation.[14]

It should be added that criticism of this sort is best offered in private.

Some mistakes are due to improper training, failure to understand instructions, or severe problems at home. In situations of this sort, the supervisor may be able to get at the root of the trouble only through skillful interviewing. And he may have to resort to formal discipline if the subordinate fails to respond to criticism and training. The problems of interviewing and discipline will be discussed in later chapters.

DEVELOPING PERSONAL RELATIONS

A subordinate is less likely to feel frustrated by the demands and restrictions imposed by his supervisor if the supervisor shows a personal interest in him. Consequently, in spite of the other demands of his job, the effective supervisor "makes" time to get to know his subordinates and to help them with their problems both on and (to some extent) off the job.

---

[14] William F. Whyte, *Leadership in the Work Team* (mimeographed, 1956), pp. 12-13.

Need for personal relations If the subordinate is convinced that his superior has a personal interest in him, he is less likely to feel overly dependent or lost in the organization. In addition, personal relations help build a more tightly knit work group and assure the supervisor of a position as an informal leader (so that people follow him because they like him, as well as because they must). When a subordinate has friendly, personal relations with his boss, he is less hesitant to bring his work problems to his boss' attention.

People like being treated as individuals. Yet, as far as the company is concerned, the average employee is nothing more than a time-card number or a job specification. The company is impersonal; only the immediate boss can make management personal. Particularly to the new employee, the immediate supervisor *is* the company, and what he does helps mold the individual's conception of the company as a whole. An insensitive supervisor can easily counterbalance all the company's efforts to create a good impression through public relations and fringe benefits.

It is generally recognized that home problems affect efficiency on the job. The good supervisor listens to his employees' problems, and in some areas actually offers assistance. Ordinarily, all he can do is listen, but even this provides some relief to the individual in distress. In any case, the more the supervisor learns about the people who work for him, the better he can understand their behavior and how to deal with it.

Even more important, good informal relations on matters that are not directly related to the job set the stage for better communication between supervisor and subordinate on problems related to work. Few employees feel completely free and easy when they are talking with their boss about the work in hand, for they are quite aware that he is the one who hands out rewards and punishments. But when they talk about the employee's fishing trip, the employee is an *expert* for the time being, even if there is no true feeling of equality between them. Some of the air of permissiveness and informality created in discussing baseball or the weather may carry over to on-the-job affairs. Once the supervisor and the subordinate know each other as individuals, both will feel freer to bring up mutual problems.

To put it another way: Earlier we said that the good supervisor tries to reduce the number of orders he gives by encouraging people to ask him questions rather than telling them what to do. For this approach to succeed, however, the subordinates must feel confident and secure enough to go to their boss when difficulties arise.

Setting the tone Obviously, it is the superior who sets the tone of the relationship, not the subordinate. First, the supervisor must make himself available to all comers. The boss who barricades himself behind a wall of formality or is always "busy, busy, busy" is not likely to develop satisfactory informal relationships. Nor is it enough to be a good fellow a few times a year. In most companies the permissive atmosphere of the annual Christmas party stands out in sharp contrast to the distant relationship that is normal for the rest of the year.

The supervisor must take the initiative by maintaining regular and frequent contacts with subordinates. Some supervisors make periodic "howdy rounds," talking to each employee in turn. Even if these chats consist only of idle chatter, still they provide an opportunity for employees to bring up problems that are bothering them. In other words, the supervisor opens up the contact and lets the subordinate decide what topics should be covered.

This technique may create a dilemma for the supervisor, however: if he spends too much time with any one individual, the others may feel left out and charge him with favoritism. Moreover, some employees are easier and more interesting to talk to than others.[15] And some who are unusually talkative or feel that they are burdened with more than their share of problems may seek to monopolize the boss' limited time. But the employees whom the supervisor should really try to contact are often the hardest to know.

Certain very real dangers are likely to arise when the supervisor develops excessively close personal relations with his subordinates, particularly in circumstances where he must rely on close rather than general supervision. A supervisor can develop friendly relations with individual subordinates and listen to their problems without losing his dignity. It is much more debatable whether he should go further and try to become part of the gang. This question will be discussed further in the next chapter.

In any case, there is more to being a good boss than being a nice fellow. Although many employees respond to the "glad-hand" approach, most are suspicious of insincerity. It is better to be naturally reserved than artificially friendly. After all, the supervisor must develop a *long-term* relationship, and over a period of time it is easy for subordinates to detect whether he is merely pretending to show interest in them. In today's cynical world people are highly suspicious of overfriendliness: they are constantly fearful of being manipulated. Unless the supervisor combines good informal "social" relations with good on-the-job relations, he will be judged a hypocrite. "He'll try to butter you up. But watch out, he'll stab you in the back."

TREATING SUBORDINATES FAIRLY

Since subordinates are directly dependent on their boss, they are understandably anxious to receive fair treatment from him. The supervisor can demonstrate his sense of fair play by letting each employee know exactly what is expected of him and by exercising consistent discipline. He can base his decisions on grounds that are accepted as legitimate by his subordinates and, above all, he can make an all-out effort to treat people equally.

---

[15] This problem has interesting complications when the supervisor is male and the subordinates are young, attractive, and female. Romance belongs in the novel, not the shop.

"Treating people equally" is not as simple as it sounds. The conscientious supervisor is torn between two conflicting, though universally accepted, platitudes: "Avoid favoritism" and "Treat people as individuals, in accordance with their special needs." He can never forget that each individual has special needs, but at the same time he must realize that what appears to be inconsistent treatment will create endless bad feeling within the group.

With all the good will in the world, the supervisor may begin to play favorites unconsciously and to follow the normal tendency of either favoring the passive, dependent, "good" employee or paying the most attention to the aggressive individual who fights for his demands, to "oil the wheel that squeaks the loudest." The supervisor must avoid both extremes.

Making exceptions What about making exceptions in special situations? Obviously, treating people fairly does not mean treating everyone in exactly the same way. It does mean that when an exception is made, it must be accepted as legitimate by all members of the group. There is a general rule, for example, that vacations must be taken during the summer months. Bill Lawrence's wife is sick, so the boss lets him have February off to take her to Florida. Is this favoritism? Only if Bill Lawrence's fellow workers think so. An exception of this sort will be accepted as fair if the group (1) knows why it was made, (2) accepts it as justified, and (3) is confident that another employee in the same situation would receive the same treatment.

Giving "breaks" In theory, the subordinate is supposed to carry out the rules and regulations of the organization to the letter—regardless of special circumstances that make it difficult or impossible for him to do so. As a consequence, the subordinate often feels hopelessly dependent. But the supervisor can reduce this feeling by "giving a man a break when he is in a tough spot"—that is, by making judicious use of exceptions and favors, provided, of course, that these "breaks" are given consistently to all.

Granting special favors when the circumstances permit not only lessens the subordinate's feeling that the organization is arbitrary and "heartless"; it may also lead to an "exchange of good turns."

> Whether you are talking about primitive tribesmen, industrial workers, businessmen, or college professors, you can make one generalization that holds without exception. If John Doe does something for you, you feel under the obligation to do something for him in return, when the opportunity arises. This sort of exchange of favors helps to build cohesive organizations. It is also one of the most powerful builders of morale that we can call upon. The supervisor in industry who neglects it does so at his peril. [16]

As a worker in an assembly plant described it:

> My foreman knows the traits of human nature and acts accordingly. . . .
> He came in one morning and it was bitterly cold. He went out to the

---
[16] Whyte, *op. cit., pp.* 213-250

cafeteria and brought two big cans of hot coffee and gave it to the men. While we can't be bought the thought was there and we appreciated it. As a result the men picked up lots of jobs that ordinarily they would have let go through to be picked up by the repair man.[17]

The assumption behind this approach is that if the supervisor does more for his men than is absolutely required, they will respond in kind. It means, for instance, that if Jack comes to work with a sprained ankle, the foreman will find him some work that he can do sitting down; if a waitress is suddenly deluged with customers, the hostess will relieve some of the pressure by setting up tables and pouring water. The hope is that when an emergency arises the subordinates will reciprocate by doing more than is normally required, by working overtime or by producing more than the usual "bogey." Thus an atmosphere is created in which both supervisor and subordinate exhibit a flexible attitude toward their mutual obligations.

There are dangers in such an approach, however. In the first place, if the supervisor constantly reminds his subordinates of his good turns, or if he seems to count them up, they will be resented rather than appreciated. As the worker in the assembly plant said above, "We can't be bought."

The supervisor should be careful to bestow favors only when the employee needs them. If, for instance, the boss decides to lend a hand at a time when the subordinate feels he is doing his job adequately, the subordinate may either look upon his help as meddling or accept it as the normal thing and complain when he doesn't get it.

Conclusion

Although the use of general supervision may minimize the occasions on which the supervisor has to resort to authority, he cannot abandon authority altogether. There are times when he must act as boss. In fact, there are some people who, because of personality or background, expect their boss to provide "firm" leadership, and there are situations where the "loose" form of supervision implied by general supervision is just not enough to get the job done. Knowing *when* (and when not) to use firmness is one of the critical criteria for effective leadership.

It is also important to know *how* to use authority: the manner in which it is used may spell the difference between resentment and acceptance. The supervisor may have to take action when mistakes are made; but he can either barge in like "a bull in a china shop" or he can try to help the offending individuals do a better job. Although the boss may have to make decisions that his subordinates dislike, they will be less resentful of his authority if they feel he is fair, understands and accepts them as individuals.

---

[17] Arthur N. Turner, "Foreman—Key to Worker Morale," *Harvard Business Review,* Vol. 35, No. 5 (September 1956), p. 77.

So far, we have been concerned with the supervisor's relationship with individual subordinates. Many supervisory problems, however, involve the supervisor's relationship with the entire group. This distinction between individual and group problems is not easy to make. Take tardiness as an example. If only a few people are ever late to work, one might assume that their tardiness is accidental or due to individual home problems. The solution obviously is to talk to each individual separately. If, on the other hand, everyone is regularly ten to fifteen minutes late, there is strong reason to believe that a group standard is in operation, and any solution to the problem must deal with the group as a whole.

In general, the supervisor who is successful in dealing with his work group makes three attempts: (1) where practical, he respects the standards and norms of behavior and value that the members of the group believe are proper, (2) he encourages the group to participate in discussing and solving problems that involve the group as a whole, both through meetings and through the informal group structure, and (3) he tries to strengthen the teamwork and solidarity

The Supervisor
and the Group

of the group. In addition, if he is to win the group's respect, he must maintain a proper social distance from his subordinates and display technical ability on the job.

Respecting Standards

As we mentioned in Chapter 3, every group has customs, proprieties, and expectations that its members believe are proper. A supervisor who violates these standards does so at his peril: the group can retaliate in numerous ways, ranging from refusal to do more than their normal share in time of emergency, to wild-cat strikes and sabotage. In contrast, the supervisor who respects the group's standards often wins its cooperation and, at times, even finds that the group will modify its standards in management's favor.

> Train crews in a marshalling yard were handling 150 trains a day. Through short-cuts (often violating safety rules) they were able to finish their work in six hours. The rest of the time they could sleep or read.

We can identify several standards in this situation: (1) 150 trains a day represent a proper work load, (2) the remaining time can be spent as the men wish, and (3) certain rules will not be enforced.

> Then management decided that since the men had so much free time they could handle 200 trains. Immediately the men began to follow all the rules. They would never move a train even a few feet without having someone go back and wave a red flag. As a result, the men put in a full day's work, but productivity fell to 50 trains a day. Soon management gave up its demand for 200.

Here management violated group standards, and the men retaliated in a way that left management helpless.[1]

THE SUPERVISOR'S BACKGROUND

Every group has definite expectations about what qualifications a good supervisor should possess. If a supervisor lives up to these expectations, his subordinates will feel that he deserves his job, that he has legitimatized his claim to authority.[2]

The fair-haired boy who is promoted solely on the basis of family con-

---

[1] What, if anything, could management have done to raise production beyond 150 trains a day? What, if anything, could management have done to enforce the safety rules without causing a substantial reduction in output?

[2] In some instances there are expectations as to the ethnic background of supervisors. If these expectations are met, men will cooperate with him; otherwise there may be restriction of output. Orvis Collins, "Ethnic Behavior in Industry: Sponsorship and Rejection in a New England Factory," *The American Journal of Sociology,* Vol. 51 (1946), pp. 293-298.

nections will find it hard to win cooperation. The outsider who is brought in over the head of someone who the group feels deserves the job will have to face strong resentment—though "proper" behavior may ultimately win him respect. Subordinates always subject a new supervisor to a period of testing and initiation to determine whether he measures up to their standards.

In the old days, the foreman was expected to be the biggest and strongest man in the shop. (Foremen often had to defend their positions in fist fights.) Today physical skill is less crucial, but, as we shall see, it is important for the supervisor to be technically skilled in the work performed by his department, even if he rarely practices this skill.

It may appear that the best way of insuring that a supervisor will be accepted by the group is to promote someone from the ranks who is already well liked—in other words, a respected informal leader.[3] But this raises the difficult and much-debated question: Should a man be asked to supervise his former equals? Among the problems to consider in deciding on such a step are:

1. Is the leader really respected by the group? Our research shows that in some disunited groups, particularly those that reject most of management's objectives, the apparent leader is often only a mouthpiece who has been selected for his ability to cause trouble, but who commands no real respect from the group.

2. Is there a basic conflict between the group and management? If the informal leader is promoted to a supervisory position and asked to work for objectives and enforce regulations that the group rejects, either (a) he will flatly refuse to do so, or (b) he will agree to work for management's goals and be considered a traitor by his former friends. In any event he will be faced with a painful moral dilemma. If the question "Which side are you on? Management's or labor's?" is asked too insistently, it is obvious that the formal leader cannot also be an informal one.

Yet we have observed many situations in which informal leaders have stepped into formal leadership with hardly a change in their relationship to the group. The supervisor remains "one of the boys," and the fact that he has become boss does not cost him the respect of his new subordinates. A highly respected foreman told this story about what happened when he was promoted:

> "A lot of young fellows who came in my department after the war came from my neighborhood and I always helped them learn their jobs. I guess since I was the oldest man in the department they always came

---

[3] There has been some rather limited but successful experimentation with the use of sociometric choice as a basis for selecting supervisors. See Norman R. F. Maier, *Psychology in Industry*, 2nd ed. (Boston: Houghton Mifflin, 1955), pp. 133-134; and Douglas H. Freyer, "Buddy Ratings: Popularity Contest or Leadership Criteria," *Personnel Psychology*, Vol. 2, No. 2 (Summer 1949), pp. 147-156.

to me with their questions. *When I became foreman I kept on doing just what I did before. My relations haven't changed since I became foreman."*

This type of adjustment occurs most frequently on jobs where subordinates enjoy a great deal of freedom and where high technical skill is required—in maintenance work, for example, or among professional engineers.[4]

There is some evidence that employees are more likely to accept a supervisor who has worked his way up through the ranks in a department where there is a well-defined status hierarchy than in one where all the employees are on the same status level. In a department where there is a step-by-step progression from unskilled to skilled jobs, all workers have a chance to move up, and the supervisor's job is just the logical top rung of the ladder. Moreover, the supervisor has legitimatized his position by demonstrating high technical skill. In departments where all the workers do the same job, however, the jump from worker to supervisor makes one, in a way, a "traitor" to his class and is more than just the logical last step toward which everyone has been aspiring.

Men who have been promoted from the ranks, of course, have the tremendous advantage of knowing both the production and human-relations problems in their departments.[5] Furthermore, they have an intimate knowledge of how the group expects the supervisor to behave.

THE SUPERVISOR'S BEHAVIOR

Over a period of time, every group develops certain expectations about how their supervisor should behave (just as the British have specific expectations as to the proper behavior of royalty). Let us look at a few examples:

In some situations a supervisor will lose face if he swears and loses his temper. In others he is "a softy" if he does not. In some offices it is traditional for the supervisor to treat the girls to lunch once a year. In industrial plants it is not uncommon for the foremen to have a drink with the boys on payday. Often executives expect their superior to entertain them at home once in a while (the same holds true for college professors and their dean). Expectations may differ radically between groups. Some groups expect the supervisor to be available every minute of the day: "He's right in there pitching." "He's always on hand when we need him." Others expect the supervisor to keep his distance: "A good boss doesn't hang over you." In groups that expect the supervisor to "act like a boss," the men take advantage of him if

---

[4] In research laboratories and in construction work, individuals are constantly switching back and forth from being a supervisor to being a subordinate. The individual who is momentarily a supervisor cannot afford to antagonize his subordinates, since he may be "given the works" when he is in the position of subordinate again.

[5] See Charles R. Walker, Robert H. Guest, and Arthur N. Turner, *The Foreman on the Assembly Line* (Cambridge: Harvard University Press, 1956), pp. 101-104.

he doesn't rule with an iron hand. In other groups it is a great compliment to say that the supervisor "doesn't act like a boss." [6] Groups also have expectations about the amount of work a supervisor should do. If he falls short of the group's expectations, he is a "lazy so-and-so"; if he exceeds expectations, he is an "eager beaver."

This much is clear: A good supervisor knows what his group expects of him, and a new supervisor should become familiar with group expectations as soon as possible. Expectations can be changed to some extent (see Chapter 12), but this takes time and may arouse anxiety and conflict.

FAIR DEMANDS

Subordinates also have strong ideas about what the supervisor can legitimately demand of them in the way of work, and it is important for the supervisor to know what these expectations are.[7] If he restricts his demands to those that the group thinks are legitimate, then obedience will be almost automatic. On the other hand, if he makes demands that the group feels are excessive, he must be prepared for resistance.

Most workers realize that they assume certain obligations when they accept a job, and acknowledge that the boss has a right to insist on a "fair day's work." But they have definite expectations as to what constitutes a "fair day's work" and, as we saw in the train-marshalling case above, they strongly resist doing more. They resent what they regard as "being taken advantage of."

A supervisor's instructions are more likely to be accepted by the group if they seem to be concerned with getting the job done rather than with the arbitrary exercise of authority for authority's sake. In general, a subordinate rejects an order as unfair if it is not reasonably related to the purpose for which he was hired. He resents rules that are imposed with no apparent reason. Thus no-smoking rules are hard to enforce unless employees are convinced that there is a real fire hazard. The supervisor must be able to justify rules as essential to getting the job done, maintaining plant safety, and so forth.

In recent years, group norms have also developed in relation to job jurisdiction. Regardless of the union contract, for example, a group may consider it unacceptable for a maintenance man to be asked to do production work—and vice versa.

---

[6] See Alvin Gouldner, *Patterns of Industrial Bureaucracy* (Glencoe, Ill.: Free Press, 1954), p. 161.

[7] See, for example, Peter M. Blau, *The Dynamics of Bureaucracy* (Chicago: University of Chicago Press, 1955), Chapter XI; and Gouldner, *op. cit.*, especially Chapters II, X, and XI.

WORK CUSTOMS

The supervisor should also be sensitive to the indirect effect of his actions on work customs. Take status for example. Assigning younger workers to the newest equipment may enable them to earn higher bonuses than their seniors, thereby splitting the work force into two hostile groups. Innocent decisions about parking lots or the arrangement of tables in the cafeteria may upset delicate relations within the group and lead to turmoil and antagonism.

Time-honored work customs sometimes conflict sharply with management's formal rules. In a gypsum board plant, for example, it was well-established practice for workers to take "extra" boards home with them for personal use. When a new supervisor decided to crack down and enforce the rules against "stealing," he helped precipitate a wild-cat strike.[8] If the supervisor is "indulgent" in minor areas that do not affect the organization's major objectives, the group is more likely to reciprocate by accepting the organization's objectives as its own.

Supervisors who ignore or flout these customs do so at their peril— *although sometimes management must take that risk.* Before doing so, however, management should pause and consider the full implications of what it intends to do, or perhaps devise an approach that will achieve management's objectives without a frontal attack on what the group feels to be its vested prerogatives. For instance, in the gypsum board case, management might decide that pilferage had to be stopped regardless of cost, or might permit employees to take home a limited number of "seconds" with the permission of their supervisors.

So far we have emphasized the negative aspects of the supervisor's relationship with the group, suggesting that he should respect group norms and expectations, or at least realize when he is violating them. Now let us turn to some more positive aspects of this relationship.

Developing Group Participation

Many high-production supervisors have discovered that they can obtain better results by giving the group an opportunity to participate in decision-making, either through consulting with the group or by allowing it to make and implement decisions by itself.

> Industrial engineers in a metal plating department had been trying for a long time to figure out an equitable way of dividing up the girls' work. The operation was unusually complex and erratic, and every time the

---

[8] Gouldner, *op. cit.*

engineers made a suggestion the girls were quick to prove that it was unfair to someone. The engineers were about to give up in disgust when the girls asked, "Why not let us decide?" In a short while they had worked out job allocations that even the engineers agreed were superior to theirs.

Naturally everybody gains from this sort of participation. The girls win the satisfaction of exercising greater control over their work environment, as well as the feeling of success from having accomplished something by themselves. Management gains in that better decisions are often made by people close to the job. There is less need for the supervisor to exercise authority or to follow the philosophy of "be strong"; individual employees are more likely to obey rules they themselves have established.

Employees who are given the freedom to regulate themselves are far more capable of making sound decisions when emergencies arise. Since they make the decisions by themselves, there is less need for them to refer every problem to the supervisor. As a consequence, he can concentrate on long-term planning and handling relations with other departments. For example, in one situation:

> [The foreman] allowed and encouraged his regular operators to take some of the responsibility for ensuring that good work was done in the section. Thus this meant that there was more interaction between operators concerning work. . . . Without waiting for the foremen or inspectors to point out trouble, the operators themselves kept each other posted about actual or potential trouble encountered in their section, and, furthermore, advised one another as to steps which should be taken to correct the difficulty.[9]

When subordinates are given the necessary freedom, they often do an impressive job of working out their own methods of scheduling, quality control, and so forth. They may even set production goals for themselves and discipline those who fail to live up to expectations. Sometimes these goals are surprisingly high.

> Groups that participate in setting goals for themselves often make higher demands for themselves than supervisors and methods engineers consider practical. A furnace cleaning job was cut from four to two days; tardiness was set at less than 3 per cent when formerly it was 10 per cent; service calls were reduced from one in 14 to one in 21 . . . repairs per man per day rose from 8.5 to 12.5 when the crew planned the service; and over a period of three years men worked more days when they decided whether or not the weather was inclement than when the supervisor made the decision.[10]

The mere fact that the group is given the power to enforce and implement rules makes the group more likely to accept the rules themselves, even rules to which they might otherwise object. In other words, whether or not

---

9 Walker, Guest, and Turner, *op. cit.*, p. 110.
10 Maier, *op. cit.*, p. 172.

a group accepts management's objectives depends not only on *what* is demanded but on *how* it is demanded.

> The superintendent of a machine operation was convinced by his Safety Department that long-sleeved shirts were a safety hazard even when rolled up. So he posted a notice that beginning the next Monday morning wearing long-sleeved shirts on the job would be prohibited.
>
> Monday morning four men showed up with long sleeves. Given the choice of working without shirts or cutting off their sleeves, they refused to do either and were sent home. The union filed a sharp grievance, asking for back pay for time lost.
>
> Then the Personnel Department stepped in. The rule was suspended for a week and a special meeting was called with the union grievance committee. The safety director explained that if a worker got his sleeve caught in a machine his whole arm might be ripped off. The union agreed to the rule provided that it was extended to include management (who originally had been exempt on the grounds that they didn't get close enough to the machines).
>
> Next Monday the rule went back into effect. A few men, forgetfully, arrived in long sleeves. The other men handed them a pair of scissors and insisted that the offending sleeves be cut off on the spot. Later in the afternoon a union vice-president and a company time-study man were treated in the same way.

Summarizing, these examples suggest that permitting the group to participate in decisions—through actually making the decisions, enforcing them, or being consulted about them—may result in genuine advantages for management. Employees take more responsibility for minor problems without constantly running to the supervisor with questions, they set production goals (at times at higher levels than would be set by management), they enforce their own rules, and they even modify their group standards in a way they might not otherwise do. In addition, of course, members of the work group gain many satisfactions from participation: a chance to be creative, to feel a sense of accomplishment, to show leadership, to let off steam, and so forth.

How can the supervisor stimulate participation of this sort? To some extent he can permit it to develop naturally, merely by refraining from close supervision. However, if he goes too far, and simply says "Take over," fumbling and confusion are bound to result. In the following two sections we shall see that supervisors can encourage the group to develop effective participation through (1) holding meetings with subordinates to consider mutual problems, and (2) working through the informal organization of the group.

HOLDING MEETINGS

Many an effective supervisor calls his subordinates together whenever he has a problem of common interest. Of course, individual problems can be discussed and worked out in private conversations, but *group* problems require *group* discussion. Such meetings need not be formal. Indeed, meetings range all the way from a regular session of the board of directors to an informal discussion between a foreman and a couple of mechanics around a machine that has been causing trouble.

Meetings of this sort may be used for three different purposes:

The supervisor makes an announcement   This is simply a substitute for posting a notice or speaking to subordinates one by one. Obviously taking the whole work force away from their job is an expensive procedure, but it insures that everyone will be notified of new directives or information which are important to the whole group. Furthermore, such meetings give subordinates a chance to ask questions, raise objections, and discuss the implications of the announcement.

The supervisor asks for suggestions   Just as the supervisor can ask individuals for suggestions on how to solve a problem (see p. 149), so he can call a meeting for the same purpose. Though the supervisor will make the final decision on whether or not the suggestions are accepted, people derive great satisfaction from knowing that their ideas are being considered and even more if they are used. A group of individuals exchanging opinions and experiences often comes up with better suggestions than any one person working alone.[11] A suggestion that has evolved from the contribution of many members of the group is more likely to be implemented with enthusiasm by the entire group than is a suggestion that is the brain child of one person, whether he is the supervisor or an individual subordinate.

The supervisor lets the group make its own decision   Just as the supervisor can delegate authority to individual subordinates to handle problems that involve them alone, so he may call a meeting and delegate authority to the group to handle problems that involve the group as a whole. Of course, there is little difference between a meeting called to solicit suggestions and a meeting called to enable the group to make decisions on its own. But, by waiving its veto power, management thrusts upon the group the responsibility for choosing between alternatives.

CAN MEETINGS BE TRUSTED?

Critics of group decision-making make this objection: "Very well, but can you be sure the group can be trusted to make what is from management's

---

11 There is considerable dispute over whether the ideas brought out by the group are of higher "quality" than ideas brought out by the same number of people working as individuals. The answer seems to vary with the nature of the problem. For instance, individuals may be more efficient than groups in devising crossword puzzles, but groups are better in solving them.

point of view the right decision? Won't subordinates avoid responsibility and try to get out of work? If given the power to make decisions, won't they wander over into areas that are none of their business?"

Actually, there are many areas in which management does not care what decision is made, so long as there is no excessive dissension. For example, management is unconcerned with how men divide up the dirty work so long as the work is done—or how rest periods or vacations are scheduled, so long as the time allotted is not exceeded. Since no vacation schedule can satisfy everybody, hard feelings are bound to result. The supervisor who can pass the responsibility on to the group saves himself a major headache.[12]

In other areas the supervisor's objectives coincide with those of the group —in matters of accident-prevention or avoiding jam-ups in the parking lot, for example. Possibly management should reserve a veto power over decisions in such matters, although it is unlikely that the group will make decisions that are, from management's point of view, far wrong.

The supervisor, of course, is interested not only in getting a sound decision but also in getting one that is accepted by the group. An *adequate* solution that is enthusiastically implemented by the group may well be better than a *perfect* solution that meets with stubborn antagonism. Thus the group-decision process is of particular value when management is more concerned with getting *acceptance* of a decision than with its *quality*.[13]

How can the supervisor keep the meeting from encroaching on areas of decision-making that are not its proper concern? One way is to set clear *limits* to the group's area of freedom. (These limits are similar to the authority-delegating limits we discussed in Chapter 6.) Suppose management is interested in refurnishing the ladies' lounge. The experienced supervisor might say, "We have $500 allowed us. How should we spend it?" rather than "What should be done?" or, even worse, "How much should we spend?" Similarly, instead of asking "How much vacation time should you get?" the supervisor might ask, "How many people can we spare at any one time during vacation and still maintain production? Who should go when?"

If there is no agreement on basic objectives, however, even this setting of limits provides no absolute safeguard against what management might regard as irresponsible decisions. Children balk at being asked, "Which do

---

[12] Note, however, that the supervisor still must preside over the process by which the men make the decision. If the supervisor merely says, "You decide," without helping to establish a procedure by which the decision can be made, there will be endless bickering and confusion. It is the supervisor's responsibility to help the group resolve its internal disputes.

[13] For a thorough discussion of this point, see Harold P. Zelko, *Successful Conference and Discussion Techniques* (New York: McGraw-Hill, 1957), p. 144. A. Whitney Griswold of Yale is supposed to have asked, "Could *Hamlet* have been written by a committee or Mona Lisa been painted by a club?" Donald W. Taylor, Paul Berry, and Clifford H. Block, "Group Participation, Brainstorming, and Creative Thinking," *Administrative Science Quarterly*, Vol. 3, No. 1 (June 1958), p. 27.

you want, milk of magnesia or castor oil?" and their parents also object to being asked to make that sort of choice. Normally a group will refuse to make a decision on "We've got to lay off twenty men. Who should they be?" unless there is some previous agreement among the parties that *someone* will be laid off. There must be a mutual acceptance of objectives before a group decision is possible.

Ideally, management provides broad areas of freedom in which subordinates can regulate their own behavior (this is simply teamwork). However, there are bound to be areas of basic conflict between superiors and subordinates, between the organization and its members. In approaching these areas, the most the supervisor can do is explain why he has made a particular decision and perhaps ask for questions. At one time or another, every supervisor must face the inevitability of making and announcing distasteful decisions.

Often great skill is required if the leader is to prevent a group decision from creating greater internal conflict than existed before. (For a discussion of conference leadership techniques, see Chapter 10). The danger of conflict is particularly great where strong vested interests are involved (for instance, when the group is deciding whether "soft jobs" should be rotated or assigned on the basis of seniority). The less cohesive the group, the greater the difficulty in reaching agreement, though experience in making decisions of this sort may help cohesion develop.

GROUP CONSULTATION ON A DAY-TO-DAY BASIS

The preceding discussion may have given the impression that the use of meetings involves a drastic change from traditional management practice. Quite the contrary. In some companies most major decisions have long been made by committees, particularly at the higher levels of management. (Sometimes this practice is called "multiple management.") And at lower levels it is now accepted practice for supervisors to hold regular meetings at which subordinates can raise questions, discuss common problems, and consider new developments. Increasingly, such meetings are being held even on the hourly-paid level, though they are still probably more common in service organizations such as restaurants,[14] hospitals, stores, schools, and libraries than in manufacturing.

Some organizations require that regular meetings be held as a standard practice at all levels. Unfortunately, supervisors may call these compulsory meetings merely because they are told to do so: they go through the motions but never become involved in the spirit of consultation. An office girl once described her experience to us:

---

[14] For a good description of such a meeting in a restaurant, see William F. Whyte, *Human Relations in the Restaurant Industry* (New York: McGraw-Hill, 1948), pp. 236-240.

"We have meetings once a month. The office manager asks us if we have any questions or suggestions. Sure we have lots of complaints, but no one has the courage to bring them up. Once in a while one of the girls who is looking to make a good impression asks some silly question, although she already knows the answer.

"Most of the meeting is spent by the office manager telling us we ought to cooperate more, we ought to be neater in our work, and so forth. Frankly I always resent these meetings—they take you away from your work. And I hate the way the office manager talks about our smooth-working loyal group when I despise her and so do the other girls."

Here, obviously, the supervisor has failed to establish an atmosphere in which the employees feel free to discuss their problems openly; instead, there is a high "wall of suspicion" and communication is difficult.

Close supervisors often regard meetings merely as an opportunity for themselves to make announcements or for individuals to ask questions, leaving little opportunity for the give-and-take of *group* participation. The distinction between the two approaches is clearly brought out by Likert and Katz:

> We found in our study of the insurance company that high production and low production groups in one situation said there was about an equal amount of discussion. But when we analyzed further, we found that in the low production groups, discussion consisted pretty much of the supervisor telling the employees what a new company regulation meant; or telling them what to do and how to do it, even though the employees at times may have known more about how to do it than the supervisor himself.
>
> In the high production groups the character of discussion was quite different. Here the supervisor made himself one of the men by saying, "Here's our problem. Here's what we've got to do." Or, "Here's a new situation. Now, what's the best way of going about it?" [15]

Even where subordinates feel free to discuss problems with their boss in private, they may hesitate to speak up in public. Until the group has had a great deal of experience in handling problems together, it is rarely enough for the supervisor to open a meeting with the bare request, "Anybody got anything to bring up?" Usually the supervisor himself has to raise questions or suggest problems to discuss. Then, once the ice has been broken, the group can move on to areas of its own choosing.

Actually, the mere act of holding formal meetings is less important than the supervisor's willingness to consult with subordinates informally when problems arise. Status differences create less of a barrier to communication when consultation takes place around the drawing board, over the machine that has broken down, or in the cafeteria—than at a formally called meeting. Clearly, the supervisor's *attitude* is more important than the motions he goes through.

---

[15] Rensis Likert and Daniel Katz, "Supervisory Practice and Organizational Structure as They Affect Employee Productivity and Morale," *Human Factors in Management,* 2nd ed., Schuyler Hoslett, ed. (New York: Harpers, 1951), p. 98.

MANIPULATION OR CURE-ALL?

The whole concept of group decision-making has given rise to great conflict in industrial-relations circles.[16] Some observers seem to feel that group decision-making is almost a cure-all for every industrial ill. There are books on human relations and supervision devoted almost entirely to this one process. Others feel that group decision-making is nothing but manipulation or even brainwashing—a device by which management imposes its will on the group without the group's realizing what is happening.

Both sides exaggerate. Group decision-making works only in those areas where management is really willing to accept the group's free decision. True, management may pretend that the group has more freedom than it really has. It may try to manipulate the decision-making process so that employees seem to agree when they really do not. Such attempts at brainwashing may be successful at first, but in the long run in a free society they are bound to backfire, giving rise to mistrust and resentment.

Working Through the Informal Organization

It would be impractical for the supervisor to call a meeting every time he has a problem to solve. Often he can work out a solution by himself, taking into account the standards and expectations of the group. But at other times the successful supervisor will make use of the informal organization of the group.

INFORMAL LEADERS

As we mentioned in Chapter 3, groups evolve their own leadership. Informal leaders play key roles in every organization, and without their co-operation management must face an uphill battle against sabotage and apathy.

> W. F. Whyte tells the story of two settlement-house recreational directors who handled the same problem in different ways.[17] The problem was this: the younger boys were to use the play center till 9 o'clock, then they were to leave and make room for the older boys. But, instead of going home, the younger boys would hang around the door, bang on the windows, and generally create a nuisance.

---

[16] For example, see Alfred J. Marrow, *Making Management Human* (New York: McGraw-Hill, 1957); Norman R. F. Maier, *Principles of Human Relations* (New York: Wiley, 1952); Norman R. F. Maier, *Psychology in Industry*, especially Chapters 9 and 13; W. H. Whyte, Jr., *The Organization Man* (New York: Simon and Schuster, 1956); Chris Argyris, *Personality and Organization* (New York: Harpers, 1957); Herbert Thelen, *The Dynamics of Groups at Work* (Chicago: University of Chicago Press, 1954).

[17] William F. Whyte and Burleigh B. Gardner, "The Man in the Middle: Position and Problems of the Foreman," *Applied Anthropology*, Vol. 4, No. 2 (Spring 1945).

Again and again the first recreational director asked the boys as a group to go away—but with no results. Faced with the same situation, the second director turned to one member of the group and merely said: "Listen, Joe, the time's up. Be a good fellow and take your gang out of here." Joe, who was the informal leader, complied immediately and the group left.

Why was the second director so successful? He recognized the informal leader's special status, and gave him an opportunity to gain still more status through proving his power to the director. Under the first director's approach, the informal leader could exhibit his power only by opposing the director's will; had the group obeyed the director, the informal leader would have lost status.

The situation is very much the same in business and industry. The supervisor can either fight the informal organization and its leaders or work with them. If the informal leaders fail to win recognition by working *with* management, they will get it by working *against* management.

Management is often heard to complain, "All our trouble is caused by a few ringleaders. If we could only get rid of them, our trouble would disappear, morale would rise, and our employees would be loyal once again." Unfortunately, these "ringleaders" are often informal leaders; the trouble they cause reflects the desires of the group. Eliminate the informal leader and the group may become still more antagonistic to management, morale may fall even lower, and new "ringleaders" will step to the fore. In a non-unionized situation it may be possible to eliminate "ringleaders" one by one till finally nothing is left but a cowed, disorganized mass of individuals who docilely obey orders. However, such individuals never show a gleam of initiative or teamwork.

What is the alternative to firing ringleaders? Working with them. There are numerous ways in which the supervisor can build up good relations with the informal leaders working under him. Among other things he can pass information along to them first, ask their advice on technical or human-relations problems, and assign them to train others.

There are, however, several dangers that the supervisor must guard against:

1. The informal leader is often hard to identify. The outstanding man who does the best work and cooperates most readily with management may *seem* to be the informal leader, whereas these characteristics may actually make him a social isolate. On the other hand, the "loud-mouth" may serve as the group's *spokesman* rather than its actual *leader*. The group may even have different leaders for different purposes. Sometimes the members of the group will follow one individual when they act in cooperation with management and another when they are antagonistic. Finally, there may be no identifiable informal leader at all.

2. The very fact that the informal leader works closely with management may result in his losing status with the group: he will be known as a "company man." This danger is particularly acute when there is antagonism between the supervisor and the work group generally and the informal leader is asked to do things that the group does not accept as legitimate.

3. Carried too far, cooperation becomes favoritism. It is one thing for the supervisor to give the informal leader information and to ask for his advice. It is quite another to give him easier work or special favors. Nothing could be more effectively calculated to drive him from his leadership position.

THE WORKING SUPERVISOR

The working supervisor is an informal leader to whom the supervisor may show special attention without giving rise to charges of favoritism. There are two kinds of working supervisor. The most obvious is "the straw boss," sometimes called the working foreman, leadman, keyman, or group chief. He is the leader of a group of men who do roughly the *same* sort of work. He shares their work and performs certain quasi-supervisory duties as well.

The other sort of working supervisor exercises his authority by virtue of his technical position on the work team, because his work is *different* from that of the others and requires more skill. For example:

> In glass blowing shops where high-quality crystalware is manufactured for the luxury market, each work team is headed by a gaffer. The gaffer is the top man in a six-step hierarchy and a craftsman of considerable skill and long seniority in his trade. He is accountable to management for the quality and quantity of the ware produced by his team and has almost complete authority over their work performance.

The supervisory power of these top-status crew members rarely receives formal recognition from management. Instead, it exists because of tradition and because supervisors have found these men to be effective assistants in running the department.

Since the working supervisor often gains status because of his seniority and technical proficiency, subordinates will be more willing to accept orders from him than from the foreman himself. This is particularly true in cases where the foreman has not come up from the ranks himself, and where coordination of the work force requires a high degree of technical skill that can be acquired only through years on the job.

We have observed situations in which management has impaired output and demoralized the work group by deliberately or inadvertently taking away some of the working supervisor's power and prestige.[18] This often hap-

---

[18] See George Strauss, "The Set-Up Man: A Case Study of Organizational Change," *Human Organization*, Vol. 13, No. 2 (Summer 1954), pp. 17-25.

pens when a college-trained foreman pays too much attention to the formal organization chart and not enough to traditional relationships between workers and management.

Actually the relationship between foreman and working supervisor is a highly personal one and cannot be established simply by top-management edict. In many cases, however, the supervisor can substantially increase his effectiveness by consulting with the working supervisor and channeling orders through him.[19]

THE UNION STEWARD

The union steward is ordinarily an informal leader who commands respect outside union matters. Provided the over-all union-management relationship is friendly, the supervisor may wish to pass on information to the steward first, use him as a sounding board for proposed changes, and even ask his advice. Again if relations are good, this consultation can be handled outside the context of formal collective bargaining and in a way that will not lead to the loss of the supervisor's power or the establishment of precedents that management may later regret. Such consultation has the great advantage of permitting the steward to participate in solving technical and human-relations problems in a constructive, positive fashion; otherwise, in order to display his status, the steward has to resort to the essentially negative activity of processing grievances. In a strongly unionized situation, the supervisor will never be able to develop cooperative relations with his subordinates if he bypasses or ignores the union.

Building a Work Team

Not long ago a nationally known concern distributed to its supervisors a pamphlet entitled "Deal with Individuals, not Groups." Its message was simple: Individuals, if properly handled, will work for management's objectives; groups will inevitably oppose management. Cater to the worker's competitive spirit, reward his individual efforts, and break up his attachment to the group, the argument ran, and you will be surprised how much work he puts out.

The fostering of competition is not the only means that management can use to break up group cohesion. As we saw in Chapter 3, groups can be made so large and heterogeneous that "team spirit" becomes difficult to develop. Similar effects can be obtained by modifying technology and work arrangements. In restaurants even the height of the counter separating waitresses from countermen affects their ability to work together.[20]

---

[19] *Ibid.;* Walker, Guest, and Turner, *op. cit.,* p. 134.
[20] Whyte. *Human Relations in the Restaurant Industry,* Chapter 6.

But is it wise for management to try to splinter the informal organization? There is no absolutely clear answer to this question. To be sure, cohesive groups show greater teamwork. Its members gain greater social satisfaction from working together. Morale is higher. Turnover and absenteeism are frequently lower.[21] Further, it may be easier to supervise a closely knit group, since the supervisor need not repeat information and orders to every member; the informal leader will act as an effective channel of communication to and from the supervisor. A quarreling, disorganized group finds it hard to work together and may direct its aggressiveness against management in the form of poor workmanship, sabotage, grievances, and wild-cat strikes.[22]

On the other hand, certain dangers arise when the work group becomes too tightly knit. Such a group may be reluctant to accept new employees as members and, though there may be more cooperation within the group, cooperation with outsiders may suffer. Thus competition and ill feeling may develop among rival groups.

But does cohesion increase productivity? Recent studies suggest that cohesive groups produce either substantially more than the average or somewhat less.[23] Particularly where the job requires close cooperation among the members of a work team, the mere existence of cohesion makes work more efficient. In general, however, cohesion results in higher productivity only if the group is interested in producing more. If the group is unified for the purpose of protecting itself against management, then greater cohesion will mean less production. All cohesion means is that the members will adhere more closely to the group standards, whatever they are.

So we come back to one of the central problems of this book: Can management motivate employees to *want* to achieve management's objectives, to produce willingly without being subjected to the policy of "be strong"?

Where management finds that there is no possibility of developing groups with goals that are compatible with the objectives of the organization, it may become necessary to resort to measures that will weaken or eliminate informal groups. Continuous movement of personnel, particularly those showing leadership potential, and supervisory patterns stressing dealing with the indi-

---

[21] Elton Mayo and George F. F. Lombard, *Teamwork and Labor Turnover in the Aircraft Industry of Southern California* (Boston: Graduate School of Business Administration, Harvard University, 1944).

[22] Cohesive groups may do the same thing, but their efforts are better coordinated, more carefully thought through, and less erratic than those of the disorganized group. Leonard R. Sayles, *Behavior of Industrial Work Groups* (New York: Wiley, 1958), pp. 7-40.

[23] Stanley Seashore, *Group Cohesiveness in Industrial Work Groups* (Ann Arbor: Survey Research Center, University of Michigan, 1954); Daniel Katz and Robert Kahn, "Human Organization and Worker Motivation," *Industrial Productivity*, L. Reed Tripp, ed. (Champaign, Ill.: Industrial Relations Research Association, 1951), pp. 161-162; Morton Deutsch, "The Effects of Cooperation and Competition on Group Process," *Group Dynamics*, Dorwin Cartwright and Alvin Zander, eds. (Evanston, Ill.: Row, Peterson, 1953), pp. 319-353.

vidual are two possible ways of keeping strong groups from developing.[24] In most instances, however, given a sound over-all program of human relations, it is in management's interest to promote teamwork.

What can the supervisor do to develop teamwork? Most important, he can develop a sensitivity to the facts of group life discussed in Chapter 3. He can familiarize himself with the social geography of the group he supervises and learn to identify the patterns of status, leadership, friendship, and cliques that exist within it. He might even draw himself a sociometric map of his subordinates' social relations—as described on pp. 67-68. Drawing such a map and understanding the relations it reveals can help him in a host of ways:

1. By carefully assigning men to work positions he can avoid putting enemies together—thus reducing the possibility of personal friction.

2. He can put friends together. True, this arrangement may lead to more talking on the job, but the evidence suggests that more work will be done too, particularly where the work requires cooperation. One study showed that carpenters and bricklayers who were allowed to choose among themselves whom they would work with outproduced those who were not permitted this choice.[25] Similar results were obtained when laundry workers were assigned on the basis of sociometric preference,[26] and where air-force pilot-training groups were selected in this fashion.[27]

3. He can provide special help and attention to isolates—the lonely workers who make no friends. Careful recognition of the position of such employees and the use of clique leaders to help them win acceptance may do much to improve their performance and to prevent them from quitting.[28]

4. He can assign men in such a way to avoid the growth of competing sub-groups.

> A study of social organization in the merchant marine suggests that watches (work teams) were most effective when (a) the entire group came from the same social background, or (b) every member of the group came from a different background. When two sharply different cliques formed, efficiency was impaired.[29]

---

[24] These were among the techniques used by the communists during the Korean War to break down the morale and cohesion of American prisoners.

[25] R. H. Van Zelst, "Sociometrically Selected Work Teams," *Personnel Psychology*, Vol. 5, No. 3 (Autumn 1952), pp. 175-185.

[26] John H. Jacobs, "The Application of Sociometry to Industry," *Sociometry*, Vol. 8, No. 2 (May 1945), pp. 181-198.

[27] L. D. Zeleny, "Selection of Compatible Flying Partners," *The American Journal of Sociology*, Vol. 52, No. 5 (March 1947), pp. 424-431.

[28] A study among naval recruits, for instance, indicated that isolates had the worst disciplinary records. R. L. French, "Sociometric Status and Individual Adjustment among Naval Recruits," *Journal of Abnormal and Social Psychology*, Vol. 46, No. 1 (January 1951), pp. 64-72.

[29] Stephen Richardson, *The Social Organization of British and United States Merchant Ships* (mimeographed; New York State School of Industrial and Labor Relations, 1954), p. 54.

5. He can cut down on excessive transfers *between* departments, within the limits of union seniority rules.

6. He can rotate jobs within the group in order to strengthen each employee's identification with the team as a whole rather than with his individual job.

7. He can try to set up situations in which the employee can make his job easier by cooperating with others.

> In restaurants we studied, management trained the waitresses to work together and help each other. They were taught to consider two, three, or more stations as a unit and to divide the work among themselves in the most efficient manner.
>
> ... The waitresses are told to help only those girls who will return the favor. ... The girl who helps nobody can get nobody to help her, and she drops behind and has trouble with her service. The girl who gives help gets help in return.[30]

8. He can provide financial incentives: group piece-work may do more to encourage cooperation than individual piece-work.

9. He can make sure that new workers are carefully introduced to the group. Many companies have a "big brother" system in which every new employee is assigned an older employee to help him become familiar not only with the formal requirements of the job but also with the informal mores of the group. In his social contacts with the group, the supervisor should be careful not to exclude the new employee.

Maintaining Proper Social Relationships

Let us assume that we have an effective, well-knit work group. What role should the supervisor play in it? Is he really a member of the group as well as a member of management? Is it a good thing for him to fraternize with his men—or should he maintain a distance? Even if he cultivates close relationships with his men on the job, should he try to develop patterns of friendship off the job?

These questions give rise to a great deal of anxiety on the part of supervisors, particularly those who have risen from the ranks. A newly appointed supervisor cannot avoid asking himself: "Can I maintain discipline and command respect if I keep up my old friendships? If I cut them off, won't the men think I am high-hatting them? But how can I keep up my old Friday night poker games with Jack and Joe unless I am equally friendly with Bill and Gus? How do I break off my old game with Jack and Joe?" (Family ties make things even harder. One foreman stated his hardest problem this way: "How the hell do you discipline your sister-in-law's uncle?")

---

[30] Whyte, *Human Relations in the Restaurant Industry*, p. 214.

We have seen that most groups have definite ideas about the relationship that should exist between supervisor and subordinate. To violate these expectations almost inevitably leads to trouble. However, such expectations differ widely from one situation to another. At sea, for instance, there has been a traditional social gap between officers and men. This distance is maintained by means of separate uniforms and separate eating and sleeping arrangements. Yet on smaller ships this traditional formality tends to break down. Moreover, there is more formality in the navy, where men are subject to danger, than in the merchant marine. And there is a decidedly different attitude in the American merchant marine, where most men rise from the ranks, than on European ships, where officers usually come from different social classes than the men they supervise.

The pattern of *off*-the-job contacts also varies widely. In a small community, for example, there are bound to be many unplanned after-hours contacts, and a supervisor's failure to meet the normal community standards of politeness will not be excused. In a large city, however, off-the-job contacts must be arranged in advance by the supervisor. Here if he goes out of his way to be "one of the boys" he may set up a pattern of expectations that cannot be maintained on the job.

Social distance is intimately connected with the supervisor's style of leadership. If he maintains informal, permissive relationships off the job, it will be hard for him to exercise close supervision on the job; on the other hand, if he avoids all social contacts not directly connected with work, he will find it difficult to develop a free and easy relationship in discussing job-related problems. Certainly snubbing people, particularly those with whom one has frequent work contacts, violates our standards of democracy. In short, any social barrier will create a communications barrier.

Undue formality increases the subordinate's feeling of dependency. And yet there are situations where the supervisor is forced to rely largely on formal authority to maintain discipline. Here he can hardly afford to be a "good guy" off the job. One reason for the carefully maintained social barrier in the armed forces is that the officers do not want their men to question decisions or initiate action.[31]

Personality factors are also important. A congenial, outgoing man will feel uneasy trying to maintain a social distance between himself and his subordinates; an introvert will feel equally uneasy trying to bridge that distance. Certainly it is as unwise for a man who has come up from the ranks to cut off his ties arbitrarily as it is for a superintendent who is new to a department to create artificial ties.

------

[31] The question of social relationships is closely tied in with technological considerations. In a scientific laboratory a premium is placed on widespread communication of information and widespread participation in solving problems. Here status differences are played down and social relationships are close. For technological reasons, just the opposite is true in a military organization.

Displaying Technical Ability

In recent years the need for the supervisor to possess technical ability has been de-emphasized. It has been argued that since the supervisor's primary job is to motivate others to work, his own technical proficiency is secondary. As one personnel director put it, "A foreman's job is to manage *people;* the people take care of *things.*" Increasingly, management is looking for generalists rather than specialists.

Symptomatic of this change has been the growing tendency to hire college graduates as foremen, thus substantially reducing the hourly-paid worker's chance to advance into management. The so-called "jet programs" for college graduates emphasize broad experience rather than specialization. Even in engineering, the best opportunities for getting ahead lie in administration rather than in jobs that require professional skill.

There are good reasons for this shift in emphasis. Certainly the evidence we mentioned in Chapter 6 suggests that it is the poorer supervisor who does the same sort of work as his men and who concentrates on the technical aspects of his job. The better supervisors are more concerned with long-range planning and development, and tend to delegate petty responsibilities. It is clearly short-sighted to promote people to supervisory positions purely as a reward for technical performance if they have shown no evidence that they can lead people.

Yet there is a danger in discounting technical skills too much, particularly in certain types of work. For example, when a close degree of coordination is required between the members of a work team—as in flying a plane, conducting an orchestra, or operating on a patient—technical ability is the crucial qualification for leadership. In all these situations there is little opportunity for participation or delegation of authority, and little freedom for subordinates to develop their own ways of doing things.[32]

Even where such close supervision is not required, technological ability helps the supervisor legitimatize his own authority. Whenever subordinates place a high value on their own skills they show little respect for a supervisor who is less proficient than they.

> Take the situation in certain air force control towers during World War II. Some of the senior enlisted men had years of civilian experience as controllers. But many of the officers were "wash-outs" from pilot training, still in their 'teens or early twenties. A workable arrangement often developed in which the officers confined their activities to signing papers prepared by the enlisted men.
>
> In one case, however, the officer-in-charge (age 19) insisted on taking a more active role. The enlisted men tried to keep him out of the tower

---

[32] In a smoothly functioning team the situation gives the order more frequently than does the leader. From observing the surgeon, the scrub nurse knows exactly when to hand him the scalpel.

by the simple expedient of insisting that whenever he was there, he would have to make all the technical decisions himself. After a few horrible mistakes (fortunately no one was injured) and a severe reprimand from the base commander, this officer confined his activities from then on to the officers' bar.

The feeling that the boss should show technical skill is particularly strong among men who take pride in their work and feel a close identification with their occupation (building tradesmen, for example, or college professors).[33] If subordinates feel that the supervisor is a master of skills they themselves regard as important, then in a way he has beaten them in a fair race: he has *earned* his job and is respected for doing so. "Unpleasant personal characteristics are often overlooked if competence is high enough. The irascible surgeon who is nevertheless highly respected for his skill is almost a legend. Colleagues and nurses judge doctors according to the mastery they exhibit."[34] (Note: The leader's technical skill need not duplicate that of his followers. A pilot can't overhaul an engine; perhaps a conductor can't play all the instruments in an orchestra; yet both derive their status from their technical ability.) Often men put a new supervisor through an initiation period in which they test his ability by asking technical questions.

Technical ability is also important if the supervisor is to perform his function of training subordinates and helping them do a better job. As one worker put it: [35]

> The foreman isn't worth a damn unless he knows what the job is all about and how to do it right. Too many of these foremen nowadays can get along with you fine, but they can't show you anything about the job.

Finally, a supervisor who is respected for his technical ability seldom needs to resort to formal authority to maintain his leadership, and consequently can permit greater fraternization between himself and his subordinates.

Conclusion

In this chapter we have tried to suggest various techniques that the supervisor can use to encourage teamwork and voluntary acceptance of management's objectives while minimizing his use of formal authority. It is too simple to say that greater teamwork in itself will lead to higher production, for the group may decide to use its strength to protect its integrity against what it feels are encroachments by management.

---

[33] Richardson points out that sailors judge the captain of a ship largely on his ability as a seaman, for two reasons: (1) his ability obviously has a lot to do with their own personal safety, and (2) sailors have little else to do but talk shop (and girls) and so are constantly comparing their present captain's ability against the ability of those they have known in the past.

[34] Burling, Lentz, and Wilson, *op. cit.*, p. 266.

[35] Daniel M. Colyer, "The Good Foreman—As His Men See Him," *Personnel*, Vol. 28, No. 5 (September 1951).

The freedom of any given set of supervisors and subordinates to develop a cooperative relationship may be limited by economic considerations, top-management policy, general union-management relations, and other environmental factors. Still the attitude of the work group toward the supervisor is to a large extent a function of his attitude toward the group. If the supervisor tries to meet the expectations of his subordinates, they will be more likely to work with him. If he engages in close supervision and denies subordinates the satisfactions derived from working together and from participating in solving common problems, they may still work together, but they will work *against* management.

In a way, the effective supervisor acts like an informal leader. He behaves in the way his subordinates think a good leader should. He respects the group standards of conduct and value. He consults with his subordinates before taking action and encourages them to make their own decisions. In handling group problems, he either meets with the group as a whole or channels his activity through the group's own informal structure. He tries to build the group into a smooth, cohesive work team. Finally, he tries to win the respect of his subordinates by the way in which he handles both social relationships and technical problems. These techniques cannot guarantee willing group acceptance of management's objectives, but they do make it more likely.

To the extent that such a cooperative relationship can be established, the gains are substantial both for employees and for management. (Notice that we say "to the *extent* that"; cooperation is never 100 per cent, never 0 per cent.) An atmosphere of cooperation provides essential need satisfactions for subordinates: the social satisfaction of working together, a feeling of identification with the group and the over-all organization, and a pride in accomplishment. Belonging to a group reduces the employee's feeling of anonymity and gives him a sense of identity.

For the supervisor, cooperation makes life a lot easier. There is less need for him to check up on his men, for they make their own rules, take care of emergencies by themselves, and may even discipline their own team members.

However, a few drops of cold water should be thrown on our idyllic picture. While there may be wide areas of supervisor-subordinate cooperation, there will always be areas of conflict as well. True, an over-all cooperative relationship will make this conflict easier to handle. Still there will be times when the supervisor *must* exert pressure to get production, even at the risk of destroying the group's cohesion or of turning the group against management. There is no one style of leadership that is equally effective in all situations.[36]

---

[36] For an excellent discussion of this point, see Robert Tannenbaum and Warren H. Schmidt, "How to Choose a Leadership Pattern," *Harvard Business Review*, Vol. 36, No. 2 (March 1958), pp. 95-101.

SUPERVISION: A Last Word

In our discussion of leadership we have tried to emphasize that there is no one pattern of supervision that is universally appropriate. Instead, the pattern of supervision that is most appropriate to a given situation depends on a number of factors:

1. The personality and background of the supervisor. Example: A supervisor who is brought in from outside the organization will almost of necessity maintain a greater social distance from his new subordinates than will one who has risen from the ranks.

2. The personality and background of the subordinates. Example: Professional engineers expect and require more general supervision than do older nurses with a rural background.

3. The type of work. Example: Assembly-line workers, who have relatively little opportunity to obtain need satisfaction from their work, may require closer supervision than do maintenance men.

4. Urgency of getting out production. Example: If quick results are required, there may be no time to develop a cooperative, cohesive work group.

5. The over-all situation. Example: If management suspects that the members of a cohesive work group might restrict output to save their jobs during a time of depression, it may resort to competition in an effort to prevent the development of cohesion.

The sensible supervisor will take all these factors into account—and many more—before he decides how to behave in a particular situation. Even in a given situation, however, there is a broad range of supervisory approaches that will be successful if properly implemented. For instance, in Example 1, a supervisor brought in from outside might very quickly develop close social relations with his subordinates and thus increase rather than decrease production. Or, in Example 3, a maintenance supervisor might get excellent production in complete violation of the principles of general supervision.

It is important to remember that many successful businessmen have violated all the principles discussed here. They have been successful in spite of their human relations—or perhaps because they have so inspired their subordinates to identify with the company and its success that employees have given their all in spite of supervisory actions that would be resented in almost any other context.

In fact, the ability to supervise is only one of the many characteristics of a good manager. The company president, for example, must be effective in dealing with his subordinates. But this is only one part of his duties: he also makes plans, evaluates the recommendations of others, represents the company to outsiders, and so forth. It has been suggested that the primary function of any top executive is to adjust the goals of his organization to the needs of his times.[37] The ability to sense the main current was the central genius of Washington, Lincoln, Franklin Roosevelt, Queen Elizabeth I, and Churchill. It is also the genius of the business executive who decides at the opportune moment to switch his company's operations from wholesaling to direct sales—or the man who steals a march on the market by making plans for the mass production of a new chemical though the laboratory tests are far from complete.

Certainly we would admit that the executive's ability to make critical decisions of this order is more crucial to the survival of the organization than his particular skill in dealing with people.[38] An organization permeated with inappropriate [39] human-relations practices, however, is unlikely to remain profitable for long, regardless of the personal brilliance of the man at the top. An organization can be successful even if some of the individuals in it, even those at the very top, lack important skills, *provided* there are others in the organization who can fill in for them. The president may be inadequate in dealing with people, but the organization will be little harmed provided he channels his contacts through someone high in the management hierarchy who is skilled in this area.

Similarly, on lower levels it would be unrealistic to expect management to promote men entirely on the basis of their supervisory abilities. What is important is not that every manager be a good supervisor, but that the structure of the organization and management policies be such as to encourage sound human-relations practices.

At this point you may complain, "A few chapters ago you seemed to state a strong preference for general supervision. Now, many hedges later, haven't you worked yourself into a position where it doesn't seem to make much difference what kind of supervision is used?" By no means. We think that the healthiest, soundest, most profitable organization will be the one in which general supervision can be used effectively. But to make it possible to use general supervision effectively, it may be necessary to revamp the whole organization through changes in organization structure, better selection, training of individuals, improved communications, and even, as we suggested in Chapter 2, substantial changes in the technological processes of production. Changes of this sort may well create cumulative changes in the over-all organization that will make general supervision possible.

---

[37] Philip Selznick, *Leadership in Administration* (Evanston, Ill.: Row, Peterson, 1957).

[38] Though we would argue that major critical decisions must be made in the field of personnel administration just as frequently as in such fields as marketing, production, or finance.

[39] Note we use the term *inappropriate*. The appropriate practice for the given situation may be the unrestrained use of authority.

As a consequence, the face-to-face relationship between supervisor and subordinate cannot be considered in isolation from the other factors that we will consider in later chapters. First, however, we should define more closely some of the skills required by the supervisor.

Problem I

The following letter was sent to the Harvard Business Review by the president of a large insurance company. The president is explaining why his company has so few immediate personnel problems in its Home Office.*

The reason lies not in the attitudes of workers but in the attitude of management. It is true that lavish offers of fringe benefits give no assurance of mollified workers. This company has gone far in the fringe area, but I have never felt that what we did accounted for the remarkable esprit de corps our people show. I feel it is how we do it.

By that I mean that for eleven years since I came to head this company my first objective in dealings with our people has been to dignify them as individuals and to express a feeling of pride in them which quickly won their recognition. This is the pattern followed by my staff. Supervisory attitudes—management's real intent—are quickly observed and evaluated by employees. My company takes this seriously.

Alex Osborn of B.B.D.&O. is an old friend of mine. You may have seen his two recent books, one captioned "Your Creative Power," and the other more recent one entitled "Applied Imagination." These books have been widely circulated among our officers and supervisory people, and many things have come out of them. For example, we took a longer look at our suggestion plan and approached it on the basis that whatever the quantity or quality of suggestions, the Suggestion Committee must deal, not only with an open mind, but liberally, with suggestions in the first year. While we get many suggestions that cannot be given dollar awards, we make sure that occasionally a good suggestion gets a walloping return. We now invest a rather substantial sum in suggestion awards, and I submit we get a great deal of genuine interest and benefit. Our plan works well and it costs us about the same as one qualified clerical person.

I am interested in the local orchestra, and a few years ago it was brought to my attention that there were several unsold boxes. I hit upon a plan evolved from Osborn's thinking that pays off three ways, and it has been most successful. Our people are encouraged to bring flowers from their garden to decorate the lobby of our building. They are given a credit line for so doing and feel good about it; secondly, our lobby is as attractive as any you will find; and thirdly, those who add to its beauty are rewarded by pairs of tickets to the concerts. The orchestra benefits as do our people. The plan appealed to every bank and insurance company in this town, save two, and there are no unsold boxes. Parenthetically, I maintain a box adjacent to that purchased for the employees. I am usually there and find an opportunity to visit either before the concert or during intermission with my people and their husbands and wives and friends.

---

* Vol. 32, No. 6 (November 1954), reproduced by permission of the author and publisher.

Perhaps the most significant thing we have done is one which has given dignity to every person in the building and it happens to be in the field of philanthropy. In 1947, I was General Chairman for the Community Chest Campaign, and the slogan adopted by the company's employees committee that year was "PAR FOR E.A.R." [E.A.R. is the president], and in that year there was 100% giving. The company became pleasantly notorious throughout the city for this 100% accomplishment; and believe it or not, with a constantly changing personnel, the record of 100% giving—every officer, every employee, every cafeteria and building maintenance worker—has been maintained through the years since. Every year the drive is completed on the first day and a telegram sent to the general chairman. In the public meetings which follow, our people are photographed and feted. Every individual feels personally responsible for the result.

Our pay scales are measured by objective job analysis and careful performance rating. Our hours are the best, our working conditions as good as any, and there is a constant effort to be humane in all matters.

We have had interesting conversations with the group acting as the Board of Governors of the "Employees' Club" over the years, and we have met every reasonable request they have made. Biweekly pay was one of the requests which we adopted costing us about 8% more in salary, smoking in work areas which we permitted, music in work areas which we maintain. We are always willing to listen to our people. If they want something that will help them in their work and in their happiness here we will go far to supply it.

Ours is not a perfect shop, and I may be lulled into thinking it is happier than I suggest, but of one thing I am sure, while most of our officers have had collegiate experiences, there isn't one who came into the world with a gold spoon in his mouth, and that may account for their interest in people and their problems.

I have a great feeling of intimacy with our employees. I write dozens of longhand letters to those who do me and this company favors, and I write a specially dictated letter to each person on his reaching a fifth, tenth, etc., anniversary.

We make a good deal of a Christmas Party that is really a family affair. There is no drinking in connection with it, though we are not opposed to drinking as such. We bring in the families and children of all people who wish to come. It is a very successful affair.

Similarly we take an interest in our retired people and annually give them the finest dinner and entertainment in the best place available. We encourage them to visit the office and to attend the functions held by active employees.

If our people should become upset about anything I am prepared to say it would be my fault, because there is nothing reasonable they could urge that we could afford to do, that we aren't doing, or be willing to do. If we could not do it my experience with them has been that we could spell out the reasons convincingly and acceptably.

We take good care of our older people and pay an extra service allowance for length of service which is quite considerable in the case of the older and, in some cases, less productive people. We have meetings in which the dignity of the individual is advanced with deliberate care.

Morale cannot be won in a day or purchased at any price. It takes a long time to develop good morale and it takes constant planning to preserve it. On the other hand, I could lose it all in one day's misbehavior. All I would need to do would be to walk through a work area and complain about the posture of a couple of people and ask whether it was necessary to burn as many lights. It would help to turn on lights but it would never do to turn one off.

The important thing is that the work be congenial; and if that is not so, liberal rules and wage scales become of less importance. Care must be taken in the employment of people and more care in the treatment of them later. We try to take that care and that I think is why we apparently do so well in our company.

1. Evaluate the effectiveness of this company's program.

2. How are the various forms of motivation, which were discussed in Chapter 5, utilized in this company?

Problem II

Bill Smith works as a tool-crib attendant at the Acme Company. A tool-crib attendant has a fairly responsible job: he has to keep tabs on who gets what tools, keep the tools in order, make minor repairs, and order new tools when the stock runs low. At the beginning and end of each shift there is a lot of work to do, but most of the time the men have relatively little to do, especially on the night shift. Nevertheless it is one of the highest-paid non-skilled jobs in the plant. (To work up to a skilled job, a man has to start as an apprentice in his twenties.)

Until last year Bill held an important union office and used his free time and the strategic location of the tool crib for political purposes. Last year he was defeated; those who opposed him felt his aggressive attitude toward the company was merely provoking trouble.

Shortly thereafter Bill was caught by his foreman reading a newspaper on the job. The following exchange took place:

Foreman: You're supposed to be working now. We're not paying you for reading.

Bill: I'm doing my job. I've got nothing to do now. How does it hurt you if I read?

Foreman: If I let you read, then the men on production will want the same privilege. If I stop them, they will say I'm discriminating against them. You pushed a grievance case just like that yourself. In fact, since I'm dealing with a legal eagle like you, I'll give you a written warning just to cover myself 100 per cent.

Bill: Why do I get the warning? I'm not the only one who's been reading papers. You're picking on me just because I made you eat a lot of dirt when I was a union official.

Foreman: No, I'm warning you because you're the first man I caught. I'll warn everyone else I catch too.

Bill: You can't give me a warning. There's nothing in the plant regulation about reading newspapers. We've never received any notice and you're punishing me for a rule you've just set up. That's poor personnel policy.

Foreman: OK, I'll post a written order too—and this warning is just to make double sure you know about it.

Bill: OK, I'm filing a grievance. By posting the notice you're admitting this is a new order. I don't want any warning in my file that you can hang over my neck from now till doomsday.

Bill filed his grievance, but his steward, who was a political opponent, never "found time" to push it. Shortly afterward, Bill's wife got a job as a night telephone operator on the 11:30 P.M.-7:30 A.M. shift. Bill's own shift ran from 8:00 A.M. to 4:00 P.M. Bill's plan was to pick his wife up after she finished work, then drive down to the Acme Company, where he would turn the car over to her and go to work himself.

Acme and the phone company were on opposite sides of town and Bill began to come in late for work. After this occurred several times, his foreman gave him a written warning that if he came late again, he would be fired. From then on, whenever he saw he couldn't get to the plant by the starting whistle, he went home, reported sick, and took the rest of the day off. Technically, management could have required a doctor's certificate from him, but this was never requested unless a man had been out of work for several days.

Finally, the situation got to be too much for Bill and he requested a transfer to the midnight shift in accordance with the seniority provisions of the union contract. The foreman turned him down on the grounds he did not possess sufficient "fitness and ability" to work the night shift since there was provision for only one tool attendant on the night shift and Bill's poor tardiness, absentee, and newspaper-reading record would mean that the company would often be caught short.

Bill did not explain the real reason for his absenteeism, fearing that it might bring him punishment. Instead, he caught the plant manager at the plant gate and said to him:

Bill: Mr. Struthers, I just asked my foreman to give me a transfer to the "mid" shift and he turned me down. I got the seniority, but he said I couldn't make the move because I've been absent too much. That's true: my wife's been sick once in a while and I've had to stay home to take care of the kids. If I can work the night shift, my sister can take over when my wife's not feeling good.

Mr. Struthers: OK, Bill, I'll see what I can do.

Next day Struthers had the following phone conversation with the foreman:

Mr. Struthers: Is it true you turned down Bill's transfer application because of his absentee record?

Foreman: Yes I did. I don't think he can be trusted on the job.

Mr. Struthers: Well, I'm willing to take the chance.

The following day Struthers told Bill his transfer would go through shortly.

Meanwhile the day-shift foreman told the night superintendent, "You're going to get a guy named Smith who will give you a pack of trouble. Watch him like a hawk."

Six o'clock the first morning of Bill's new shift, the superintendent dropped in on him, sure that Bill would be asleep. Instead Bill had spent the whole evening washing down the walls and building a new cabinet for his equipment. Since that time the superintendent has checked on him only at infrequent intervals. Bill is fairly satisfied with the new work:

"Of course, it is just as boring as can be. I hand out about ten tools a night. I've repainted and completely straightened out the crib, but you can't do that forever. I can't read my paper in the spare time, so lots of times I go to sleep, often for six hours. I have an arrangement with the fellows in the shop that if anybody from management comes they'll make some noise and wake me up."

1. Was management wise in instituting the no-newspaper-reading rule? List the arguments that could be presented for and against this course of action.

2. What was wrong with the way the order was issued? What would you have done?

3. Suppose you were night superintendent and word came to you through the "grapevine" that Bill was sleeping on the job. Would you have done anything? What? Why?

4. Comment on the foreman's interviewing technique.

5. Go through the rest of the case and point out the mistakes you feel were made at the different levels of management.

Problem III

While walking through your department, you notice that one of the operators a couple of aisles over seems to be working with the safety guard up. However, as he catches your eye, he fumbles with a piece of stock and knocks the safety guard into place—at least that is how it looks to you. This is a serious offense. When an employee commits this violation (often in order to speed up his operation and make it a little easier), the usual penalty is a three-day layoff. Several people have been seriously injured by failure to use the safety guard.

1. How would you approach the employee?

2. What would you say?

3. What would your objectives be in your discussion with him?

Problem IV

Jane Smith has been a slightly better-than-average employee, though not an outstanding worker. Recently, the quality of her work has been declining, for no apparent reason. You have just checked some of the parts she has been working on and decide that nearly half of them are unsatisfactory. This is about the worst performance you have ever spotted.

1. How would you approach Jane?

2. What would you say first?

3. Should you first compliment her on her work?

Problem V

"Our work load in stock control has increased enormously in the past few months. I liked the job and even started taking work home, just one or two nights a week at first, but even more later on so that we wouldn't fall behind. I knew the boss was anxious to make an outstanding record and I was anxious to show him that I could hold up my own end.

"Then one day I extended my lunch hour to get a haircut. Probably no one would have noticed it, but the barber gave me a real close cut. When my boss came by my desk later on he bawled me out for taking company time for personal business, asking me what I thought I was paid for. He pointed to the company policy book which said that employees were forbidden to take time off during work hours. I started to tell him how much time I had been putting in extra, on my own, but he cut me short, saying that he was referring to company time."

1. What did the boss do wrong here?

2. How is the subordinate likely to react?

3. In view of the company policy, what would you have done if you were the boss in this case?

Problem VI

Through the years your company has had a no-smoking rule that has been largely ignored. Recently some of your departments have begun working with rather inflammable material, though there is still almost no fire danger in most of the departments. You are plant manager.

1. Describe the steps you would take to handle the danger of fire and yet maintain sound human relations.

2. Why would you take these steps rather than others?

Problem VII

Management has been having a great deal of trouble in the cone-making department in the MM plant. Cone-making used to be done entirely by hand and required considerable skill. Today much of the skilled work is handled by machinery, but the cone-makers still put in a good deal of physical effort in feeding the machines, and the work process involves heat and fumes. The department is isolated from the rest of the plant in an older, rather dilapidated building.

The cone-makers have traditionally been a tight-knit group, and for years management has pretty much let them have their own way, though, on occasion, the men have gone on slow-downs or wildcat strikes over petty grievances. Their foreman, Mike Malone, has looked upon his job chiefly as that of protecting his men from management pressure. In recent years, productivity has tended to fall and costs in this department are considerably higher than in comparable departments in other plants. Malone is ready to retire and management must find a successor. Among the possibilities are:

a. *John Callahan*, age 50, has been with the department for 33 years. He knows cone-making backwards and forwards, is well liked by the men, and has been union steward for years.

b. *Gus Nowak*, college graduate, age 32, has done an outstanding job in cutting costs as foreman of the assembly department, a department of low-skilled workers which includes many women and has always had considerable turnover.

1. What are the relative strong and weak points of each candidate? Which one would you select?

2. Assuming Nowak is selected, what advice would you give him?

3. Assuming Callahan is selected, how should the plant manager try to handle him?

Problem VIII

Hospital orderlies are often homeless older men who accept hospital work in spite of its low pay because it offers them free room and board. Their duties normally include various sorts of dirty work, such as moving beds and carrying stretchers—work that is too hard for women.

In some hospitals each orderly is assigned to a ward or group of wards where he works under the direction of the head nurse and does any work that the nurses, student nurses, practical nurses, and nurses' aides on the floor ask him to do. When he is through with one assignment, he waits around for another.

In other hospitals all orderlies work out of a central orderly room. When a head nurse wants an orderly, she calls the head orderly, who dispatches men as needed. When they finish their tasks, they report back to the orderly room.

1. What needs do the orderlies satisfy in each of these situations?

2. What human-relations problems would you anticipate in each situation? In particular, how would the relationship between the orderlies and the nurses vary in each situation?

3. What special skills would be required by the head nurses in dealing with the orderlies in each situation?

Problem IX

The Merrimac Corporation sells, rents, and services electronic data-processing equipment and employs a large staff of servicemen to keep its customers' equipment in order. The 30 servicemen who work out of the St. Louis district office (which covers most of the Midwest) all live in the St. Louis area and are often required to travel to customers in distant locations; usually they travel by air. A given trouble call may take several hours or even days of work.

A problem has arisen from the fact that when an assignment is completed the men fly back to St. Louis and often arrive home late in the evening or even after midnight. Under these circumstances management has always allowed the servicemen to take a few hours extra sleep and not report to the office the first thing in the morning. Recently there are signs that the men have begun to abuse this privilege. A few men have developed the habit of taking the entire morning off after every out-of-town trip, even if they arrive back at their home by 5:00 the previous evening. And other employees are beginning to wonder whether they might do the same.

Management has considered imposing a hard-and-fast rule that all servicemen must report for work at 9:00 A.M. regardless of what time they got in the night before. But in some cases this would impose an obvious hardship, and it might encourage the servicemen to spread their work out so that instead of finishing their job in the afternoon and returning home late they would slow down and work through the next morning, returning home in the afternoon.

Above all, management is anxious not to disturb the employee's high morale and interest in his work. These servicemen are paid a salary, receive liberal fringe benefits, and have always been treated more like members of management than like ordinary factory workers.

1. Advise management on how to handle this problem.

SUPERVISORY SKILLS

In this section we shall look more closely at some of the skills that the effective supervisor must possess. Obviously before a supervisor can supervise his subordinates he must be able to communicate with them. Yet communication is not a simple matter. The words uttered by the sender of a message may have a different meaning for him than for the man who receives them. Particularly when subordinates are insecure, hostile, or suspicious of their superiors, they may ascribe unintended meanings to messages from above. To prevent misunderstanding, the senders of messages, at all levels of the management hierarchy, must be careful to fashion them so that their meaning is clear to the receiver. This is the problem we shall discuss in Chapter 9, "Communications."

Effective communication is a two-way process. The good supervisor is also a good listener. Interviewing, which is merely deliberate listening, is an essential skill if the supervisor is to get to know his subordinates. In addition, merely by listening the supervisor may help subordinates solve their own problems or at least induce them to become more receptive to what he has to say (Chapter 10, "Interviewing: The Fine Art of Listening").

The supervisor must deal with groups as well as individuals. Committee meetings and informal conferences are becoming increasingly important as a means of communication in industry. The skills of conference leadership are closely akin to the skills of interviewing (Chapter 11, "Conference Leadership").

Chapter 12, "Introducing Change," considers a problem that is directly influenced by the quality of communications within the organization: introducing change. As we shall see, it is the meaning that is communicated by a proposed change that most often leads to resistance. Effective use of communications, interviewing, and conference leadership—as well as of some of the supervisory skills discussed earlier—helps insure that change will be readily accepted.

What happens when change is rejected? When subordinates refuse to obey new rules—or, for that matter, old rules too? Then discipline is required (Chapter 13, "Discipline"). In a way, discipline is also a form of communica-

tion: the message that management is trying to transmit is that it really intends to enforce certain rules. To make discipline accepted and meaningful, the rule and its penalty must be carefully communicated, and the offender must be made to understand that the reason for his being disciplined is the fact he broke the rule, not personal animus on the part of the supervisor.

Considered together, these are some of the skills that an effective supervisor uses in implementing the philosophy which we discussed in the preceding section of this book.

But I didn't think you meant I was to inspect *every* unit."

"How did I know he was serious about quitting?"

"Our employees are always misinterpreting what we say...."

"You can't trust management to tell the truth."

There is hardly an aspect of management's job that does not involve communications. Serious mistakes are made because orders are misunderstood. Casual kidding leads to a grievance. An off-hand remark by the big boss leads the plant manager to adopt a get-tough attitude with the union. All spring from a breakdown in communications.

In this chapter we shall be concerned largely with face-to-face communications between individuals. In Chapter 14 we shall look at communications in terms of the over-all organization.

On the surface, face-to-face communications would seem to be simple. Have you ever listened to two old friends talking together? Rarely do they use complete sentences; often a single word, a grunt or a groan, or a raised eyebrow communicates as much meaning as lengthy speeches would

9

Communications

convey between casual acquaintances. Since each of the friends is aware of the other's frame of reference, key words or signs are all they need to transfer ideas. A few syllables go a long way.

But this may suggest that successful communication takes place automatically whenever two people get together. Let's examine a situation more typical of business life, however. The shop-clerk tells his boss with pride, "This is the heaviest day we've ever had." But the boss thinks the clerk is lazy and looking for an excuse not to unload new stock. So he answers angrily and the subordinate concludes that the boss is an overbearing, ungrateful so-and-so.

The basic problem in communications is that the meaning which is actually received by one person may not be what the other intended to send. The speaker and the listener are two separate individuals living in different worlds; any number of things can happen to distort the messages that pass between them.

The human sensory apparatus does not transmit an exact duplicate of reality from the outside world into the mind of the observer. Our needs and experiences tend to color what we see and hear. Certain "messages" are repressed—those we don't want to accept. Others are magnified. Still others are created out of thin air (for example, the "faults" in a person we dislike) or are hideously distorted from their original reality.[1]

What are the causes of breakdowns in communications? What can be done to overcome them? We shall consider each of these questions in turn.

Why Communications Break Down

WE HEAR WHAT WE EXPECT TO HEAR

What we hear or understand when someone speaks to us is largely shaped by our own experience and background. Instead of hearing what people tell us, we hear what our mind tells has been said. These may be the same things—or very different. We all tend to have preconceived ideas of what people mean; when we hear something new we tend to identify it with something similar that we have experienced in the past.

> The supervisor tells an employee that the company has lost some important orders. Now this employee has had other jobs, and whenever a company has lost business he has been thrown out of work. So he "hears" the supervisor's statement as, "You can expect to be laid off in the near future." When the man announces that he has quit to work elsewhere, the supervisor may be surprised to learn that the man thought his job was in danger.

Most of us resist change. We tend to reject new ideas, particularly if they conflict with what we already believe. In many ways our communications

---

[1] Our discussion is greatly influenced by Alfred Korzybski, *Science and Sanity* (Lancaster, Penn.: Science Press, 1933).

receiving apparatus works like an efficient filter. When we read a paper or listen to a political speech, we tend to note only those things that confirm our present beliefs. We may even comment that it is "good to get that additional information." On the other hand, we tend to ignore anything that conflicts with our beliefs; sometimes our filters work so efficiently we don't hear it at all. And even if we do hear it, we either reject it as a fallacious notion or find some way of twisting and shaping its meaning to fit our preconceptions. Because we hear and see what we *expect* to hear and see, we are rarely disappointed.

One of the best examples is our tendency to think in stereotypes. We grow up believing that Rarutanians (or some other group) are shiftless and lazy. Bill Jones is a Rarutanian. When Jones comes up with an intelligent short cut on his job which took a great deal of time and energy to develop, we take it as proof that "he's always looking for a chance to loaf, just like all the rest of them." Though ridiculous, such stereotypes are stubbornly preserved even in the face of conflicting evidence.

WE HAVE DIFFERENT PERCEPTIONS

Take the case of a supervisor who is watching a group of employees laughing.

1. To the supervisor who believes that work must be painful in order to be productive, the laughter communicates to him that time is being wasted, and perhaps assignments are too easy.

2. To the supervisor who believes that contented employees work harder, the laughter communicates that he is succeeding as a manager.

3. To the supervisor who is personally insecure, the laughter communicates that the men are ridiculing him.

This story emphasizes the obvious fact that people interpret the same stimulus in different ways, depending on their previous experience.

We find this problem arising in the "economic education" programs conducted by many companies. These programs try to give workers an understanding of how profits and productivity are related to job security and high wages, and an awareness of the advantages of our economic system over others. It has been estimated that companies are investing $100,000,000 each year in such attempts.[2]

Here again the difficulty is that the management which sponsors these programs and the employees for whom they are produced live in different worlds. Abstractions like "profits," "capital," and "productivity" have real meaning in the world of management, but they may have little meaning to the employee (or very negative associations).

---

[2] William H. Whyte, Jr., *Is Anybody Listening?* (New York: Simon and Schuster, 1952), p. 7.

> Fundamentally, [the typical program] is based on the attractively plausible idea that the cure for negative attitudes and misinformation is information. Unfortunately, in matters where sentiment enters too, it is not. . . . Since business' mass-education efforts have dilated heavily on how good business has been to everyone, "the facts" can often provoke an even more negative reaction. . . . [The educational literature] . . . must read to many people as unsolicited apologia, or, worse yet, as undeserved self-approbation.[3]

Clearly, the group with which we identify ourselves—the "reference group," as psychologists call it—tends to shape our interpretation of the communications we receive. As advertisers discovered long ago, the individual rarely changes his mind by himself. His attitudes toward politics, music, recreation, work pace, and all his other activities and interests are largely colored by the group with which he identifies. As we mentioned in Chapter 8, the supervisor is wasting his time trying to convince an individual employee to work harder when there is a strong group standard to the contrary. The employee would be risking ostracism if he went along with the supervisor's request. Management often uses slogans and posters to indoctrinate workers with the idea of safety, cutting scrap losses, making suggestions, or engaging in good housekeeping. They even send personal letters to employees' homes. The trouble with these efforts is that they are directed to the *individual,* whereas the basic attitudes and convictions are determined by the *group.* Thus if an employee's fellow workers see the supervisor as harsh and unfair, chances are he will feel the same way.

In a large organization, the difficulties of perception are compounded. An announcement may go to dozens of groups with different occupational and status interests. What each group "hears" depends on its own interests. An announcement that the company has purchased the plans for new products that will be manufactured in a new plant on the West Coast may be heard in these different ways:

> *Design engineer:* "This may be an indication that the company prefers to go outside the organization for new ideas, and that is bound to hurt our status."
>
> *Production engineer:* "This new product will mean more work for us. Some of us may have a chance to move out West."
>
> *Worker:* "The new products aren't going to be manufactured in the home plant. That means if business should get slack, we're likely to get laid off. A bad trend."

One researcher has compared the problem of getting every group to hear the same thing with the language problem in the United Nations,[4] where it is necessary to use a system of simultaneous translations. In the same way,

---

[3] *Ibid.,* pp. 13-14.

[4] Jay Jackson, "The Organization and Its Communications Problems." Paper presented to the Society of Public Health Educators, Atlantic City, N.J., Nov. 10, 1956.

every business organization needs some sort of translation system to overcome misunderstandings.

WE EVALUATE THE SOURCE

"The first time I met Bill Smith he tried to impress me that he was a
big shot. Ever since, I have discounted everything he says because I know
what kind of blowhard he is."

Not only does the receiver evaluate what he hears in terms of his own
background and experience, he also takes the sender into account. How reliable is he as a source of information? Does he have an axe to grind?

Often the receiver ascribes nonexistent motives to the sender. This is
particularly true in labor-management relations. Many union members, convinced that management is trying to weaken the union, interpret every company statement as an attempt to deceive them. Similarly management often
regards every union grievance as a political maneuver designed only to win
votes. Both sides are sometimes right of course. But this mental set makes
mutual understanding and agreement more difficult.

One experimenter clipped a cartoon from a union publication illustrating
"The Four Goals of Labor" and pasted it up with a caption indicating that
it had come from a publication of the National Association of Manufacturers.
When the clipping was shown to union members, they were overwhelmingly
critical of it as an unfair, biased representation of labor's goals. Having accepted the source as anti-labor, they automatically drew the "obvious" conclusions.[5]

This is one of the reasons why company newspapers (so-called "house
organs") find it difficult to gain worker acceptance. Once employees become
convinced that the paper is just a management mouthpiece, many will believe nothing it prints, no matter how objective or verifiable. So, too, with
pamphlets and other give-aways. If these are tagged as propaganda, all the
information they contain becomes suspect, even useful information about
health and household safety.

Similarly it is hard for a supervisor to shed a reputation for being hard-
boiled or unfair. Suppose he goes through a training program and emerges
with every intention of turning over a new leaf. Subordinates may well be
extremely suspicious of his motives and assume that his new approach is just
a trick. If so they will distort and misconstrue every move he makes.

A manager who receives a suggestion from a colleague or subordinate may
assume one of two things: (1) here is an alert, intelligent employee who is
anxious to make a contribution to the efficiency of the organization, or (2)
here is somebody who is trying to show me up by suggesting something he
figures I was too foolish to think of myself. And which of the two motiva-

---

[5] Whyte, *op. cit.*, p. 23.

tions he attributes to the subordinate will have a substantial effect on what he actually "sees" in the suggestion.

In short, it is extremely difficult for us to separate what we hear from our feelings about the person who says it.

WE IGNORE INFORMATION THAT CONFLICTS
WITH WHAT WE ALREADY KNOW

Communications sometimes fail to have the desired effect because they run counter to other information that the receiver possesses. Management may insist that the company must reduce costs if it is to survive. Everyone is urged to work harder and cut expenses to the bone. But some of the employees shrug off the announcement, for they know that salesmen still receive lavish allowances for "entertainment expenses." These expenses may be justified as a means of obtaining orders, but this is something the employees are in no position to appreciate. The same reaction would set in if they saw wasteful methods of manufacture countenanced week after week without being corrected.

Similarly, statements that hard work leads to promotion are likely to be ignored in a company where promotions in fact often are made on the basis of seniority or favoritism. A guarantee that "the company never cuts an incentive rate because employees are earning too much" is disregarded if rates have in fact been cut as a result of minor engineering changes. Even if the company is perfectly justified in retiming a job after the method or product has been changed, the employees may be convinced that this is simply an excuse for cutting the rate.

WORDS MEAN DIFFERENT THINGS TO DIFFERENT PEOPLE

This is the so-called "semantic" problem. Essentially language is a method of using symbols to represent facts and feelings. Strictly speaking we can't convey *meaning;* all we can do is convey *words.* And yet the same words may suggest quite different meanings for different people. The meanings are in the people, not in the words.

When management says that profits are essential if the business is to survive, it is thinking of profits as a means by which the company can buy new equipment, expand, and provide more jobs. To management, profits mean a successfully operated, growing enterprise. But to employees, the word profit suggests a picture of excess funds piled up through paying inadequate wages. No matter how often management explains the need for profits, employees may persist in attaching the meaning of "excess," "unearned," or "unfair" to the term. Any attempt to communicate about profits must surmount the barrier of established meanings attached to the word.

This problem is especially acute with abstract terms. But even simple concrete words and phrases often lead to trouble, again because the sender and receiver live in separate worlds. For instance:

> The foreman spots oil on the floor and tells a machinist, "Get that oil wiped up as soon as you can; it's a real safety hazard." The machinist nods that he will. Ten minutes later an inspector slips on the very same spot.
>
> The supervisor is enraged by this needless accident. When he prepares to penalize the machinist for failing to follow instructions, he is told, "But I was going to do it *as soon as I could,* as you told me. I thought you could see that I was working on a delicate cut, and I had to finish that first."

To the supervisor "as soon as you can" meant immediately; to the operator it meant as soon as it could be done without endangering his work. It is foolish to try to decide who was right. Here we see the fallacy of the simple "tell them what you want them to do" approach. Simply telling people isn't enough when the sender and the receiver give the words different meanings. Confusion arises even when words are selected with great care.

WORDS HAVE SYMBOLIC MEANINGS

For some people, a particular word may have a symbolic meaning that others overlook. When we use words of this sort, we may find ourselves communicating things we had no intention of saying.

> When the manager tells a new supervisor that the parking lot is too crowded for him to have a parking sticker, something more is being communicated than simple information on parking conditions. What the new supervisor hears may be this, "You are not accepted as a member of management, and everyone will soon know it."
>
> Or when a group chief tells an employee that the division head wants to see him in his office next morning at nine, something extra is communicated. For the rest of the day the employee dawdles at one unimportant task after another, apparently unable to accomplish any real work. He has interpreted the request as a threat of punishment to come, for this is the meaning that "main office" has for him.

In both these instances, the supervisor's statement carried far more meaning than he had intended.

Observers of collective bargaining have noted that violent antagonism develops in discussions about "management prerogatives" or the "union shop." Again, these are terms that have great symbolic significance. While the manager is talking about prerogatives to the union, he is really trying to say that the very basis of the managerial function and perhaps of the free-enterprise system is involved. Similarly, the union leader arguing for the union shop feels that acceptance or rejection symbolizes the real place of the union in the plant—is it a permanent, accepted institution or merely a temporary nuisance that is being tolerated? Compromise on such issues is difficult, for both parties feel that their vital interests are at stake.

OUR EMOTIONAL STATE CONDITIONS WHAT WE HEAR

When we are insecure, worried, or fearful, what we hear and see seems more threatening than when we are secure and at peace with the world. Rumors of all sorts spring up when management makes a change of any kind without adequate explanation, even a change as simple as moving desks around the office. This is particularly true during an economic recession. Then statements and actions that under less trying circumstances would have passed unnoticed become grounds for fear. "Yes, Joe might be right, they are going to double the work load." "I saw the foreman looking at the seniority list; I guess the rumors are right, a lot of men will be laid off because of the new equipment."

By the same token, when we are angry or depressed, we tend to reject out of hand what might otherwise seem like reasonable requests or good ideas. Our gloom and despair color everything we do and see.

WE DON'T KNOW HOW THE OTHER MAN PERCEIVES THE SITUATION

This is one of the most serious sources of friction in industry. With all the sincerity in the world, we try to frame a message that will break the communications barrier and carry an appropriate meaning to those to whom it is directed. But in many instances we know too little about their point of view, and our efforts miscarry.

The trouble may be simply that the subordinate doesn't understand what sort of information his boss wants him to supply. Consequently, the subordinate has no way of knowing what he should tell his boss, or when or where he should speak. Inevitably, the boss complains that vital facts have been kept from him or that he is being deluged with useless information.

The reverse situation is just as troublesome. In training a subordinate, the superior often tries to communicate information before the subordinate is ready to understand it.

In conclusion, it is very difficult to understand information that is outside our experience, no matter how simply and clearly the information is presented by the sender.

SUMMARY

Barriers to communications among members of an organization cause breakdowns, distortions, and inaccurate rumors. They plague the daily life of the manager who must depend on accurate transmission of orders and information for efficient operation. The implication is clear: Don't assume that every message you send will be received in the form you intended.

Overcoming Barriers to Communication

Up to this point we have purposely presented a discouraging, one-sided picture: pervasive problems and no solutions. But the picture need not be this bleak. We now know many techniques for improving communications, though—it should be emphasized—none is a cure-all. Perfect understanding between people is impossible.

We shall devote the rest of this chapter to a discussion of several methods by which the alert supervisor can maximize his success in communicating. At first glance, these techniques may appear mechanical substitutes for mutual trust and understanding. However, a wide variety of research confirms the efficacy of considering communications as a type of engineering problem—the problem of transmitting information from one point to another.

UTILIZE FEEDBACK

Perhaps the single most important method of improving communications is *feedback*. This term, adopted from engineering,[6] refers to the ability of certain complex machines (technically: systems) to check on their own performance and to correct it if necessary.

We all use this principle of feedback in our human communications—perhaps without realizing it. Even in casual conversations we are constantly on the alert for cues to whether we are being understood (e.g., attentive nods from the other person). Similarly, a good teacher is always interested in audience reaction among his students. If they seem confused or drowsy, he knows his lecture isn't getting across. The good supervisor is equally conscious of the need to determine his subordinates' reactions to what he is trying to communicate.

An interesting study conducted by Dr. Alex Bavelas illustrates the importance of feedback.[7] Two students were placed in different rooms and one was asked to communicate to the other the position of an interconnected series of dominoes placed on a grid. Both had identical grids in front of them. The sender was permitted to explain to the receiver, in any way he saw fit, the relative positions of the dominoes. It was impossible to complete the task successfully when the receiver was forbidden to respond—that is, when com-

---

[6] For sophisticated analyses of how principles of electronic communications may be applied to human communications, see Norbert Wiener, *Cybernetics* (Cambridge, Mass.: Technology Press, Doubleday, 1954); Colin Cherry, *On Human Communication* (New York: Wiley, 1957).

[7] As described to his students at M.I.T.

munications were entirely one-way. No matter how painstakingly the sender explained the pattern, the receiver never understood all of it. Apparently some opportunity to ask for further information, at least to answer "yes" or "no" to the questions of the sender (e.g., Did you understand what I said?), is essential if complex information is to be communicated. Without feedback, false perceptions creep in, and even a small error that goes uncorrected may become magnified into a major distortion.

Bavelas' experiment also revealed that communications gain in speed and efficiency as more and more feedback is permitted. Limiting the receiver to "yes" or "no" responses is less effective than allowing him to expand his comments to whatever he deems appropriate.

MAXIMIZE FEEDBACK BY USING
MANY CHANNELS OF COMMUNICATION

How do we know if the person to whom we are communicating understands, agrees, or sympathizes with us, or is indifferent, hostile, or confused? There are several techniques for maximizing feedback.

Observation   In a face-to-face situation, we can observe the other person and judge his responses by his total behavioral set. We can watch for nonverbal cues—the expressions of puzzlement, anger, or comprehension that flicker across the face of the listener, or the subtle body motions that reveal impatience, animosity, or agreement. These cues give eloquent expression to attitudes that the receiver may be reluctant or unable to express in words.

Indeed, by their posture and facial expression, the set of their lips, the movement of an eyebrow, people often tell us more than they do in hours of talk or scores of written memoranda. A subordinate is seldom eager to challenge the orders of his superior. But in the course of informal, face-to-face discussion, an alert supervisor can detect the subordinate's lack of enthusiasm by his tone of voice and his general physical behavior.

Few of us appreciate just how much valuable information these nonverbal cues transmit. As one social scientist has observed, "When communication is at peak efficiency, in the most intimately shared situations, words are often superfluous. Good examples of this are the hospital operating room, the jazz band, and some small interdependent work teams in industry." [8] The close coordination necessary for these groups to achieve their goal is attained exclusively through occasional nods and glances.

Listening with a "third ear"   We must listen carefully if we are to discover what a person is trying to say. Though few of us can qualify as psychiatrists, we can learn to listen with a "third ear" by asking ourselves such questions

---

[8] From a lecture by Dr. Robert N. Wilson, Executive Development Program, Cornell University, 1952.

as: "What did Joe really mean when he told me he was 'fed up'? Was it his assignment? His family? His chances for promotion? Me, as his boss? Why did he remain silent when I asked him for details?"

There is a hidden content in many communications that can only be inferred by the listener. (This non-logical element is frequently referred to as the *latent* content as distinct from the *manifest* content.) While the listener should keep his imagination in check, he should try to go beyond the logical verbal meaning where there is some evidence that emotional feeling is involved. Most communications are in fact a combination of fact and feeling.

A good example of this hidden content is provided by the word "communications" itself. An office manager complains to the personnel director that all his human-relations problems stem from "poor communications." If the personnel director wants to be of assistance, he will try to get behind the manager's use of the word "communications." The manager might mean that there are divisive cliques that tend to distort his orders or that he, the boss, never hears the "real truth" about what is going on in the office. He might be using the word communications to mean that cooperative teamwork is lacking, or to mean many other things. The point is that the words used by a speaker may not be very informative until we have an opportunity to question him on what he really means in terms of actual observable behavior. The listener must try to get back to the *referents* of the speaker and to avoid the easy assumption that both people are attaching the same meaning to abstract words.

Checking on reception   The speaker himself may have to initiate queries to insure that the message he is transmitting is actually being received. For instance, he might ask the receiver to repeat complex verbal orders. Or he might simply ask, "Do you understand? Is this clear?" (This is one of the functions of the classroom recitation.)

Feedback is particularly hard to obtain in a large organization. When top management wants to discover whether its directives are being understood, face-to-face exchanges are often impossible. Morale surveys and suggestion systems sometimes help to bridge the gap between top management and subordinates, but, as we shall see in Chapter 17, the best way to promote feedback is through changes in organizational structure and over-all supervisory attitudes.

USE FACE-TO-FACE COMMUNICATIONS

Face-to-face communications are superior, under most circumstances, to written orders, printed announcements, or newspaper articles. Only when the sender is able to experience direct feedback from the receiver can he really know what the receiver is hearing and what he is failing to hear. How else can the sender become aware of the hidden meanings—the symbolic significance the receiver is ascribing to his words? How else can he bring out into the open contradictory information already in the receiver's mind that may cause him to reject or ignore the communication?

Another reason for the greater effectiveness of voice communications is that most of us communicate more easily, completely, and more frequently by voice.

Probably the greatest advantage of voice communications is that they provide immediate feedback. Merely by looking at the audience, the skillful speaker can judge how it is reacting to what he is saying. If necessary he can modify his approach or vary the intensity of his voice. (The human voice can provide a wider variety of emphasis and pace than any printed page, regardless of the number of type fonts used.)

Even better feedback is possible if the recipients of the message are allowed to comment or ask questions. This gives the supervisor an opportunity to explain his meaning or to consider unexpected problems. (Printed material can provide explanations, but few writers can anticipate all the questions that might be asked.)

Furthermore, we usually ascribe more credibility to what we hear someone say than to words attributed to him in print. Employees conditioned to the "slick" releases of public relations offices tend to discount many of the printed announcements they read. Actually hearing the boss say that the company is in serious trouble, however, may carry a great deal more weight than would a statement in the house organ, particularly if employees have an opportunity to ask the boss direct questions.

When the late John Foster Dulles was asked why he flew away from Washington so frequently, he replied:

> Well, I fly because I go to meet heads of government, foreign ministers of other countries, and in a few minutes or at most a few hours of personal consultation you can achieve a much better understanding than you can possibly achieve by going through notes and writing to each other.
>
> It is just like you and me talking here, today. We understand each other, I am sure, a lot better than if you were writing me a letter and I was to write you a letter back.
>
> Now, it is the same thing that happens on a broader scale in the field of international relations.[9]

Does all this mean that written messages have no place in the organization? Not at all. In fact, they are often indispensable. Lengthy, detailed instructions must be put in writing so that the person to whom they are addressed can have a chance to study them at leisure. The spoken word exists only for an instant, and then vanishes. The written message provides a permanent record to which the receiver can refer to make sure he understands what has been said, and to which the sender can refer as evidence that he has in fact

---

[9] Dana Adams Schmidt, "Instant Diplomacy and the New Diplomats." *Columbia University Forum* (Fall 1958), p. 36.

said it. Frequently, too, the relative formality of written communications gives the message greater weight than it would have if it were delivered orally.

For very important messages, both the spoken and written word may be used in combination. For instance, if a new procedure is to be introduced, the supervisor might call a meeting of his subordinates to give them a rough outline of the change. At this point he could (1) explain why the change is necessary, (2) answer their questions, and (3) perhaps make adjustments to meet objections. Once general agreement has been reached, the new procedure can be reduced to writing for future reference.

BE SENSITIVE TO THE WORLD OF THE RECEIVER

It is extremely difficult to get through to a listener when what we are trying to communicate contradicts his expectations and predilections. If our typist has been in the habit of preparing only a single carbon, we must stress our request for two carbons. If being sent to the front office is regarded by employees as a sign of impending discipline, we must take pains to communicate that this is *not* the reason, if in fact it is not.

In short we must be sensitive to the private world of the receiver and try to predict the impact of what we say and do on his feelings and attitudes. The greater the gap between our background and experience and that of the receiver, the greater the effort we must make to find some common ground of understanding. If the supervisor really wants to communicate with the sweeper, for example, he must find a way of (a) fitting his remarks to the sweeper's attitudes and beliefs, (b) making some appeal to the needs of the sweeper, and (c) constantly testing (via feedback) whether his message is being received.

This same problem arises when management attempts to communicate to employees through company newspapers (house organs) or reports. Management often relies on such publications to tell employees about personnel changes, the company's economic condition, cost problems, cost-reduction programs, future prospects for company business, how company products and services are being used, and the "why" and "how" of doing things throughout the organization. For obvious reasons management thinks these are matters of importance and wants all employees to understand as much as possible about them. Unfortunately, however, management is often insensitive to the world of the employees and tries to project its own interests onto them. The employee down the line may be bored by information on the sources of company funds or the painstaking engineering that lies behind the company's products, though these are subjects of great importance to management.

Management often spends a great deal of time and money to present information of this sort in a way that will capture the interest of the employees when they read the house organ. But what happens is that the carefully worded story simply passes over the heads of the majority of employees whose interest in the subject is limited or downright nonexistent.

Many companies try to get around this problem by including information that *is* relevant to rank-and-file employees—information on their own world of activities and interests. They feature news of company-sponsored athletic events, social notes, announcements of weddings, births, retirements, and so forth. Departmental correspondents are appointed to broaden the coverage. The objective is to improve morale and enhance employee identification with the company.

The Detroit Edison Company has adopted an interesting approach. Its house organ features a "rumor clinic" in which top management deals candidly with questions raised by employees on such subjects as: alleged pay and vacation inequities, why some employees receive company-bought clothing and others do not, the quality and price of cafeteria food, and the reasons for layoffs or overtime. In answering questions submitted by workers, management has an opportunity to communicate information about the company's economic condition, engineering and sales problems, and so on—and in terms of direct interest to employees.

BE AWARE OF SYMBOLIC MEANING

As we have seen, symbols play a vital role in the "private world" of the listener. Here is a case in which effective communication was blocked until symbolic meanings were taken into account:

> To help in the preparation of market analyses the District Sales Manager asked the salesmen to compute correlation coefficients from their records. These coefficients could be calculated quite simply and painlessly by use of a simple formula. But the salesmen refused to do what they were asked. One excuse followed another: the computations were too complicated, it was clerk's work and not part of their job description, the coefficients were really useless, and so on. There seemed to be no way to convince the men to perform this simple task, and their persistent refusal seemed out of all proportion to the issue at hand.
>
> Why was this modest request greeted with such stubborn resistance? The very degree of the salesmen's reaction was the key to the problem. Investigation revealed that coefficient correlations had been tried three years earlier, when the department was headed by an inept supervisor who had earned the universal dislike of his subordinates. Among other things, he had tried to revamp all the departmental procedures and in the process had introduced this statistical technique. Ever since, the salesmen had associated the term "coefficient correlation" with autocratic supervision. To them it had become a symbol of oppressive management. Once the company had plumbed this seemingly irrational attitude, it was a simple matter to develop a different terminology for the operation, to conduct training in how the computations should be carried out, and to gain ready acceptance for the whole activity.

The moral of this story is clear: if there is extraordinary, unexpected resistance to a proposal, try to find out whether some symbolic meaning is associated with it.

TIME YOUR MESSAGES CAREFULLY

We have already noted that our current beliefs often distort the meaning we ascribe to what we hear or see. There is an analogy here to the concept of "noise" as used by the communications engineer. The supervisor must recognize that when he is trying to tell his subordinate something, other things are being heard simultaneously that may distort his message.

One way of limiting the amount of noise or distortion is to communicate your message before those other beliefs or attitudes come into play. Then the communication will meet less resistance and your chances of getting it accepted will be greatly increased.

> Management announced that Foreman Green would retire in a few months and would be replaced by a man named Williams from another department. One of the men felt that Williams had done him an injustice years ago, and spread the word among his fellow employees that Williams was a tyrant who played favorites.
>
> Long before Williams set foot in the new department, a petition was sent to top management requesting that a different foreman be assigned. And once Williams showed up, everything he said and did was fitted into the picture the employees had already established. Every job assignment he made was scrutinized for favoritism. Even harmless statements were often interpreted as threats.

A situation like this is an ideal breeding-ground for misunderstanding and unrest. Yet management could have minimized the problem by taking positive action before the picture of the new supervisor got established, perhaps by having the employees meet him as soon as the announcement was made.

REINFORCE WORDS WITH ACTION

Words by themselves are suspect. Employees are more likely to accept new propositions when they observe an actual change in behavior or participate themselves in the process of change. For example, supervisors in one company were told that they would have the final say in granting individual pay increases. This was a radical departure from past practice. Most of the supervisors were skeptical about whether management really meant what it said. But this feeling disappeared when they began filling out recommendation forms themselves and sending them to the Personnel Department (a minor clerical job that in the past had been done in the superintendent's office). The consistent reinforcement of verbal announcements by action increases the likelihood that the communication will be accepted.

Management must be careful not to allow supersalesmanship techniques to dominate its thinking in communicating to employees. Because employees are able to judge for themselves the quality of the relationship they enjoy with a company, sustained repetition of slick slogans will not be effective. One cannot advertise one type of personnel program and deliver another. In the same vein, low-pressure statements are probably more effective than high-pressure pronouncements. Instead of telling workers how generous their pension benefits are, it may be more effective to give them the facts (comparative data on pension plans for the industry or community) and let them draw their own conclusion. It is difficult if not impossible to communicate "values"; facts can be transmitted with some success, but even facts are subject to distortion.

Once management has acquired a reputation for accuracy and reliability in its communications, it can do a more effective job of communicating information on new problems. The British learned this lesson during the war.

> Early in World War II, when the radio stations of most countries were widely suspected of distorting the war news, the British Broadcasting System adopted a policy of frankly reporting Allied setbacks. This gave the British a morale and tactical advantage over their enemies when the tide turned in favor of the Allies, for Europeans of all nationalities were ready to believe the news of the German rout—simply because it came from a source that had proved itself trustworthy.

USE DIRECT, SIMPLE LANGUAGE

Written communications should be as intelligible and readable as possible. Rudolf Flesch, one of the foremost proponents of simple, clear, direct writing and speaking, urges that multisyllable and erudite words be avoided, that lengthy sentences be broken down into more manageable units, and that metaphors, irony, and other indirect devices be shunned.[10] He has developed various scales by which the readability of material may be related to the education and comprehension level of different groups of readers.[11] Flesch and others who have specialized in research of this sort also advocate the use of words and phrases that personalize the material and make it more concrete and immediately intelligible.

Every manager must insure that his announcements, public statements, and directives are couched in simple, direct language. Government agencies have been the favorite butt of jokes about "gobbledegook," but many private organizations also are guilty of torturing simple statements into complicated puzzles, and of using specialized and complex jargon. Low readability is

---

[10] Rudolf Flesch, *The Art of Plain Talk* (New York: Harpers, 1946), and *The Art of Readable Writing* (New York: Harpers, 1949).

[11] For instance, the Flesch index for this section is 5.45 or difficult. According to Flesch, it should have a potential audience of 24 per cent of all readers. *The Art of Plain Talk,* p. 205.

undoubtedly a factor in the breakdown of communications. (And since most people talk more simply than they write, it is another reason for using face-to-face communications whenever possible.) High readability, however, is not an answer in itself to the fundamental barriers to communication that we have discussed.

INTRODUCE PROPER AMOUNT OF REDUNDANCY

Communications engineers have developed techniques for measuring the amount of "redundancy" in a message—roughly the amount of repetition it contains. The supervisor who wants to give a direct order or transmit technical information should make sure that his message includes substantial redundancy. Then, if any word or phrase is misunderstood, there are other elements in the communication that will carry his point.

> To give a very simple example: a firm manufacturing several thousand varieties of chemical compounds used a numerical coding system to refer to each of the products. Increasingly, management found that mistakes were creeping into the ordering system. When a supervisor requested a shipment of compound #28394, a clerical error would occasionally result in a wasted shipment of #23894. Each digit was crucial, and the slightest mistake was costly. Eventually the firm adopted individual names for each compound and these words had a great deal of built-in redundancy, as do nearly all words. If a clerk ordered "calitin" instead of "calithin," the shipping department knew what he meant.

If each word is crucially important, it pays to say the same thing in several ways. In giving complicated directions, for example, it is wise to repeat them several times, perhaps in different ways, to guarantee successful transmission.

At times, however, the manager may want to avoid redundancy, and concentrate instead on introducing novelty or originality into his communications.[12] We tend to ignore many of the messages we receive simply because they sound so familiar. Most of us are guilty of repeating our favorite clichés to the point where people no longer listen to what we say because it is all so predictable. ("I know what the boss is going to say the minute he starts on that line about us all being one big happy team.")

There is some need for surprise, in modest doses to be sure, if we are to gain the attention of those with whom we wish to communicate. This is particularly true when our message contains something that contradicts expectations. For instance, to repeat our previous example, if our typist has been in the habit of preparing only one carbon, we must stress our request for two carbons.

Thus the supervisor needs to balance carefully the redundancy and surprise elements of his communication.

---

[12] Cherry, *op. cit.*, p. 14.

Conclusion

The swiftest, most effective communication takes place among people with common points of view. The supervisor who enjoys a good relationship with his subordinates has much less difficulty in explaining why air-conditioning equipment cannot be installed for another year than does the supervisor who is not trusted by his men. When people feel secure, they can talk to one another easily. Where discontent is rife, so is misunderstanding, misinterpretation, rumor, and distortion. In this sense, communication is

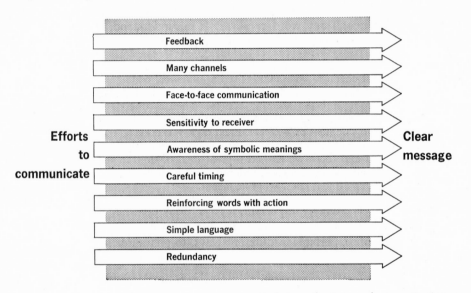

Techniques for improved communication.

a dependent variable. Where human relations are good, it is easy; where they are poor, it is almost impossible. Therefore the communications area is *not* the place to start improving supervisor-subordinate relationships.

Nearly every aspect of personnel work and of supervisor-subordinate relations involves communications. Even the structure of the organization—affecting as it does status relations and the number of levels between top management and the worker at the bottom—has a most significant effect on the ability of people to communicate easily and quickly.

The personnel programs that we shall discuss in later chapters also have a profound effect on communications. When a selection policy is geared to admit people with similar backgrounds and interests, some of the problems we have discussed in this chapter are minimized. Similarly, carefully planned training and orientation programs help establish a common point of view and thus tend to reduce the misunderstandings that arise out of differing frames of reference.

Nevertheless, the problem of communicating accurately and effectively in each contact makes the supervisor's job more difficult. He must guard against the natural inclination in our highly verbal society to assume that simply *telling somebody* is enough to insure successful communication. Fortunately, as we have seen, the supervisor can resort to a number of techniques to facilitate the transmission of understanding between people in their day-to-day activities.

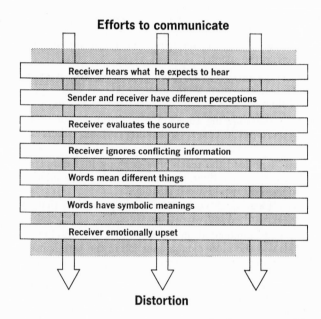

Efforts to communicate

Receiver hears what he expects to hear

Sender and receiver have different perceptions

Receiver evaluates the source

Receiver ignores conflicting information

Words mean different things

Words have symbolic meanings

Receiver emotionally upset

Distortion

Barriers to successful communication.

Communications is a matter of both transmitting and receiving. This chapter has emphasized transmitting. In Chapter 10 we will consider one of the most useful techniques for receiving information: interviewing.

Problem I *

In October 1956, construction was begun on a new can manufacturing plant that was to be ready for production in June 1957. Starting in December 1956, eight machinists and five other mechanics were hired over a period of five months and sent to various eastern and midwestern plants for training. As a group they were above average in intelligence and craftsmanship and performed superior work in the plants they visited.

---

* We are indebted to Mansfield Elkind for this case.

By late spring of 1957 it was realized that construction difficulties would force the postponement of the plant opening until the early fall. In view of this, management decided to recall all the men from field training in late June and early July. The reasoning was that excessive training costs would be eliminated, intensive machine training could be provided locally, and management would have an opportunity to observe their men first hand.

Although the factory building was not completed, a large temporary warehouse on the premises was in operation. There was considerable activity consisting of unloading and trucking cartons of cans from freight cars and truck trailers into the warehouse, and loading other trucks with cartons of cans for shipment to local customers. Management intended to use the returning men for daily part-time labor in the warehouse during the periods they were not attending equipment school.

After the first group of seven men arrived, they were put to work in the warehouse under the direction of the foreman. The following comments were made about introductions to the plant.

> *Machinist* (Larson): "Nobody told us who we were working for."
>
> *Supt.:* "When the men were brought in we first explained what was expected of them."

From the outset the shipping foreman was dissatisfied with the work of the machinists. Some were put in boxcars unloading cartons. Others were put to work inspecting cans.

> *Foreman:* "I noticed the machinists dogging it. I didn't say anything because I knew it wasn't their type of work. I didn't mind if they worked slowly, if only they would work steadily."
>
> *Machinist* (Larson): "We were all slightly shocked that we had to go to the boxcars. We griped but we did the work."

The superintendent commented on the work of a few machinists who were inspecting cans. This was the most monotonous job in the warehouse. The men were compared to those working in the boxcars.

> *Supt.:* "It seemed to me they weren't doing the same job as the other machinists. They didn't have their heart in it.
>
> "I had built-in resentment against some of the men from what the foreman told me about them. I didn't speak to any of them about it, however, because I feel a guy should have only one boss. I heard they were giving the foreman smart answers."

In school the men were divided into three groups and given very little supervision. They first received job instruction training and instructors were chosen from the group. The equipment they worked on was new and they had the responsibility of pooling their knowledge and developing written adjustment and set-up instructions for each machine. There was considerable group participation and the men were enthusiastic.

When the new group of six men reported for work the personnel supervisor requested them to come in about an hour late so as to give the foreman a chance to get his department running.

> *Machinist* (Larson): "Some of the men came in late for work because the personnel supervisor asked them. A few days later during morning roll call the foreman mentioned this fact that the men came in late and asked—Who's supposed to pay you guys for that time? The personnel department better pay for it—as if there was a dividing line between shipping and maintenance men. He talked as if the money was coming out of his own pocket."

In the days that followed the machinists began returning late from morning and afternoon breaks. Larson quoted the foreman's comment on this practice.

Foreman: "My men get back from breaks on time so why can't you?"

Machinist (Larson): "He [the foreman] always made that distinction between his men and us."

Due to scheduling difficulties it was sometimes necessary to put three men in a boxcar instead of two.

Foreman: "I saw three men doing the work of one man. I told them it was a one-man job. Perhaps I was a little sarcastic when I said it. It's a bad idea to have them working in groups."

Machinist (Larson): "We used to take pride in emptying the cars in about five hours. We kept on making a target for ourselves.

"When you work together it isn't so boring because you can talk and work at the same time."

Foreman: "My men started making cracks about the maintenance men. They would say—Look at them [the machinists]. I guess it's going to take a couple of days for them to unload that car."

Some of the machinists were unloading cartons of cans from the boxcars. The cartons could not be handled roughly due to the danger of damage to the cans. They were transferring the cartons to the railroad platform.

Foreman: "The men were tossing the cartons. I told them,—Don't toss the cartons, just place them.—I came back 15 minutes later and they were doing the same thing. This time I gave them a direct order and said that I wasn't kidding. I guess I had a nasty look on my face and I meant it.

"It was indicative of the type of work they were doing."

Machinist (Larson): "There was a big space between the dock and the railroad car. It was dangerous to keep walking across the space. We figured out a way of making sort of a fire line and handing the cartons out easier and faster than we could do the regular way. It was also safer because we didn't have to walk across that space. The foreman said we were throwing the cartons but we really weren't. He made us go back to the old way and we couldn't understand why."

1. Note all the communications breakdowns that occurred in this situation and explain the source of the problem.

2. In each case, explain how the difficulty could have been avoided.

Problem II

Carlin Mailaway specializes in reproductions of New England antiques and sells them by means of a nationally distributed catalog. The company, located in Great Barrington, Massachusetts, has won a dominant position in the market it serves.

Recently Carlin instituted a more formal inventory system. The results were appalling to the General Manager, James Coffin. According to the second quarterly inventory, at least $2,000 worth of merchandise had disappeared "mysteriously" during the preceding three months. Almost simultaneously the warehouse supervisor found several pieces of merchandise wrapped as trash in a refuse barrel—as though they had been placed there by someone who intended to retrieve them later.

As soon as the figures were confirmed by a sample rechecking, Coffin dictated a letter to the Warehouse Supervisor, and sent copies out to every one of the 28 employees working in the warehouse. The letter read as follows:

> Our auditing procedures have just disclosed a shocking loss of goods in our warehouse. In the future, no unauthorized personnel are to be allowed into the warehouse section of our building and all employees working in the area will be expected to refrain from carrying packages in or out of the department and permit close scrutiny of their persons as they leave work.
>
> In no sense should any of our loyal, faithful employees interpret this as a slur against their characters. We know that they would want these stern provisions to be introduced to eliminate any possibility that they might be implicated.
>
> We will appreciate your cooperation and thank you for your help in the past.

1. As a long-service employee in this department, how would you "interpret" this letter? Would others interpret it differently, do you think? Which ones and why?
2. What would you think the General Manager's motives were in writing this letter?
3. What alternative procedures might have been considered? What would their shortcomings and advantages be?
4. Might the Manager's letter have been better conceived and written?

Problem III

For many years the Brace Machine Works had employed Negroes only in menial jobs. After deliberation, and in part as a result of the passage of new state legislation, top management decided to adopt an unambiguous policy of offering equal employment opportunities for members of all nationality, racial, and religious groups.

The president of the company called in the personnel director for his counsel on how to announce this new policy in a way that would not only assure Negroes of equal employment opportunities but would also guarantee that they would not be discriminated against in opportunities for promotion to better-paying, more skilled positions.

1. If you were the personnel director, what advice would you give the president?
2. In helping him frame his approach, what questions would you ask, what information would you need, and what knowledge about the company would be useful to you?

My boss doesn't give a hoot about me. As far as he is concerned I am another piece of machinery."

"I'll say this about my boss: No matter what your problem is, he'll hear you through."

"Though I'm supposed to be in charge of this department, it's my people who do the work. I try to remember that to himself each person is absolutely different from anyone else. He wants special recognition. So I try to pay attention to him, listen to his problems."

Effective communication requires effort both by the sender of the message and the receiver. The last chapter was devoted largely to the sending of messages. In this chapter we shall be concerned with an important aspect of receiving them—with listening.

Listening is one of the most important of all management tools, for it is of tremendous help to the supervisor in maintaining good relations with his superiors, his subordinates, and his equals. Yet even though people learn to listen before they learn to talk, relatively few ever master the fine art of listening—that is, the art of *interviewing*.

10

Interviewing:
The Fine Art of Listening

What do we mean by "interviewing"? Most people think of interviewing in the sense of the formal interviews connected with getting a job. By interviewing we mean much more than this: we mean deliberate, active listening whose purpose is to draw the other person out, to discover what he really wants to say, and to give him a chance to express himself fully.

Effective interviewing is not easy. It requires self-control and training. Yet because the skills of interviewing produce such valuable results, the effort to learn them is very worth while.

Historical Background

Management first became aware of the value of interviewing in industrial relations during the 1920's as a consequence of studies conducted at the Hawthorne plant of the Western Electric Company.[1] These studies were primarily concerned with the determinants of morale and productivity. However, in their attempts to uncover basic feelings regarding these factors, the researchers found that direct questions designed to find out how the subjects felt about specific aspects of their jobs result in superficial, "lifeless" answers. Even worse—or so it seemed at the time—instead of giving "straightforward" responses, some of the people interviewed tended to talk about what interested them most at the moment.

Following this clue, the interviewers tried a radically new experiment: they sat back and decided to let the interviewees direct the interviews. Now they discovered that people began to express their *feelings* as well as give factual answers. Employees launched into long tirades (to which the interviewers patiently listened) revealing attitudes that might otherwise have been kept carefully guarded. In fact, some employees expressed attitudes that they had not been consciously aware of themselves. As a consequence, the interviewers got a much better picture of the psychological geography of the plant. They discovered surprising relationships about which they would never have learned by asking direct questions.

More important: the employees benefited greatly as well. Just by talking freely in the presence of a sympathetic listener, they got their problems off their chest and felt better. They experienced what psychologists call *catharsis* (from the Greek: to make pure). In addition, merely by talking things over, the employees began to gain insight into the nature of their own problems. Once they had relieved their feelings by speaking openly in a receptive

---

[1] For the most thorough review of these studies, see F. J. Roethlisberger and W. J. Dickson, *Management and the Worker* (Cambridge: Harvard University Press, 1939). For a critical analysis of these studies in the light of later research, see Henry Landsberger, *Hawthorne Revisited* (Ithaca: New York State School of Industrial and Labor Relations, 1958).

environment, they were able to look at their problems more objectively. And their clearer understandings, supplemented by further discussion, often enabled them to work out solutions (at least to those problems that they were in a position to solve themselves).

Impressed by the value of the Hawthorne experience, Western Electric instituted a program of formal counseling.[2] Specially chosen counselors were trained in the use of _non-directive_ interviews. (By non-directive interviews we mean—as we shall explain later—a type of interview in which the interviewer encourages the interviewee to express his own thoughts with considerable freedom—as contrasted to directive interviewing, in which the interviewer asks direct questions and tries to keep the discussion within predetermined limits.)

These "free-floating" counselors were given no regular supervisory duties; they were completely separate from the normal management hierarchy. Their function was merely to listen to employees' problems without giving advice or taking action.

Other companies rapidly followed Western Electric's example. Particularly during World War II counseling was very popular. Many employers assigned "free-floating" counselors throughout the company, especially to help women workers.[3]

The counselors faced a tough ethical problem of what to do with the information they received. If they repeated to management what they had been told, the workers would no longer trust them. On the other hand, if they could use their information in a discreet manner, they might be able to eliminate the causes of trouble. Often the counselors compromised by giving management general reports without revealing details that might identify individuals.

In recent years the use of such counselors as a personnel tool has declined. It was discovered that this technique had many drawbacks, including the following:

1. Although counseling might help an individual make a better adjustment to a poor environment (say to an inept supervisor) it didn't improve the environment itself. Employees often began to feel that they were wasting their time talking to a counselor who could do nothing for them, and ended up almost as frustrated as before.

2. Counseling is directed almost entirely toward changing _individual_ attitudes and behavior, in spite of other evidence from the Hawthorne study itself that group attitudes are often more important than individual attitudes.

---

[2] Jeanne L. Wilensky and Harold Wilensky, "Personnel Counseling, The Hawthorne Case," _The American Journal of Sociology,_ Vol. 57, No. 3 (November 1951), pp. 265-282.

[3] See Douglas Arbuckle, "Differences Between Clinical and Industrial Non-Directive Counseling," _The Personnel Journal,_ Vol. 26, No. 10 (April 1948), pp. 374-376.

3. The counseling system gave subordinates a chance to bypass and tattle on their supervisors. Naturally, the supervisors objected.

4. In some cases employees began to compare the "good" counselor with the "bad" supervisor. Supervisors felt they were entitled to the undivided loyalty of subordinates.

5. The counselors discovered that they were spending most of their time with a few disturbed individuals who really needed deep psychotherapy rather than counseling.

The basic trouble with "free-floating" counseling was its separation from line management. Line management emphasized downward communication: "I'll tell you what to do. I don't particularly care what you think about it." Counseling provided upward communication. But the two forms of communication went along different channels. The solution was to transform supervisors into counselors, to look upon counseling as a normal function of supervision. As a consequence, modern management is beginning to train supervisors in the technique of interviewing so that they can do their own counseling, rather than assigning specialists to the job.

Listening as a Management Tool

Effective communications must go both ways. Upward communication and downward communication, listening and order-giving, are both more effective if done by the *same* person. Furthermore, if they are merged into the same process, something new and better emerges. Thus there has come the realization that counseling or interviewing or listening (which are really all the same thing) is not a special technique for use by personnel experts only, but a vital aspect of good management generally.

To list the circumstances where interviewing is useful would be almost like listing the functions of management itself. Indeed, all through our discussion of general supervision and methods of correcting mistakes we constantly emphasize the importance of listening. Here are a few examples, however, of what might happen when this approach works at its best.

Making a work change   Suppose you are a division manager and you want to introduce a new system of quality control. Although you have not as yet consulted with the production supervisor, you have heard through the grapevine that he has strong objections to the new system. Yet his cooperation is essential if the system is to succeed.

You feel pretty certain that your plan is good and that the production supervisor's objections are not well grounded. You are the boss, of course, and you could give him a direct order to put the plan into effect. (Question:

How would the supervisor react to this order? How loyally would he carry it out?)

Instead, you decide to listen to his point of view. In spite of the grapevine you can't really be sure you know what his objections are until he has spoken to you personally. If you are at all sincere, you must admit to yourself that his objections may have some merit. (Question: What would happen if you had already made up your mind, and just went through the formalities of listening?)

So you explain the proposed change to him, being careful to emphasize that you still have an open mind, and ask him to comment. You listen attentively and encourage him to express himself fully. As he speaks, he relaxes and explains his point of view with more balance and restraint than he would if he felt he were on the defensive. Instead of trying to answer his arguments, you encourage him to tell you everything he thinks and feels about the change. When he finishes, you briefly summarize what he has said to make sure you understand—and also to indicate *to him* that you have understood.

After speaking his piece, the production supervisor feels free to listen to your point of view—which may have changed since you heard his objections. You fill in some of the areas where you feel he was mistaken, indicate the points on which you have changed your own thinking, and explore with him any adjustments that seem necessary. Even if he is still not fully convinced of the wisdom of your plan, he is more willing to try it out and probably feels pleased that you consulted him and listened to his objections.

Handling a problem supervisor   The union complains that one of your supervisors has been antagonizing his employees by the gruff way in which he gives orders. Your own observation indicates that the complaint is to a large degree justified. You decide that bawling the supervisor out would do little to help matters—and yet he is too good a man to discharge. So once more you use the interview.

The supervisor comes to your office on the defensive; he knows all about the situation and expects to be bawled out. Instead, you ask his advice on how to handle the complaint. At first, he lets off steam against the union and the uncooperative workers. Gradually, as you encourage him to talk, he admits that perhaps he might be somewhat at fault—at least that these workers are so uncooperative that he doesn't know how to handle them. He seems to have gained some insight into his own inadequacies.

You help him go as far as he can by himself. Then you ask him how he might handle certain specific situations, hoping that his new insight will enable him to draw practical conclusions.

You ask him to go over alternative solutions to a couple of problems, weighing carefully the advantages and disadvantages of each. He decides that although a more tactful approach might have its disadvantages in certain cases, the tactless one would be even worse.

On other problems you very tentatively make your own suggestions and ask for his comments. In listening to his objections, you may modify your own ideas. You don't force him to accept any approach—after all, in-grown attitudes are hard to change.

Certainly you haven't made any earth-shaking change in this one interview. But it is likely that the supervisor feels greater confidence in both you and himself and may be willing to experiment with some of the techniques you have discussed. He feels that you are someone who will help him rather than punish him.

These two examples indicate the flexibility of the interview technique (though we must emphasize that the results are frequently not as good as we have pictured). It is obviously well suited to formal interviews, such as those used for hiring, exit, and requests for transfer. But it is also appropriate in less formal situations, such as the following:

> *Low morale:* finding out the cause of employee dissatisfaction, turnover, or absenteeism.
> *Discipline:* discovering why employees are performing unsatisfactorily and helping them to evolve means of correcting themselves.
> *Order-giving:* getting reaction to and acceptance of orders, to see that the person who receives the order really understands it.
> *Resistance to change:* gaining acceptance of new techniques, tools, procedures.
> *Merit rating and evaluation:* helping an employee correct his weaknesses.
> *Training:* finding out how much an employee knows and what difficulties he experiences in learning.
> *Grievance-handling:* finding out the real causes of a union grievance and getting the union officers to agree to a constructive solution.
> *Settling disputes:* finding out the causes of the disputes between employees and getting them to agree to settlement.

The interview approach is not something to be applied only when dealing with specific problems. It is a general attitude which the supervisor can apply day in and day out in his dealings with fellow supervisors, subordinates, and his boss. In a nutshell, it is a matter of always being ready to listen to the other fellow's point of view and trying to take it into account before taking action oneself. If this attitude is absent, then communications may become blocked, as they did in one company:

> The most frequent complaint was that although orders and instructions about work traveled easily enough, it was difficult to take up ordinary feelings, especially if they were critical about the job or about life in the factory. The main stumbling block in getting such feelings resolved was the reticence about communicating them upwards. The reticence was said to be due to the fact that if a person tried to express to his superior his feelings about the job, or about the superior himself, it was all too likely that

the superior would argue with him and try to show him that his feelings were unreasonable and that they did not tally with the facts. Having the existence of one's feelings denied in this way only made things worse. The person was not only left with the original feeling but in addition had a resentment against his superior for not understanding him and not helping him get at what was disturbing him.[4]

ESTABLISHING CONFIDENCE

The supervisor must take the initiative in encouraging subordinates to come to him with their problems. He must show that he is willing to hear them out. Otherwise minor irritations may grow to tremendous proportions, even before the supervisor has become aware of the danger. For example, the supervisor does something the subordinate doesn't like. The subordinate doesn't feel free to talk about it. Gradually his irritation grows and he begins to see his superior in a new light. Everything the supervisor does may now seem threatening and unfair. The subordinate's antagonism grows stronger and stronger, until at last there is a serious breakdown in his relationship with the supervisor.

If the initial interview is a pleasant experience for the subordinate, he will come back more freely and more regularly when new problems arise. If it has been an unpleasant experience and if he feels he has been "put on the spot," he will be reluctant to reveal what is on his mind in the future.

The supervisor should be aware that some of the men who report to him will be easier to get to know than others. Some will talk to him quite freely and easily. Others will hold back because of fear or natural timidity. The supervisor must be careful not to spend all his time with those to whom it is easy to talk.

To avoid the charge of favoritism, and to insure that he is able to deal with the problems of all his employees, the supervisor must go out of his way to make contact with employees who are reluctant to come to him. The supervisor must recognize that there is an invisible barrier which separates him from his subordinates. For some, this status difference is of little importance, but for many it makes effective upward communication much harder. In working with these employees, the supervisor may have to initiate many, many contacts in which little seems to be accomplished before they will open up to him. The supervisor must earn the confidence of his men, and the best way to do this is to show, through *listening*, that he values their feelings and ideas. He may not agree with everything they say, but he must indicate that he is willing and anxious to listen to them with sincerity and respect.

---

[4] Elliott Jaques, *The Changing Culture of a Factory* (London: Tavistock Publications, 1951), p. 133.

OFF-THE-JOB PROBLEMS

Supervisors sometimes use interviewing to help employees solve personal off-the-job problems. Normally stable individuals may have unexpected trouble and seek to use their supervisor as a wailing wall. However, the supervisor should be careful not to give advice or get himself saddled with the responsibility for running his subordinates' personal lives.

> Suppose, for instance, a girl tells her supervisor a long involved story about how her boy friend has proposed to her, and then asks, "Should I marry him or shouldn't I? What do you think?" Regardless of what advice he gives her, he is running quite a risk. If he says "Yes" and the girl takes his advice, he will get the blame if the marriage turns out unhappily. Similarly he will be blamed if he says "No" and the girl later regrets turning the proposal down—and, in addition, the boy friend will be justifiably angry at the supervisor for meddling in matters that do not concern him.

The supervisor should be particularly cautious when sensitive areas are reached in the course of an interview. In situations like this what most people want is a sympathetic, understanding listener rather than an adviser. They may ask for advice, but actually they want only a chance to talk. Even when advice-giving is successful, there is the danger that the employee may become overdependent on his supervisor and run to him whenever he has a minor problem.

The supervisor should be still more careful when deepseated personality problems are involved. In such a case it is wise to refer the person to a professionally trained specialist rather than to play amateur psychologist. Moreover, genuinely disturbed individuals may take up more than their share of the supervisor's limited time.

The Use of the Non-directive Approach

The type of interviewing we shall discuss here has been called "non-directive"—because it emphasizes permitting the interviewee (rather than the interviewer) to direct the interview, at least in the early stages. What can the non-directive interview accomplish? When should it be used? The non-directive interview has three functions:

1. From the point of view of the interviewer, it helps provide clues to what the interviewee is really thinking and what lies at the root of the problem. Thus, if the supervisor is the interviewer, the interview is a means of getting *information* on which he can base decisions.

The first answer an employee gives to an involved question may not be the whole truth. He may not be exactly lying, but he finds it difficult to express just how he feels. True, if the supervisor starts to fire direct questions, he will usually get direct answers, and they may *sound* reasonable. But they may represent only a small, inaccurate sample of the interviewee's total feelings.

Most of us have trouble expressing our real feelings to others. In part this is because we are fearful or ashamed of what the other person will think. We want to make a good impression. This reluctance to reveal our true attitudes is also a product of our inability to understand our own complex, often conflicting, and even unconscious feelings. Consequently we often say things we don't really mean.

Patient, prolonged, skillful listening is required to help the other person express his feelings. Good interviewing, then, is essentially a technique to encourage expression which is uninfluenced either by the preconceived notions of the interviewer or by the need of the interviewee to make a good impression.

2. It helps the interviewee achieve catharsis, a feeling of relief. There are many sources of frustration in modern industry, and unless frustration is relieved it may lead to aggression, regression, and other undesirable responses. The interview provides a channel through which frustration may be partly drained away, even though the causes of the frustration remain.

3. Non-directive interviewing helps a man develop greater insight into his own problems. Turning his questions back and encouraging him to talk enables him to answer them himself. We all have a tendency to think better when we think out loud—when we have to organize and weigh our thoughts —than when we are thinking to ourselves.

In arranging his thoughts before presenting them to a sympathetic listener, the interviewee may bring his problem into sharper focus and, without additional help, actually change his own attitudes. This is when you hear comments such as, "You know, the more I talk about this, the more I think I have been on the wrong track." Solutions reached in this fashion are much more likely to be implemented with enthusiasm than are those suggested by the supervisor.

STAGES IN AN INTERVIEW

In understanding how the non-directive approach should be used, it is helpful to think of the interview as running through three stages: feelings, facts, solutions.

1. Feelings The interviewee is encouraged to release his feelings; the interviewer is concerned with helping the interviewee express himself. This stage is the most purely non-directive, for the interviewer still has little idea where the discussion will go.

2. Facts Having blown off steam, the interviewee is now ready to look at the facts rationally. In this stage the interviewer can be more directive and may even use "probes" (to be discussed later) to bring out information that the interviewee has not already volunteered. In fact, the interviewer may contribute additional information on his own.

3. Solutions   Once the facts have been assembled, the interviewee is in a position to weigh alternate solutions and pick the best one. As we have mentioned frequently, it is preferable to help the interviewee work out his own solution; however, the supervisor may have to be rather strongly directive to make sure that the solution is consistent with the needs of the organization.

These, then, are the three major stages of the interview, although it may switch back and forth from one stage to another as different problems are considered. Still it is important that on a given problem the interviewer stick to the order indicated: feelings, facts, solutions. Certainly he should avoid the common human tendency to jump to a solution before getting all the facts.

Equally important, he should not waste his time trying to isolate the facts before the interviewee has had a chance to express his feelings, to blow off steam. Why? Because feelings color facts, and as long as a man is emotionally excited he is unlikely to approach problems rationally. Furthermore—and the point is subtle—the feelings of the people concerned in the situation are themselves facts that must be considered. For instance, the foreman has been having trouble getting Jones to do a full day's work. The most important *fact* in this situation may be the foreman's intense dislike of Jones as a person. Until the foreman's feeling is recognized as a complicating element, every "fact" he presents will be distorted by his antagonism toward Jones.

Does this mean that the interviewer should never express himself—that he should never try to correct the other person if he is wrong, or try to change his opinion? Of course not. It may be enough for the psychiatrist or the professional counselor merely to listen. The supervisor must also take action. But in most cases before he takes action he should wait until he has heard the interviewee's whole story.

Suppose a subordinate comes to you and says, "Boss, you've got to transfer me from this job. I can't stand it any more." If he insists in his request, you will have to give him some kind of answer. Only antagonism will result if he gets the impression that you are trying to put him off. But there is no need for you to commit yourself *before* you have heard him through.

The non-directive approach is not a magic solution to all personnel problems. There are times when the supervisor may have to be quite firm and directive in the solution stage of the interview to make sure that the solution is consistent with the needs of the organization. For instance, the supervisor may listen patiently to the subordinate's objections to a new rule; the subordinate may persist in his resistance; and the supervisor may still have to overrule him, explaining why, and insist that the system be used. However, the subordinate will have had the satisfaction of being consulted, of knowing that he had his day in court to present his side of the story.

How to Interview [5]

Skillful interviewing is an art, and like all arts it requires training and experience. It can be learned better by practice than by reading a book, especially when the practice is supervised by an experienced instructor. Fortunately, one can gain unsupervised practice every day of the year.

Each interviewer must develop a style that is comfortable for him and that fits his personality, but he should avoid using the same technique with all people and for all purposes. An interview held for disciplinary reasons will naturally be different from an interview held for the purpose of order-giving.

Regardless of the form of the interview, here are a few hints that may prove useful.

ENCOURAGING INTERVIEWEE TO TALK

Your primary objective is to get the interviewee to talk freely, *not to talk yourself.* The best way to find out what the other person wants to say is to listen, and the best interview is usually the one in which the interviewer talks least.

But listening is not easy, for our natural impulse is to talk. This is particularly true when we feel threatened by what is being said to us—for instance, when we are being criticized. Under these circumstances we are interested above all in defending ourselves, in expressing our point of view, and it is very difficult to listen to what the other man has to say.

Listening is more than just not talking, however. It requires an active effort to convey that you understand and are interested in what the other person is saying—almost that you are helping him say it. A friendly facial expression and an attentive but relaxed attitude are important. A good interviewer also makes use of phrases such as "Uh-huh," "I understand," "That explains it," or "Could you tell me more?"

Even silence can be used to keep a man talking. When he pauses in his

---

[5] Three excellent and very different treatments of interviewing are: Carl Rogers and others, *Client-Centered Therapy: Its Current Practice, Implications and Theory* (Boston: Houghton Mifflin, 1951); Robert L. Kahn and Charles E. Cannell, *The Dynamics of Interviewing* (New York: Wiley, 1957); David Riesman and Mark Benney, "Asking and Answering," *Journal of Business*, Vol. 29, No. 4 (October 1956), pp. 225-236.

discourse, he is either being polite and giving you a chance to talk, or else he wants you to comment, to evaluate what he is saying. Merely by not taking up his challenge, by waiting through his pause, you indicate that you have nothing to say at the moment, that you want him to continue talking.

Still another way of encouraging a man to resume talking after he has come to a temporary halt is to repeat his last phrase. An employee says, "The reason I want to quit is that so-and-so foreman keeps pestering me. He won't give me a chance!" Then he stops, wondering whether he has got himself into trouble by saying too much. Your response, "He won't give you a chance?" encourages him to tell the rest of his story, but it does not commit you in any sense.

REFLECTIVE SUMMARY

One of the most effective devices to encourage the other person to talk is the *reflective summary*, in which you try to sum up the feelings a man has expressed, disregarding the factual details and incidentals. For example:

> *Employee:* "Yes, I'm thinking of quitting. I can't seem to get the hang of this job. I don't think I'm fitted for it. I'm always making mistakes that no one else makes. I'm disgusted."
> *Supervisor:* "You feel you aren't making much progress?

Such a summary serves a number of purposes:

1. It shows the worker that you are giving his ideas careful consideration and that you understand him—in other words, that you are being fair.

2. It gives him a chance to restate and elaborate his attitudes if he feels that you haven't quite grasped his point.

3. It serves to highlight what he has really been saying. Often people are surprised to learn what their words have meant to someone else, and are rewarded with deeper insight into their own attitudes.

The reflective summary is particularly effective if you reflect not only what the man has actually said, but can somehow put into words what he has tried, unsuccessfully, to express. Be careful, however, not to hear more in his words than he intends to put into them. For if he finds you reading things into his words that he did not mean to be there, he will be doubly careful to watch what he says.

Be careful, too, that you frame your reflective summary in a way that will invite the interviewee to go on. You are doing much more than merely asking whether you have understand him correctly.

Your summary should indicate neither approval nor disapproval of what the interviewee is saying. It should simply indicate that you are listening attentively. For instance, he says, "It's got to the point where I may lose my temper and take a poke at the foreman." If you were to say, "Well, that's quite understandable," you would almost be inviting him to carry out his threat! A far more satisfactory response would be, "You are really sore at him because. . . ."

PROBES

The "free-floating" counselor is interested primarily in getting at the interviewee's underlying feelings. And as a supervisor you too are interested in the feelings of your subordinates. But if you know that you must act on the basis of what you learn in the interview, you will also want to get all the facts, the whole story. This means that after the feeling stage has passed, you should to some extent direct the interview. Tactfully and calmly, you should steer the conversation, but without forcing the interviewee into an area he does not want to enter, and with no hint that you have already made up your mind.

One way to direct the interview is to build on what the interviewee has already said. By repeating certain words selected from what he has said, you can indicate that you would like him to talk more about this particular area. This device is called a "probe." For example, in explaining how a fight started between himself and another employee, the man being interviewed says, "Joe was always riding me. When he picked up my lunch bucket, that was the last straw." Now if the supervisor wants to find out more about what Joe has done to arouse this man, he has a good chance to insert a probe: "You say Joe was always riding you?" Then he stops and waits for the man to go on. Notice that the interviewer does not say: "What did Joe do to make you so sore?" Rather, he simply repeats the employee's own words. Chances are this approach will encourage the man to tell more about the "riding" than he would if he had been asked a direct question.

Less subtle probes are: "Could you tell me more about . . . ?" or "I am interested in what you said about. . . ."

Another useful probe might be called the "I-am-a-stranger, could-you-explain-this-to-me?" approach. You are questioning an employee about how he happened to pile up so much scrap on one operation. In order to get at the details, you might start out by saying, "I haven't done that operation myself in years. Just how does it run now?"

WEIGHING ALTERNATIVES

Sometimes it is enough if the interview helps you find out how the employee feels about the situation and what the essential facts are as *he* sees them. In other instances, however, you may wish to help him devise a solution. How can you do this without seeming to impose your own ideas on him? The following approach may be useful both in individual interviews and in group meetings:

Let's go back to the foreman who was antagonizing his employees by his gruffness. First, you might encourage him to list all the possible alternative courses of action—without judging which one is better. Second, you could go over each alternative, one by one, asking, "What would happen if you did this? What good effects would it have? What bad effects?" In other words, your objective would be to encourage the foreman to make a systematic and open-minded examination of each alternative.

The foreman's first suggestion, for example, may be that he should go right out to the shop and fire the chief troublemaker. If you keep asking for additional suggestions, he may suggest transferring to another department all workers whose productivity has not been up to par recently. Finally, he may come around to suggesting certain changes in his own behavior.

Now, after the foreman has offered all these suggestions, you would attempt to get him to examine each one:

> What would its probable effect be?
> How would the men react?
> How would it help him solve his problem?

By helping the interviewee think through his problem, you may succeed in having him come to a conclusion that is *his,* not yours. And if it is his, he will be much more likely to act on it with enthusiasm.

Things to Avoid

TOO MUCH WARM-UP

Many people feel that before getting down to the subject of an interview, particularly if it is an unpleasant one, they should try to place the interviewee at ease by discussing some irrelevant topic—baseball, fishing, the traffic problem, or what have you. Thus a foreman calling a man in to lay him off may chat about the Dodgers for a few minutes before settling down to the nasty task.

This approach may relieve the foreman's anxiety, but it intensifies that of the worker, particularly if he has some idea of why he has been called in. While he is on the "hot seat," he may be thinking, "Why doesn't this character get down to business? Why does he have to play cat-and-mouse? What's going to happen? Am I going to lose my job? Why does he have to pretend to be my friend and talk about baseball at a time like this?"

Such "warming-up" is useful at times; however, the interviewer should be careful to use it only when it actually reduces anxiety. Often when the supervisor initiates the interview, "beating around the bush" merely increases the suspense. Similarly, if the employee comes to the supervisor with a problem, he probably wants to get down to business without delay.

Even if you plan to use the non-directive approach, it is vital to set the stage properly, to indicate to the interviewee what you want the interview to cover. For example, if you wish to talk to a worker about sloppy work, you might start with, "Bill, you seem to be having a little trouble with the blue-edge gadgets."

DIRECT QUESTIONS

One of the most frequent errors made by inexperienced interviewers is transforming the interview into a game of "twenty questions." A man has fallen into the habit of coming to work late and his supervisor is anxious to straighten him out before discipline becomes necessary. Having had some training in human relations, the supervisor suspects that a home problem is involved. His end of the conversation may run something like this:

> "Bill, why are you late so often?"
> "Do you have trouble starting your car?"
> "Is there any trouble at home?"
> "Does your alarm clock go off on time?"
> "Did you have a drink too many last night?"

To each question Bill replies, "No, it isn't that." And to himself he says, "That's none of his business." And then another question is shot at him.

Here the foreman, not Bill, is directing the interview. Note that every one of these questions is phrased in such a manner as to put Bill immediately on the defensive and make him over-cautious in what he says. Some of the questions, such as, "Did you have a drink too many last night?" he may feel are insulting.

The interviewer rarely knows the right questions to ask; if he did, he would probably know the answers as well. The problem is usually more complex than it seems at first glance, and direct questions tend to narrow it down too quickly.

To complicate matters, most subordinates try to say what they think will please their supervisor. Direct questions often imply the kind of answer the supervisor wants, or at least give the subordinate an "out." For instance, the question "Did you have trouble starting your car?" provides a ready excuse for the tardy worker.

If the supervisor wants to find out what the subordinate really has on his mind, he should leave the situation as free as possible to permit the subordinate to emphasize the things that are important to *him*.

If possible, the interviewer should avoid questions that can be answered with a simple yes or no. "Well, do you like your job?" "Do you think the tools are in bad shape?" Questions of this sort shut off discussion because they can be answered by a relatively meaningless "Oh, I guess so," "I suppose you might say that."

PREMATURE JUDGMENT

The interviewer should avoid giving any indication that what the subordinate says either pleases or displeases him. In other words, he must refrain from passing judgment. This restraint is extremely important because subordinates look for verbal or facial cues that will tip them off to what the superior wants or does not want to hear. (Of course, unconsciously we are always forming impressions, even on the most meager facts. However, the supervisor should be aware of his predispositions and try to keep them from warping his judgment or his communication.)

Criticism or moralizing puts the interviewee on the defensive. Even if he does not argue back, he will begin to edit what he says in order to win the interviewer's approval. He will concentrate on proving that he is right rather than on giving an honest explanation. Certainly putting a man on the defensive makes it harder to find out what he really thinks.

Even praise or sympathy should be avoided until the end of the interview, for it makes the interviewee think his present approach is correct and encourages him to avoid the hard work of thinking the problem through.

ARGUING

Little is gained from argument, at least in the early stage of the interview. Yet everyone has a strong human tendency to correct the other person when he says something that is obviously wrong. Moreover, if the interviewer himself is attacked personally, he must exercise tremendous restraint not to answer back.

For example, an employee says he is having trouble doing the work because the stock has been changed. "The company must be buying cheaper material these days." Now if you know that there has been no change whatsoever in the materials, you will be strongly tempted to "set the employee straight" on this point, although his complaint may be a symptom of something much more basic. If you give way to this temptation, you may simply transform the interview into a fruitless argument. If you just continue to listen, however, the employee may move on to genuine problems and difficulties that he finds more troublesome to discuss.

ADVICE-GIVING

When you finally get the complete picture as the employee sees it, you may be able to provide advice or information that has not previously been available. But again it is often better to help him work through his own problems. In any event, you should hold off giving advice until *after* the interviewee has told his entire story—until you have all the facts.

MASTERMINDING

Many people go through the motions of the non-directive interview but violate its spirit. They hope by asking shrewd questions to manipulate the interviewee into believing that he is thinking through his problem by himself, though the way questions are worded inevitably forces the interviewee to arrive at the interviewer's own predetermined conclusion.

Masterminding is used with various degrees of sophistication. One of the less subtle forms makes constant use of the "leading question," the "don't you feel?" approach: "Don't you feel it would be better for the company and your own future if you came to work on time?"

Questions like this usually permit only one answer. They are thinly veiled forms of advice, judgment, or just plain bawling out. They are even more directive than an overt, straightforward statement. The interviewee is often free to reject outright advice, and even if it is clear that he must accept it (in other words, when the advice is really an order) he may be unhappy about it, but willing to be a good soldier. Masterminding, however, not only requires the interviewee to do what the interviewer wants, but also to say that he likes it. The interviewee is treated like a child and the alleged interview degenerates into a form of brainwashing.

There are subtler forms of brainwashing in which the interviewee may actually feel convinced of something at the time of the interview, only to realize that he has been duped after he has had a chance to think things over. Conversion at a forced rate seldom lasts. As the poet Robert Burns once said:

> He who is convinced against his will,
> Is of the same opinion still.

People change their attitudes slowly, and only when they are ready to do so.

Conclusion

Interviewing is a form of communications, and like other forms of communications it is most effective when it is two-way. A good interview is more than a one-way process in which the interviewee tells his story to the interviewer; the interviewer must in turn be constantly communicating his interest in the interviewee as a person and in what he has to say.

It is not enough for the supervisor to understand his employees; he must also give them the feeling that he is sincerely trying to help them. The supervisor must not only listen, but must also communicate the feeling to his employees that they are being listened to.

The basic purpose of non-directive interviewing is to enable the interviewer to find out how the individual sees the problem or situation at issue, and then to help him think and, above all, *feel* his way through to a solution. The goal of this whole philosophy is for the supervisor to be perceived as a source of help—as a man who can assist the subordinate to develop and do a better job.

It has been argued that the interview approach would be fine if the supervisor had nothing else to do all day except serve as a wailing wall, but that in practice he just doesn't have time to do much listening. Realistically, pressure and other demands may make him abrupt and unsympathetic in his dealings with subordinates. And yet the supervisor who "makes time" to listen may find not only that his human relations are better, but that in the long run he will save enough time by having fewer personnel crises to deal with.

The non-directive interview is not a cure-all for every situation. Effective interviewing requires considerable skill, and even a good interviewer discovers that many people find it difficult to discuss their problems. Moreover, many problems involve several people and require group discussion. Finally, certain problems cannot be decided at the supervisor-subordinate level. Still in spite of these reservations the interviewing technique is a useful tool for every supervisor.

Problem I

In each of the following cases, which of the responses suggested would be more likely to lead to a constructive solution of the problem? Remember that these represent the opening of the interview.

1. You have come home from a hard day and your wife greets you with:
   "What a day I've had. The baby was crying all morning. The washing machine broke down and I had to do the things by hand. Then I went downtown to buy a hat and had to wait twenty minutes for a bus. I couldn't find a thing I liked and everybody was so pushy and the store was so crowded. When I got back the baby-sitter had let the stew burn—and I'd worked on it so hard. I'm so mad I could cry. And I've got to go downtown tomorrow again to look for a hat."

   a. "You must have had an awfully hard day."
   b. "Your old hat looks pretty good to me."
   c. "I'm tired too. You should hear what happened to me. First...."
   d. "Don't say another word. Put on your glad rags and I'll take you out for dinner and don't mention it."
   e. "You know, maybe we ought to get another baby-sitter."

2. A worker has been late three times in the last two weeks. You ask him why and he replies:
   "I just can't seem to get up in the morning. Frankly, I've lost my enthusiasm for the job. It doesn't interest me any more. So when I do get up I've got to rush like mad to get here."

   a. "Don't you think you are letting the company down?"
   b. "Do you have an alarm clock?"

    c. "You've got to lick this problem or I've got to lay you off and give you some time to think it over."

    d. "The job doesn't interest you any more?"

    e. "Are you having any trouble at home?"

    f. "Have you thought of going to bed earlier?"

3. A worker who has been making little progress tells his boss:

"I just can't seem to get the hang of things. I try to find out what I'm supposed to do, but no one tells me. The other guys don't pay any attention to me and I can't figure it out by watching. Maybe I ought to quit."

    a. "Why don't you give the job a chance? Most people take a while to learn it."

    b. "Why don't you try harder? You can't get ahead without hard work."

    c. "If I were you I would ask the other fellows to help you."

    d. "Do you have any ideas why the other fellows don't help you?"

    e. "I'll assign one of them to instruct you."

    f. "You feel that the other fellows don't pay any attention to you?"

4. A toolmaker tells his foreman:

"I've had ten years' experience and no one ever told me I did a bum job. Sure I make a few mistakes, but why do I get all the blame?"

    a. "All I want you to do is be a little more careful in your work."

    b. "You feel the standards are too high?"

    c. "I'm not saying it is your fault. I am just asking you to please do the piece over."

    d. "You feel you get blamed for everything that goes wrong?"

Problem II*

SCENE I

Mary, a salad girl, is seated at a table backstage by herself, thumbing through a magazine. She is off duty. Miss Jones walks on stage from the right and stops at Mary's table.

Miss Jones: Mary, may I speak to you for a moment?

Mary: All right.

Miss Jones: It's about your work. I feel that you're a hard worker but there are times when you seem to grow a bit careless. I've noticed lately that sometimes your salads are a trifle sloppy in appearance, and you don't always check your recipes carefully enough. For example, the fruit salad calls for two halves of plums. I saw you putting three on some of the salads today. If you just check up on things like this, you'll do the job I think you're capable of.

(Mary does not answer. She shuts the magazine, gets up, and walks away. Miss Jones looks startled, then walks toward the office of Mr. Black, the manager, downstage left, and knocks on the door.)

SCENE II

Black: Come in. (Miss Jones walks in and sits down.) Hello. What is it, Miss Jones?

---

* We wish to express our thanks to Professor William F. Whyte for permission to use this case, which was prepared by him.

Jones: I'm worried about Mary Stevens. I thought maybe you'd want to talk to her.

Black: What seems to be the trouble?

Jones: Well, she's a hard worker, but sometimes she just doesn't seem to have her mind on her work. Now that wouldn't be so bad if she'd let us correct her, but the girl won't take criticism. I just asked her to be a little neater in putting up her salads and I checked her on putting an extra half plum on the fruit salad. I put it just as tactfully as I know how, but she wouldn't even answer me. She just sat still until I was finished and then walked right out on me. It was a deliberate insult.

Black: Yes, that's bad. . . . Do you think she is quitting?

Jones: Well, I don't know. But I don't see how I can use her when she behaves that way.

Black: Do you want to get rid of her?

Jones: Well, you know how short we are at that station. I can't really spare her and she can do a very good job when she wants to. Maybe it's some trouble at home. I don't know. But I thought you might be able to help her.

Black: I'd be glad to talk to her for you. She'll be coming in for her paycheck tomorrow. I'll see her then.

Jones: Thanks. That'll be a big help to me.

SCENE III

(Black's office. Black at desk; Mary comes in.)

Black: I was hoping you'd come in to see me. Won't you sit down, Mary?

Mary: (hesitates, then sits down) Well, I suppose you know all about it.

Black: Miss Jones told me something about it, but I want to get your side of the story. After all, we want to be fair with you. I've always done my best to see the employee's point of view. We want you to feel satisfied with your work here, and if there is some problem I can help out on, I want you to feel free to talk things over with me.

Mary: Well, I don't suppose I should have walked out, but I just couldn't take it.

Black: You mean, you can't take criticism?

Mary: Well, not exactly. But this is such a nerve-wracking job. And Miss Jones is always picking on you. She doesn't seem to appreciate the work you do.

Black: Mary, don't you think you're being a little unfair to Miss Jones? Now, I happen to know that she thinks very well of you. She wants to help you.

Mary: She doesn't act that way. I mean—well I know she has to see that the work gets done right, but it seems she's always looking over your shoulder to catch you or something. And such little things, too, she—

Black: Mary, you have to remember that the little things add up together to make something pretty big. If we neglected the little things, we wouldn't be in business very long. Now that extra half plum—it may seem like nothing at all to you, but we have to work out the prices and portions to make a small profit on that salad. If we put in an extra half plum, we're really giving it away. If we sell 100 of those salads a day, that mounts up. We're doing all the work for nothing. Now, I'm not criticizing you, but I just want you to understand the importance of these things. Do you see what I mean?

Mary: Well, if I did put on an extra half plum, it was only on 2 or 3, not 100. I don't remember every one, but I know it was only 2 or 3.

Black: Sure, that's what I'm getting at. You were just a little careless. That's all. Miss Jones was trying to correct you. Now, you don't blame her for trying to see that the work is done right do you?

Mary: Sure, she wants it done right, but she doesn't realize what we're up against. It's one thing to know just how to make a salad. It's another thing to have to make hundreds of them in a rush, like I have to. If Miss Jones had ever worked behind the counter like the rest of us, she'd know what it's like.

Black: But Miss Jones did work behind the counter when she was getting her training.

Mary: That's different. You weren't so rushed then like we are now.

Black: Yes, that's true. But I'm not trying to defend Miss Jones to you. I'm just trying to help you to get this thing straightened out. Now, you didn't like the way Miss Jones criticized you. But let's look at both sides of it. Do you think you were fair to her?

Mary: I know what you think. You think I wasn't polite to her. All right, I wasn't. I lost my temper. If I had said anything, I would have told her what I thought of her. So I thought it would be better not to say anything. Well, what of it? It's done, and I'm through now. Give me my paycheck and let me out of here.

Black: Your check is here for you, Mary, but let's not be hasty about this. Remember your aunt has worked here a long time. She hoped you'd fit in too. If you just walk out this way, it'll be quite a blow to her.

Mary: I don't care about her or Miss Jones or you either. I've got my own life to live. I'm tired of having people always pick on me and tell me what to do. I know what I want to do now. I want to get out of here. Give me my check!

Black: Well, if that's the way you feel about it—(hands her the check).

1. Comment on how Mr. Black handled his conversation with Mary.
2. How should he have handled it?
3. What mistakes did he make?

Among the most valuable skills of the modern executive is the ability to function as an effective conference leader or committee chairman. In fact, meetings have become so common in modern industry that many observers are worried lest "group think" replace individual initiative. In some companies all important decisions are based on group consensus, never on the strength of one man's judgment. The standing joke is, "All we do is meet all day and never get time for work."

Why this emphasis on meetings? As we have seen, one reason is the growing realization that people are more enthusiastic about carrying out plans that they have helped draw up than they are about implementing plans that are simply announced from above. Moreover, as business activities grow increasingly specialized it becomes more urgent to coordinate departments and encourage subordinates to volunteer advice.

Conference skills are useful, of course, even when the participants are not sitting around a table at a formal meeting. The supervisor needs these skills in his day-to-day activities whenever he is talking to a group of subordinates or equals and trying to reach some sort of agreement.

Conference Leadership

Conference techniques are valuable in working through differences in a wide variety of human relationships. Suppose three workers are quarreling over their vacation schedules and come to the foreman for a solution. He could listen and play judge. But it would be better if he could somehow get them to work out a schedule themselves that they could all accept.

In Chapter 8 we distinguished between three types of meeting: those called for purpose of giving information, those called to elicit suggestions, and those called to arrive at decisions. Although we shall be primarily concerned with decision-making meetings in this chapter, the skills we discuss are useful in the other types of meeting as well.

Let us start with an example:

> The Plant Manager has called a special meeting of his top staff to consider whether a new cafeteria should be built. The present cafeteria is forty years old and too small for current needs.
>
> It is 5:00 and the meeting is getting nowhere fast. It has been in session since lunchtime and the participants have been alternately bored and annoyed with each other. There has been lots of hot air but little real progress. Everyone has his pet point of view and so far there has been no semblance of agreement.
>
> Of course the Plant Manager could put a stop to all this talk by proclaiming his own opinion, but at least on this issue he doesn't want to act without the close support of his staff. To this moment he has failed as a conference leader. Yet unless he can induce the group to accept a common solution there will be no new cafeteria.

Why all this trouble? What are the pitfalls that make running a meeting such a difficult art to learn? For one thing, there are invisible currents in every discussion that must be recognized and mastered if agreement is to be reached. It is the ability to identify these currents and to direct them into proper channels that constitutes the strength of a good conference leader.

The success of any meeting, particularly one called for the purpose of decision-making, depends largely on three interrelated factors: (1) the development of unity and teamwork within the group, (2) the chairman's ability to handle the meeting, particularly his skill in maintaining the proper degree of looseness or tightness of control, and (3) the participants' observance of an agenda designed for the orderly consideration of the problem at hand.

Many of the concepts we shall discuss in the following pages were developed by R. Freed Bales of the Harvard Laboratory of Social Relations,[1]

---

[1] Over the years Professor Bales, using a room with one-way glass to permit observation of meetings in session, has developed ingenious devices to measure interaction among committee members. See R. F. Bales, *Interaction Process Analysis* (Cambridge: Addison-Wesley, 1950), and R. F. Bales, "In Conference," *Harvard Business Review,* Vol. 32, No. 2 (March 1954), pp. 44-50. See also E. D. Chapple, "Measuring Human Relations: An Introduction to the Study of Interaction of Individuals," *Genetic Psychology Monographs,* Vol. 22, No. 3 (1940), p. 147.

by the Research Center for Group Dynamics, and by the National Training Laboratory for Group Development [2] (sometimes called the "Bethel group," after Bethel, Maine, where the Laboratory conducts an intensive summer training program).

Internal Unity and Teamwork

In addition to carrying out their formal tasks, the members of every meeting carry on an informal social life among themselves; if this informal life is unsatisfactory, the formal tasks will not be performed successfully. In other words, before we can have a smoothly working committee we must have a smoothly working social group.

As we discussed in Chapter 3, a new group is a collection of strangers, each of whom is anxious to establish a position that meets his personal needs.

> When people are confronted with each other, they must first find the place where they fit in. This involves being in or out of the group, establishing oneself as a specific individual, and seeing if one is going to be paid attention to and not be left behind or ignored. This anxiety gives rise to individual-centered behavior such as overtalking, extreme withdrawal, exhibitionism, recitation of biographies and previous experience.[3]

Much of the early history of a group consists of attempts to establish pecking orders or status hierarchies. Only when these relationships have coalesced and a well-defined informal organization has been established can the group settle down to work. Gradually the members of the group develop friendships and teamwork, and the aggregation of self-conscious individuals grows into a real group.

The success of the conference depends a great deal on the needs and interests of the people who take part in it. "The problems on the conference table are really not as difficult to deal with as the people around the table." [4] Let us look at some of these needs and interests, using as an example the cafeteria meeting we mentioned earlier.

Oustide commitments of the members   It is just human nature for committee members to think first about how a new proposal will affect them and the people with whom they work. Mr. A, the assistant controller, is worried lest he give the impression that he has committed his boss (who is not

---

[2] See Leland Bradford and John R. F. French, eds., "The Dynamics of the Discussion Group," *Journal of Social Issues*, Vol. IV, No. 2, and *Explorations in Human Relations Training: An Assessment of Experience* (Washington, D.C.: The National Training Laboratory in Group Development, 1953).

[3] William C. Schultz, "The Interpersonal Underworld," *Harvard Business Review*, Vol. 36, No. 4 (July 1958), p. 132.

[4] William M. Sattler and N. Edd Miller, *Discussion and Conference* (Englewood Cliffs, N.J.: Prentice-Hall, 1954), p. 149.

present) to spend money on the cafeteria.⁵ Mr. B, from the main office, wants the cafeteria located near where he works. Even though the arguments for building it elsewhere are very persuasive, he is worried about how those who work for him will react to having to take a long walk to lunch.

Differing perceptions of the issue   Mr. C has been sold on the desirability of a new cafeteria for a long time and feels that the only question left is how to design it. Mr. D, on the other hand, feels pressured by any discussion of design, since he hasn't been convinced that a new cafeteria is needed in the first place. Mr. C and Mr. D have obviously started out with different assumptions as to the purpose of the meeting. These differences will undoubtedly lead to friction.

Equally troublesome are the differing perceptions of the assistant controller and the personnel director. One thinks purely in terms of cost, the other in terms of improving morale. Moreover, different commitments are likely to cause differing perceptions, so that people see the same "facts" differently.

Obviously what is needed at the outset is an agreement on the basic nature of the problem (or, in most cases, problems) and the setting up of an agenda so that each problem will be considered in turn. Certainly the chairman should refrain from stating baldly, "Gentlemen, *this* is the problem," for his perceptions may differ from everyone else's. Instead, he should find out from the participants what *they* think the fundamental issues are and then try to establish a common basis for discussion.

Personality needs   People do not stop acting like people just because they are at a meeting. They abandon neither their personal idiosyncrasies nor their status position in the organization. Mr. E has just had a fight with his wife. Mr. F is an assistant division manager and *expects* to receive respect. Mr. G wants to show up well in the discussion so that he will be promoted. Mr. H enjoys an argument of any kind. Mr. I is just shy.

Reactions to individuals rather than to ideas   Mr. J talks too much; consequently the group habitually rejects his ideas. Mr. K is disgusted by all this chatter and keeps his mouth shut. Mr. L, who is on the opposite side of the political fence from Mr. M, is almost automatically against whatever Mr. M is for and would love the chance to make M look silly. L and M are leaders of opposing cliques. When cliques develop in a group, the members tend to evaluate a new idea on the basis of how it will affect their prestige rather than on the basis of its real merits.

Thus members bring to the meeting what sociologists call their respective roles—their points of view and patterns of behavior. It is the chairman's

---

⁵ In a situation like this it is sometimes a good idea to adjourn the meeting for a few days before trying to reach final agreement—or else make it clear that "representatives" do not bind "principals."

job to handle these various roles in such a way that individual viewpoints are dovetailed for the good of the group—in other words, so that teamwork develops.

So long as a committee has an unsatisfactory internal life, the members will go out of their way to look for matters of substance on which they can disagree, to make mountains out of molehills. On the other hand, a closely knit group will not be disrupted even by differences of policy. Each member feels assured of the acceptance and respect of colleagues. Social activity and good-natured kidding help build solidarity. Mr. J's need for security no longer forces him to talk all the time. Mr. I's shyness no longer prevents him from offering suggestions. All the members show willingness to listen to each other's points of view, and to accept each other's foibles. Furthermore, once a matter has been fully aired, the minority is willing to go along with the majority, for there is group pressure to conform. At the same time, the majority respects views that are strongly held by the minority and is reluctant to override them.

Once the members begin to experience the subtle transformation that marks the emergence of an effective team, they begin to take on new roles related to the functioning of the meeting itself. Some of these roles have to do with the *content* or subject matter of the meeting. Others have to do with the *process* by which the discussion is carried out. Here is a suggestive, though by no means complete, list of these roles (note that not all of them are constructive): [6]

Content Roles

Initiator—makes suggestions
Information-seeker—asks questions
Blocker—objects to other people's suggestions for action
Expert—knows the facts
Destructive critic—tears other people's ideas apart

Process Roles

Summarizer—summarizes where the group stands
Task-setter—tries to get the group to move on, emphasizes what still has to be done
Decision-announcer—announces decisions after the group has reached agreement
Traffic cop—decides who talks when
Encourager—encourages others to contribute
Mediator—tries to narrow differences
Playboy—kids around (and sometimes reduces excess tension)

---

[6] See "Training in Member Roles," *Adult Leadership*, Vol. 1, No. 8 (January 1953), pp. 17-23; and Kenneth D. Beane and Paul Sheats, "Functional Roles of Group Members," *Journal of Social Issues*, Vol. 4, No. 2 (Spring 1948), pp. 41-50. Note that although we are using the same types of role as Beane and Sheets, we are categorizing them differently.

(In addition to the roles we have mentioned, there are also inactive roles, such as follower, listener, and daydreamer.)

Does this mean that every member of the group plays only one role at a time? Not at all. Members frequently switch from one role to another and may play several roles simultaneously. Similarly, any one role may be played by several people at once.

If certain key roles are neglected—that of initiator or summarizer, for example—the whole meeting will suffer. But overemphasis on any single role should be avoided. Clearly, everyone cannot serve as an initiator or a harmonizer. In fact, a meeting in which everyone is careful not to step on anyone else's toes never accomplishes anything. Similarly, "rigidity of role-taking" [7] is undesirable, for team spirit is shattered when one person insists on always acting as destructive critic or demands parliamentary procedure regardless of the situation.

One of the responsibilities of the chairman is to help people fit their roles together for the good of the group. He wants to insure that the meeting will enjoy the full benefit of Bill's skill as a summarizer, Joe's expert knowledge, or Dick's special skills by calling on each at the *proper* time.

In summary, a successful meeting requires that members subordinate roles based on personality needs, outside commitments, and so forth, and accept team roles, both content and process, which will help the meeting move toward its objectives. In other words, from an aggregation of individuals a work group arises which both satisfies the social needs of its members and works in reasonable harmony in solving problems.

The Chairman

The chairman himself plays a variety of roles: traffic cop, mediator, decision-announcer, and so forth. Indeed the success of the meeting depends to a large extent on the skill with which he plays these roles.

The so-called "autocratic" chairman plays both content and process roles: that is, he acts as an advocate of one point of view and also tries to get the meeting to reach agreement. His "democratic" counterpart is concerned primarily with process and tries to remain neutral when it comes to a question of content. But even the democratic chairman will be flexible in how he uses process roles, depending on the kind of problem being considered, the nature of the group, and the amount of time available. At times he must keep tight control over the meeting (that is, keep many of the process roles for himself); at other times he may exercise only loose control and try to spread responsibility throughout the group.

---

[7] Beane and Sheats, *op. cit.,* p. 47.

With this brief introduction, let us look more closely at various approaches to the chairman's responsibilities.

SHOULD THE CHAIRMAN ASSUME CONTENT ROLES?

It has been argued that the chairman's job is to help others express their point of view while keeping his own to himself. His function has been defined as "interviewing the group," helping it work through its own problems and reach its own decisions. Like the interviewer, the chairman needs to be permissive and unbiased. He is a catalyst who serves to bring out ideas already present in the group.

Certainly it is true that if he takes sides or expresses his own opinions other members may hesitate to take issue with him (particularly if the chairman happens to be the boss). In fact, any value judgment offered by the chairman may inhibit or distort communication.

> We have observed this problem at union meetings where the local president serves as presiding officer. The president seems to have a split personality. During most of the month he must act on his own initiative, like the commander of an army. Here his success depends on personal forcefulness, ingenuity, and ability. But in the meeting he is expected to be completely impartial even when his policies are under attack. Such switches in role are extremely difficult to make. The members are confused too. Bob Jones starts to criticize the president's activities as chief executive at the wrong point in the agenda—and is then called out of order. Bob can hardly avoid suspecting that the president is being less than impartial.

There are times, however, when it would be unrealistic for the chairman to remain completely neutral. Naturally, it would be foolish for the chairman of a three-man committee to keep his opinions completely to himself (although at times this is what a mediator does in labor relations). And if the chairman is an expert on the subject under discussion, it would be senseless for him to withhold his factual knowledge and his informed opinions—though if the subject is touchy he should be careful to distinguish his role as expert from his role as chairman.

What about the meeting in which the chairman is also the boss and has already made up his mind about what he wants to do? Should he pretend to remain impartial throughout the meeting, even though he knows very well that he may ignore the group's recommendations as soon as the session is over? Or should he try to mastermind the group into thinking that his ideas are really their own? Experience suggests that it rarely pays for the chairman to play cat-and-mouse with the group, for people resent being manipulated. Nor is it wise for him to exaggerate the amount of freedom that is actually being bestowed on the group. In such a situation, it is probably best for the chairman to open with something of this sort: "I'm thinking of doing so-and-so. What are the loopholes in this plan? Will it or won't it work?" The chairman should then try to answer questions and objections and must be willing to accept constructive suggestions.

In meetings where the members in fact enjoy a wide range of freedom, the chairman should normally try to stay neutral. However, it is often hard for a chairman to restrain himself, particularly where he is also boss. Feeling that he is expected to act as a vigorous initiator and decision-maker, the boss may fear that if he were to sit back and listen his behavior would be interpreted as a sign of weakness and indecision. And so, if the chairman is really anxious to let his subordinates make their own decision, he must learn to control his desire to take a dominant role.

With the exceptions noted, then, the chairman is usually wise to avoid assuming content roles. What about process roles?

SHOULD THE CHAIRMAN ASSUME PROCESS ROLES?

It has been argued that the chairman should not assume process roles. When the field of group dynamics was first explored, there was a great deal of interest in what are known as "leaderless groups." It was felt that in a really mature group there would be no need for a formal chairman. Instead, every member would share the responsibility for steering the meeting and would automatically exercise the self-discipline needed to make the meeting a success. Strong leadership, it was argued, is undemocratic and tends to prevent the group from reaching its maximum potential.

Leadership groups have proved useful in psychotherapy,[8] as a technique for selecting leaders (see p. 445) and in what is known as sensitivity training (see p. 560). And almost every day we all participate in groups that get things done with only informal leadership or with no apparent leadership at all.

Nevertheless there is strong evidence that if a group must meet over a period of time, "there is need for a stable structure of group organization if the group is to move ahead on the tasks before it. . . . When the leadership is in doubt, the members will become preoccupied with the leadership problem and with their relations with each other in general, and they will not be able to move ahead towards their goal until progress can also be made in the development of a regular pattern of interaction." [9]

In other words, the chairman performs an essential function in developing a pattern of teamwork that will lead to the efficient handling of problems. Sometimes an informal leader, acceptable to all the members of the group, will emerge naturally—though there is always the danger there will be a long, nasty struggle for power. But usually time will be saved if a chairman is formally elected or appointed.

---

[8] See, for instance, a series of articles by W. R. Bion in Vols. 1-3 of *Human Relations*.
[9] William F. Whyte, *Leadership and Group Participation*, Bulletin 24, New York State School of Industrial and Labor Relations, pp. 19-20, 25.

One study has suggested that groups without formal leaders are less effective in solving mathematical problems than groups with leaders.[10] Apparently the significant difference between such groups is that the formal leaders give minority opinions a chance to be expressed, and often it is the minority opinions that lead to a correct solution. In leaderless groups, however, minorities have less opportunity to speak up. Another study showed that as leaders become better trained, the quality of group discussion improves.[11]

Thus it seems that the chairman makes an important contribution to making discussion effective. Now let us look more closely at what he does.

THE CHAIRMAN'S DILEMMAS

The chairman is beset by dilemmas. The goals of a meeting are to (1) devise what seems the best solution to the problem under consideration, (2) with the greatest amount of unanimity, (3) in the shortest period of time. Obviously these three goals sometimes conflict.

1. The quality of the final decision depends both on the amount of time devoted to hammering it out and on the degree of freedom the members enjoy to make comments and suggestions. Too much haste or too zealous an attempt to work out a compromise acceptable to everyone may result in an unsatisfactory solution.

2. It is wise to give everyone a chance to participate in decision-making, particularly when the committee members are expected to implement their own decisions. "A few words [on each member's part] will serve to express and solidify his involvement, and to avoid his subsequent dissatisfaction." [12] The chairman should try to persuade the minority to go along with the majority, or, at times, try to induce the majority to accommodate objections that the minority feel to be extremely important. But this takes time and may result in a less satisfactory solution.

3. Most business meetings run under a time limit—either implicit or explicit. Even where there is no limit, the members become bored or frustrated if the meeting lasts too long. However, time can be saved only at the cost of less participation and a less carefully considered solution.

These conflicts among the basic goals of the meeting present the chairman with some perplexing problems. He must somehow manage to obtain general participation, but he must *also* keep the discussion relevant and directed toward the agenda, and he must *also* insure that the meeting will move

---

[10] Norman R. F. Maier and A. R. Solem, "The Contribution of the Discussion Leader to the Quality of Group Thinking: The Effective Use of Minority Opinions," *Human Relations,* Vol. 5, No. 3 (August 1952), pp. 277-288.

[11] Norman R. F. Maier, "The Quality of Group Decisions as Influenced by the Discussion Leader," *Human Relations,* Vol. 3, No. 2 (June 1950), pp. 155-174.

[12] Bales, "In Conference," p. 46.

steadily along toward its ultimate purpose—the making of a decision. How can the chairman keep all these balls in the air at the same time?

OBTAINING GENERAL PARTICIPATION

Probably the chairman's hardest job is to encourage nonparticipants to speak up and to persuade those who talk too much to give others a chance to be heard. The man who sits cloaked in silence all through the meeting is often either apathetic or secretly opposed to the solution being discussed. Bring his objections out into the open and they may either be answered or the program may be modified to gain his support. Only through active participation can he get the feeling that *we* made the decision.

This does not mean that the conference leader should strive for absolutely equal participation by all members. Naturally on any given subject some people are likely to be better informed or to have stronger feelings than others. Furthermore, evidence suggests that the man who talks most in a conference tends to have the best ideas and tends to approach problems in the most constructive manner.[13]

How can the conference leader stimulate participation? His general attitude is important. He should accept everyone's contribution without judgment and should seem to want everyone to participate. He should try to ask questions that are specific enough to stimulate a spirited response, even controversy. Once discussion is underway, he can use the reflective response to keep it going: "Jack thinks we can afford new equipment only if we can count on a large increase in sales. What do the rest of you think?" As in interviewing, here the reflective response serves to acknowledge Jack's contribution and to spur the others to join in.

A more elaborate technique for involving everyone in the discussion is the so-called "buzz session," in which the conference is broken down into small committees, each meeting in a separate part of the room. Each committee is instructed to discuss an assigned question and report back to the meeting as a whole after a specified period of time. Among the advantages of the buzz session are: it forces people to think for themselves, it gets people to talk who would remain silent in a larger group (in fact, it is the only way in which all the members of a very large group can participate), and often it saves time because a lot of discussion gets boiled down into a brief report. Buzz sessions are particularly useful in a larger conference.

Another technique of eliciting discussion is for the chairman to start at one side of the room and ask each conferee in turn to give his thoughts about the problem at hand. This device is particularly useful at the beginning of the meeting.

What can be done if, in spite of all the chairman's efforts, one man still

---

[13] R. F. Bales, "How People Interact in Conferences," *Scientific American*, Vol. 192 (March 1955), p. 18.

declines to get into the act? First, the chairman can try to discover why this member is holding out. The chairman might ask him a question on which he is known to have expert knowledge. Or in directing general questions to the group, the chairman might glance at him frequently. And if the member does start talking or indicates that he would like to, the chairman should be sure to recognize him before his more loquacious colleagues.

What about the noisy member who talks too much? Although again it is helpful to know what motivates him, there are certain tactful techniques that make it easier to handle such an offender:

> ... Don't recognize him if someone else wants the floor.
>
> ... Thank him for his contribution and ask if anyone else has something to say.
>
> ... Before he begins, say, "Would you mind keeping your remarks brief? I'd like to give everyone a chance to talk."
>
> ... Put him in a blind spot where it is easy not to recognize him.
>
> ... Make a half-joke of telling him to shut up.
>
> ... Before the meeting starts, explain tactfully that you would like his cooperation in giving others a chance to talk.

Of course, obtaining general participation is not the chairman's responsibility alone. Cohesive, well-functioning groups are quick to censure over-talkative members by ridicule, ostracism, or more subtle techniques.

STICKING TO THE AGENDA

The chairman must also keep the meeting from wandering off into a discussion of irrelevancies. Otherwise progress will be slow and morale will fall.

One of the most effective techniques for keeping the discussion moving along in the right direction is to record on a blackboard or flip chart [14] both the original agenda and the essential steps that are taken as the meeting progresses. Keeping a visual record of the unfolding discussion serves three functions: (1) it acknowledges contributions and encourages people to speak up, (2) it prevents repetition of what has already been said, and (3) it encourages participants to ask themselves whether their contribution will be relevant before they start talking.

Other, more specific techniques (besides the blunt "You are out of order") may be used by the chairman to keep the session marching along at a brisk pace:

---

[14] A flip chart, sometimes called a "chart easel," is a jumbo-sized pad of paper displayed on an easel so that the whole conference can see it. The chairman writes with colored crayons, and when a page is finished he can either flip it over or detach it and hang it up. Flip charts have an advantage over blackboards in that the pages can be saved for reference. However, for the chairman who needs lots of space in which to write, the blackboard is preferable.

... Comment, "That's a good point. Do you mind if we take it up later?" (And perhaps point to the appropriate spot on the posted agenda.)

... Repeat or write down only the relevant part of each contribution.

... Ask, "How does this fit in with what we are discussing?" (Perhaps you yourself are at fault for not recognizing its relevancy.)

... Summarize what the group has accomplished and what still must be done, so that the participants can decide for themselves what is relevant at the moment.

... Ask a member to do the summarizing, thus spreading responsibility for keeping the discussion on the track.

The chairman should not be too dictatorial in ruling people out of order. It is not easy to decide what is irrelevant. After all, what seems irrelevant to the chairman may seem perfectly relevant to the majority of the members. And even an apparent irrelevancy may spark a completely new approach to the problem. In fact, to the man who made it, the contribution must have seemed relevant or at least associated in some manner with the problem under discussion. If the chairman cracks down on a member now, he may inhibit this member's contribution in the future. Moreover, some irrelevancies, such as wisecracks or funny stories, actually help relieve tension and create a relaxed atmosphere.

KEEPING THE CONFERENCE MOVING TOWARD ITS GOAL

As we have pointed out, the chairman faces a dilemma in keeping the conference moving toward its proper goal. If he moves too fast, some of the participants may feel pressured and resentful, and may not feel involved in the group's decision. On the other hand, if he moves too slowly, some members may grow restless and apathetic. The fact that most conferences operate under the pressure of a time limit helps the chairman keep the discussion moving, but it also obliges him to be less permissive than he would otherwise be.

As we shall see, a carefully prepared agenda helps the group progress, particularly when it is supplemented by periodic summaries to remind the group of what is still to be accomplished. A blackboard listing of matters still to be covered can gently coerce participants to move faster.

Through experience, the chairman learns when is the opportune time to move on to the next point. Certainly it is time when the members start repeating gossipy irrelevancies. Having decided that the discussion has stalled, the chairman may resort to various techniques to motivate the group to move on. Note the difference in urgency between "Does anybody want to add anything" and "Unless someone has something else to say, I'd like to take up...." Which technique is used depends on the pressure of time at the moment. A short summary also helps close off one topic and lead the way to another.

THE CHAIRMAN'S TIGHTNESS OF CONTROL

How tight should be the chairman's control over process? To refer back to our discussion of process roles, certainly the chairman must perform the function of traffic cop. In addition, he may decide to assume all the other process roles: mediator, encourager, task-setter, and so forth. But if he does, he must realize that he will be exercising extremely tight control over the meeting, and he will run the risk of appearing dictatorial. Even if he does this in a highly benevolent fashion—by drawing others out, acknowledging contributions, and so on—the members may become resentful under his paternalistic rule.

Perhaps the best solution is for the chairman to try to induce the members to accept a share of the procedural responsibilities. The more fully the members share in the work of making the decision, the more likely they will be to carry it out with determination.

The following comparison suggests some of the differences between groups in which the leader exercises tight control and groups in which the leader exercises loose control.

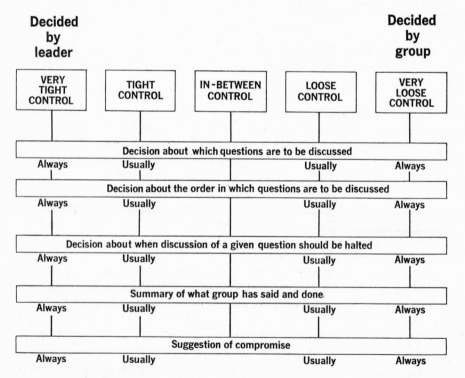

The chairman can exercise tight or loose control in a number of different ways.

The Agenda

The chairman is responsible for steering the group step by step toward the final decision.[15] Before the meeting gets underway he should give careful thought to his over-all strategy—to his agenda. But he must not insist that his plan be followed rigidly, for he cannot predict exactly how the members will react to the questions that come up. Consequently he must be flexible enough to adjust his strategy to the ever-changing demands of the group. He must remember that what may seem to him the most efficient way to analyze a problem may not meet the psychological needs of the group.

The chairman who exercises tight control normally decides on his over-all plan in advance, even though he may apply it with flexibility. He may even circulate copies of the agenda before the meeting as a means of helping the members prepare for the discussion. The chairman who exercises loose control may let the group itself decide on the agenda. Or he may listen to a preliminary discussion of the problem and then propose an agenda that seems to cover the main issues raised.

The productive meeting seems to pass through successive stages of development. If these stages are ignored or taken in the wrong order (for instance, if there is an attempt at decision-making before the facts are evaluated), the meeting will take longer and be less productive.

There are certain standard procedures for analyzing problems, such as (1) assemble facts, (2) evaluate them, and (3) make a decision. But such neat formulas are often too simple to be of any real value. Instead, the course the discussion takes should be determined by the chairman's (or the group's) evaluation of what are the crucial issues. Here, for example, are three alternative agendas for a discussion of the problem of tardiness.

Agenda I
1. Should we have a firm rule against tardiness?
    a. What advantages?
    b. What objections?
2. How could such a rule be enforced?

Agenda II
1. Why are people late?
2. What can be done to handle each reason for lateness?
3. How can these suggestions be put into effect?

Agenda III
1. How much of a tardiness problem do we actually have?
2. What can be done about it?
3. What are the advantages and disadvantages of each suggestion?
4. Which one should we adopt?

---

[15] One experiment showed that groups which follow "developmental" plans for discussion (that is, agendas) came up with higher-quality decisions than groups which per-

Note the difference between these three agendas. Agenda I concentrates on one solution of the problem: a definite rule. Agenda II tries to find the basic causes of the problem and makes it possible to explore alternative solutions. Agenda III goes even deeper by exploring whether a serious problem really exists. Each of these agendas will lead to a different kind of discussion. Which agenda is best, of course, depends on the immediate situation.

With this warning against the dangers of too standardized an approach, let us sketch roughly the steps through which a typical problem-solving meeting might progress. (Note that we do not say *must*.)

PREPARATION

There is no need to repeat the standard injunction that the chairman should make sure of his arrangements beforehand—a suitable room, a blackboard, and so forth. But it is just as important for him to remember that advance briefing of the members on the main topics that are likely to be covered may stimulate them to do some thinking before the meeting. A preliminary caucus of those who are most concerned with the problem may be useful, provided it does not suggest to the others that the meeting has been rigged.

SOCIAL WARM-UP

Remember that a committee cannot become an effectively functioning work group until it has first become a comfortable social group. An opportunity must be given for new members to be introduced and for old members to go through the standard social ceremonies of banter and kidding (though when the participants see each other regularly, this period may last only a few seconds). To regard such social activities as disruptive or extraneous is to misunderstand completely what happens within a normal group. If the opportunity for socializing is not given before the meeting, chances are that it will occur during it.

STATEMENT OF THE PROBLEM

The chairman's initial statement of the problem sets the stage for what is to follow. If there have been earlier meetings, he may simply summarize what has transpired so far. If it is the first meeting on a particular problem, the chairman's opening statement may cover: the general nature of the problem, its importance, its background and history (if necessary),

---

mitted "free discussion." Norman R. F. Maier and P. A. Maier, "An Experimental Test on the Effects of 'Developmental' v. 'Free' Discussion on the Quality of Group Decisions," *Journal of Applied Psychology*, Vol. 41, No. 5 (October 1957), pp. 320-323.

the range of freedom the group will have in making a decision, and, possibly, a tentative agenda.

FREE DISCUSSION

There is real value in having a free, unrestricted discussion before settling down to the systematic analysis necessary for decision-making. By free discussion we mean a chance for the participants to talk about those aspects of the problem that seem most important to them, regardless of whether the comments have any logical relevance to each other. In our tardiness conference, for example, A may brag that there is no lateness in his department; B may insist that he can't stop tardiness in his department until the other supervisors do something to put their departments in order.

Many a member comes to the meeting burning with a pet idea that he *must* get off his chest before he starts listening to anybody else. He is bound to bring it up at the first opportunity, even when it is obviously not relevant to the topic of the moment. (Thus, even if the chairman tried to start the discussion by asking, "Why are people tardy?" Mr. C would insist on talking about the side issue of how to enforce rules.)

Unrestricted discussion of this sort makes it easy for people to warm up to the problem and to start participating. It gives the chairman a chance to survey the psychological atmosphere, so that he can plan his strategy and anticipate the crucial issues. Finally, the free-discussion period provides an opportunity for participants to get to know each other's position; it is in every sense a warm-up before people start "keeping score."

ADOPTING THE AGENDA

When the free discussion has served its purpose, it is time for the chairman to propose an agenda or ask the group to suggest one. In either case it is important that the agenda be made explicit.

GETTING THE FACTS

Too often meetings flounder because members are arguing from conflicting factual premises. Facts may be hard to obtain but at least they are subject to objective inquiry, and it is usually easier to get agreement on facts than it is to get agreement on opinions. Actually, one may lead to the other.

> A rich background of common facts lays the groundwork for the development of common inferences and sentiments, and out of these common decisions can grow. No decision rests on "facts" alone, but there is no better starting point.[16]

---

[16] Bales, "In Conference," p. 47.

LISTING ALTERNATIVE SOLUTIONS

Logically, the next step is for the group to suggest alternative solutions to the problem at hand. The chairman will normally want to elicit as many suggestions as possible, to insure that no good idea is overlooked and that no participant feels neglected.

In recent years a technique known as "creative thinking" has come into use as a means of stimulating suggestions. Although it has had its most enthusiastic following in advertising and public relations, its principles are sometimes useful in other fields. The advocates of this approach insist that all alternatives should be listed before any attempt is made to evaluate them, since premature judgments may interfere with getting the maximum range of ideas.[17]

The heart of creative thinking is "brainstorming," a process in which the members throw out ideas as they occur to them. No attempt is made to evaluate the suggestions. Instead, the chairman writes them down as fast as they are made. The emphasis is on unorthodox, "free-wheeling" ideas, or on "hitchhiking"—that is, using another person's ideas as a springboard for a completely different one of your own. On a question such as "What can be done to stimulate sales of government savings bonds?" a good group can think of as many as a hundred ideas in five minutes. "Brainstorming" has been compared with free association in psychoanalysis, where the patient is expected to give expression to everything that comes into his mind. It should be noted that brainstorming has been criticized as leading to fewer suggestions than would be produced by the same number of people working alone.[18]

EVALUATING ALTERNATIVE SOLUTIONS

Having listed the alternative solutions, the next step is to evaluate them. Although the method of evaluation will naturally depend on the nature of the problem, evaluation normally proceeds by stages. One approach is to discuss the advantages and disadvantages of each proposal in turn (along with suggestions on how to overcome difficulties), and then to compare one proposal against another.[19]

Notice how this approach differs from typical parliamentary procedure,

---

[17] The creative-thinking movement is largely the brain-child of Alex Osborn, co-founder of the advertising firm of Batten, Barton, Durstine and Osborn. See his *Applied Imagination* (New York: Scribner's, 1953).

[18] Donald W. Taylor, Paul Berry, and Clifford H. Block, "Group Participation, Brainstorming, and Creative Thinking," *Administrative Science Quarterly*, Vol. 3, No. 1 (June 1958), pp. 24-47.

[19] This is an elaboration of the "risk technique," which is discussed in Norman R. F. Maier, *Principles of Human Relations* (New York: Wiley, 1952), pp. 62-73.

in which each suggestion is considered separately and accepted or rejected :n turn with no explicit consideration being given to possible alternatives.

During this evaluation period the chairman should try to help the group guard against the normal human tendency to think only of objections without trying to figure out how they can be overcome, or to take a black-and-white position for or against each idea, without trying to weigh alternatives realistically.

NARROWING THE ALTERNATIVES [20]

The group's function is to narrow down the many conceivable alternatives to the one or more on which general agreement can be reached. Normally, the more adequate the evaluation has been, the easier it will be to reach agreement. Yet the process is not automatic.

The first step is to determine which alternatives can be eliminated by unanimous consent. The remaining alternatives, which presumably have some supporters in the group, can then be narrowed down (1) by their proponents becoming persuaded that they are wrong, (2) by mutual concession—that is, by a negative compromise in which everyone gives up something, or (3) by synthesis—that is, by a constructive or positive compromise that incorporates what every member regards as significant and that leaves out nothing that anyone feels is important. Probably the third alternative is the best, and the second the worst.

In the process of working out a solution, the chairman may take entirely upon himself the function of conciliator or "middleman." But there will be greater acceptance of the final decision if there are other "middlemen" in the group who assist in finding a constructive synthesis or compromise.

One of the chairman's most difficult problems is to help the minority surrender its position without loss of face. Agreement is easier to achieve if the chairman is able to convince each of the factions that the final decision incorporates some of their ideas and that each has won a partial victory.

At times agreement is not reached because the members misunderstand each other's position, or because they disagree over the facts themselves. To forestall unnecessary stalemates, the chairman may ask "Is this what you mean?" There are enough clear-cut problems to be settled without letting semantics cloud the issues.

> People often think they disagree when actually they simply are not talking about the same experiences. In such cases they do not draw each other out enough to realize that, although they are using the same words, they are talking about different experiences.[21]

---

[20] Note that the techniques suggested here are the same as those listed by successful labor-management mediators.

[21] Bales, "In Conference," p. 49.

The chairman can also invite the protagonists to restate their position in a constructive, positive form (avoiding criticisms of their opponents), by asking clarifying questions, or perhaps by summarizing the various positions in a way that will emphasize the areas of agreement. If none of these work, it may pay to refer the problem to the committee, or to recess while the members think things over.

One observer has proposed a "procedure for coercing agreement" to be used when the chairman feels the conference is bogging down in emotional argument. Here the chairman takes a firm stand and entertains only questions and answers designed to ascertain facts, to clear up details, and to distinguish one proposal from another.[22]

TAKING A VOTE

Should the chairman insist on working through to a unanimous agreement no matter how long it takes, or should he terminate the discussion by taking a vote? Traditionally, voting has been regarded as the democratic way to make decisions, and the practice has taken on almost ceremonial overtones. In fact, a vote is often taken even where there is no opposition, just to show the group's solidarity.

And yet it can be argued that voting sometimes makes agreement more difficult to attain, since it plays up the differences among members and makes side-taking unavoidable. The trouble is that once a man has publicly committed himself to a position it becomes awkward for him to change his mind. Moreover, the man who is flatly overruled by a vote will be less likely to carry out the group's decision with enthusiasm. The public recording of each member's position tends to split the group into opposing factions, and encourages the members to pay more attention to the arguments of those who are on "their side" than to the arguments of the opposition.

It can even be argued that in a sense majority rule is actually undemocratic, since it shows no respect for minority. The Quakers, for example, insist on unanimity, and any member can block a decision until he is convinced of its validity. Consequently, whenever action is finally taken it enjoys unanimous support.

> If [the group] can reach unanimous consent . . . the effort is well worth
> while, for there will be no disgruntled minority which refuses to support
> or reluctantly supports group action. The search for unanimity places a
> premium on trying to understand a person rather than arguing him down.[23]

---

[22] See Irving J. Lee, "Procedure for 'Coercing' Agreement," *Harvard Business Review*, Vol. 32, No. 1 (January 1954), p. 39. For criticism of this approach as being autocratic and mechanical, see Harold P. Zelko, *Successful Conference and Discussion Techniques* (New York: McGraw-Hill, 1957), pp. 152-153.

[23] Frank S. Haimon, "Group Think or Group Thinking," *Adult Leadership*, Vol. 1, No. 10 (March 1953), p. 12.

Insistence on absolute unanimity, however, has certain disadvantages: (1) it makes for unduly long meetings and delays essential action, (2) in a sense it lets the dissenter make the decision (since he decides whether there will be a decision or none at all), and (3) the common-denominator compromise that suits everybody is rarely bold, imaginative, or capable of arousing enthusiasm. The unanimity rule may work well enough in a religious community (particularly one in which the members have a strong sense of social values) [24] but in industry quick decisions are often of the greatest importance.

The chairman should seek unanimity whenever possible, of course, and on most issues this is not too hard to obtain. The chairman can usually sense when agreement has been reached, and then he needs only to state the "decision" and ask if everyone agrees. Unanimity should not become a fetish, however. If the cost in time and frustration promises to be too great, the leader should call for a vote. A minority that loses after having had ample opportunity to sway the majority frequently accepts the results without too much ill feeling. To do otherwise in our society is considered poor sportsmanship.

RELEASING TENSION

Arguments, decision-making, and undertaking commitments naturally result in the building up of tension within the group. The Bales study has suggested that after a decision has been reached it is important to give people a chance to release this tension by relaxing and engaging in informal social activity. The chairman who ignores this need by rushing the members back to work will find that until they let off steam they just won't settle down to business.

Self-evaluation

Successful group cooperation does not occur spontaneously. Group members must learn to work together. This learning process can be speeded up if the group sets aside some time to examine the effectivness of its own activities—in other words, to learn from itself. Self-evaluation enables the group to improve its performance constantly.

Evaluation of this sort is usually more successful if there is some sort of feedback.[25] For example, one member of the group may be designated as a "process observer." He takes no active part in the meeting; instead, he makes

---

[24] Even Quakers, however, sometimes feel frustrated because of a hold-out objector. See Whyte, *Leadership and Group Participation*, p. 35.

[25] See David H. Jenkins, "Feedback and Group Self-evaluation," *Journal of Social Issues,* Vol. 4, No. 2 (Spring 1948), pp. 50-60.

a series of running notes on what is happening and then reports his observations during the evaluation period.

> The observer can act as the "eyes" for the group leader, who, because of his own responsibility for discussion, is unable to attend as closely to the difficulties in the group process and to be as objective about his own feelings.[26]

A typical observer's report might start this way:

> "Discussion was slow at first. No one was sure what the problem was. Then Bob presented his ideas and almost everyone started contributing. Jack sidetracked us a bit by talking about . . . and the rest seemed bored until Jim (the chairman) very tactfully suggested that Jack defer his comments until later. I notice that Gus and Mike have been very quiet."

Even this small segment of the report would provide plenty of meat for self-evaluation:

1. How could the problem have been stated better at the beginning?
2. How did Jack feel about being called out of order? (When discussed in the evaluation session, this would permit Jack to let off steam, might persuade him to show more self-discipline next time, and would help the chairman evaluate his handling of Jack's irrelevancies.)
3. Why were Gus and Mike so quiet?

Indeed, the chairman can interrupt the meeting for a special report from the process observer whenever he thinks discussion has bogged down. The role of the observer should be rotated in order to give everybody a chance to observe the group from outside.

Another aid to self-evaluation is a "post-meeting evaluation form," which is filled out by each of the members. A simple form might include questions such as these:

1. On the whole, how did you regard the meeting?
   Excellent—— Very Good—— Good—— Fair—— Poor——
2. What was good about the meeting?
3. What was bad about the meeting?
4. Was the chairman too strict? Too easy?
5. Do you feel you had sufficient opportunity to talk?

Parliamentary Law [27]

Parliamentary law is a formalized procedure designed for large deliberative bodies. Consequently it rarely has much value in small committee

---

[26] *Ibid.*, p. 57.

[27] For a sharply contrasting view on the value of parliamentary law, see Malcolm Knowles, "Move Over Mr. Robert," *Adult Leadership*, Vol. 1, No. 2 (June 1952); Robert W. English, "General Robert Replies," *Adult Leadership*, Vol. 2, No. 2 (June 1953), p. 29; and Zelko, *op. cit.*, pp. 151-152.

meetings, and even in large meetings it should be applied with flexibility. If a group tries to follow the letter of the law, it will fall into interminable, meaningless wrangles, resulting in the frustration of everyone concerned.

Strict observation of parliamentary law demands that the group vote for or against each proposal, with no provision for making a systematic comparison of alternatives. Parliamentary procedure is supposed to save time and to produce a more orderly meeting, but its rigid rules often do just the opposite, particularly since few people understand their intricacies.

Nevertheless parliamentary procedure does have one major advantage for large meetings: it keeps control over process firmly in the hands of the members themselves. Only the group as a whole can decide when to stop debate, to make a decision, or to move on to the next question. The chairman's power is restricted to recognizing speakers and calling members out of order (and even this is subject to appeal).

Conclusion

The ability to act as an effective chairman or a productive committee member is becoming increasingly important in management. The same basic rules of conference leadership apply when the company president sits with the board of directors in mahogany and velvet surroundings as when the foreman calls his men together in the locker room to discuss a production technique.

Good meetings don't "just happen." They require skillful leadership on the part of the chairman and sincere cooperation on the part of the members. When the members are unable to integrate their individual needs and roles, meetings tend to degenerate into futile wrangles. A feeling of solidarity and common purpose is required before members will evaluate ideas on their merits rather than in terms of self-interest.

The chairman plays a variety of roles, depending on the purpose of the meeting. The more effective chairman minimizes content roles. If he is a strict chairman he will assume strong process roles; if he is a loose chairman he will not.

The chairman faces a constant dilemma in deciding how tight a rein to keep on the discussion. Too tight control may frustrate the natural development of ideas, force people to conclusions before they are ready, and generate resentment. Too loose control may result in a feeling of aimlessness and confusion.

The chairman must constantly keep in mind that the goals of meetings (high-quality decisions, general acceptance, and economy in time) often conflict with each other. He must encourage participation and yet at the same time keep the discussion both relevant and moving toward a conclusion.

The successful meeting proceeds smoothly from stage to stage. The chairman senses the invisible currents at work within the group and decides on the proper moment to move on.

If a meeting is to achieve its objective there must be a carefully devised agenda to insure an orderly, efficient procedure for discussion and decision-making. An effective agenda takes advantage of the natural stages through which a meeting passes, and is flexible enough (1) to meet the needs of the particular problem, group, and time limit, and (2) to be modified during the course of the meeting as the need arises. An agenda that has been accepted by the members serves many purposes: it insures that every point of view has been considered; it allows for maximum participation, and (hopefully) it enables the meeting to make its decision within the time allowed.

In a broad sense, the first three chapters of this part have been concerned with communication problems: those involving transmission of messages (Chapter 9), the reception of messages (Chapter 10), and improving the flow of messages among members of a meeting (Chapter 11). In each of these areas, as the following table illustrates, certain principles have emerged which dovetail neatly with similar principles from other areas.

Communicator	Interviewer	Conference Leader
1. Directs message to the world of his audience.	Tries to understand how interviewee sees problem.	Helps each member understand how others see problem.
2. Pitches remarks in terms audience can understand; takes into account what words mean to the audience.	Tries to understand what the words of the interviewee mean to him.	Helps members understand what each other's words mean.
3. Tries to discover the audience's emotional state and takes this into account in framing message.	Helps interviewee release feelings before getting down to consider facts.	Allows group to express feelings before getting down to decision-making.
4. Tries to indicate to audience that he understands their problem.	Tries to indicate that he understands interviewee's problem.	Tries to indicate that he understands conference members' problems.

Problem I

Craig, President of the Craig Toy Company, has called a special meeting of his top officers—his plant superintendent, his comptroller, and his methods engineer —to discuss the installation of a new conveyor system which the plant superintendent (who has been with the company only six months) wants to install in the paint department. Under his proposal workers will receive the toys on a conveyor system of hooks, remove them, spray them, and then return them to the conveyor hooks so that they can be carried to the drying ovens.

The following are the attitudes the men bring to the meeting.*

---

* We are indebted to Mr. Richard Gordon for permission to use this problem.

Craig—President

You feel that Smith, the comptroller, will oppose the introduction of the machine. Smith won't accept any suggestion that means spending money without a lot of convincing. You've had occasion to thank him for this atttitude in the past. It has saved you a lot of money. However, you know that Smith doesn't think too much of Jones, the new superintendent. He considers Jones an upstart, and too big for his breeches.

Johnson, your methods engineer, may not prove too cooperative either. He has made similar suggestions in the past which you have not accepted because the time was not ripe. Nevertheless, now you feel the time is ripe. Demand has increased to the point where the increased production is warranted. Also, you want to give Jones the encouragement of having another of his suggestions accepted.

You have called the meeting with your three top men to get final confirmation before introducing the conveyor system. You feel it's an important move but you also feel that you must get the cooperation of your staff if the introduction is to be successful.

Jones—Plant Superintendent

Naturally you are anxious to introduce this new system. You figure it will cost about $12,500, but will increase production about 50 per cent and save the company about $40,000 in a year. In addition, the employees will not have to work as hard.

You have talked over the idea with Johnson, the methods engineer, and he advised you that you wouldn't get anywhere with the suggestion. He said he has made similar suggestions at least three different times in the last five years. Each time it was turned down without the courtesy of a decent explanation. Well, it looks as though you've done better than he has. You've always said that anything can be sold if you do it the right way.

The fellow who really has to be sold is that old codger, the comptroller. He guards the company's money as if it were his own. No wonder the equipment in this plant is twenty years behind the times. You'll get things on the ball, though. That's what they hired you for.

Johnson—Methods Engineer

Jones has talked the conveyor belt idea over with you and it's a good one. In fact, you have proposed it at least three times in the last five years. It has been rejected, without discussion, by Craig every time. Suddenly, the golden boy, Jones, makes the suggestion and the idea is up for discussion. Jones was brought in from the outside to become plant manager. Outside ideas are o.k. but ideas by old-time employees aren't worth a hoot.

Jones' figures show the system will lead to a 50 per cent increase in production. You estimate he may even be a little conservative.

If anybody else but Jones had come up with the idea, you'd be all for it. Trouble with this plant, they're not keeping up with the times. The plant could turn out twice as much if Craig would take some of your suggestions. No, he says, the old way is the best way.

Smith, the comptroller, typifies this attitude. All he wants to do is make money. He never wants to spend a dollar to make a dollar. You're with him on turning down this proposal. Anything to keep from supporting that newcomer Jones and see him get the credit for one of your ideas. He's been with the company six months and acts as if he owns the place. Craig should assert his authority more and put this new fellow in his place.

Smith—Comptroller

Twelve thousand five hundred dollars, that's what it will cost. They sure can think up more ways to spend money around here. If it weren't for you, the company would be bankrupt. Mr. Craig would spend more money than he could earn. He takes suggestions from every Tom, Dick, and Harry.

Over twelve thousand dollars for a conveyor system to speed up painting. The toys can't be passed along by hand. It makes the employees too tired. Supposed to increase production 50 per cent. That Jones, he's been in the plant six months as plant superintendent and has spent more money than the old superintendent, Peterson, did in three years. Everything is supposed to double production and cut costs in half. You haven't seen it in the balance sheet yet.

He's worse than Johnson, the methods engineer. Johnson is always coming up with new ideas, too. However, you could always get Peterson or Craig to turn them down unless they were outstanding. But this new fellow, Jones, has Craig's ear. Craig listens to him more than he does to you. It's up to you to save Craig from himself. This whiz-kid Jones will bankrupt the company with his crazy ideas. You've turned down better ideas than this kid ever thought of.

You'll make a stand on this item for sure. You think Johnson, the methods engineer, will support you. He won't like this young fellow stealing his ideas and presenting them as his own. The old-timers will have to stick together or this young fellow will be in control for sure.

A full $12,500 for a conveyor system. Huh! !

1. What problems will Mr. Craig face in reaching an agreement? What techniques should he use?

2. Role-play this case.

3. How can Jones best put over his plan?

We live in a world of change. We Americans in particular have learned to expect change as part of our everyday life. We pride ourselves on being modern and up-to-date in our habits and behavior. Still we may be more traditional than we think. To be sure, we accept and even welcome changes in terms of material things, such as household gadgets or cars. But we tend to resist changes in our interpersonal and job relations, because these changes threaten the security of the orderly and familiar ways we have known in the past.

If a company is to survive today, it must be able to react to changing conditions by changing itself. In fact, it *must* anticipate environmental changes by altering its own policies and structure in time to meet these new conditions as they arise. The ability to introduce change with a minimum of resistance is one of the key skills of the administration. In this chapter we shall discuss (1) why there is resistance to change and (2) what can be done to overcome it.

12

Introducing Change

Types of Resistance to Change

Of all the types of resistance to change perhaps the one most commonly recognized is the resistance of many employees to technological change—to automation, for example. Such resistance is readily understandable. In some instances, technological change means that employees must agree to work on faster machines with increased workloads.[1] In others it requires the acquisition of new skills and even a new approach to work; to cite automation again, the worker must learn to watch and adjust equipment rather than to operate it manually.[2] In still others it may mean the loss of work altogether.

In many companies one hears constant complaints about "old fogies" who are hampering progress. Take the case of a clothing store, once famous for its high-quality merchandise, which is located in an area from which the high-income customers have moved. A new owner resolves to introduce a lower-priced line and to induce his salesmen to engage in high-pressure salesmanship. Naturally the salesmen react violently.

Resistance to change is sometimes as violent at the managerial level as it is at lower levels. We shall explore elsewhere (see Chapter 24) the problems involved in re-educating managers to improve their supervisory practices, to give higher priority to accident prevention, and so forth. Indeed, managers tend to resist the introduction of almost any new personnel practice. They may regard a new system of job evaluation as a threat to existing status relationships, or the introduction of tests in hiring as a threat to their traditional prerogative to hire whomever they wish.

Resistance to change may show itself in unexpected ways—for instance, in aggression, regression, and in all the negative reactions discussed in Chapter 5. Aggression, perhaps the commonest reaction, may be expressed either against specific changes or against the organization as a whole. One clear sign of resistance is a series of apparently "emotional" or "irrational" objections to minor changes; these often indicate that more deep-seated problems are involved.

Some problems, of course, provoke more resistance than others—and some provoke no resistance at all. Few people object to a pay increase, but almost everyone objects violently to a pay cut. Model changes are enthusiastically accepted by automobile dealers—the resistance would come if these changes were eliminated.

---

[1] The problem of getting acceptance of increased workloads has been intensively studied, particularly in the New England textile industry. For example, see Richard C. Nyman and Elliot D. Smith, *Union-Management Cooperation and the 'Stretch Out'* (New Haven: Yale University Press, 1934).

[2] See Charles R. Walker, *Towards an Automatic Factory* (New York: *Harpers,* 1957); Bernard Karsh, "The Meaning of Work in an Age of Automation," *Current Economic Comment,* Vol. 19, No. 3 (August 1957), pp. 3-13.

What causes resistance to change? How can it be eliminated or at least minimized?

What Causes Resistance to Change?

ECONOMIC FACTORS

The most obvious reason is economic. Workers resist automation because they fear they will lose their jobs; they are unimpressed by arguments that in the "long run" there will be more jobs in other parts of the country. What concerns them most is the economic welfare of themselves and their families.[3]

Similarly, a craftsman may fear that new developments will reduce the economic value of his skills. In the same way, managers themselves oppose a change that helps the company as a whole but hurts their individual promotional opportunities.

Sometimes the economic factors underlying resistance to change are obscure and not immediately apparent. In one plant the employees began to damage parts they were sending to a new plant overseas; formerly the parts had been shipped to a domestic plant. Was this blind resistance to change? Not at all. Investigation revealed that the employees were afraid the company was shifting more and more of its operations to the overseas plant and feared that eventually they would lose their jobs.

We must, however, guard against the common misconception that workers generally—and particularly their unions—blindly resist all forms of technological progress. The Hat Workers and Clothing Workers unions, for instance, have developed special programs designed to encourage management to introduce such changes. They recognize that only through rising productivity can their wages be raised. Similarly, John L. Lewis and the United Mine Workers cooperated with coal-mine owners in an extensive mechanization program which has resulted in substantially fewer jobs in the coal fields, but higher earnings for those who remain. Foreign visitors to this country express surprise at the extent to which American workers have learned that technological change redounds to their benefit and is the source of rising wages. There is, however, a significant gap between the intellectual recognition of this relationship and the acceptance of change in a particular case.

---

[3] For similar reasons, workers may object to bigger workloads, even when there is no demand for greater physical effort. They reason that they may work either themselves or their friends out of a job.

INCONVENIENCE

Equally understandable is the resistance to change that threatens to make life more difficult. A worker fights the assignment of extra duties; he has learned his old job so well that it requires no attention any more, while the new job requires surface attention. Similarly, executives dislike the inconvenience of being reassigned from one location to another. Even if the company pays their expenses, there is the bother of buying and selling houses, packing, and readjusting to new work and a new environment.

All of us develop a vested interest in our usual way of doing things. Our everyday habits provide us with a certain security in our life. Some of these are quite trivial: we drive to work by a fixed route every day, even though other routes are equally good. When our usual route is temporarily blocked, we are annoyed by the inconvenience of having to change our pattern.

Learning new ways requires the expenditure of energy, and human beings are generally lazy. Even for the simplest job there are "tricks to the trade" that take time to learn. When a man is thrown into a new situation his tricks no longer apply and he loses the security of the familiar.

UNCERTAINTY

The new way is always strange, threatening, and laden with uncertainties—even if it is an improvement over the old. We have a chance for a new job at higher pay. Should we take it? Maybe not. How hard will it be? How long will it take to learn? Will we be able to meet the challenge? Who will our friends be? The opportunity may be very good indeed, yet there is a strong tendency to let well enough alone.

One reason for this fear is the lack of factual information. We know the old circumstances; we don't know what the new ones will be. Some people are gamblers by nature, but the average person hesitates to venture into uncharted waters. The uncertain is always threatening.

New equipment is introduced into the plant. What will it mean to our job, our status, our security? A new boss is assigned to the department. What will his policies be? How will they affect us?

Uncertainty caused by lack of information may be corrected simply by providing answers to questions—assuming that management is aware of what questions are being asked. But there is another kind of uncertainty that cannot be dissipated by providing information: the anxiety that springs from the individual's fears about how *he himself* will react to the new situation. Every draftee is assailed with doubts the night before his induction. What will army life be for me? Every veteran is delighted to provide information, but no one can predict how *I* will react. For this sort of uncertainty there can be no quick remedy.

THREATS TO SOCIAL RELATIONSHIPS

As we mentioned in Chapter 3, anything that disrupts the customary social relationships and standards of the group will meet with strong resistance. In particular, employees oppose changes which threaten their status.

For example, vests and coats in one clothing center are made by separate groups of tailors, though to an outsider their skills seem readily interchangeable. In recent years the demand for vests has fallen off while there has developed an acute shortage of skilled coatmakers. Yet in spite of the combined urging of union and management, the vestmakers refuse to transfer to coatmaking. As a result the vestmakers lose over $30 a week. Why do they persist in this apparently illogical attitude?

The vestmakers are a small, tightly knit clique of friends who are proud of their skill. They have a long-established union local of their own. They fear that if they were transferred to coatmaking their clique would be broken up, they would become the *least*-skilled coatmakers rather than highly skilled vestmakers, and they would lose the protection of their local. Thus the change is a threat to their prestige, their ability to meet their social needs, and their union protection.

Even when no change in physical location is involved, most changes tend to upset social relations. Take the situation in a small firm that had just hired a new purchasing agent. Previously each department head had ordered his own supplies. Now the department head merely filled out a purchase order and the purchasing agent decided on the supplier and negotiated the price. Though this saved the department heads from being pestered by salesmen and saved the company money, the department heads were highly antagonistic. They missed the feeling of importance that came from dealing directly with salesmen; the purchasing agent was far less obsequious to them than the salesman had been, and he threatened their authority by suggesting at times that they might use cheaper, lower-quality material. This fact may help explain why they began complaining about red tape and about how the purchasing agent made their jobs harder, not easier.

Every supervisor develops patterns of informal relations with his subordinates. And every new supervisor requires a long period of initiation before he is accepted by his subordinates, in part because they fear that he may not follow his predecessor's patterns of informal relations. In fact, *any* new member of a group has a hard time until he develops satisfactory relations with his colleagues—and one of the reasons why people resist being transferred to new jobs is that they dislike the disruption of old relations and the work of establishing new ones.

Other changes may threaten a man's opportunity to provide leadership. For instance, before automation a crew chief on a press directed the men who worked with him; after automation there was less need for teamwork

and less opportunity for him to issue orders. Or the change may mean that
the man who used to call the signals waits passively for someone else to take
the initiative. Under the old scheme the maintenance man scheduled his own
work; under the new scheme he must wait until someone calls him, thus
reducing his discretion and status and substantially changing his social relationships with others.

Individuals adjust their pattern of social relations to fit their own special
personality needs, just as they adjust other elements of their life in the
formation of habits. Over a period of time, assuming an employee is not
anxious to quit his present job, he has probably developed a good fit between
his personality needs and the requirements of the job. The man who wants
to boss others around, even if he is not officially a supervisor, has probably
found a position in the work group that permits him to initiate activity; the
worker who wants to avoid social pressures has probably found a job
where no one can push him, not even the man who works next to him.
Changing work procedures and systems, and introducing new equipment,
upsets these convenient, pleasant job patterns. The sequence of work may
be so drastically changed that the man who was formerly isolated must
now work with a high-pressure colleague, and the leader is left with no one
to lead.

SYMBOLS

Symbols raise special problems. It will be remembered from Chapter 9
that a symbol is something which stands for something else. The flag
symbolizes one's country, the Bastille pre-revolutionary oppression in France,
the supervisors' parking lot their special status, the restaurant's white table
cloth its general excellence. A symbol cannot be eliminated without threatening in people's minds the things for which it stands.

> The new manager of the Integrity Insurance Company had little diffi-
> culty with his "modernization" program until he decided it was a waste of
> money to print policies on high-quality parchment paper. His proposal to
> substitute a cheaper but still durable paper led to a storm of protest from
> the company's insurance agents: the new paper wouldn't look or wear
> well, it didn't look right, the customers would think it cheap. Investigation
> revealed that to the agents the parchment paper was a symbol of Integ-
> rity's reputation as a leader in the industry. They began to fear that these
> changes would mean that Integrity would be just like any other insurance
> company.

Small changes may symbolize big ones, particularly when employees are
uncertain about how extensive the program of change will be. When a
situation begins to shift, subordinates search for indications of what lies
ahead. For Integrity's agents, the cheaper paper was a convincing sign that
management intended to degrade the company's prestige. A symbol repre-

sents a whole framework of treasured relationships and values; subordinates unite to protect it against attack just as if everything it represented were actually in danger.

RESENTMENT OF NEW ORDERS AND INCREASED CONTROL

Whenever management institutes change, it must substantially increase the number of orders it gives to subordinates. This in turn may well lead to resistance.

Many people resent taking any orders at all. Others have become accustomed to a certain level of control from higher management but resist any attempt to strengthen that control. On routine jobs or on jobs where employees are used to being their own boss, direct orders from management are relatively rare. When change occurs, they become subject to all sorts of unusual pressures from supervisors, engineers, and the big boss. Suddenly they find that someone is checking up on them and barraging them with far more orders than usual. This sharp increase in control reduces their feeling of autonomy and self-reliance. It emphasizes their dependence on management.

When told that they *must* change their behavior, people sometimes become stubborn. They seek to defend themselves and become more committed than ever to their old attitudes. As we shall see, change is easier when the people who are to be changed are consulted beforehand or have a chance to participate in making the decision—and thus do not feel pushed.

It has been argued that one of the main problems in introducing change is to keep it from being introduced in an intermittent fashion. The organizations that have greatest difficulty are often those that make changes only once in a while. The trick, it is claimed, is to make change almost continuously, to make change for the sake of change, even if there is no compelling reason for change at the moment. Perhaps this suggestion is too extreme. Still it does emphasize the point that living under change is very different from leading the same placid existence day after day.

UNION ATTITUDES

Unions are also likely to resist change unless management consults with them, either formally or informally. It is not enough to inform individuals or consult with them. Every union has certain institutional needs that must be met if it is to retain its members' loyalty. If management makes a point of working with the union, the union may cooperate in introducing the change. If management ignores the union, the only way the union can preserve its status is by opposing management.

What happens when management decides to introduce new equipment that will require men to learn new jobs and assume new responsibilities? The typical approach in some companies is for the industrial engineer to make all the necessary plans, perhaps in consultation with the foreman. When the equipment arrives, the foreman assigns men to the new jobs and the personnel department computes the new pay rates. Almost inevitably, the union will find something wrong with the change and will file a grievance— and perhaps even sponsor a slow-down or wildcat strike. Why? If the union were to accept management's action passively, it would in effect be abandoning what it regards as its proper role. The only way to save face is to fight the proposed changes.

In other companies, management customarily informs the union of proposed changes long before they are made, asks for suggestions on how the seniority clause should operate when men are transferred, bargains over wage rates for the new jobs, and even invites the steward to make suggestions on where to place the new machines. The union's status is preserved, and it assumes responsibility for resolving what might be a bitter dispute over who will be assigned to the new jobs. Of course, in bargaining over wages the company may have to make concessions, but the over-all cost may be less than the expense of trying to force the change over the union's objection, for workers are in an ideal position to insure that unwelcome change will prove unsuccessful or costly.

Reducing Resistance to Change

Back in Chapter 5 we pointed out that management always has two ways of changing behavior, either by (1) raising the pressure to *overcome* forces of resistance, or by (2) *reducing* the forces of resistance themselves. We compared method 1, overcoming resistance, to trying to stop a car by slamming on the brakes without taking our foot off the gas. This method leads to tension, uncertainty, and attempts to insulate oneself from pressure. Method 2, on the other hand, involves an attempt to discover and reduce the forces of resistance to a particular change. It can be compared to permitting a car to slow down to a halt without applying the brakes. Though method 2 (reducing resistance) frequently cannot be used without some of method 1 (overcoming resistance), method 2 is the one that places least strain on human relations.

In overcoming resistance, management seeks to apply enough pressure on a man to induce him to do what is expected. For instance, the most obvious way to overcome resistance to change is simply to threaten to fire a man if he doesn't change, or promise to pay him more if he does.

But this threatening approach leads to all the problems we discussed in Chapter 5 under "authority and punishment." A man may respond to threats either by quitting altogether, by sabotaging the change once it has been introduced, or by implementing it in a half-hearted manner.

What about trying to deal with resistance by promising a man an economic reward if he will accept the change? If the reason for resistance in this case is largely economic—and in many cases it is—obviously an economic reward is a good answer, for its helps reduce the cause of resistance and thus helps get the change accepted with less tension.

On the other hand, economic rewards are less successful if the reason for resistance is non-economic. For instance, an executive may be offered a salary increase to move to a new location. Let us assume that the executive's immediate reaction to this offer is that the new location is very unpleasant and that he has misgivings about the type of work he will be doing and the type of men he will be associating with.

Confronted with such a choice, the executive will probably experience painful indecision. And indecision is always frustrating even between attractive alternatives. He may even try to get the salary increase without leaving town, perhaps by going to work for another company. And regardless of what he decides, for years to come he may resent having been forced into the decision at all. If he stays, he may deplore his economic sacrifice every time he pays a bill. If he goes, his attitude may make it difficult for him to adjust to the new situation.

A large chemical company with many laboratories throughout the country used quite a different approach in manning a new laboratory in a remote section of the country. Their approach emphasized reducing causes of resistance. First, the company publicized the importance and challenge of the new laboratory's work and hinted broadly that assignment there would offer great opportunities for promotion. Then it invited a small core of experienced engineers to accept positions in the new lab and told them that they could invite less-experienced men to join them. However, management made it clear that those who were invited were free to reject the invitation. The new men and their families were brought together from all over the country at the site of the new lab and were given a chance to get to know one another and to investigate housing possibilities. As a consequence, they had no trouble recruiting able men to work in the new location.

In the discussion that follows, we shall seek to emphasize methods of reducing, rather than overcoming, resistance.

THROUGH ECONOMIC INCENTIVES

As we mentioned earlier, much of the resistance to change has an economic motivation. Either men hear that the change will result in an immediate loss of job or earnings, or else they fear that it will affect their long-run job security or chances for promotion. The easiest solution in such a case is simple but expensive: guarantee that these fears are groundless. For instance, if a man refuses to work on a new machine merely because he fears a loss of piece-work earnings, management might guarantee him that his earnings will be no lower on the new machine. Certainly, too, if new equipment is to be introduced that will displace men, the change should be made in a period of expanding employment when the displaced employee can be offered another job that offers equally good security and pay.

Such guarantees are extremely useful in smoothing over change. The difficulty is their expense. The very reason for change may be the desire to cut costs because of economic necessity. Even in such a case management may reduce resistance if it can truthfully show that the change will be an improvement in the individual's own (not just the company's or the other workers') economic prospects in the long run.

Though the bulk of this chapter is concerned with non-economic means of handling resistance, the reader should not draw the wrong impression from our allocation of space. *Economic motivation is very important in our society.* And when the cause of resistance is economic, all the non-economic techniques that we are about to discuss will be meaningless. True, an employer may successfully manipulate an employee into acquiescing to a change that is not in the employee's best interest. But in the long run in a free society such attempts at brainwashing tend to backfire against their instigators. We emphasize this point because there are employers who feel that if proper "human relations" are applied, employees will be willing to do without a fair wage. Such misuse of human relations is, in our opinion, highly immoral; fortunately, it is rarely successful.

THROUGH TWO-WAY COMMUNICATION

Resistance to change that springs from fear of the unknown can be reduced simply by providing appropriate information. This information should explain not only *what* is to happen but also *why*. And it should be sent to the whole organization, both to those directly and indirectly involved.

This question of communications raises all the problems that we discussed in Chapter 9, particularly: (1) Is the information really understood? And (2) does it answer the questions actually being asked? Here, as in most areas of human relations, only *two-way* communication will serve the purpose. When major change is contemplated, supervisors and subordinates should sit down and discuss the proposed plan in a way that will bring doubts and questions out into the open where they can examine and answer them.

THROUGH GROUP DECISION-MAKING

One of the most effective techniques of reducing resistance to change is to permit the individuals affected to share in the making of decisions. In recent years a great deal of interest has developed in group decision-making as a means of changing both attitudes and behavior.[4]

One of the classic studies in this area involved a pajama factory that was subject to constant changes in style and production methods.[5] These changes were met with great opposition from the workers. Their opposition was reflected in several facts: on the average, employees transferred from one job to another took longer to learn the new job than did completely new employees; moreover, 62 per cent of the transferred employees either failed to attain a satisfactory level of production or else quit altogether.[6] The causes of this resistance were: frustration over loss of status, difficulty in learning new methods, and fear of never regaining their old rate of speed. Economic pressures were less important, for although the girls were on piece-work they received a liberal learning allowance during the period of adjustment.

An experiment was set up involving four groups, each of which was subjected to change in method which involved elimination of certain frills and affected less than 10 per cent of their total work.

Control group. The control group followed the standard routines that had been developed for instituting change. They were called together as a group, told that competitive conditions made the new method necessary, informed of the new piece-work rate, and given an opportunity to ask questions.

Partial-participation group. In the second group, all the operators were called to a meeting in which the need for the change was explained as dramatically as possible. Management pointed out that the elimination of frills would make it possible for the company to produce its products more competitively. The members of the group, having agreed in principle to the change, elected a committee to help management make the necessary plans and to establish the new piece-work rate.

Total-participation groups. The last two groups were smaller than the partial-participation group. The same procedure was followed with these groups except that all the operators participated in planning the change. "In the meetings with these two groups, suggestions were immediately made in such quantity that the stenographer had great difficulty in recording them." [7]

Production dropped substantially in the control group, and there were "marked expressions of aggression against management, such as conflict with the methods engineer, expression of hostility against the supervisor, deliberate restriction of production, and lack of cooperation with the supervisor. There were 17 per cent quits in the first forty days." [8] The experimental groups cooperated very well, and achieved a very rapid re-

[4] Many of the benefits of group decision-making can be obtained by letting individuals make decisions for themselves too.

[5] Lester Coch and John R. P. French, "Overcoming Resistance to Change," *Human Relations*, Vol. I, No. 4 (1948), pp. 512-532.

[6] The resistance revealed itself in different forms, depending on the degree of internal cohesion in the group whose work was changed. Cohesive groups restricted output and engaged in aggressive acts against management. Members of noncohesive groups quit the job altogether: their turnover was almost three times as high as among cohesive groups.

[7] Coch and French, *op. cit.*, p. 521.

[8] *Ibid.*, p. 522.

learning curve. Soon production was 40 per cent higher than in the control group. There was no turnover at all in experimental groups.

Several other such experiments have pointed to the same conclusion: group decision-making is an effective method of reducing resistance to change in some circumstances.[9] Why is this approach effective in some instances?

Two-way communication   In the pajama-factory case, management explained what change it intended to make and why the change was necessary. It encouraged employees to ask questions and gave them an opportunity to bring their doubts out in the open.

Involvement   We have seen that most people have a strong desire to participate in decisions that affect them directly. Group decision-making involves subordinates actively in the process of introducing change and enhances their sense of control over the environment.

> One group-decision experiment was made with girls who were learning machine-paced work and who were failing to keep up with the required pace.[10] In discussions with their foremen, the girls requested that they be allowed to determine the pace themselves. A dial was installed that allowed them to set their own speed. It was discovered that the girls set up a work pattern which varied with the time of day, but that the *average* speed was considerably higher than the *constant* speed previously set by engineers. Yet the girls reported that their work was easier, and their total output was between 30 and 50 per cent higher than expected.

Unfreezing attitudes   People often resist change because they hold certain fixed attitudes or stereotypes to which they adhere in spite of all evidence to the contrary. Group decision-making helps them *unfreeze* these attitudes so that they can be re-examined.

> An example occurred in the pajama plant we discussed above.[11] During World War II the company's staff psychologist tried to persuade management, in view of the general manpower shortage, to abandon its policy of not hiring workers over 30. The top-management group immediately opposed this suggestion, insisting that older women took too long to train, had a higher absenteeism rate, and never worked at top speed. When the staff psychologist mentioned the good performance of older women currently employed, management dismissed them as exceptional cases.
>
> Shifting to another approach, the psychologist tried to involve management in a minor research project to find out how much money the company

---

[9] See, for example, Kurt Lewin, "Studies in Group Decision," Dorwin Cartwright and Alvin Zander, eds., *Group Dynamics* (Evanston, Ill.; Row, Peterson, 1953), pp. 287-301; and various articles in *Journal of Social Issues*, Vol. 1, No. 3 (1945). It should be noted that not all the "group-decision experiments" have been able to be duplicated.

[10] William F. Whyte and others, *Money and Motivation* (New York: Harpers, 1955), Chapter 10.

[11] A. J. Marrow and John R. P. French, "Overcoming a Stereotype," *Journal of Social Issues*, Vol. 1, No. 3 (1945), pp. 33-37.

was losing through employing older women. Management itself determined the criteria to be used (production rates, turnover, absenteeism, and learning speed) and also decided how the data were to be gathered. In short, management became actively involved in the project. To management's surprise, the data showed that older women were better on all counts. Highly excited by these findings, management changed its policy and even spread the word of its shift to other companies.

Notice that the psychologist failed when he tried to attack management's stereotypes head-on. But he succeeded when he induced management to unfreeze its old attitudes by engaging in the research study. By doing this management opened its mind to objective evidence. In a sense the approach used involved a form of double-clutching. Instead of switching directly from one attitude to another, the group went first into "neutral" before taking up its final position.

Establishing new group standards   In Chapter 3 we mentioned that groups develop certain standards of proper conduct and that individuals who fail to live up to these standards are subjected to pressure to conform. When an individual member of a group decides to accept a change imposed from above, he fears that his fellow workers will criticize him for playing along. But when the entire group is involved in the decision leading to the change, just the opposite occurs: the man who *refuses* to accept the change is pressured into accepting the group decision. In effect, group decision-making may lead to the establishment of new group standards that are rigidly enforced.

Commitment   Group decision-making commits each member of the group to carry out the decision that is agreed on. Even if a member has reservations or second thoughts, he is under strong pressure to implement the decision. Providing employees with information and arguments may influence them one way or another, but they themselves must decide whether to accept or resist a proposed change if they are to experience any commitment to the ultimate decision.

In summary, group decision-making may serve as a powerful tool in reducing resistance to change. But it is not a cure-all for management's problems. It works effectively in areas where management is relatively indifferent to what the group decides; for instance, management may not care how the work is divided up so long as the job is done. Group decision-making may also prove effective when management and employees have overlapping but not conflicting interests: in the pajama-factory case, for example, management wanted more ouput and the employees wanted greater earnings and prestige. But when no community of interest exists, group decision-making is of little use in reducing resistance to change. Under such circumstances bargaining may be more appropriate.

THROUGH BARGAINING

How does bargaining differ from group decision-making? In group decision-making management gives the group freedom to make its own decisions (though within limits). Bargaining implies a willingness to talk things over and to make compromises in an effort to get the group's approval of proposed changes. However, management does not agree in advance to accept any decision made by the group. Normally, it accepts only some of the group's proposals and only as a *quid pro quo* in exchange for the group's accepting the rest of what management wants.

Sometimes bargaining is implicit (as we mentioned in Chapter 5)—that is, unspoken understandings are reached on how much management will demand in the way of change, and subordinates in effect agree to accept a limited amount of change as long as management is "reasonable" in its demands.

Often explicit, open bargaining is more useful, particularly in a unionized situation. As we have seen, unions insist on being consulted on every matter that affects the welfare of their members. Some changes, such as pay cuts, may clearly require union approval. In other instances, management may have the power to make a change on its own, but may be caught up in a swarm of grievances if the union does not approve of what was done. When workers are transferred from one job to another, for example, the union may charge that the seniority clause of the contract has been violated. When workloads are increased, the union may charge that there is a violation of the health and safety clause of the contract or of established past practices.

Many managements insist on their "prerogative" to make all decisions by themselves. When the union attacks their actions, they try to limit the discussion to the strictly legal question of whether the contract was in fact violated. They feel that once the union is given a say, it will be difficult or impossible to operate efficiently or to make any decisions at all.

There are times when management probably should stand on principle, particularly to show that unrelieved obstinacy on the part of the union can provoke equal obstinacy on the part of management. But management should set an example of reasonableness—at least to the extent of listening to the union's point of view.

Management loses little of its essential power when it informs the union well in advance of proposed changes and shows a willingness to listen to objections. But these gestures may not be enough in themselves. The union is seldom satisfied just to be informed or to be given an opportunity to air its objections, if these objections always prove fruitless. If management wants to win the union's support in introducing change, it must give careful, open-minded attention to grievances brought up by the union. And, as we will note in Chapter 28, it may even let the union participate in the decision-making process itself.

In either case, management must be prepared to make concessions and to accept union suggestions that it may not feel are fully desirable, on the theory that a reasonably adequate solution enthusiastically supported by the union is better than a perfect solution strongly opposed by the union.[12]

Many of these same principles apply to dealing with non-union groups. The interests of management and subordinates often conflict. Regardless of how assiduously management uses the techniques of consultation and group decision-making, there will be occasions when subordinates are unwilling to accept everything management wants. Under these circumstances it is only common sense for management to make some concessions to the subordinates' strongest objections, if only as a means of winning more complete acceptance of other aspects of the proposed change.

Collective bargaining is difficult with non-union groups, for there is no established mechanism to rely on. With small non-union groups, however, it is at least possible to discuss problems with the group as a whole, and with larger non-union groups management can deal with informal leaders or specially selected committees. It should be emphasized, though, that such meetings are useless unless all participants feel free to express their objections openly.

In conclusion, we repeat that management is under no obligation to bargain over every change it wants to initiate. On occasion it must push proposals through without regard to the objections of subordinates. But whenever management acts this way, it should be fully aware that it may be preparing the way for costly resistance later on.

MAKING CHANGES TENTATIVE

When the individuals concerned are permitted to participate in making the final decision on whether or not to accept a change, it is sometimes useful to ask the group to go along with the change on a tentative, trial basis at first. This approach has two advantages:

1. It enables employees to test their own reactions to the new situation, and provides them with more facts on which to base their decision.

2. It helps to "unfreeze" their attitudes and encourages them to think objectively about the proposed change. A change introduced on a trial basis is less threatening and generates less resistance.

---

[12] This is not the place to enter into a full discussion of the techniques of collective bargaining. We might observe, though, that in dealing with unions it is rarely wise to adopt a take-it-or-leave-it attitude. In fact, if the union is to survive politically it must win some sort of "concession." Management may sometimes adopt an extreme position at first, just to give the union a chance to win an apparent victory. Also, management should not insist that the union give immediate answers to its proposals; rather, it should give the union leadership a chance to consult with its rank-and-file membership.

However, where the individuals concerned do not participate in making the final decision, tentative changes may be unwise. They prolong the period of uncertainty and tension and the length of time in which the group is supervised closely. And there is always the chance that employees will "participate" in the final decision—by resisting it or sabotaging it.

HANDLING SYMBOLS

How can management minimize resistance when it becomes necessary to change or eliminate some feature that has acquired symbolic meaning? First, management should indicate clearly that changing the symbol is not the same as attacking the values for which the symbol stands. Thus in switching from parchment paper for insurance policies (see case on p. 268), the sales manager might emphasize that the change will help create the modern, up-to-date atmosphere that customers of the Integrity Company expect.

Sometimes it is possible to replace one symbol with another: when a new state is added to the Union the old flag is discarded, but a new one takes its place. Similarly, if it becomes necessary to move the foremen's cars from the front to the rear parking lot, special areas might be reserved for them, marked with special signs.

> We have been told of an interesting example of this technique used by the administrative staff of a hospital.[13] Members of the resident medical staff often had guests in the hospital cafeteria for Sunday dinner. Due to crowded conditions they often found it impossible to find a whole table for themselves. They had the cafeteria director place a sign on a group of tables: "Reserved for Medical Staff." Immediately several other high-status groups asked for similar consideration. To avoid the inflexibility and embarrassment that would arise if a majority of tables were specially reserved, the director changed the notices to read: "Medical Staff Are Requested to Use These Tables." This request could be justified on the grounds that it would make doctors easier to reach in case of emergency calls—and also minimized the feeling that this was an additional symbol of the doctors' higher status.

SLOW CHANGE OR QUICK?

Should change be introduced slowly or quickly? The answer is not clear. Many people believe in "making haste slowly," on the grounds that slow changes are less disruptive than fast changes and provide greater opportunity for adjustment. Given time, the new will blend with the old—as, for example, in the British constitution.

Fast changes, if forced on people, may lead to violent resistance, and the resulting shock may disrupt the entire organization. There may be some resistance to slow change, but it will be less intense at any given time. Indeed,

---

[13] We are indebted to Dr. Robert Wilson for this case.

if the change is introduced slowly enough, it may not even be perceived—
or else the organization may become accustomed to constant, gradual change
as a natural process, as the fashion industry has.

Slow change entails certain dangers of its own, however. Every change
has widespread ramifications, and it is bound to be less effective if it is just
patched onto the existing set of practices. In introducing change it is far
better for management to consciously re-examine the entire process to determine what adjustments should be made. Unfortunately, however, when
management introduces slow change this sort of total re-evaluation is rarely
made (often because management wants to avoid "trouble"), and practices
are continued that are no longer appropriate to the changed situation.

> The story is told of how during World War II the British army ordered
> a time study of their standard procedure for firing artillery.[14] Most of the
> operation seemed efficient enough, except that just before the gun went off
> two men came to attention. When the time-study man asked why, he was
> told, "We've always done that." Only after considerable research did he
> discover that the original purpose was to keep the horses from jumping.

When change is so gradual that people do not recognize that it has occurred,
they may well continue to behave in a way that was appropriate only to the
old situation.

> We observed this tendency in a factory where management sought to
> strengthen the power of the foreman. Formerly the set-up men were the
> ones who gave orders to the operators; the foreman had little direct con-
> tact with his men, concerning himself chiefly with over-all administration.
> It was decided to make this change gradually, "so they won't realize what
> is happening," and the foreman began giving all the orders on his own and
> to refuse to support the set-up men's decisions.
>
> As time passed, both the set-up men and the operators became increas-
> ingly confused. The set-up men tried desperately to maintain their tradi-
> tional prestige and resisted the foreman every inch of the way. They met
> each new slight to their authority with growing indignation. Production
> gradually slumped until the foreman himself gave in and began once more
> to channel his orders through the set-up men.

If change is to be made slowly, management would be wise to give everyone concerned an over-all picture of what is eventually intended. Otherwise
employees will begin to wonder, "Something is happening, but we don't
know what," and exaggerated fears will arise about where the change is
leading.

Actually, if employees fully understand and accept the change, there is less
reason not to make the change rapidly. Adjustment is required only once,
and there is less likelihood of anachronistic holdovers from a former period.

---

[14] Elting Morison, "A Case Study of Innovations," George Shultz and John R. Coleman, eds., *Labor Problems: Cases and Readings,* 2nd ed. (New York: McGraw-Hill,
1959), p. 264.

Fast change eliminates the need for the constant series of adjustments which are required by slow change and which leave the organization in an endless state of turmoil.

OTHER TECHNIQUES

One of the most common and most difficult problems in introducing change is that of bringing in a new manager to head up an existing department in an established company. Ordinarily, if the old manager has been well liked, the new one will have two strikes against him, for none of the employees will believe that he can be as good as the old one. At the outset, everyone wonders what changes the new man will make. Thus his most inconsequential acts are carefully examined for clues to his future policy, and may be exaggerated into forebodings of future disasters. His subordinates may resent him as an outsider and prepare themselves to reject everything he does.

Let us examine this problem and how it was handled in a specific situation; our example will illustrate several techniques that may be helpful in introducing change in a wide variety of situations. W. F. Whyte describes how a new supervisor was introduced into a large restaurant: [15]

> Since the old supervisor had developed warm relations with her subordinates, the restaurant manager was afraid that her departure might have a bad effect on the morale of the whole organization. Consequently he prepared the way for her successor with great care. First, he discussed the problem of a replacement with both the old supervisor and the chef, her chief assistant. The chef proposed a candidate for the job; though this candidate had to be rejected, the reasons for the rejection were fully explained to the chef.
>
> When the new supervisor was finally selected, she was introduced to her subordinates at a general meeting. The manager announced that the old supervisor was leaving and went on to say how much she meant to the restaurant. The old supervisor spoke with great emotion about how sorry she would be to leave her associates. Then she introduced the new supervisor, extolled her virtues, and asked her employees to show the new woman the same cooperation they had given to herself. Finally, the new supervisor promised to do her best to follow in her predecessor's footsteps.
>
> For the next few days the new supervisor followed the old one around, getting to know people and trying to learn the supervisor's routine and methods of dealing with people. On the old supervisor's last day, the whole kitchen staff gave her a farewell party.
>
> Although the new supervisor decided that she would eventually make certain changes in the operation, she spent her first few weeks trying to follow the human-relations pattern established by her predecessor. Only after she was fully accepted by the group did she begin making changes.

---

[15] Adapted from *Human Relations in the Restaurant Industry* (New York: McGraw-Hill, 1948), pp. 319-331.

What techniques were used here to win acceptance for the new supervisor? How might these techniques be used in other situations?

Consultation   The manager respected the key position of the chef in the informal organization and requested his opinion on the change. When he felt the chef's opinions had to be rejected, he was careful to explain why.

Other organizations may use similar techniques to involve key subordinates in the selection process and thus substantially increase their acceptance of the final decision. Universities, for instance, typically appoint faculty members to the committees that choose presidents or deans. Earlier we mentioned that some companies are using sociometric choice as a helpful technique in choosing supervisors.

Induction   The old supervisor was careful to introduce the new supervisor to all key personnel and to explain the customs of the organization. Doubtless this did much to save the new supervisor from making social *faux pas,* to help integrate her into the social pattern of the organization, and to minimize the amount of disruption caused by the change in command.

Ceremony   The meeting at which the new supervisor was introduced, and the farewell party for the old supervisor, both served a ceremonial function. They formalized the fact of change and helped the old supervisor pass on some of her prestige to the new.

There is a tendency in our cynical society to play down the importance of ceremony. Yet it is no coincidence that throughout history every strong, stable institution—be it church, state, university, or company—has been noted for the ceremonies by which it helped focus individual loyalty on the organization as a whole.

Ceremonies are particularly important in time of change. Take, for example, the traditional ceremonies observed at the crucial moments of our life: birth, graduation, marriage, and death. The presence of relatives and friends and the giving of gifts and flowers help symbolize friendship and the unity of families. By involving ourselves in the formalized rites of the ceremony, we somehow protect ourselves from some of the fears and pains of moving from one stage of life to another. The heightened emotional atmosphere helps prepare individuals for major changes in their relationships with others. Indeed, we have learned to expect really important changes to occur in this way.

Probably more important, the use of ceremony is a public proclamation that in spite of apparent change the basic values remain the same; the new pays obeisance to the old. The English cry, "The King is dead; Long live the King." The French say, "Plus ça change, plus c'est la même chose." In primitive countries, oil companies may hire medicine men to sprinkle holy incense on new oil wells—thus showing their willingness to come to terms with the older culture.

Avoiding change until acceptance is assured   The new supervisor avoided making changes until she had developed informal, social relations with her subordinates. This is in conflict with the old adage that a new broom should sweep clean—or that a new manager should make all his changes at once. True, as we suggested earlier, it is sometimes (but certainly not always) desirable to complete change quickly rather than to let it drag on. Even so, it is usually wise for a new manager to wait before taking action until he knows more about the organization and the people with whom he is dealing.

In earlier chapters we distinguished between the supervisor's formal and informal authority, pointing out that the first arises from his official position, the second from the respect accorded his technical and leadership skills. The man who has both informal and formal authority can win acceptance of his ideas more easily. But the new manager has only formal authority and in effect must force his ideas on his subordinates. After a few months he begins to accumulate informal authority; as he becomes trusted as an individual, his ideas meet with less resistance.

Building on the past   In the restaurant case cited above, the new supervisor made it clear that she had no intention of throwing out past practices wholesale. As anthropologists and missionaries long ago discovered, it pays to learn the customs of the people with whom one works, particularly their ceremonies, symbols, and expected ways of doing things. Changes can be introduced more easily if an adjustment is made to the past. There are times, of course, when one may wish to cast out all the old patterns of behavior and start completely from scratch. However, in doing this one also casts out the good with the bad, the baby with the bath.

Conclusion

The normal tendency of most managers is to ignore the widespread existence of resistance to change. They fail to recognize that even a seemingly small change may have profound ramifications. Yet people resist change even when it is apparently in their own interest. They have vested interests in the old ways; they fear the uncertainties of the new. They give strange meanings to change, and dislike having their traditional customs, status, and symbols violated. People seldom resist change just to be stubborn; they resist it because it hurts them—economically, psychologically, or socially.

Management often regards resistance as essentially irrational, forgetting that apparently irrational attitudes or behavior may be symptoms of deep-seated problems. The first step in dealing with resistance is to bring the real problems out in the open, to establish genuine two-way communication. Only by learning the genuine causes of resistance can management deal intelligently with them. Often resistance can be successfully handled through the skillful use of economic rewards, bargaining, or group decision-making. At times, however, management's best efforts may fail and it may be necessary to resort to the exercise of authority or the imposition of discipline.

Problem I

A small, fashionable store with long-service employees has always catered to the wealthy classes. Traditionally it has closed at 5:00 P.M., but a new manager is considering whether it might be more profitable to stay open two nights a week until 9:00.

He is concerned about how he would distribute evening work, particularly since each salesclerk has her own clientele. Also, he is far from sure whether any of his present customers would prefer to come in during the evening.

1. Advise him on what he should do about the employee-relations aspect of his projected change. In particular, discuss why the employees might resist this change and what might be done to overcome their resistance.

Problem II

You have recently been hired by the Winspear Corporation as Marketing Research Director with instructions to rejuvenate the entire research program. When your predecessor started the program 30 years ago, he had advanced ideas, but in the years prior to his retirement he seemed to slow down both physically and mentally. He handled a few projects himself, but the rest of the staff (12 employees) gradually began to look for guidance to Heath Bailey, Assistant Marketing Research Director. Bailey ran the department in a competent but unimaginative manner.

Your talk with your new subordinates indicate that they are quite capable, and in general get along together well. However, two of the youngest men in the department, Bob Hertel and Jim Delevan, seem restless and anxious to try out new ideas.

At present Bailey handles all administrative matters himself. Following the practice developed under your predecessor, the staff reports to him, he hands out assignments, makes decisions, and then at long intervals tells you what he has done.

By now you have a number of research projects that you would like your research staff to begin. Some are quite different from anything the staff has done before, and several require a good deal of travel—which is also new.

1. Are the human relations in this department sound?
2. Should you try to change Bailey's key position in the organization? Why? How would you go about making the change?
3. What sort of relationship would you like to develop between yourself, Bailey, and the rest of the staff?
4. How should you handle Hertel and Delevan?
5. How do you intend to introduce the new research programs?

We have purposely left discipline to the end of this part so that we could discuss other problems first. Discipline is required only when all other measures have failed. Suppose you have clearly instructed an employee on his duties, have listened to his problems, have tried to help him to do better, and have tactfully criticized his performance—yet he still fails to meet standards. Then what? Then, reluctantly, you are forced to resort to discipline.

But can discipline be made consistent with what we have said about general supervision? We think it can.

In the first place the best discipline is self-discipline, the normal human tendency to do one's share and to live up to the rules of the game. Once people understand what is required of them, they can *usually* be counted on to do their job effectively and with good cheer. Yet some people (perhaps most of us) find that the possibility of discipline lurking in the background helps our "better selves" win out over our "lazier selves." As one man put it: [1]

[1] Daniel M. Colyer, "The Good Foreman—As His Men See Him," *Personnel,* Vol. 28 (September 1951), p. 142.

13

Discipline

> If you can get away with small things you keep trying to get away with bigger and bigger things until, finally, you are caught and you are in trouble. Just for example, if you can sneak nuts and bolts out of the plant in your lunch box, you start trying to take spare parts and accessories out next. . . . It's much better if you know that they are going to check your lunch box every night and you can't even take out the smallest thing. Then . . . you don't get into bad habits.

Ordinarily, if employees feel that the rules by which they are governed are reasonable, they will observe them without question. That is to say, they will respect the rules not because they fear punishment, but because they believe in doing things the *right* way. Coming to work on time; following the supervisor's instructions; avoiding fighting, drinking, and stealing at work; punching the time clock—all these are accepted by a majority of workers as reasonable rules, as necessary conditions of work.

When new rules are introduced, management must make every effort to convince employees of their reasonableness and legitimacy.[2] For instance, as we mentioned in Chapter 8, management should avoid introducing too many rules or rules that seem unrelated to doing the job at hand. No organization would survive if its only means of winning acceptance of correct procedures was to discipline all violators. Our disastrous experience with Prohibition shows the futility of trying to enforce a law that the majority feels to be unreasonable.

In other words, management should try to establish what has been called "positive discipline," an atmosphere in which subordinates willingly abide by rules which they consider fair. In such an atmosphere the group may well exert social pressure on wrong-doers and reduce the need for the "negative" punitive discipline discussed in this chapter.

Standards accepted by the group are frequently enforced by the group. (See for example our story on page 168 of how machinists enforced the rule against long-sleeved shirts.) Still it is useful for management to back up the group when it is seeking the same objectives as management. The following quotation from a worker on an automobile assembly line illustrates a common feeling:

> "If a man is late all the time, the guys just try to avoid him. They have no use for a guy like this. He just makes it hard for us all because the utility man [the substitute for all jobs on the lines] cannot do the work as well as the regular man, and so we have to work harder just to keep the work up. Of course, if a guy is just trying to give a smart aleck foreman a hard time, we are all for him. . . . But if the fellow is just a slacker, the foreman should straighten the man out for the sake of everybody."[3]

---

[2] One of the problems of introducing new industries into underdeveloped areas is that the new industrial employee, fresh from the farm, has no conception of factory "etiquette." In India, for example, employers find it difficult to teach employees that they have to report to work regularly.

[3] Colyer, *op. cit.*, p. 143.

A plant superintendent told us this story:

> "The union has been complaining about that girl too. She's so pregnant she can't do her work and they say she's holding everybody else up. I guess I've got to tell her to take maternity leave."

Most employees are tolerant when a man has an occasional off day, provided he does his part the rest of the time. But they resent seeing someone else "get away with murder" while they are doing a full day's work. As one man said:

> "[Management] should be able to trust men, not have to watch them all the time. But you don't like to do your best and work hard while the other guy goofs off, loafs, and is always "busy" while you swing the job. It burns you." [4]

In fact, unless the culprit is disciplined the rest of the group may adjust to his low level of performance.

Thus consistent proof that all rules are being enforced serves to strengthen the informal group's efforts at correction. Clearly, good supervisory practices will vastly reduce the need for discipline. But if employees realize that infractions of rules will be disciplined, good supervision will become even better.

Types of Discipline

How severe should the penalty for wrong-doing be? In recent years many companies have provided what is called "progressive" or "corrective" discipline, which calls for increasingly severe penalties each time a man is disciplined. Except for very serious wrong-doings, an employee is rarely discharged for a first offense. This is particularly true if the firm is unionized, since arbitrators insist that a man be given a second chance. Ordinarily, the sequence of penalties under "progressive" discipline is as follows:

1. Oral warning.
2. Written warning.
3. Disciplinary layoff.
4. Discharge.
5. demotion

Oral warnings, as a form of correction, were discussed in Chapter 7. When a man fails to maintain standards, or has broken a rule, a clear oral warning that repetition may eventually call for discipline is in order. The supervisor should, of course, concentrate on helping the subordinate figure out ways to prevent his troubles from recurring.

Written warnings are the first formal stage of progressive discipline. Psychologically, perhaps, they are not different from oral warnings, but they are made part of the employee's record—and they can be presented as evi-

---

[4] *Ibid.*

dence if more serious penalties follow or if the case is taken to arbitration. Written warnings, sometimes called "pink slips," are often prepared in four copies—one each for the foreman, steward, personnel department, and the disciplined individual.

Disciplinary layoffs (to be distinguished from layoffs caused by lack of work) are next in severity. Usually they are for several days or weeks; layoffs in excess of a month are uncommon. Some companies skip this stage of discipline altogether, particularly when it is hard to find a trained replacement on the grounds that it is too cumbersome to replace a man for just a few weeks. Moreover, the disciplined employee is likely to return from his layoff in an even nastier mood than when he left. There are some employees who pay little attention to oral warnings, but to whom actual punishment, such as loss of income, is convincing proof that the company means business. For them a layoff may be the shock that brings them back to their sense of responsibility.

Discharge remains the ultimate penalty, and one that is being used less and less commonly. The expense of training a new employee makes the loss of an experienced man very costly to the company, and the hardships that face a man who has been discharged make arbitrators and unions increasingly unwilling to permit its use. Many arbitrators, indeed, refer to discharge as "industrial capital punishment"—and for good reason.

> Consider the impact of a discharge on a man of say 55, with 30 years' seniority. In the first place, he may lose pension rights worth $5,000 or more, plus substantial vacation benefits. Few high-paying employers would be willing to hire a man of his age, especially after they check his references and discover his discharge. Certainly he can expect less pay than he was getting from the job to which his 30 years' service had carried him. Further, as a low-seniority man, he is now fully susceptible to all the winds of economic misfortune. Assuming he loses $1.00 an hour for the rest of his life, his financial loss may be as high as $50,000.

No wonder one arbitrator told us: "I am very reluctant to let a man be fired unless I feel the company's grounds are justified, both morally and legally. I think the employee should have every chance to mend his ways." Faced with this attitude among arbitrators, companies are being forced to place greater emphasis on their selection and training programs. Workers who are discharged today are often individuals who simply don't care for their jobs, younger employees with no family responsibilities, or persons with severe behavior problems, such as alcoholics or psychotics.

Because of the serious implications of discharge in the modern economy, some companies authorize their foremen only to "suspend" employees for a five-day period, and reserve to higher management the final decision on whether they are to be discharged.

Demotion is seldom used as a disciplinary measure; it is ordinarily re-served for situations in which an employee has been mistakenly promoted or is no longer able to perform his job. As a disciplinary measure, demotion has a number of disadvantages. Losing pay over a period of time is a long, slow form of constant humiliation, as compared with the sharp slap of a layoff. Also, if a company is going to retain a trained man in any capacity, it makes more sense to use his highest skill.

The "Hot-Stove Rule"

Inflicting discipline puts the supervisor in a dilemma. How can he expect his subordinates to continue to regard him as a source of help, when discipline is by nature painful? Can he impose discipline without generating resentment? We think so—through what Douglas McGregor calls the "hot-stove rule." This rule draws an analogy between touching a hot stove and undergoing discipline. When you touch a hot stove your discipline is *immediate, with warning, consistent, and impersonal.*

Let's look at these four characteristics as applied to discipline. When you burn your hand you are angry with yourself. Sometimes you are angry with the stove too, but not for long. You learn your lesson quickly, because:

1. The burn was *immediate.* There is no question of cause and effect.

2. You had *warning.* Particularly if the stove was red hot, you knew what would happen if you touched it.

3. The discipline was *consistent.* Every time you touch the stove you are burned.

4. The discipline is *impersonal.* Whoever touches the stove is burned, no matter who he is. Further, he is burned not because of who he is, but because he touched the stove.

In short, the act and the discipline seem almost one. You are disciplined not because you are bad, but because you have committed a particular act. The discipline is directed against the act, not against the person. There will still be resentment against the source of the discipline, but the more automatic the discipline becomes, the more this resentment is reduced. As one worker put it:

> "I really had it coming to me. I was looking for trouble. I can't blame the foreman. His job was to enforce the rules. That's what he is paid for."

Put another way, "the purpose of discipline should be to obtain compliance with established rules of conduct—that is, to correct improper conduct. It should not be punitive in nature, that is, to discipline solely for the purpose of getting even with the employee." [5]

Let us see how the "hot-stove rule" works out in actual practice.

---

[5] H. D. Garrett, *Building a Responsible Work Force* (Ann Arbor, Mich.: Bureau of Industrial Relations, University of Michigan, 1955, multilith).

IMMEDIACY OF DISCIPLINE

The supervisor should begin the disciplinary process as soon as possible after he notices a violation of the rules. (Of course, if he has lost his temper he should wait until he has cooled down.) Note what happens if he delays action:

> Joe Jones has a bad tardiness record. He comes in a half-hour late, but thinks the foreman hasn't noticed it. By noon, Joe decides he has nothing to worry about.
> The supervisor *has* noticed it, but he is busy on another problem and he figures it might be a good idea to let Joe "stew awhile." Late in the afternoon, just before closing time, he calls Joe into the office to give him a two-day layoff.

Naturally, Joe feels he has been treated unfairly and resents both the discipline and the foreman. He assumes the supervisor has been saving his grudge instead of "having it out like a man." In the future, he will never feel secure with the supervisor and will always wonder, "What's he going to pull on me next? Why does he have to play this cat-and-mouse game with me?"

Further, the more quickly the discipline follows the offense, the more likely the offending person will be to associate the discipline with the offense rather than with the person imposing the discipline—that is, the more automatic the discipline will seem.

Of course, immediate discipline does not mean that a man should be judged without full investigation. But it does mean that the supervisor should take notice of the offense as soon as possible and push the investigation with all due speed.

> For instance, a man comes in to work after two days' absence. According to your records, he never called in to report sick, and, therefore, he is subject to discipline. "Immediate discipline" requires that you call him into your office for an explanation as soon as he gets to work. However, if he claims he was unconscious under a doctor's care during this period, you obviously are not going to discipline him until you have a chance to investigate. Even here you should push your investigation as rapidly as possible.

When the facts of the case are not clear, and yet immediate action is necessary, many companies provide for suspension. The employee is told that he is "suspended" and that he will be informed later about what discipline will be imposed. This technique may be used where tempers are so high that calm appraisal is impossible, or where the guilt is obvious but the amount of penalty can be determined only after further investigation. Suspension also makes possible consultation among various levels of management before the final penalty is determined. Since suspension is a form of layoff, however, it should not be used unless the offense calls for at least a layoff. If the suspension is longer than is justified by the offense, arbitrators will usually order back-pay.

FOREWARNING

If discipline is to be accepted without resentment, both the man who is being disciplined and his fellow workers must regard it as fair. And *unexpected* discipline is almost universally considered unfair. This means that (1) there must be clear warning that a given offense will lead to discipline, and (2) there must be clear warning of the amount of discipline that will be imposed for a given offense.

Assume that a rule has been posted for several months but that the supervisor has never disciplined anyone who violated it. Clearly, no one expects that the rule will be enforced in the future either. Now the supervisor grabs one man and makes an example of him. The victim might well cry, "Why me?" Discipline without warning violates the workers' expectations of fair supervision.[6] Further, if the case were taken to arbitration the company might lose.

Does this mean that once an order is laxly enforced the company can never again enforce it? Perhaps, for the arbitrator may rule that a *precedent* of no enforcement has been established. If, however, there has been at last some enforcement of the rule (that is, if the company has not given clear evidence of its acquiesence to non-enforcement), the company can begin strict enforcement once it has issued clear warning of the change in policy.

> Suppose, for instance, the company has been very lax in requiring men to be at work on time. Before starting to penalize tardy workers, the company should give clear warning that it is tightening up on enforcement. The foreman might call the men together and, after appropriate discussion and explanation, say "From now on I'll expect you to come to work on time. Anyone who is more than five minutes late without adequate excuse will receive a written warning. If you receive more than two written warnings in any 30-day period, you will get a day's layoff."

Warning is also provided in what we have referred to as "progressive discipline." The first time a man commits an offense (unless it is a major one), he receives a minor penalty plus a warning that repetition will bring more serious discipline. The minor penalty is particularly effective with those who are not much impressed by words, for it indicates that management really means what it says. Continued infractions bring more severe penalties. Yet, except where a major offense, such as stealing, or assaulting the foreman, is involved, there is strong expectation among other workers that the culprit will get a second chance.[7]

---

[6] See Alvin Gouldner, *Patterns of Bureaucracy* (Glencoe, Ill.: Free Press, 1954), p. 170.
[7] *Ibid.*

We have already discussed the need for effective communications within the organization. Once more, let us emphasize management's responsibility to make sure that all employees really know what the rules are and how they are to be enforced. A failure to communicate such information deprives employees of clear warning. A communications program might include, among other things, the following:

1. Upon induction, the immediate supervisor can explain the rules to all new employees, perhaps with the help of the personnel department.

2. Notices can be posted on the bulletin board, and handbooks distributed to employees.

3. In some cases, lists of penalties can be included in the union contract.

4. When rules are changed, the immediate supervisor can call a group meeting or notify individuals informally.

5. When a rule is about to be violated, or actually is violated (provided it is a minor, first offense), the supervisor can issue an informal warning.

Many arbitrators, interpreting the legal meaning of the contract, might say that posting a notice on a bulletin board constitutes clear warning. But from the point of view of human relations, this is not enough. Written communications should be supplemented by oral communications. The better job management does of explaining a new rule and why it is necessary, the easier it will be to enforce it—simply because workers will be more likely to accept it as reasonable. Regardless of the legal requirements of arbitration, management is clearly to blame if the men unwittingly violate rules because they don't know what is expected of them. Good communications pay off by significantly reducing the amount of discipline that must be imposed.

CONSISTENCY

If two men commit the same offense and one man is more severely disciplined than the other, naturally there will be cries of favoritism. One of the quickest ways for a supervisor to lose the respect of his subordinates and to lower the morale of the work group is to impose discipline in a whimsical, inconsistent way. Consistent discipline is considered fairer and is far more likely to be accepted by the workers involved. Indeed, consistency is basic to good human relations.

Management must always keep in mind the educational function of discipline (and also of non-discipline). Consistent discipline helps to set limits (that is, to inform employees what they can and cannot do); inconsistent discipline inevitably leads to confusion and uncertainty.

Every individual wants to know the limits of permissible behavior, and one way to establish these limits clearly and dramatically is to punish those who exceed them. We all tend to be unhappy and insecure in a situation where we are not sure what is expected of us. Child psychologists, for instance, have learned that children are not necessarily happier when they are given absolute freedom. One reason they get into so much mischief is that they are trying to find out how much they can get away with, at what point Daddy will spank. Grown-ups are the same way. They want to know "How far can I go? What can I do? What can't I do?"

Consistent discipline, however, is essential if the work environment is to be kept stable. When some rules are permitted to go unenforced, employees may either (1) decide to ignore all rules, or (2) bcome confused about what is really required of them.

> Whenever we are speeding on the highway, we must feel this same sort of anxiety. After all, we are breaking the written rule; on the other hand, it isn't often enforced. Maybe this is a place, or a set of policemen who don't take the rule seriously, and we can speed a little. But still there is a lurking insecurity, because the police may, at any time, decide to enforce this particular rule.[8]

For instance, one day the boss lets Mary, his secretary, get by with handing in a report that is full of erasures. The next day he bawls her out for a sloppy report that is actually less sloppy than the previous day's. Under the circumstances, it is hard for Mary to know what standards are expected of her. She may well decide that the discipline has nothing to do with her act and "learn" only that the boss has a personal grudge against her. Not only won't she learn the rules, but she will be resentful as well.

Consistency is hard to maintain. Some people we like—others we don't. Sometimes we see a rule violation as a personal insult, a direct challenge to our authority. Other times, prompted by our natural instinct to be understanding and kindhearted, we are tempted to tell the rule-breaker, "Well, I'm going to let it go this time, but don't do it again."

Dissatisfaction may arise over excessive leniency as well as over excessive harshness.

> The office had a rather strictly enforced rule that employees could not leave without permission until the end of the work day. Braden was caught by his supervisor in the hall heading for the exit about ten minutes before quitting time. Upon review the normal penalty of a one-week layoff was suspended because the following week was Christmas. However, a petition was signed by the other employees protesting this decision as showing favoritism and thus being discriminatory! They felt that since he was obviously guilty, he should receive the same penalty others had received.

One source of inconsistency is management's tendency to be stricter in slack times and to ignore rule violations when manpower is short.

> Crawford had a terrible absenteeism record. He missed work for two days without a legitimate excuse. Normally, given his record, his offense would justify an immediate two-week layoff. However, Crawford's services

---

[8] Mason Haire, *Psychology in Management* (New York: McGraw-Hill, 1956), p. 60.

were badly needed on a rush job. No one else could take his place. So the supervisor added the incident to Crawford's personnel record and warned him that a further violation would lead to discharge.

Keeping Crawford on solved the immediate problem of maintaining production. But the long-term effects might have been more serious. What did Crawford and the other workers learn from this incident? One of several things: (1) the absentee rule was not to be enforced strictly, (2) the supervisor was playing favorites, or (3) strict discipline in time of slack work was merely a dodge to get around the seniority provisions of the contract. In any case, the employees' respect and trust for their supervisor probably nose-dived.

Often a supervisor finds it easier to transfer a problem employee to another department than to face the hard task of disciplining him. In one case a man who had consistently failed to live up to plant rules had been transferred eleven times without any record of disciplinary action appearing in his personnel folder. This employee could hardly be blamed for not knowing what standards of behavior were expected of him. No one had taken the trouble either to help salvage him or to rid the company of a constant expense.

Consistency in enforcing discipline may be expensive in terms of lost production, but inconsistency may be even more so. Although the evidence is incomplete, it would appear that automobile plants which are most hesitant about enforcing rules against wildcat strikes (work stoppages not officially authorized by the union) have had the worst record of such strikes. If a whole department goes on strike, it may be very costly to discipline everyone. Not only will the company lose the production of that department, but the men in other departments may walk out in sympathy.

Wildcat strikes are set off by a variety of causes (frustration with the work or slow handling of grievances, for instance). Obviously it is better to eliminate the causes than to punish the symptoms.[9] Still, if no discipline is imposed, the men "learn" that they can engage in such strikes with impunity. Companies that have been willing to sustain the short-run costs of low production have found that wildcat strikes have decreased over a period of time. Further, when management takes a firm stand, the union finds it easier to discourage its members from taking matters into their own hands. Many union leaders have told us candidly that they find it hard to observe the "no-strike" provisions of their contracts when management doesn't take the initiative in disciplining violators. "We can't be more against strikes than management."

Consider another problem involving consistency of discipline. We have heard foremen say, "I can only catch a small proportion of the rule violators,

---

[9] Indeed if workers are prevented from wildcatting they may release their aggressions in other ways—through slowdowns and absenteeism, for example.

but those I catch I punish severely." Is this fair? Many men consider it a form of "Russian roulette." Adventurous souls may make a game of this procedure and try to see how much they can get away with. Furthermore, scattered instances of discipline hardly constitute clear warning.

If a rule is on the books, the supervisor should make an effort to enforce it (and enforce it uniformly). If he finds it impossible to do so, the rule may have to be revised or dropped altogether. Sloppy enforcement of one rule encourages employees to disregard other rules.

In some situations, of course, 100 per cent consistency is impossible. For instance, unless everyone is searched as he leaves the plant, stealing may be impossible to stamp out. However, such searches are expensive and deeply resented by employees. The company may have to rely on stern punishment of anyone who is accidentally caught stealing. Since workers generally accept anti-stealing rules as reasonable, there will be little resentment of this policy, inconsistent though it seems.

Does consistency require that the penalty should be determined entirely by the offense, regardless of the personal history and background of the person who committed it? Of course not. We have already said that it is common industrial practice to be more lenient on first offenses. Arbitrators are reluctant to let "industrial capital punishment" be imposed on a man unless a reasonable effort has been made to rehabilitate him. Certainly each case should be considered on its own merits. As a top industrial-relations executive put it:

> There is no precise mechanical formula. . . . Each instance of misconduct must be viewed . . . individually. . . . This, of course, is a matter of judgment, but . . . four principal factors should be taken into consideration . . . first, the seriousness and circumstances of the particular offense; second, the past conduct record of the employee and his length of service; third, the lapse of time since his last misconduct for which disciplinary action was taken; and fourth, the plant practice in similar cases.[10]

For example, three employees are caught gambling. One has been disciplined for the same offense before, the other two have not. The first man is discharged, the other two are given written warnings. This, we would argue, is being consistent, not inconsistent as it may first appear. Although each case should be considered on its own merits, the over-all disciplinary program must be kept consistent. Certainly if two individuals with the same personal histories commit the same offense, they should be treated equally.

How long should a rule violation be held against an employee? Current management practice tends toward disregarding offenses committed more than a year or two ago. Thus an employee with a poor absenteeism record would start afresh if he maintained a good attendance record for a year.

---

[10] Garrett, *op. cit.*, p. 5.

The rules of fair warning and consistency require that discipline be neither greater nor less than expected. If the degree of discipline comes as a surprise, the company may have failed to give adequate warning; if it is less than expected, the company will have difficulty in gaining acceptance of a more serious penalty in the future. When there is uncertainty and misunderstanding as to whether the offense is to be punished and how much the punishment is to be, then the policy is inconsistent. If the rule-breaker sees the supervisor as wielding arbitrary discretion, then he may blame the supervisor for his discipline rather than himself.

There has been considerable discussion in industrial-relations circles about whether or not good personnel policy requires the posting of all rules and the setting of standard penalties for violations. For example: "Rough-house: First offense, warning. Second offense, one-day layoff. Third offense, one-week layoff. Fourth offense, discharge."

Those who favor such lists argue that they provide effective warning and greater consistency. Those who oppose them feel that they make it harder for management to distinguish between various degrees of guilt. Mandatory discharge for stealing would mean that the employee who is seen taking a box of safety clips would receive the same penalty as one who was caught robbing the safe. One company with a rigid series of penalties was obliged to impose only a two-week layoff on an employee who had doctored his output records—this was the standard penalty for inaccurately reporting production figures. Actually, the employee had been doctoring his records for years and had received hundreds of dollars in unearned incentive payments as a result. Had the company not set up a specific penalty in the rule book, it could have imposed a far more severe penalty.

Some companies insist that unless they maintain a uniform list of penalties they are unable to justify discipline to the union. Others say that such lists enable the union to force the company into excessively legalistic decisions on discipline. For instance, if the company had no specific rule against loafing, legally it couldn't discipline a man no matter how lazy he was.

IMPERSONALITY

We have said that a good supervisor encourages his subordinates to express themselves freely and tries to play down differences in status. He tries to build up the feeling that he and the worker are on the same team. Doesn't the imposition of discipline seriously endanger this relationship? It may. In fact, the disciplined employee might easily murmur, "That so-and-so. I thought he was my friend. I'd rather have a foreman who wasn't such a hypocrite and then you'd know where you stand."

It is not easy to impose discipline without causing the person disciplined to feel resentful and aggressive. But the supervisor can minimize the danger to the relationship by imposing discipline in as impersonal a way as possible. Once more, "It ain't what you do but the way that you do it."

> Discipline is most effective and has least negative effect on individuals, if the individual feels that his behavior at the particular moment is the only thing being criticized and not his total personality.[11]

In its opening stages, the disciplinary interview is not much different from most other forms of interview. First, state the problem as you see it; then encourage the subordinate to state his point of view. Let him tell you his story. Ask *how* it happened, not *why*. Give him every chance to explain himself. Try to avoid this sort of exchange:

> *Foreman:* Late again, I see. Didn't I tell you yesterday, if you were late once more this month, I'd give you a layoff. . . .
> *Employee:* But . . .
> *Foreman:* (ignoring him) Well, you've had your last chance. You better go home.
> *Employee:* But I did get here on time—only the superintendent called me in to his office to discuss the Savings Bond drive.

Instead, do your best to draw the man out and try to discover the real story. Use the interview technique. Don't ask him for his excuse, but concentrate on the *basic* reasons for his rule violation. Is he having trouble at home? Has he been poorly instructed on the job? Has he lost his motivation? Why? (Of course, you should have asked yourself some of these questions long before the employee's misconduct led to discipline.)

Sometimes your interview will give you all the facts you need. In other cases you may need to investigate further, perhaps by checking with other members of management. Avoid making a decision until you have the whole story, but reach your decision as soon as possible.

Once you have decided what discipline is appropriate, impose it quietly and impersonally. For example, suppose in an absenteeism case that the employee shows general irresponsibility, and that his only excuse for his latest tardiness was that he forgot to set his alarm clock.

> *Supervisor:* Well, I can see how it happened. But from the company's point of view, not setting your alarm clock is not an adequate excuse, particularly since this has happened three times this month.
>
> (Pause—in which to listen to objections.)
>
> You have already received two written warnings this month and the rules now require that you receive a day's layoff.
>
> (Pause—again for objections.)
>
> Jim, you've got to figure out a way to get here on time. You do a fine job when you are here, but the rule is that if this occurs again within 30 days you will receive a week's layoff and if it occurs again you will lose your job. I don't want this to happen. Now what can be done about it?"

[11] Chris Argyris, *Executive Leadership* (New York: Harpers, 1953), p. xiii.

(Then discuss positive means of avoiding trouble in the future. Try to get him to suggest a workable plan—or suggest one yourself. Even if this doesn't work, end with:)

Jim, will you try harder to get here on time in the future?

(The answer is bound to be "yes" and you have, for what it is worth, a positive end to the interview and a positive commitment to do something.)

Note that the discipline here has been imposed impersonally and the employee has been given every chance to express his objections. After imposing discipline the supervisor reverts to his role of *helping*. The interview ends on a positive note.

After we have disciplined a subordinate, we tend to avoid him or to alter our attitude toward him in subtle, hardly noticeable ways. These shifts in attitude are particularly dangerous, for they generate corresponding alterations in the subordinate's attitude. He concludes, "You hurt me and you know it." Eventually, the whole relationship may be destroyed. By contrast, if we treat the man as we always have, we indicate that by-gones are by-gones, that it was the act that was punished, not the man.

Simple as this advice may seem, it is hard to carry out in practice. Both parties are upset at what has happened. It is easy to understand why the person who has been disciplined is resentful, but the act of imposing discipline is also emotionally distasteful to the person who imposes it. Most of us hate to hurt other people, and when we do so we feel guilty—even when such a feeling is not justified. To protect ourselves from guilt feelings, we have to build up a feeling of anger. But, since we fear the anger of the person we have disciplined, we become unapproachable and cold after we have imposed the penalty. As a result, we seem to be disciplining the other person *as a person*, rather than as the violator of a specific rule. Naturally, his response is, "He doesn't like me."

Two mistakes are common in imposing discipline: the supervisor either apologizes or bawls the offender out.

Apologetic discipline

Supervisor: Jim, I'm sorry I have to do this, but the rule says I must. How would the other fellows feel if I didn't do something?

Subordinate: (to himself): Even the boss doesn't think it's a good rule. Boy, I sure have tough luck.

Or: He doesn't have guts enough to back up his own rules. *Or:* Why does he worry about the other fellows? I know they won't care if I get off.

Personal bawling out

Supervisor: I've given you every chance, gone out on the limb for you, and you haven't helped at all. You told me last time that you would really make sure you'd leave home early, and you broke your promise. Well, I've done all I can for you. You are letting the company down. You aren't being fair to them or to the other men. You've got to wise up or you'll really be in trouble, and I won't bail you out.

In the second case, the superintendent is being overpersonal, possibly because he feels a little guilty. There is no need to remind the employee over and over again of what he has done, to rub his nose in the dirt. Instead, it is much better for the supervisor to make it clear that he wants to let by-gones be by-gones and that he assumes the man will mend his ways.

It requires a great deal of maturity to approach discipline without a sense of guilt or hostility, particularly if we feel that a man's disregard of the rules is a reflection on our own supervisory abilities.

The Role of the Union

As yet we have said little about the role of the union in matters of discipline. We have observed in our research that unions rarely object strongly to discipline provided it is applied consistently and provided the rules are clearly publicized and generally considered reasonable. Of course, union officers may go through the motions of filing a grievance at the request of a disciplined member, much as a lawyer defends a client even though he is wrong. But in doing this, they often feel as this union officer did:

> "I've got to go to this grievance meeting and fight for that so-and-so. He had it coming to him and got what he deserved. How can he think he is so much better than anyone else he doesn't have to follow the rules?"

Along the same lines, in our discussion of wildcat strikes we implied that management normally cannot expect the union to discipline members who violate the contract.[12] When the union does impose discipline, it is abandoning its traditional role as the worker's defender, and management is failing to assume its responsibilities. A management spokesman makes this point:

> The union cannot maintain its proper function of representing the employee and protecting his interests if it assumes any part of management's function of setting disciplinary penalties. If the union agrees with management as to what a proper penalty should be in a particular case, it forecloses its right to protest the penalty. Union representatives should be in a position to protest any disciplinary action taken by management against an employee on the grounds that the discipline is unfair, unjust, discriminatory, lacks cause, or is too severe. Any procedure which forecloses the right of the employee to have his case aired in the grievance procedure is basically unsound.[13]

Management must also be realistic about the union leader's political position. Often union leaders feel obligated to defend members whom they themselves think are guilty; to do otherwise would be to risk defeat at the next election. Once management recognizes that union leaders must often perform

---

[12] There are a few exceptions in the building and clothing trades, where powerful unions may discipline members who violate the contract.

[13] Garrett, *op. cit.*, p. 1.

what is for them an unpleasant job, life becomes a good bit easier for both management and the union.

Management may be able to reduce the number of grievances prompted by disciplinary action by bringing the union into the earlier stages of the disciplinary procedure.

> Bill Jones has been absent frequently. According to accepted plant practice, after five no-excuse absences, he can be laid off for a month. Jones' foreman informs the department steward that he intends to enforce the rule against absenteeism and that the steward might try to "straighten Jones out" before he gets into real trouble. Where the foreman-steward relationship is a good one, the steward will often warn the man that continued violations may lead to a penalty that the union will find difficult to get reduced.

In this way the union is given an opportunity to play a constructive role without being burdened with the responsibility for applying discipline.

QUASI-LEGAL PROCEDURES

The presence of a union need not impair management's efforts to maintain a satisfactory disciplinary policy. But it may force management to adopt what might be called a "quasi-legal" procedure.

Most union contracts require (1) that the company may discipline employees only for "just cause," and (2) that any employee who feels he has been unjustly disciplined may appeal to higher management through the grievance procedure, and, if management's answer is unsatisfactory, to arbitration. The arbitrator makes the final decision on whether the discipline was for just cause. He may be able to sustain the company's action completely, or reduce the penalty, or decide the penalty was entirely unwarranted and eliminate it altogether.[14]

The grievance procedure provides a valuable protection to the individual worker, awkward though it may be for management. Since Magna Carta, an established principle of Anglo-Saxon law has been that an individual shall not be judged by his accusers. Management has the right—one might even say the *duty*—to establish the rules under which the organization shall operate. But a channel of appeal must be kept open from management decisions on whether or not these rules have been violated. Thus the grievance procedure operates as a means of enforcing consistency.

In our Anglo-Saxon tradition, a man is assumed innocent until proved guilty, and in establishing guilt the burden of proof is almost entirely on management. For instance, to prove that a man has been loafing on the job, more than the supervisor's unsubstantiated word is required. Management must be able to produce objective, factual data which show that other em-

---

[14] For an excellent discussion of how arbitrators handle discipline problems, see Paul King, "Tips to Successful Discipline," *Factory Management and Maintenance* (June 1958), pp. 78-87.

ployees on comparable jobs consistently produce more than the alleged offender. And it must show that the worker's low production was not due to poor material or faulty equipment. Similarly, the union may challenge any rule that has not been clearly communicated to the employees or consistently enforced.

As a consequence, disciplinary matters must sometimes be handled in a legalistic, courtroom manner, particularly when they reach the arbitration stage. Unfortunately, both union and management may find themselves devoting more energy to legal intricacies than to dealing with the human problems involved. Each side tries to build up an air-tight case and to poke loopholes in the case of the opposition. The billowing clouds of legal technicalities often serve as a smoke screen that obscures the underlying human problems. Fortunately, the company that maintains a generally fair disciplinary policy as part of its standard procedure is less likely to become involved in the legalisms of arbitration.

The existence of the grievance procedure means that the supervisor's disciplinary penalty may be reduced or eliminated, either by higher management or by an arbitrator. It is even possible that a man, who the supervisor is sure has flagrantly violated the rules, may be totally exonerated. Under these circumstances the supervisor naturally may feel frustrated when his decision is not "backed up." However, such possible miscarriages of justice are the price that must be paid for development of a judicial system which permits every accused employee to have his "day in court." A basic tenet of our society is that it is better for a guilty man to go free than for an innocent man to be convicted.

The reason why "guilty" employees are acquitted at higher stages of the grievance procedure is usually that the supervisor has failed to gather evidence, to be consistent in his application of discipline, or to communicate the requirement of the job to employees. Hence it is important for higher management to train and advise supervisors on the requirements of a sound disciplinary policy.[15]

Conclusion

Basically, discipline is a form of training. When disciplinary problems arise, it may be as much management's fault as the workers. Many disciplinary problems grow out of management's failure to inform employees what is expected of them.

On the other hand, effective discipline depends on more than one-way communication in which the supervisor tells employees what to do and pun-

---

[15] For a good analysis of the problems of effective disciplinary policies in unionized companies see Orme Phelps, *Discipline and Discharge in the Unionized Firm* (Berkeley and Los Angeles: University of California Press, 1959).

ishes them if they don't. Employees may be aware of a rule, yet refuse to accept it. For instance, if there are large numbers of employees taking extra-long lunch hours or using sick leave as a vacation, the problem is not to punish the guilty but to get group acceptance of a new standard. We must initiate discipline by winning acceptance of the standard (a process discussed in Chapter 8). Once this has been accomplished, discipline will be provoked only by the small minority of recalcitrants.

For discipline to be accepted, the rules must be effectively communicated and the penalties inflicted must be consistent. Discipline helps employees learn the requirements of their job; and if discipline is applied impersonally, without personal animus, the respect shown the supervisor by his subordinates may actually be increased.

Problem I

Suppose an employee has been making a series of small mistakes. Is it better for the supervisor to (1) discuss each mistake with him as it occurs, or (2) discuss his *over-all* record with him from time to time?

Problem II

Dave Thatcher comes to work drunk. The foreman sends him home with another man, intending to speak to him when he is sober. As soon as Dave comes in the door the next morning, he drunkenly picks up a high-pressure hose and squirts the foreman in the face. The company discharges him for insubordination, assault with a deadly weapon, intoxication, and violation of company rules. There are no posted rules or penalties.

The union doesn't deny that Dave was pretty high. However, it alleges that (1) he has been having trouble with his wife, (2) his record has otherwise been excellent, (3) he was sent home but not otherwise given a warning on the first day, and (4) in other cases of drunkenness that occurred this year the men were referred to Alcoholics Anonymous.

The company answers: (1) Dave has had no previous disciplinary record but his work has not been good, (2) Dave was in no condition to appreciate a warning the first day, (3) the men referred to Alcoholics Anonymous were quiet drinkers who hadn't committed major violations of company safety rules, and (4) Alcoholics Anonymous is for alcoholics and there is no evidence that Dave is an alcoholic.

1. Was the company's position correct?

Problem III

The company has posted this rule: "No smoking will be allowed on company property. Violators will be punished by discharge." Every employee has been informed of this rule orally and in writing.

Nevertheless management has reason to believe that some workers are smoking in the men's room stalls. The fire insurance company's inspector has noticed butts on the floor and insists that something be done about it.

Despairing of other methods of enforcement, management bores small holes between the stalls and stations foremen in the stalls before the men report to work.

Each foreman can look into the stall to his left and his right. Every time he sees a man smoking, he puts his name on a list. At the end of the day 17 names have been taken. Next morning all 17 receive one week's layoff.

1. What do you think of the company's approach? What would you have done?
2. If the case were brought to arbitration and you were the arbitrator, how would you rule?

Problem IV

The company's employment application says "Falsification of this form will be grounds for immediate discharge." Among the questions on the form is this one: "Have you ever been convicted of a crime?" Howie Bowman was employed three years ago and has a perfect record. Suddenly the company finds out that 15 years ago, when he was 17, Howie was convicted of stealing an automobile and given a suspended sentence. He had not mentioned this fact on his application.

1. Should Howie be disciplined?
2. How long should the company hold this rule violation against him?

Problem V

The foreman catches two men fighting. Smith had been kidding Jones about his hillbilly background. Jones took a poke at Smith. Smith hit back. Both have had a good record in the past.

While some companies try to determine who really started a fight, others feel they will get nowhere trying to settle personal feuds between workers, but should exercise discipline only when one party resorts to his fists to settle differences.

1. What do you think? Should both men receive equal punishment? Should Jones be punished more severely for starting the fight—or Smith for provoking it?

Problem VI

A foreman says, "We have rules posted against gambling. Of course, we don't enforce them against small bets and there is some card-playing for money in the washroom at lunch break. However, we have the rules posted as a standby measure if things get out of hand."

1. Do you agree with this foreman's approach?

Problem VII

A company has a posted rule against gambling. Six months ago two men were given written warnings about shooting dice. One day the local police arrest two other men on plant property for bookmaking. There is evidence that they have been collecting bets on horses in the plant. The men plead guilty before the judge, who gives them a suspended sentence. When they return to the plant they are discharged. To date, both men's records have been perfect.

1. If this case were carried to you as an arbitrator, what would you decide?

ORGANIZATION

Up to this point we have been talking about some of the components of the organization: individual workers and their jobs, supervision, informal groups, and unions. Each of these is an integral part of the organization, but there is a missing element still to be considered: the organizational system itself, within which all these components interact. In this section, therefore, we consider the impact of the organization on human behavior.

As long as people work in small groups where they see each other almost continuously, little thought need be given to defining in advance how they are to relate to one another. They develop patterns of relationship almost spontaneously: few formal plans need be made except to insure a high quality of supervision.

As more and more people are added to the organization, however, the management of personnel becomes more complex. In order for work to be done efficiently, an orderly pattern (or system) of human relationships must be evolved. This pattern is commonly referred to as *organizational structure*. A company such as General Motors, for example, must coordinate the activities of hundreds of thousands of people doing thousands of different tasks in dozens of locations. In large organizations, merely giving consideration to the needs of *individual* workers and the requisites of face-to-face supervision is not enough.

Our primary questions, then, are these: What patterns of human relationships enable an organization to function most efficiently? What problems arise in the attempt to establish these patterns? What type of organizational structure is most likely to motivate people to work toward management's objectives? How can structure be evaluated in human-relations terms?

In a very real sense, an organization is a set of human relations. Every organization has a hierarchy of authority. The men at the top give orders to the men beneath them and so on down the line. The purpose of the hierarchy is to make it possible for a large number of people to work under the over-all control of a relatively small number of managers.

Organizations also spread out horizontally. Rather than having one person do the total job—for example, make a pair of shoes—many people are brought together and their activities are coordinated so that, although each does only a small part of the total job, at the end finished pairs of shoes are produced. This is the familiar principle of division of labor. By assigning only a limited number of tasks to each specialist, the organization hopes to attain greater productivity than when each person does the whole job by himself.

These two principles—(1) control exercised from the top down through successive levels of hierarchy, and (2) specialization of function—are the source of a host of challenging human-relations problems that management must somehow solve. Indeed, failure to develop an adequate organizational structure may nullify the benefits of effective supervision. Careful planning in this area must precede any other personnel program.

Within the broad field of organization, we shall concentrate our attention on several types of problem. Perhaps the most obvious one, but certainly not the simplest, concerns the ability of a many-leveled organization to control itself—the ability of upper levels of management to direct the efforts of employees whom they never contact directly and probably do not even know. Chapter 14, "The Impact of the Hierarchy on Human Relations," discusses these "vertical" relationships, the passing down of orders and information through a series of levels, and the efforts of management to develop systems by which information from below will flow upward to these same levels.

A special problem within this larger one of organizational hierarchy concerns the first-line supervisor. The co-

hesiveness of his subordinate group and the expectations of his own superior make the supervisor's position especially difficult. Observers sensitive to his predicament have referred to him as "Supervisor: Man in the Middle," the title of Chapter 15.

Many organizations that resort to the use of specialists in their attempts to achieve maximum productivity find that the alleged benefits of specialization are simply not forthcoming. Coordinating all the specialized parts so that they fit together neatly into a productive organization gives rise to many human-relations problems. These problems of coordination are described in Chapter 16, "The Impact of Specialization on Human Relations."

A number of answers have been proposed to the human-relations questions associated with large organizations. These proposals are analyzed in Chapter 17, "Minimizing the Human Problems of Large Organizations." We shall devote particular attention to efforts to provide greater decentralization, whereby lower levels of the organization are assigned self-contained tasks that limit their need for contact with other levels of the organization.

Another type of relationship characteristic of the contemporary organization is that between staff and line. Staff activities represent an extension of the specialization principle to the creation of special departments that assist and help regulate the work of the regular "line" departments. Again, coordination problems are created by this type of specialization, particularly since staff and line often have overlapping responsibilities. Because our main interest lies in personnel administration, most of our examples of these problems will have to do with the staff personnel department and its members. Chapter 18 is a discussion of "Personnel as a Staff Function."

The purpose of hierarchy is to make it possible for one person or a small group of people to control the activities of a large number of employees. But there are limits to the number of subordinates any supervisor can manage effectively; consequently, the larger the number of people in the organization, the greater the number of supervisory levels that will be required.[1] In large companies it is not unusual to find ten levels separating the hourly-paid workers at the bottom from top management.

What difference does the number of levels make to human relations? What is the difference between the functioning of a small organization in which the owner-manager supervises everyone and the functioning of General Motors or General Electric?

In a situation such as the one diagrammed on page 306, Bill is responsible to Henry, Henry reports to Tom, Tom reports to Dick, and Dick reports to Fred, the organization head. Why should it make any difference if Bill reports to Fred—or

---

[1] Of course, the number of levels in the organization is also dependent upon the number of subordinates who report to each supervisor, or what is called the "span of control" of the supervisor.

14

The Impact
of the Hierarchy
on Human Relations

continues to be one of Fred's employees, but with several "layers of organization" and other supervisors in between?

First, let us stop and rethink what an organization really consists of. When we draw boxes and connect them with lines, we have a tendency to believe that the system we design will function like a physical model—that is, we think of an organization as though it were a system of interrelated pipes and reservoirs. Water starting at the top always reaches the bottom in exactly the same quantity and quality as when it started out—if everything is connected correctly, that is. Thus, the model suggests that someone at the top issues an order or makes a policy decision, and the next person in the hierarchy passes the instructions along to the men who report to him, and so on down the line.

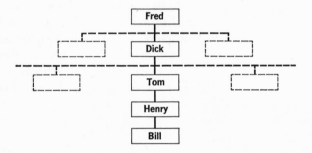

Similarly, significant information from "down the line" is reported upward through the same system of "pipes" so that those at the top will have at their finger tips all the information they need to administer the affairs of the organization. This constant circulation of information up and down the chain of command provides the lifeblood of the organization and keeps it in a healthy state of alertness and efficiency. Each employee at the bottom is supposed to respond in some predictable way to plans originated at the top, regardless of the number of linkages through which orders must flow before reaching him, and regardless of how many layers his ideas and experiences must pass through before reaching the top again.

But an organization is not made up of mechanical parts or pipes. It consists of *people,* whose attitudes and behavior are affected by the system of human relations in which they function. These people upset the simple mechanistic working of the hierarchical model. They introduce distortions in both the downward and upward transmission of information. In this chapter we shall concentrate our attention on these distortions and on the human-relations problems they create.

In a sense, we are now dealing with the problem of exercising good supervision where there are more than two levels of authority. As we shall see, the supervisory practices we recommended previously appear simple in contrast to the complexities of motivating and directing people in a multi-level structure.

Patterns of Downward Communication

In an efficiently operated organization top-level managers make decisions and give orders that are then passed *downward* through their subordinates and on down to the lowest level in the structure. Unfortunately, this vital process may be disturbed, and decisions may be dangerously distorted as they are communicated downward.

DISTORTIONS DOWNWARD

Let us start with an example. Top management decides that racial discrimination in employment shall be eliminated. What happens as this policy is passed down the line through successive stages of the hierarchy? By the time the policy reaches the individuals who do the actual hiring, it may have been transformed almost beyond recognition, for example: "Hire *some* Negroes at each location, so that the company appears to be non-discriminatory."

In part, this sort of distortion is caused by the communications problems we discussed in Chapter 9. People may "hear" the new policy in ways unintended by top management. The result is wide differences in interpretation, which grow increasingly wider the more broadly the policy is communicated.

But the organization itself complicates matters further. The order-giver is a long way from the final recipient. You may have played the game in which a story is passed from person to person in a group. Each person alters the facts slightly to fit his own needs and preconceptions, often without intending to do so. When the story finally re-emerges, it has been distorted beyond recognition. Information passing through many levels of an organization can be even more confused.

Complex statements of policy, whose accuracy depends on subtle shades of meaning, are particularly vulnerable to distortion as they move "down the line." A fairly simple company decision to grant every employee with more than six months' service a two-week vacation with pay could probably be communicated down through several levels without major alteration. But an announcement of policy on union matters, or on promotions, is often badly mangled or downright misleading by the time it filters down through the levels of the organization.

Two sorts of distortion are particularly common. The first is *exaggeration*. Every subordinate is highly dependent on his boss' goodwill, for the superior has countless ways of making his job either easier or harder. Consequently, most subordinates are highly sensitive to the boss' every whim and seek to anticipate his desires before they are expressed. This constant search for clues to what the boss wants often leads to strange results.

> Nearly every company is familiar with what happens when one of the members of top management makes a visit to an outlying installation. If local management hears through company gossip that the visiting dignitary is likely to be impressed by the physical appearance of the organization, a sudden redirection of effort takes place. Employees are taken away from their regular jobs to do housekeeping chores which are normally neglected. Equipment and buildings take on an unusual "shine."

Many a subordinate asks the boss' secretary, "What is he gunning for today? Is it safe for me to mention . . . ?" The authors once observed a personnel department hectically preparing to run a morale survey (though the department doubted that it was a good idea) purely because a top official had read a short article in a popular management magazine and had remarked to the personnel director, "This looks like a good idea for us."

The second common type of distortion is just the opposite: the *playing down* of directives. Lower management drags its feet in carrying out an order, or follows the letter but not the spirit. For example, we once observed the reaction of middle and lower management to a top-management directive to install a supervisory performance-evaluation program. This program required each superior to rate his subordinates every six months, and then to discuss his ratings with them. With few exceptions, the managers were reluctant to adopt this new program, which they felt would breed more antagonism than good will. So they procrastinated, in the hope that the program would gradually be forgotten by all concerned.

Distortion of this sort occurs when the subordinates as a group feel strongly opposed to a new policy and feel that top management is not really serious about implementing it. Many subordinates show sheer genius in endlessly evading directives without becoming overtly insubordinate, making sure that nothing can be "pinned on" them.

To summarize, as the organization grows larger, communications become increasingly difficult, and top management finds it harder and harder to maintain firm control over the lower levels of the hierarchy simply by issuing orders. Top executives are never really sure of what is happening below, and those at lower levels become uncertain about what is expected of them. As a result, management's decisions often become vitiated or distorted as they move down the line.

SHORT-CIRCUITING THE LINES OF COMMUNICATION

In an effort to improve the effectiveness of communication, top management frequently introduces modifications into the organizational structure

decentralized a lines of communication are shorter than in a centralized form.
distortion - because of large numbers of link in a chain.

that depart radically from the model we described earlier. In the model, you will remember, every order is passed down the line of command, from Fred to Dick to Tom and so forth; it is assumed that no steps are omitted, and that every bit of information is passed upward in the same way. But in real-world situations, management's fear that it has lost contact with lower levels often leads to the short-circuiting of many of the steps pictured in the model.

Bypassing   A manager may become so frustrated by the time-consuming process of going through channels and the apparent inability of subordinates to carry out instructions precisely as they were intended, that he bypasses intermediate levels and goes straight to the men involved. For instance, the superintendent goes directly to an employee to find out why a new machine is producing so much scrap, or the division manager calls in a salesman to tell him to give special attention to a customer who is threatening to take his business elsewhere. Often top-management expediters are sent as temporary replacements for lower managers who are in trouble. Here is a description of a top executive (President of Curtiss-Wright) who is particularly well known for taking direct action and cutting through red tape:

> Hurley is chief expediter at C-W and chief executioner of good ideas with bad cost records. He seldom "moves through channels." He figures that the division manager doesn't have any more idea than he has of what is wrong or the figures would not have been negative in the first place. So instead of waiting for a briefing, Hurley moves directly to the spot, right down to the machine on the floor if that is the heart of the problem. Many a division manager has discovered hours later that the boss has been in his department and long since moved on. And many department heads have discovered that an important job has been given to an employee they hardly know, and without consulting them. Hurley spots a man who seems bright and says, "You do it." That the job may be completely unrelated to the employee's work is of no concern to Hurley.[2]

As we shall see later, bypassing has its dangers as well as its advantages. It threatens the leadership position of the supervisor who has been bypassed and creates confusion among his subordinates. Attractive and dramatic though bypassing may seem, we must remember that sticking to the formal channels has one great advantage: it insures that everyone who is supposed to be informed actually is informed.

Personal contacts   In an effort to recreate the personal intimacy between hierarchical levels that characterizes small organizations, many managers try to cultivate the feeling of "one big happy family." They resort to such devices as:

> Personal appearances by top management before employee groups.
> Special, personal letters from the company president to employees on birthdays, anniversaries with the company, birth of children, etc.

---

[2] William B. Harris, "Curtiss-Wright Throws Away the Book," *Fortune,* Vol. 57, No. 1 (January 1958), p. 115.

Want to achieve control

Christmas parties, bowling teams, golf tournaments, and other events at which various levels of the organization meet informally.

All these efforts are designed to counteract the impression that the company is impersonal, to give the feeling that top management consists of flesh-and-blood individuals who are genuinely interested in the welfare of the people who work for them. As General Electric puts it, the purpose is "to endow qualities of friendliness, consideration, fairness and competence." [3] At best, this approach helps subordinates to identify with the organization as a whole (just as Britishers feel a surge of patriotism when they see their Queen). But two factors seriously limit the effectiveness of this approach as a means of communication:

1. As we noted in our discussion of communications, the lower levels may suspect or distort management's motives. Here are two not untypical comments made at a lavish annual company picnic: "Today is 'Be Nice to the Children Day.'" "Look at the big boss over there, surrounded by apple polishers. He really thinks he's one of the boys. Ha!"

2. This type of communication is directed primarily downward. Printed messages or talks before large groups provide little opportunity for feedback. Even picnics and bowling leagues are poor devices for eliciting a sampling of employee opinion.

The manager of one large plant made a daily recording of a "management-to-management message of the day" which any supervisor could listen to by dialing a special number in the plant phone system. One foreman said, "That's the typical kind of conversation we have around here: *they* tell *us*. But when that so-and-so finishes, I always cuss him out. I sure hope that really is just a recording."

As with other aspects of supervisory behavior, such personal contacts by higher management cannot be evaluated in isolation; they take on meaning only in the over-all context of the personnel program. If the president's "personal" birthday card fits into the employee's previous perception of his relation to the president, fine. If not, the birthday greeting may seem hypocritical. Similarly, it is waste of effort for the boss to be a mass of smiles at the annual picnic if he is completely unapproachable at other times of the year. Under such circumstances, gestures that are intended to be warm and personal may well be perceived as merely mechanical or hypocritical.

Mass communications In many companies the word *communications* refers not to the transmission of orders and information through normal hierarchical channels, but to what we would call mass communications: the company

---

[3] *Employee Communication: Executive Summary* (New York: General Electric Company, 1952), p. 23, as cited in Reinhard Bendix, *Work and Authority in Industry* (New York: Wiley, 1956), p. 321.

newspaper ("house organ"), bulletin-board announcements, direct mailings to employees, fillers in pay envelopes, movies, a loudspeaker system, and so forth. Almost every large company has a special staff assigned to preparing material of this sort.

Mass communications are seldom used by themselves to convey messages that are really important. When management wants to raise production or cut costs, it sends clear, unmistakable orders down the line, and makes sure that every subordinate understands them. Mass-communications techniques are used chiefly in areas that are peripheral to management's main job of getting the production out—areas such as safety, personnel policies, suggestions, scrap reduction, and the company's financial position.

Why are mass-communications techniques used so widely in these areas? There are several reasons:

1. Often the information to be transmitted is of a technical nature. If details of a new insurance scheme, for example, are transmitted by word of mouth from top management through the various levels of supervision, they are bound to be badly distorted by the time they reach the rank and file. Further, management may feel that the foremen are not qualified to explain such involved matters as why depreciation must be deducted from profits to given an accurate picture of the company's financial position, therefore top management must communicate directly with employees.

2. Since messages of this sort do not have A-1 priority, management wants to insure that they will not be distorted or forgotten by lower supervision. Lower supervision is chiefly interested in getting out production, and messages relating to "fringe" areas may be laid aside or given perfunctory attention. The supervisor tells his men at the end of a meeting, "And, of course, as you know, I'm supposed to tell you once a week to be sure to wear your safety hats."

Many of the messages sent through mass-communications channels are sponsored by staff departments, such as finance or personnel. And these departments have learned through sad experience that if they have to trust line management to carry their messages, the information will never reach lower-level employees.

3. Finally, in contrast to what we said earlier, some messages are so vitally important that it is essential that details are not distorted by transmission through channels. For example, new regulations of the Internal Revenue Service may require a substantial change in the way salesmen report their reimbursable expenses—especially prepared new forms must be used. The requirements and details of this new procedure might be outlined in a mimeographed announcement distributed to all sales personnel and their supervisors. For the same reason, after V-E day the details of military discharge policy were revealed simultaneously to servicemen throughout the world by means of movies.

As is probably already clear, it is unwise for management to rely excessively on mass communications.[4] With the exception of movies and loudspeaker announcements, mass communications involve the printed rather than the spoken word; they are always one-way rather than two-way. You will remember from our discussion in Chapter 9 that printed one-way communications lack flexibility and the opportunity for the feedback of the face-to-face spoken word. A man can't ask questions of a bulletin board, nor does a letter repeat itself if the reader is drowsy or inattentive.

If the message is of any importance at all, the use of mass communications tends to reduce the status of the immediate supervisor. In effect, top management is saying, "We don't trust you to explain complicated problems." Often, too, if the message is of importance, the subordinate has questions to ask about it. If his boss can't answer them, then the subordinate's respect for him will drop even more.

On the other hand, the fact that messages are sent through mass communications channels rather than through the line may indicate to the employees that the message is really not important. If the boss says "work faster" and the bulletin board says "work safer," the subordinate will be more likely to pay attention to the boss than to the bulletin board.

Improved mass-communication methods In order to overcome these difficulties, many companies are using mass communications with greater finesse. For example, top management may (1) give higher supervisors advance notice before relaying messages to lower levels, (2) urge the immediate supervisor to add a few words to supplement the formal message, and (3) encourage subordinates to address questions concerning these materials to their immediate boss. Such efforts preserve the advantages of specificity and uniformity, enable the immediate supervisor to retain his status, and encourage feedback from subordinates.

Of course, these procedures also mean that management must devote more time and effort to its attempts to disseminate information through the normal hierarchical channels of communication. As an expert in this field put it:

> If the general manager is planning a direct-mail letter to all employees, explaining the new working requirements resulting from the defense program, the foreman should know about it before some employee on the morning shift brings it to him with a question. The foreman or immediate supervisor should know in advance, not only that certain information is about to be given to employees, not only the mere content of the letter or article or bulletin, but a substantial amount of explanatory and supple-

---

[4] For a good discussion by successful executives, see Alexander R. Heron, *Sharing Information with Employees* (Stanford, Calif.: Stanford University Press, 1942), and Neil McElroy, *Communications: A Way of Working with People* (Cincinnati, Ohio: The Procter and Gamble Company, n. d.).

mental data to make him a respectable source of answers for questions employees may raise.[5]

Let us look at a few examples of how this works in practice.

In an effort to explain past performances and future prospects, some companies have experimented with movies to dramatize the annual financial report. These often fail to accomplish their objectives since there is little tie-in between the accomplishments of the company as a whole and those of any particular department. In an effort to provide this tie-in, some companies have supplemented the movies, with a verbal report by the immediate supervisor on prospects for the department for the coming year. (Naturally he must be briefed to answer questions on company finances.)

For years a chemical company had tried to enforce a no-smoking rule throughout its plant. It had met with little success, however, since many parts of the plant presented no safety hazard. Even supervisors made a practice of slipping into corners for a cigarette when no higher-up was looking. This laxity made enforcement in the really dangerous areas extremely difficult. After consultation with lower levels of supervision, top management decided to abandon the plant-wide rule, to mark very clearly certain limited areas in which the no-smoking rule would be strictly enforced, and to permit those who were regularly employed in these areas to take periodic smoke breaks outside the area. Management wanted to emphasize that this was a plant-wide policy that was to be enforced by all levels of supervision. Each supervisor called his subordinates together, explained the new policy to them carefully, answered questions, and then handed out a written statement of the new policy that had been prepared by the personnel department.

Notice that in both these cases mass communication was effectively supplemented by personal contacts by the immediate supervisor. The supervisor's status was enhanced rather than impaired.

The grapevine Though this last device for short-circuiting the hierarchical channels is not consciously designed by management, it is frequently more effective than any of the others. "Being flexible and personal, it spreads information faster than most management communications systems operate. With the rapidity of a burning powder train, it filters out of the woodwork, past the manager's office, through the locker room, and along the corridors."[6] Often subordinates learn of top management's decisions through the grapevine long before anything is put into writing. And when formal messages are transmitted, rumor "helps" explain and interpret them. Since the grapevine is personal, spoken, and permits feedback, it often has a far stronger impact on the recipient than do other forms of communication.

---

[5] Heron, *op. cit.*, p. 191.
[6] Keith Davis, *Human Relations in Business* (New York: McGraw-Hill, 1957), p. 244.

Many managers feel that rumors should be stamped out, on the grounds that they are often false, exaggerated, malicious, and even give away management secrets. Yet the grapevine performs a very useful function: it tends to correct some of the shortcomings of formal communication. Mr. A is never officially told about something that vitally affects him; he finds out about it through the rumor channel. Bill and Joe are in totally different divisions of the organization, but their work is closely tied together. A change is made in Bill's department that will vitally affect Joe. It may take weeks for the message to go up through the formal channels of communication and then reach Joe—possibly much distorted. But if Bill passes the word along to Joe on the job, the message is transmitted efficiently and accurately.

Actually it is unrealistic to expect that rumors can be stamped out. The grapevine fills a vital human need. Gossip gives people a social outlet and a chance to exercise their imagination. As we noted earlier, it gives them an opportunity to relieve their fears of the unknown by expressing their anxiety in the form of stories. Above all, it allays curiosity.

The grapevine is bound to exist in any organization. If facts are available, it will transmit them effectively, though often with some distortion. If facts are not available, the grapevine may invent them. From a few clues, vastly perverted images may be constructed. Rumors rarely cause trouble where facts are readily available.

The best way to minimize undesirable rumors is to improve other forms of communication. Untruthful rumors rarely get started if the boss announces his intentions in advance, and if his subordinates feel free to ask him questions.

We have been talking about four somewhat different techniques used to short-circuit formal downward channels of communication: by-passing, personal contacts, mass communications, and the grapevine. More generally, we have been discussing the whole process of downward communication as a means of coordinating people in the organization, the reasons why this communication sometimes fails, and what can be done to improve it.

COMMUNICATION AND SUPERVISION

It is useful, for a moment, to look at the relationship between hierarchical communication and patterns of supervision. The supervisor who uses the policy of "be strong" may have difficulty even in communicating *downward* (it is obvious that he will have trouble with *upward* communication). In the first place, subordinates may be afraid to ask their boss questions even when they fail to understand what he has said. Sometimes they seek to impress the boss by doing more than they think he has requested and thus exaggerate his orders. Alternatively, they may object to the boss' order, yet fear to express their objections openly. Instead, they "play down" the order and systematically sabotage it or give it only token compliance.

Lacks trust and confidence of the employees

In the first and third instances, it should be noted that the boss' failure to encourage upward communication makes downward communication more difficult.

In practice, this type of supervisor is not anxious to encourage downward communication, particularly through the regular channels, because he has little confidence in his subordinates. He doesn't trust them to convey information or orders and, not trusting them with information, he doesn't see why they need more than the minimum amount required to do their job. His idea of good communication frequently is in terms of what we have called mass communications.

Rules as a Form of Communication

ADVANTAGES

Few organizations rely solely on a series of specific orders directed from top to bottom. Rather, control is exercised through rules (or "policies") designed to shape the behavior of subordinates over a period of time. Rules are an essential element in the chain of authority, part of the downward stream of communication to which subordinates are expected to respond. Though many people disparage rules as "red tape," they are essential if the organization is to operate effectively.[7]

Establish consistency   Particularly in larger organizations, rules serve to make the behavior of the parts consistent with the needs of the whole. They reduce the possibility that personal feelings rather than organizational objectives will predominate in decision-making. For instance, top management may want individuals hired on merit, not on the basis of race or religion. Since actual hiring may be done by hundreds of individuals, the way to accomplish this objective is to set standards to guide the behavior of lower levels. The alternative would be to have one man do all the hiring.

Save time   Rules save time for an executive. His subordinates do not have to consult him on routine matters, for the rules lay down principles in advance. Thus decisions can be made more quickly and at lower levels.

Provide standards for evaluation   Rules are in effect standards by which the behavior of subordinates may be evaluated. They make possible supervision by results and provide a basis for discipline. Without well-publicized standards of behavior, subordinates have no way of knowing what is expected of them.

---

[7] For an excellent discussion of the relationship between rules and organizational efficiency, see Alvin Gouldner, *Patterns of Industrial Bureaucracy* (Glencoe, Ill.: Free Press, 1954), pp. 167 ff.

Make possible general supervision   The existence of rules increases the job satisfaction of employees. Without rules no one would know how much discretion he had to make decisions; theoretically everything would have to be referred to higher levels for approval. But well-thought-out rules establish limits within which supervisors are free to act on their own. Higher levels step in only when one of these limits is violated, or when a question comes up that is not covered by existing policy. As a result, the leadership position of managers is strengthened all down the line.

Help individuals know where they stand   Rules are also useful in defining employees' duties and responsibilities. They enable subordinates to predict the consequences of their actions—an ability that is essential to personal security. In the small company the new employee learns by word of mouth what is expected of him in terms of daily conduct. In the large organization such informal means of communications cannot be relied on to provide new employees with adequate indoctrination. Word of mouth must be supplemented by rules.

Until about twenty-five years ago, there were few explicit personnel rules in most companies. Each supervisor was free to hire, fire, or promote as he wished. The coming of unionism shocked management into recognizing that many abuses and inequities in the handling of personnel had developed in their own organizations through the years. For example, there were great disparities in the manner in which employees were treated from department to department. In order to correct these abuses, management centralized the handling of personnel problems, often in personnel departments. As we shall see later, this development assured higher management a better over-all picture of personnel developments. But it also brought about a severe reduction in the authority and prestige of the individual supervisor. Today, companies are seeking a happy mean between all-out centralism and near anarchy through establishing general policies or guideposts which, like the other rules we have been discussing, can be administered with some measure of flexibility.

EXCESSIVELY RIGID RULES

Rules may be too specific and detailed, however, and they may be applied too rigidly by subordinates who fail to use good judgment in handling specific cases. This is one symptom of what some people call "bureaucracy" (though sociologists apply this term to any hierarchical organization that makes use of uniform policies).

Unnecessary rules are difficult to enforce, and inadequately enforced rules may lead to a general breakdown of discipline. Even when obeyed, too many rules result in the attitude that if a man lives up to the minimum requirements of the rules, he has done all the company can reasonably require of him. Particularly when the reasonableness of the rules is neither self-evident nor well explained, they tend to make a man feel restricted, breed resentment and aggressiveness, and at times provoke a desire to break the rules just to prove one's independence.

Excessively rigid rules also discourage individual discretion and initiative, and make it difficult for the organization to adapt to changing conditions. They give the petty tyrant a shield behind which he can vent his vindictiveness. They provide the inept supervisor with a crutch to lean on, and enable him to avoid the conflicts and uncertainties of making decisions on his own. They subject the able supervisor to endless frustration and make it impossible for him to operate with the flexibility required for peak efficiency. At the very least, they lead to red tape and wasted effort. Here is the way the personnel director of a small branch plant described the effect of excessively rigid rules:

> The company employment procedures require us to check all references. This may be OK for some of the big plants with operations different from ours. But in this community with our type of work it is silly. We have written the top office a dozen times asking for an exception to be made for us. All they say is that it has to be uniform throughout the company. Why? Well, we go through the motions, but it really is a waste of time. *And in my job this kind of thing happens again and again.*

Similarly, the introduction of automation into a major steel company was almost a failure because top management insisted that the standard-incentive (piece-work) system be used, though it was obvious to everyone on the spot that this system was inappropriate for the new method of production.[8]

Rules have a tendency to become ends in themselves, particularly if those who carry them out forget the reasons for which they were promulgated in the first place.

> In order to prevent salary increases from getting out of hand, top management decides that one per year is the limit for any employee. An exceptional employee does an outstanding job. To prevent him from accepting a better offer from another company, his supervisor tries to offer him an extra salary raise. The personnel department automatically turns the supervisor's request down and the man quits.

We have no way of knowing, of course, whether this particular man should have been given an extra increase; we would need additional facts before deciding that. But it is clear that some investigation was called for.

Rules give the insecure supervisor a means of "passing the buck" for unpleasant decisions: "The office just issued a strict new policy—no more days off unless a man is sick; my hands are tied." The supervisor hopes, by

---

[8] Charles R. Walker, *Toward the Automatic Factory* (New Haven: Yale University Press, 1957), p. 168.

blaming higher managers with whom the subordinate does not have any regular contact, to maintain his own good relationship with his subordinate. The result is a general weakening of the immediate supervisor's leadership position as well as damage to the employee's respect for the organization.[9]

CORRECT USE OF RULES

Rules are designed to set a general direction, to insure some measure of uniformity and consistency. But the basic reason for rules is not to restrict the individual, but to further the general welfare of the organization and the attainment of its goals. When a given rule prevents this organizational objective from being attained, then it must give way, an exception must be made.

The important point is that the exception must be clearly identified as such. A rule is like setting the course of a ship.[10] There may be times when the ship runs off course—in bad weather, for example—but the ship's officers need to know when and where they are departing from the prescribed course and by how much, if the ship is to reach its destination.

In summary, intelligently devised rules grant the individual in the large organization considerable freedom to make decisions on his own. To insure that his decisions are not completely unfettered, however, his actions need to conform to the goals of the total organization. This insurance is provided through setting limits—that is, through establishing rules. These rules or policies can free higher-level managers from the necessity of handling many time-consuming aspects of the routine business of the organization. The next level of manager *up* in the organization only steps into a problem situation when one of the pre-established limits has been violated by a subordinate or when a case comes up that is not covered by existing policies. Thus, properly handled, rules can strengthen the satisfaction and leadership position of supervisors all the way down the line. Supervisors do not have to check back with their boss each time an action or a decision is called for—they know the limits within which they can operate. The danger is that the existence of rules makes it possible for the inept or autocratic supervisor to avoid his responsibility for making difficult personnel decisions by interpreting rules in an excessively narrow fashion and "passing the buck."

---

[9] Note that we are *not* saying that the existence of such a rule or its enforcement is necessarily bad. That could not be assessed without knowing more facts. The point here is that a supervisor cannot use the rule simply as a crutch to avoid discussing an employee-relations problem and then making a decision on his own responsibility.

[10] Peter Drucker, *The Concept of the Corporation* (New York: Day, 1956).

Patterns of Upward Communication

A healthy organization needs effective upward communications as much as it needs effective downward communications—and for two primary reasons:

1. *Obtaining information* Top management depends on a steady stream of information from subordinates in order to make intelligent decisions. How well are we doing on Line 7? Is that new quality-control man working out OK? Are we going to have to hire some more junior engineers? Without some sort of reporting system, top management can never find out what orders are needed or how effectively its orders are being carried out. Effective upward communication furnishes management with quick and accurate reports on what is happening at lower levels.

Successful upward communication requires that management's questions be truthfully answered. More than this, it requires that vital information be transmitted upward even if management has never requested it; it requires that *management be willing to listen to unsolicited messages.* The men on the top do not always know the right questions to ask or the right instructions to give. Subordinates frequently have useful suggestions to make, questions to ask, or problems of which their supervisors are ignorant. Unless subordinates feel free to communicate these matters upward, management will lack some of the data essential to sound decision-making.

2. *Maintaining morale* It is psychologically unsound for the initiation of contacts to run in only one direction—always from superiors to subordinates. No one is happy when he is always on the receiving end. We all want some opportunity to express ourselves, particularly to those who control our activities and welfare. When we are disturbed or under pressure from others—for example, when an earlier deadline has been unexpectedly imposed, or another department is demanding speedier service from us— the need to express ourselves becomes even more urgent.

DIFFICULTIES IN UPWARD COMMUNICATION

Effective upward communication is difficult to obtain, particularly in larger organizations. In a small firm, the informality that usually prevails between the employees and the top boss produces a feeling of intimacy and personal satisfaction. A mechanic in a small auto shop can easily tell his problems to his boss; it is infinitely harder for a worker to complain to the president of General Motors. Let us examine this difference in detail.

Covering up Subordinates have a natural tendency to withhold unfavorable information from their superiors, or to filter the information as it is passed up along the line. This tendency is intensified when subordinates have learned through experience that the supervisor is more interested in fixing blame than in helping his men work out their difficulties.[11]

Even where there is no willful attempt to withhold damaging information, a subordinate may hesitate to submit detailed reports for fear that they may not be what his boss wants to hear, or that they are too trivial to be worthy of his attention. Or the subordinate may have learned that "seeing the boss is a sure way to get into hot water." Even worse, the superior may encourage this attitude by assuming that every employee who wants to discuss a problem with him is a trouble-maker.

Subordinates are eager to win the approval of their superior in order to gain promotion and advancement. In their desire to make a good showing, they may try to paint a rosy picture of current operations—far rosier than the facts justify. Often they conspire to hide unpleasant realities from superiors. For instance, a foreman and his supervisor may decide to hush up the fact that they have had to destroy a large batch of chemicals because rust got into the vats. Many times a subordinate will fail to ask for help when he needs it from his supervisor for fear that he might give the impression that he can't do his job.

This tendency to cover up unfavorable information sometimes leads to confusion and injustice in the handling of grievances.

> A drawing-mill operator claims that his customary work load has been increased in violation of the union contract. The supervisor insists that the operator has always operated three drawing machines. On the supervisor's word, his boss rejects the grievance. Just prior to arbitration, the final stage of the grievance procedure, top management discovers that the man has been operating only two machines for more than a year. The supervisor had permitted the employee to do this, in violation of company policy, in order to get him to work with inferior materials at a time when high-quality materials were unavailable. The supervisor had not reported this fact because it was a violation of policy, and had even refrained from admitting it in the early steps of the grievance procedure.

The subordinate's fear of sending unfavorable information upward also reflects his lack of certainty concerning what top management wants. Recognizing the imperfection of downward communication, and not sure of what is expected, he tries to avoid reporting anything that might give an impression of failure. (Thus poor downward communications often makes upward communications harder.)

Status problems In an effort to maintain his superior position, and to ration his scarce time, the manager may isolate himself from his subordinates

---

[11] One would expect upward communication to be much more effective in a company that practices general supervision. Here subordinates are more likely to feel free to discuss problems with their bosses without fear of being bawled out for mistakes. The close supervisor, on the other hand, tends to build a wall of suspicion between himself and his subordinates.

by setting up barriers. An advance appointment, appropriate dress, passing the scrutiny of an officious secretary—all may be necessary before a man can ask the boss a modest question.

A department head calls in one of his subordinates to give him special instructions on handling an important project. The instructions are confusing, but the subordinate makes no attempt to ask clarifying questions. Why? Simply because he is afraid that the supervisor will interpret his questions as evidence of slowness or stupidity. He is not sure that the questions he will ask will be "good ones"—that is, the kind of question an intelligent, competent man is supposed to ask. So rather than risk hurting his reputation, he remains silent.

Strangely enough, this common cause of breakdown in upward communication is also one of the easiest to remedy. The solution is simply for the supervisor to encourage questions, indicating that they are expected and appropriate—in fact, giving the subordinate the feeling that asking questions indicates a high degree of alertness.

IMPROVING UPWARD COMMUNICATION

In a small organization the manager can see for himself how his decisions are being carried out. In the large organization, managers can "see" only through the eyes of others. Top management normally relies on the reports of managers at the next level in the hierarchy, who in turn must rely on those reporting to them, and so on down the line of command. But top management finds it very difficult to discover what is really happening on the levels below. One often hears executives asking, "We wonder what our employees really think of us?"

Quite revealing are the apocryphal stories about the efforts of navy captains to learn what is happening below decks. In the typical tale the captain disguises himself as a seaman and wanders through the ship, or invites a seaman to his cabin for drinks and talk.[12]

On the other hand, employees are often anxious to bring their problems to the attention of higher management. Joe feels that his manager is discriminating against him and wants a fair hearing from someone higher up on why he has been denied a promotion. Jack has thought up a new fixture that he is sure will cut machining time by one-third, but his foreman brushes him off with a curt rejection. Bill feels at ease with his immediate supervisor, but realizes that it is pointless to complain to him about his salary when someone higher up makes the decisions. In effect, all these men are saying, "If only someone in top management would listen to us!"

Numerous techniques have been tried to facilitate and encourage upward communications.

---

[12] James F. Downes, "Environment, Communications, and Status Change Aboard an American Aircraft Carrier," *Human Organization*, Vol. 17, No. 3 (Fall 1958), p. 17.

The open door Some companies have experimented with the "open-door" policy. Every employee is guaranteed the privilege of walking into the office of any manager at any level in the organization to voice his complaints. In some companies this policy has succeeded in opening up a worth-while channel of appeal. More often, however, subordinates take advantage of the privilege only rarely. Why? One reason, of course, is the deterrent of social distance—the fear that keeps the buck private from complaining to his colonel that he has been assigned to KP too often, even though the colonel makes himself available. More than this, the subordinate realizes that once he exercises the privilege of appeal, he will have jeopardized his whole future with his superior.

Understandably, the supervisor is upset when a subordinate decides to go over his head with an appeal to a higher level in the organization—this behavior spotlights his own deficiencies. The supervisor also begins to worry lest the subordinate reveal practices or mistakes that he has carefully tried to cover up. And he recognizes that if the top boss does decide to grant the complainant's demand, a steady stream of complaining subordinates will carry appeals over his head, and thus seriously endanger his leadership position.

Thus the subordinate knows intuitively how his supervisor feels about the open door. He calculates that if he walks through this portal he has only a slim chance of winning anything and a good chance of losing a great deal. After all, the immediate supervisor controls many things that the complainant holds important—job, salary level, work assignments, and so forth. The risk is too great, and the open door is rarely entered.

Particularly where there is no union, however, an employee needs some channel for contacting managerial levels above his immediate boss. Otherwise he has no opportunity for appeals—no chance to obtain a review of a crucial decision affecting his immediate well being. Realistically, although a supervisor tells his subordinates that he will always hear appeals on his decisions, a boss is not likely to reverse himself. The reasons are obvious.

In spite of what we have just said, a boss can always, if he wishes, encourage employees to bring problems directly to him, by-passing their direct supervisors. Many times a higher-level manager will be contacted informally —perhaps while he is walking through the office—by an employee who has a special request or protest. The frequency with which this occurs depends more on the attitudes of higher management than on any formalized "open-door" policy.

What is a boss to do when the subordinate of one of his supervisors comes to him with a problem? If such by-passing is encouraged, the effect on the supervisors' morale may be disastrous. Yet if it is completely banned, the effect on the workers' morale may be equally harmful. Probably the best approach is to listen to at least a summary of the problem and then to suggest tactfully that the subordinate see his immediate supervisor.

But suppose the man has already seen his supervisor? One solution would be for the boss to call the supervisor and subordinate together and hear them out. Such a meeting, however, might aggravate the tension between them, and inhibit both of them from talking freely. The supervisor might have had confidential reasons for taking the disputed action. Above all, the fact that the subordinate is implicitly making charges against his supervisor tends to make the supervisor feel that he is on trial, that he must defend his every action. To make a meeting of this sort successful would require unusual human-relations skills on the part of the boss.[13]

Probably a better approach is for the boss to listen carefully to the subordinate's problem, without committing himself one way or the other, and then promise to discuss it with the supervisor.[14] In his meeting with the supervisor, the boss should try to minimize his interference with the supervisor's freedom to make decisions within the limits of his delegated discretion. If the problem is serious enough, the boss may use the nondirective technique to help the supervisor talk through his difficulties. If possible, however, he should leave the final decision to the supervisor. In the event that he feels compelled to reverse the supervisor's decisions, he should be careful to give the reasons why. Further, in order to preserve the supervisor's prestige, he, not the boss, should be the one to explain the final decision to the subordinate.

Attitude surveys Many companies use morale or attitude surveys as a means of finding out how their employees feel about their job, their supervisors, specific policies, or the company as a whole.

Today the making and interpretation of such surveys is a growing but specialized field. Psychologists in colleges, in management consulting firms, and in individual companies have become highly skilled in preparing, administering, and evaluating questionnaires.

Some experts argue that standardized surveys (which can be purchased from firms specializing in psychological services) are the best, for they make it possible to compare firms and departments and to point out significant deviations from "norms" that have been developed on the basis of experience elsewhere. Other experts argue that special questionnaires should be devised to meet the needs of each particular company.

Most surveys consist of written questionnaires that may be filled out on the job or at home. (As might be expected, a high percentage of the "take-home" questionnaires are never returned.) In either case, care is taken to preserve the secrecy of the response.

---

[13] For an example of a boss who was able to make such meetings successful, see William F. Whyte, *Human Relations in the Restaurant Industry* (New York: McGraw-Hill, 1948), pp. 298-300.

[14] For examples of the problems involved in this technique, see Problem I at the end of this chapter.

Many questionnaires require the employee to indicate the degree of his feeling in regard to each point. For example:

I feel fairly well satisfied with my present job: [15]

_____ strongly agree	_____ disagree
_____ agree	_____ strongly disagree
_____ undecided	

Other questions may invite the employee to choose among various alternatives:

The following items describe different conditions that may be bothering you in your work. Check the ones that need to be improved: [16]

Ventilation	( )	Unpleasant noise	( )
Lighting	( )	Faulty unsafe equipment	( )
Too cold	( )	Dirty work station	( )
Too hot	( )	Lack of sanitation	( )
Drafts	( )	Too far from rest room	( )
Sun glare	( )	Unpleasant dust	( )
Dampness	( )	No union	( )
Unpleasant odors	( )	Other _____	( )

Some surveys try to elicit more detailed (and perhaps deeper) answers through so-called "open-ended" questions, such as, "What would you say are your most serious dissatisfactions with your present job?" A modification of this technique is the sentence-completion procedure, in which the respondent is requested to complete sentences like "The most serious complaint I have about my present job is _____."

Because employees are sometimes reluctant to reveal their deeper feelings and may not even be able to express them, attempts have been made to adapt psychiatric techniques to industrial use. For example, rather than using verbal questions, the respondent may be shown cartoons of people in the organization, talking with the traditional little "balloons" over their heads. The respondent is asked to fill in the balloons with what he thinks the people are saying to each other. These more sophisticated forms of survey are much more expensive to score than the check-your-answer forms, and are less frequently used.

Once the forms have been filled out, the results must be tabulated and analyzed. Simple, so-called "straight runs" (e.g., 70 per cent of the men like their jobs) are usually less useful than cross tabulation, such as:

	Among men who like their jobs	Among men who dislike their jobs	Total
Foremen speak to them often	85%	15%	100%
Foremen speak to them rarely	45	55	100

---

[15] Roger M. Bellows, *Psychology of Personnel in Business and Industry*, 2nd ed. (Englewood Cliffs, N. J.: Prentice-Hall, 1954), p. 155.

[16] *Ibid.*, p. 146.

The survey results are then presented to top management, which sometimes disseminates them to lower levels. Indeed some companies use survey results as a springboard for supervisory training. On occasion, the results are specific enough to dictate immediate action, as in the case of a survey which revealed that many employees misunderstood the details of a new pension plan. More often the results are ambiguous. They raise a host of questions but the answers, if any, must be found through a careful re-examination of policies and behavior in the affected areas.

Thus surveys point up broad problems, but rarely suggest solutions. They are a rather artificial form of upward communication and their findings are subject to serious forms of distortion. Employees may purposely or unconsciously misinterpret questions and give misleading answers. By their very design, these surveys make no provision for communicating the specific problems of specific employees. Often they are expensive and time-consuming. For all these reasons, attitude surveys are a valuable adjunct to, but not a substitute for, more unambiguous, direct means of upward communication.

Committees   Management sometimes sets up special conference groups or committees to find out what is on the minds of employees. These committees give lower-ranking personnel a chance to express their attitudes directly to top management, thus by-passing intermediate levels. For example, the first-line supervisory group may elect representatives to meet weekly or monthly with the general manager to discuss current problems. The representatives are encouraged to ask about the rumors floating about on their level, ask questions, ventilate gripes, and give management some idea of the unsolved problems in their departments.

Some companies have used similar devices for hourly-paid personnel.[17] Here caution needs to be exercised to insure that these committees do not conflict with existing unions or violate the provisions of the National Labor Relations Act, which prohibits employers from assisting in the formation of employee organizations with union-like functions.

Other techniques   Suggestion systems are used by many companies as a means of collecting specific ideas for improving company efficiency. Ordinarily suggestions are presented in such a way as to by-pass the intermediate levels of management.

> The experience of one company highlights the manner in which suggestion plans by-pass normal communication channels. An employee suggested that the installation of a coin-operated coffee machine would reduce the half-hour coffee break to a few minutes. The employee wrote out his proposal and dropped it in the "Suggestion Box." It was the first indication that top management had ever had that half-hour coffee breaks were being permitted at lower levels.

---

[17] For a description of how one company makes use of overlapping committees that blanket the entire organization, see Elliott Jaques, *The Changing Culture of a Factory* (New York: Dryden, 1952).

In a sense, the union itself provides a very important channel of upward communication by bringing the average worker's problems directly to the attention of top management. The Scanlon Plan, which grew out of a program of union-management cooperation, brings committees of workers face to face with top management in discussions of production problems.

Effective upward communication is essential both to organizational efficiency and to individual job satisfaction. Top management needs to know what is happening on lower levels, and subordinates feel helpless unless they have some opportunity to talk freely to their own bosses and to make direct contact with the decision-makers at higher levels.

Of course, a great deal of information passes upward through the ordinary channels of the hierarchy. This is particularly true when supervisors at the various levels (1) encourage subordinates to speak freely about their problems, and (2) make a vigorous effort to represent their employees' problems to higher levels of management. As we have suggested, the effectiveness of communication through an organization is directly related to the supervisory practices of the individual managers. With general supervision pervading the entire organization, each subordinate feels free to talk to his own boss, and communications tend to flow upward more efficiently and with less distortion than under close supervision.

Even with highly effective supervision, however, upward communication through many levels of hierarchy is inefficient and subject to some degree of distortion. For this reason some sort of short-circuiting or appeal channel is required to permit individuals to give vent to their feelings and to preserve the health of the organization. Since excessive short-circuiting tends to undermine the position of intermediate management, however, these techniques should be considered chiefly as auxiliary aids. It is more important that each supervisor be sensitive to the problems of those on the levels below him.

Statistical Controls

Now let us explore what is probably management's most effective means of upward communication—statistical controls. Normally, management introduces statistical controls in order to pinpoint responsibility and find out what is actually happening at the operating level. Since figures are harder to distort than subjective reports, higher management insists on receiving a constant flow of data on production, sales, costs, scrap, grievances, salary increases, turnover, and so forth.

Through cost accounting, for example, "standard costs" are developed for every item produced or service rendered. If the standard cost of an item is 35 cents and the foreman can make it for 33 cents, he is making a "profit" (part of which may accrue to him, personally, as a bonus). If he spends 37 cents to make it, he is incurring a "loss." These departmental profit and loss accounts, called *variance accounts,* provide standards by which higher management can measure departmental efficiency. Other standards may be set in terms of quantities produced, man-hours expended per unit, sales, scrap loss, turnover, and so on.

To insure that these data reach headquarters rapidly and without distortion, they are ordinarily collected by staff departments, such as accounting, quality control, and personnel. Because these departments operate at least semi-independently of the line, the data can be reported directly to the top without being filtered through intermediate steps of management that may have reputations to protect. Electronic data-processing apparatus, such as UNIVAC, enormously increases the amount of data that can be assembled and the speed with which they can be transmitted to top management.

In addition to providing top management with the information it needs for decision-making, statistical controls serve many other functions (see Chapter 6).

Supervision by results   Statistical controls eliminate the necessity for close, detailed supervision, and provide the evidence needed for supervision by results. Through reports on profits, sales, and so forth, top management can evaluate the effectiveness of subordinate departments without checking on every detail of their work. Without satisfactory statistical controls, decentralization is difficult.

Standards   Statistical controls also make it possible for management to set standards of achievement and to emphasize areas that require special attention. For instance, if top management is anxious to focus attention on a scrap-reduction program, all it need do is ask all subordinate departments to report each month how much they have reduced scrap losses over the preceding month. Thus statistical *controls* are a means of downward communication and exerting pressure. In turn, they help develop goals and provide motivation and measures of success for those whose work is measured by controls.

Personnel evaluation   Statistical controls that measure individual performance provide a means for selecting, appraising, and compensating employees.

DIFFICULTIES IN MEASUREMENT

Yet statistical controls should not be considered as a magic cure for all organizational ills. Improperly handled, they may create as many problems as they cure. Elements like department costs, efficiency, and productivity are difficult to measure fairly, while the very act of measurement may distort effort. Furthermore, controls are often perceived as pressures, leading to all the problems the theory of general supervision seeks to avoid.

Naturally if employees are to be evaluated largely in terms of their success or failure in meeting these goals, it is important that the goals be fair and reasonable. Establishment of such goals is a highly technical and often inaccurate procedure.[18] It is all too easy to set standards that are too "tight" or too "loose." (It should be obvious too that the greater the reliance on statistical measures of efficiency, the greater becomes the power of the staff departments which prepare them—but more of this later.)

Many types of work are so general and intangible that it is almost impossible to devise an adequate technique for measuring them. How is one to measure the effectiveness of the personnel department?[19] Surely not in terms of cost, because low cost may simply mean that nothing is being accomplished. Not in terms of turnover, number of strikes and grievances, productivity, and so forth, for all these things are related to over-all plant policy or the organization as a whole.[20] Roughly the same sort of objections can be raised against any direct rating of staff departments. And there are other departments, such as research, where meaningful results become apparent only in the long run.

In talking to engineering supervisors in a large research organization, we heard this common complaint: supervisors had a hard time evaluating their subordinates, and subordinates didn't know what was required to get a pay raise or promotion. One supervisor put it this way: "An engineer is constantly making decisions in which he is balancing time against efficiency against cost. It is practically impossible to know whether his judgment is good. Also, if a man doesn't get results, how are you to know whether he has been 'goofing off' or been up against a streak of bad luck?"

Even more severe problems arise in attempts to make a comparative rating of various departments. How does one rate costs in division A, which makes the same product year after year, against division B, where the product is always undergoing change? Some department stores try to measure departmental efficiency in terms of sales and profit, but the level of sales in

---

[18] In Chapter 26 we shall talk about some of the limitations of time-study procedures involved in establishing standard costs—one type of statistical control.

[19] Or how does one measure the efficiency of a university professor? By the number of students who take his courses? But this may depend on whether the professor makes it a "snap course" or on the nature of the subject matter (witness the rise of physics). By student rating? Perhaps, but teaching ability is more than being a good showman. By relative scores on an identical exam which is jointly graded and given to all students in the same course? Possibly—but note the motivation this gives the professor to cover only those points likely to be on the exam. In many colleges promotion is largely based on the number of scholarly articles published with an obvious effect on the relative time spent on research as against teaching. How does one compare the relative efforts of a classics professor with one in chemistry? Obviously direct measurement has its limitations in the university as well as in industry.

[20] Note: Our objections apply more strongly to the measurement of the personnel *department* than the personnel *program*. This is in line with our philosophy that the personnel program is the responsibility of management generally.

any department may depend on its location in the store, the weather, and the business cycle more than on the individual efficiency of the department manager.

DISTORTING BEHAVIOR

If excessive emphasis is placed on statistical controls, compared to other forms of upward communication, the very act of measurement may lead subordinates to distort their efforts and work less efficiently.

Overemphasis on the items measured   Departments will normally concentrate on the items that are being measured rather than on the job as a whole. Successful banks realize that good customer relations are vital and that a very poor impression is created when a teller refuses to serve a customer until he has finished adding up his figures. Yet "the teller has found all his rewards in the past for careful balancing of the books. . . . He has never been rewarded or punished for his treatment of customers." [21]

Token compliance   Supervisors may greet statistical control with token compliance—that is, by striving to *look* as if they were meeting their standards. Unfortunately, the effect of keeping up appearances may well be to lower over-all performance.

As part of a drive to cut excess inventory, the divisional superintendents in one company were required to give a monthly report of supplies on hand. What happened? There was a scramble to use up all the stock before the end of the month and to insure that no new supplies were delivered until after the beginning of the next. But the average inventory over the month remained just about the same.

Inefficient scheduling of work   Sometimes the existence of standards results in a long-run deterioration of real performance, *even on the items being measured.*

> Because management in one company paid so much attention to end-of-month efficiency ratings, department supervisors left no stone unturned to get as many units into finished stores as possible. They even resorted to such expensive and disruptive processes as "bleeding the line"— that is, stopping operations in order to complete more units by the deadline. This process is summarized by what another foreman said:
> "For the last two weeks of the month we're driving hell out of the men. We have to get pieces out and we are always jammed up at the end of the month. . . ." [22]

Even where employees are not subjected to such hectic pressures, the mere existence of standards may induce them to schedule work less efficiently.

---

[21] Mason Haire, *Psychology in Management* (New York: McGraw-Hill, 1956), p. 17.
[22] Frank Jasinski, "Use and Misuse of Efficiency Controls," *Harvard Business Review*, Vol. 34, No. 4 (July 1956), p. 107.

A claims adjuster once told us, "Of course, some claims are harder to handle than others, but as far as the quota is concerned they all count the same. So I always try to keep a few easy cases aside to handle at the end of the month if it looks like I won't be able to meet the quota without them. I try not to turn in too many cases in any month or they'll always expect me to work that hard." Piece-workers in particular have a tendency to build up "banks," as we shall see when we discuss incentives.

Emphasis on short run rather than long run   The use of statistical controls often produces short-term results at the expense of the organization's long-term good. Managers often complain that supervisors are "department-centered" and show no loyalty to the organization as a whole. For instance, department managers in retail stores are rewarded for high sales and profits in their *own* departments. By pushing shoddy merchandise they can sometimes get high sales for themselves at the expense of the goodwill of the entire store. Yet under these circumstances, what other sort of motivation could be expected? Similarly, salesmen, conscious of the importance of an impressive sales record, may ignore the store's public relations—showing themselves unwilling to spend time with indecisive or dissatisfied customers —in favor of the easy, free-spending customer.

Supervisors are supposed to maintain both high morale and high productivity. Morale is intangible and difficult to measure, but productivity and costs can presumably be measured to a tenth of a decimal place. As a consequence, productivity comes first; good employee relations are a luxury to be enjoyed only when there is nothing wrong with output. Measuring factors such as costs, output, and scrap alone may encourage short-sighted supervisors to overemphasize short-run production results at the expense of human assets and longer-run efficiency. One authority suggests: "There is only one solution to this situation: obtain adequate periodic measurements of the character and quality of the human organization . . . which will penalize managers financially and otherwise when they permit the quality of the human organization under them to deteriorate." [23] And many companies do attempt to measure the state of their human relations through turnover figures, morale surveys, and other techniques.

False records   Faced with the necessity of having to look good on paper, the natural impulse of employees is to try to "adjust" the reported statistics. At times plain lying is sufficient, but sometimes it is necessary to hide the evidence. In one department the men put defective parts in refuse cans and covered them over—with the foreman's full knowledge. In another, the foreman himself came back to the department at night to pick up damaged equipment and drop it in the local quarry.

---

[23] Rensis Likert, "Measuring Organizational Performance," *Harvard Business Review*, Vol. 36, No. 2 (1958), pp. 41-50.

In the midst of a safety campaign, one employee suffered a slight injury at the end of his shift which might have kept him home for several days. The foreman begged him:

> "If you can possibly come to work tomorrow I will guarantee you will not have to do a lick of work until you really feel up to it. I'll pick you up at home and drive you back. But for the love of Mike, let's not have a lost-time accident on our record."

In another large company, maintenance and repair charges assessed against production departments were "adjusted." Departments that were "friendly" to maintenance received low charges, while unfriendly departments received not only their own charges, but those left over after the special reductions.[24]

Passing the buck   Another unfortunate by-product of excessive emphasis on standards is an added inducement to pass the buck. If parts turn out defective, there is always an argument about which department should be charged with the cost of repair. Similarly, there may be endless haggling over whether time spent in training new employees, or in the handling of grievances, should be charged against the particular department or against the personnel department.

In a well-known national company, accident-prevention is so strongly emphasized that regular tribunals have been established to determine whether an accident will be "charged" against the foreman of the department in which it occurred. In one case, all sorts of internal political pressures were used to influence the panel members in their decision. These tribunals seem more concerned with fixing responsibility than in determining and eliminating the causes of accidents.

Impaired teamwork   Statistical controls and supervision by results rest on the assumption that each individual supervisor should be held responsible for the efficiency of his own department. Within limits it is healthy to encourage individual responsibility. Yet overemphasis on individual performance may lead to excessive individualism and selfishness, particularly in departments that are highly interdependent.

Reduction in discretion   Insofar as statistical data are used as the basis for evaluating the success or failure of managers and departments, they serve to reduce the discretion of the immediate supervisor. As one researcher has noted:

> The evaluation of subordinates is a major responsibility of supervisors. If this evaluation were based entirely on statistical indices, this responsibility would be reduced to a clerical task, the application of a mathematical formula to a set of data. This would not only make the job of supervisor

---

[24] Melville Dalton, *Men Who Manage* (New York: Wiley, 1959), p. 37 ff.

less interesting for him but also undermine his authority over subordinates.[25]

Another expert points out the need for preserving supervisory discretion:

> The practical effect of this high-handed behavior [excessive reliance on statistical controls], oddly enough, is not to make top management the boss, rather, the accountant with his rows of figures, becomes the dominant voice in the company. He becomes a manager by default, as it were, because knowledge is power, and the knowledge on which action is based is what the accountant puts into his reports.
>
> The fact is that the day accountants can devise a balance sheet or graph which encompasses total reality, we can do away with executives—but not until then.[26]

Effect on centralization   The introduction of electronic data-processing apparatus has a similar effect on the position of the supervisor. Such equipment makes available to top managers vastly more data than they have ever had before, and permits them to make detailed decisions affecting the smallest department in the company—thus completely by-passing middle management.[27]

Some observers, however, believe that improved processing of statistical control data can strengthen the decision-making ability of lower levels of the organization. Used properly, computers can also process information that communicates directly to first- and second-level supervisors rather than to higher management. One manager of data-processing operations described the situation in his company:

> [In the old days] many decisions were of necessity made at the plant manager's level because the superintendent didn't have the local facts.
>
> Now the superintendent makes the decisions and they're better decisions because information is more complete, more accurate and available when the manager needs it.
>
> Take the foreman. Decisions he used to make about stock each day were based on not much more than experienced intuition. Now that he knows the answers these decisions are easy—almost automatic. He can concentrate on areas like personnel relations, performance, on schedule and operating efficiency.[28]

Standards as a form of pressure   Without question, management uses standards as a means to apply pressure. The techniques, of course, vary with the supervisor, as these contrasting quotations indicate:

> "I go to the office and check the budget every day. . . . If it's OK, I don't say anything. But if it is no good, then I come back here and give the boys a little—well, you know, I needle them a bit."

[25] Blau, *op. cit.*, p. 41.

[26] Jasinski, *op. cit.*, p. 111.

[27] Edward L. Wallace, "Top Management Decisions and Their Importance to a Program of Automation," *Automation for Senior Officers* (Chicago: University of Chicago, 1956).

[28] *For Line and Staff Supervisors*, National Foremen's Institute, New York, July 1959.

"You know, it is a funny thing. If I want my people to read the budget, I just lay it on my desk and leave it alone. They'll pick it up without doubt." [29]

Notice that both approaches use standards as a form of pressure. Basic to both is the assumption that failure to meet a quota is prima-facie proof of falling down on the job. In effect, the standards are transformed into an extremely arbitrary boss. Many a supervisor says, "I don't want excuses, just get the job done." It does little good for the subordinate to reply, "But I did get the job done—only the profit figures don't give the complete picture." When standards are boss, all explanations are regarded as excuses.

> Perhaps one of the [supervisor's] greatest criticisms of budgets was the fact that they never included the reasons *why* they were not achieved. . . . Supervisors disliked intensely the fact that their departments would look "sick" in the budget while the reasons for the "sickness" were never published along with the results. [30]

Controls are not omnipotent In most organizations there are other pressures at work "balancing off" the pressures exerted by the use of standards. As we have observed, the work group, unions, and colleagues have standards or norms of their own which may conflict with the requirements being imposed by top management. Then the supervisor, charged with the responsibility of making a good showing in the eyes of his boss, finds himself caught "in the middle."

This phenomenon even occurs in totalitarian states, where consumers, community groups, and employees can exercise some influence because of their ability to withhold or give enthusiastic cooperation. For example, a re-cent study shows that in Russia the factory manager tends to resist standards imposed from *above* because of informal pressures being exerted from *below*

> These informal pressures constitute standards of which the manager must take cognizance, pressures to which he must adjust, in order to maintain such relations with his "working community" as will permit him to meet standards directly set and enforceable by superiors. . . .
>
> [The manager reacts to pressures from above by] providing for a safety factor; simulation, or feigning the meeting of standards, and *blat*, or the use of personal influence to obtain favors. [31]

IMPROVED USE OF CONTROLS

The use of control measures is an essential part of management's job in any large organization. No top manager can know everything he needs to know without quantitative data that summarize what is happening and that

---

[29] Chris Argyris, *The Impact of Budget on People* (New York: Controllership Foundation, 1952), p. 24.

[30] *Ibid.*, p. 11.

[31] Andrew G. Frank, "Goal Ambiguity and Conflicting Standards: An Approach to the Study of Organization," *Human Organization*, Vol. 17, No. 4 (Winter 1958-59), p. 9.

compare actual results with expected or planned results. When carefully presented, these data enable him to detect trouble-spots almost instantly, without reviewing every facet of day-to-day operations. All he need do is look for the variances, the departures from the quantitative limits that he has set for his subordinates—the number of units to be processed, the amount of permissible over-time, the number of merit increases, and so forth.

The challenge for the manager is to develop methods of using control channels of communication that do not have the serious drawbacks described above.[32] If he is successful, the rewards can be substantial—greater autonomy, job satisfaction, and better performance for subordinates at each level.

One test of good usage is the organization's response when a man fails to meet standards. Is his failure regarded as evidence of incompetence, perhaps meriting discipline? Or is it just a cue for management to find out how badly he has fallen down, to help him find out why, to stand ready to give him whatever assistance he needs? Management must decide whether to use controls as a means of "catching" people, or as a means of identifying problems and allocating the resources of the organization to provide assistance. Management's choice is dictated in part by its approach to setting standards in the first place. Standards are probably most effective when they are set by the supervisor and subordinate working together. They are least effective when they are imposed by staff officials or top managers who have relatively little understanding of the specific department. Standards are particularly troublesome when they are used as a basis for setting compensation (as in a bonus system) without appropriate appeal channels.

In summary, statistical data do not necessarily give a complete picture of "results." Failure to achieve "results" should always raise the question "*Why?*" "What has happened to cause this departure from what we anticipated?"

"In the words of the old saw, 'Figures don't lie.' Maybe they don't lie, but that doesn't mean that they are capable of dictating action without the aid of managerial judgment bolstered by information gleaned from multiple sources." [33]

Conclusion

Organizational structure is more than a series of interconnected boxes and lines on a chart. It is a pattern of human relationships—planned and unplanned—that has evolved over a period of time in response to the human and technical problems of the firm.

The manager of any large organization faces a most difficult task in getting all employees (frequently including many levels of supervision as well) to coordinate their efforts and to follow his leadership and direction. To accom-

---

[32] Staff groups are frequently utilized in the application of these standards as management "controls." Their role in this application is discussed in Chapter 18.

[33] Jasinski, *op. cit.*, p. 106.

plish this objective he must make use of both downward and upward channels of communication—he must both give orders and assess their effectiveness. Yet the systems of human relationships that he depends on for transmission are far from foolproof. Organizations often do not function as planned. Serious distortions are introduced by the necessity of communicating through many levels; interpersonal contacts inevitably are limited and restrained between employees at different levels.

In an effort to duplicate some of the communication advantages of the smaller organization, modifications are introduced in the hierarchical structure. These include, among others, techniques for by-passing and short-circuiting, such as mass communications, open-door policies, special committees, and appeal channels. However, there is a danger that these modifications can be as injurious to the organization as the problems they are supposed to remedy. Usually they threaten the leadership position of the immediate supervisor.

Two distinctive features of large, many-leveled organizations are the use of rules (or policies) and quantitative controls. Poorly administered rules and controls can throttle initiative, destroy job satisfaction, and create debilitating inflexibility. However, they can be used to advantage by the administrator who is sensitive to their impact. Rules and controls developed with care insure that employees will know what is expected of them, what criteria they will be judged on, and what discretion they have to make decisions. All the way up the line, supervisors are relieved of the time-consuming and morale-damaging necessity of interfering in the work of subordinates in order to make sure it is going as planned. Personnel policies in particular, since they are among the most important *rules* established by higher management, can be either a source of good human relationships in the organization, or one of the factors responsible for their deterioration. The last sections of this book will consider the problems of developing adequate personnel policies in large organizations.

Problem I

Telephone Conversation—(General Superintendent phones, somewhat excitedly, to one of his superintendents)

Gen'l Supt.: "Say, this morning when I was walking through one of your departments, one of the setup men, Joe Smith in Department X, stopped me and said the fixture he was using on his machine was no good. It had to have a couple extra clamps on it which slowed his production down by a third. What are you doing about this?"

Supt.: "I don't think I know anything about the situation you're talking about. I'll have to check into it."

Gen'l Supt.: "But the setup man said that this has been going on for a week now. Haven't you heard anything about it?"

Supt.: "No, I guess I wouldn't hear anything about it unless it involved a problem that the foreman out there thought he couldn't handle."

Gen'l Supt.: "Well, get on it as soon as you can, and let me know what you find out as soon as you do."

In Superintendent's Office

Supt.: (to Foreman) "I've called you in to ask whether we are having any serious trouble with the fixtures over in Joe Smith's area."

Foreman: "Well, I've been with Engineering on this. They're designing an entirely new-type fixture, so we're getting along with this the best we can in the meantime. I know it's costing us something to limp along this way, but I figured it was cheaper than ordering a replacement for the old fixture at a couple hundred dollars and have it become obsolete in the couple weeks it would take them to develop the new one. I feel this new design is going to really save us some money. Why, is there anything wrong?"

Supt.: "Yeah, the boss wants to know what we are doing to take care of it. Maybe this is something I should have known about since the setup man was griping to the boss."

Foreman: "Oh yeah, I remember yesterday when the boss came through; Smith and he started talking. I guess I should have gone over to see what was up. And the next time, on something like this, I'll check with you immediately."

Supt.: "Did the setup man know what was being done with Engineering about the fixture?"

Foreman: "Sure. I told him about it last week. He knows the whole story. I wonder what he's trying to pull—griping to the boss."

Supt.: "Well, I'll call the boss and you take care of Joe."

Foreman: "O.K."

1. Why was the General Superintendent disappointed that the Superintendent did not know about the malfunctioning fixture? Should he have been upset?

2. What effect did the General Superintendent's call have on the methods of supervision that would be used in the future? Describe the probable changes in the relationship between the General Superintendent and Superintendent, between Superintendent and Foreman, and between Foreman and setup man.

3. Did the Foreman handle Smith correctly? Is there anything the Superintendent can do to review this problem with the Foreman that will not discourage the Supervisor in taking responsibility and initiative?

4. Assume that the whole incident could be repeated. What should the General Superintendent do after learning about the operating troubles in Department X? Be specific in describing what should take place in the contacts between:
   General Superintendent and setup man
   General Superintendent and Superintendent
   Superintendent and Foreman
   Foreman and setup man

5. What might Smith's motives have been in this case?

Problem II

Bill Adams was hired to fill a new job as assistant to Alfred Grozia, the laboratory head and research director. Adams' assignment was to handle all the administrative details for a very busy executive-scientist.

After about six months on the job, Adams was on good terms with nearly everyone in the lab. In the course of a conversation, Adams learned that one of the ablest metallurgists, Isaac Carroll, was seriously considering quitting. Carroll's boss, Felt, a project director who reported directly to the research director, had been giving Carroll a great deal of extra routine work to do. Not only was Carroll finding it difficult to complete his regular research activities and earn recognition for the quality of his performance, but he also found the additional work tedious and unsatisfying. Carroll had asked for a technician to serve as an assistant, but this request had been turned down.

Adams was unsure of what to do. He was convinced that Felt was unaware of Carroll's extreme dissatisfaction. Felt had a reputation for "pushing" people, although he was technically competent. But Adams was reluctant to broach the question to Felt; the two had never hit it off, and Felt had made it clear that he wanted no interference from the boss' assistant. Moreover, Adams was reluctant to speak directly to Grozia, for fear that he might be regarded as a "spy," and cause Carroll serious embarrassment. If word got out, Felt would feel that Carroll had gone over his head. At the same time, Carroll's resignation would be a serious and needless loss to the organization.

1. How would you handle this situation if you were Adams?

Problem III

Eggert is the general manager of a large eastern department store, with responsibility for directing most of the operating departments. For years, two of these departments—packaging and merchandise-marking (ticketing)—have been afflicted by a high turnover rate, failure to meet deadlines, and employee grievances.

Recently the situation in marking has improved significantly, although it is still far from satisfactory. Apparently the present supervisor in the marking department, Elsohn, is doing a good job—at least the selling departments are no longer complaining about incorrect ticketing or failure to have merchandise ready for floor display on time.

Recently Colson, the head of the packaging department, complained to Eggert that all sort of disciplinary problems were being created by the way Elsohn was running his department. The two departments were physically adjacent, and Colson's employees noticed that the people in marking consistently stopped work 15 to 25 minutes before the end of the day to freshen up, gossip, and relax. There was a clear store rule that all personnel were to work until the closing bell had rung; ample time was provided during the day for employees to take breaks.

Colson said he could hardly enforce this rule in his own department so long as it was being flagrantly violated next door. Eggert promised to "look into the situation."

1. What would you do if you were Eggert? What information would you need? What criteria would you use in evaluating new data?
2. What are the dangers here?

Problem IV

The company president has received a long letter from an employee in the shipping department, complaining that he did not get a promotion to which he felt himself entitled. The reason, claims the employee, is that his supervisor has a grudge against him. Moreover, he claims, the supervisor's judgment cannot be relied on. In his letter, he discloses a number of violations of company policy that the supervisor has countenanced, and a number of private deals that have been worked out in the department.

1. What should the company president do with this information?

Every supervisor, except for the company president, belongs to two groups: the work group of which he is the leader, and the higher-management group of which he is the immediate representative. The supervisor is thus a man in the middle, endlessly beset by conflicting loyalties and demands. The ineffective supervisor allows himself to be squeezed by these conflicting pressures; the effective supervisor resists them and serves as a communications link between those above and those below him.

The Supervisor and His Boss

Our emphasis in earlier chapters—and the emphasis in current research, training, and management thinking—has been on the relationship between supervisors and their subordinates. In actual day-to-day activities, however, many supervisors spend less time with their subordinates than they do with superiors, staff, and other supervisors at their own level. And there is empirical evidence that the effective foreman spends a

The Supervisor:
Man in the Middle

greater proportion of his time on upward and horizontal contacts than does the ineffective supervisor. The General Electric study, discussed in Chapter 6, reported the following results:

Percentage of Time Spent on Personal Contacts *

	High-rated Foremen	Low-rated Foremen
With staff and service people	32%	20%
With own subordinates	19	17

* Quentin D. Ponder, "The Effective Manufacturing Foreman," *Proceedings of the Tenth Annual Meeting* (Madison, Wisc.: Industrial Relations Research Association, 1957), p. 50.

And yet the amount of time a supervisor spends on any one activity is not the only important criterion. One must consider his skill in using that time. The effective supervisor is successful in maintaining good diplomatic relations with his boss and with other departments. The University of Michigan studies suggest that high-productivity supervisors, as compared with low-productivity supervisors: [1]

1. Receive general rather than close supervision and have authority delegated to them
2. Know where they stand with the company and the boss, particularly in regard to promotion
3. Stand up for their men and are able to win benefits for them

In addition, the effective supervisor is usually responsible to only one boss; he is not subject to conflicting supervision.

Let us consider each of these points in turn.

TRANSMITTAL OF SUPERVISORY STYLES

Supervisory styles are handed down from level to level; good supervision at the top is reflected by good supervision at the bottom. The evidence suggests that those who receive general supervision are more likely to practice general supervision themselves, and that those who are supervised closely will supervise their subordinates closely. [2]

---

[1] See Rensis Likert and Daniel Katz, "Supervisory Practices and Organizational Structure as They Affect Employee Productivity and Morale," Personnel Series 120 (New York: American Management Association, 1948); Daniel Katz, Nathan Maccoby, and Nancy Morse, *Productivity, Supervision, and Morale in an Office Situation*, Part I (Ann Arbor: Institute for Social Research, University of Michigan, 1950); Robert Kahn and Daniel Katz, "Leadership Practices in Relation to Productivity and Morale," *Group Dynamics*, Dorwin Cartwright and Alvin Zander, eds. (Evanston, Ill.: Row, Peterson, 1953).

[2] See Edwin Fleishman, "The Description of Supervisory Behavior," *Journal of Applied Psychology*, Vol. 37, No. 1 (February 1953), pp. 1-6; Edwin Fleishman, "Leadership Climate, Human Relations Training, and Supervisory Behavior," *Personnel Psychology*, Vol. 6, No. 1 (Summer 1953), pp. 205-222; Charles R. Walker, Robert Guest, and Arthur N. Turner, *Foreman on the Assembly Line* (Cambridge: Harvard University Press, 1956), p. 25.

It is perfectly natural for the supervisor to reflect the supervisory style of his boss, for the boss is the one who hands out rewards. His actions are looked upon as clues to the behavior he expects from his subordinates. "To a greater or lesser extent, any assigned job becomes, in this medium, two jobs: one job is to carry out the assignment; the other (but not always the secondary) job is to please the superior." [3] The subordinate imitates his boss' work hours, his sense of humor, perhaps even his car, and certainly his style of supervision. (The implications for training will be considered in Chapter 24.)

If the supervisor is subjected to pressure by his own boss, he has a strong tendency to pass it on to those below. Transmitting pressure—and perhaps increasing it a bit in the process—is a time-honored way of relieving frustration and soothing a wounded ego. Moreover, when the boss applies pressure on the man directly below him, he is saying in effect that he wants immediate results regardless of the long-run effects on subordinates farther down the line. As a consequence, many supervisors decide:

> "I can't afford to have any mistakes made in my department or my boss will get me in trouble. Also, he's likely to quiz me on everything that happens. So I better check up on everything and have all the facts and explanations at my finger tips. This means I have to keep close tabs on my men."

Yet "keeping close tabs" on the men may generate widespread frustration, aggressiveness, and other negative reactions. One general foreman made this shrewd observation:

> "Some people . . . have got to recognize the fact that by putting too much pressure on the foreman, you are only going to drive him to do things that lead to friction on the job. . . . As for myself, I have a thick skin, and I absorb a lot of the pressure and only pass on what I think should be passed on." [4]

Ineffective supervisors often "develop into pompous, petty bureaucrats. . . . Their outstanding trait is a Janus-like subservience to their superior—combined with a thirst for unrestricted power over their subordinates. . . . They are extremely status conscious, they prefer subordinates who are bootlickers." [5]

Furthermore, no supervisor can permit his subordinates to exercise freedom in areas in which he does not have freedom himself. Some top managements, for instance, issue strict rules which describe in detail what they want subordinates at all levels to do in almost every conceivable situation. Under such circumstances the supervisor has little discretion himself and cannot delegate any at all.

---

[3] Harold Leavitt, *Managerial Psychology* (Chicago: University of Chicago Press, 1958), p. 264.

[4] Walker, Guest, and Turner, *op. cit.*, p. 25.

[5] Robert N. McMurray, "Recruitment, Dependency, and Morale in the Banking Industry," *Administrative Science Quarterly*, Vol. 3, No. 1 (June 1958), p. 90.

On the other hand, the supervisor who receives general supervision from above feels free to let his subordinates make decisions by themselves. Knowing that he will be judged by over-all results, he encourages his subordinates to experiment and does not penalize them for making unintentional mistakes. He is confident that his own boss will back him up when his judgment is questioned, whether by subordinates, by other supervisors, or even by top management. Here we have an extension of the principle of delegation of authority. In effect the boss is saying, "I really mean it when I tell my supervisor that I am giving him authority. I won't interfere with his decisions so long as the final results are good."

KNOWLEDGE OF STANDING

The effective manager knows pretty well where he stands—and it is usually pretty high. He recognizes that as long as he produces results his boss will back him up and refrain from meddling with petty details. Imbued with a sense of confidence and freedom, he operates in what we have called an "atmosphere of approval."

One reason for the ineffective manager's poor performance is his personal insecurity. Uncertain about where he stands in the eyes of his boss and his company, fearful that the axe will fall any minute, and anxious to avoid the boss' displeasure, it is little wonder that he is reluctant to experiment or to encourage his subordinates to develop their own ways of doing things.

REPRESENTING SUBORDINATES

By definition, a supervisor is the man to whom formal authority has been delegated to run a department. But the effective supervisor goes beyond this purely formal role and performs another series of functions: he acts as spokesman and protector for his subordinates, and represents their interests to higher management. (You will remember that in our discussion of informal leadership in Chapter 3, we mentioned that the informal leader functioned as "an outside contact man" for the group. The effective supervisor fills a similar role.)

In a sense, the effective supervisor serves as a shock-absorber, shielding his men from outside influences that jeopardize their welfare and productivity. As one foreman put it:

> "If I treat a man right and he figures a way of doing a job which gives him a little rest, then so much the better for him. My boss doesn't understand that, so that you might say I am a concrete wall between the general foreman and the men. I have to take it one way, but not give it out the same way." [6]

---

[6] Walker, Guest, and Turner, *op. cit.*, p. 26.

He accepts responsibility when things go wrong. When the boss asks for explanations, he doesn't say, "That's Joe's fault; I'll speak to him." Instead, he takes the "rap" himself rather than involving Joe with higher-ups. (Whether Joe knows about this specific favor is irrelevant; the group will know the results of the policy, and that is what is important.) He tries to ameliorate the rigid requirements imposed by higher management, in an attempt to make life easier for his subordinates. In short, he *humanizes* management.

Moreover, he speaks out for the interests of his men when he thinks that management has made a wrong decision. He acts as spokesman for subordinates who have less opportunity to contact higher levels of authority. Note what one worker said:

> "My present foreman is the nicest guy I ever worked for. The other foremen respect him also. I saw him stick his neck out with the general foreman over work loads. . . . He'll argue a point with the general foreman if he thinks he is right." [7]

What this means in practice is dictated by the situation. To the average soldier or sailor, a good commanding officer is a man "who will look out for his men." One observer described a typical case in the Navy:

> The personality of the captain was an important factor maintaining morale and efficiency despite the tensions among the enlisted men. The captain was extremely popular with the men who looked upon him as their active protector against higher authority. . . . Although many of the 3,000 men aboard seldom saw their captain, there was a growing body of lore concerning his disregard of naval formalities and his concern for enlisted men. [8]

In other cases, acting as spokesman for the group may mean fighting for promotions, getting better heating for the men in winter, cutting red tape to get an employee immediate benefits under an insurance plan, getting a larger appropriation (in a government agency), pointing out to the time-study engineers that their controls are too "tight" or (in an engineering firm) battling for the special interests of the department against interference from other departments that wish to put their plans first.

However, the manager cannot fight for his men or take a critical attitude toward management decisions if his boss forces him to be a "yes man." In battling for the interests of his group, the manager may have to tread on a lot of toes; he may even have to disagree with the boss himself. But he can behave in this way only if his boss permits him to do so: If he listens to his suggestions and backs him up when he gets into trouble with other departments.

Much depends on the supervisor himself, of course. Being a spokesman for

---

[7] *Ibid.*, p. 27.

[8] James F. Downes, "Environment, Communications and Status Change Aboard an American Aircraft Carrier," *Human Organization*, Vol. 17, No. 3 (Fall 1958), p. 14.

the group is not enough. The supervisor must be successful in getting results.[9] This means he must have the skill to make effective presentations to his boss and to other departments: he must be a good listener and a good communicator. And, since it takes time to develop good relations, he must be able to plan his work and train his men well enough so that he doesn't have to be constantly present in his own department.

Thus the effective supervisor has what has been called "influence"[10]— that is, other levels of management respond to his requests. When the supervisor is successful, the confidence of his men is reinforced. When he is perpetually turned down, his men become disillusioned with his effectiveness in exerting influence.

In fact, general supervision *without* influence may lead to poorer results than close supervision *with* influence (or at least to more dissatisfaction).[11] Why? Take the case of the general supervisor who commands no influence. He calls a group meeting to discuss a common problem. Then he takes the group's suggested solution up to higher management, only to find that it is rejected out of hand. A group that goes through this experience several times sinks into frustration and cynicism; it becomes antagonistic toward the company and disrespectful of the supervisor. Subsequent attempts by the supervisor to practice general supervision will be interpreted merely as weakness. Finally, the men may decide that, since trying to work *with* management has failed, they might as well try working *against* it. They may choose to by-pass the supervisor altogether and seek to challenge higher management directly, either through their union or through an independent wild-cat strike.

The effective supervisor, on the other hand, is able to persuade management to satisfy the group's legitimate requests. This kind of activity helps build reciprocal loyalty between supervisor and subordinates. "Since our supervisor stands up for us, we'll stand up for him." As a consequence, the subordinates are more likely to comply with his requests.

Do effective supervisors feel greater loyalty to their subordinates or to their boss? Often members of management complain, "We've got to make our foremen feel they are company men. They're always taking the employees' point of view." This may not be too regrettable a situation. There is evidence that at least on the foreman level the good supervisor identifies as closely with his subordinates as he does with management.[12]

In the Prudential study, supervisors were asked questions designed to de-

---

[9] At Prudential, supervisors of the less productive departments were more likely to *recommend* promotions; but supervisors of the more productive departments won the promotions. Katz, Maccoby, and Morse, *op. cit.*, p. 27.

[10] Donald Pelz, "Leadership within a Hierarchical Organization," *Journal of Social Issues*, Vol. 7, No. 5 (1951), pp. 48-55.

[11] Nancy Morse, *Satisfactions in White Collar Jobs* (Ann Arbor: Survey Research Center, University of Michigan, 1953), p. 164.

[12] Katz, Maccoby, and Morse, *op. cit.*

termine whether they identified more closely with company or with employees. As the following table indicates, employee-identified supervisors had the more productive sections: [13]

	Identified with	
	Employees	Company
High-production supervisors	9	2
Low-production supervisors	4	8

This same company had separate dining rooms set aside for supervisors. The high-productivity supervisors, reflecting the attitude of their employees, objected to this form of segregation. The low-productivity supervisors went along with it.[14]

Still, the supervisor's loyalty is not undivided. He is also loyal to management—or, to be more precise, he is motivated to carry out the assignments that have been delegated to him. As a result, he may sometimes find himself in conflict with the men he supervises and have no choice but to act restrictively. And yet he must somehow manage to keep his dual role intact, for he will sacrifice his effectiveness if he becomes too interested either in meeting management's production demands or in safeguarding the interests of his men.

> If management fails to recognize this duality and attempts to enlist a supervisor's undivided loyalty, he may lose his ability to act as a representative of his employees and eventually his effectiveness in helping management gain its objectives.[15]

Too Many Bosses

According to organizational theory, every employee should be answerable to one and only one boss. This arrangement eliminates the possibility that employees will receive conflicting instructions, preserves the authority of the boss, and makes it possible to hold one man responsible for the output of each section of the organization.

In practice, however, the typical supervisor receives orders from many people. Sometimes his boss' bosses give him orders directly. A piece of equipment breaks down and the plant manager descends on the foreman to de-

---

[13] *Ibid.*, p. 23.

[14] *Ibid.*, p. 25. High-producing foremen in a tractor factory were more critical of company policies and their bosses than were low-producing foremen. Kahn and Katz, *op. cit.*, p. 222. Higher-rated Forest Service supervisors were more likely to be critical of their superiors than were lower-rated supervisors. A. L. Comrey, J. F. Pfiffner, and H. P. Beem, "Factors Influencing Organizational Effectiveness: The U. S. Forest Service," *Personnel Psychology*, Vol. 5, No. 4 (Winter 1952), pp. 307-328.

[15] F. C. Mann and J. K. Dent, "The Supervisor: Member of Two Organizational Families," *Harvard Business Review*, Vol. 32, No. 6 (November 1954), p. 112.

mand an explanation, bypassing the general foreman and causing frustration.

Orders from staff are even more common. In theory, staff members do not give orders, but in actuality (see Chapter 18) they give advice that is almost impossible to ignore. The personnel director advises on how to handle a grievance; the safety department suggests new guards. Even the guise of advice-giving is often abandoned: quality control prescribes inspection standards, industrial engineering determines work methods. All these staff departments establish policies that the supervisor must enforce.

There is bound to be dissatisfaction if the engineering department decrees that machines should be run faster or the comptroller institutes a new set of accounting forms. Or perhaps the big boss turns down a pay increase for an executive's secretary, or the comptroller turns down a superintendent's urgent request for new loading equipment. Though the immediate supervisor has had no responsibility in making these decisions and may even have violently objected to them, he has the burden of answering complaints and trying to smooth things over so that the decisions will be accepted with a minimum of bad feeling. As one office manager commented, "Staff makes the decisions, but we have to live with them."

Often staff will contact subordinates directly, by-passing the line manager and jeopardizing his authority and prestige. For instance, a manufacturing superintendent once told us, "My foremen have learned that they can get action a lot faster if they go to staff than if they see me. Except when there is trouble I am pretty much a figurehead—and then I am the one who has to bear the blame."

Caught in this dilemma some managers take the easy way out—they pass the buck to higher management and to staff. In effect, they say, "Don't blame me. Blame the other guy."

Sometimes this device is necessary and useful. But used to excess it becomes a crutch for weak supervision. It makes subordinates lose respect for their supervisor and breeds distrust in the organization as a whole.

The problem of too many bosses is really the same as that of by-passing, which we discussed in the preceding chapter. Certainly there are circumstances when by-passing is justified. A subordinate may have a greater feeling of identification with the total organization if he has a chance to talk to members of higher management as well as to his own boss.[16] If he has the opportunity to contact several levels of the organization at once, he will feel less dependent on the whims of his own boss.

Thus, while the supervisor resents being by-passed himself, he has rather mixed feelings about having more than one boss.

---

[16] Walker and Guest ascribed low morale in an automobile assembly plant in part to the fact that many workers "had neither met nor knew the name of the general foremen, or of the supervisors above them." They contrast this with the greater feeling of identification in a steel mill. *The Man on the Assembly Line* (Cambridge: Harvard University Press, 1952), p. 158.

The Special Problem of the First-line Supervisor

First-line supervisors probably suffer more from being men-in-the-middle than do the members of any other supervisory group. Their subordinates, whether they are production workers, office girls, or engineers, do the actual work of the organization. These subordinates have no one to supervise and often little chance for promotion. As a consequence, even if they are paid salary or commission, they are less likely to identify with management. In fact, since they normally do not compete with one another, they have a tendency to join together in defense against higher management.

The first-line supervisor can ignore this potentiality for revolt only at his own peril. His subordinates, as a group, are in a strategic position to embarrass him. By following his instructions too literally and by failing to use common sense, they can spoil work, damage equipment, and waste materials. By slowing down in unison they can prevent him from meeting schedules; through a hundred different subterfuges they can increase his costs and make him look bad in the eyes of his superiors. Thus, though the first-line supervisor is subject to many pressures from above, he cannot pass these pressures down to lower levels; if he tries to do so, he will only make matters worse.[17]

The inevitable result is that the first-line supervisor must somehow come to terms with his subordinates. He must be particularly careful to insure strong, continuing motivation, primarily through bargaining and on-the-job need satisfaction. Often, too, he must make deals with the union steward involving special concessions to the men in return for their implicit agreement to keep production high.

As might be expected, expedient arrangements such as these are rarely acceptable to higher management. Consequently supervisors sometimes become "two-faced," turning one face to management and another to their subordinates. Caught inescapably in the middle, they must cope with all the problems of higher levels of management and at the same time resolve all the problems that are peculiar to their own position in the hierarchy.

THE FOREMAN AS MAN IN THE MIDDLE [18]

The role of the first-line supervisor has been changing in recent years. In order to get a better understanding of his role as a man in the middle, let us look at the historical evolution of a typical first-line supervisor—the pro-

---

[17] For a description of the reaction of foremen in a situation where higher management imposes pressures which they cannot pass on, see Chris Argyris, *Executive Leadership* (New York: Harpers, 1953), Part II.

[18] For useful discussions of the foreman's changing role, see Burleigh Gardner and William F. Whyte, "The Man in the Middle: Position and Problems of the Foreman," *Applied Anthropology*, Vol. 4, No. 2 (Summer 1945), pp. 1-8; Fritz J. Roethlisberger, "The Foreman: Master and Victim of Double Talk," *Harvard Business Review*, Vol. 23, No. 3 (May 1945), pp. 283-298; and Floyd G. Mann and James K. Dent, *op. cit.*

duction foreman. Many of his problems are faced by the office supervisor as well.

Fifty years ago   A half-century ago, the foreman had almost absolute power. He did all the hiring (there were no personnel departments in those days) and he expected his men to show gratitude for being selected. If he picked friends or relatives, no one was in a position to object. The workers were completely dependent on him and naturally catered to his every whim. Often they even felt obliged to give him Christmas presents. As one old-timer put it:

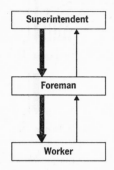

Foreman fifty years ago.

> "In the old days the foreman used to be King —he really *was* a big shot—he'd walk down the plant floor like he really owned the place and you better do what he wanted fast—or you'd be looking for another job."

He had the sole power to discharge employees, for unions were rare and personnel standards nonexistent. If the stories of old-timers are to be believed, it was not uncommon for a foreman to fire a man "just to show who was boss and to keep people on their toes." Single-handed, he took care of all the activities that are now called scheduling, methods, safety, wage administration, and quality control (though many foremen of those days would not have known what those terms meant).

Scientific management   The first blow to the foreman's prestige was the scientific management movement. The doctrine of specialization preached by its apostle, Frederick Taylor, meant that the foreman's job would be bro-

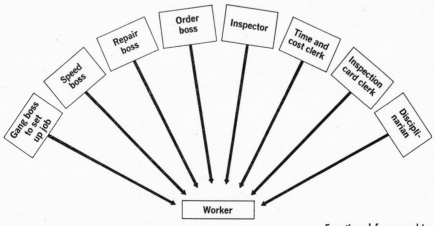

Functional foremanship.

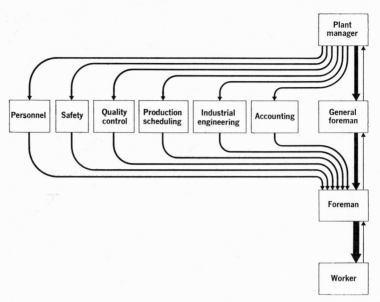

The growth of staff.

ken up into functional specialties. Instead of one foreman, every worker would be supervised by eight different supervisors, each of whom performed a different function: one set up the work, another handled repairs, a third served as disciplinarian, a fourth acted as inspector, and so forth. Each of the eight could give the workers orders. "Functional foremanship," as it was called, was not widely adopted; it caused too much confusion and overlapping of responsibilities, and encouraged buck-passing. Many of its features, however, persist in the modern staff system.

By 1930 many of the foreman's functions had been taken over by staff departments. *How* men worked was decided by the methods department; the *sequence* in which they handled products was decided by production control. Quality-control inspectors came into the foreman's shop to check on quality. A special organization arose to handle safety, and another was set up to take care of maintenance. In many cases even the hiring of workers—the foreman's traditional prerogative—was taken over by the personnel department, thus usurping one of the foreman's main sources of prestige and loyalty.

The union During the 1930's the union made its first appearance in many plants. No longer was the worker obliged to humor the foreman in order to protect himself from being fired. Union membership sapped the loyalty of employees to their immediate supervisor, making it harder for him to make his orders stick. A radically new style of supervision was required, to which it would take the foreman years to adjust.

Worse, another official was added to those who could give the foreman

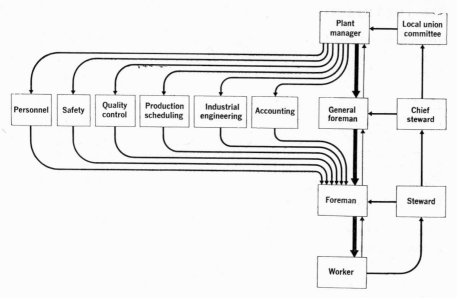

The advent of the union.

"orders"—this was the union steward, who was technically the foreman's subordinate.

Furthermore, largely as a means of protecting itself against the union, management began to centralize the functions of discipline, promotion, and salary administration in the personnel department. Management's reasoning went this way: The union filed grievances whenever the foreman violated the contract or showed favoritism; and whenever a foreman in one plant made an unfortunate decision, the union regarded it as a precedent that could be used against the company in its other plants. Very well, said the company, we will centralize all these functions in the hands of experts, to insure a uniform, consistent policy.[19] What little power the foreman had left was now restricted by specific rules.

As a consequence, the foreman was exposed to conflicting orders and pressures from all sides. His fall from power was almost complete.

Loss of opportunity for promotion   The next blow fell when the foreman was deprived of his opportunity for promotion into higher management. More and more companies now began to recruit their future executives from among college graduates. In some companies the foreman was faced with a dead-end job.

The war   Next came the war period, with its frantic pressures to perform miracles with untrained help. And then the final blow: The advent of wage

_____
[19] Even non-union companies adopted this policy, in an effort to eliminate possible causes of unionism.

controls meant that in many cases the foreman's wages fell below the wages of some of the men he supervised, particularly the men on piece work. By the end of World War II foreman morale was at an all-time low.

The foremen join a union   To protect themselves against this steady erosion of their prestige and power, a number of foremen decided to establish a union of their own. The Foreman's Association of America spread like wild-fire.[20] The foreman reasoned that if other workers could bolster their position by joining a union, he would be foolish not to do the same thing himself. He felt himself excluded from management, relegated to the status of a mere messenger boy.

Management rediscovers the foreman   The rapid spread of the Foreman's Association came as a traumatic shock to management. It was bad enough to lose workers to the union; if the first-line foremen were to defect as well, how could management hope to control its men?

Management's first reaction was an all-out attack on the Foreman's Association. The biggest battle was at Ford, where after a lengthy strike the Association was completely crushed. (Some companies are still suspicious of foremen's clubs of any kind, even those run by the YMCA.)[21]

On a more constructive level, measures were taken to induce foremen to feel once again as though they were members of management. One measure was largely social: management clubs, management dinners, and other activities were arranged at which foremen could mingle on a supposedly equal level with their superiors. Management also made an effort to improve downward communications by means of newsletters and meetings designed to help the foreman feel that he was "in the know" on company developments—hopefully, before the union learned of them.

But management's major efforts to rehabilitate the first-line foreman were in the area of training. At the least sophisticated level, the newly instituted training programs consisted of trite exhortations to feel and act like management (though, as one foreman put it, "it is more important to be treated as management than to be told that you are management"). The better-conceived programs helped to equip foremen with the attitudes and skills necessary to lead men rather than drive them (see Chapter 24).

More substantial than any of these measures was the decision taken by some companies to cut down on the power of staff and restore it to the foreman. In many instances foremen were given the final say over hiring, disci-

---

[20] This was the period during which the National Labor Relations Board gave it the same status as other unions, a condition that was reversed by the Taft-Hartley Act. See U.S. Bureau of Labor Statistics, *Union Membership and Collective Bargaining by Foremen*, Bulletin 745 (Washington, D.C.: Government Printing Office, 1943).

[21] At times with reason: we were present at one foreman club's "annual gripe session," to which management was invited. The interchange sounded remarkably like collective bargaining.

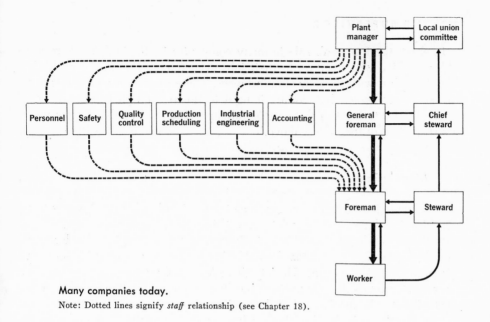

Many companies today.

Note: Dotted lines signify *staff* relationship (see Chapter 18).

pline, and promotion. Often the safety and quality-control departments were made purely advisory, with the foreman exercising actual control.

Moreover, as higher-level supervisors began to grow familiar with participative techniques of supervision, they started to consult with their foremen on important matters. Foremen conferences were conducted according to democratic procedures, and the foreman at last got a real chance to communicate upward.

Many companies also instituted a policy of recruiting their foremen from among college graduates. Years before, the argument for taking power away from the foreman was that he was insufficiently trained to handle such technical problems as personnel and industrial engineering. The new theory was that the foreman's job was, above all, to handle people. If a foreman lacked the necessary skills, management reasoned, it was better to change the foreman than to change the job requirements. Consequently, in many companies the older, less flexible men were often replaced by college graduates.

The general results of this shift in attitude were beneficial. Yet management sometimes underestimated the importance of technical skills, and tended to assume that a college degree was an automatic guarantee of good human-relations skills. Sometimes, however, the young college graduate had neither the age nor the technical skill to command respect; frequently he was led into costly mistakes by his failure to understand group norms or to speak the same "language" as the men he supervised. On the other hand, the old-style pusher or the man who is strictly a technician is obviously incapable of coping with the conditions that prevail in modern industry.

In short, the foreman's role in many companies is still in flux. There are older foremen who hang on to their jobs even though they are completely unable to deal with the new circumstances. There are others who are trying to make the change, but finding it hard to do so. And there are younger men who are trying to practice general supervision with subordinates who are suspicious of their every move.

Conclusion

The ability of the supervisor to motivate his subordinates depends to a considerable degree on his relations with his boss. The evidence suggests that the boss who is most likely to have effective supervisors under him practices general supervision himself, delegates authority, and backs up his subordinates' decisions. He lets them know where they stand and encourages them to make suggestions; he allows them to function as spokesmen for their subordinates instead of demanding unquestioning obedience.

Particularly at the level of the first-line foreman, the role of the supervisor is changing. No longer has he absolute power to issue orders on his own, for his authority has been curtailed by the rising power of staff and union. It is becoming increasingly important for him to be a leader rather than a technician, an expert on men rather than an expert on things. Yet the change is slow and painful, and endlessly frustrating for many supervisors.

Problem I   *Clarence has "influence"*

"I'm the manufacturing superintendent of the Snyder Division of the Amherst Corporation. I've been on the job in this plant for six months and I have a big problem—my boss, Clarence Akron, who has been Division Manager for about fifteen years. Clarence loves his job and he loves people. He knows all 700 employees in the Division by name and he spends a great deal of time wandering about, listening to people's problems and helping supervisors out of trouble. He's even pitched in on the assembly line when we've had a tight schedule.

"All this is fine—except for two things. He spends so much time talking to individual employees and to first-line supervisors that he never has time to spare for his office work and the long-range problems. And his whole approach makes my job—keeping the manufacturing end of the Division going—much harder. I never know what he has told the men—so in a way he's more on top of *my* job than I am. I'm just a figurehead. Frankly, I'm ambitious. I'd like to do a good job here, but his attitude makes it hard—though he's always been friendly and personally helpful to me. The other men on my level, the chief engineer, the sales manager, and the office manager, all have the same troubles I have, though they've been here longer and have got used to it.

"What should I do? Should I talk to Clarence alone? What should I say to him? Should I try to get the rest of management to see him as a delegation? Should I talk to the Vice President (I know him rather well) next time he pays us a visit from Corporation headquarters? Or is there some other approach?"

Seldom is an organization composed of people who all do the same type of work. The typical pattern is for individuals and groups to *specialize* in one function or activity, leaving other functions to their colleagues in other departments or divisions. In fact, specialization has become so common in contemporary life that we tend to take it for granted—it has come to seem the "natural" way of doing things. In this chapter, however, we shall see that the use of specialization as a means of increasing output and efficiency has many repercussions for human relations within the organization, some of which pose complex problems.

As we move down from the top of the organizational pyramid, we find that the functions performed change from one level to the next. The top levels typically devote themselves to broad policy matters. They make the decisions that determine the over-all objectives of the organization. Lower echelons decide *how* these goals will be attained and set the appropriate course of action. Below these levels the *how* is converted into detailed instructions in terms of *who, when,* and *where.* Finally, at the bottom, are the workers who actually perform the operations—the selling, the manufacturing, the processing.

16

The Impact
of Specialization
on Human Relations

Thus the Board of Directors might decide that the company will expand its output by 50 per cent by adding additional facilities. At intermediate levels this decision is converted into detailed plans; next, work schedules are set up; and finally the first-line supervisors assign the men to do the work.

Notice that the amount of discretion diminishes as we move down through the hierarchy. The decisions of the officers at the top are limited only by law and economic forces, but the worker at the bottom has almost no discretion.

This vertical specialization is sometimes carried too far. Many companies have found that stripping their employees of discretion has transformed the work into a painfully monotonous routine and has destroyed both initiative and productivity (see Chapter 2). It is to overcome this problem that management employs such techniques as supervision by results and job enlargement.

Advantages of Specialization

More commonly, however, when we use the term specialization we are referring to the breaking down of a single job into several separate jobs. The concept behind specialization is simple enough: it is more efficient to have each worker perform a single function than to have everybody do a little of everything. For example, as soon as a service station has built up a big enough volume of business, one man concentrates on selling gasoline, another on lubrication, and others on repairs.

More specifically, specialization has these clearly recognizable advantages:

1. It reduces training costs, for a worker learns more quickly when he concentrates on a single function.

2. It avoids the waste of time involved in shifting a man from one kind of job to another, and enables each man to fully develop his skills for a particular job.

3. It makes unnecessary the duplication of equipment that would otherwise be used on only a part-time basis.

4. It enables the company to purchase more specialized equipment.

5. It simplifies the problem of developing job controls.

6. It reduces wage costs by making it possible to hire less-skilled workers.

As the organization grows larger, the degree of specialization steadily increases. It becomes economical to restrict employees to a single task. The jack-of-all-trades may be useful in the home; he finds few openings in a large business. Individual employees, realizing that the way to advance themselves and to improve their marketability is to develop specialized skills, push the level of specialization even higher. No longer is a man just an engineer, or even a mechanical engineer; now he becomes a specialist in tool design, or in strength of materials, or in any of a dozen narrow fields. Whole departments are built around these specialists: community relations, industrial engineering, wage and salary administration, testing, technical recruitment, and countless others.

In fact, any large organization—U.S. Steel or the U.S. Air Force—is an amalgamation of highly specialized, semi-independent units, each with its distinct functions, needs, and internal life.

Problems Created by Specialization

At first glance, specialization would seem to be an unmixed blessing for the organization—at least so long as it can afford to hire enough experts. And yet specialization creates certain severe problems in the organization. Here we shall consider four such problems: (1) specialization tends to increase the amount of red tape in coordinating adjacent departments; (2) specialization encourages departments to compete for power and prestige, often destructively; (3) specialization usually means that the flow of work cuts across departmental lines, causing substantial problems in maintaining cooperation; and (4) specialization impedes coordinated decision-making among mutually dependent work groups. In fact, specialization makes it difficult for subordinates to comprehend the relationship of their unique activities to the total objectives of the organization.

GOING THROUGH CHANNELS: THE RED-TAPE PROBLEM

The typical large company has not one but a number of separate hierarchies with parallel lines of upward and downward communication. Each hierarchy represents a specialty. Since, in theory, these specialties are completely independent of one another, except for coordination at or near the top, one might think that there would be very little need for contact between them. Nothing could be further from the truth.

Take a typical problem: A group of plumbers are working on the air-conditioning equipment in the accounting office. The men stop work a half-hour before quitting time and engage in extensive "clean-up" operations. After this has been going on for several days, the clerks begin to grumble that they should have the same privileges.

How can the accounting supervisor handle this problem? In theory, he must report the matter to his supervisor and so on up the line until it reaches the common boss over both accounting and maintenance. Then the matter descends down the maintenance chain of command till it hits the plumbers.

In this case it might take six supervisory contacts before the problem could officially come to the attention of the supervisor who is directly responsible. If there were a need for frequent adjustments between the accounting section head and the plumbing foreman, the number of contacts would soar astronomically.

In one sense, this cumbersome procedure is very desirable. If the accounting supervisor were to start giving orders directly to the plumbers, the plumbers would be subject to all the evils of "too many bosses." Confusion would set in and the plumbers would suffer a loss of autonomy. A clearly defined sequence of supervisory contacts, by contrast, helps to bring order into interpersonal relations.

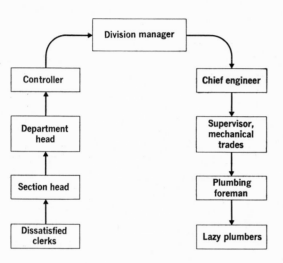

But in emergencies the need to go through channels can be costly in terms of managerial time and may only complicate the problem. Days and weeks may pass before a serious problem can be attended to. Think what would happen in a hospital: ". . . Suppose a piece of oxygen equipment goes out of order. If the nurse were to report it to the head nurse, she to the chief engineer, and he to the repairman, the patient would probably be dead before the equipment was fixed." [1]

As you can see, it becomes more difficult to move swiftly and effectively on challenging problems within the specialized organization. Particularly in large companies, the burden of going through channels, in terms of the sheer number of interactions that must take place for every problem, tends to slow the organization and creates endless frustrations and conflicts. It is under these circumstances that one hears that "red tape" or bureaucracy is defeating the purpose of the company.

As a result, there is a widespread temptation to short-circuit the chain of command. In the case above, the accounting supervisor might go directly to the plumbing foreman. But those who are left out—those who get "short-circuited"—are understandably resentful of such violations of the chain of command.

---

[1] Temple Burling, Edith Lentz, and Robert N. Wilson, *The Give and Take in Hospitals* (New York: Putnam, 1956), p. 323.

COMPETITION BETWEEN FUNCTIONS

As emphasis on specialization increases within an organization, the various specialists begin to identify themselves with their respective groups rather than with the organization as a whole. One reason, of course, is that the members of each group interact with one another more frequently than they do with persons outside the group. This identification with an informal group provides an important need satisfaction for employees who might otherwise feel lost in the larger organization (see Chapter 3). It enables them to relieve themselves of pent-up hostility and bolsters their self-confidence. These satisfactions can contribute to over-all efficiency, but, as we shall see, a price must be paid for these advantages.

What happens when groups of specialists concentrate on their own narrow interests rather than on the interests of the organization as a whole? Each group is intent on growing as large as it can. Each seeks to impress its own point of view on the total organization. Each wishes to enhance its relative status or prestige. Though the competitive struggle may help keep each group on its toes, it may also get out of hand, lead to destructive friction between groups, and do serious injury to the organization as a whole.

Parkinson's Law   There is a tendency (which has recently come to be known facetiously as "Parkinson's Law") for every unit to try to build up its importance by expanding the number of its personnel. C. Northcote Parkinson argues with adroit satire that the number of people employed in a given department within an organization has no relationship to the amount of work that needs to be done. In order to improve their own position vis-à-vis others in the organization, managers are motivated to expand their staffs needlessly: "An official wants to multiply subordinates, not rivals." However, this grand strategy for self-aggrandizement rarely reveals itself because the new personnel make work for one another—with the organization's strong propensities for division of labor. Parkinson describes how seven officials can keep busy doing work that was formerly handled by a single employee:

> For these seven make so much work for each other that all are fully occupied and A is actually working harder than ever. An incoming document may well come before each of them in turn. Official E decides that it falls within the province of F, who places a draft reply before C, who amends it drastically before consulting D, who asks G to deal with it. But G goes on leave at this point, handing the file over to H, who drafts a minute that is signed by D and returned to C, who revises his draft accordingly and lays the new version before A.
>
> What does A do? He would have every excuse for signing the thing unread, for he has many other matters on his mind. Knowing now that he is to succeed W next year, he has to decide whether C or D should succeed to his own office. He had to agree to G's going on leave even if

not yet strictly entitled to it. He is worried whether H should not have gone instead, for reasons of health. He has looked pale recently—partly but not solely because of his domestic troubles. Then there is the business of F's special increment of salary for the period of the conference and E's application for transfer to the Ministry of Pensions. A has heard that D is in love with a married typist and that G and F are no longer on speaking terms—no one seems to know why. So A might be tempted to sign C's draft and have done with it. But A is a conscientious man. Beset as he is with problems created by his colleagues for themselves and for him—created by the mere fact of these officials' existence—he is not the man to shirk his duty. He reads through the draft with care, deletes the fussy paragraphs added by C and H, and restores the thing back to the form preferred in the first instance by the able (if quarrelsome) F. He corrects the English—none of these young men can write grammatically—and finally produces the same reply he would have written if officials C to H had never been born. Far more people have taken far longer to produce the same result. No one has been idle. All have done their best. And it is late in the evening before A finally quits his office and begins the return journey to Ealing.[2]

Department in-breeding As times goes by, each specialized group—the salesmen, the production men, the engineers, the grinders—comes to adopt a distinctive point of view or "organizational character."[3] Each develops a certain dominant value or goal that shapes its entire way of doing things.

For instance, the results of job evaluation may be quite different depending on whether the evaluation is handled by Industrial Engineering or by Personnel. Industrial Engineering may be more interested in the technical accuracy and scientific validity of any job-evaluation study it conducts, whereas Personnel is more likely to come up with results that can be "sold" to the union.

The "in-breeding" that develops within these specialized units makes it difficult to hammer out common agreement on interdepartment problems. Since each specialty has been conditioned to think in a characteristic way, they find it hard to work together as a team. (As we discovered in Chapter 11, these outside commitments present the committee chairman with one of his most difficult problems.) Here is a good description of what happens:

> We've refused to recognize or admit that the various components of our industrial machine are driven by different people with different motives. Sales, for example, is always looking for something to add to the product in order to gain competitive advantage . . . sales presses for changes to get an edge over competitors. Engineering wants changes too, but for an entirely different reason. They're always fighting for easier, cheaper production. Where Sales wants to add to the product, Engineering wants to simplify it. Production has a totally different idea. They

---

[2] C. Northcote Parkinson, *Parkinson's Law* (New York: Houghton Mifflin, 1957), pp. 5-6.

[3] For an excellent discussion of this point, see Philip Selznick, *Leadership in Administration* (Evanston, Ill.: Row, Peterson, 1957), pp. 38 ff.

know that their salvation lies in keeping the men at the machines doing the same thing over and over again. Any production man will tell you how and why repet:ive work is the secret of mass production. And he'll fight changes at the drop of a suggestion.

Thus we have three major divisions of one business looking at the same product from three conflicting points of view. Each of them tries to impress on top management that its contribution is the most important and in the process it pushes under the rug anything that might lower its own status, and slyly points up the faults of its "competitors."

Is it any wonder that we have friction? And, mind you, this friction exists when people are working together with the best intentions.[4]

A sociologist looking at the same problem draws a similar conclusion, but in somewhat different terms:

> The over-all managerial problem has become more complex because each group of management specialists will tend to view the "interests of the enterprise" in terms which are compatible with the survival and the increase of its special function. That is each group will have a trained capacity for its own function and a "trained incapacity" to see its relation to the whole.[5]

Status hierarchy and anxieties   Normally a status hierarchy develops among the various specialties, even among those who are, organizationally speaking, roughly on the same level. For example, production work may carry less prestige than office work; accordingly, production supervisors enjoy lower status than office supervisors.

Ambiguous situations in which the status position of each specialized group has not been clearly established are particularly troublesome. Take plant clericals, the men who do paper work on the production floor. These men insist that they should be considered as office workers and resent any personnel policy that includes them among plant workers.

> Office workers in the X Company are permitted to visit the cafeteria during morning coffee break. For production workers, management sends wagons through the plant with exactly the same kind of food as that sold in the cafeteria. Employees can make their purchases on the spot and take a break as long as the one office workers take. Though the food wagon stops within 100 feet of their work area, the plant clericals have been agitating for the right to go to the cafeteria.
>
> Management, in response to these pressures, has granted the plant clericals what it thought would be a compensating advantage. They were told that the white shirt and ties customary in office areas would no longer be expected of clericals working in production units. Much to management's surprise, this announcement created additional resentment. Not

---

[4] Bernard Davis, "The Pill's Grim Progress," *Esquire*, British edition, Vol. I, No. 3 (August 1954), p. 55; cited by Lt. Col. Lyndall F. Urwick, "The Span of Control—Some Facts about the Fables," *Advanced Management* (November 1956), p. 11.

[5] Reinhard Bendix, "Bureaucratization in Industry," *Industrial Conflict*, ed. A. Kornhauser, R. Dubin, and A. Ross (New York: McGraw-Hill, 1954), p. 170.

one clerical took advantage of the "privilege" of wearing open-neck sport shirts.

Cases like this confront management with a dilemma. Management argues that each groups should be treated "equally," but if status distinctions are ignored, this is bound to generate trouble. Certainly, as we mentioned in Chapter 8, each manager should get to know the "status map" of his organization if he is to avoid causing friction through ignorance. The manager's problem is complicated by the fact that "underdog" departments may be struggling to get ahead and raise their relative status in the organizational community.

Competition for improvements in working conditions and benefits appear to be most frequent among groups that are halfway up the status ladder. Their position is somewhat ambiguous; they are almost the best, but not quite. Members of these groups seem to be carrying a chip on their shoulder. They seize on real or imagined slights that they can protest through the grievance procedure, and never miss a chance to put pressure on both union and management. They are always looking for ways to improve their position: making the job a little easier, loosening the incentive standard, or perhaps eliminating some of the less desirable operations. Their special sensitivity marks them off as sources of danger for both union and management, who must treat them with extra care if turmoil is to be avoided.

Struggles between groups   To some extent every specialized department is engaged in a continuous struggle with other, similar departments for such advantages as higher pay, a larger staff, more power, or more prestigeful treatment (such as more secretaries, a "higher-status" work place, or assignment to a special parking lot). Such struggles may be observed at all levels of the organization—for instance, in the competition between plants and divisions to be allocated new functions or capital for expansion, and in the fights between groups of hourly-paid workers to receive higher relative pay through job evaluation, or "looser" piece-rates through time study.

In theory, management decides between such conflicting claims purely on the basis of their merits; in practice, power politics play an important role. Such power struggles among white-collar and managerial groups are often kept under cover. Among groups of hourly-paid, unionized workers, however, they frequently operate openly.

What sorts of weapon do hourly-paid employees use in fighting each other? [6] They send representative delegations to the personnel department and to top union officials to call attention to their needs; they reinforce their claims by writing a constant series of grievances; they engage in union politics, fighting to place members of their group in power; at times they

[6] See Leonard R. Sayles and George Strauss, *The Local Union* (New York: Harpers, 1953), Chapter 5.

even engage in wild-cat strikes or slow-downs designed to embarrass the union and put pressure on management. Similar though more subtle techniques are used by white-collar and managerial groups.

Which groups win out? There are a number of factors at play.[7] Among others: (1) the most militant, most "outraged" groups (often those who suffer from what we have called "status inconsistency") normally fight harder than those who do not *feel* so aggrieved (regardless of the objective situation); (2) cohesive, successful groups are more successful than those that are internally divided; (3) employees (such as maintenance mechanics or design engineers) whose activities are of critical, immediate importance to the organization's goals find it easier to win concessions from management than those whose services *seem* more dispensable (such as personnel departments); and finally (4) departments that report directly to top management are in a position to better themselves more than those that contact only intermediate echelons.

Thus excessive competition may be a harmful by-product of the compartmentalized organization required by specialization and large size. Management needs to be particularly careful that powerful, united groups in key positions do not create serious inequities in areas such as wage and salary administration, seniority privileges, work schedules and assignments, and fringe benefits.

WORK-FLOW PROBLEMS

Specialization creates many problems of coordination. The theory is that each specialized unit operates independently; in practice, however, a great many contacts are required in the normal flow of work if all the units are to complete their jobs successfully. For example, coordination is simple to achieve in the supermarket when the same girl acts as both cashier and bagger. But once these functions are divided between two people, there is always the possibility that the cashier will get ahead of the bagger and thus create a jam, or that the bagger will get ahead of the cashier and have time on his hands. Obviously, defective coordination is a rich source of friction.

Below we will consider four work-flow problems that arise from specialization. Each of these involves relationship problems that arise as a result of the division of labor in the organization—the fact that an employee *cannot* complete his job, nor can a department, without the help and collaboration of other groups in the organization.

Who is at fault? Friction is normal on any job, for work rarely goes as planned. When things go wrong, there is a temptation in a specialized organization to avoid accepting responsibility and to pass the buck to others involved in the work sequence. For example:

---

[7] See Leonard R. Sayles, *Behavior of Industrial Work Groups* (New York: Wiley, 1958).

The accounting department is criticized for failure to meet its schedule for making reports. It blames the production department for failing to provide needed data on time.

A shortage of material develops on the night shift. When asked why, the night-shift workers protest that the day shift failed to keep the material bins full. They insist the day shift never does its share; they just use up the stocks provided by the night truckers.

Sales criticizes credit for being too harsh in reviewing customer credit ratings, thus causing sales to drop and making it impossible to meet the annual sales quota.

This natural tendency of each group to defend its own interests hurts the organization as a whole. Groups sometimes devote more energy to proving that another group is at fault for some problem than in trying to solve the problem itself.

When higher management pressures subordinates for results at any cost, and imposes heavy penalties, the stage is set for passing the buck. Thus the system of rewards built into the organization frequently motivates its members to think only of their own personal interests. In so doing they make it more difficult for others to do their job.

Bottleneck operations Intergroup competition may manifest itself in a struggle to corral as much as possible of a "scarce resource." The incident below involving interdepartment competition for scarce maintenance facilities, described by a departmental supervisor in a large industrial plant, will help illustrate what we mean:

Whenever we need equipment repaired, we put a tag on it saying what we think is wrong and send it to the Repair Department. We have a series of different-color tags which we can use. We use a white tag for a routine job. Yellow tags mean important but not top priority. A red tag means the repair is highly urgent and production will be held up until the piece is returned. Well, we suddenly burned out one vital unit and I sent it down with a red tag because we needed it back desperately. When I didn't hear from them for several days, I really got mad and decided to check on what was holding us up. Well, you can imagine how burned up I was when I entered the Repair Department to see that every piece they had down there was red-tagged.

This approach, of course, simply makes scarce resources become scarcer. When one supervisor decides that he may not have all the supplies or repair facilities available that he might need in the future, he takes steps to build up an ample reserve. When other supervisors follow suit, a potential shortage becomes an actual scarcity and the whole priority system breaks down.

This kind of situation strains relations among the groups that are competing for the scarce resource, and each accuses the other of selfishly trying to grab more than its share. Needless to say, the common supervisor to whom these groups report constantly will have to mediate among them and resolve intergroup disputes.

Unbalanced pressure   In organizational terms, pressure springs from the efforts of *others* to originate action for you. Pressure is great when one person repeatedly and consistently attempts this (the supervisor who comes back constantly to ask why a certain job has not been completed), or when a relatively large number of people come to you with conflicting demands (as was the case in the repair department described above, and in most service departments). Next-door departments act like irate customers constantly demanding quicker service.

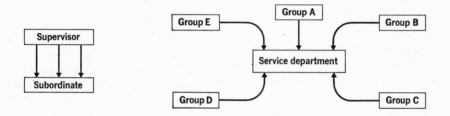

In either instance, the endless pressure is bound to keep you in a state of unrelieved discomfort. Look back to the "Case of the Red Tags" from the point of view of the repair department. Imagine the pressure the repairmen are under who control the scarce resource! Here is an example of a job subjected to constant pressure, as described by the supervisor in charge:

> We are part of a special purchasing division that services the engineering department. It is our job to order parts and materials for the various research projects the engineers undertake. Well, it has gotten so that nothing is routine anymore. The engineers are always engaging in rush projects—you know, someone gets a brainstorm and they want to get it underway immediately. So they come down with the orders they want filled. First they try to get you to tell them it will be done within an hour. By the next morning they're calling the boss to complain you are not working on it fast enough, and by the next afternoon they are in the office themselves trying to get you to put their order ahead of someone else's. They can't seem to understand that it all takes time and we've got lots of other rush jobs. It seems as though we are always under pressure; someone is always asking for greater speed than we can give them. Let me tell you, I have never experienced such tension; I don't know how much longer we can take it.

Normally, higher-status employees give orders to lower-status employees, and not vice versa. This is true throughout life. We expect to have to respond to persons of higher prestige than ourselves; in fact, we are often very reluctant to try to approach them first. We wait to be approached, and similarly we expect to initiate action to people we feel occupy positions of less prestige than ourselves.

Sometimes the work-flow patterns *reverse* this normal relationship. We have all seen situations such as this:

> A clerk or office boy is sent by the department head to ask a skilled craftsman in another group if it would not be possible to speed up his work on a particular job. The employee bristles when approached in this manner by a mere "clerk" and may, if anything, slow down his operation.

This is a critical source of human-relations difficulties in the restaurant industry. Whenever female waitresses give orders to male bartenders, or when pantry personnel give orders to veteran chefs, periodic blow-ups hurt productivity as well as job satisfaction.[8]

Intermittent pressure   Most people want to achieve some equilibrium in their dealings with others: they don't want five people asking them to do something one day and twenty-five the next. Employees are willing to tolerate a certain amount of variation in this contact pattern from day to day as the work load varies; however, this range of tolerance can be exceeded only at the expense of much tension and discontent. Unfortunately, work rarely flows evenly through the organization. There are usually periods of crisis when everyone feels under tension, tempers are short or nonexistent, and normally suppressed conflicts break out into open hostility.

Some of the crises are periodic. At the end of the month clerks in the billing department work under high pressure; store clerks rush to spruce up their displays before the monthly visit of the district manager. Many organizations go through annual cycles. In a toy company, for instance, design changes must be made in the winter; production works hardest from July to October, while shipping is under greatest pressure till the first of December.

Other crises are unplanned. A vital piece of equipment breaks down, a rush order comes in from an important customer, the "brass" from the main office arrives on a surprise inspection trip.

In each of these situations the normal level of contacts is left far behind as members of the organization scurry around to get other individuals and groups on whom they depend to get their work out faster, cheaper, or more impressively. When work routines are interrupted, management becomes worried, and frequently many levels of the hierarchy descend simultaneously on some small group of employees. The pressure created by these many managers only serves to make matters worse.

Reaction to pressures   The tensions created by these pressures take their toll on departmental efficiency. The rate of personnel turnover is often high,

---

[8] William F. Whyte, *Human Relations in the Restaurant Industry* (New York: McGraw-Hill, 1948), pp. 105-108,

while those who stay usually resort to the following patterns of defense or adaptation:

1. Some workers affect an air of resignation, though they may be seething inside; they work off their tensions on their families, friends, or themselves (in terms of psychosomatic illness).

2. Others fight back. They give vent to their frustration by dealing with their tormentors in an aggressive fashion. One observer has related a classic case of how a group defends itself against excessive pressure from other groups:

> The Ship's Store department on a large ship found that certain groups were always demanding rapid service on complicated requisitions. The Ship's Store workers, moving with speed and efficiency, merely announced that these offending groups would have to fill out in perfect detail the multi-copy, excessively complicated formal requisition sheets that were required by an official, but rarely observed, rule. These same pressuring groups also were denied their share of the special goods and goodies that were distributed, in part, at the discretion of the Stores department: stationery, film, etc.

Unfortunately, this response may further reduce organizational efficiency and lead to additional pressure.

3. Still others develop a cordial personal relationship toward the offending groups in the hope of cutting down the pressure. The expert at this approach uses a mixture of kidding, sympathetic listening, and sincere concern. This is the approach followed by the men's store that hires a delectable blonde to handle complaints.

4. Finally, some workers establish their own system of priorities and firmly resist all efforts to violate it. This is what the rushed butcher does when he asks his customers to take a number and wait until it is called.

Employees who work side by side day after day often work out their own systems for accommodating the demands they make on one another. These systems may be reinforced by group norms that forbid fellow members to push or pressure one another.

Large, specialized departments, however, even when they are located close together, seldom develop such informal patterns of accommodation.

The supervisor's responsibility   The alert supervisor is sensitive to the impact of the organization, particularly the work-flow, on his subordinates. In analyzing personnel problems, this is one of the areas he explores: the repercussions of the specific specialization pattern to which his employees are exposed. What can he do when this is the source of trouble? Here is one easy solution:

> Joe Santini was in charge of the industrial engineering department in the central offices of a diversified manufacturing company. As one of their miscellaneous duties, some of his men were assigned the job of

moving office equipment when departments were relocated. Santini discovered that one of his most loyal subordinates, in charge of this operation, was about to quit, claiming that he couldn't take the "strain of his job any more." This seemed strange, since the man had exhibited no previous difficulties. Through good interviewing and investigation the supervisor discovered that the man who was ready to quit had been subject to a series of conflicting pressures. The company had been undergoing rapid change and expansion. In the process everyone wanted their facilities moved at the same time, each claiming that their job had priority and that the "President is vitally interested in our getting into our new quarters as soon as possible." This man had no way to resist their demands—he was many levels below all the managers who came into his office to get service. Santini's solution was a direct one: he got top-management approval for a new policy: all requests for moves were to come directly to his office and he would assign a priority to them based on date of submission and company needs. Because of Santini's relatively high position in the organization, he could not be intimidated as his subordinate had been, and in turn, the subordinate found that his job no longer was pressureful.

This solution represents just one small example of reorganizing the flow of work and the pattern of interpersonal contacts required by the division of labor as a means of solving certain morale problems. The next chapter will describe these types of change in more detail.

Other remedies for failure to work together for common goals involve incentives for intergroup cooperation. People need to be rewarded for helping others. As we shall see in Chapter 28, group piece-work and production bonuses based on over-all plant performance help provide this motivation. Job rotation between departments and interdepartmental meetings also help. Finally, the attitude of individual supervisors tends to set the pattern either for cooperation or for unbridled competitiveness. Are they on the lookout for evidence of teamwork among subordinates? Do they reward teamwork? Or do they emphasize getting results in one department at the sacrifice of everything else?

COORDINATION

Sometimes problems between specialized departments arise not from the actual flow of work but from the need to coordinate decisions. Here we are faced with many of the problems we have already discussed, plus some others that we have not as yet considered.

There are circumstances in modern industry where the work of each department is so closely coordinated with that of the other departments in the organization that each department's decision affects all the rest; and yet no department can make a decision without knowing what the others are doing. Problems of this sort resemble simultaneous equations, where no one part of the problem can be solved without solving all the rest. In industry, such problems often arise in large engineering laboratories that design new products, or in "job shops" that are constantly planning the production of items to the customer's special order. Each department or group controls a part of the "answer"—but these parts must be assembled before the organization's problem is solved.

To see these problems in action, let us look at the process of designing a new-model TV set, as we observed it in one company. The Engineering Department is, of course, the one most directly concerned, and it consists of five sections. *Electrical* determines in theoretical terms how the set will be made (technically: what the over-all "system" will be). *Mechanical* tries to fit the components together; it often finds that Electrical's theoretical plans are impractical or even that one Electrical engineer's theoretical suggestions are incompatible with those of another. *Chassis* designs the cabinet; close coordination is required if the components are to fit into the cabinet. This is not as easy as it sounds, since Electrical and Mechanical are constantly designing improvements which give better reception, but which conflict with the company's over-all goal of producing an ever-thinner, lighter set.

Automation designs the machinery which makes the printed circuits and attaches the tubes to it; in contrast to Electrical, which wants an ever-more "sophisticated" set, Automation wants one that is simple enough to be reduced to printed circuitry and put together mechanically. *Industrial Engineering* determines the techniques by which the set will be manufactured (other than the operations that are 100 per cent automated). Like Automation, it seeks to eliminate what it feels to be unnecessary frills.

Further complicating over-all coordination are the pressures brought by outside departments: Sales wants an attractive product that will sell easily, and Manufacturing wants a set that is easy to put together. And management as a whole is interested in keeping costs low, profits high.

Note that in this case no one section can make modifications without affecting all the others. A change in cabinet, for instance, may require adjustments by every other section, yet each adjustment may in turn require further compensating adjustments elsewhere. Each section has its own vested interest. Electrical, with its goal of technical perfection, conflicts, for example, with Industrial Engineering's goal of manufacturing ease.

Since a new model must be designed each year, intergroup conflicts tend to reach a crescendo as the time for a final decision approaches. During the early part of the year there is little pressure to resolve agreements, and each section is free to work on its own pet projects. As the deadline draws near, an increasing number of compromises and adjustments must be made, tempers grow raw, and human-relations problems begin to complicate the technical ones. Each engineer likes to feel that he has *completed* his end of the job and hates to reconsider his position just to please another section. No engineer likes to sacrifice his own brainchild.

Complicating all these problems are the changing status relationships between departments. When TV was new, the major problem was to design a workable set, and Electrical was the highest-status section. Today the emphasis is on sales appeal and manufacturing ease. Electrical still thinks its function is the most important one, but management seems to favor other sections when it makes critical decisions and hands out promotions.

We have gone into the problem of this TV engineering department at some length because we think its problems are typical of many in management. When an organization is small, and specialization at a minimum, the problem of coordination can be solved by one man who keeps all the details in his head and can predict by himself all the possible ramifications of each possible change. Once the organization passes a certain size, however, no one person can keep track of all the variables. At this point, good communication among the specialists becomes all important—both to enable each person to get all the information he needs to make a decision, and also to help preserve organizational morale. The usual hierarchical form of communication, in which information flows upward and downward, is less efficient where long, sustained teamwork is required to solve challenging problems.

The value of lateral communication in solving such problems was shown dramatically in an experiment designed to compare various communications nets.[9] Among others, the two below were compared:

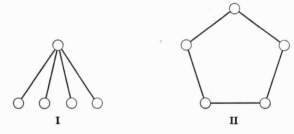

I   II

Note that though both nets permit intercommunication, the arrangements and numbers of channels differ, in a way somewhat analogous to the patterns of communication within industry.

---

[9] The subjects in this experiment were assigned to solve various problems while isolated in cubicles, which were ingeniously arranged so that the experimenters could control with whom the subjects could and could not communicate. Each member of the group held an essential clue to the final solution of the problems, and until the clues were assembled no complete solution could be attained. See Harold J. Leavitt, "Some Effects of Certain Communications Patterns on Group Performance," *The Journal of Abnormal and Social Psychology*, Vol. 46, No. 1 (January 1951), pp. 38-50; Alex Bavelas, "Communications Patterns in Task Oriented Groups," in *Group Dynamics*, Dorwin Cartwright and Alvin Zander, eds. (Evanston, Ill.: Row, Peterson, 1953), pp. 493-506. See also: George Heise and George A. Miller, "Problem Solving in Small Groups Using Various Communications Nets," *Journal of Abnormal and Social Psychology*, Vol. 46, No. 3 (July 1951), pp. 327-355.

Which of these nets was more efficient? The answer depends on what is meant by "efficient." With simple problems, net I gave the fastest and most accurate results. However, net II resulted in higher over-all morale (after all, the man on the top is the only one who has much feeling of accomplishment in I). But as more complicated problems were introduced, I's relative accuracy tends to fall. Also, preliminary experimental evidence suggests that I is slower in adjusting to new situations and less accurate or speedy in handling problems (such as are faced in real life in the TV engineering department) where each member of the group needs all the information available to everyone before he can make a realistic decision himself.

Possibly a network like this, where every member can communicate with every other member, might be most efficient in handling complex, ever-changing problems. However, we should not be too sure of this. Unless some natural leader arises who can coordinate and systematize the flow of communication, too many channels of communication may lead to chaos.

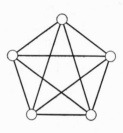

We can conclude that as problems of coordination become increasingly complex, more and more attention must be given to providing carefully designed, *systematic, lateral* communication between specialized departments (in contrast to communication upward and downward through the hierarchy). Too little communication, as we have seen, may result in reduced efficiency; too much communication means that each manager must spend most of his day in committee meetings, in writing or reading reports, and in interoffice correspondence. To minimize these problems, management must study the requirements of each situation with extreme care in order to design a communication pattern that will be best for that situation.

Organization and Personality

What we have been saying about division of labor, and our earlier observations concerning the existence of fixed policies, have important implications for the individual's ability to express his personality.

In terms of strict organizational theory, the way each specialized job is performed is supposed to be independent of the personality of the man who fills it. Thus it should make no difference whether the position "Product Engineer for Special Fabrics" is occupied by Mr. Ross or by Mr. Jones. Each should do it in exactly the same way, because that is the way the organization is designed to function.

But practice differs enormously from theory. The organization will undoubtedly not function the same way when Ross has the job as it did with Jones. Each man's personality will reveal itself in the way he works with his colleagues, his boss, his subordinates, and other departments. As a result, when the incumbent on a job changes, everyone has to adjust to a whole series of changes in the way work is accomplished.

In spite of organizational theory, it is naive to assume that employees fit themselves into the strait jacket of the job specification. As they try the job on for size they begin squirming a bit, pulling in here and pushing out there, until the job begins to fit their personality needs. The result is that the organization functions differently from the way the planners of the structure envisioned.

> Brown as purchasing agent is supposed to spend about half his time analyzing sources of supply and negotiating terms of purchase, and the other half managing the employees in the purchasing office. Brown enjoys negotiating, but is unhappy handling what he calls these "darn petty personnel problems." So he spends less and less time supervising and more time buying. Gradually the job of running the office is assumed by his chief assistant, since the employees need someone to turn to with their problems.
>
> In contrast, Smith is supposed to spend nearly all his time drawing up engineering specifications. However, he has a flair for dealing with people, and he soon finds that other engineers are coming to him with their personnel problems. He begins to represent them directly in contacts with the division head. As his reputation as a fixer grows, upper management uses him as a trouble-shooter. He does less and less engineering and more and more human-relations work. At the same time, his own boss, the section head who prefers puzzling over blueprints to worrying about employee relations, is by-passed and gradually loses authority.

Two important points are suggested by this example:

1. Every effort should be made to find the man with the right human-relations qualifications as well as the right technical qualifications for the job. If the top man is a skilled technician, then perhaps his assistant should be good at handling people, and vice versa.

2. Top management should permit subordinates to exercise enough flexibility to meet their own needs. For instance, the human-relations ability of Smith, the engineer, would have been wasted had he been tied down to his desk, while morale and efficiency might have been seriously impaired if his blueprint-loving boss had been required to make all the personnel decisions.

Thus both the work-flow-coordination problems that are a function of the degree of specialization, and the superior-subordinate problems flowing from the hierarchical nature of the organization, are in an important and critical way modified and influenced by the distinctive personalities of those filling the various jobs. One cannot realistically consider the human-relations problems of the organization without giving attention to the individual who is the incumbent of each block in the organizational chart. How the organization operates will vary as a function of these personalities.

Conclusion

We do not question the contribution of specialization of labor to our national productivity. However, this chapter has emphasized that a manager's problems do not end when he has broken a single job into parts that can be handled by specialists. Managerial success depends on being able to put these parts together again, on developing coordinated cooperation among various individuals and sub-groups in the organization so that the total organizational goals can be achieved.

Specialization is the source of many human-relations problems. Employees learn to identify with their own specialty and frequently lose sight of the over-all organization. Employees who are supposed to integrate their work activities so that ideas, materials, or papers pass smoothly from department to department often engage in struggles for their "fair share" of rewards and prestige. The weapons used in these intergroup struggles are techniques that enable men to avoid responsibility, to "pass the buck." Extreme specialization increases the likelihood of bottlenecks in the work flow, and those who are caught in the bottlenecks are subject to heavy pressures from fellow employees, such as mutually conflicting demands from other departments for quick service. All this pressure leads to bickering between departments and a breakdown of morale.

We have suggested certain "short-term" remedies that may help to ameliorate some of the pressures arising from specialization. In the next chapters we shall consider the possibility of making basic changes in the organizational structure designed to eliminate some of the underlying causes of discontent.

Problem I

You were just promoted to the position of Purchasing Agent for the newly acquired Dooley Division of the General Products Company.

As you left your old boss in central purchasing, he cautioned you, "Be careful now. Remember that division was pretty much a one-man firm till we bought them out. Tom Dooley would never have sold out to me if he didn't need capital for expansion. His outfit is a money-maker and as Division Manager he is still the boss there. As long as he brings in the profits no one from headquarters is going to interfere with his decisions. He's never had a PA and you are the only man sent from headquarters except the controller. He asked for a PA, but I'm not sure if he knows what purchasing is all about."

You arrived at the new plant—miles away from the main office. Dooley showed you around, or tried to, because it seemed that he couldn't take a step without someone running to him for a decision—mostly on technical questions. The administrative problems he seemed to push off on Bob Wallace, the manufacturing superintendent.

When Dooley left, Wallace sat down with you and began to speak haltingly. "To tell you the truth, I'm not sure why you are here or what you are supposed to do. We never had a PA before. We are really a very small outfit with only 150 people and we just don't believe in paper work. We have always worked so well together that we really don't need it. Now as I see your job it is to keep the salesmen off Tom's and my shoulders—except for the few with whom we have very good relations—and to buy our supplies at the lowest possible cost."

Before you could comment he was off on an errand, having instructed a general foreman to show you around. You asked what you felt were shrewd questions about costs and output, some of which the general foreman seemed reluctant to answer. You noticed several parts that it would seem better for the company to buy rather than make. When you suggested this, the general foreman answered, "This is a small firm, mister, and a lot of people depend on this work."

You tried to talk to the chief engineer. He showed a lot of interest in your background, your family, your housing arrangements, but he seemed to freeze up when you mentioned his work. "It's highly technical . . . making big advances which are hard for a layman to understand. . . . Yes, we make up the blueprints and tell the shop what to make. They're a good lot. All local boys, been with us a long time, take care of the troubles before they come up. . . . Specifications? Well, insofar as we have them we draw them up with Dooley, he tells Wallace what to buy. . . . I guess you'll be helping Wallace on that. He needs help. Things have been getting pretty busy recently."

The controller gave you a different picture. "I'm going crazy here. Been trying to get some sort of cost analysis, but don't make any progress because there are no records kept of anything. If I want specific information I can usually get it from Dooley or Wallace, they keep it in their heads, but I can't develop anything systematic. If I try to pin Dooley down on a new system of some type, he seems to listen, but he's off on a new problem before I get an answer."

Next day Wallace started giving you instructions. "Get in touch with some of the coal firms in town and see what price you can get it for. Maybe we can buy it cheaper. Call up Louhurst Bros. and ask them to send over 10 gallons of Sherwin-Williams paint."

You asked if a purchase order was needed. He answered, "No. When the bill comes in, Mary in the office will call Jack in receiving, and if it came in OK, she'll send out a check. . . . Oh, Tom or I sign it."

Just then the phone rang. It was Dooley, the boss. "I'm sending over a salesman from the MM Company, who is going to make some widgets for us and it's a big order, so make up some kind of agreement with him—he'll tell you what we agreed on—and send it to me to check over and sign."

1. How much could you realistically expect to accomplish in the near future on your new job?

2. What problems might arise in getting a real purchasing program accepted?

3. How would your problems be complicated by the personalities and vested interests of Dooley, Wallace, the general foreman, the chief engineer, and the comptroller?

4. What plans could you make for handling each of them?

5. What mistakes did you make at the outset?

6. How had the absence of specialization, rules, procedures, and so forth helped and hindered the Dooley Division?

Problem II

Just before their pre-Christmas business reached its maximum, the Cantor Toy Company installed a new conveyor line which provided a more mechanized means of spraying and drying their toy soldiers. Simultaneously they placed the operation on a three-shift, round-the-clock basis to meet the heavy influx of customer orders.

A group of six sprayers worked on individual fixtures and placed the sprayed soldiers on a conveyor belt which went into a drying chamber. The drying cycle took about two hours, so that the same sprayers were able to take off dried units and box them. The job description and the incentive plan under which the sprayers worked took into account the fact that each sprayer was both a sprayer and a packer. There were continuous shifts so that the next shift would package soldiers that had been sprayed during the last couple of hours by the previous shift and so on.

Management observed that during the first hour or so of each shift the sprayers always seemed to be in trouble and behind their quota (if they were to actually make a bonus for the day). On closer examination it became apparent that each shift was normally careful to place sprayed soldiers on the conveyor belt in such a way that they could easily be removed for packaging without interrupting the spraying operation. However, toward the end of the day, when the sprayed units would no longer be packed by themselves (because the drying cycle would take them into the next shift), they grow careless in their haste to make their own quota. The next shift would then find them bunched and unevenly spaced, would fall behind, and, in turn, would take a careless attitude toward the spacing of the pieces they rushed through to make their quota during the last couple of hours.

1. To what extent is this production problem due to poor attitudes toward work and to what extent is it the result of the technology—the organization of work?

2. Have you any suggestions for eliminating this problem?

Problem III * *Look at*

The Bellows Chemical Laboratories were engaged in the development and production of a number of organic chemicals used in the printing and textile industries. As a result of the growing acceptance of the company's product line, the research laboratory experienced a major expansion.

In this company the job classification of "laboratory technician" referred to persons who performed routine tests at the direction of professionally trained employees. A variety of tests were involved, and many of the tests required considerable skill to execute. All the technicians had completed high school and several had attended college for one or two years. Several technicians had also worked in the factory and had been transferred to the laboratory at their own request. The professionals in the laboratory were all graduate chemists or engineers.

The work of the laboratory was organized under the "project" system. The work was authorized by management, as required, and assigned by the head of the laboratory to one or, at the most, two professionals for execution. When the work was completed, the chemists or engineers involved were given new assignments.

Until recently, the size of the laboratory (both professional and technician groups), was small enough so that frequent interaction among the entire staff was possible. Desks of all personnel were located within a single "conversational" area, and everyone had fairly accurate knowledge of the goals and work requirements of the various active projects. When a chemist or engineer had a series of tests to

---

* We are indebted to one of our former students, Mr. E. W. Coleman, for the outline of this case.

be run, he would ask the technician who seemed least burdened with work at the time to undertake the assignment. On the whole, this arrangement worked smoothly. Delays in the work and manifestations of discontent among the personnel were infrequent.

Recently the demands on the laboratory have increased markedly. The number of active projects has increased by a substantial margin, and the number of professionals employed has approximately doubled. Also, several additional technicians have been assigned to the laboratory.

When it became apparent that the informal arrangement for scheduling technician time would not function adequately with the larger group, a "technician pool" was created and put in the charge of a senior technician. Professionals who desired tests run were to route their requests through the head technician, who in turn would assign technicians from the "pool."

The new arrangement has had two unexpected results. First, the number of technicians per professional employee has had to be increased to get the required work completed on schedule. Second, a considerable degree of discontent has developed among the technician group and to a lesser extent among the professionals. Not infrequently, conflict arises over priority in the use of equipment. Availability conflicts between the head technician and the chemists over technicians are becoming more numerous. One of the technicians has requested that he be transferred out of the laboratory. Whereas the old informal scheduling of technician time had become cumbersome and inefficient, the new technician "pool" has resulted in still further loss of efficiency and in open conflict.

1. To what extent were the new problems involving the allocation and assignment of technicians an inevitable product of expansion in the laboratory?

2. Why didn't some of these conflicts over priorities emerge when the laboratory was smaller? It is unlikely that there was a surplus of technicians, even then, and there must have been times when a chemist or engineer could not obtain personnel when they were needed.

3. "Pools" are used to conserve many scarce resources in the organization. They are supposed to insure that everyone has an equal opportunity to use facilities and that the facilities are not wasted. Why doesn't this reasonable explanation enable everyone in an organization, like the laboratory, to accept temporary shortages and inconveniences, since the total group is probably benefiting by the arrangement?

Problem IV

The Wilton Company manufactures a small replacement part sold by automobile accessory dealers. The company is in a highly competitive industry, and recently has been losing ground to other manufacturers whose product sells for slightly less than that manufactured by Wilton. The Executive Committee of the company has decided to try to decrease their unit labor costs. The plant manager has indicated to the two division heads who report directly to him (the superintendent for fabrication and the superintendent for assembly) that they will be held responsible for tightly adhering to new output standards, which require about 5 per cent more work for approximately the same wage cost.

During the first week after the application of the tighter standards and the closer checking of department cost figures, a major disagreement arose between the two division heads. Since the matter of quality standards was also involved, the plant manager invited the head of the inspection department to attend the meeting. The chief inspector also reports to the plant manager, and serves in a staff capacity to the production departments.

The following exchange took place during the meeting:

Plant Manager: "I have called this meeting to find out what we can do about this awful production situation. As you know, it was just a week ago that we decided to try to up our output by about 5 per cent. I am certainly shocked at the results of our program. As you probably know by now, the figures for the week indicate that instead of some increase in output we actually suffered a 9 per cent decline over our average for the past two months. Apparently, a large share of this poor performance is due to low-quality work and scrap. How do you explain this?"

Superintendent for Fabrication: "I know what's holding us up! It's simple. Jack, here [superintendent for assembly] is sending back nearly one out of five parts that we send to him, claiming that they are not perfect, and he can't use them in his assembly operations. This is ridiculous; we are utilizing the same tolerances we've always utilized. There is no such thing as perfection, as he knows, but all our parts are within limits."

Superintendent for Assembly: "All I know is that we can't continue to meet our old output standards, no less meet these new ones, if we're going to have to use parts that are finished like these have been. If my foremen are going to be able to insist that each employee work along at 100 per cent efficiency, those employees have got to have parts that don't jam when they try to fit them together. Sure, if we had all the time in the world, we could fuss around with them to make them fit—they wouldn't have to be remachined—but we don't have all the time in the world and we've got to have good parts if we're going to have any decent level of output."

At this point the plant manager asked for an opinion from the chief inspector. His response was brief, and somewhat unexpected.

"All I want to say is that in the past week my inspectors have been under more pressure from both of your foremen than they have ever endured. Both in fabrication and assembly the inspectors have been pressured to pass work that was really borderline, if not below standard. I can assure you that we haven't succumbed to any of these pressures, but our job has just been made that much more difficult. I don't see why your production foremen can't stick to the standards and leave it up to our inspectors to find out whether or not the parts fit."

1. How do you explain the sudden drop in quality at the fabrication stage?

2. What is likely to be the effect on interdepartmental relations of this attempt to increase output?

3. What do you see as the basic problem in the manufacturing organization of the Wilton Machine Company? Do you have any suggestions for improving the organizational structure?

We have been looking at some of the problems that stem from extended lines of authority and the division of labor in the contemporary organization. By this time you may have decided that the "game is not worth the candle"—that too heavy a price must be paid in terms of human relationships to win the advantages of large-scale organization. There are those who look back nostalgically to the "good old days" when companies were small, when the boss knew all his employees intimately, when everyone worked together and did a whole job, when problems of coordination and communication were at a minimum. Neither horizontal nor vertical cleavages were particularly significant, and the work group and the company were synonymous.

Many studies have shown that employee morale is higher in small groups than in large ones.[1]

---

[1] See R. Marriott, "Size of Working Group and Output," *Occupational Psychology*, Vol. 23 (1949), pp. 47-57. In comparing large with small groups in British industry, Marriott found the latter superior in output by a factor of 7 per cent. See also Mason Haire, *Psychology in Management* (New York: McGraw-Hill, 1956), p. 28. Professor Haire also has included a stimulating section on the interrelationships of organization size, shape (structure), and functions. (*Ibid.*, pp. 191-201.)

17

Minimizing the Human Problems of Large Organizations

Supervision and job satisfaction are all easier to achieve in the more intimate setting.

The technological and economic advantages that come with size, however mean that large organizations are here to stay. Size makes possible many of the economies of specialization (*e.g.*, mass production) and the introduction of expensive equipment (*e.g.*, electronic data-processing). As the organization grows, it usually gains what economists call "economies of scale"—that is, money can be borrowed at lower interest rates, supplies purchased in larger quantities, and so on.

Fortunately, larger companies have pioneered in introducing personnel programs designed to eliminate many of the sources of unrest common to smaller companies. They have sought to regularize employment, to develop training and promotion programs stressing merit rather than nepotism, to introduce equitable wage and salary administration programs that adjust income to job responsibility, and to provide retirement and insurance programs to reduce the fear of illness and old age.

The basic problem is this: How can organizations gain the advantages that come with size without paying a heavy price in terms of reduced employee and managerial effectiveness? In the small organization where face-to-face relationships predominate, a manager of goodwill who likes and respects people may prove highly successful. In the large organization, good intentions are not enough; human relations need to be planned to insure an environment conducive to productivity.

It is a mistake to assume that there need be any *rigid relationship* between the number of people working for a given company and the quality of the human relations within the company. Only after a company has realized that its *organizational structure*, as well as its patterns of supervision and the quality of its personnel, affects productivity and effectiveness, can it consider ways of modifying the structure to its advantage.

How can organizational structure be designed to minimize human friction? In answering this question, we shall try to show that the manager who plans his organizational structure intelligently and realistically can:

1. Reduce the number of levels in the organizational hierarchy, even though he does not reduce the total number of employees.
2. Improve the efficiency with which the immediate work group solves the difficult work-flow problems of coordination and cooperation.
3. Improve cooperation between groups within the organization.

Fewer Levels of Supervision

In Chapter 14, we mentioned that the existence of many levels within an organization complicates the problems of management. The individual employee feels lost because he is many steps removed from the key decision-makers who control his welfare, and both top management and the worker feel isolated from one another. Orders and information have to pass up and down through so many levels that there are countless possibilities for breakdowns and distortions in communication.

It is not uncommon for large corporations to have ten to twelve levels intervening between the hourly-paid employee and top management. And yet the number of levels required by the organization is *not* automatically determined by the number of employees. For instance, Sears Roebuck reported in 1950 that with 110,000 employees in their retail division, there are only four levels of supervision *between* the president of the company and the salespeople in the stores.[2] This "flat" structure is not accidental; it is a reflection of deliberate management policy to maximize the number of subordinates (the span of control) reporting to a given supervisor. The result is that the levels of supervision in the organization are kept to a minimum.

A simple exercise will demonstate the relationship between the span of control and the number of levels in an organization. Assume that a company employing 2000 people wants to determine how many managers it needs. Each first-line supervisor has 20 subordinates, and each second-line supervisor has 5 foremen reporting to him. There will thus be a need for 100 first-line supervisors and 20 second-line supervisors. In addition, the 20 second-level manager will require 4 third-level supervisors who in turn will report to the head of the company. This gives us *four* levels of supervision in the organization. However, if each supervisor handles double the previous number of subordinates, we need only three levels in the organization.[3]

IMPACT OF FLAT VS. TALL ORGANIZATIONS ON HUMAN RELATIONS

Fortunately, the Sears Roebuck Company has analyzed the effect of its organizational setup on human relations within the company. Sears operates many stores that have an almost identical number of employees doing highly similar jobs. In some of these stores, 32 department managers report directly to the store manager; in others, the department managers report to 5 or 6 division managers, who in turn report to the store manager.[4] Obviously the

---

[2] James C. Worthy, "Factors Influencing Employee Morale," *Harvard Business Review*, Vol. 28, No. 1 (1950), p. 69.

[3] There are other organizational techniques for reducing the number of supervisory levels, which we shall not detail here. The interested reader will find a description of them in an excellent case study of reorganization at the International Business Machines plant in Endicott, N. Y.: F. L. W. Richardson, Jr., and Charles R. Walker, *Human Relations in an Expanding Company* (New Haven, Conn.: Labor and Management Center, Yale University, 1948), pp. 32-48.

[4] A good summary of the Sears experience may be found in William F. Whyte, *Modern Methods in Social Research*. Prepared for Office of Naval Research under Contract NOM-401 (2), pp. 25-28, undated, processed.

first is a relatively *flat* type of structure; the second, a *tall* type. What has Sears observed in the operations of these two quite different organization patterns?

The tall organization tended to encourage close supervision. With a relatively small number of subordinates, each supervisor, whether he was the store manager or the division manager, was able to give very detailed instructions to and exercise strong control over every one of the people in his unit. But in the flat organization the relatively large number of subordinates made this type of supervision physically impossible. Each supervisor was obliged to rely on general supervision and good training; he just didn't have the time to keep a close watch on everyone. The delegation of responsibility in these stores encouraged subordinates to work on their own initiative and learn from their own mistakes. Since the supervisor could not make a decision on every problem that arose, subordinates achieved a high degree of self-reliance. The results showed themselves in the higher profits, better morale, and greater number of promotable executives produced by the flat organization.

Another obvious advantage to the fewer-leveled organization is the saving of managerial time: problems are handled more quickly. Equally important are the better human relations associated with fewer levels. Communication is expedited; the individual employee finds it easier to identify with the work of his part of the organization.

Not every organization, of course, can arbitrarily increase the number of subordinates reporting to each of its supervisors. The ability of Sears to make use of a relatively "wide" span of control is a function of the following factors:

1. It was possible to develop efficiency measures (controls) for the various departments so that a manager could be left to make nearly all his own decisions and only have to account for the final results: in other words, supervision "by results."

2. Department store personnel receive a good part of their compensation in the form of commissions and bonuses based on sales performance. These incentives provide them with a high degree of motivation and decrease the need for close supervision.

3. No great amount of coordination between department managers was required in these stores. In effect, each department could be operated relatively independently of the others, thus reducing the amount of supervision required by the store manager.

Building Integrated Work Teams

In an organization where employees can work relatively independently of one another, management can reduce the height of the organizational pyramid and bring managers and employees closer together by broadening the span of control. Where closer coordination and thus more supervision are required, the same objective can be obtained by reorganizing the components of the face-to-face work group.

THE AJAX COMPANY: CUSTOMER-ORDER PROCESSING DEPARTMENT

To illustrate how this reorganization can be accomplished, we shall describe a case in which changes in organization substantially altered the human relations of the situation. Notice particularly that the original emphasis on functional specialization, a characteristic of modern organizations, as emphasized in Chapter 16, was the chief source of the difficulty. The division of labor employed *before* the change looked logical and reasonable on paper;

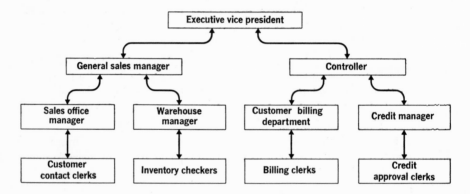

but when real people filled the jobs that had been created, continuous personnel conflict and inefficiency arose. Management's mistake was in assuming that people behave like the rectangles and lines of an organization chart.

Before

The Ajax Company manufactured small home appliances which it sold to retail outlets. Every order sent in by salesmen in the field had to be processed by four different groups of employees in the home office.

a. *Customer contact clerks* communicated with the customer if the salesman's order was unclear, if the merchandise ordered was unavailable, or if price changes had taken place.

b. *Billing clerks* checked the arithmetic on the order and entered correct charges and credits on the customer's account.

c. *Inventory checkers* checked to make sure that goods ordered were available for shipment.

d. *Credit approval clerks* examined the customer's credit status in order to authorize shipping.

The Ajax Company placed each group of employees under separate supervisors, as in the figure above.

Thus each customer order passed through four distinct departments (and two divisions). Each specialist belonged to the organizational unit to which his function was *logically* related.

You can probably predict what happened. The design of the organization made no provision for the cooperation and communication required to complete the *total job* of customer-order processing. There was constant conflict among employees. Inventory checkers complained that they had to track down merchandise that might later be dropped from the order as a result of the discovery of a salesman's clerical error or inadequate customer credit. Customer contact clerks were in a constant dither because their letters were rendered obsolete by the work of the credit clerks or the inventory checkers. Responsibility for delays in processing orders were "passed" from one group to another. The billing clerks complained that the inventory checkers were always late with their information, and the inventory checkers retorted that their delays were the result of faulty information from customer contact clerks.

Higher management was always being called in to settle disputes. When conflict arose between an inventory checker and a customer contact clerk, for example, each would contact his superior, who in turn would take the battle up to the General Sales Manager. When the billing clerk complained that he couldn't get up-to-the-minute information from the customer contact clerks (and thus made embarrassing errors in customers' accounts), the problem might have to go to the Executive Vice President, who was their common supervisor. Even the Sales Manager and the Controller were constantly blaming one another for difficulties in each other's departments.

After

In a reorganization of these functions, all employees processing customer orders were placed under a single general office supervisor, who in turn had first-line supervisors for the various geographic areas served by the company. The new organization looked like this: [5]

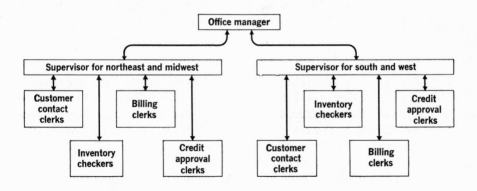

---

[5] We have omitted from our description of the changes that took place the new staff responsibilities of the sales, warehouse, and credit managers. Each manager became responsible for establishing standards of performance for the clericals who did work in-

Under each of these supervisors, the same specialists continued to do much the same job they had done before. Now, however, any dispute could be settled face-to-face within the immediate work group, or, in exceptional instances, by the first-line supervisor. No longer was it necessary to channel complaints up the line through two or three levels of management. The new scheme saved a great deal of executive time, and made it possible to settle most problems by horizontal work-flow contacts between the employees themselves. The arrangement increased output enormously by eliminating many petty frictions.

REDUCTION IN NUMBER OF LEVELS

In the past, Ajax had spent a great deal of management time and energy trying to solve the coordination problems that inevitably arose *between* its functional specialists. The sales office manager, the warehouse manager, the head of the customer billing department, and the credit manager were constantly becoming involved in work-flow problems. Furthermore, many questions had to go even higher, to a third level in the hierarchy: to the general sales manager and the controller. In this type of "functional" organization any difficulty in one group is immediately communicated to every other group.

Under the new arrangement, on the other hand, nearly every decision, and all information that has to be communicated, is handled either at the work level, among the employees themselves, or between them and their immediate supervisor: one of the two geographic office supervisors. The organization of this part of the business now consists of two relatively autonomous divisions, each of which can function almost entirely on its own. In effect, this unit has become much "flatter"—that is, the lowest level of the hierarchy is much closer to the highest level.

In short, what happened at Ajax was this: (1) Management reduced the number of levels of supervision that had to participate in the solution of normal, daily work problems. And (2) it created more inclusive work teams that could handle problems on a face-to-face basis with a minimum of friction.

IMPROVED COMMUNICATIONS AND COORDINATION

Recall the recurring struggle and frictions among the customer contact, billing, and credit approval clerks and inventory checkers. There was little of the mutual help, loyalty, and protection that we described as characteristic of the informal work group in Chapter 3. Why? The employees who had to interact with one another in order to complete the assigned work of processing customer orders did *not* belong to the same group. The billing clerks, for example, may have had a fine relationship with one another, but unfortunately the people they had to work with were not other billing clerks.

volving their respective special interests, and for checking to be sure that these standards of performance were being observed. These types of staff relationship will be considered in the next chapter.

They were working with employees in other departments: inventory checkers, customer contact clerks, and so on.

The manner in which work activities are organized influences the quality of communications within the work group: people who work near one another and identify with the same group find it far easier to share the information they need to coordinate their jobs than do people who have infrequent contact with one another. In fact, much of our earlier discussion of flow-of-work problems could just as logically have appeared in a discussion of "communications problems." When two work groups have so much trouble understanding each other that communications are misinterpreted or go astray, or when top management complains that lower levels fail to understand the needs of the business—these are usually indications that the groups that make up the organization are too far apart. Because they report to different supervisors, they develop unique interests. Their separate worlds, their special skills, their special desires and activities, create barriers to effective communication.

Vast quantities of information are required to perform many of the jobs within the large organization, and the superior-subordinate relationship cannot possibly carry the burden of communicating all of it. If every employee had to rely exclusively on his immediate superior for information about the company and his particular function within it, the supervisor would have to spend full time "communicating" information.

Students of organization are often surprised by the amount of work-oriented information that is communicated during what appear to be social contacts. During a coffee break it is not unusual to hear a conversation of this sort:

> "Say, Joe, just out of curiosity, tell me what your guys are doing to mangle those parts we're supposed to put together in a minute and a half in our assembly operation."
>
> "Bill, you've got the wrong villain. Orders came down from the plant manager's office to loosen up on our tolerances. They figure we were rejecting too many out-of-limits parts and wasting money. In fact, they claim that you guys have been having it too soft with our perfect parts; now you'll have to just work a little harder to put 'em together."

These semi-social contacts, which are normally a product of membership in the same group, are an indispensable supplement to the more formal channels of communication.

Mining example [6]   Let us examine what happened when a natural work team in a coal mine was broken up. At one time all the operations at the mine face were performed by a small team which worked together on a single shift. Since they were in close contact with each other, it was easy to devise

---

[6] E. L. Trist and K. W. Bamforth, "Some Social and Psychological Consequences of the Long Wall Method of Coal Getting," *Human Relations,* Vol. IV, No. 1 (1951).

solutions for problems as they arose. Each member of the group felt responsible for the entire operation.

In the mistaken belief that it would increase efficiency, management combined these small groups into much larger ones working over larger areas. For example, one crew did nothing but prepare the new "face" for blasting. Others handled the recovery of the coal that came down after the dynamite had been set off; another crew worked on timbering and moving rail lines. This new division of labor was carried out on a three-shift, 24-hour cycle: each shift performed a different function. Each worker became a specialist. As a result, no single group of workers felt responsible for the total operation; as problems arose, each shift developed the habit of shrugging them off and passing the buck to the next shift. Communications, which at best are very troublesome in a mine, were further complicated by the workers' being separated from each other in time and space. Previously, the small groups were almost self-supervising (motivated as they were by a group incentive plan); now, coordinating the various individual workers, none of whom had much motivation, became a complex management task. Even new equipment did not compensate for production losses due to work-flow problems.

Similar problems arise even when employees are not separated into different time shifts.

Textile mill example [7]   An Indian textile mill, which had undergone intensive "job re-engineering," did not attain satisfactory output levels. Each occupational group in the mill was assigned a work load based on a careful study of all the job components. For example, in one room containing 240 looms, the following assignments were made to the 12 types of specialist:

1. Each weaver tended approximately 30 looms.
2. Each "battery filler" served about 50 looms.
3. Each "smash hand" was assigned some 80 looms.
4. Each of nine different categories of maintenance men was responsible for from 120 to 240 looms.

All these occupational tasks were highly interdependent, and the utmost coordination was required to maintain productivity. But the assignment of work loads militated against coordination. In effect, each weaver came into contact with five-eighths of a "battery filler," three-eighths of a "smash hand," and even smaller fractions of the other nine workers on whom he was at least partially dependent to keep his looms operating.

When the work was reorganized so that all interdependent workers were made part of the same work group, production soared. Work groups were reconstructed so that a single group of workers was responsible for the operation of a given bank of looms. The new interaction pattern produced regular

---

[7] A. K. Rice, "Productivity and Social Organization in an Indian Weaving Shed," *Human Relations*, Vol. VI, No. 4 (1953).

relationships and communications among workers and led directly to the increase in output.[8]

The conclusion to be drawn from these studies is that in designing the organization the administrator should provide each work group with a relatively autonomous task. Only under such circumstances can competent *internal* leadership and group responsibility develop.

Ideally, the individual worker should be permitted to coordinate his activities by himself (i.e., through job enlargement). If the same girl does both the typing and the filing, problems in integrating the two processes are unlikely to arise. The next best thing is to have the coordination take place within the immediate work group, where each individual feels loyalty and responsibility to his fellow workers and is willing to adjust his pacing, the quality of his work, and his over-all efforts to the needs of the others.

AVOIDING THE MORALE PROBLEMS OF LARGE, HOMOGENEOUS GROUPS

The type of organization rearrangements we are considering have another valuable by-product. The new groups that are created are more likely to have high morale than are large, highly specialized work groups.

The nature of a work group has a profound effect on the job satisfactions derived by its members. An employee who is just one of many, all doing the same operation, which operation in turn is only a small part of some larger activity, feels little sense of accomplishment or identification with the larger unit. However, in the semi-autonomous groups we have been describing, in which people who do complementary tasks are brought together:

> Employees have a much better opportunity to know each other, so that cooperation between individuals and departments can develop on a more personal, informal basis and not be so largely dependent on impersonal systems and administrative controls. Employees can see much more readily where they themselves "fit" into the organization and the significance of their jobs in the whole scheme of things.[9]

Where large numbers of people doing similar work are brought together in a single department, particularly if their work is unchallenging, personnel difficulties are likely to multiply. Typing pools, departments filled with hundreds of draftsmen or engineers doing identical tasks, all are sources of serious morale problems. To be sure, such a scheme may mean that the work can be scheduled more efficiently and that complex and labor-saving equipment can be used to handle the work of the entire organization. Yet the concentration of a large number of people, all doing the same job, tends to isolate them from the total organization. These groups become conscious of areas

---

[8] See L. R. Sayles, "Human Relations and the Organization of Work," *Michigan Business Review,* Vol. VI, No. 6 (November 1954), pp. 23-24.

[9] Worthy, *op. cit.,* p. 68.

where their needs conflict with the rest of the organization. We have seen an occupational group that was satisfied with its pay and working conditions become a sore spot in the organization when the entire group was concentrated in the same department.

> In one large automobile manufacturing company, the draftsmen became a source of friction after they were all moved into one department instead of being scattered around among the departments that used their services. The new department became known as "Siberia."

Improving Coordination Between Groups

It would be unrealistic, however, to assume that completely autonomous work groups can be developed. In the modern organization, work groups and departments have to cooperate with one another if the objectives of the enterprise are to be attained. Consequently, management has a responsibility to innovate organization changes that further intergroup cooperation.

Large Organizations

1) LAYOUT

Excessive physical distance among groups almost invariably reduces their opportunities to cooperate.

> "As accountants, our job is to help department heads improve their procedures and records to make their jobs easier and the results more effective. Oftentimes, however, we are not called in early enough when a new project gets started or some change is contemplated. The fault lies in our location—the laboratory accounting office is located in a small rented building several miles from the nearest research or development group. Being far away they never get around to calling us until their plans are already fixed; it takes so much longer to undo things than to get in on the ground floor. When we used to be located in the same building, these problems never occurred."

One way to improve opportunities for contact between groups that need to coordinate is to revise office and work-floor layouts. At the same time, the manager may also want to separate groups that do not need such intimate contact. Too easy access between such groups may encourage them to make unnecessarily frequent demands on each other.

Where for one reason or another such physical shifts are impossible for the manager to arrange, he may be able to devise special procedures to bring groups together that have to coordinate their activities but that are part of separate organizational families. We observed one company in which such procedures were hit on by chance. Two groups of engineers who reported to separate departments but who were working on interrelated drawings found that they needed to see each other more frequently than the normal flow of work allowed. Since there was no company cafeteria, the members of the two groups developed a car-pooling arrangement for traveling to and from lunch so that they could discuss their problems on the way.

2) COMMITTEES *(size affects committees)*

Special committees are useful in facilitating exchange of information between groups that normally have little contact with one another:

> The members of one department were upset by another group's habit of sending in requests for "rush orders" that put tremendous pressure on everyone to do the impossible. They couldn't understand why these last-minute needs could not be predicted earlier in the day. It was only when cross-department staff meetings were held that they learned about certain inherent technical problems in processing that made additional supplies necessary at the last minute.

Under the direction of a skilled chairman, committee meetings provide an opportunity for systematic, face-to-face discussion of problems and dissemination of information. Unfortunately, however, some companies waste the time of their supervisors by insisting on excessive use of committees. Care must be taken not to make committees too large, for as a rule the larger the committee the longer it takes to handle a problem. Also, each time it sets up a committee, management must ask itself, "Are we passing problems along to the committee which might be better handled by a sharper division of individual job responsibilities? Could this problem be more easily handled by individual supervisors?"

3) REPORTS

Properly designed reports improve organizational efficiency by keeping each group informed of what other groups are doing and by enabling each group to dovetail its activities more effectively with those of other groups. The bureaucratic tendency to require too many reports, however, wastes the time of the people who draw them up and of those who must read them. Once we made a study of paper-work flow in a seemingly well-organized organization in which the average executive had to go through over 100 pages of interoffice memos, reports, correspondence, and so forth, each day. Of these 100 pages less than 25 per cent were of any direct use to the executive in question, yet all had to be read and almost half had to be filed.

4) CONTROLS

The good manager evaluates the status of intergroup relationships as part of his regular supervisory pattern. He seeks to identify potential and actual points of friction in the organization and to determine whether they are the result of poor organization design, personality problems, bad placements, or temporary operating problems.[10]

5) TRAINING (size)

As we have seen, many of the problems of coordination in specialized organizations arise out of the fact that each group has its own "vested interest," its own typical point of view or approach to problems. The engineer is interested in quality, for instance; his training and the nature of his work give him little interest in cost reduction. The accountant has just the opposite point of view. Such differences are inevitable (in fact, properly utilized by management they contribute to organizational strength).

An effective training program can help the engineer put himself into the accountant's shoes. It can show each group how its own actions sometimes cause unwitting but unnecessary affronts to other groups. It can show each group how it can communicate with others in understandable terms.

Clearly, then, provision must sometimes be made for communicating across department lines even though the departments normally have little in common, and even though they report to separate parts of the organization. Realistically, of course, this type of communication can never be as effective as face-to-face communication between members of the same work group.

The Meaning of Decentralization

efficiency — morale, satisfaction + production measured by

Some of the types of reorganization we have been describing might appropriately be called shifts toward greater *decentralization*. Large, amorphous organizations in which nearly every decision must go up through many levels are highly *centralized*. They are the ones cursed with the problems of many-leveled hierarchies and specialization described in earlier chapters (like the Ajax Company before it was reorganized; see pp. 380-381).

And yet centralization is not just a product of a particular managerial or supervisory philosophy, such as: "Close supervision is useful because people can't be trusted." Centralization also results from the design of the organization itself. When operations are highly specialized and departments finely subdivided, decisions *must* be made by higher levels in the organization, and rigid rules *must* be employed. The reason, of course, is that no supervisor, any more than a single employee, is in a position to be "on his own." Because only a small part of the total job is done by any one employee or department, upper levels of management must step in to insure cooperation and coordination.

These centralized organizations are based on the principle of functional

---

[10] Techniques for assessing these problems are described in Eliot D. Chapple and Leonard R. Sayles, *The Measure of Management* (New York: Macmillan, 1960).

specialization—that is, everyone performing a similar function is placed in the same department or division. All the punch-press operators are in one group, all the typists in another, all the chemists work under the same supervisor, and so on. The familiar problem of these organizations is strikingly described by James Worthy of the Sears Roebuck Company:

> Where the work of the organization is broken up into so many functional divisions again, cooperation can no longer be achieved spontaneously. After all, each functional unit was set up as a distinct entity in order that it might achieve a more efficient system. Each unit, therefore, tends to operate primarily in terms of its own system rather than in terms of the needs of the organization as a whole. Each unit becomes jealous of its own prerogatives and finds ways to protect itself against the pressures and encroachments of others. Conflict develops on the employee level as well as the supervisory level, thus forcing an extra administrative load on higher levels of management because of the need for constantly reconciling differences.[11]

Under decentralization, by contrast, management considers a very different set of variables in deciding on organization structure. Rather than grouping employees together because they do similar work, management assesses the number and type of contacts required to complete a total operation. It designs work groups to facilitate coordination and cooperation between people who must interact frequently. When interrelated jobs are carefully grouped together, the supervisor can be left pretty much to his own devices. He can serve as an effective leader, since he has autonomy himself and can in turn delegate some autonomy to his subordinates.

There is some evidence that American industry is moving in the direction of greater decentralization. The Vice President of Manufacturing in a large oil company has described the organization of one of the company's new refineries in these terms:

> In this refinery all the men except the accountants and laboratory technicians are part of a single operating team. There is only one department—the Operating Department. The men have been trained somewhat as the crew of a submarine, in that every man can fill almost any breach. They are not concerned whether someone is doing their work, or whether they are doing someone else's work. Their interest lies, as a team, in keeping the operation going. All of the operating work is their work.
>
> There are ten on each shift. They run the entire refinery, including crude distillation, catalytic cracking and reforming, product testing, blending and shipping of products, and the utilities.[12]

---

[11] James C. Worthy, *op. cit.*, p. 71. Harold Leavitt titles an interesting description of this dilemma "The Jigsaw Puzzle of Responsibility," in his text *Managerial Psychology* (Chicago: University of Chicago Press, 1958), pp. 266-269.

[12] Clarence H. Thayer, Vice President in Charge of Manufacturing, Sun Oil Company, Philadelphia, Penn., "Automation and the Problems of Management" (address to the Wilmington, Delaware, Chapter of the Society for the Advancement of Management, delivered on October 14, 1958).

Decentralization can be effective at every level of the organization. The manager of a single plant of a larger corporation can exercise more effective leadership if *all* the functional specialties he needs to operate profitably report directly to him—that is, if staff groups like Personnel, Engineering, and Purchasing (which we will be describing in the next chapter) come under his jurisdiction rather than reporting to some higher level of management.

Decentralization means shifting "downward" the point at which all the employees necessary to do a complete job come together and report to a common supervisor. Again, this shift means that more responsibility can be delegated to the supervisor. Building the organization structure around the flow of work permits the large company to enjoy the human-relations advantages of the small company. All the operations that need to be integrated come under a common supervisor at the lowest possible level. This supervisor is able to communicate directly with everyone who has any impact on his ability to meet the goals assigned him. Workers and managers who must coordinate their activities are made members of the same team. Each employee is able to contact directly his real boss—the man who makes the important decisions.

In other words, the organization should consider its needs for *horizontal* communications before constructing its *vertical* or *hierarchical* lines of communication.

LIMITATIONS OF DECENTRALIZATION

This technique of decentralization is not a cure-all for human-relations problems, however. While companies like General Motors,[13] Sears, duPont, and others are enthusiastic about its virtues, others, like Chrysler, have tried it and moved away.[14]

One of the reasons for this difference in experience may be that decentralization requires unusually able personnel—managers and employees who can accept delegation and general supervision and the responsibilities these entail. This means that management must devise good selection procedures by which it can accurately identify supervisory talent (see Chapter 19) and must also provide for effective on-the-job training (see Chapter 24). Decentralization demands that all managers in the company share a common understanding of the methods and objectives of the organization; otherwise autonomy may lead to anarchy.

There are other limitations that make decentralization something less than a cure-all for organization ills. Decentralized organizations may not be as effective in making quick decisions or in adjusting to rapid environmental changes. For example, it may be hard to get separate units to agree to man-

---

[13] See Peter Drucker, *The Concept of the Corporation* (New York: Day, 1946), pp. 41 ff.

[14] Chrysler Faces Up to Its Troubles," *Business Week*, May 3, 1958.

power cutbacks unless the change is imposed from above. Many organizations are composed of parts that are too interdependent to allow for a great deal of autonomy—the opposite of the Sears Roebuck case described earlier. Interdivisional cooperation may prove deficient when each division concentrates primarily on its own objectives rather than on those of the organization. One division may be unwilling to share scarce technicians with another, although the needs of the latter are more pressing. A research laboratory that is completely autonomous may fail to coordinate its activities with the needs of the manufacturing divisions. In turn, the manufacturing divisions may fail to appreciate how they can make use of research.

Conclusion

If we want to understand how an organization functions and what sources of personnel problems lie within it, it is not enough to look at the formal organization chart. We need to observe the actual operation of the organization: who comes into contact with whom in the course of getting the work done—at whose initiation and how frequently and for how long. These interpersonal relationships are the life blood of the organization.

Unfortunately, some managers believe that the prime requisite for a smooth-running organization is a clear-cut, symmetrical organization plan which shows each man who his boss is and what his responsibilities are. Or they assume that the most logical scheme is to bring together under a common supervisor all employees who do similar work—that is, to organize personnel according to a "functional" pattern.

The results of such approaches to organization may have a disastrous effect on efficiency and human relations. They consume a great deal of managerial time simply because many levels of supervision are regularly involved in the day-to-day problems of getting work done. They encourage intergroup struggles and make it difficult or impossible for supervisors to use the techniques of general supervision. Supervisors are compelled by the difficulties inherent in the organization structure to resort to close supervision and rigid rules; they cannot afford to delegate much responsibility. But the mere piling up of pressures, rules, and controls does not guarantee that all the parts of the organization will do "as they are told" and coordinate their activities effectively.

We have endeavored to show how some of the problems stemming from large, impersonal hierarchical structures based on the principle of division of labor can be ameliorated or solved. Care needs to be taken to insure that both work groups and department jurisdictions encompass as many as possible of those jobs that are closely interrelated. Cooperation that arises spontaneously out of the structure of the organization is far easier to maintain than that which is imposed by rigid rules, control, and close supervision.

Furthermore, decentralization leads to an enormous saving in managerial time and energy. It means that more of the day-to-day work problems can be solved by the immediate supervisor, rather than having to be carried up through one or even several levels to a common supervisor.

In short, organizations should be constructed from the *bottom up*, rather than from the *top down*. In establishing work-group boundaries and supervisory units, management should start with the actual work that must be performed, an awareness of who must coordinate his job with whom, when, and where. Making work groups as inclusive as possible discourages close supervision and fosters downward delegation. Rather than an amorphous institution in which people cannot understand the relationship of their jobs to the objectives of the business, the organization then takes on some of the desirable characteristics of the informal group.

We have traveled a rather long road to prove our point. At the outset, you will recall, we emphasized that to a substantial degree the human relationships in an organization are a product of its structure, as well as of the type of people, jobs, and supervision that make it up. In outline form, this is the pattern we have tried to develop:

Structure of the organization

Size
Number of levels
Type of specialization ——➤ *marketing, finance, sales, & production*
Degree of centralization
↓ ↓ ↓

Shapes the pattern of human relations or interaction

Social (informal group) contacts
Up- and down-the-line contacts
Flow-of-work (horizontal) contacts
↓ ↓ ↓

Whose product is

Quality of teamwork
Degree of cooperation
Type of leadership
Personal motivation

This structure of human contacts and communications provides the framework within which problems of personnel policy and decision-making can be realistically understood and dealt with.

We have neglected one important element in the large organization: the position of staff personnel. This is such an important topic that we have devoted a separate chapter, which follows, to the implications of the staff role to the conduct of personnel matters in the organization.

Problem I *

You head a division of your company that will perform three primary functions or operations; "A work," "B work," and "C work." Since no major equipment is involved (i.e., there are no economies of scale), each of these types of work is divisible into any size; however, the finished service or product requires one unit each of "A," "B," and "C." (One example might be machining, assembling, and inspection.) The total volume of output required of the department is such that there is need for three units of "A work," three of "B work," and three of "C work."

The organization could be structured in one of two quite different ways:

1. All of each type of work could be placed under a common supervisor, one unit having all the "A work," one all the "B work," and one all the "C work." Each of these supervisors would report to a common second-level supervisor, a superintendent.

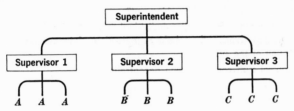

2. Alternatively, these nine units could be placed under three supervisors, each of whom managed one unit of "A work," one unit of "B work," and one unit of "C work." Again, these supervisors would report to the superintendent.

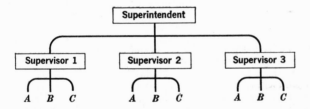

Compare the relative advantages of these two systems of organization. Consider the impact of each on the problems of supervision, coordination, the ability of the superintendent to delegate to his subordinates, the quality of personnel required for the various supervisory jobs, the amount of management development that would be accomplished.

Problem II

The Freshway Supermarkets prided themselves on their policy of decentralization. Each store manager's bonus depended on the profit performance of his store. In general, each manager controlled his own purchasing, advertising, display, and

---

* This case is taken from material presented by James Worthy in his paper, "Some Aspects of Organization Structure in Relation to Pressures on Company Decision-Making," *Proceedings of Fifth Annual Meeting, Industrial Relations Research Association*, L. Reed Tripp, ed. (Madison, Wis.: Industrial Relations Research Association, 1953), pp. 72-76.

clerical activities. The corporate offices of the chain provided certain essential services through pooled purchasing and staff assistance in technical areas: equipment selection, employee testing, techniques for reducing food spoilage, for improving advertising copy, and so forth.

Harry Alpert, the manager of the South Dayton store, earned the highest bonus of any of the midwestern managers. To a large extent this was the result of Alpert's technical ingenuity. By means of several inventions he was able to reduce the cost of his refrigeration equipment and to keep his fruits and vegetables looking fresher longer (thereby avoiding the waste of markdowns). He also developed a stock-handling system that was a significant improvement over the method recommended by the central staff industrial engineering department. In fact, Alpert violated several of the routine procedures that had been established by central staff groups. However, he was careful not to disclose his techniques or deviations to others.

1. From the point of view of the organization as a whole, how was Freshway's policy of decentralization working out?

2. Is there any way of rewarding individual managers for their initiative and ability that will not deprive the whole organization of innovations developed in any single unit of the system?

3. Is a central staff consistent with decentralization?

Problem III

Jane Hall, Director of Market Research for the Summertime Fabrics Company, looked out of her office to see why her secretary had not responded to the telephone-flashing signal. She was surprised to see three executives hovering around the secretary, obviously discussing some matter of great importance. After three-quarters of an hour had elapsed, the men left and Miss Hall was able to call her secretary. When asked what all the commotion was about, this is the story the secretary told:

"Since we have expanded the use of our sales office customer questionnaires, I am beginning to accumulate them in droves. They no longer fit in the file cabinets we have in the office, so I asked Mr. Frank, the office manager, if I could have another file. He said he would call Purchasing, and request that a new one be ordered. Apparently they told him they could not authorize the purchase without the approval of the Systems and Procedures Department. Mr. Frank then called them and they sent Mr. Otto over with a slide rule and lots of tables that tell you what shapes and sizes are most efficient for storing things. As Mr. Otto and Mr. Frank were interviewing me on just what items I wanted to keep in the files, their size, and how often I would be using them, Mr. Helpton came down from Purchasing. He said that frequently the most scientific file either wasn't readily available or was much higher in cost, and he usually found it moved matters along if he could get the Systems people to compromise on a unit they regularly order from a reliable supplier. Mr. Frank stayed in the conversation because he said that while he didn't want his budget to be charged with any fancy, unnecessary equipment, he wanted me to have the right file cabinet now, when I needed it. It took the three of them the good part of an hour to come to an agreement on what kind of file I should have."

1. What organization problems do you see here?

2. What is their source?

3. What organization changes could be introduced that would eliminate or minimize this type of situation?

Having looked at the function of the organization as a whole, we must now ask, "Where does the Personnel Department fit in?" In answering this question, we shall first examine the position of staff groups in the over-all organization (a subject of critical importance in itself) and then review the place and function of the personnel specialist.

What Is a Staff Department?

Accompanying the growth of large organizations in the American economy, the trend toward specialization, and the emphasis on scientific management, has been the evolution of staff departments. The term "staff department" designates a group in the organization that is not charged with the responsibility for the primary activities —as distinct from *line* departments. Staff departments are auxiliary units that perform some specialized service to help the line departments do their job. The evidence suggests that the size and number of these departments are still increasing.

supplies - information & advice

staff - advisory & information; has power

18

Personnel
as a Staff Function

In current organizational practice "staff" departments frequently provide the following services:

> *Information and advice*—e.g., the legal department interprets legislation and appraises the liabilities the organization will be assuming under specified conditions.
>
> *Services*—e.g., purchasing acquires supplies from outside vendors.
>
> *Controls*—e.g., inspection checks the quality of goods produced.

Technically, these activities are subsidiary to the central operating functions of the organization, but this does not mean they are necessarily less important. Wise purchasing can save enormous sums of money; astute legal advice can make the difference between success or failure in many business transactions.

It is easy to visualize the members of staff departments as aides, advisers, and counselors of line administrators with special problems. But the pattern of the actual relationship in any specific situation is most complex, and, under many circumstances, the dividing line between "line" and "staff" becomes somewhat hazy. In certain types of institution the normal relationship between line and staff may be reversed. In universities, hospitals, and some research organizations, for example, the central administration may provide staff services to the various specialists—the professional scientists, physicians, or teachers. Here the major work of the organization is carried on by specialists.

As we explore the relationships between staff departments and the line organization, we shall concentrate our attention on the personnel department. We believe that the most important determinant of the effectiveness of the personnel department is its ability to develop a good working relationship with line managers. This ability is even more important than the knowledge possessed by members of the department, the adequacy of their specialized techniques, and their individual abilities as experts. In turn, the usefulness of a staff department like personnel to the line manager, the supervisor, or the president is largely dependent on the quality of the line-staff relationship that prevails.

Evolution of the Personnel Department

What actual work is performed by the staff department? The case of the personnel department will illustrate the variety of responsibilities that rest with a staff department and the conflicts that sometimes arise among these responsibilities.

On the facing page is an example of the internal organization of a personnel department in a medium-sized company. To understand how all these functions have gravitated to a single staff unit, we need to look at the historical development of the personnel department.

THE RECORD-KEEPING STAGE l

Historically, the personnel department made its first appearance as a record-keeping department. It maintained employment records for workers and managers, including such factual material as date hired, background information, successive jobs held in the company with dates and wages received, disciplinary penalties imposed, and other events in the relationship of the individual to the organization. Sometimes it maintained time and production records for the purpose of preparing payrolls, and kept a record of the rates paid for various jobs. These were relatively routine clerical tasks that the line members of the organization were probably glad to have taken from their shoulders. These functions are still important, of course, in view of the growing emphasis on pension and insurance programs, seniority benefits of all kinds, and in-company promotion and management-development programs.

THE EMPLOYEE-SERVICES STAGE 2

Then during the 1920's the whole concept of personnel was vastly expanded in response to a new theory of industrial relations: many managements believed that the threat of union organization and "un-American influences" required a direct frontal attack on employee discontent. The new emphasis was on employee benefits—giving employees cafeterias and better

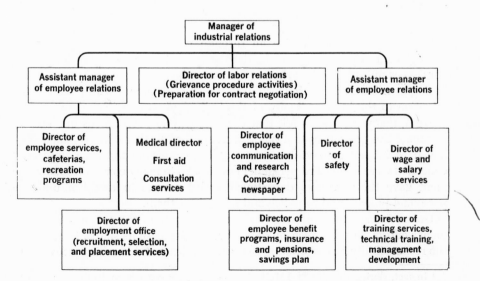

Internal organization of a personnel department in a medium-sized company.

rest rooms, baseball teams, company stores where they could buy products at a discount, social-work counselors, medical aid, and clubs whose representatives could discuss employee "grievances" with management. All these benefits, designed to make workers "happier," had a strong tinge of "paternalism." [1]

As a consequence, personnel took responsibility for an increasing number of activities that did not fit into any of the regular departments of the organization. As time passed, many personnel departments became "catch-all" units. Plant-protection activities (guards), fire-fighting services, in-company telephone services, and reception-desk activities—all tended to find their way into the personnel department.

As a result of this historical development, many personnel departments today are large, unwieldy, disjointed operations, with little internal unity. Furthermore, all these miscellaneous responsibilities compete for the time of the senior executives of the department, at the expense of more pressing responsibilities that may directly affect the success of the total enterprise.

THE PERSONNEL DECISION-MAKING STAGE 3 *(threat of unionism)*

During the 1930's there was another shift of emphasis: in many companies the personnel department (with its title often expanded to read "industrial relations department") was now expected to take direct charge of all employee and union relations. Often it was given full responsibility for hiring, firing, wage determination, handling union grievances, and determining who should be transferred or promoted.

Why did the personnel department suddenly gain so much power? Partly because of a widespread recognition by management of the importance of human elements, but probably the threat of unionism was the chief factor. Unions were on the offensive all through the late 1930's. They charged management with setting substandard wages, with discharging long-term employees unjustly, with harboring foremen who acted as petty tyrants, with basing transfers and promotions purely on favoritism, and with paying little attention to the human dignity of the individual worker. Faced with such charges, many companies felt that the best way to keep unions out was to eliminate the grievances that made workers turn to them. Management believed that inept supervisors were largely responsible for what observers conceded were haphazard personnel policies. So in many companies management gave the personnel department broad powers to establish uniform personnel policies and to police and administer them.

Unions came into many large companies in spite of the personnel department's efforts. But this invasion only served to increase its status. Now it had the responsibility for negotiating the labor contract and handling grievances.

---

[1] In fact, during this period YMCA directors, athletic coaches, and others in similar occupations were regarded as having the best qualifications for personnel work.

And since unions constantly seek out chinks in management's armor and try to establish precedents in one department that can be used elsewhere, the personnel department was given still further centralized control over personnel activities throughout the organization.

At the same time, as we saw in Chapter 15, other parts of the supervisor's job were being shifted to other staff groups. The industrial engineering groups took on the determination of work loads and methods and production scheduling. The accounting department won the power to question wage expenditures, and quality-control specialists assumed the job of setting and checking quality standards.

Yet as the supervisor's standing as a leader declined, the question of the staff's proper role in the organization was asked more and more persistently. To the supervisor the enhanced power of the staff meant a usurpation of his authority, a weakening of his relationship to his own subordinates, and a forced dependence on a department that did not share his responsibility for meeting cost and production objectives. The demoralized supervisor complained that he was being asked to run his department without any effective power to select, discipline, or reward his subordinates. Furthermore, the industrial-relations department overruled his decisions so frequently that he often gave up all attempts to exercise supervisory judgment.

At present the pattern is not clear. Many companies continue to use staff departments like personnel to substitute for the skills of line supervisors. In these organizations, personnel departments make critical decisions concerning such matters as selection, wage and salary administration, and discipline. Other organizations have become concerned with the impact of this fragmentation of the supervisor's job on his ability to exercise effective leadership. These companies believe that staff groups like personnel should restrict their activities to advising and counseling supervisors who request their assistance. A small number have attempted to experiment with giving first- or second-line supervisors their *own* staff assistants so that they can have fuller control over what happens in their own departments.

What should be the role of the personnel administrator as a staff man? What problems will he face in fulfilling this role? There are three types of staff activity in most modern organizations: (1) advising and counseling line managers; (2) controlling (auditing and evaluating and sometimes making decisions for line managers); and (3) special services. Let us explore the human-relations problems inherent in each type of activity.

Advising and Counseling Line Managers

Precisely how can the personnel department help a line supervisor make important decisions and at the same time maintain harmonious relationships with him? In actual practice we find rather extreme answers to this question. On the one hand there is the manager who interprets the activities of the personnel department this way:

> "Why it's simple. We use personnel people to deal with all our human problems—you know, managing people. Most of us know plenty about engineering and what makes equipment work and how to schedule and go out and sell, but we need someone to handle the people. This way we can be free to concentrate on the technical problems."

Then there is the manager with quite an opposite point of view:

> "The Personnel Department is there for help if you want it. If you don't want it, they leave you alone. They are sort of like a doctor—you don't have to go for a check-up, but it's good that you do."

Does either of these appraisals of the staff role of personnel in the organization provide a pattern worth emulating?

TENDENCY FOR STAFF TO DOMINATE LINE DECISIONS

In theory, the staff man merely provides advice and information for the supervisor; the line makes the decisions. How realistic is this distinction?

Blurred distinctions   This theory rests on the assumption that a sharp distinction can be drawn between the three categories of advice, information, and decision-making. In practice, this distinction is blurred.

When the staff man is providing information, he simply furnishes the facts that will help the line manager make sound, well-informed decisions:

1. The disciplinary clause of the union agreement means so and so.
2. The "going rate" for engineers like Jones in our present labor market is $650 per month.
3. Other companies in the metropolitan area require their carpenters to move small machinery when it is necessary in the course of their work.

Or the staff man may play a more active role and furnish advice:

1. You are likely to provoke a wildcat strike if you give Bill Williams a disciplinary lay-off.
2. On the basis of the record, Jones looks like a better bet for the promotion, since the man on the job will have to assume a good deal of initiative without close supervision.
3. If you hire Smith at that salary, you are going to have some dissatisfied older employees in your departments.

Sometimes there is a very narrow line between providing facts and providing advice. By selecting his facts carefully, the staff man can actually sway the line manager's decision one way or the other.

Finally, the staff can make decisions:

1. Don't discharge Brown; give him a warning slip.
2. Hire Green to replace the man who left.
3. Pay White $100 per week for that new job.

Actually, these neat distinctions break down in practice. As we shall see, what is given as "advice" may be interpreted by the supervisor as a decision.

Staff are experts   We have mentioned the tendency of management to turn over more and more functions to well-trained experts who have specialized knowledge in a relatively narrow field. When staff officials were first used to supplement the skills of line supervisors, the distinctions between information, advice, and decision-making were rarely made. Further, management showed a readiness to accept staff decisions, for it was anxious to avoid giving aid and comfort to the union. Often the industrial-relations department, for example, actually *told* supervisors whom to hire, what to pay them, and how to answer their grievances. As we have seen (Chapter 15), the result was often disastrous to the prestige and status of the supervisor.

In practice, it takes a strong-willed staff man to resist the temptation to become a decision-maker. Once he has grown accustomed to providing advice and counsel, he may find himself irresistibly taking the next step and actually make the decision—e.g., "Bill Williams should be given another chance, not discharged."

It is not surprising to find that staff groups seek to broaden the number of questions on which they will be consulted. A new personnel man in a company may be hired just to give expert advice on employment and training problems. It would be a safe prediction that he will soon seek to have his expertise used for a broader range of questions, such as wage and salary questions, grievances, and reorganization problems.

Sometimes these pressures are the result of the desire of a staff department to get more work for itself, justify bigger staffs and budgets, and take on more status in the organization. This reflects the competition between departments that we earlier observed as one of the by-products of specialization in the organization.

Even when the staff man is careful not to usurp the responsibility of the line supervisor, his actions may still be misinterpreted. The following case illustrates this problem:

> A grievance was filed against Gus Homes, a departmental supervisor, for failing to divide overtime equally. Homes argued that employees who failed to meet production standards on regular work should not be given overtime. The union contract said nothing about overtime, although general plant practice sanctioned equal division. The personnel director of the company, anxious to avoid any union bargaining on the overtime issue, urged Homes to change his mind. Homes refused.
>
> Some weeks later, Homes was transferred to a less desirable job. The plant "grapevine" reported that the manager had "given him the axe" on the recommendation of the personnel director. The truth of the matter was that the manager had believed for some time that Homes should be removed from his department. The overtime situation was just one among many reasons that seemed to justify the move.
>
> From this point on, other supervisors in the organization thought twice

about refusing the "advice" of the personnel director. His recommendations had become cloaked with real line authority; he had become another boss.

Capitulation by the line organization   Up to this point we may have given the impression that staff members aggressively seek to broaden their responsibilities and in the process thwart the line organization's efforts to maintain its unity of command. This is not always the case, however, for the line officials may themselves encourage the growth of staff activities.

The willingness of the personnel man to help out on a difficult problem, for example, may provide the supervisor with welcome relief from burdensome responsibilities. In effect, he says to the personnel man, "Good. You handle the personnel and I'll take care of all the technical problems." Then if something goes wrong, if a decision backfires, the line supervisor can simply point out that it was not *his* decision, it was a *staff* decision. And what a pleasant relief this provides.

The readiness with which line officials surrender responsibility for unpleasant personnel matters has been described by Mason Haire:

> If we are assembling widgets we usually know just what to do.... However, at the next step up the hierarchy the job is very different. Now, although the superior is responsible for the number of widgets turned out, he can't assemble them himself. He must accomplish the production through a very uncertain medium that intervenes between him and the widgets themselves—the people on the production line. It is a medium that is changeable, unpredictable, and intractable. It is a little like trying to pick a cherry from the bottom of a tall glass with two wobbly straws. It is easy to see what you are trying to do, but the instrument with which you are working is very hard to control. In many cases it seems likely that it is because of the difficulty of the medium through which production must be accomplished that managers turn away from the medium itself, in an unconscious effort to escape the problem, and say, My job is production—I'll hire an expert staff man to worry about the people.[2]

The line supervisor's reluctance to question the staff's expertise is easy to understand. After all, top management has identified staff members as specialists who have *the answers* to difficult problems. The subordinate manager who challenges their ability feels that he is running the risk of making a bad decision for which he will have to bear all the responsibility. He may even be anxious to interpret "advice" as a decision in order to avoid assuming responsibility and in order to "pass the buck" to the expert.

Paradoxically, a line official may complain that a staff group is pressuring for increased recognition and at the same time grumble that the staff is failing to take responsibility for decision-making. As one supervisor expressed it:

---

[2] Mason Haire, *Psychology in Management* (New York: McGraw-Hill, 1956), pp. 49-50.

"We stay away from the industrial relations department as much as possible—they're always trying to sell you on some new program or new way of doing something that makes more work for you. But then when you go to them with a problem you can't get a straight answer from them; they won't tell you how to handle it." (Interviewer's reply: "But what do they tell you then?") "Oh, they give you a lot of pros and cons and stuff that leaves you more confused than when you went in."

In short, the tendencies we have been discussing all lead, through one route or another, to the staff's taking on more and more responsibility in the typical large, specialized organization.

Are the results of these pressures on staff good or bad?

EFFECT OF STAFF DECISION-MAKING

Staff sees only part of the picture   Unfortunately, most supervisory problems do not lend themselves to staff decisions, largely because a single staff expert, by virtue of his job and his training, sees only part of the picture. Often a seemingly trivial decision concerning something like the change of one man's work schedule may involve questions of cost, production balancing, safety, quality, work-group stability, and a host of special circumstances that can only be known to the immediate supervisor in the department where the question has arisen. The supervisor can call on one or more experts for advice on parts of the problem, but rarely can the expert solve the whole problem.

The line official can seek the advice of the various staff "experts" on the impact of the alternatives under consideration. They can suggest to him the likely ramifications, advantages, disadvantages, and even methods of implementation. But they should not tell him what he should do—not just because they do not have the formal authority to make such decisions, but, more important, because they can speak with authority only about the one or two variables that lie within their own sphere of competence.

Furthermore, the staff expert does not have responsibility for the *total end result*. There are few decisions that the supervisor can make just by finding out the facts. Most involve elements of uncertainty, probability, and risk; for example, another salary increase for Jones will put his earnings out of line with those of the other engineers in the department, but if we don't give it to him he may quit. The balancing of all the pros and cons, the estimating of the "calculated risks" involved—these are the province of the line executive, and he must not surrender them.

For line officials to capitulate to staff destroys the most important aspect of the line organization: namely, accountability, or responsibility. They assume, mistakenly, that the supervisor's job can be departmentalized into a whole series of specialized skills, and that some of these skills can safely be assigned to others. The fact is that nearly every decision the supervisor makes has certain personnel implications, and certain quality, safety, and other implications as well. Trying to isolate all the separate "functions" only serves to destroy the responsibility of the supervisor.

Impairs line responsibility A further problem is that the line supervisor abdicates an important part of his job when he accedes to staff decision-making. If the personnel department "rules" that Bill Williams should *not* be discharged when the supervisor asks its "advice," the supervisor may be inclined to shrug off responsibility for the future performance of Williams: "After all, I really wanted to get rid of him, but they made me keep him," reasons the supervisor. The supervisor, as we noted above, has many difficult and risky decisions to make. This one may cause a work stoppage and that one may lose a valuable man. If management wants the supervisor to face up to the consequences of what are inevitably difficult, unpleasant decisions, staff groups cannot take a strong hand in influencing these decisions.

Who is the boss? Another serious ramification of staff decision-making is the potential erosion of the supervisor's leadership position. As employees begin to detect that staff groups are determining how hard they should work and at what rate of pay, who is hired and who is fired—they find little reason for dealing with their direct supervisor as the "boss." He, in turn, will find it increasingly difficult to motivate or control the behavior of his subordinates, since he no longer controls the rewards and penalties or determines the basic decisions in his department.

Often the personnel department becomes the "good boss" when employees discover that they can obtain relief from their supervisor's decisions by taking them "to personnel." In other cases the supervisor "passes the buck" to the personnel department; he tells a subordinate, "I'd be glad to give you that raise, but they (the personnel people) won't let me."

In either case the supervisor's relationship to his men is damaged. His subordinates decide that the personnel department, not the supervisor, has the power to influence their standing in the organization, and bend their efforts to finding ways of influencing the personnel department.

INTRA-MANAGEMENT FRICTIONS

These ambiguities in the position of staff in the organization set the stage for severe human-relations problems between staff and line officials. These two sets of management representatives are often antipathetic toward one another and their feelings of distrust handicap cooperation. Friction and bad feeling also impair the quality of communications between the groups, and the actions of one come to be misinterpreted by the other.

Just as we observed that departments or employees adjacent to one another in the organization can pressure one another (Chapter 16), so staff

groups like personnel and engineering can exert pressure on their line colleagues. Efforts to convince a manager that he ought to change the way he is
doing some part of his job nearly always eat into his time and energy, and
inevitably create a source of irritation. Furthermore, since the suggested
changes throw a spotlight on the manager's skills and ways of doing his job,
he regards them as a threat to his security.

To understand the antipathy that often crackles between staff and line
managers, we must also take into account personal jealousies. This is an
example of the struggle between the specialist and the generalist—the man of
ideas and the man of action. The line official, who has over-all responsibility
for some activity, feels that the specialist can't really understand his problems because he is interested in only a narrow area. Over and over again the
protests and suggestions of personnel men are greeted by a "Yeah, but
you don't have to get out the production!"

To complicate matters, line and staff men customarily have quite different
backgrounds. The line official is more likely to have worked his way up
through the organization, more on the basis of experience than of formal
training. The staff specialist, on the other hand, usually has had advanced
training outside the organization, and has often been appointed directly
to his present job. This difference in background introduces another element
of dissimilarity that may breed suspicion or at least antipathy on both sides.[3]

Another problem results from differences in the "height" of the hierarchies
to which each reports. In theory, within a given organization, a staff man
may be the equal of a line supervisor (i.e., they both appear at the same
level on the organization chart). In fact, the staff hierarchy may be substantially shorter. As a result the staff man may take a case involving a
difficult supervisor to his boss, who in turn has access to the very top of the
organization. On the other hand the line supervisor may be five or six levels
below the top management level. Staff people move more freely about the
organization and can contact more influential levels in management without
appearing to "go over somebody's head" than can their equivalents in line
management. This is a result of their more loosely defined job descriptions
and their need for more mobility within the organization. The staff's advantage in "contacts" serves to irritate the less mobile line supervisor, who may
in turn feel coerced by the staff.

In most companies, however, there is a balancing asset on the side of the
line. Usually promotion to top-level positions requires line experience, and
the line executive is the one who receives the important promotions. Therefore to move into top management most staff people must expect to shift
to a line job, and they recognize the wisdom of staying on good terms with
that side of the organization.

---

[3] Melville Dalton, "Conflicts Between Staff and Line Officials," *American Sociological
Review,* Vol. 15 (June 1950), pp. 342-351.

TECHNIQUES FOR HANDLING THE STAFF ADVISORY FUNCTION: INFLUENCE WITHOUT AUTHORITY

How can a staff department exert influence without resorting to the use of authority? To put it another way, how can the staff man gain acceptance for his ideas without forcing them on the line manager under threat of punishment or promise of reward? Let us look at a typical case and then explore possible solutions:

> The personnel department has noticed that turnover is very high in Chet Anthony's department. Chet's boss, the vice president in charge of sales, urges the personnel director, Phillips, to do something to halt the loss of valuable personnel. What should the personnel director do? How should he approach Anthony?

What happens if he calls on Anthony to say that both he and the vice president are worried about his high turnover rate? Chances are that Anthony will react this way:

> "Here is someone representing the vice president. Phillips carries the boss' authority. All right, what do they want me to do? If they're willing to put up the money for higher salaries or take the responsibility for putting in some new-fangled ideas, that's up to them; it's no skin off of my teeth."

Clearly, the battle is lost before it has begun, for Anthony has no intention of telling Phillips what his problems really are. From this point on, Anthony may "cover up" as much as possible and try to shift the blame for any future problems onto personnel.

And if Phillips makes suggestions, Anthony may term them "too theoretical" or "impractical," or else accept them superficially (perhaps just to settle the issue), only to destroy them in practice through subtle sabotage. For example, he may agree to introduce some technique of general supervision and even hold meetings with his subordinates and ask for their advice, but continue to hold the threat of punishment over the head of anyone who does not immediately accept his point of view.

How then can the personnel director influence the department head without "pulling rank"? Primarily by persuading Anthony to regard him as a *source of help*. Anthony has certain objectives that he is trying to achieve. He may be anxious to establish a record that will earn him a promotion, or to win prestige in the eyes of his fellow managers, or to minimize the amount of administrative red tape. Phillips can exert influence by convincing Anthony that his skills and knowledge will help him reach his goals.[4]

---

[4] We are indebted here to the excellent analysis of the role of the staff expert first presented by Douglas McGregor in his article, "The Staff Function in Human Relations," *Journal of Social Issues*, Vol. IV, No. 3 (Summer 1948), pp. 6-23.

The staff expert must keep in mind that Anthony's way of handling his department has evolved over a long period of time in response to his own particular needs. For any real change to take place, Anthony must discover for himself that his behavior is inadequate to the situation, and must be genuinely ready to accept help.

Phillips should concentrate on creating an atmosphere that will permit a free and easy discussion of all the facts in the case and the possible alternative solutions. By means of a counseling interview (see Chapter 10) he can help the line supervisor to know himself better. If this interview is handled properly, the supervisor may feel free to discuss his own shortcomings without covering up—as he might do with his own boss.

Phillips might start the discussion by commenting that he has noticed a rise in the turnover figure and is curious about what it signifies. Is Anthony having any trouble training replacements? What makes so many people quit so quickly? Is it just coincidence? Is there anything the personnel department can do to help? Using this as an opening, Phillips might encourage Anthony to explore the problem. While Anthony talks, Phillips should avoid seeming to judge him, or to be imposing a solution on him. Instead, Phillips should make it clear that he is merely trying to find out how the problem looks to Anthony and perhaps help Anthony view his problems and himself more realistically.

In the process of working together on a variety of problems, Phillips can learn Anthony's attitudes toward his job and its problems. He also can present a picture of personnel's role and position in the organization. He can make it clear that the goals of the personnel department are to help other groups and individuals help themselves to deal with their human-relations problems, and to provide specific skills and techniques when they are called for by the line managers.

Next Phillips might encourage Anthony to consider the alternative solutions to the problem, and the probable success of each. This is the most crucial point of all, for Anthony must work through for himself the ramifications of suggested changes. He must regard as his own any programs that are developed, and must assume responsibility for implementing them. "Role-playing" (Chapter 24) can be used in the conference to "try out" various solutions to a delicate personnel problem. Such training, counseling, and try-outs should be designed not only to increase the line official's skill but also to bolster his confidence in himself.

In effect, Phillips should try to use all his knowledge of individual needs and informal group behavior, of supervisory skills (such as interviewing and discipline), and of labor relations to *help* the line supervisor make *his own* decision.

In this case, Anthony may decide that his own supervisors need a training program to improve their managerial skills. But he would prefer to have the whole program handled by the personnel department—after all, this is "out of his field" and personnel are the experts. Phillips should be wary of such efforts to shift the responsibility to the staff group. Lacking responsibility for the program, Anthony would never be sure that it was exactly what he wanted; the supervisors participating in the program would not associate it with the "boss'" attitudes and desires.

Of course, Phillips must not be merely a passive listener. He must provide information and evaluations, when asked—though only as a means to help Anthony make a realistic decision. For example, he might reveal some of the dimensions of the problem by probing more deeply into the turnover statistics: Who is leaving—what age groups, from what occupational groups? How does turnover here compare with turnover in other departments? What are the possible causes: wages, supervision (including Anthony's), other factors in the work environment? Personnel, like any other staff group, has specialized tools at its command—in this case, perhaps, a community salary survey or a review of department employment records.

Thus a simple "yes" or "no" answer—a "do this" or "do that" response— by the staff man to line problems wastes an important opportunity. Research in learning suggests that training is more effective and individuals more highly motivated to learn when they have immediate problems that they want to solve. The best time to help train a supervisor to make better decisions in the future is when he has an immediate problem.

Over time, subsequent discussions with the personnel department should enable Anthony to handle his personnel problems by himself, and to ask for help only when especially difficult problems crop up. The end result should be a better-informed supervisor with considerable skill in applying the knowledge developed by personnel experts to his day-to-day problems.

Using personnel as our example, let us summarize the elements that seem to characterize a healthy supervisory-staff relationship:

1. The supervisor turns to the personnel man for help with his problems largely on his own initiative, with a feeling that he can discuss them freely with a sympathetic listener who is not in the line of authority.

2. The supervisor comes to understand the role and to utilize the skills embodied in the personnel group, and, in turn, the personnel staff grows familiar with the special interests and needs of the supervisory group it services.

3. The supervisor is helped by personnel to understand the dimensions and alternative solutions of his problems, and is helped to develop skill in evaluating alternatives.

4. The supervisor increases his own ability to cope with the human problems of his group. He regards problems as means of developing new abilities and insights.

5. The personnel staff develops greater acceptance for its ideas and points of view, not through putting pressure on the line supervisor to change

"or else," but through developing confidence in the staff's "helping" role and through proving in practice that it can contribute to the supervisor's effectiveness.

6. The line organization receives credit for any improvements that result.

You will have realized, of course, that we have been describing an ideal staff-line relationship, one that is difficult to achieve in practice. Staff groups like personnel actively struggle within the organization to gain recognition and acceptance for their points of view and skills. While their efforts to contribute ideas and programs often fall on deaf ears, top management may still hold them responsible for evident failures in the company's personnel efforts. As a result, staff officials are caught in a dilemma: How can we exert influence and help ward off personnel problems in the organization when we don't have authority to get our recommendations adopted by the supervisors whose actions determine the company's personnel relationships? Efforts to escape this dilemma take many forms: attempts to "educate" supervisors or their bosses, guarded threats to report ineffective supervisory actions to higher levels in the organization, and a host of subtle or overt lobbying activities.

The Control Functions of a Staff Department

In Chapter 14 we observed that management uses controls as a means of regulating the activities of subordinate levels. Staff groups are the ones usually assigned the function of "controlling" or monitoring certain aspects of the day-to-day activities within the organization. For example, accounting departments check to see that departmental expenditures are consistent with approved budget allocations; inspectors test finished parts or products to insure that agreed-upon specifications have been met; a wage and salary specialist within the personnel department approves salary increases to insure that individual salaries do not violate predetermined ranges; industrial engineering approves all new layout plans and equipment purchases.

The function of controls is to guarantee that the organization will conform to official policies, particularly those that might be slighted in the heat of day-to-day operating pressures. Staff, being somewhat removed from the battle line, may be in a better position to evaluate how the organization is functioning—perhaps by identifying problem areas and pinpointing sources of waste and inefficiency. For example, a division might be tempted to use excessively high salaries as a means of attracting and retaining personnel. Of course, this practice would eventually have an impact on salaries in other departments. Thus the regular checks carried on by staff, such as quality and wage and salary control, serve as the eyes and ears of management, particularly top management.

ESTABLISHING THE STANDARDS FOR CONTROLS

Behind these control activities is the assumption that the organization has *standards* or *criteria* on which to base the evaluation of supervisory or department performance. For example, checking to see that the salaries paid for engineers in Department Z are "appropriate" requires that there be such policies. The same holds for appraisals of productivity, safety, and the results of labor negotiation.

Staff departments are often asked to develop indices that will keep upper levels of management informed. Personnel specialists, for example, develop measures of turnover that will enable individual departments to compare their records with those of other departments in the same company as well as in other companies. The same holds for accident records, absenteeism statistics, number of grievances, and similar personnel data.

Recently some staff groups have tried to make more use of concepts that had formerly been restricted to the field of quality control.[5] Statisticians have provided tools by which inspection groups can determine whether deviations in the quality of finished products are due to normal, chance variation, or to some special, non-random factor, such as a machine or material problem or poor workmanship. The inspector can make this distinction by plotting the results of his quality tests on control charts, which show the ideal specifications and allow entries to be made indicating departures or deviations from the standards. Statisticians have found that for many processes, variations from standards that exceed three times the expected or "normal" random deviations are an indication of trouble. A deviation of this magnitude could not be due to the usual, chance variations that are always occurring; rather, they must have an assignable cause.

In the future it is conceivable that personnel may extend this method in an attempt to identify parts of the organization that are "out of control." That is to say, personnel's auditing responsibility requires them to look for trouble spots in the organization. Every supervisor is going to have a certain amount of personnel difficulty: quits, requests for transfers, grievances, poor workmanship, and absenteeism. However, it is not sufficient to know that Department A has more quits than Department B. The two may employ entirely different types of people on different types of job—A has young girls doing clerical work who are always getting married and resigning; B has long-service toolmakers. More significant is detecting when a department is shifting from one position to another—for example, moving from a medium-turnover record to a high-turnover position.

---

[5] See Eliot D. Chapple and Leonard Sayles, *The Measure of Management* (New York: Macmillan, 1960). The authors illustrate how quality-control principles can be used to control a variety of managerial processes.

The value of the quality-control principle is that it enables management to know when a real shift has occurred, and to distinguish results that indicate a new source of trouble from results that indicate a normal, expected variation from the standards.

Although staff groups have technical expertise in activities of this sort, it is our view that they should *not* be permitted to establish the organization's criteria for supervisory success. All the policies, objectives, and standards of the company are so integrally related to one another that line management —and line management alone—must retain responsibility for determining them. The staff can provide information on which line can base its decisions, of course. For example, in establishing a salary policy for a branch unit in a new community, personnel department surveys of labor supply and salaries paid for comparable jobs will be an indispensable component of the final policy decision. But line management should decide what salary policy the company will adopt.

TECHNIQUES OF CONTROL

What role does the staff play in administering these controls or audits of line management's activities? Several quite different patterns of staff behavior are discernible:

Advance approval   In some areas the staff is made responsible for approving proposed supervisory actions *before* they are put into effect. For example, some companies require that supervisors receive approval from the personnel department for all salary increases. Here the staff is administering a salary policy that sets forth certain limits within which individuals can receive merit raises.[6] As long as the projected increase falls within these limits, approval is granted.

When the action does not conform to these predetermined rules or policies, the staff may take a variety of steps. The simplest is informing the supervisor that his action cannot be approved. Should the line manager wish to pursue his original plan, both parties may appeal to higher levels in the management hierarchy to resolve the dispute.

Regular, continuing checks   As the "eyes and ears" of upper management, the staff may also initiate a series of continuing checks on line activities. Personnel departments maintain running observations of turnover statistics, grievance and accident records, requests for transfer, numbers of merit raises, and similar events. Again the purpose is to detect situations that are going "out of control," in the terminology of quality control.

---

[6] We are, of course, assuming that management has thought through and established a policy in this area. See Chapter 25.

Where they detect a manager or a department that is getting into trouble, the staff originates action to the line. This may just be a matter of telling the line supervisor that the control data indicate a problem, and then leaving it to him to decide what to do. If the staff group believes that the situation is serious enough, it might go further and advise the line manager on what action he might take. This further step is taken, of course, if the staff believes that effective line action will not be taken without prodding.

In many cases the source of the immediate difficulty may not be readily apparent. For example, if a department develops a serious employee-relations problem, personnel may be asked to use its skills and technical knowledge to analyze the cause of the problem. It may discover that the difficulty lies in selection or placement, inadequate supervision, wage administration, or some other area. In any case, once the source of trouble has been identified, close cooperation between staff and line personnel is essential if a realistic solution is to be devised and put into effect. And cooperation depends on the existence of a reservoir of good will built up by the staff group in the past through its efforts to help the line meet its objectives.

When cooperation is impossible between staff and line, the staff may just report its findings to higher management, which in turn must decide what action should be taken—e.g., discipline, further investigation, or no action.

Periodic audits   Some large companies use staff groups like personnel as outside auditors to make periodic investigations of various departments and prepare an over-all evaluation of each unit's effectiveness. Here, of course, there is no semblance of line-staff cooperation. Management, in fact, expects the staff investigators to avoid developing close relationships that might bias their findings. The reports themselves go directly to top management, although the line managers involved may receive copies.

REACTIONS OF SUPERVISORS TO STAFF CONTROL ACTIVITIES

The staff is responsible for directing management's attention to trouble spots and for helping to develop remedial actions. But it can do neither job unless it enjoys a good working relationship with the line officials who must institute changes. Unless this relationship exists, the staff can prepare any number of lengthy reports and analyses, but they will automatically be filed away and never referred to again.

Line management may look upon staff control activities as just another form of pressure designed to make their life more difficult. At the operating level, the supervisor has to cope with informal groups, he has to adjust to the demands of his subordinates if he is to get them to accept his demands— and this means that he must often depart from the plans, procedures, and policies that top management has established. Understandably, he regards staff control activities as a threat to his established ways of doing things. Line managers are motivated to hide their methods of operation, to juggle figures or seek excuses or shift responsibility in order to cover up deviations from standards. In the process, they develop an antipathy for the "checkers" who do not "understand the problems we face on the firing line." Further, staff proposals for improvements often call for drastic changes in work methods that will upset status relationships in the informal group and violate well-established group norms.

Additional problems are created when management uses staff control activities to exert "pressure" on the line organization. The staff's formal and informal reports are often used to spur the supervisor to more effective efforts, as well as to provide top management with information.

The most serious problems of staff-line relationships develop when the staff takes this point of view: "Our job is to dig up dirt, and that is the way to get promotions, too." This attitude makes the objectives of the staff almost incompatible with those of the line departments on which the controls are being imposed.

Fortunately, the line-staff relationship is not always as unpleasant as we have suggested. Successful staff personnel have learned that they are more effective in improving line performance if they discuss the results of their evaluations with the supervisor involved *before* they send them on to higher management. This gives the supervisor a chance to improve his performance before the boss learns that he is doing a poor job. Rather than a pressure mechanism, the staff report then becomes a device to help the supervisor remedy defects in his operations and meet the standards established by top management. When most of the problems uncovered by staff investigations are remedied without recourse to higher levels of the organization, one usually finds that staff and line groups work together harmoniously.

Line managers will be more willing to accept a staff control report if they can see how its contents will help them achieve their objectives. An accountant provided a good example of this constructive technique:

> "Management has given us the responsibility of getting department heads to use special procedures in purchasing materials and supplies from other departments within the company. Many supervisors don't like to fill out these forms in advance—claiming that they are just a lot of red tape. When we detect this situation, we spend some time with the supervisor, showing him how his work will actually be made more difficult if he fails to use these procedures. It is easy to show that he will have to do much more paper work later on in accounting for these and getting requisitions approved than if he does it ahead of time. While this may take an hour or so of our time, it gets better results than just telling him, 'This is to be management's policy.'"

In summary, control responsibilities may make it more difficult for staff members also to serve as "advisers" and "counselors" to line supervisors.

Some policemen, skilled in human relations, manage to develop this type of relationship with the people "on their beat," but it is admittedly a difficult task. The fact is that many inconsistencies are inherent in the two roles. Of the several techniques of staff control, periodic auditing appears to be the least compatible with the development of any counseling relationship; staff responsibility for giving advance approval to line decisions is probably most compatible.

Staff Service Activities

In practice, it is impossible to draw a neat dividing line between staff responsibilities for carrying out *control* responsibilities and staff responsibilities for carrying out *service* functions. The identification of a recurrent line problem often leads directly to the development of a new service program. We are using the term "service" to refer to activities that are carried on exclusively by the staff department itself; service activities are another example of division of labor within the organization. For example, such jobs as recruitment, the administration of employee records and insurance programs, the operation of company cafeterias, and the supervision of company guards are often turned over completely to the personnel department. Functions such as purchasing, legal counsel, and engineering are given to other staff groups, which make their services available to the total organization. In assigning service activities to the staff, management hopes to enjoy the benefits of high technical competence and the economies of specialization.

In performing a service activity, the staff department does something *for* the line department. Usually the relationship is quite amicable, for line departments have little interest or ability in these specialized areas and are glad to have staff relieve them of what they feel are "nasty headaches." The division manager is glad to have the public-relations department write press releases for him, and the sales manager is pleased to have personnel handle his personnel records.

There are times, however, when the service relationship leads to friction between line and staff.

1. The line department may ask the staff department to perform services that the staff feels are excessive or unnecessary.

2. Several line departments may compete with one another for a larger share of the staff department's services.

3. In contrast, the line department may resent the staff department's performing a particular service, either because line feels it can handle the service more effectively itself, or because it feels that the so-called "service" actually makes its job harder.

LINE ASKS FOR TOO MANY SERVICES

At times line management requests services that staff believes are unnecessary or ill-advised. For example, a line department may ask the personnel department to run a training program for first-line supervisors, even though the personnel department is convinced that such a program will be useless until higher management itself participates in such a training program.

Often line tries to get staff to assume responsibilities that line should handle itself. A supervisor may pass the buck to the personnel department in the handling of a ticklish disciplinary problem. Or line management may ask the personnel department to make the final decisions on union grievances, or even to handle the negotiations for a new contract.

Some of the services requested by line may actually appear wasteful to staff. A training program is not always the answer to employee-relations problems. A bigger and fancier house organ may actually intensify the problems of poor employee-employer relations.

Staff should try to persuade line departments not to request unnecessary services. In the last analysis, however, staff may have to provide such services if the line authority insists—at least, if line is willing to pay for them out of its budget. The skillful staff official, without seeming to shirk his responsibilities, is able to demonstrate to the line official why a special new program will not answer his problems.

CONFLICTS OVER SCARCE SERVICES

When line's demand for staff services becomes too great, the staff must somehow ration its limited time and energies among rival claimants. Department A wants personnel to devote more of its efforts to recruiting engineers; Department B thinks personnel should concentrate on finding better accountants. Production departments are constantly jockeying to get their "proper share of maintenance." The staff department must show great tact in setting priorities, for every time it turns down one department's request for services it hurts its advisory relationship with that department. Preferably line-management establishes standards for these priorities.

RESISTANCE TO STAFF PERFORMANCE OF SERVICES

Some line departments, imbued with the "do-it-yourself" philosophy, object to having staff perform certain services. They feel that they could get much more effective service if they could do their own purchasing, instead of having to channel their requisitions through the purchasing department.

Certainly when the line department has direct control over a service, it does not have to compete with other departments for "scarce resources." Furthermore, line may feel that staff does not understand its special needs. Thus the engineering department may feel that it should recruit its own engineers, since "the average personnel man doesn't know what makes a good engineer tick." Purchasing insists on using a supplier who quotes the lowest price, while a particular line department prefers another vendor who responds to requests for special services and quick delivery. Often, too, line supervisors are suspicious that staff wants to take over a service in order to increase its own importance and the size of its budget and its staff. Line's resistance is intensified if management charges the cost of the new service against the line department's budget, or if it requires line managers to spend time and energy on the new activity.[7]

> We once watched the difficulties encountered by the personnel department in one company that attempted to introduce a new management-development program. Line officials tried to sabotage the program, even though it was designed to help them develop more promotable subordinates. However, in another company an almost identical program was welcomed by line managers. Why the difference?
> In the second company, the firm's president had indicated that one of the new *controls* he would begin watching was the number of promotable executives produced by each department and the vigor with which each department set up training programs. Aware that this new factor would enter into their own appraisal, the line managers asked the personnel department to *help them* create management-development programs. In the first company, the initiative had come exclusively from personnel.

In short, line managers welcome staff activities that promise to help them achieve their own goals and resist staff activities that do not seem intimately related to their needs.

STAFF INITIATES PROGRAMS

Staff departments sometimes find themselves engaged in service activities that they feel should really be handled by line simply because line refuses to accept responsibility for them. At other times, staff throws its energies into service activities seemingly as a compensation for its failure to develop satisfactory advisory relationships with line. One personnel director told us:

> "I handle grievances myself. I know you professors think this is wrong—it detracts from my supervisors' prestige and so forth. But I can't trust them to handle grievances properly—every time I let them try it I get into trouble. I've tried training programs, but I can't get them to change their ways. Some day our present supervisors will retire and I'll let the new

---

[7] It is common accounting practice to prorate the cost of service programs to all line departments according to some criterion like number of employees or gross sales.

men handle the responsibility. But for the moment I can't risk ruining my union relations just to back up a theory."

Staff often retreats into service activities because they do not require such close working relations with line management as do more advisory relationships. For example, a safety director may have tried in vain to get supervisors to attend a safety course, or to induce them to discipline employees who engage in unsafe practices. In despair he resorts to a safety poster campaign —not because he thinks posters can compete with a supervisor's order in changing employee behavior—but because he knows that no one will object to posters and at least he will have a sense of achievement and something to show management in the way of "activity."

> [One company] reports that it has developed an automated suggestion box which senses an employee who is approaching the box. When this occurs a music box attachment is "set off," playing a stimulating march tune and then a taped "pep talk" on the value of suggestion, and finally a shoe-shine device is activated which gives the employee at the suggestion box a free shoe shine.[8]

Company resources are wasted frequently in these efforts.

SPECIAL PROBLEMS IN DECENTRALIZED ORGANIZATIONS

Staff departments in decentralized organizations face special difficulties: Their immediate supervisor is usually the line manager who heads the branch operation, but they also have a "functional relationship" to the central-office staff group. Thus a personnel man in the Akron office of the Superior Insurance Company takes his orders from the District Manager in that office, but his chances for promotion also depend on whether or not he pleases the Vice President for Personnel in New York City. Conflict often arises when the central staff tries to get some new program adopted throughout the organization—for example, an employee appraisal system. The local personnel man is urged by New York to lobby for the new program, but the management in Akron is far from enthusiastic about having New York interfere in local employee relations. The local staff man is caught up in a "role conflict," since he must try to satisfy the incompatible norms or standards of two distinct groups.

Appropriate Staff-Line Division of Labor

The following table represents what we feel is an appropriate division of labor and responsibility between staff and line in one area of company

---

[8] *Industrial Relations News*, March 7, 1959

activity—employment. As you check the distribution of responsibility between staff and line, try to analyze the reasoning behind it.

Employment [9]

Personnel—Employment Specialist (staff)	Department Supervision (line)
1. Develop sources of qualified applicants from local labor market. This requires carefully planned community relations, speeches, advertisements, and active high-school, college, and technical-school recruiting. [Second step.]	1. Prepare requisition outlining specific qualifications of employees needed to fill specific positions. Help create reputation that will attract applicants. [First step.]
2. Conduct skilled interviews, give scientific tests, and make thorough reference checks, etc., using requisition and job description as guides. Screening must meet company standards and conform with employment laws. [Third step.]	2. Interview and select from candidates screened by Personnel. Make specific job assignments that will utilize new employees' highest skills to promote maximum production. [Fifth step.]
3. Refer best candidates to supervisor, after physical examinations and qualifications for the positions available have been carefully evaluated. [Fourth step.]	3. Indoctrinate employees with specific details regarding the sections and jobs where they are to be assigned—safety rules, pay, hours, "our customs." [Seventh step.]
4. Give new employees preliminary indoctrination about the company, benefit plans, general safety, first aid, shift hours, etc. [Sixth step.]	4. Instruct and train on the job according to planned training program already worked out with Personnel. [Eighth step.]
5. Keep complete record of current performance and future potential of each employee. [Tenth step.]	5. Follow up, develop, and rate employee job performance; decide on promotion, transfer, layoff, or discharge. [Ninth step.]
6. Diagnose information given in separation interviews, determine causes, and take positive steps to correct. [Twelfth step.]	6. Hold separation interview when employees leave—determine causes. Make internal department adjustments to minimize turnover. [Eleventh step.]

Conclusion

The growth of staff personnel activities is a reflection of the increasing importance of specialized departments in the functioning of large organizations. And yet the staff role in personnel, as well as in other areas, poses a number of special problems beyond those created by specialization as a principle of organization. The most difficult is the relationship of staff personnel to line personnel. This is not the simple superior-subordinate relationship we are used to in the ordinary work group.

The success of the personnel activity depends on a very tenuous relationship between line and staff. Line administrators faced with difficult problems in the management of people will turn to the personnel man for advice if they regard him as a source of help. But, since the staff expert often can exercise

---

[9] Robert Saltonstall, "Who's Who in Personnel Administration," *Harvard Business Review*, Volume 33, No. 4 (July-August 1955), pp. 75-83.

power over line supervisors by virtue of his specialized knowledge and his ready access to higher levels of management, he can easily destroy this relationship. On the other side, if the staff man allows himself to be shifted to a decision-making position, many supervisors will abdicate responsibility for personnel decisions and use him as a crutch. Yet it is the line supervisor, not the staff man, who is ultimately responsible for meeting the production and efficiency goals prescribed by management, and he must not abdicate that responsibility.

Staff departments are often assigned responsibility for certain control and service activities, which call for a very different type of relationship with line supervisors. The staff may be asked to serve as the "eyes and ears" of upper management by checking or auditing supervisory effectiveness, and the reports submitted by staff may be used as a source of reward or punishment for members of the line organization. Clearly this function may prove incompatible with staff's role as adviser and consultant.

Staff jobs require unusual personalities—executives who can conscientiously identify organization trouble spots and work with line management without creating antagonisms and without using threats. This job is made particularly difficult by differences in background and training between the line and staff officials within a given company.

One way of viewing the total staff job is to consider it as a training relationship—that is, staff should try to improve the line manager's ability to detect and solve organizational problems. As we shall see in a later chapter, the motivation to learn is heightened when the learner is aware that he has a problem. As auditors, staff members are conscious of the difficulties faced by each supervisor in meeting the standards set for his unit by top management. By enhancing the supervisor's own awareness of his difficulties, and by providing him with new skills and techniques in coping with them, staff can discharge its responsibility for training.

Sometimes the answer to an organizational problem may lie in a totally new staff program or service. For example, recurring shortages of qualified applicants might be dealt with by a recruiting *service* developed by the Personnel Department. Other service functions, such as handling company pensions and insurance plans, are centralized in staff groups to avoid duplication of people and facilities.

Ideally, management should take full advantage of the technical expertise of staff departments, but it should keep the basic responsibility for managing the organization firmly and unambiguously in the hands of department supervision. Both line and staff must work together, and their activities must intermesh; but their roles in the organization should not be permitted to shift over time. Because line supervisors are charged with the task of "getting out the work," they must make most of the basic decisions involved in setting standards and executing plans.

Students who plan to make a career in the staff personnel field should become familiar with some of the following publications:

Personnel, published by the American Management Association, is an easy-to-read means of keeping abreast of new developments. For a broader discussion of management problems, the following university publications are excellent: the *Harvard Business Review, The Journal of Business* (published by the School of Business, University of Chicago), the *California Management Review*, and the University of Indiana's *Business Horizons*. A more academic, sociological approach is presented by the *Administrative Science Quarterly*. For technical discussions, see *Personnel Psychology* and the *Journal of the American Society of Training Directors*.

The Industrial and Labor Relations Review presents scholarly discussions of union-management problems, many of which are related to personnel administration questions. Trends in wages, government policy, fringe benefits, and collective bargaining are ably reviewed and analyzed in the U. S. Department of Labor's *Monthly Labor Review* and the National Industrial Conference Board's *Management Record*. Prentice-Hall publishes a loose-leaf service for personnel executives that reviews company personnel practices, current legislation, and current personnel problem areas.

Questions of personnel administration involving public employees are considered in *Public Administration Quarterly*.

The *Labor Law Journal* is also very helpful in this field, and adequate summaries of recent legal developments are provided by the *Monthly Labor Review*.

University research in the social sciences, some of which has a direct bearing on personnel problems, is well represented in the following journals: *American Journal of Sociology* (sociology); *American Sociological Review* (sociology); *Human Organization* (anthropology); and *Journal of Applied Psychology* (psychology, with some emphasis on the testing field).

Problem I *

Many companies have set up departments to analyze such paper-work activities as billing operations, interoffice correspondence, inventory control problems, and various file systems. This type of department is usually placed on a staff level and is called the Methods Department or Industrial Engineering Department.

In the Rajah Comptometer Company this department is called the Systems and Procedures Department. On a staff level, it is directly responsible through its department head to the vice president in charge of marketing. As Systems and Procedures increased in size and in the scope of activities it undertook, line personnel began to regard it as in the same category as the company's financial auditors. Depending on what line people you talked to, Systems and Procedures was called everything from a bunch of "idiotic college-bred snoopers" to "a necessary evil." Almost every branch manager, salesman, and plant foreman has heard by word of mouth that the department raises havoc with normal work techniques when it undertakes investigations, that its remedies cause more work

---

* We are indebted to a former student. Stuart Pennels, for the outline of this case.

than the original method employed, and that the cost of maintaining it outweighs the cost "cutbacks" that result from its work. "Maybe we are even paying their salaries by our efforts," has been a frequent comment.

When department employees went out into the "field" to conduct an investigation, the local branch manager decided with whom they could talk and work. This rule inhibited the Systems and Procedures people, since the branch manager did not always let them talk to the personnel who were close to the problem they were investigating. Moreover, since their visits were always announced in advance, line personnel met them with a "hale fellow, well met" attitude. And yet line had a great many misgivings, feeling that the investigation would be an inconvenience and that the resultant suggestions would be "half-baked" at best.

Recently, two men from the Systems and Procedures Department were ordered to make a cost analysis of the paper work involved in receiving and answering a typical comptometer service repair call in the Columbus, Ohio, District Branch. They arrived early one Monday morning to spend the week with the repairmen who did the work. The first morning they spent with the manager, who had been forewarned by a letter from the comptroller's department and another from the home office general service manager. The local manager was not too happy to see people from the home office, simply because their presence implied some deficiency in his managerial ability. (Branch offices operate on the theory that no news from the home office is good news.) After a long lunch, paid for by the "visiting firemen" because they were on an expense account, the manager spent the afternoon trying to discover what the Systems and Procedures men were "really" trying to do. After they had assured him that his office had been selected for the investigation only because it typified small district offices and for no other reason, the manager told them that he did not want his service department upset, and that his foreman had been there fifteen years and was very touchy about criticism. "The men in my service department are the best in all the Midwest." Then the manager said that it was getting late and he felt he would like to talk to the service foreman first before the Systems and Procedures men did, so that he could "smooth the way."

Tuesday morning the Systems and Procedures men finally were able to see the service foreman. He seemed very reluctant to listen to their explanations of the investigation, let alone cooperate with them. The six servicemen who worked for him were equally unresponsive; they had obviously been warned not to give away any branch "secrets."

The servicemen of Rajah Comptometer are talented, skilled mechanics. The speed and efficiency with which they respond to service calls has won them an enviable reputation in the trade. Few of them have college degrees; most are high-school graduates. And they look askance at anyone who is (1) a college man and (2) doesn't know how to repair a comptometer.

The Systems and Procedures men spent the second day vainly trying to justify their trip to the service foreman, and trying to communicate with the group as a whole. The third day was almost equally unsuccessful, although their casual revelation that there would be a new comptometer model in the spring did alleviate some of the tension.

The two Systems and Procedures men spent Wednesday night trying to figure out how they could gain access to the service department group. They realized that they were hampered by the fact that they were newly hired, college-trained employees who didn't know how to repair a comptometer or even know the names of its parts. So they spent three hours memorizing the names of various parts out of a service linebook they happened to bring along. To win acceptance from the foreman, since all the servicemen seemed to take their cues from him, they also decided to appeal to his interest in gardening and rare flowers.

1. How would you evaluate the situation faced by the two Systems and Procedures men in the Columbus branch office?

2. Given your evaluation of the situation, what alternative courses of action are open to them? What do you think of the course they chose?

3. Can this problem be worked out in the "field"? Or is it an over-all company problem that cannot be solved by staff representatives?

4. What objectives should these men set for themselves in their field work?

Problem II

The finishing department in a large paper-manufacturing plant has been the source of many grievances. The personnel director of the plant has evidence that the superintendent of the department is in part at fault. The superintendent, a member of the "old school," assigns heavy disciplinary penalties for the slightest violation of shop rules. The most recent grievance, which almost resulted in a strike, concerned a two-week layoff he had given to a man for "loafing on the job." Caught smoking in the washroom, the man had insisted it was common practice for workers to leave their machines for brief intervals when setup men were changing rolls. The union won its grievance and the employee received two weeks' back pay for the "unjustified" layoff.

This was just one of a series of such instances. To date, the finishing department has had two wildcat strikes and several slowdowns.

It is common knowledge in the company that the personnel director has had several discussions with this superintendent about his handling of disciplinary problems and his dealings with the unions.

The plant manager is primarily concerned about maintaining output levels. Competition is severe and stoppages impair the company's ability to fill orders. For this reason the plant manager has decided to transfer the superintendent of the finishing department to a considerably less important job. In doing this, he points out to the superintendent that the transfer is a direct result of his failure to follow good personnel practices, and that he has had ample opportunity to "mend his ways" with the help of the personnel director.

Word quickly spreads through the organization that the "word of the personnel director is law" and that supervisors violate his "suggestions" at the risk of transfer or discharge.

1. How can the personnel director, under these circumstances, retain his staff status and avoid "undermining" the authority of line supervisors?

Problem III

A Case for Role-playing:
Dealing with a Supervisor Accused of Discrimination

Role for Personnel Director   You are convinced that the supervisor of the receiving and marking room is discriminating among his employees. There is now a union grievance on your desk charging that he has failed to equalize overtime in the department as required by the union contract. Two girls were passed over for Friday night work that involved an extra four hours (or pay for six hours), which amounts to about $10 lost wages for each girl, Miss Smith and Miss Jenkins.

The supervisor claims that he asked the girls on Friday whether or not they would like to work and they said they wanted to get an early start for a weekend trip. The union claims that the supervisor purposely waited until late Friday before announcing the opportunity in order to discriminate against these particular girls. In the past, the supervisor has indicated that he was dissatisfied with their work and attitudes.

In "playing" the role of personnel director, have clearly in mind the objectives you want to accomplish through your discussion with the supervisor.

Role for the Supervisor   You have been pressed to cut costs. Your department is a sort of "graveyard" to which women who have failed elsewhere are transferred. You don't like to admit this, however, because it lowers your prestige. In fact, you yourself may have been put in this department for the same reason! Where possible, you try to give the girls who do accomplish something a little extra break, feeling that it is the only way to encourage them, since all jobs pay the same. The work is unpleasant, though relatively easy and not fatiguing. The two worst shirkers are Miss Smith and Miss Jenkins. They are always baiting you and you are pretty sure they are telling other people in the department false things about you behind your back.

You did wait until late in the day hoping that they would refuse. You don't see how you can face them if they win the grievance and get back pay. You feel that would destroy any chance of improving the morale and efficiency of your department.

Role play the personnel director's interview with the supervisor.

1. Role play the personnel director's interview with the supervisor.

2. Assuming that the personnel director is unsuccessful in his interview with the supervisor, what should be his next move?

Problem IV

You work in the university president's office for the personnel director, who is a subordinate of the president. Your boss has given you the following assignment: Personnel records disclose that Dean Ella Cather's office in the Home Economics School has the highest turnover of clerical employees, the highest clerical costs per student and per teacher, and the greatest number of requests for transfer. This is the first real problem that has been disclosed by the new record-keeping system devised by the personnel office, and the personnel director has convinced the president that attention must be given to Dean Cather's office. You have been selected by the president to work as an administrative assistant to the Dean, although you will continue to have a functional relationship with personnel.

After one interview with your new superior, the Dean, you learn these facts: The Dean is very unhappy about this appointment; she accepted the president's idea with great reluctance. She is aware of her performance but does not believe that the records disclose anything very valuable. Her school has just had a streak of bad luck in acquiring a number of clerical employees who lack aptitude and interest in this type of work. Were it not university policy to avoid discharges, and were it not so difficult to hire replacements in the present "tight" labor market, the Dean believes she would have no problems.

1. How would you handle this assignment?
2. What would you do about the Dean's skepticism concerning the validity of the new controls being used in the president's office—i.e., the personnel records?
3. Try "role-playing" your next meeting with Dean Cather.
4. If you are unsuccessful, what would you do next?

MANPOWER

AND EMPLOYEE DEVELOPMENT

We are now ready to consider the more traditional areas of personnel management. Since each supervisor faces almost identical problems in developing and maintaining effective employee relationships, and since the actions of one supervisor have an impact on all others within the same organization, progressive companies try to establish and publicize systematic policies for the treatment of personnel questions. These, in turn, regulate personnel decisions.

Few organizations can take for granted that there will always be enough workers available to fill all the jobs that must be manned. Consequently, one of the most pressing responsibilities of management is to attract to the firm and develop within the organization enough people to handle present positions and to move into vacancies created by changes in the company's business, retirement rate, and other factors.

A stream of qualified personnel must be kept flowing into the organization and through the various promotional, training, and transfer channels designed to allocate scarce human resources. This is a continuing responsibility, for no organization is static: employees are always leaving; and shortages are always developing at certain points, surpluses at others. In this section we shall examine alternative methods for developing this "stream of manpower" and various criteria for judging the effectiveness of these methods.

The sequence of chapters in this section reflects the movement of employers through the organization: Chapter 19, "Recruitment and Selection Policies," discusses ways of bringing new personnel into the organization; Chapter 20,

"Promotion, Transfer, and Seniority Policy for Non-managerial Employees," takes the newly hired employees along the pathways by which they are assigned to appropriate jobs and rewarded for performance and service. "Technical Training," Chapter 21, concentrates on the psychology of learning as applied to the development of specific job skills, again at the non-managerial level. The next three chapters are concerned with the assessment and development of managerial talents: "Management Development," Chapter 22; "Performance Evaluation," Chapter 23; and "Management Training," Chapter 24.

In no one of these areas are there any pat formulas or fixed principles. However, there are methods of analysis that enable the manager to develop solutions consistent with his needs at a particular time, in a particular place. Thus in the chapters to follow in this section and in the next as well, we shall be emphasizing the questions that management must ask itself when seeking to develop policies and procedures. Personnel problems are never solved easily or permanently. Company-wide methods may minimize the human-relations problems of each supervisor, but each method has its limitations and requires constant adjustment.

Our objective is to ask the "right questions"—to identify the potential sources of difficulty in each situation, to know what data are necessary, and what method of analysis, to provide a workable (but, to be realistic, not a permanent) solution. Knowledge about the components of an organization—its people, jobs, unions, and structure—as well as an understanding of the skills of supervision, are necessary ingredients in gaining acceptance of these manpower policies.

In addition, these policies provide a fertile ground for employee misunderstanding. Tenure and promotion arrangements are matters of vital concern to all, for they have a direct effect on each employee's sense of security and progress. Unless management uses effective means of communication, bolstered by clearly defined, widely available, written statements of policy, rumors and half-truths will circulate freely throughout the organization. And in the murky atmosphere of rumor, both productivity and morale languish.

Logically, the first step in the development of a firm's personnel policy is to acquire the personnel to operate the organization. Not only is this first in theory, it is one of the most critical steps in the establishment and growth of a business. The supply of qualified people limits the success of a business just as sharply as the supply of money, materials, or markets.[1]

On closer examination, this area of policy emerges as an interrelated, ordered series of decisions:

1. Whom should we look for: what type of personnel and in what numbers?
2. Where should we look? Inside or outside the firm? Or both?
3. What methods should we use to encourage the "right" people to come to us seeking employment?
4. What methods should we use to decide what applicants to choose for what positions?

---

[1] See Peter Drucker, "Integration of People and Planning," *Harvard Business Review*, Vol. 33, No. 6 (November-December 1955), p. 36.

19

Recruitment and Selection Policies

Whom Should We Look For?

This is not a simple question to answer. It is difficult to project man-power needs into the future, and a firm's decisions must take into account the realities of the labor market. There is little point trying to attract stenographers at $45 a week if the going rate is $90.

Farsighted companies make careful analyses of their manpower needs. They consider their existing work force, their promotional ladders, and the future vacancies that will be created by predicted turnover (via quits, discharges, deaths, and retirement) and growth. The results of this analysis should provide time tables of acquisition needs, specifying:

1. The skills required in new employees.
2. The potential (for personal development) required in new employees.
3. The jobs to which new employees will probably be assigned.

Decisions also must be made on whether to hire all new employees at the bottom and then train them for promotion—or whether to hire people directly from outside the organization for all levels and skills. The objective is to establish a kind of dynamic equilibrium that will enable the organization to avoid being stampeded into promoting people in times of labor shortage, but at the same time will enable it to avoid building up glutted areas with inadequate opportunities for advancement or even for tenure. The ideal is a work force perfectly balanced in terms of age, seniority, and promotion potential.

There are two problems that must be given particular consideration in determining the company's manpower policy: turnover, and the present composition of the work force.

DEFINING THE RECRUITMENT PROBLEM

Turnover   The recruitment problem differs enormously from one organization to another. A department store with a relatively large percentage of young, unmarried girls on its payroll may find that it has to hire two or even three times the total number of its employees each year. Not that everyone who is employed at the beginning of the year will have left before the end. Rather, some newly hired personnel will leave almost immediately, thus obliging management to hire several people to fill a single job for the year. On the other hand, in a large utility with a high percentage of male employees with at least fifteen years of seniority, the recruitment problem is almost nonexistent.

Present composition of the work force   Historical factors also enter into management's approach to recruitment. Here are some typical problems:

During the war, when labor was in very short supply, Company A hired a great many people with very limited potential for advancement. As a result, the bottom rungs of the company's promotional ladders are now filled with incumbents who are unlikely to advance. Consequently, the company must plan to recruit an unusually great number of people for the higher levels (both in terms of pay and responsibility).

Company B enjoyed a period of rapid growth twenty-five years ago, and then fell into a period of decline. As a consequence, a high proportion of its employees have very long service and are relatively old. A radically changed technology is now eliminating the jobs for which these employees are suited, yet they lack the flexibility to adjust to the new jobs that are being created. How can the company bring in new employees with needed skills without penalizing the older group?

Where Should We Look?

Every firm has an *internal* supply of manpower which is a function of its promotion, transfer, and training activities. (See Chapters 20, 21, and 22.) The external labor market, however, is the major source of manpower for most organizations.

LABOR-MARKET CONCEPTS

Economists study the labor market just as closely as they study the finished-goods market and the capital market. In recent years empirical studies have revealed that neither employers nor employees behave like the buyers and sellers in other types of economic market. There are many rewarding discussions of this subject; here we can simply summarize some of the findings that are relevant to recruitment policies.[2]

What is a labor market? A labor market consists of *geographic* areas in which the forces of supply (people looking for work) and demand (employers looking for people to hire) interact and thus affect the price of labor (wages and salaries). The actual boundaries of the market depend on the type and number of job candidates being sought. The labor market for certain unusual skills may be half or all of the United States. Top-quality hotel chefs may move from resorts in Maine to Florida when appropriate openings

---

[2] Students interested in further exploration of labor-market problems as they affect recruitment may consult the following: Lloyd G. Reynolds, *The Structure of Labor Markets* (New York: Harpers, 1951); Charles Myers and George Shultz, *The Dynamics of a Labor Market* (Englewood Cliffs, N.J., Prentice-Hall, 1951); Richard A. Lester, *Hiring Practices and Labor Competition* (Princeton, N.J.: Princeton University, Industrial Relations Section, 1954); Gladys Palmer, *Labor Mobility in Six Cities* (New York: Social Science Research Council, 1954); and Herbert S. Parnes, *Research on Labor Mobility: An Appraisal of Research Findings in the United States*, Bulletin 65 (New York: Social Science Research Council, 1954).

occur. At the other extreme, female clerical personnel may be unwilling to take jobs that are not within a few miles of their home.

Why this interest in the boundaries of the labor market? Certainly in locating new units, in deciding whether to expand or contract existing facilities, or in launching any plan that will call for the recruitment of new employees, a firm must consider the available supply of qualified personnel. Many times the personnel director will draw a line around the work location and attempt to estimate the number of potential applicants who live within that area. The line will rarely describe a perfect circle, since few employees commute to work "as the crow flies." In fact, it may be more appropriate to define the area on the basis of transportation lines and commuting time. Over the years the time spent in commuting has tended to remain constant—that is, as transportation speeds have increased, people tend to live farther away from their work.[3] Thus it is possible to rough out the area of potential labor supply in terms of mileage. Many companies find that about half their employees come from the community in which the company is located and the other half from outside the community. Rarely do more than 10 or 20 per cent of the employees commute more than 30 miles.[4] At times, of course, a company planning to open a new operation that will employ a relatively large number of people may find that people will be willing to commute very long distances and eventually shift their residences to take advantage of opportunities vastly superior to any nearer home.

Estimating potential applicants   Once the labor market has been identified, the next step is to assemble estimates on the number of potential applicants in the area. In larger cities, those presently unemployed but seeking work are likely to be registered with state unemployment insurance offices. Chambers of Commerce, utilities, city and state departments of commerce and development, and larger firms in the area all accumulate statistics on both the numbers and types of workers within the geographic areas they serve.

Recent estimates of future changes in the labor force suggest that recruiters will have to give greater attention to sources of labor that have ordinarily been neglected. As the table on page 431 shows, the most significant increases in available manpower will be among the younger and older workers, both male and female.

Traditionally, industry has been loath to employ older workers, on the assumption that they are less energetic, more accident- and grievance-prone, and more costly in terms of welfare payments. But evidence indicates that they compensate for some of their liabilities by virtue of their mature judgment, long experience, and steady application. Similarly, women have been discriminated against on many jobs. Yet women are becoming one of

---

[3] See Daniel Bell, *Work and Its Discontents* (Boston: Beacon Press, 1956), p. 4.

[4] See Leonard Adams and Thomas MacKesey, *Commuting Patterns of Industrial Workers* (Ithaca, N.Y.: Cornell University, Housing Research Center, 1955).

the most important sources of labor, since their role as wives and mothers no longer inhibits participation in the labor market:

> At the turn of the century, half of the women never worked outside the home and the average work life for all women was about eleven years. Today almost all women work at some time during their lives, and on the average a young girl can look forward to working at least twenty-five years.[5]

In fact, many companies find it useful to direct their recruiting efforts toward groups that are not commonly regarded as comprising the work force in a given area. Labor economists refer to a "secondary labor force" consisting of people not now employed or actively seeking employment. Housewives, semi-retired workers, and very young people will respond to attractive, close-at-hand jobs when they are brought to their attention.[6]

Labor Force (in Millions) by Age and Sex *

	Actual 1955	Estimated 1965	Estimated 1975	Net Change 1955-65	Net Change 1965-75
TOTAL	68.9	79.4	92.6	10.5	13.2
Male					
14-24 years	8.2	10.9	13.8	2.7	2.9
25-44 years	22.3	22.2	25.8	—.1	3.6
45 years & over	17.5	19.7	21.4	2.2	1.6
Total	48.0	52.9	60.9	4.8	8.1
Female					
14-24 years	4.4	5.9	7.4	1.5	1.5
25-34 years	4.3	4.3	6.0	0	1.7
35 years & over	12.1	16.3	18.3	4.2	2.0
Total	20.9	26.5	31.7	5.7	5.2

* *Labor's Economic Review,* Vol. 13, No. 10 (October 1958), p. 59.
Source: Bureau of the Census and Bureau of Labor Statistics.

In considering available manpower, it would be unrealistic to neglect implicit and even explicit discriminatory barriers based on race, religion, or nationality. A company may deprive itself of many good candidates by refusing to hire workers on these grounds, or by considering members of minority groups for only the most menial jobs. True, a number of states have Fair Employment Practices laws prohibiting discrimination in hiring

---

[5] Eli Ginzberg, "The Changing Pattern of Women's Work: Some Psychological Correlates," *The American Journal of Orthopsychiatry,* Vol. XXVIII, No. 2 (April 1958), p. 314. See also his *Womanpower* (New York: National Manpower Council, Columbia University Press, 1957).

[6] See Richard C. Wilcox, "The Secondary Labor Force and the Measurement of Unemployment," in National Bureau of Economic Research, *The Measurement and Behavior of Unemployment* (Princeton, N.J.: Princeton University Press, 1957), pp. 167-210.

procedures, and there have been efforts at federal legislation and control as well. But arbitrary and highly subjective criteria continue to enter into employment practices. Companies that reject discrimination and prejudice open up a potentially rich source of new recruits.

Most companies are not primarily interested in the gross number of workers available in the labor force. They want to know instead: (1) What skills are available? (2) How many workers with these skills are likely to apply at the rate we offer? (3) What are the attitudes toward the company of potential job-seekers in the community?

What skills are available?   Few companies hire "labor"; rather, they hire specific kinds of worker. Many large offices that move out of cities to sub-urban areas find that although there is a readily available labor supply, there may be a severe shortage of young girls with clerical skills. Companies that want to hire large numbers of highly skilled tool and die makers must locate in areas where these tradesmen have established homes.[7] Where fully trained workers are required, a new firm may have no choice but to locate near the plants of competitors. Auto stylists are most likely to be found in Detroit, and photographic engineers in Rochester, New York.

How many applicants are likely to apply?   Potential employees find some organizations far more attractive than others. Company A is engaged in an expanding, profitable industry and can afford to pay high wages. It guar-antees steady employment, high wages, rapid promotions, clean work, and attractive fringe benefits. This company may never really have to recruit, for a steady stream of prospective employees will come seeking work. When an opening does occur, the personnel department need only look through its files of applications and select the most likely candidates. Company B is in a highly competitive industry in which profit levels and wages are rela-tively low. The company has a reputation for unsteady work, and many of the jobs it offers involve dirty, dangerous work. This company has a difficult time recruiting employees, particularly in times of relatively full employment.

There is another variable affecting recruitment: economic conditions in the labor market itself. A new plant located in a depressed labor market may be swamped by unemployed workers. On the other hand, a firm trying to establish itself or to expand in an area where few qualified workers are out of work has quite a different recruiting problem.

Companies that require relatively large numbers of a particular type of employee often have a severe recruitment problem. If a firm needs only a single bookkeeper, it usually has little trouble finding one—even though it pays less than competitors and has a poor reputation in the community. But

---

[7] Recent research suggests that skilled workers are even less mobile than non-skilled workers; therefore, a company could not expect an influx to satisfy unfilled demands. Palmer, *op. cit.*

in an insurance company, for example, which must hire hundreds of stenographers every year, relative wages and working conditions are critical.

Community attitudes   Communities differ in their appeal to new personnel, and many companies believe that communities also differ in their attitudes toward industry, work, and management—in what is sometimes called the prevailing "business climate." Some companies, for example, seek to avoid areas with a history of labor-management conflict.

Ethnic problems in the community may also spill over into the company. A union official in the textile industry once commented off the record that one of his union's problems was the heritage of bad feelings between "New England Yankee" Protestants, who dominated management, and French-Canadian Catholics, who made up most of the work force in the textile mills. In our own studies of unions we have noted friction between workers with different religious and nationality backgrounds.

The firm must also remember that unattractive communities will repel applications; locations with a good climate, attractive recreational facilities, plentiful housing, fine schools, and decent government will attract applicants from a wide radius. Increasingly, professional and managerial employees are demanding good living conditions as a job prerequisite.

What Recruitment Methods Should We Use?

Once we have decided what workers we want and where we expect to get them, the next question is this: How can we induce qualified applicants to apply for employment? To answer this question, we must look at how workers seek employment.

THE SEARCH FOR WORK

The new worker taking his first job   The new, inexperienced worker has only a sketchy idea of the labor market and of his own capacities. Studies indicate that he is likely to take several jobs during his first five or six years of employment (the "trial period," as it is called) in his search for the kind of job that is compatible with his expectations and personality. His final settling down is likely to be as much a result of growing family responsibilities as of his finding genuine job satisfaction. The job held by his father, the ambitions encouraged within his family, and his level of education all exert a major influence over what jobs he regards as acceptable.[8]

The already employed, but dissatisfied employee   Firms that require special skills often recruit workers who already are employed but who are

---

[8] For a careful review of the influences on occupational choice, see Delbert Miller and William Form, *Industrial Sociology* (New York; Harpers, 1951), pp. 636-762.

looking for a "better job." Every job has its disadvantages; we all rebel to some extent against authority; and we are convinced that our talents are going unrecognized and uncompensated. Consequently, we might expect that most employees would constantly be on the look-out for a better job. The fact is, however, that most employees do not actively seek other jobs. Recent studies indicate that only a small percentage of employed workers actively compare their present job with any actual or potential alternatives.[9]

Family and friendship ties deter the worker from searching for opportunities outside his immediate neighborhood, and seniority and fringe benefits that are tied to length of service also reduce the motivation to look elsewhere. Furthermore, the early job-hunting experiences of a worker and his friends may have convinced him that good jobs are scarce, and that whatever its disadvantages a job in hand is worth innumerable possibilities in the bush. It is a striking observation that even those new employees who quit voluntarily do not usually have a specific alternative in mind.

There is one exception to this generalization, however. During periods of what has come to be called "over full employment," when companies actively compete for labor and when jobs are remarkably easy to get, employees may begin to consider alternatives. Stories spread about how well Jim Jones did when he walked across the street to an employment office or answered an advertisement, and gradually other employees who are not over-committed to pension, insurance, or tenure guarantees begin to follow the same route.

> As a general rule, then, one can say that dissatisfaction with the present job does not make the worker search actively for a new job. It does make him more receptive to tips, rumors and actual job offers which come to him. If none of these look promising enough and if his present job continues to be unsatisfactory, he will eventually (during a period of high employment) quit his job. *Active search for work usually does not begin until after he is unemployed.*[10]

A small percentage of the labor force consists of perpetual malcontents, who, for one psychological reason or another, are never satisfied with their work and cannot tolerate the normal restrictions imposed by life in an organization. They move endlessly from one job to another. In a sense, these workers fit the economist's model: they do indeed try to maximize the net advantages they receive in return for their labor, and they actively compare the benefits offered by various employers.

Another group of potential dissidents is made up of new employees. Longer-service employees have usually adjusted to their job and typically expect to stay with it for some time to come; the newly hired employee has made no such adjustment. He is still trying to accommodate himself to his

---

[9] Reynolds, *op. cit.*
[10] Lloyd Reynolds and Joseph Shister, *Job Horizons* (New York: Harpers, 1949), p. 37. (Emphasis ours.)

fellow workers, to supervision, to the pace and work requirements of a specific job, and to the organizational "climate" of a particular company. Voluntary quits are highest by far during the first year of employment on a new job. (It is for this reason, it might be added, that turnover is particularly costly. In order to replace one long-service employee who quits, the company may have to hire two or three or even four new employees.)

The practice of hiring employees from other companies raises the question of "raiding." The connotations of the term itself suggest that many employers consider this practice unethical. Some companies scrupulously refrain from recruiting employees from other firms in their community or industry. They may even require clearance from a potential recruit's present employer before they will accept his application. In actuality, however, so-called "no-raiding agreements" are honored more in theory than in practice. In order to avoid the stigma of "raiding," employers sometimes use intermediaries, such as consulting firms, to make contacts for them.

The unemployed worker   Ordinarily, the unemployed worker is a man who has been laid off because of slack times, or because of an infraction of company rules, or because of the permanent closing of his employer's business. If he has been laid off because of slack times, a company may hesitate to hire him for fear that he will return to his original employer as soon as possible in order to enjoy the seniority benefits he has accumulated there.[11] Of course, firms are suspicious of those who have been discharged from another job.

The unemployed worker is no more systematic in his search for a job than the potential recruit who is currently employed and is under less economic pressure. As one study concluded:

> Where the worker does not hear of a job through friends within a reasonable time [when seeking employment] he frequently resorts to direct application at a plant which is conspicuous because of its size, closeness to his home, or some other reason. In most cases, however, he knows little about conditions in the plant before applying for work.[12]

METHODS OF RECRUITMENT

Clearly, then, the mere availability of jobs will not bring applicants into the employment office. True, a firm with an outstanding reputation in the community (and size contributes to ready visibility) may have a steady stream of applicants. But most companies must engage in active recruitment. What techniques of recruitment are most useful?

---

[11] Reynolds found that 88 per cent of his sample of laid-off workers in New Haven, Connecticut, planned to return to their previous employer. (Reynolds, *op. cit.*, p. 88.) Most seniority policies limit recall privileges to one or two years.

[12] Reynolds and Shister, *op. cit.*, p. 106.

Word of mouth Tips from satisfied friends and relatives are among the best sources of recruitment that a firm can have. Many companies conduct regular programs to encourage their employees to speak to friends about job openings in the company; some even give bonuses to employees who introduce applicants who are actually accepted for employment.

Word-of-mouth recruiting has a real disadvantage, however, for it may lead to an undue emphasis on nepotism, particularly in management positions. Such an emphasis may arouse resentment in the present staff and may impair morale and long-run efficiency.

Employment agencies State employment agencies are located in nearly every major city. In the past, many employers turned to these agencies only as a last resort, or as a source of unskilled labor; now, however, public employment agencies are winning a reputation for carefully screening applicants for the needs of a particular job in a particular company, including a wide range of manual, technical, and professional occupations. They charge neither the employer nor the prospective employee for their services, for they have a public responsibility to serve both.

Private employment agencies tend to specialize in specific occupations and skills—clerical, manual, craft, or technical, for example. Sometimes the employer pays the fee, sometimes the employee; in either case, the fee may be quite substantial. Recently, management consulting firms have entered the business of finding specialized high-level talent for their clients.

Advertisements Advertisements in daily newspapers, over local radio stations, in trade journals, and in the magazines of professional associations usually attract applicants in great numbers but of highly variable quality. A more homogeneous group will respond to an advertisement in the *Journal of the American Chemical Society*, for example, than to one in the community's local newspaper.

Although newspaper advertisements have no built-in screening mechanism, they do serve a useful purpose. When a company opens a new plant, for example, and requires a large work force, advertisements in the local papers provide an excellent means of announcing the fact that openings are available.

School recruiting Increasingly, companies are sending representatives to interview seniors in high schools and colleges. This technique enables the company to paint an attractive picture of its employment opportunities and to do advanced screening of candidates. The better candidates are then invited to visit the company for further consideration. In addition, good contacts with school placement officials help in channeling suitable candidates to the company.

The union as recruiter   In certain occupations the worker feels a stronger attachment to the industry as a whole than he does to an individual firm. This is particularly true in the building trades, in longshoring, and in the maritime industry (and one might include college teaching). In these occupations, the union is the traditional clearing-house for jobs, and both employer and employee have come to accept the union hiring hall as a combination employment agency and recruiting office. To a lesser extent the union provides this service (and frequently demands its use by the employer) in the printing and entertainment industries, restaurants and hotels (when union-organized), and sometimes in men's and women's clothing manufacturing.

Notice that these are all industries in which there is a certain instability of employment—in fact, in some there is even what might be called casual employment. Clearly it is to management's advantage to be able to tap a ready supply of skilled, experienced workers merely by lifting the phone and calling the union. This saves management the expense of recruiting and screening, and also means that management will be less hesitant to lay off a skilled worker. The union's stock-in-trade becomes its ability to maintain a full complement of readily placeable skilled tradesmen.

Selection Methods

Attracting qualified job applicants is only the first step in the process of acquiring new employees. Next, the firm must develop techniques for selecting who, among these applicants, will be accepted for employment. This is a very important decision, since most employees do not leave their employer voluntarily after the completion of their "trial period." Hiring and training costs may be substantial, and no firm wants to lay out more money than it has to. Further, union standards and employee and community expectations serve to limit management's ability to discharge employees. Therefore, it is reasonable to expect that once hired, a given employee is likely to remain with the company for a long time.

It should be noted, however, that most organizations use a probationary period as a check on their selection system. The newly hired worker does not become a regular employee until he has successfully completed a one- to three-month or even a one-year trial.

ALTERNATIVE SELECTION POLICIES

Organizations tend to develop hiring methods that are consistent with their over-all philosophy of selection. These methods differ significantly from company to company.

Screening out applicants who don't fit The primary objective of the selection procedure may be to screen out applicants who "obviously" don't qualify for the type of job typically available in the company. Such procedures endeavor to fit people to the organization as a whole rather than to specific jobs.

For some companies, "don't qualify" means that the applicant is in general unsuited to the company. These criteria are usually discriminatory, and are based on the questionable assumption that there is a "right type" for the firm—that is, "right" in terms of physical appearance, background, degree of "drive," and similar characteristics. One researcher, for example, has found that banks try to maintain a very homogeneous group of employees, all of whom place security above advancement, lack aggressiveness, and prefer a job in which they are left alone.[13] Brokerage houses often favor applicants with an "ivy league" college background. Some companies seek handsome, white Protestants to fill most of their jobs.

There is evidence that even when the company sets up no formal restrictions, an informal self-selection process will operate. Certain types of people gravitate to and find working in certain kinds of organization compatible with their own personalities. This pattern has been observed among operators in clothing manufacturing plants,[14] retail store personnel,[15] and government employees. Thus there may be some justification for attempting to avoid mismatching by weeding out those who will be uncomfortable in their new work environment. On the whole, however, these "right-type" criteria usually represent irrational discrimination.

There are other, more concrete, general selection criteria that may appropriately be utilized as screening variables. Where most jobs in the firm require technical ability, some minimal education requirement may be imposed on all entrants—e.g., completion of high school or college. (Of course, there is the real possibility that a good candidate may have achieved equal proficiency through less orthodox channels.)

Fitting jobs to people Alternatively, management can go in the opposite direction and seek to adjust the jobs themselves to the people who are available to fill them. For example, during World War II, many male jobs were, with slight modifications, made suitable for women. Great progress has been made in recent years in modifying or redesigning jobs for those who are blind, infirm, or incapacitated. Experiments in adjusting working hours to permit housewives to be employed for split shifts have proved successful. Skilled craftsmen's jobs have been broken into components that could be learned by relatively untrained novices.

---

[13] Chris Argyris, *Personality and Organization* (New York: Harpers, 1959), p. 85.

[14] Margaret Chandler, *Labor Management Relations in Illinois City*, Case Study 3, Garment Manufacture (Champaign, Ill.: Institute of Labor and Industrial Relations, 1953).

[15] Eliot D. Chapple, "Contributions of Applied Anthropology to Institutional Psychiatry," *Human Organization*, Vol. 13, No. 2, p. 14.

Psychologists in particular have been active in a field that has come to be called "human engineering." While industrial engineering has stressed fitting people to satisfy the time and motion requirements of machinery and production schedules, these psychologists have sought principles and methods to make equipment design better adapted to typical human characteristics.[16]

Fitting people to jobs Perhaps more common is the selection program designed to fit applicants to particular jobs—to match jobs and people. This selection philosophy assumes that the requirements of a given job, and the characteristics of a given applicant, are sufficiently unique and explicit to make possible an intelligent match between them. Most of the rest of this chapter will be devoted to discussing the problems involved in implementing this philosophy.

ALTERNATIVE SELECTION TECHNIQUES

The first concrete step in carrying out any selection program is to develop adequate job descriptions for the positions that are to be filled.

Obtaining job descriptions Job or occupational titles in themselves often give a misleading impression of the actual content of a job. A "milk deliveryman," in addition to being able to drive a truck, must also handle customer accounts and sell the company's products. An engineer may have to spend most of his time *selling* department heads on the importance of using standard parts. Many so-called "clerk" jobs embrace a range of duties that are unrelated to the simple tabulating or recording activities one might associate with the job title. Company records may fail to specify the real duties that supervision expects of a given employee in a specific job. Consequently, those who are responsible for selecting applicants need to make a careful investigation if they are to discover the true nature of each job.

Once we have a complete description of the duties that must be performed, we can construct a personnel requirement list for each job. This would include the type of education and/or experience an applicant should have; what skills he must possess; what physical attributes he needs (e.g., stamina, height, and so forth); and what personality requirements are desirable. The list should also specify the types of relationship he will be expected to undertake and maintain with other people.

Careful descriptions produce certain valuable by-products. First, they give the applicant an accurate picture of the job and reduce the possibility that he will be unpleasantly surprised by the duties expected of him after he has started to work. Second, job descriptions are useful in setting wages and

---

16 See Ernest J. McCormack, *Human Engineering* (New York: McGraw-Hill, 1957), and Organization for European Economic Cooperation, *Fitting the Job to the Worker,* EPA Project No. 335 (Washington, D.C.: OEEC, 1958).

salaries through job evaluation, and as a check list against which to measure job performance. (See Chapter 25.)

When the company knows what it is looking for in a potential employee, it is ready to explore alternative methods of assessing the characteristics of candidates. Of the many techniques used, the following are some of the best known:

Application forms   The *application form* is a traditional, widely accepted device for recording information on such biographical items as: age; marital status and number of dependents; previous education (subjects and grades) and training; previous work experience, including nature of duties, salary, length of time on the job, and reasons for leaving; and such personal items as association memberships, police records, if any, outstanding debts, and home ownership.[17] It also tests the candidate's ability to write, to organize his thoughts, and to present facts clearly and succinctly. The information recorded on the application blank provides interviewers with leads and points of departure for a formal job interview, and it provides the company with data for its permanent employee record. The application indicates, further, whether the applicant has consistently progressed to better jobs, and whether his education and occupational experience have been logically patterned.

Efforts have been made to convert the application blank into a more formal test, with the various questions weighted and scored according to their predictive value.[18] A statistical analysis is made of the relationship of various items on the application blank to the actual job success of candidates who have previously filled out these blanks.

Interviews   The *interview*, unlike the application blank, is a selection technique that enables the person responsible for hiring to view the total individual and to appraise the person and his behavior directly. The objective of the interview is to measure the applicant against the specific requirements of the job and to decide whether there will be a good "fit." It also permits the applicant to ask questions about the organization and the job.

The interview is a widely used selection technique. Does this mean that there are also widely accepted standards of what constitutes good and bad performance on the part of the interviewee? Not at all. Moreover, the practices and the competency of those who conduct interviews differ widely. Since interviewing is both expensive and time-consuming, it would be well

---

[17] The "Fair Employment Practice" laws adopted by many states make it illegal to ask questions about an applicant's religious affiliation, wife's maiden name, parents' names, "race," and similar points, on the grounds that such questions constitute either direct or indirect attempts to ascertain race, religion, or nationality, and provide a basis for discrimination.

[18] See Edwin E. Ghiselli and Clarence Brown, *Personnel and Industrial Psychology* (New York: McGraw-Hill, 1955), pp. 180-184.

for most organizations to take stock of how much benefit they are deriving from the practice.

Ideally, the interview provides a valid sample of the applicant's behavior. Even though the applicant is "on guard," careful to present the best picture possible, the skilled interviewer can draw him out far more successfully than can an application blank. Furthermore, the interviewer can uncover clues to the applicant's motivation, to his attitudes toward himself and to the kinds of situation he finds troublesome and satisfying. Using the information recorded on the application blank, the interviewer can guide the applicant into explaining why certain jobs appeal to him and others do not, and into speaking freely about the influence of family and educational experiences. By getting the applicant to talk about himself, the interviewer can get some inkling of the candidate's level of aspiration (what is he "shooting for" in the long run as well as what types of job would be acceptable in the short run), his ability to deal with interpersonal situations, and his readiness to take the initiative in conversation and in dealing with strangers.

The interview is a flexible tool; it can be used for many different types of job and with many different kinds of personality. It can emphasize the applicant's formal qualifications or seek to plumb the depths of his personality. Interviews differ in their amount of internal structuring. Many interviewers make use of a fixed pattern of specific questions; others use a more non-directive approach relying on broad, general questions which let the interviewee introduce topics.[19] For example, the interviewer may start by asking the applicant why he is applying for a job in this company, or what he liked and disliked about his previous jobs.

Nevertheless, even at its best, the interview is not a precise technique, and skillful interviewing is difficult to conduct. Candidates react very differently depending on who is interviewing them and how the interview is handled. Since there are no fixed criteria for success or failure, the prejudiced interviewer can easily evaluate the interviewee's performance in accordance with his own stereotypes. (If the applicant is interviewed by several people, it may be possible to cross-check observations.) Unfortunately, there are still people who believe that they can assess other people on the basis of the type of necktie they select, their tone of voice, or whether they "look you straight in the eye."

Physical examinations   Many jobs require unusual stamina, strength, or tolerance of unpleasant working conditions. Physical examinations reveal whether or not a candidate possesses these qualities. Furthermore, the com-

---

[19] The military and various private organizations have experimented with efforts to standardize the interviewing procedure by means of a fixed format and the use of a panel of interviewers. The applicant is evaluated, not only in terms of the content of his answers, but also in terms of his reactions to the stress introduced by the situation.

See also Arnold Judson, "New Approach to Executive Selection," *Harvard Business Review*, Vol. 32 (March-April 1954), pp. 127-136.

pany's responsibility (both legal and ethical) for employee health and safety encourages widespread use of physical check-ups. Thorough physical examinations also provide valuable records in the event of accidents.

Formal Tests

To many people, tests are synonymous with selection methods, although many companies do not employ formal testing procedures in their selection programs. Tests have been developed in an effort to find more objective means of measuring the qualifications of job applicants, as well as for use with employees who are candidates for transfer or promotion. One of their major advantages is that they may uncover qualifications and talent that would not be detected by interviews or by listings of education and job experience. Tests seek to eliminate the possibility that interviewer or supervisory prejudice, instead of potential ability, will govern selection decisions. Because of their importance, we shall look closely at their design and their limitations, as well as at some of the policy problems involved in applying them to personnel selection and placement.

MAJOR TYPES

First we shall examine some of the more commonly used types of tests and the objectives they set for themselves. With this as background we shall consider the limitations of formal testing, stressing the extreme care that must be used in evaluating results.

Performance tests   The simplest and perhaps most obvious type of testing procedure is the work-sample or performance test in which the applicant is asked to demonstrate his ability to do the job. For example, prospective typists are asked to type several pages and their speed and accuracy are then calculated. Or a prospective machinist is asked to interpret a blueprint and to make certain adjustments on the equipment he will be expected to operate.

But how about jobs like sales representative or control room attendant? Here the characteristics that make for success are less obvious, the requisite skills not so easy to test.

Intelligence tests   On the assumption that quick-learning, alert, bright people can learn almost any job more quickly and successfully than those who are less well endowed, many companies use general intelligence tests. The most accurate and reliable intelligence tests require many hours of careful professional administration, and they are expensive and cumbersome. Therefore most organizations make use of shorter paper-and-pencil tests which give a rough approximation of the I.Q. (Intelligence Quotient) of the applicant.

Psychologists are not unanimous in recommending the use of these abbreviated tests, nor is there general agreement on the concept of "intelligence" itself—that is, on what is being measured by the test.

Aptitude tests In a sense, an intelligence test is a kind of aptitude test—measuring the *potential* ability of a candidate to learn a new job. However, psychologists have developed a large number of much more specialized aptitude tests which seek to predict the likelihood that an applicant can learn a certain type of job effectively. Individuals differ markedly, for example, in their ability to learn work involving precise eye-muscle coordination, such as the work done by the skilled shop craftsman or mechanic. It is difficult for some people to learn to do jobs that involve quantitative computations or that require the ability to visualize solid objects in space. Tests have been developed to assess the degree to which an employee who is not now qualified to do a skilled job can profit from training, given his basic mechanical abilities.

Personality tests Many observers feel that more employees fail on the job because of personality defects than because of lack of aptitude or physical ability. A psychologically well-adjusted employee who is highly motivated to do a good job may be worth more to the company than a man with great potential who is emotionally upset or lazy. At times, personality affects job performance in the most unexpected ways.

> During World War II, when great numbers of trained technicians were in demand, it was assumed that those who had mechanical aptitude would make good airplane mechanics. A careful analysis of this assumption proved otherwise. It turned out that a good shoe clerk in civilian life would become a better mechanic for military purposes than someone who had fixed cars most of his life and learned on a Model-T Ford. The critical trait was not mechanical aptitude but the ability of the trainee to follow instructions. The Army then worked out its instruction manuals so meticulously that the best recruit turned out to be a mildly obsessional person who could read and follow directions. The last thing they wanted was someone with his own ideas on how to fix equipment.[20]

In fact, for management jobs, personality tests may well be the equivalent of work-sample tests, since the most important component of many managerial jobs is the ability to deal effectively with people. In 1954, *Fortune* magazine checked a sample of 63 American corporations and found that 60 per cent of them were using personality tests to assist in selection and placement.[21] There are hundreds of consulting firms who specialize in providing

---

[20] Edward T. Hall, *The Silent Language* (Garden City, N.Y.: Doubleday, 1959), p. 94.

[21] William H. Whyte, Jr., "The Fallacies of Personality Testing," *Fortune* (September 1954), p. 117. Support for such programs is provided by Albert Micherson, who notes that in a survey of 76 companies, 9 out of 10 executives discharged were fired because of personality defects, not because of lack of skill. *Saturday Review of Literature* (November 21, 1953), p. 38.

testing services for these companies, as well as large numbers of full-time staff psychologists who conduct elaborate testing programs in the larger companies.

The most popular personality tests are also of the pencil-and-paper variety; [22] the applicant is given a test booklet in which he writes his answers. A standard key is provided with these tests to enable employment department technicians to process them with ease and with limited training and expense.

Here are some questions typical of those asked on paper-and-pencil personality tests:

> a. Do you ever feel that people are staring at you and laughing at your appearance? Yes _____ No _____
> b. Do you frequently wake up in a "cold sweat"? Yes _____ No _____
> c. Most people get into trouble because they have never been punished and don't know the meaning of discipline. Yes _____ No _____
> d. My mother was the greatest influence in my life. Yes _____ No _____
> e. I find it difficult to work when people are talking. Yes _____ No _____

Most of these paper-and-pencil tests claim to give a well-rounded picture of the applicant's personality, but many observers argue that they are superficial, inaccurate, and misleading. Clinical psychologists favor depth interviews and projective tests that require many hours to administer and that must be interpreted individually by trained experts.[23] Originally, these tests were developed to analyze the abnormal or deviate personality. Only recently have they been used to assess the more "normal" personality.

Situational tests   Situational tests combine aspects of both performance and personality testing. They are designed to observe how job applicants react to stressful but realistic real-life situations.

During World War II,[24] the Office of Strategic Services initiated a testing program that was a radical departure from traditional test forms and interviews. Candidates for special assignments were placed in true-to-life situations and asked to work through actual problems. For example, a candidate might be told to complete a small construction project with the help of an assistant who had been carefully briefed in how *not* to cooperate without actually refusing to obey orders. The key measures in such tests were the

---

[22] Some of the more widely used are: Minnesota Multiphasic Personality Inventory, Washburne Social Adjustment Inventory, Thurstone Temperament Schedule, Adams Personal Audit, Bernreuter Personality Inventory, Guilford and Martin Personal Inventory, Herman Wadsworth Temperament Schedule. (Among the traits these tests try to measure are: level and quality of activity typically maintained; degree of patience, ambition, nervousness, etc.; attitude toward life and associates; decisiveness; self-confidence; purposiveness; introversion; extroversion; compulsiveness; optimism.)

[23] Two well-known projective personality tests are the Rorschach "Ink Blot Test," and the Thematic Apperception Test. (These tests place little emphasis on measuring specific traits. Rather, they try to assess the dynamic relationships within the total personality. They are harder to fake, since there are no obvious "right" answers.)

[24] Strategic Services Assessment Staff, *Assessment of Men* (New York: Rinehart, 1948).

applicant's reaction to the obstreperous assistant, his ability to undergo stress, and his demonstration of ingenuity under pressure. In industry, there has been some effort to apply this technique in "leaderless-group" situations. Several candidates for managerial positions are presented with a problem that requires group collaboration. Observers note which men are able to exercise and gain acceptance of leadership skills.

One other situational test which is a departure from the paper-and-pencil personality tests, but retains their ease of use and scoring, is the Chapple Standardized Interview. Here the applicant is evaluated on the basis of the *pattern* of his behavior. The interviewer is trained to speak for given lengths of time, to interrupt the applicant, and, on occasion, to refrain from making any response whatsoever. The interviewee is observed in terms of the length of time he speaks without break, how quickly and how often he takes the initiative in the conversation, and his tolerance for and response to the stress of ceaseless interruptions or the absence of response. These time distributions are precisely measured by an instrument called an "Interaction Chronograph." The resulting profile is said to predict the applicant's reaction to similar situations that he will encounter on the job.[25]

EVALUATION OF TESTING PROGRAMS

It is not difficult to develop or purchase selection tests that will give numerical data concerning some of the characteristics of job applicants. However, management must assess the relative usefulness of this information, particularly in relation to its cost and in comparison to other selection methods. Numerical results, such as those provided by testing programs, often look deceivingly objective and valid to the casual observer. Let us look at some of the assumptions that lie behind formal tests, and the techniques employed in developing and using them in industry.

UNDERLYING ASSUMPTIONS OF TESTING PROCEDURES

1. Testing procedures assume that there are significant differences in the extent to which individuals possess certain characteristics—such as intelligence, finger dexterity, knowledge of blueprint reading, and motivation.

2. Testing procedures also assume that there is a direct and important relationship between the possession of one or more of these characteristics and the individual's ability to do certain jobs. This relationship should enable the manager to predict the candidate's eventual job performance.

3. Finally, testing procedures assume that the organization can measure selected characteristics practically and evaluate the relationship between test results and job performance.

---

[25] Eliot Chapple, "The Standard Experimental (Stress) Interview as Used in Interaction Chronograph Investigations," *Human Organization*, Vol. 12 (1953), pp. 23-32.

At first glance, all these assumptions seem perfectly reasonable. Actually, however, they often lead an unsuspecting management into trouble. For example, in some instances the degree of individual differences does not justify a testing program. As one psychologist points out, it would be wasteful to try to test differences in color discrimination among female applicants for inspection jobs, because "Color blindness in women is about as rare ... as appearances of Halley's Comet." [26] Similarly, a self-selection process, by which people themselves decide whether or not to apply for a specific job in a particular company, may minimize applicant differences to the point where they are hardly worth the expense of testing.

The fact that some jobs can be handled successfully by more than one type of person throws doubt on the assumption that there is a close relationship between certain employee characteristics and job performance. For example, the older worker, who is slower and less agile, may compensate for his liabilities by displaying greater attention, persistence, and energy.

The validity of the last two assumptions can be evaluated only after we have additional knowledge about how tests are actually developed for use in industry.

TEST DEVELOPMENT

Useful tests cannot be developed in a vacuum; a method must be found to relate performance in the testing situation to some outside criterion. From the point of view of management, that criterion should be job success—the justification for using tests as a selection device.

Validating a test   The best technique for validating a test is to administer a series (battery) of tests of different types to potential employees or candidates for a given position. The results of the tests are *not* used at this point to make hiring or placement decisions. Rather, the scores are filed, and then, after some extensive period of time has elapsed, the job-performance records of those who took the tests are examined. The test scores are then compared with the performance records to determine which, if any, of the tests helped predict who would be successful on the particular job. After this comparison has been made, and assuming that one or more of the test results did have a significant correlation with performance on the job, a new battery is developed using those tests or parts of tests that were shown to be useful predictors.

This appears to be a straightforward and reasonably simple procedure. Unfortunately, it is not. Most companies have neither the facilities nor the patience to undertake this type of program. As a result, they begin giving a test and use the results immediately to make selection decisions. This means

---

[26] Mason Haire, "Use of Tests in Employee Selection," *Harvard Business Review,* Vol. 28, No. 1 (January-February 1950), p. 44.

that the evaluation data are "contaminated," for there is no way of knowing how those who were not hired, because of poor test scores, would have performed.

When the results of the testing program become generally available to supervisors before the test is *validated*, the test scores themselves may influence managerial decisions. Employees with relatively high scores may be given more personal encouragement and opportunities for promotion. Understandably, these high-scoring candidates are evaluated as being "superior" to those who came through with lower scores. Since, at best, supervisory evaluation of personnel performance is a subjective process, test results may introduce a strong biasing factor, and thus make it impossible for the organization to obtain any truly independent evaluation of the usefulness of the test.

Another short cut followed by some companies is to give present employees the test and see how the scores of "good" employees compare with the test scores of "poor" employees. However, this procedure may not give an accurate reflection of the population from which actual selections have to be made. Furthermore, employees who were hired years ago may have faced job and supervisory conditions very different from those that will be faced by employees hired now.

The use of any predictive method assumes that the organization can identify who is successful and who is not, distinguishing "good" from "poor." Actually, however, performance evaluation is one of the most frustrating elements in any personnel program.[27] Most organizations rely on the judgments of supervisors, although these may be quite inaccurate. Fortunately, for some jobs it may be satisfactory to distinguish the employee who is still on the job from those who quit or were fired. Still, the generally low level of reliability of most measures of employee performance seriously limit attempts to assess a testing program.[28]

Companies frequently rely on the reported success of other organizations with a particular test battery. But test adoptions of this sort may be based on fallacious reasoning, for the other companies may have quite different jobs to fill, even though they carry the same job title. A more serious shortcoming is that enthusiastic users of a test may have failed to undertake carefully controlled validating procedures. They may have used short cuts in deciding that the test was valid for them, and may have failed to apply objective criteria to ascertain whether or not the employees chosen by the testing procedure actually performed in a superior fashion to those who were

---

[27] The subject of performance evaluation is treated systematically in Chapter 23.

[28] See S. Rains Wallace, "Contributions to Business and Industry," in American Institute for Research, *Planning for Progress* (Pittsburgh: A.I.R., 1956), pp. 13-19. Dr. Wallace, who is research director of the Life Insurance Agency Management Association, deplores the lack of objective criteria for judging selection programs in the insurance industry.

rejected. In many companies, moreover, there is a strong tautological bias—that is, when a testing program succeeds in producing a number of candidates who bear a close resemblance to employees whom supervisors have previously judged to be "superior," everyone is pleased. No one knows whether or not the testing program is really able to select employees who will do better than those selected by other means. Used in this fashion, the tests simply confirm existing prejudices.

Thus an organization that intends to use testing must be willing to go through the time-consuming and expensive routine of independently *validating* the tests. Surely the types of test to be tried out can be suggested by the experience of other organizations. However, to avoid the supervisory temptation of "seeing" improved selectivity that doesn't really exist, there is no substitute for rigorous validation.

Test reliability   In assessing the value of a test, management must consider its reliability—that is, the degree to which it produces stable results. If the test produces results with low reliability, management must be cautious about what use it makes of them. Some tests are more easily faked than others, for example. While psychologists have taken pains to build internal checks into many paper-and-pencil personality tests, individuals can usually vary their response to specific items in their desire to give answers the tester wants. Obviously such test results are useless.

Use of too general criteria   Management sometimes becomes discouraged by the difficulty of proving that given personality attributes or aptitudes as revealed by test scores actually contribute to job success. Criteria for success in salaried positions, particularly managerial jobs, are very difficult to obtain. Consequently, there is a growing tendency to use personality tests to screen out people who look "different" from those now employed in similar jobs. Lacking proof that the test scores are significantly related to job success, management simply assumes that unusual personality traits will probably be a universal handicap, and that people with these characteristics will be more difficult to absorb into the organization. Since white-collar jobs require people who can work closely with other people, management decides to look for "adaptable, conformist" personalities.[29]

There may be a measure of truth in this approach, particularly in selecting lower-level white-collar personnel. But there is an obvious danger inherent in this type of reasoning. Not only is there no proof that these attributes are desirable characteristics, but by emphasizing them management runs the risk of excluding creative, imaginative talent:

---

[29] Unfortunately, some consulting firms that specialize in evaluating candidates for managerial positions concentrate on attempting to fit applicants to the over-all "climate" of the organization or to the personality of the top executive. It is assumed that they will "fit in" easily and not be troublemakers.

Personality tests . . . are loaded with debatable assumptions and questions of value. The result . . . is a set of yardsticks that reward the conformist, the pedestrian, the unimaginative—at the expense of the exceptional individual whom management most needs to attract.[30]

OTHER LIMITATIONS OF TESTS

Statistical rather than individual predictions   Test scores can never make firm predictions on what will happen if a specific individual, Mr. Jones, is hired. Rather, test scores simply tell management (assuming that the tests have been validated) that a greater proportion of the people who score above a certain point will be successful than those who score below that point.[31] However, test results can never predict precisely that Jones himself will succeed or fail. The testers tell management that, in general, people whose test results look like Jones' are successful or are not successful. The degree of accuracy of their prediction depends on how closely the test scores are correlated with job-performance evaluations, and these correlations are never perfect. Thus, some people who do poorly on the test will do well on the job, and some people who score well will fail on the job.[32]

Test are more useful when many similar jobs must be filled. The military, for example, will derive more value from the use of testing procedures for pilots than will the XYZ Company that wants to hire one advertising manager.

Labor market limitations   The use of tests assumes that the supply of recruits is so large that management can afford to reject those who don't pass, even though some of them might have proved satisfactory employees. Un-

---

[30] William H. Whyte, Jr., "The Fallacies of Personality Testing," *Fortune* (September 1954), p. 118. Whyte's point of view is also presented in his book, *The Organization Man* (New York: Simon and Schuster, 1956), pp. 171-201. For a systematic rebuttal of Whyte, see Stanley Stark, "Executive Personality and Psychological Testing," *Current Economic Comment*, Bureau of Economic and Business Research, University of Illinois, Vol. 20 (May 1958), pp. 15-32.

[31] We are touching only superficially here on what is a complex problem of statistical analysis. During the test-development program, so-called "cut-off scores" are determined by correlation techniques. Hypothetically, after correlating test performance with job performance, the test-development group may say to line management, "If you insist that everyone hired for this job have a combined test score of 80, the validity of your hiring predictions will be improved 20 per cent over what they are now. If you raise the minimum required score to 85, you will improve the quality of hiring predictions by a factor of 30 per cent." That is, the test will be more selective and fewer employees will be hired who will fail. Of course, in the process of making the test more selective by raising the cut-off scores, management is increasing the costs of the testing program and requiring a larger number of candidates to be recuited, but more of this shortly.

[32] An exception to the statistical nature of testing results is found in the clinical personality tests referred to above as "projective" personality assessments. These endeavor to examine the single individual as a dynamic whole, interrelating the various drives, inhibitions, and values of his personality. However, the results are not directly relatable to job characteristics, nor can they be easily validated.

fortunately, this assumption conflicts with the conclusion that tests are more useful when many identical positions must be filled. The job of filling a great many such position often taxes the recruiting skills of the organization. For example, large department stores must hire large numbers of salespeople. The problem is made more acute by the high turnover associated with jobs that attract young, unmarried women. The introduction of a new selection requirement—for example, all applicants must pass an employment test— may mean that the company will have to double or even treble the number of applicants recruited in order to find enough who can meet the new requirement. But conditions in the labor market may make this possible. Unfortunately, the amount of improvement that tests can generate is a function of the number of applicants that can be *rejected!* Of course, where the supply of applicants greatly exceeds the number of openings, test programs become more economical.

Insofar as tests reduce turnover, this variable becomes less important.

Costs   Testing is a specialized technical field that requires professional training, usually in psychology. If a company intends to develop, validate, and administer its own testing program, it must hire well-trained, high-salaried professionals. Moreover, most of the commercially available test batteries contain copyrighted elements, for which a fee must be paid each time they are used. Even companies that use outside consultants to administer and score tests incur substantial expenses. Simple paper-and-pencil tests cost only a few dollars to administer, but the information they provide is minimal; clinical psychological testing, including projective tests and other personality assessment techniques, may cost several hundred dollars per candidate. Also, as we have noted, additional recruiting costs may be incurred.

On jobs where training costs are high and the employee has considerable discretion in how to perform the job, the cost of testing programs is easier to justify than on jobs where these conditions do not prevail.

An important expense item that is frequently neglected because it is difficult to measure is the impact of testing on employee effectivness, particularly where tests are used for promotion decisions.

TESTS FOR PRESENT EMPLOYEES

So far, we have been talking about the selection of new employees. Some of the techniques we have mentioned, however, may be used to test existing personnel. Increasingly management is using interviews, group rating, and tests in deciding whether to promote or transfer an employee to a position with different job responsibilities from those of his present post.

The use of tests for such purposes may detract from the leadership position of the immediate supervisor. If good test performance is required for promotion in the organization, what happens to successful job performance as an incentive? As Whyte observes:

> ... The weight now being given test reports makes it clear that for those who aspire to be an executive the most critical day they may spend in their lives will be the one they spend taking tests.[33]

Employees often resent the great weight given to the results of tests that they do not understand and may even regard as inaccurate measures of eligibility. The problem is further aggravated by the statistical nature of test results. It is difficult to use test results to explain to an employee why he did not get a given promotion. At best, one can say that, "In general, those with scores like yours are less successful than those with higher scores."

Management also has to justify its decision to use specific tests. Many times the material covered by a personality or aptitude test bears little logical relationship to the job to which the employee aspires. And those who develop the tests are not much help here; as one expert in this field remarked candidly in a lecture at Columbia:

> "All we look for are correlations between test items and our criterion of job success. We don't care whether it is the height of the applicant's grandfather or how much he likes fish. As long as it correlates, we will use it in the battery."

The depth projective tests in particular probe into rather personal areas of the individual's life and mind—his attitudes toward his parents and his family, for example, or toward sex, and life and death. These responses are highly confidential and are subject to serious misinterpretation except in the hands of a trained clinician; moreover, their very possession by a business organization raises serious ethical and moral issues. Employees are justifiably disturbed when their test results fall into the hands of supervisors, and many companies have begun to question the practice of recording certain test findings in employee files. Where outside psychological consultants are employed to administer the testing, they may keep all the records and relay to management only their interpretation of them as they relate to specific job requirements.

Need for distributing information   A company that bases its promotion decisions primarily on test results must be prepared to inform employees how and why the tests are used. Otherwise it will be faced with serious morale problems, for employees will feel that they are subject to mystical forces and that hard work counts less than test-writing and interviewing skills. As many employees have said, "The head-shrinkers decide which way you go in this company."

If the testing program has been carefully chosen and well administered,

---

[33] Whyte, *op. cit.*, p. 174.

management can justify it to employees. Personality tests, for example, uncover talent that would otherwise go to waste. An immediate supervisor may overlook or be prejudiced against the abilities of a given subordinate, but an impersonal test may bring these abilities to the attention of higher management. Moreover, management can make it clear that test results are not the *sine qua non* for advancement, but only one type of evidence that is used. And the employee can be made to realize that tests are valuable for his own purposes, for they identify attributes that suggest types of jobs and training that he will find satisfying and rewarding.

Above all, management must assure employees that test results will not be made freely available to any curious party in the organization. A policy decision must be made, to which the personnel department should contribute, on how much, what types, and in what form such information is to be disseminated. Adequate safeguards must be introduced to protect confidential information.

However, the most important element in any employee information program is deciding who should make selection decisions.

IMPACT OF TESTING ON SUPERVISORY
RESPONSIBILITY FOR SELECTION

We have spoken before about the relative authority of staff and line executives. Since selection procedures contribute significantly to the supervisor's effectiveness, responsibility for decision-making must reside with the line. Personnel specialists can help the supervisor select his subordinates by recruiting and screening appropriately qualified candidates. But the final decision on whom to hire for a specific job must rest with the supervisor.

Unfortunately, the supervisor may try to shirk this responsibility. Selecting personnel is a difficult job in which the intangibles always seem to outweigh the tangibles, and the supervisor is tempted to pass the job along to some sort of testing procedure that provides numerical, apparently objective answers. Unaware of the fallibility of test scores, he may place far too much reliance on them.

When a test claims to measure the "impulsiveness" or "self-sufficiency" of an applicant, the supervisor may ignore the fact that these are just labels ascribed to test results, and that a given applicant who scores high in these categories may or may not possess the corresponding personality attributes in any heightened degree. For example, even psychologists are not agreed on any absolute definition of *intelligence;* most frequently, *intelligence* is defined in terms of scores on specific tests.

If the supervisor is to discharge his responsibility for making selection decisions, he must understand the use and limitations of testing procedures. The personnel department may send him back a report on Mr. "X," whom he is considering for promotion, that looks something like the figure on p. 453.

For his own needs, as well as to reassure employees that personnel decisions are being made by line management, the supervisor should know how data of this sort are derived and what confidence can be placed in them, particularly in their predictive power.

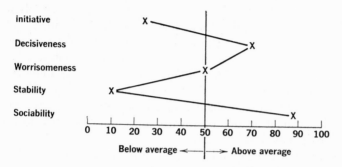

Personality profile of Mr. "X."

The danger is that managers tend to ascribe more validity to test scores than test specialists do. The specialists readily admit that test results do not guarantee success or failure; they know that test scores are simply another set of data to be added to information about the applicant's previous experience, training, work evaluations, interview information, and the impressions of those who know him.

Conclusion

In order to survive, every organization must attract an adequate supply of employees and must then assign them to the jobs for which they are best suited. In administering its recruitment program, the company must determine its personnel needs and the methods it will use in seeking to fill them. It must devise specific programs tailored to the numbers and skills to be recruited and to prevailing conditions in the labor market. Moreover, it must make a systematic evaluation of alternative selection techniques in light of their relative advantages and costs.

When psychologists first began to explore individual differences, the application of their research to selection promised to introduce a new era in employee relations. Theretofore, employee failures had been attributed to laziness or recalcitrance; now it could be argued that the real fault lay in trying to force square pegs into round holes. Testing enthusiasts claimed that careful appraisal of individual capabilities would solve most personnel problems. Placing the employee in the right job would assure a high level of performance and eliminate employee discontent.

These predictions have proved somewhat extravagant. The individual human being has shown himself to be more difficult to appraise and categorize than was anticipated. Frequently an employee with the requisite skills and learning potential has failed for lack of motivation. Personality attributes particularly, the most difficult characteristics to encompass by simple test measures, frequently seemed more important in explaining job success or failure than the more tangible characteristics of the individual.

Nor are jobs themselves easy to classify, particularly the more complex managerial positions. As we mentioned in Chapter 16, different people will handle the same job in strikingly different ways. The requirements of a job may change radically when a new supervisor takes over, and there is no way of predicting organizational changes of this sort. Jones, who was selected to work in a department headed by Brown, finds himself unable to work effectively under the new head, Smith.

But we must not relegate all selection techniques to the dust bin just because they have serious limitations. Personnel programs are characteristically somewhat less than perfect, and the effective supervisor must learn to work within the limits set by his tools and techniques.

Many organizations concentrate on trying to fit jobs to people, rather than trying to fit people to jobs. This approach calls for the development of soundly based recruitment programs, techniques for screening out the obviously unqualified, and effective means of *finding* or *adapting* jobs within the organization for those who have been hired.

Problem I

Colton, Langenberg and Harford is a large, successful advertising agency. One of the reasons for its success has been its ability to produce fresh, creative, eye-catching copy. The company employs about 60 copywriters working in 15 different departments.

The department heads, who are responsible for hiring, have different ideas on what makes a good copywriter. Their predilections are based pretty much on chance experience and ingrained stereotypes. One supervisor will tell you: "I can tell a good copywriter right away—all you have to do is to give him two minutes to come up with an original advertisement for something like condensed milk and see what he does." Others use this criterion: "I have him bring in all the ads he has ever written and ask him for his 10 favorites and 10 worst. Then I spend the next evening reading them all over and comparing my judgments to his." Others are influenced by the candidate's physical appearance and manner of speech; still others, by his resemblance to copywriters who have proved successful in the past.

The results of this haphazard approach to selection have not been good. At present the company needs five new copywriters, and one-third of the present staff have not worked out well. The agency's personnel department would like to use a more systematic procedure for evaluating applicants, including some technique for testing writing skill. The new program would be costly, however, and there would be little point in setting it up if the department heads ignored its findings.

1. If you were head of the agency, how would you set up an improved selection procedure that would not detract from the department heads' responsibility for turning out high-quality copy?

2. What information would you need before deciding on such a new policy?

3. How would you introduce and gain acceptance for the new approach?

Problem II

Frank Lorette has been an average employee, in and out of trouble, during his five years with the Parcel Trucking Company. Recently, inadvertently, the company learned that Lorette had lied on his application blank by indicating he had never been arrested. Lorette had been charged with petit larceny and convicted ten years before coming to his present job.

As a truck driver delivering department store packages, Lorette has a position of some trust. Although there have been no obvious thefts on Lorette's routes, there have been the usual number of mysterious disappearances of packages.

1. What should the company do with its newly discovered information?

2. How much responsibility does the company have to check the application blank prior to accepting a new employee?

3. Should the employee's "just-average" work record be taken into account in evaluating what steps to take?

Problem III

The Firstway Aircraft Company has just received a government contract to develop a new military transport plane. At least 75 additional engineers will be needed to initiate this program, although it is uncertain how long the contract will remain in effect. The funds will be cut off unless Congress increases the military budget at the end of the year.

Management is faced with several problems in recruiting the personnel required by this program:

1. Because of the recent cancellation of other projects by government cutbacks, the company has been left with a surplus of engineers. Unfortunately, however, they will not have completed their present assignment until one or two months after the new program is scheduled to get underway. Further, most of them are experienced in designing fighter aircraft but one not familiar with transport planes. What criteria should management use in deciding whether or not to select engineers from the anticipated surplus to staff the new activity?

2. The new program may be short-lived. But if the company publicizes this fact, it will hamper its recruiting activities in a tight labor market. Is the company under any obligation to disclose that the work may be short-term? If so, how can it discharge that obligation?

Problem IV

Alfred Elkind had been with the Consolidated Electronics Company for seven years when he requested a six-month leave of absence to travel to Florida to visit his mother, who had an incurable disease. When Elkind returned, company policy required that he take a medical examination. The company doctor's examination disclosed what his fellow employees had known for more than two years. Elkind had become almost totally deaf as a result of a disease of the central nervous system. Hearing aids would do him no good.

Management refused to take Elkind back and placed him on an indefinite sick leave. The department supervisor and higher management felt that Elkind could not work efficiently and safely with such poor hearing.

Elkind appealed to the union, which filed a grievance including these arguments:

1. The supervisor had known for more than a year about this condition and had taken no action. A leave of absence is not supposed to prejudice a man's employment rights. It was taken with company approval for a pressing matter of justifiable family concern. A man should not be penalized for visiting his dying mother.

2. Elklind's job as an electronic tester does not require him to work closely with other people, and the supervisor can "find ways to communicate to him."

3. Elkind's personal doctor has given him a signed statement indicating that he is healthy enough to engage in all the work relating to his present job.

4. The company President, Mr. Vaughan, once signed a Chamber of Commerce policy statement indicating that "hiring the handicapped is good business."

5. The company has a moral and legal obligation to workers with seniority. This action is discriminatory and in violation of the contract.

On reviewing the case, the general manager told the union that the company would try to find some job for Elkind but it could not guarantee to find one that required equal skill and that paid as well as his present job. "His present job, however, is too critical to the company's reputation as a producer of quality equipment. There are many instances when the supervisor and/or other employees have to discuss work problems centering on the workmanship and electronic characteristics of certain components and a man with a hearing problem cannot fill that part of the job description."

1. If you were the general manager, how would you evaluate the specific points raised in the union's grievance?

2. What steps would you have followed had the case been presented to you after the report of the company's medical director had been received?

Problem V

The Phillips Paint Company trains the salesmen it hires to sell its product line to retail stores. The company seeks personable young men who have the energy and initiative to make the requisite calls on customers and the ability to speak enthusiastically and intelligently about the company's products. Flexibility and patience in meeting a wide variety of people, and accuracy in transferring orders to order forms, are also important requirements.

James Henry has applied for a sales job. The interviewer who is going to talk with him has noted the following entries on his application blank:

Henry is 26 years old.
He has completed one year of college, at a small teachers' college in the Midwest.
He was divorced after three years of marriage, no children.
He has held five jobs since leaving school; he had had no work experience prior to that time. The jobs were:

1. Shipping clerk, small tool and die company (6 months), New York.
2. Bus driver, inter-city bus company (1 year), Albany.
3. Laboratory assistant, Memorial Hospital (2 years), New York.
4. Credit manager for collection agency (2 years), Buffalo.
5. Milk deliveryman (6 months), Albany.

No job is listed for one year. James notes on his application that he was recovering from an illness during that period.

1. If you were the interviewer, what objectives would you set for your interview with James?
2. How would you phrase your questions?

Problem VI

You are the executive vice president of a large "high-style" women's dress manufacturing organization. Your firm finds it increasingly difficult to find candidates for custom-tailoring positions. These craftsmen, in the past, at least, have been apprentice-trained in Europe, and most of the better American tailors have been immigrants.

1. What proposals would you make to your company concerning means of increasing the supply of custom-tailors available to your organization? (You employ about a hundred of them, many of whom are nearing retirement.)
2. In your proposal, consider the sources of information and the channels of communication you would explore in developing a proposal with reasonable chances of success. Remember that costs are a significant factor.

You have been asked to assist the executives in charge of food-preparation activities for a large hotel chain. Top-quality chefs, with skill in the preparation of a variety of dishes, are in short supply. These specialists, too, have been largely trained in Europe.

1. How would you develop a source of supply for this type of personnel?
2. Would your answers to questions of this sort differ if you were a member of a dress manufacturers' or hotel trade association? In what respects?

Once an employee has been selected and inducted, he does not stay put on a single job for the duration of his tenure with a particular company. Hopefully, he will be promoted; transfers are always likely; and if conditions are unfavorable he may be demoted or even laid off. The development of policies governing these movements through the organization are the subject of this chapter.

PROMOTION POLICY

Internal Promotion or Outside Recruitment?

Promotional policy is a crucial area of personnel management, both for the organization and for individual employees. For the organization it insures a steady supply of trained people for higher-level positions, and for employees it provides a powerful incentive to win advancement by improving their performance. There is satisfaction in knowing that one can improve one's position without leaving the firm. Let us look at these three objectives more closely.

Promotion, Transfer, Seniority Policy for Non-Managerial Employees

INTERNAL RECRUITMENT

No organization can rely on outside recruitment to fill all the internal openings that occur. True, certain jobs are similar from one organization to another (janitors, electricians, tool-makers, typists, salesclerks), but most jobs have distinctive characteristics and require specialized knowledge that can be obtained only through experience within a particular firm. When we look closely even at those jobs that do not seem to be unique, we find that they require familiarity with the people, procedures, policies, and special characteristics of the organization in which they are performed.[1]

But beyond the storehouse of information and the special skills that employees bring to the new jobs into which they are promoted, internal recruitment also provides an excellent means of selection. We have already seen that most selection procedures, such as interviewing and testing, are far from perfect in furnishing an accurate appraisal of a new applicant's potential worth to the organization. Seeing a man in action, however, over a period of years in a less important position, enables management to make a realistic assessment of both the person and the attributes he brings to his work.

Promotion also provides a process of "selective socialization." Over a period of time, those whose personalities and skills enable them to get along in the climate of human relations characteristic of the organization tend to stay on; those whose personalities conflict tend to leave—either voluntarily or involuntarily.

ON-THE-JOB INCENTIVES

The knowledge that successful performance of one's job may lead to more remunerative assignments is a powerful incentive. The individual gains additional job satisfactions through his own efforts and in a manner consistent with the goals of the organization itself. Management provides the opportunity for attaining the kind of satisfaction that comes with more challenging, interesting work, higher pay, and more desirable working conditions; the employee himself, however, must attain this satisfaction through his own efforts.

Employees have little motivation to work harder if all the better jobs are reserved for outsiders, particularly on jobs where production incentive plans make no sense, and where merit increases have only limited value.

JOB SATISFACTION FOR THE INDIVIDUAL

The opportunity to keep moving ahead is a highly important source of job satisfaction for Americans. Additional responsibilities and recognition

---

[1] There is some evidence that jobs in the middle range of the promotional ladder are most likely to be unique to a particular company. Unskilled work and highly skilled jobs are more likely to be similar from one company to another.

from superiors may provide some of this satisfaction, but tangible evidence of progress in the form of higher-ranked jobs is an essential requirement for many employees.

As we noted in the last chapter, after completing the trial-and-error period of finding a satisfactory job in a satisfactory company, most workers look forward to unbroken, continuous service. They like to feel that they can get ahead in their own company without having to turn elsewhere.

BRINGING IN OUTSIDERS

Every organization needs to make a basic policy decision: Which jobs should be filled from inside the organization (and, by implication, from outside only when it is clear that there are no qualified candidates on the payroll), and which jobs should be filled from outside the organization?

Just as many organizations seek outsiders to sit on their boards of directors in order to introduce new perspectives, so they reserve certain lesser positions for newcomers. This infusion of "new blood" contributes to the health of the organization—it keeps the members from growing stagnant, repetitious, and overly conformist. This is probably of less importance in hourly-paid jobs than in staff and managerial jobs, however.

Another reason for recruiting outside the firm may be to avoid the expense of training new employees. Many employers find it more economical to hire employees, particularly skilled tradesmen, from the outside than to undertake expensive training and upgrading programs. Some of these programs are feasible only for large firms that can afford the expense.

There is another pitfall in the rigid adherence to a policy of promotion from within. In many companies this policy means that every new non-managerial employee must start out in the job of an unskilled laborer, even though he has the potential to rise to a top job. For example, some advertising agencies require all newly hired personnel to start in the mailroom, and some airlines encourage everyone to start as a ticket-seller. Many highly motivated and able candidates may be discouraged by the prospect of having to work at menial jobs and by the long time-lag before they can work themselves up to a relatively skilled position. On the other hand, the companies that practice this policy can assure their workers that all the better jobs are filled by "our own people, not by outsiders." Furthermore, when a man reaches the top rungs of the promotional ladder he is more widely trained in company operations and is able to assume a greater range of positions. If business declines, he will be easier to reassign, because he is intimately familiar with lesser-skilled jobs "below" his present position.

Organizations that are failing to expand, or that are actually contracting, have special problems in filling higher-rated jobs. In one case known to the authors, a large agricultural plantation was changing over from a set-up that had used primarily unskilled field hands. Since the industry had been suffering from overproduction for several years, this organization had recently done no new hiring, and many of its present employees were over 40 years old. Most of these men had been hired when secondary schooling was less common than it is today, and few of them were qualified to take over the new jobs that were being created. So the company found itself in the difficult position of trying to hire new employees from outside at the very time it was laying off men with more than ten years of seniority.

This is one of the acute problems raised by automation, for many employees fear that their education and experience will not qualify them for the new and perhaps better jobs that are replacing their present ones. Only when management can assure these workers that adequate training facilities will be provided will they accept the new processes ungrudgingly. Historically, the unions that have been most receptive to technological change have been those whose members were not thrown out of work by innovations. They were either craft groups whose members were able to take over the new equipment at about the same wages they had been earning before, or industrial workers who could shift easily to the new processes.

DIFFERENCES BETWEEN MANAGEMENT'S
AND EMPLOYEES' CONCEPT OF PROMOTION

Many managers tend to project their own feelings about promotion onto their employees, forgetting that not every employee wants to be promoted—at least not in the terms in which management typically conceives of promotion. Employees differ greatly in their "level of aspiration."

In some industries, technology has made it difficult to satisfy the desire of older employees for easier jobs—for the majority of jobs are fast-paced and demanding. This is more true of the automobile industry, for example, than of the chemical industry.

Some companies rely so heavily on the promotion-from-within procedure to fill their manpower requirements at higher levels that they cannot afford to keep people who do not qualify or are not desirous of moving ahead. Even many universities follow the practice of "up or out," which simply means that instructors and assistant professors must either earn a promotion or seek employment in another institution.

Management sometimes makes the mistake of using a highly unpopular job as the required stepping-stone to higher positions. As a result, serious shortages may develop in the jobs "above," because few candidates are willing to spend time on the undesirable rung of the promotional ladder.

Similarly, when an employee enters into an apprenticeship program, he is often required to accept a reduction in pay for two or three years before he wins a craftsman's rating. Management officials assume that employees should be willing to make short-run sacrifices in return for long-run benefits, but they forget that their own time perspective may be quite different from that of their employees.

What management regards as a substantial promotion may not seem like a promotion at all to the employee himself. In research work in the natural sciences, for example, or in nursing, an employee who is "promoted" into a supervisory position may feel that administrative work is a real hardship rather than an advancement. Not only does it force him to spend his time in activities that are less interesting than his own professional work, but it may even cost him the confidence and respect of his professional colleagues. Organizations that employ such specialists must somehow provide promotional opportunities that do not demand the sacrifices of primary interests.

Finally, there is always a group of employees who are quite content to stand still, who prefer the known to the unknown. Unwilling to risk what they have in hand, they want to stick close to the people they know and the responsibilities they are familiar with. To these people, *improvement* means regular wage increases and perhaps a better security position—for example, growth in seniority credits.

Because of these differing conceptions of what constitutes a promotion, management faces several problems in establishing a sound promotional policy. It must provide realistic opportunities that will encourage promising employees to take the risks involved in moving upward. It must not discourage valuable employees from seeking advancement by making service in an unpopular job a prerequisite to promotion. It must provide realistic alternatives for professionals who are reluctant to assume supervisory responsibilities. And it must provide for employees who do outstanding work but are unwilling to take on new and additional responsibilities.

Selecting Who Is to Be Promoted

Although significant exceptions exist, there are usually more candidates for promotion than there are openings to be filled. How does the organization select the most desirable candidate?

MERIT

Since we want promotions to provide an incentive for employees to improve their performance on their present job, it would seem logical to select the candidate who has the best record in terms of output, skill, cooperation, and so forth. Actually, however, this principle is not easy to follow.

Certainly simple measures of output do not tell the whole story. How much a given factory worker is able to produce depends on many factors outside his own control: the condition of his machine, scheduling delays, and special assignments he may receive. The same is even more true outside the factory. Two department store clerks, for instance, may show very different sales totals because of the different physical location of their counters.

Because of the shortcomings of a simple measure of output, many organizations ask their supervisors to rate their subordinates periodically on a number of criteria such as cooperation, dependability, output, and housekeeping. Such formalized systems of evaluation—often called merit rating—have many values: above all, of course, they help the supervisor take all factors into account in making a promotion and thus reduce his personal bias; in addition, they encourage him to scrutinize the work of his subordinates more closely and broadly and thus improve the quality of his own supervision; they make it easy for him to provide "feedback" to his subordinates on "how they are doing"; and they force him to keep more careful records of employee behavior for use in case of disciplinary action.

Performance evaluations are all subject to numerous distortions—as we shall see in Chapter 23, however. It is worth while to note here that to handle such evaluations successfully the supervisor must learn to do a better job of observing his employees—and to take into account not only how well a man performs, but also what can be done to improve his performance. An employee's poor performance, and his failure to progress, may be the result of inadequate supervision.

ABILITY

Unfortunately, promotion cannot always be offered as a reward for present performance. Jones may be doing fine on his present job but lack the ability to do the work on a higher-ranked job. Smith, on the other hand, may be doing poorly on his present assignment because of inadequate supervision or the unchallenging nature of the work. Put him on more difficult work and he may blossom out.

There are longer-term factors to consider as well. An employee who has a great deal of seniority and the ability to move one more step up the promotional ladder may seem the most deserving candidate at the moment. And yet, from a long-run point of view, the organization may wish to promote a younger man who can go far beyond the immediate opening. Thus management must consider two separate questions: Who is best fitted for the present vacancy? Who has the greatest potential not only to handle this job but also to move into positions of greater responsibility?

How does one determine ability? It will be remembered from our earlier discussion of testing that ability is difficult to measure. The specific traits, attitudes, personalities, configurations, and skills that make up ability are frequently ambiguous. For this reason we must often rely on objective measurements—years of education, for example—which presumably give us some estimate of how a candidate is likely to perform in the future.

The years-of-education criterion used to be more helpful than it is at present, however. Twenty-five years ago, an employee who completed high school was somewhat exceptional. Such an accomplishment indicated that he was probably competent to handle difficult assignments and also that he possessed a high degree of motivation. So much of modern "education" is automatic that it is no longer an index to unusual drive, perseverance, or general ability.

Another problem in determining ability is that some of the people in an organization may be given special opportunities to acquire valuable skills and knowledge, whereas others are not. Certain jobs give employees an opportunity to move about freely, bringing them into contact with high-level personnel whose opinions are crucial in promotion decisions. They "learn their way around the organization," and are on the spot when a promotional opportunity turns up.

What we are saying, then, is that the concept of ability is, like that of merit, surrounded by subjective elements that may create inequities. However, it is still important to make an effort both to measure and reward merit and ability. Organizations that have failed to reward excellence in service, or that have relied too heavily on personal relationships or length of service, suffer in terms of both efficiency and morale.

Furthermore, even when an employee lacks the desire or the ability to advance, he wants to know that others who are more able and more ambitious than himself are receiving appropriate recognition. Some cultures assume that advancement should be based on ties of family or friendship, but Americans are loath to accept such a criterion. For example, we regard nepotism (favoritism shown to relatives) as somehow unethical or immoral. In part, this attitude reflects the relative absence of rigid class boundaries and strong restrictions on the individual in our national experience. We believe that an individual should be able to move ahead on his own merits, regardless of his family background and early life.

Opinions of fellow employees   Some organizations give considerable weight to the opinion of employees who work closely with the prospective candidates. Management may either poll these employees informally or make use of a sociometric questionnaire (see Chapter 3). This technique is of particular value in picking a person for promotion to a supervisory job.

SENIORITY

One of the most controversial criteria for selecting individuals for promotion is length of service. Unions have probably put the greatest stress on seniority, but it is also emphasized among unorganized groups and within management itself. Let us look at some of the arguments that are mustered in favor of seniority as a criterion for promotion.

Objectivity   The use of such subjective criteria as performance evaluation, selection tests, and the opinions of highly fallible supervisors leads many employees to challenge and resent promotional decisions. As soon as a decision is announced, charges of favoritism and discrimination ring out on every side, and the ensuing conflict can cause a drop in productivity as well as morale.

To avoid this sort of difficulty, it is often suggested that promotions be based on some objective criterion, and that the only truly objective criterion is length of service. When management knows that it is going to promote the employee with the longest service, chances are that it will give him the training he needs to move into the new job. Management will also tend to perfect its initial selection procedures, for once an individual gets into the organization his future will be relatively assured. Moreover, an objective criterion like length of service eliminates one of the sources of friction between managers and subordinates, and reduces unprofitable discussions and disputes to a minimum.

Most unions regard seniority as the only really valid criterion for promotions. They recognize that as long as managers have the power to select the most suitable candidate for promotion, it is a simple matter for them to discourage ambitious employees from becoming "too interested" in union affairs. With professional groups, such as engineers, however, the unions are faced with a serious dilemma. The membership sincerely believes that promotions should be based on merit. But union leaders realize that they are weakening their own position when they permit management to retain the unilateral right to evaluate merit and to select candidates for promotion on the basis of such evaluations. True, the merit evaluations themselves can be made more objective, but the element of personal choice continues to operate.

Cultural factors   In certain primitive societies, the oldest men invariably occupy the highest positions; although we do not follow this practice rigidly, we still feel that it is appropriate for the senior people within an organization to occupy higher positions than their juniors. True, we make a good many exceptions: the long-time employee who is clearly incompetent, and the young man who is a genius. However, ours is at least partially an "age-graded society" where age, position, and prestige are positively correlated.

Excessive emphasis on seniority, however, may violate employee attitudes about the "right" way of getting ahead:

> The top-skilled members of glass- and steel-making crews are typically men who have worked their way up through a lengthy, informal apprenticeship system. In the old days they worked long hours, often without pay, under the far from tolerant tutelage of a craftsman who would put up with his younger assistants only in return for numerous services. It was a long, hard, grueling road to the top, and those who have made it frequently resent the rather automatic manner in which men can now work themselves into similar positions primarily by accumulating seniority.

They resent the fact that others can reach their position without comparable initiation periods.

The promotion of incompetents solely on the basis of length of service clearly violates a strongly entrenched cultural attitude that rewards should be somehow commensurate with accomplishment.

Contribution to ability The third defense of length of service as a criterion for promotion holds that ability increases with service on lower-level jobs in the promotional ladder. Although research is lacking in this important area, the effect of length of service on an individual's promotability seems to differ from job to job.

Recent research among production workers suggests that the employee with the longest service often is better prepared for promotion than management is initially willing to admit. When management is forced by the union and the arbitration process to promote the senior worker, even though it prefers another employee, the promotion may still work out rather well.[2] For many jobs, particularly those at the lower levels, differences in ability from one employee to another may be less than management tends to think. Consequently, the gain in morale derived from promoting the most senior employee may more than offset any slight loss of efficiency.

Up to some undetermined point, it seems likely that an employee's promotability does increase as he gains more and more experience at a given job —that is, the longer he works at one job, the more qualified he becomes for promotion to the next-higher job. This correspondence undoubtedly diminishes as length of service increases, however. The length of time for which the relationship holds depends on how much learning is actually taking place on the job and how much is required to do the higher-rated job. Beyond a certain level, continued service brings very little gain. And a point may well be reached after which increased length of service actually *reduces* an employee's ability to move on to the next job, producing in him what is often referred to as "a trained incapacity." He becomes so imbued with the problems and procedures of his present job that he is unable to adjust to new circumstances and situations. The expert simply becomes too expert at what he is doing. Too often the best accountant in an organization, or the best salesman, or the best nurse, fails when promoted to a position in which the highly detailed information he or she has accumulated is no longer particularly useful. Each organization needs to assess, for each job, the relationship between readiness for promotion and length of service.

Reward for loyalty In a sense, to grant promotions on the basis of seniority is a way of rewarding employees for loyalty to the organization. In an organization that wants to hold on to its employees and avoid costly turnover,

---

[2] James J. Healy, "The Ability Factor in Labor Relations," *Arbitration Journal,* Vol. 10 (New Series), No. 1 (1955), pp. 3-11.

a type of guaranteed promotion plan may be an effective personnel policy.

No one would deny that loyal service deserves reward. But the question is how many loyal employees become discouraged about their future with the organization when they realize that they can be promoted only as fast as length of service permits?

STRIKING A BALANCE

Every organization is faced with the problem of ascribing relative weights to merit, ability, and seniority in making promotion decisions. Even when company policy or the union contract sets up merit and ability as the prime determinants, many an organization succumbs in time to the presumably more objective criterion of seniority. At first, supervisors may seek to promote the most able man instead of the most senior one; but if management refuses to back them when the union files a grievance challenging such decisions, they soon learn that it is safer to use seniority as the criterion. And even a supervisor who knows that his decisions will be backed up by his superiors may believe that relations with his subordinates will be easier if he promotes the most senior employee. In practice, almost all companies give some weight to seniority, although companies that are unionized give it greater weight than those that are not.

We can draw a straight line to represent the whole spectrum of criteria on which promotional decisions are based, ranging from "pure" merit and ability to "pure" length of service:

Merit and ability	Ability plus seniority	Seniority plus ability	Minimum length of service	Seniority except for incompetents	Length of service
a	*b*	*c*	*d*	*e*	*f*

a. At the extreme left, management tries to choose the man with the *greatest merit and ability* from among all eligible candidates. No weight is given to length of service.

b. Here management selects the *most senior* employee from among the *most able* candidates. Ability is still very important; but where the ability of the candidates is about the same, the one with the longest service receives the promotion.

c. At this point on the continuum, the organization selects the most meritorious and able employee for promotion *only* if he is "head and shoulders" above those with longer service.

d. Here, near the middle of our continuum, management follows a promotional policy which states that a certain *minimum length of service* is required before an employee becomes eligible for promotion, regardless of the merit and ability he demonstrates.

e. This represents a management decision to exclude the obviously incompetent from consideration before selecting the man or woman with the greatest length of service. Although definition of terms is a problem, "incompetent" refers to employees who by their own admission or by a substantial consensus lack the qualities demanded by the higher-rated job.

f. Finally, we reach the other extreme of the continuum, where length of service is the sole determinant of selection for promotion.

In weighting all these criteria, most organizations are interested in what effect their promotional decisions will have on over-all efficiency.[3] Left to its own devices, management would often prefer to stay very near the left end of the scale (weight given to merit and ability), but union and employee pressure serves to move the decision farther to the right.

THE PROBATIONARY PERIOD

Companies that emphasize length of service in making promotions usually require a trial period of from one to three months in which to assess the ability of the worker who has been selected for a higher-rated job. This practice benefits both the employee and the company. It gives the employee an opportunity to prove himself, and it gives the company a chance to test its decision. In practice, of course, disagreement sometimes arises over whether the worker's performance during the trial period has been satisfactory and how much training or assistance the employee should receive while "trying out."

Administering the Promotional Program

DEALING WITH THE INDIVIDUAL

Handling employees who are unlikely to be promoted A supervisor must be able to predict what members of his group will be the most likely candidates for promotion when openings occur. And he must try to keep those who are unlikely to be promoted from taking it for granted that they will soon be moving up the ladder. For example, an employee with seniority may feel himself well qualified for promotion and yet lack the basic experience or training, or some specific ability, that would justify his promotion. If the supervisor waits until an opening actually occurs before informing such a person that he is not qualified, the individual will feel sharply disappointed and frustrated and may become highly emotional and aggressive. Moreover, his colleagues may press him to assert himself and protest the seeming injustice. Even a man who recognizes his own shortcomings may be pressured by his colleagues to demand the right to try out on the new job.

Problems of this sort can be avoided if the supervisor makes a point of

---

[3] U. S. Wage Stabilization Board, *Companies' Presentations Before Special Panel, Wage Stabilization Board* (*in matter of United Steelworkers of America, CIO and various steel and iron ore companies*), *Steel Industry Case D-18-C, 1952* (New York: January-February 1952), Vol. II. Presents a good summary of company arguments.

discussing with the hopeful candidate the exact nature of the new responsibilities *long before the opening actually occurs.* Then, if the employee is clearly not qualified for the promotion, he may be brought around to accept his unsuitability. The supervisor may be able to suggest a way in which the employee can supplement his background or improve his performance so that he will eventually become eligible for a promotional opportunity. If he shows himself unwilling to make the extra effort required, the job of winning his assent to being "passed over" becomes much easier.

Once a department has begun to buzz with gossip over "who is going to get the nod," it is too late to undertake an individual counseling program. Expectations have already built up, and frustrations are unavoidable. Furthermore, a junior employee who wins a promotion that the group feels should have gone to another man may not be able to gain the group's cooperation. This is a serious problem when the promotion puts him into a supervisory position.

Handling employees who are likely to be promoted   When should an individual be notified that he is likely to be promoted? There is a middle ground between notifying likely prospects too early and waiting until the last minute to make the selection. A candidate will often be anxious to undertake additional training to prepare himself for the new job, and tensions in the group may be reduced when the decision is reached. Such notice also permits good candidates to fill in any deficiencies in their training and experience and thus qualify themselves for a new promotion.[4] However, selection of likely candidates in advance, when the time period is too great, may appear unfair and discriminatory.

Dealing with the employee who doesn't want to be promoted   In our culture, anyone who does not want to advance is regarded as somehow queer or lazy. Many individuals take on higher-level jobs even when they are not suited for additional responsibility; but the cost is high to themselves and to the organization. In fact, people who really should not be promoted may come to feel that a failure to show interest in advancement is a black mark against their record. Actually, a clear recognition of each employee's psychological and intellectual limits is valuable both to the organization and to the individual.

Every company needs to provide promotional opportunities, both as a source of skilled employees for higher-rated jobs and as a source of greater on-the-job motivation. But the employee who has reached the limit of his ambitions or abilities also has a vital role to play. The armed services have discovered the value of the "old-line" master sergeants who stay with a par-

---

[4] A good example of this procedure is described in the example in Chapter 21, in which older nurses were encouraged to take additional formal training to qualify for promotion.

ticular unit while its commissioned officers come and go. These men provide stability and continuity, give new officers and enlisted men a sense of what has come before, and explain how old policies influence the present behavior of the unit. So, too, members of an organization who have been in one department for a long time may help to break in newcomers, particularly new supervisors.

Many organizations make it clear to employees that they do not have to try for a given promotion, and that they will be given other opportunities if they decide they want to be considered for future openings. But non-mobile people must not be permitted to monopolize the training jobs in which more suitable candidates can be prepared for higher positions. These stepping-stones must be reserved for employees who are equipped to move upward.

Helping the unsuccessful candidate　Supervisors should give special attention to hopeful employees who have been passed over, or who try and fail on a new job. These men have undergone a trying emotional experience and they are worthy of special counseling and perhaps special consideration.

Helping the successful candidate　The real problems, however, are experienced by the man who *does* move up into a new position, particularly if it involves supervision. Unless he has been with the group for a long time, and unless the group has concurred in his promotion, he is bound to encounter some measure of fear and resistance. At first, his subordinates are uncertain about what his new leadership will mean to their future. He needs to be coached and cautioned by his superiors.

The employee who is promoted to a non-supervisory position has his problems, too, for he may be facing new responsibilities for which he is not wholly prepared. We tend to forget how long it took us to learn all the details of our present positions; we assume that we do everything almost automatically, without thinking, as if we were driving an automobile. But nothing is "automatic" in a strange job, and the new man is under great strain. In worrying about what he should do and how to avoid mistakes, he may become so tense that he performs clumsily or forgetfully. If his supervisor is aware of these strains, he can provide the understanding that will help the new man over the hump of the first days on the job. This is a *must* when the employee is undergoing a trial period to test his fitness for the job.

IMPACT OF DEPARTMENT BOUNDARIES ON PROMOTION

The existence of department boundaries affects the administration of any promotion policy. The number of potential promotions and the number of qualified candidates may not be distributed equally throughout the organization. This creates problems that management must solve if it is to establish an effective program.

Willingness to consider candidates from other departments   Companies find that they often overlook good candidates who do not happen to be in the department where the opening occurs but who do have relevant experience and appropriate abilities. Consequently, it is important to set up some device for communicating the existence of promotional opportunities throughout the organization. The personnel department can act as a clearing-house, or the company can use "posting": that is, employees from any department in the firm can formally "bid" for jobs that are advertised on bulletin boards. The advantage of this procedure is clear: it enables management to choose the right man for a job from a much larger pool of prospective candidates.

Many organizations are also drawing up careful personnel inventories which list the complete qualifications of each employee. Those who are responsible for selecting men to fill job openings are encouraged to scrutinize these inventories for qualified candidates who might otherwise be overlooked. Of course, as we shall see, such advance manpower planning is even more widely used at managerial levels.

The current interest in psychological testing reflects the desire to avoid overlooking a good candidate, particularly for management positions. Testing, it is hoped, will reveal valuable employees whose formal duties have not called them to the attention of their superiors.

Inequality in promotional opportunities   If opportunities for promotion differ greatly from one department to another, employee morale may be seriously impaired. It is a simple matter for an organization to calculate the number of promotional opportunities that are likely to be available at any given level in each unit. Some departments are notorious for the lack of promotional opportunities they offer to employees. In one company, we found that participation in a new union was inversely correlated with promotional opportunities: the group that enjoyed the fewest opportunities for promotion was the most anxious to engage in union activities. Here experienced, skilled men felt frustrated by their inability to move ahead.

A seemingly innocent change in management policy within a given department sometimes wipes out the promotional opportunities of a whole group of workers. For example, a sudden decision that specialized training will be required for promotion may disqualify most, if not all, of the present group from consideration. Whyte describes such a case:

> In view of the rapid scientific and technical development of the company [the Vice President of the department] decided that only college graduates should be appointed as foremen. The new ruling hit the HI-Test plant particularly hard, for some of these men had been singled out as especially able and promising. . . . They were at the top now with no place to go. . . . It was common to hear them say, "We're just bumping our heads against the ceiling here." [5]

[5] William F. Whyte, "Engineers and Workers: A Case Study," *Human Organization* (Winter 1956), p. 5.

When management finds that there are so-called "dead-end jobs" in the organization where promotions are unlikely, it should either try to open up these dead-ends or else fill them with employees who have neither the capability nor the desire to move ahead.

Manpower hoarding Departments sometimes try to hoard more employees than they need, particularly employees with scarce talents; engineers, for example, were hoarded during the shortage of the 1950's. Understandably, employees grow restless when they realize that the opportunity to advance is being blocked by the piling up of excessive people in existing positions. When promotions are more rapid in one unit than in another, resentful employees may ask to be transferred to the units that are expanding and where promotions are more rapid. Fearful that the supply of trained manpower may be depleted, managers tend to discourage such transfers or, if policy permits, actually refuse to let such requests go through.

Interdepartment competition may also be a factor in restricting promotional opportunities. For example, a department that was carrying on a full-scale training program for tool-makers refused to honor requests from employees who finished the course to accept a promotion in another department, claiming that the other department was "too cheap" to do its own training. On the other hand, there are situations in which everyone recognizes that certain departments will train workers for other departments. The important thing is to insure that the organization's evaluation systems, such as cost accounting, reflect this contribution. Clearly, any department that does a substantial amount of training for other groups will have higher operating costs, for it must constantly take on new people and then surrender them as soon as they become promotable.

Management must insure that all the supervisors throughout the organization display the same degree of willingness to release people for other jobs and that adequate replacements are available. If some supervisors are reluctant to let their trained workers move on to higher-rated jobs in other departments, serious inequities are bound to develop in the promotional system.[6]

At the heart of every one of these problems is the need to predict future needs and to plan to have people in training and in lower-level jobs who can eventually be promoted to higher-ranking positions. During the period of expansion after World War II, many companies found that they needed more skilled workers but that they had failed to develop enough promotable talent through their training programs.

Thus the organization needs to guard against a situation in which pockets of promotable personnel build up in some areas where promotions are "slug-

---

[6] Some companies have even considered using the protests of a man's department when a promotion is in the offing as an important criterion of promotability!

gish"—and a dearth of promotable personnel builds up in other areas where promotional openings are more numerous.

In a sense, the opportunity for promotion is a function of the "width" of the promotional ladder. When management insures that men can transfer easily from a unit in which they are blocked to a unit in which there are more openings, without sacrificing their accrued benefits, inequities are less likely to occur in the promotional system. One way of widening the ladder is to tie together "families" of jobs that call for common skills and common experience even though they are not related on the organizational chart. Such a policy also widens the perspective and loyalties of employees by inducing them to see the problems of the organization from a less parochial point of view.

What usually happens, however, is that an employee must sacrifice his seniority, and in a sense start all over again, when he moves into another department where the opportunities for promotion are greater.[7] Barriers to promotion may also result in poor distribution of qualified personnel, for historical factors may have enticed many able people, anxious for promotion, into a unit that is no longer expanding and may even be contracting. Only by making it possible for them to shift to other units without undue sacrifice can this defective distribution of personnel be corrected.

HOW MANY PROMOTIONS?

So far we have said nothing about the absolute number of promotions that are desirable in an organization during a given period of time. The organization can, more or less at will, increase or decrease the number of promotional openings in any department or in the organization as a whole.

The number of promotions is in part determined by the number of different wage or salary grades in existence. In an office employing 50 clericals, for example, it is possible to have, at the extremes, either none or 50 promotional steps. In practice, of course, neither would be likely. By de-emphasizing the differences in job duties, the company could place nearly all jobs in the same salary grade. Or, by carefully noting every conceivable difference between jobs, one could justify paying each employee a slightly different salary, thus making possible the 50 promotional steps.

What is the optimum number? Too few promotional steps may injure morale by eliminating the sense of personal progress and accomplishment, an important source of job satisfaction to many workers. However, unduly numerous promotional steps may be equally injurious. Not only do the distinctions become increasingly difficult to justify, but the department must constantly spend time and effort selecting the right candidate, gaining acceptance for the choice, and shifting employees. The result may be chaos.

---

[7] Why such moves should entail loss of seniority credits will be explained in the last section of this chapter.

Somewhere there is a middle ground where the unrest caused by an excessive number of shifts is kept at a minimum and where an optimal number of promotional openings remain to provide individual satisfaction. It is difficult to say just what the ideal frequency of promotions is, for there has been little research on this subject. We do know that employees often have trouble shifting from the regular semi-annual "promotions" they have been used to in school and college to the less regular pattern of promotions in industry.

In approaching this question of frequency of promotions, we must be careful to distinguish between promotion to a better job and periodic wage or salary increases. In both industry and government, fairly regular *merit increases* have become common practice. Year after year, perhaps for as long as five or six years, the employee derives a sense of progress from these "raises" which, though they are somewhat related to effort and accomplishment, are often almost automatic. Under this system, a true promotion serves to establish a higher ceiling on the regular raises.

In many salary plans, however, the top wage level in one job is actually higher than the starting level in the next higher-rated job. And, though it is highly undesirable practice, an employee is sometimes promoted to a job that carries with it added responsibilities but not a higher income. We shall return to problems of this sort after we have dealt with wage and salary administration in Chapter 24.

There is a good bit of ambiguity, particularly on professional jobs, about when an employee has actually moved to a more important job, for job definitions are often quite elastic. An engineer, for example, may be required to work on a more difficult assignment for several months before the change in his job status is officially recognized by what we would call a promotion—that is, a job title with more prestige, and the increased income that goes with it.

The distinction between an engineer doing "more responsible" work and an engineer doing somewhat "less responsible" work is often vague. The jobs of both may change over time as new projects come in and old ones are completed. When a man is officially promoted to a more responsible position may be simply a matter of supervisory judgment.

Confusion of this sort is bound to affect the employee's feelings about his rate of advancement. Often he enjoys a sense of progress for the first five or ten years in the organization, and then finds that additional progress becomes more and more difficult. The number of higher-rated jobs has diminished, and the competition for them has increased. Furthermore, a man must turn out truly outstanding work if he is to obtain recognition at the higher levels, and it becomes increasingly difficult for management to identify the really high performers. Clearly, such a situation is fraught with potential morale problems.

There are two points, then, at which crises are likely to develop: just after the transition from the school system, with its regular "promotions," to the job situation, where promotions are less assured; and after the employee has run through the course of easier, lower-level promotions. These are the times when the employee begins to wonder whether he should continue with an organization where "you can't get ahead." The organization should be alert to the likelihood that these two transition points will give trouble, and should stand ready to help individuals adjust to the realities of the situation. It is impossible to set up precise prescriptions for dealing with this problem, but it is helpful to encourage supervisors to regard the anxieties of their more ambitious subordinates during these periods as understandable and worthy of attention.

HORIZONTAL AND DOWNWARD MOVEMENTS IN THE ORGANIZATION

Life would be much simpler if all movements of employees in an organization were upward, to higher-skilled and more responsible positions. In actuality, both because of the changing needs of the company and the shifting desires of employees, there is a great deal of horizontal movement (transfers between jobs paying approximately the same rates) and downward movement (downgrading and lay-offs). In this section we shall look briefly at the reasons for these movements, but we shall concentrate on the kinds of problem they pose.

Transfer Policy

SHORT-RUN TRANSFERS

Rarely are the operations of any organization so smoothly and successfully scheduled that surpluses or shortages of personnel never develop. One of the typists is ill in the Purchasing Department; a sale of men's ties draws more customers than predicted; a machine breaks down, resulting in a surplus of machinists. What problems must be met in dealing with these short-run emergencies?

1. The employee resents being wrenched out of his normal work routines and assigned—even temporarily—to a new and unfamiliar job. In particular he objects to being forced to leave his old job uncompleted. Where possible, an employee should be allowed to come to a natural breaking point in his present job—to type to the end of the report or to fill the tote box with finished parts—before he is ordered elsewhere.

2. The employee may object to being transferred out of his old informal social group to another social group, which may well be hostile to all newcomers. To minimize this problem, the supervisor should carefully introduce the temporary employee to the group and explain why and for how long the transfer is to be made.

3. The employee may object that he is being discriminated against by being given more than his "fair share" of distasteful work. Here again the supervisor needs to remember that jobs with equal pay may not have equal social status, and he may have to rotate undesirable assignments or resort to other techniques to eliminate charges of discrimination.

4. The employee may be inadequately trained to handle the new job. For organizations that have frequent short-run transfers, the obvious solution is to train all employees to handle several jobs.

5. The employee may complain that he is being made to do work that is "out of his job description" (work that he did not expect to do on the basis of the original description of his duties)—that is, he may experience *craft-consciousness*. This problem is so serious that we shall devote a separate section to it.

CRAFT-CONSCIOUSNESS

Craft-consciousness—the feeling that no one should work outside his narrowly defined job duties—has traditionally been strong in the construction and maintenance trades. A carpenter will refuse to do any work but carpentry, and he will refuse to let other employees do carpentry work—even if this means that other employees must stand idle or be laid off.

There is considerable evidence that craft-consciousness is spreading from the building trades into industry generally. Many groups that lack the traditional craft status of the building trades are trying to erect barriers around their particular skills. The primary motivation seems to be job security, for workers feel that if they can prevent other men from doing their work, they will be able to make their own jobs more secure. Unions in general encourage craft-consciousness, because they look upon it as a means of restricting management's power to make transfers. And every time management gives in to a union demand to make craft boundaries more sacred, a "past practice" is established, which is in a sense "frozen" into the union contract.

> In one company, machinists were prohibited from picking up any material that had fallen on the floor. This was the janitors' work! Even valuable parts were sometimes swept away by the clean-up crews because the machinists refused to pick them up.

Management itself, by carrying specialization and division of labor to extremes, may be responsible for proliferating an unwieldy number of narrowly defined jobs. Employees, taking their cue from management, then proceed to erect artificial barriers that inhibit flexible transfers designed to expedite the flow of work and to even out work-load inequalities.

Where jobs are defined narrowly, each with a limited number of highly specific duties, the problem of shifting employees is accentuated. Unless management takes precautionary steps, workers will tend to erect protective barriers around their jobs.

> "I am the only girl in the office who can run this mimeograph machine. It's not easy, let me tell you; it's old and has got lots of tricks to it that it takes years to learn. I don't want other girls using it; this way I know they really need me around here. When we occasionally run out of work on the machine, I don't think it's fair for me to have to do other odd jobs. After all, this is what I am getting paid for."

At the extreme, this is the attitude of the craftsman who insists that a long apprenticeship and membership in a union be a requirement for admission to the job. But in less extreme form this attitude may develop in any job and militate against flexibility in the work force.

Reducing craft-consciousness How can management deal with excessive craft-consciousness? First, by accepting as natural the work group's efforts to protect its members. Very little is accomplished by accusing employees of "feather-bedding," for employees, like companies, are anxious to strengthen their security.

A second, more specific, way of meeting this problem is to develop new job descriptions, in which all jobs are defined in terms of the work that needs to be done rather than in terms of abstract craft skills. For example, rather than listing the traditional skills of a welder, the job description should emphasize the skills and responsibilities associated with maintaining one or more pieces of equipment. In short, job duties must be determined by the requirements of the work process, not by traditional concepts of what a craftsman is.

Of course, employees will probably resist such efforts, fearing that their skills will no longer be highly valued and that they may lose their jobs to less well-trained workers. But this resistance may be minimized by skill in introducing change (see Chapter 12). At the very least, adequate safeguards must be provided to protect employees from arbitrary treatment. The conversion of a worker from one type of job to another requires patience and time.

When the supervisor is inducting new employees, he should try to instill in them the broadest possible definition of their jobs. This is also a function of recruitment and training policy. Employees with diversified skills and good training are more easily transferred.

The usefulness of transfers is controlled by the division of labor. Obviously, as jobs become more complex and the learning period for them is lengthened, short-run transfers become more difficult. This is one of the costs the firm must take into account in introducing new methods and equipment which require highly trained employees.

There is some evidence that automation and other recent technological developments that require a smooth flow of work are tending to eliminate sharp distinctions between jobs. In order to do their work successfully, employees need to be trained in a variety of related skills. A study of a steam-generating plant recently equipped with automatic controls revealed that many of the jobs had been enlarged as a result of the new procedure:

> Each of [the new operators] is expected to have most of the skills and, especially, the knowledge and information previously held separately by the skilled boiler, turbine, and electrical operators. [These new operators] must be capable of running all of the major parts of the production system. The [lesser-skilled employees beneath their level are] . . . in the process of acquiring proficiency in all operations.[8]

Under a program like this, we would expect that the transfer problem would be significantly reduced, because the employees are no longer divided up into pockets of specialists who must be transferred formally to meet the demands of scheduling. Furthermore, since automation requires that all parts of the system function at approximately the same level of activity, the need to shift personnel from one job to another is reduced. Instead, the individual worker allocates more time to one function and less to another, *within* his own job, and no formal changes in assignment are necessary.

LONGER-RUN TRANSFERS

So far, we have been talking about temporary changes in job assignment necessitated by the normal day-to-day problems of scheduling, workload balancing, and breakdown. Transfers may also be used to solve more enduring problems.

Remedial transfer   The most obvious use of this sort of transfer is to shift an employee who has failed to make a satisfactory adjustment to his job—perhaps as the result of faulty assignment or of a personality conflict with the supervisor or another employee. Transferring the employee to another department may be the most satisfactory solution to the problem.

A word of caution, however: There are many possible reasons for a worker's poor performance. His supervisor may be doing a poor job; he may be suffering from inadequate training or inconsistent discipline; or he may be the target of prejudice or petty discrimination within the work group. Under these circumstances a remedial transfer may be a mistake because the conditions that caused the problem will persist and lead to future problems, even more serious ones.

At the other extreme, management may have to encourage supervisors to request remedial transfers by assuring them that they will not be criticized for recognizing and rectifying mistakes in placement.

---

[8] Floyd C. Mann and L. R. Hoffman, "Individual and Organizational Correlates of Automation," *Journal of Social Issues*, Vol. XII, No. 2 (1956), pp. 12-13.

Changing manpower needs   Changes in the over-all organization may also create a need for long-run transfers. With shifts in technology or in the company's pattern of business, the manpower needs of some departments may decline while the needs of other departments increase. In order to safeguard the jobs of long-service employees and to avoid losing the skills of trained personnel, most companies make every attempt to transfer employees to other jobs. Moreover, a company that follows a liberal transfer policy and provides retraining for employees who are transferred to new jobs has less difficulty in introducing technological and organization changes.

Downward Movements: Seniority and Layoffs

Jobs cannot be absolutely guaranteed in a free economy. When layoffs are necessary, some priority system is needed to determine who will lose his job first. (Of course, an employee who is laid off usually has hopes of regaining his job when business improves, but we shall discuss this expectation later in detail.)

Most employers probably would prefer to give major weight to *ability* in determining which employees to retain and which to lay off during periods of declining business activity or labor surplus. However, largely because of union pressure, *seniority* is the primary factor considered in unionized companies and to a considerable extent in non-unionized concerns as well. Even so, there is pressure from management for some exclusions from the hard-and-fast seniority rules, and union contracts sometimes permit small groups of employees (e.g., 10 per cent) who would otherwise be laid off, to keep their jobs during layoffs.

CALCULATING LENGTH OF SERVICE: SENIORITY SYSTEMS

Even when a company and union agree that seniority shall be the main factor considered in deciding on layoffs, the question remains: How shall seniority be calculated? This is a deceptively simple question. Here are several possible answers:

1. Seniority is the length of time an employee has worked for the company ("company-wide seniority").

2. Or seniority is the length of time an employee has worked in a particular department of the company ("department seniority").

3. Or seniority is the length of time an employee has held a specific job in a particular department of the company ("job seniority").

The method by which seniority or length of service is calculated obviously has a significant effect on which employee is laid off when, for example, there is a surplus of clerical help in the Accounts Receivable Department.

The "youngest" employee (with least seniority) under formula 1 might be a recently hired stenographer in the Engineering Department of the Company. The employee with the least amount of service in the company within the Accounts Receivable Department might be transferred into the Engineering Department to take the job of the laid-off stenographer.

The employee with least service under formula 2 might be a secretary who has been with the company for several years, but who recently transferred into the department when an opening occurred. (She will probably regret having shifted jobs!)

Under formula 3, the company would be required to lay off the youngest employee doing the specific clerical job in the Accounts Receivable Department where the surplus existed.

Bumping At this point we must introduce another complication: *bumping*. The application of seniority principles to a situation where a company has a surplus employee does not imply that only one employee moves from his job. A whole series of moves may be generated by the requirement for a single layoff.

Let us look again at our earlier example. Under formula 2, the following would be a typical sequence of events: The Accounts Receivable Department has too many stenographers. The stenographer with the least service in the department would lose her job. However, she would have the privilege of taking another job she could perform in the department which is currently held by an employee with less department service than her own. Thus, the girl first displaced might "bump" a tabulating clerk with less service. In turn, the tabulating clerk may find that there is a file clerk with even less seniority than hers, and she will exercise her privilege of taking that job. The process repeats itself as long as employees who are displaced can find other workers with less seniority than themselves occupying jobs that they are able to perform. Larger companies find that cutbacks in manpower may generate thousands of job shifts, which in turn create massive record-keeping and personnel problems. Since every employee is anxious to safeguard his own interests, shifts of this sort are bound to provoke countless grievances and complaints about alleged inequities in the demotions. In actual practice the seniority rights of a given employee are often ambiguous.

SELECTING FROM AMONG ALTERNATIVE SENIORITY SYSTEMS

Which seniority system is best from the point of view of the firm? Unfortunately there is no simple answer; it depends on the circumstances. However, there are certain criteria that management can apply in arriving at a solution.[9]

---

[9] We estimate that, in practice, perhaps one-third of the companies that weigh seniority in matters of tenure do so on the basis of departmental service, about one-third use plant-wide or company-wide service, and the balance have a system combining elements of both and perhaps job seniority as well.

Reducing frequency of movement   One criterion to apply in evaluating a seniority system is whether or not it will minimize the frequency of job-shifting. Shifts create grievances, and they also give rise to training and efficiency problems. Although management may require that an employee be able to perform the job for which he exercises his "bumping" privileges, making an accurate measure of competent performance is subject to the same ambiguity and disagreement that surround the appraisal of merit and ability. Under the pressure of events, employee job shifts inevitably result in workers being displaced from jobs which they do efficiently and being placed on jobs for which their performance is marginal. "Bumping" works best when the movement takes place down a promotional ladder and where everyone in the department has worked his way up from the bottom jobs. In summary, to satisfy this criterion, management often favors a relatively "narrow" seniority unit, as suggested by formula 2 or 3 above.

Retaining valuable employees   The use of these "narrow" seniority units may be costly to the company, however. Assume that the need for machinists has declined temporarily. Under a system of job seniority, the company would be required to lay off machinists with long training and experience. Then, when the present period had passed, expensive recruiting and training would be required to acquire new machinists. Obviously, management would like to shift these employees to other jobs, and allow less valuable employees, on less skilled jobs, to be laid off. Many times some form of department seniority is a good compromise solution to a problem of this sort.

Encouraging requisite mobility   In our earlier discussion of transfer policy, we saw that employees evaluated the effect of a transfer on their job security. "Narrow" seniority units militate against transfers, for seniority is transferable. Thus, where a company must depend on horizontal employee movements to provide a flexible work force, it needs "wider" seniority units: department or company-wide seniority.

Providing equity   Management is also concerned with making equitable decisions. Fairness is important for its own sake, and also for the sake of employee morale. What is equitable, however, may not be easy to determine.

In theory, employees and unions favor "wider" or more inclusive seniority units than does management, on the grounds of equity. They argue that it is unfair to lay off employees with 15 years of seniority in one department, when there are employees with only one year of service in another department. Unions have sometimes sought corporation-wide seniority agreements to enable an employee whose job is terminated in one company location to shift to another; on occasion, they have even demanded that moving expenses be provided.

In actual practice, employees very often favor narrow units much as management does, only for quite different reasons. All the non-managerial employees of a company are not bound together in a single homogeneous group with unified goals and common interests, even when they are union-ized. Rather, employees tend to cluster into informal groups, many of which are organized around the job itself. Because the employee tends to consider his job as a piece of "property," even though management has a very different interpretation, he seeks out the help of his fellow workers who share the same or nearby jobs to help him protect this valued possession. The result often is a demand for a very narrow seniority unit. This is in direct conflict, of course, with the more orthodox union view toward senior-ity: the protection of the longest-service employee. The drive for security is a strong one, however, and it frequently triumphs over more philosophical beliefs, such as "equity." [10]

Special problems of equity and seniority. The importance of seniority and the careful calculations of self-interest that go into employee decisions impinging on this area are revealed by the following case:

> In the ABC Chemical Company, John Jones was seriously injured in an explosion. The company sought to transfer him, after his recovery, to a department where the resulting physical impairments would not be as much of a handicap to him as they were in his present job. The workers in the new department, even though they were aware of the reason for the transfer, filed a grievance that their rights were being endangered. Since plant-wide, not departmental, seniority determined eligibility for layoffs, and this injured worker had very long service, each of the employees with less service felt that his position and job security would be worsened by this move.

Either management or the union may seek modifications in existing senior-ity regulations when changes in technology or in the company's business threaten whole groups or departments with loss of their jobs.

> The Furst Corporation is eliminating its consumer product lines. Under the terms of the existing union-management agreement, even employees with 30 years of service expecting to retire in six months or a year will have to be laid off since the seniority clauses forbid interdepartment "bumping." Recently hired young men in adjacent departments will retain their jobs while these senior employees are separated.

These are very delicate problems of equity and contract. The union finds it difficult to make up its own mind on what to ask the company, because inevitably some of its members will be injured and others will benefit.

Thus the criterion of seniority is a two-edged sword. It represents a vic-tory over management: namely, the elevation of length of service to the prime

---

[10] For a survey of the machinations of work groups seeking to manipulate seniority provisions of the union-management contract to increase their job security, see L. Sayles, "Seniority: An Internal Union Problem," *Harvard Business Review,* Vol. XXX, No. 1 (January-February 1952), pp. 55-61.

determinant of job security. But simultaneously, winning this guarantee opens the door to countless problems of what constitutes the appropriate seniority unit; and many of these problems create major internal conflicts for the union as its members struggle with one another to improve their relative position.

Swift return to normal production   After the need for layoffs has passed, management seeks to return to normal production as quickly as possible. Naturally, key employees must be the first to be recalled. The operation of the seniority system tends to insure that they are the first by specifying that those who were laid off last will be the first to be called back.[11] Presumably the more senior workers will have held the more important positions. This correlation is not always a perfect one, however, and management frequently asks for exceptions to the regular recall procedure. It may prove more efficient, for example, to recall employees whose skills are essential to the resumption of production, even though they are not the most senior workers.

A quick return to normality also demands that the employees who were laid off are standing by waiting to be recalled. When the cutback is temporary, chances are that most of them will still be available when they are needed again. But when layoffs are prolonged, many valuable employees are lost for good because they find permanent employment elsewhere. The most ambitious, well-qualified workers are those most likely to be lost, of course.

TERMINATION OR LAYOFF?

When a layoff is permanent, or when it is assumed to be so, management has a responsibility to inform the employee of this fact. The union will scrutinize such layoffs carefully to insure that the company has not eliminated a job as a device to discharge an unsatisfactory employee whom it was reluctant to discipline through normal channels.

Most union-management agreements and company policies specify that an employee's right to be recalled, with a priority determined by his length of service, will not continue beyond one or two years. Thus, if the layoff persists for this length of time, the employee also loses his claim to other employment benefits associated with accrued service. If he is rehired, he will come back as a new employee.

It is becoming increasingly common for companies to pay some *severance* or *termination* allowance when an employee loses his job through no fault of his own. This allowance, usually based on a formula that increases with

---

[11] This last out-first back method means that newer employees are most directly exposed to the threat of unemployment—another reason why employees seek to build up seniority.

length of service, assists the employee during the period in which he is seeking new employment.

REDUCED HOURS OR LAYOFFS?

Depending on the nature of the work process and the number of surplus workers, a company can sometimes choose between reducing the workweek for everyone or else laying off the least senior employees, keeping the remainder fully employed. Sharing work—which is what reduced working hours implies—means in effect that unemployment is distributed equally. Depending on circumstances, this may or may not be an advantage to the firm. Sometimes the exact procedure is specified in the union-management agreement, thus eliminating the need for a discretionary decision. These agreements often require that working hours will be cut back to some minimum figure—for example, 30 hours per week—after which time, if there is still a surplus of manpower, layoffs will begin.

What criteria does management use in deciding which procedure to favor? The nature of the industry itself is a critical factor in this decision. A department store could not arbitrarily reduce the hours it is open to the public without seriously damaging its business. Other firms have more flexibility in resorting to a reduced schedule when business warrants.

Naturally enough, longer-service employees are likely to pressure for the laying off of short-service personnel, in an effort to secure higher income for themselves. This is another potential area for internal union conflict, and the frictions generated here, if not quickly attended to, may spill over and affect production and efficiency.

Sometimes it is desirable to resist laying off any workers at all, particularly if the firm can predict that the need for reduced manpower will be short-lived. Such restraint minimizes the direct and indirect costs of employee movements, and eliminates the risk of losing good workers to other employers during the layoff period.

The availability and the magnitude of *unemployment insurance* benefits may also influence the choice between laying off employees and reducing work hours.[12] At some point it becomes more desirable, from the point of view of the employee, to accept these insurance benefits and avoid the expenses and effort associated with reporting to work for relatively brief periods.

---

[12] At the present time, about 80 per cent of all non-agricultural employees are covered by joint federal-state unemployment insurance. Employers pay up to 3 per cent of their payroll to the plan, a percentage of which goes to the federal government, which in turn reimburses the states for their expenses in operating the plan. The participation of the federal government is designed to insure uniformity among the benefits paid by the states. The benefits paid are geared to the previous period of employment and the amount of earnings of the laid-off employee. For many firms, these payments are supplemented by special funds created in collective bargaining, *supplementary unemployment benefits*. which are designed to increase the income of laid-off workers.

Regularization of Employment

Many of the state unemployment insurance plans, as well as company-sponsored supplementary benefit plans, are designed to penalize the employer with a record of unstable employment. In addition, the process of laying off and rehiring is expensive to administer, and valuable employees may eventually be lost to other employers. Changes in employment levels involve shifts of workers within and between departments, with the attendant costs of retraining and supervision. Just the fear of layoff may encourage employees to consider "stretching out the work" as they mark time, waiting to see "who will be the next to go." Disagreements over seniority criteria result in costly, time-consuming grievances.

All these possibilities provide a stimulus for the firm to seek means of avoiding employment instability. While external market fluctuations may be beyond the company's control, there are internal management measures that may minimize the impact of economic conditions. The following represent a sample of some of the techniques currently utilized by progressive firms seeking to attain this objective:

1. Try to develop a more flexible work force through careful selection and training, supplemented by contractual provisions that permit relatively free transfers between departments.

2. Avoid hiring permanent workers to meet the needs of peak volume periods. Use temporary employees in such periods so that layoffs of permanent employees will not be necessary when the peak passes.

3. Take on additional products or service lines whose variable demand will complement the demand for existing products. For example, if peak demand occurs in the summer, seek products that are used primarily during the winter months.

4. Explore the possibility of improved warehousing practices during periods of slack demand, and offer new incentives for customers to stockpile during normally slow periods or order longer in advance.

5. Contract-out work that would require the employment of new people who might not be needed when the job is completed—for example, maintenance or construction work.[13]

With effective administration of such programs, the company may find that it can extend certain guarantees of full employment over the year to a significant number of its employees (e.g., those with at least five years of employment). When management is able to tell employees that they are not being hired by the hour, the week, or even the month, but on the basis of a

---

[13] For a survey of the problems involved in using this method, see Margaret Chandler and Leonard Sayles, *Contracting-Out: A Study of Management Decision-Making* (New York: Graduate School of Business, Columbia University, 1959).

much longer term, many of the insecurities associated with the employment relationship disappear.[14] Restriction of output, resistance to technological change, and many union-management conflicts stem from employee fears that their jobs and livelihood will be endangered by management activities. Blue-collar workers particularly are sensitive to their inferior status and are jealous of the white-collar employee who is hired on the basis of a monthly salary or an annual salary.

Of course, caution must be exercised to insure that such guarantees do not commit the firm beyond its capacity to stabilize production—particularly in the more volatile segments of industry. The effect of extending such assurances can be estimated by looking at past employment records and by evaluating the effect of future activities on the regularizing of employment.[15]

Conclusion

Only at great peril can a company neglect the development of adequate policies governing promotion, transfer, and layoff. These areas affect the vital processes of the firm as well as employee motivation.

The effectiveness of these policies determines whether or not the firm will be able to draw on an available reservoir of adequate manpower. Each company needs to strike a balance between internal sources of personnel (through promotion) for higher-rated positions and external sources (through recruitment). Similarly, it must strike a balance between merit and ability as against length of service as criteria for promotability. The inevitable changes in personnel requirements that arise among departments and in the firm as a whole must be prepared for by means of well-planned transfer and layoff procedures. The firm that fails to develop satisfactory procedures must be prepared to pay a severe penalty in terms of administrative costs, misallocation of personnel, low morale, and ineffectual performance, both among nonmanagerial employees and their supervisors.

Unfortunately, these are not problems that can be solved once and then forgotten. All the policies we have discussed must undergo constant revision in light of shifts in the company's business and in the type and location of employees working in the organization. Finally, as we noted particularly in the case of seniority policies, few rules or systems provide automatic answers to specific employee grievances or specific managerial decisions. Only through untiring concentration on personnel matters and through careful, intelligent investigation and assessment can management cope with the ambiguities inherent in matters of promotion, transfer, and layoff.

---

[14] See Fred H. Blum, *Toward a Democratic Work Process: The Hormel-Packinghouse Workers Experiment* (New York: Harpers, 1953).

[15] See A.D.H. Kaplan, *The Guarantee of Annual Wages* (Washington: Brookings Institution, 1947).

next time

Problem I

When Bill Jones, with six years' seniority, was promoted to the position of straw boss, Al Smith complained. Smith, with fourteen years in the department, argued that he could do the job himself, and furthermore the company in the past has promoted the senior man to such jobs.

As divisional superintendent, you are notified by the Industrial Relations Department that a union grievance is pending. Here are the two sides of the case:

Supervisor's argument: The job of straw boss requires good judgment in making work assignments. Jones has held the job temporarily several times and has demonstrated this competence. Smith, on the other hand, some years ago in another department, failed when he was promoted to a foreman's position. His records were always "mixed up"; he used poor judgment in requesting repair help, assignment of men, and so forth. Furthermore, Smith is not a good "leader" from the point of view of his own colleagues. He was appointed to fill a vacancy as a union steward, but was not elected when he ran at the next regular election.

Smith's argument: He has never been given a chance to try out as a leader— Jones always was given these chances. His "failure" took place ten years ago when he was young and less mature. The supervisor has never criticized his work; the company and the supervisor are discriminating against him because of his union record. While he was steward, he fought through many difficult grievances that embarrassed management. He lost the election because he was Polish and a majority of the department are of Italian descent. In general, it is company practice to promote by seniority unless there are overwhelming reasons favoring the less senior man, although the contract states that management will give substantial weight to merit and ability and will use seniority as a criterion only when there are no significant differences in ability.

1. How would you investigate this case?
2. What further information would you need? How would you assess the facts you now have?
3. What responsibilities does the supervisor have in this case?
4. What criteria would you use in making your decision?

While you are evaluating this situation, the Industrial Relations Department reports the following comments to you—from another company supervisor in a different department:

"Sure, our union contract says that management can promote the employee with the most ability, and only when there are no substantial differences do we have to take the most senior. But try and do it! I have tried it. The men get together and almost force the oldest guy to file a grievance, and then the union opens up on you. As a supervisor, you are put into the position of having to come up with solid-gold proof that the senior man isn't as good as the man you selected, and believe me, it is hard to get such proof. Sure there are no problems when the older man has been constantly absent, drunk, or a troublemaker. But if he has 'kept his nose clean,' the union can put up an awfully good case that you are discriminating against him for something he did 15 years ago. Then during the grievance procedure your relations with the rest of the men in the department are strained; it's like a cold war. In the end, the Industrial Relations Department may reverse your decision anyhow because they feel that they can't win the case in arbitration or for some other reason. Then you swallow your pride and take the man off the better job whom you promoted (and is he upset!), and put the other guy on the job whom you first turned down—and his feelings toward you are nothing to write home about either. Your reward for following the contract out to the letter of the law is poor morale and a lot of lost time for yourself in grievance meetings, and in the Industrial Relations Department. Do you blame me for taking the easy way out?"

1. Does this statement alter your evaluation of the case?
2. As the divisional superintendent in this company, how concerned would you be if these sentiments were prevalent in the organization?
3. If you wanted to change the situation, what steps would you take?
4. Does the prevailing situation mean that the union-management contract is not really a contract?

Problem II

Myers was a mechanical engineer himself before being promoted to supervise a department of engineers. The new job provided a great deal of challenge. Time, however, was always a problem. While Myers believed in delegation, he couldn't resist getting involved in the technical problems of the work in his department, and this took time away from the daily round of administrative questions that came to him, largely on personnel and scheduling problems. Therefore, when Myers found that one of his subordinates, a young engineer by the name of Thompson, was eager to take on new responsibilities and handled them well, he began assigning certain administrative detail work to him. Thompson filled the job of assistant supervisor, which appeared nowhere on the department's organization chart, and he handled many of the work-assignment decisions and relationships with other departments.

After four months, in which this informal arrangement had worked well in relieving the pressures on Myers, the supervisor requested a formal promotion for Thompson to a managerial job classification. While Myers' superiors were willing to add an additional manager to the division, they turned down Thompson as being too inexperienced and lacking in adequate formal education (Thompson did not have a college degree).

Myers was left with a difficult problem. He could not get a salary increase or change in status for Thompson, although he had pressured for this. Should he take away the additional duties from Thompson, although his subordinate did not request him to do so, or should he encourage him to seek a job in another division of the company that would recognize his managerial capacities and not discriminate against him for his lack of a college degree?

1. What should Myers' decision be?
2. Did Myers handle the informal upgrading of Thompson appropriately? (Remember that Thompson liked his administrative work, wanted additional responsibility and was, in fact, receiving good training.)
3. Are there circumstances that justify a "promotion" without a commensurate increase in income and status?

Problem III

The Frank Home Oil Service has had a long-standing tradition of promotion from within, largely on the basis of length of service. Men were hired as laborers and moved up through several promotional ladders to higher-paying positions, including maintenance work. Older workers typically "bid" on the mechanics' jobs when there were openings, because this work was easier than delivery and pumping jobs. Recently the company became concerned that its maintenance mechanics were less skilled than those of its competitors. As new and more complicated equipment was purchased, the company found itself without adequate maintenance personnel.

The company was finally able to negotiate an agreement with the union permitting it to use aptitude tests in selecting new mechanics. The steady stream of older workers bidding on these jobs was now halted. To fill openings as they occurred, the company for the first time was able to go outside the organization and hire young trade-school graduates who quickly learned the requisite skills. Over time the older mechanics who had come into their jobs "unscreened" were shifted to the less-skilled work in the department—largely building-maintenance work.

The immediate problem is that declining business is forcing a cutback in the size of the maintenance department. Normally, department seniority is used to determine who will be laid off. The result in this case will be that nearly all of the relatively new and more able younger mechanics will be laid off, except those who have enough seniority to "bump" the few unskilled laborers in the department. The company fears that its maintenance work will be crippled, and that a good share of the mechanics will leave the company permanently to take jobs elsewhere.

1. How would you analyze the company's problem? What mistakes have been made that other organizations can profit from?

2. What are the alternative solutions, and how would you go about trying to put any of them into effect?

Problem IV

Bill Allen accepted a new promotion with mixed feelings. He was proud of having his work recognized, but he had some doubts about how he would like the new work. His former job had involved regular contacts with salesmen—trouble-shooting, helping them with special customer problems, and so on. His new job in market research was essentially a research job, working with population data, industry marketing reports, and the like.

Bill missed the routine of his old office and the men he had worked with. He had a private office now, but he felt he really did not have the educational background for the job. When he submitted his first report, the division head was nice enough—suggesting some changes that in fact meant that Bill had really used the wrong approach. His boss said not to worry, "We all have to learn a new job." The more Bill thought about it, the more he wanted to go back to the old job. But he hesitated for fear that he would be considered a failure by management and thus disqualified for any further promotion.

1. If you were Bill's boss, what could you do to correct this situation?

2. What would your objectives be?

3. Could this situation have been avoided altogether? How?

The efficiency of any organization depends directly on the ability of its members to do their job—that is, on their training. Newly hired employees almost always need some training before they can take up their work, while older employees require training both to keep them alert to the demands of their present job and to fit them for transfers and promotions.

Training also motivates employees to work harder. Employees who understand their jobs and what is expected of them are likely to have higher morale. And the very fact that management is confident enough of their abilities to invest in training provides a sense of assurance that they are valued members of the organization. This is particularly important in dynamic companies undergoing changes in technology and methods. Such changes as automation are resisted when workers fear that they will not be competent to assume the new jobs that are being created.

For these reasons, American companies spend enormous amounts on training. In this chapter we shall be concerned with technical training, and in Chapter 24 with management training.

Technical Training

Training complements selection. If the personnel department can recruit well-qualified candidates, there will be less need for training inside the organization, if it can recruit only poorly qualified candidates, then training must try to fill the gap. And yet training cannot do everything, for some candidates may be so poorly qualified that they lack the ability to learn.

Because of differences in company rules, equipment, and methods, it is rare to find jobs that are absolutely identical in any two organizations. A journeyman printer, a bricklayer, or an actor, however, may move from one organization to another with a minimum amount of training. Some industries, in fact—such as construction, the maritime trades, the theater, and, to a lesser extent, industries with fluctuating employment levels like printing and clothing manufacture—can count on drawing fully qualified employees from an industry-wide pool and therefore do little training themselves. At the other end of the spectrum are companies with highly unique jobs that have no counterpart in any other organization. For example, the XYZ Mills are having a special processing unit built to their order, and the crew chief in charge will have to undergo extensive training before being qualified to operate the new equipment.

The Nature of Training

At one extreme, training consists of a few hours (or only a few minutes) of induction by the supervisor, who gives the new employee a skeleton outline of company policies, the location of the locker room, and a summary of work rules. At the other extreme, training consists of formal courses designed to develop qualified specialists over a period of years. In between these extremes are countless programs tailored to fit the needs of particular organizations: short courses on local safety hazards, or on customer uses of company products or services; instruction in writing sales slips or insurance policies; and courses in sales techniques, automobile repair, mechanical drawing, or internal auditing.

But it is misleading to think of job training purely in terms of formal courses and programs. Almost everything that happens to an employee after he joins a company serves as a training experience. That is to say, the worker learns what is expected of him in a new situation through the experiences he undergoes. Those elements in an employee's repertoire of behavior that are rewarded and thus provide him with satisfaction tend to be repeated; those that are punished tend to be abandoned.

There are many people within the organization who provide these rewards and punishments in addition to those who are formally assigned to train employees. The informal work group, with its clearly defined codes of behavior, has a potent influence on its members; formal groups like the union also exert a strong effect. Many times the supervisor may be training his subordinates without even being aware of it. The acts that provoke discipline or that fail to provoke discipline tell an employee what is expected of him and what he can do with impunity. Good housekeeping practices that are praised and slovenly workmanship that goes uncriticized both serve as a source of training. Similarly, the methods, short cuts, and routines practiced by fellow employees all carry important meanings that are assimilated by the novice as he makes his way in a new job situation.

The training derived from all these informal sources may be in sharp conflict with the prescribed ways of doing things. But it is the sources of information and advice that prove most consistent and most satisfying that will have the most profound effect on the employee. So management must be careful to see that the impact of casual, day-to-day experiences does not nullify the practices stressed in the more formal training sessions.

Who Should Train?

In many companies training is very informal. It consists of assigning new employees as helpers to old employees, or telling an old employee to "show this fellow what he should do." At times the results are excellent, but often the old-timer fails to train adequately. Sometimes the failure reflects the old-timer's indifference or even hostility to "breaking in a new employee," a job he feels he isn't being paid to do or that may create a competitor for his own job. More often, the old-timer fails because he is unable to communicate and lacks systematic knowledge of learning principles.

Increasingly, management is making formal provision for training, either through holding line management directly responsible or by hiring training specialists, and sometimes both. Sometimes these training specialists report directly to line management; more frequently, a special training section is established in the personnel department.

As a staff expert, of course, the training specialist faces the problems of staff men everywhere: line management may resent his efforts as interference; he may try to teach employees methods that conflict with those their boss wants them to use (either because in practice line doesn't follow standard company procedures, or because the trainer has not kept pace with developments "out on the floor"). Conflicts often arise when the training specialist insists on telling employees who are under the direction of line supervisors, how they should do their job. Equally unfortunate, once a training specialist has been appointed, the line supervisor may decide to pass the buck and give up all responsibility for training. Some companies have tried to create an amicable division of responsibilities by having the staff trainer conduct classes off the work floor and advising the line supervisor on how to do better training on the floor (in a sense the staff trains the trainers), and by holding the line supervisor responsible for all training in production areas.

Even when staff assistants are available, however, the main burden of training must fall on the supervisor. Each time there is a change in the work situation workers have to adjust. Whether it is called "training" or not, nearly every instruction or correction given by the supervisor is a form of training, and the more familiar he is with the principles of learning, the better will be the results of this training.

Types of Training Program

INDUCTION TRAINING

Progressive companies have long recognized the need for properly introducing a new employee to his job. Not only do they familiarize him with the tasks he will be expected to perform, but they also provide him with information about company rules and personnel policies, introduce him to his fellow workers, and give him an idea of where his job fits into the total operation of the organization. A carefully planned orientation-induction program helps the new employee to identify with the organization and its procedures and gives him some feeling for the significance of the work he will be doing. Efforts of this sort contribute substantially to his future job satisfaction and help him overcome the fears and anxieties that are bound to arise on a new job.

Unfortunately, the busy, hard-pressed supervisor tends to neglect what he considers the mere formalities of induction training and concentrates exclusively on the immediate job assignment. Haste and lack of sensitivity at this early stage, however, will spawn unnecessary personnel problems later on.

> Mary was hired as a secretary in the Purchasing Department. She came to the company fully trained and with eight years of experience in similar work. The supervisor told her the first day that he was sure the work she would be doing was comparable to what she had done elsewhere and that she would have no trouble mastering the "details of the job." During her fifth week of employment, the supervisor asked her to assist the girls in the adjacent mimeograph room in collating processed materials, explaining that it was their usual practice to have the secretaries "pitch in" when they had the time and there was an overload in another work group. Mary immediately resented what appeared to her to be an unfair imposition on her time and energy. Furthermore, the additional work was "degrading," because it required little skill. Mary quit shortly thereafter, primarily because she believed the supervisor was taking advantage of her by assigning her "extra work," when she had worked hard to complete her regular work.

Where employee duties are clearly and completely described at the outset, such misunderstandings are unlikely to develop. Furthermore, proper induction training makes it unnecessary for the employee to unlearn methods and procedures that prove unacceptable. Unlearning is both difficult and time-consuming.

Realistically, of course, no supervisor can expect to communicate everything about a new job at the outset. And some of the information he presents is bound to seem meaningless and confusing to the inexperienced subordinate, who simply has not had enough experience to appreciate the significance of what is being told him. Cashier trainees in department stores report that they found much of their induction training meaningless because, never having been on the job, they knew nothing of the situations to which the information would apply. Once they had gone out on the job, however, and started receiving mutilated, faulty sales slips, they felt a need for the training they had once felt was worthless. Clearly, if the employee is to be given useful training early in his work experience, some attempt must be made to simulate actual on-the-job problems. Only then will information on "what to do if this problem occurs" be worth while.

VESTIBULE TRAINING

Supervision must make another important decision in training the new employee: Should the training take place in the normal work location or off the job?

Where the job is difficult, where mistakes or slowness will materially impair production schedules or methods, and where very special coaching is required, off-the-job or *vestibule training* is called for. On certain jobs, placing the new employee in the work situation immediately would endanger his own safety and the welfare of others, and would risk damage to costly equipment.

So-called "simulation devices" are an invaluable form of vestibule training. For example, Link Trainers permit novice pilots to learn how to handle complex problems of instrument flying without ever leaving the ground. Experiments are being conducted to develop comparable equipment that will simulate the controls of utility generating stations and complex automation equipment. With training devices of this sort, the trainee can run through typical problems and crises without danger, and management can evaluate his performance and reaction time. The learner is shielded from the pressure of the actual job situation and the demands of supervisors who are primarily interested in getting out production.

While the logic of off-the-job training is apparent, it does have certain disadvantages. Many skills simply cannot be learned in "slow motion." In effect, doing a task slowly may transform it into an entirely different kind of task; this is particularly true of certain difficult muscular-sensory coordination jobs. Also the noise and other distractions of the real work-place may be factors that the trainee must learn to accommodate, just as he must also master specific body motions and intellectual responses. Finally vestibule training is expensive to administer, and the employee is being taught by instructors who will not work with him and evaluate his performance when he moves on to the actual job.

REMEDIAL TRAINING

When an employee fails to measure up to established standards, his performance may signal the need for additional training. Over time, an employee may forget the methods and procedures he learned during the induction process, or he may neglect correct techniques in favor of slipshod short cuts that require less energy and thought. Or management itself may introduce new procedures and equipment that alter the employee's job. Thus training is not a one-step process; it is a continuing responsibility of supervision.

Training employees with some experience on the job may be a more difficult task than giving them induction training, however. They may resent being told that they can't do their job, or may suspect that the training is an attempt to "show them up," perhaps for disciplinary reasons, or to step up output—all at their expense. Telling an employee that he needs remedial training may embarrass him before his colleagues, for it is an implied threat to his status as an intelligent, competent workman.

As an alternative to remedial training for individuals, some companies use regular refresher courses in such areas as safety, job methods, and housekeeping. This practice avoids spotlighting the poor performers and may head off the tendency to slip into less effective methods and short cuts which injure quality and quantity. Periodic training also permits the regular introduction of new methods and techniques. New accounting practices, new company products or engineering standards, new equipment—all require explanation. If these explanations are presented regularly, the possibility that important changes will be overlooked is substantially reduced.

ADVANCEMENT TRAINING

Effective training may also serve as a mechanism for mobility within the organization by enabling individuals to climb promotional ladders to more responsible and better jobs. (Of course, this is the function of all education in a free society: to permit individuals to advance on the basis of their merit and ability.) Careful ordering of jobs in promotional ladders also permits individuals to learn, primarily through observation, some of the skills of higher-ranked positions while doing their present jobs. Filling-in for higher-ranked colleagues during vacations or absences also provides a type of informal on-the-job training.

Many companies have developed their own school program. Organizations that employ skilled tradesmen like machinists or printers, for example, may conduct formal apprenticeship programs. Here, on-the-job training, directed by skilled journeymen, is supplemented by classroom and laboratory activities supervised by trained instructors. Smaller companies that cannot afford programs of their own often join together to sponsor community-wide training programs, usually in collaboration with unions and the public-school system.[1]

Trade unions that represent skilled craftsmen also have a strong interest in the formulation and conduct of training programs. Above all, they want to keep down the number of men trained, so that excessive competition for job opportunities can be avoided.[2] In fact, many agreements specify a definite ratio between the number of journeymen and apprentices, thus limiting the number of trainees.[3]

After World War II a long, bitter dispute took place in the automobile industry, both within the unions and between the unions and management. Employees who had been upgraded to skilled tradesmen's jobs during the war, and who had learned their skills without going through the formally prescribed apprenticeship program, sought to maintain the status they had earned. Employees who had completed formal apprenticeship programs contested the rights of these "upgraders" to claim skilled tradesmen's status.

Advancement training is not limited to the skilled trades, however. For example, companies employing accountants and engineers find that employees need training that will enable them to advance more rapidly. Accordingly, they make available special courses in financial policy or nuclear physics taught by specialists within the company or by teachers from nearby schools. Other companies provide their salesmen with an opportunity to learn more about the technical problems associated with their customers' organizations and with the products they sell.

In recent years, more and more formal education has been required of hospital nurses; as a result, many nurses who received their training years ago are no longer qualified for promotion. Some hospitals have tried to correct this injustice by giving older nurses extra time off so that they can take additional training. This training does not guarantee that they will be promoted, but it puts them on an equal footing with younger nurses and it enables hospitals to take advantage of the older nurses' years of experience.

In mass-production companies, employee resistance to technological change has been reduced by company guarantees that retraining opportunities will provide equivalent jobs for workers displaced by new equipment. Older employees, of course, may still fear that they will not be able to absorb the new

---

[1] See "BAT and Community Apprenticeship Programs," *The Journal of the American Society of Training Directors* (November 1958). The Federal Bureau of Apprenticeship and Training works closely with state and local agencies to encourage training of all sorts.

[2] See George Strauss, *Unions in the Building Trades* (Buffalo, N.Y.: University of Buffalo, 1958), Chapter 3.

[3] *Ibid.*, p. 10.

knowledge, particularly when the training program assumes previous education, such as high-school mathematics.

Forward-looking companies have also discovered that they can encourage self-development by paying part or all of the tuition charges incurred by employees taking special courses after hours or on leaves of absence. These payments are made both for vocational courses offered in high schools and trade schools, and for college credits.

Two policy questions arise when a company utilizes these types of advancement training. Perhaps the most obvious has to do with the economics of training. How much can a company afford to spend on developing employees who may leave at any time, permitting another firm to harvest the fruits of the effort? Some companies have no choice in this matter: their needs are so acute and the supply of trained personnel so meager that training programs are an absolute necessity. For other companies such training is optional; these firms must insure that their wage and salary levels, the quality of their supervision, and their working conditions are sufficiently attractive to hold trained personnel. They cannot assume that their employees' gratitude for the training received will outbalance genuine disadvantages. In fact, those employees who are most ambitious and most eager to grasp educational opportunities are the very ones who will be most alert to other job offers.[4]

Evidence provided by recent studies of the job histories of apprentices is somewhat encouraging, however. Not only do most apprentices continue in the trade for which they are trained, but a high proportion have worked for only one employer since completing their apprenticeship.[5]

The second policy decision has to do with the amount of "credit" the company will assign to an employee who has successfully completed a training program, particularly if the training has been taken during uncompensated time. Should those who undertake extra training be guaranteed advancement in preference to those who do not elect to do so? If so, all employees should be made aware of the policy and its implications. In one organization, we observed that certain off-premises, evening courses were designated as "voluntary" and "optional," although attendance was a prerequisite to promotion.

Principles and Techniques of Training

Whatever type of training management decides to provide, it can insure high-quality results only by paying attention to the principles of learning,

---

[4] This is the continuing problem in the armed forces, since many recruits leave after a short term of service during which the government may have invested as much $20,000 in specialized training.

[5] United States Department of Labor, *Career Patterns of Former Apprentices*, Bulletin No. T-147 (Washington, D.C.: U. S. Government Printing Office, March 1959). If data from the construction industry were excluded, this percentage presumably would be significantly higher.

most of which have been formulated by psychologists. Some of the principles that are of particular value to the trainer are summarized below.[6]

MOTIVATION

The indifferent, reluctant student will learn very little, even from a brilliant instructor. For an employee to benefit from training, he must be anxious to improve his abilities and his job performance and thus enhance his opportunities for advancement. Clearly, the amount of return the company receives from its investment in training will depend upon the over-all level of morale in the organization and the extent to which supervisors have developed a sense of job satisfaction.

On the other hand, overly intense motivation may actually inhibit learning. If an individual becomes too tense, or if he sets goals for himself that are beyond his ability to attain, the result may be acute disappointment and loss of motivation.

REINFORCEMENT

Related to motivation is the need for *reinforcement*—that is, for learning to take place, the individual must receive some encouragement or reward. The reward need not be tangible. All the individual needs is to experience some feeling of progress, either through the teacher's comments or through his own observation that he has done well.

Such positive rewards for progress appear to have a much better effect than punishment or the threat of punishment when mistakes are made. Most people have only a limited tolerance for failure. If punishment for failure is excessive, the phenomenon of "fixation" may develop, in which the same unsuccessful response is repeated over and over again.

Obviously, the trainee will not always be successful in his attempts to learn. But his ability to tolerate failure will still be a function of the success he has achieved and the degree to which his correct behavior has been reinforced.

FEEDBACK

For reinforcement to be effective in improving performance, there must be feedback, or *knowledge of results*. Imagine how difficult it would be to improve one's marksmanship without being able to see the target. If self-correction is to take place, the trainee must know the relationship between

---

[6] Additional references to the field of learning are: Richard Bugelski, *The Psychology of Learning* (New York: Holt, 1956); Charles E. Osgood, *Methods and Theory in Experimental Psychology* (New York: Oxford, 1953); Ernest Hilgard, *Theories of Learning*, 2nd ed. (New York: Appleton-Century Crofts, 1956); Harold Leavitt, *Managerial Psychology* (Chicago: University of Chicago Press, 1958).

his behavior and the impact, or result, of his behavior. Unless he knows how close his achievement is to the desired standard of good performance, he will not be able to improve his performance, no matter how hard and how frequently he tries. This means that the supervisor should resist the temptation to contact the subordinate *only* when he has made a mistake. The learner also needs to know when he has made the right decision. And when he has made a mistake, he needs to recognize *why* and *how* he went wrong and how close he came to doing the work properly. Feedback of results should be provided as quickly as possible after the trainee's performance.

Here are two examples of the effective use of feedback in improving job performance: [7]

> Previously, furnace crews had no measure of the effectiveness of their work. When gauges were installed to indicate the efficiency of individual boilers graphically, it was estimated that $333,000 was saved in fuel costs.

> A recording device was invented to show employees their cutting patterns on a foot-operated abrasive wheel used to cut tungsten discs. The device revealed learner errors so dramatically that training time was cut almost in half.

Finally, feedback should be presented in a non-threatening environment; the learner should be made to realize that mistakes will not cost him too dearly and that difficulties in learning are natural and expected. It is the supervisor's responsibility to provide this feedback, not just during the so-called training period, but on a continuing basis.

LEARNING BY DOING

Learning is most efficient when the learner is actively involved in the learning process, rather than merely listening to a description of it. In fact, the greater the number of senses involved, the more effective the learning. To learn a poem quickly and accurately, it is much more efficient to recite it aloud than to read and reread it silently. Doing rather than just seeing or hearing also means that the individual is more likely to devote more of himself to the task; he becomes more *involved* in the learning process. It has been suggested that motor activity (muscular movement) directly stimulates the higher mental processes, such as learning. [8]

This principle has obvious implications for the supervisor's role in training. Instead of relying exclusively on lectures, or on training films and manuals, he should encourage the employee to try out new jobs, to ask questions, and to go through all the requisite motions. Of course, he watches for mistakes

---

[7] Both examples are adapted from James N. Mosel, "How to Feed Back Performance Results to Trainees," *Journal of American Society of Training Directors* (February 1958).

[8] See Gordon Allport, "The Psychology of Participation," *Psychological Review*, Vol. LIII (May 1945).

and insures that they are corrected, but he reinforces the correction by having the trainee repeat the activity properly. Active repetition is useful only when the training situation permits the trainee to try out alternative approaches in the full assurance that he can make mistakes and learn from them.

REPETITION

Active repetition should not be continuous, however. Many experiments have shown that *spaced repetition*—that is, learning periods distributed through time—are more efficient than attempts to learn "all at once." Apprenticeship programs, in which the trainee learns by repeated doing, are an excellent example of this approach. Another obvious value of repetition is that it serves to inhibit forgetting. Without practice, learned skills gradually disappear.

REALISTIC GOAL-SETTING

Realistic goal-setting is another requirement of efficient learning. Few of us can tolerate endless defeat; we need some sense of success and progress if we are to maintain our motivation. If either the trainer or the trainee sets his sights too high at the outset, frustration, discouragement, even resignation, will set in. Goals that are too low are also inefficient, because they fail to provide adequate challenge.

LEARNING BY PARTS

Learning is expedited when the total process or skill to be mastered is broken down into small, "digestible" segments. This approach contributes to the trainee's motivation; he obtains satisfaction from reaching each of the subgoals, and these, in turn, help him to reach his objective of total mastery of the activity. Whether or not this type of training is possible depends in part on the technology. For example, the electrician can learn simple wiring and the associated arithmetic and then gradually move in logical steps to more complex circuitry.

On other jobs, this progression is hampered by the indivisibility of the work. Student nurses on medical wards, occupied chiefly by chronically ill patients, complain that they are always doing unimportant jobs that teach them nothing: custodial duties like bed-making and water-carrying. On the surgical floors, however, where each patient requires one or more of the "nursing arts," every student and assistant gets assignments commensurate with her growing ability.[9]

---

[9] T. Burling, E. Lentz and R. Wilson, *The Give and Take in Hospitals* (New York: Putnam, 1956), pp. 252-253.

LEARNING BY MASTERING LARGE SEGMENTS

Learning is inhibited if the segments to be mastered are too small, however. Anyone who has learned to swim knows how difficult it is to combine leg movements with arm movements. If a job is broken into fragments, each of which must be mastered by itself, the problem of learning to integrate them into a whole activity, as a smooth, continuous process, becomes extremely difficult.

But how "small" a part of the job is "too small"? Wherever possible, the learner should try to master as a single unit all those activities that must be performed in a smooth, continuous sequence. In this way, each sub-part becomes an internalized "cue" that stimulates the next part of the sequence. The trainer may have to encourage the learner to try out what seems at the outset to be an impossibly large segment. But it is more efficient in the long run for him to make many mistakes in trying to master a logically constituted unit, to fumble badly because of the number of coordinations required, than to concentrate on learning the parts as if each were to be performed in a vacuum.

In addition, emphasis on these larger segments of the job may de-emphasize the trainer's tendency to assume there is only "one best way." When arm, hand, finger, and body motions are taught individually, in violation of what is easiest and most natural for the trainee, the training degenerates into an artificial, stilted ritual. Further, when these theoretically correct motions are combined, the resulting behavior pattern may be unsuited to the idiosyncrasies of the individual worker's nervous and muscular system.[10]

GIVING THEORY

One of the more controversial questions in training technique concerns the amount of *theory* or *background* the trainee needs to learn most effectively. Obviously the electrician, or even the electronics technician, has no need to go back to quantum mechanics. However, the effectiveness with which he learns repair or maintenance methods will be materially enhanced if he has some knowledge of electrical theory. The theory itself may not be essential to the specific tasks he will be performing, but it will help him to *transfer* his knowledge to new jobs, equipment, and processes. If the employee is to develop insight into new problems that arise during the course of his work, he must achieve more basic understanding of his activities than that provided by the "this-is-how-you-do-it" type of training. "Logical" training is always more effective than "rote" training—at least for jobs that call for any degree of sophisticated performance. As we noted in our discussions of

---

[10] See Chapter 26, which discusses some of the industrial engineering problems of job design.

supervison, the supervisor explains *why* when he gives directions, to insure that the employee will be able to handle unusual, unanticipated situations.

Typical Learning Patterns

Supervisors need some understanding of the pattern in which new skills are learned—of what are called "learning curves" (see figure below). When the employee first begins to learn a new job or a new skill, he is likely to find himself unusually clumsy or inept—"all thumbs." This can be very discouraging, particularly to a man who prides himself on his agility and ability; and so, during this early stage, the learner needs the supervisor's support and encouragement. (This, of course, is one justification for conducting certain kinds of training off-the-job.) The duration of this first stage is a function of the complexity and newness of the skill being learned—it may be only a few minutes or a few weeks.

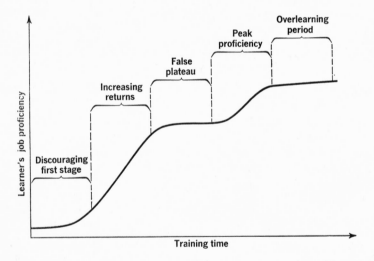

Hypothetical learning curve.

After this period, the typical learning rate is rapid. This is the stage of increasing returns, in which small additional amounts of practice by the trainee produce substantial increases in job-proficiency. During this second period, the employee's confidence and satisfaction rise.

After more training time has elapsed, many observers have noted that a "plateau" develops. Now additional training time does not result in very significant increases in proficiency, and both the supervisor and the learner may be deceived into thinking that the maximum of improvement has been attained. Ghiselli and Brown cite the case of a taxi-driver whose performance increased by a factor of 50 per cent in seven weeks' time, but then remained constant for 12 weeks. Over the succeeding 10 weeks, additional training brought about another 50 per cent improvement. They conclude, "Mistaking the intermediate plateau for the final plateau would have led to the conclusion that learning had been completed long before the worker actually had attained his maximum performance." [11]

These plateaus seem to be the result of two factors: (1) a loss of motivation as early surges of progress are dissipated and as further progress becomes more difficult, and (2) the trainee's need for substantial blocks of time to develop new and improved skills. Initially the employee may be forced to learn a new job in segments, thinking consciously about each part of the job. A great deal of practice is required before a real "break-through" takes place that permits these separate parts to become merged and the motions or movements to be joined into a single, coordinated sequence of actions. Ghiselli and Brown describe this stage as follows:

> Through practice, certain phases of the action patterns are automatized, superfluous activities are dropped out, precision of movement and smoothness of coordination are effected, excess tension is eliminated, the energy requirements of the total performance are greatly reduced, and the trainee develops self-assurance and confidence in his performance. [12]

The employee who has achieved this level of training is obviously of greater value to the organization. Not only does the well-trained worker become less fatigued, but he can also devote his energies to the genuinely important aspects of his job. When we are learning to drive, nearly all of our efforts are directed to completing the hand-foot coordinations. But a seasoned driver can concentrate on road conditions, predicting the reactions of other drivers, and similar problems.

The supervisor must be aware of these aspects of the "learning curve" if he is to help the employee weather the difficult, stressful experiences of the early days on the job and maintain his motivation to continue practicing. This motivation, as we have noted, is a prerequisite of learning.

The supervisor must also be wary of assuming that the employee's training has been completed once he has achieved peak skill. Continued repetition needs to be encouraged so that *overlearning* will take place. An experienced automobile driver can refrain from driving for six months or even six years, and still be able to drive when the occasion demands. This is largely the result of overlearning, which diminishes the likelihood that forgetting will take place. Apparently, the reflex sequences that relate muscular responses

---

[11] E. E. Ghiselli and C. W. Brown, *Personnel and Industrial Psychology*, 2nd ed. (New York: McGraw-Hill, 1955), pp. 385-386.
[12] *Ibid.*, p. 384.

and sensory stimuli become more deeply ingrained when the individual continues to practice even after he has reached top performance.

One note of caution: the learning curve of all employees is not the same. On the contrary, there are profound differences in native ability to synchronize muscular movements, to effect eye-hand coordinations, and to sense subtle differences in tactile and muscular responses. When these individual differences are added to differences in motivation and morale, they result in wide disparities in learning rates.

These differences pose serious problems for the supervisor. Should the highly motivated employee with less ability who achieves the same level of performance as the less highly motivated employee with greater ability receive the same or greater rewards? Would your answer be the same if you knew that the more gifted employee was working less hard and performing at a lower level of accomplishment than he would if he were to exert himself? (Professors face such questions every day!)

Job Instruction Training

Job Instruction Training (J.I.T.) was developed in World War II to provide a simple, quick training method that could be easily applied by new supervisors. This method embodied many of the principles we have just been discussing. Here are the main stages in a J.I.T. training program:

1. A job description is worked out that breaks the job down into a series of motion sequences that can be described. The trainer identifies the special techniques required, the special precautions that need to be taken, the criteria that indicate whether the job is being performed correctly, the quality and safety levels required, and so forth. These are the *key points* of the job.

2. At the beginning of the training session, the equipment and supplies are arranged in the way in which the worker is expected to keep them.

3. The trainer puts the learner at ease, finds out what he already knows, explains the relationship of his job to other jobs in the organization, and shows him the correct working position.

4. The trainer describes the job completely, stresses the key points, and then performs the job, describing "what" and "why" at each step. The learner is encouraged to ask questions.

5. The learner then tells the trainer how the job is to be done and the trainer follows his instructions.

6. The learner does the job, explaining to the trainer at each step "what" he is doing and "why."

7. The trainer follows up with periodic checks and tells the trainee where he can go for help if he runs into difficulty.

The J.I.T. program carried a simple admonition: "If the worker hasn't learned; the instructor hasn't taught." This is an appropriate philosophy for the entire training area, for the supervisor must share the responsibility for a trainee's failure to learn.

Conclusion

Training means changing behavior patterns, and this is always a difficult task. An individual's method of doing a job, the skills he employs, the energy and thought he applies, the checking and coordinating with other people he undertakes—all are a reflection of his personality and the needs he has brought to the work situation. The supervisor must assume that the employee's old pattern of behavior brought certain satisfactions—else he would have abandoned it. Since a change in work methods will be a threat to these satisfactions, the employee will resist new learning. This resistance may be bolstered by his desire for the approbation of his work group and by his psychological needs for security and a sense of accomplishment. Efforts to increase productivity through teaching better work habits may run counter to group-enforced production "bogeys" based on a fear that increased output will lead to layoffs and demotions.

The success of any training program is a direct function of the success of other aspects of the personnel program. Where employees are already highly motivated and closely identified with the goals of the organization, well-conceived training programs will lead to better performance. On the contrary, where morale is low and employees are suspicious and resentful of management programs, training will be ineffective in improving performance. For example, in one company a course in work-simplification was seriously handicapped because it was associated in the workers' minds with the widely disliked time-study department.[13] If the trainees fail to see how they will benefit by adopting the techniques being taught, no amount of good teaching will change their behavior.

Nevertheless, the satisfactions an employee derives from his work experience depend on his knowing what to do and how to do it. The employee who lacks confidence in his ability to perform successfully can never do his job well, no matter how vigorously management pursues the other aspects of its personnel program. Successful training policies, therefore, are a prerequisite to high productivity and job satisfaction. But training is not merely a matter of techniques, formal programs, and instructions. Well-conceived promotional ladders and transfer procedures supplement training.

---

[13] Harry C. Triandis, "Attitude Change Through Training in Industry," *Human Organization,* Vol. 17, No. 2 (Summer 1958), pp. 27-30.

Problem I

Draw up a complete J.I.T.-type training instruction guide for teaching a trainee to swim or to operate a slide rule. Be very specific in outlining the progression of steps, including directions for the trainer and the learner.

Problem II

Wilma Granger works in the accounts receivable section of a large department-store billing department. Her supervisor has found a large number of mistakes in a random check of the accounts she is responsible for, and her over-all output of work is lower than the department standard.

1. What "checks" should the supervisor make in evaluating whether this poor work is due to inadequate training or other causes?
2. If this investigation discloses inadequate training, how should he introduce remedial training?
3. How should the training be carried out?

Problem III

The packaging department was the most troublesome department in the U.S. Auto Parts Company. The employees' job in this department was to watch high-speed, semi-automatic packaging machines and make adjustments and compensations for unexpected operating difficulties. Though the work was simple and easily learned, productivity was low. Employees frequently neglected obvious danger signals and failed to make the proper adjustments.

Management tried all sorts of solutions to this problem: employees were disciplined for making mistakes (they objected violently); supervisors were sent through a training program; a new incentive system was introduced. When all these efforts failed, management decided to experiment with a retraining program. Some of the employees may have forgotten their initial training, or perhaps it had been inadequate. In any event, many employees were using clearly inefficient, fatiguing motions on the job, and improved job performance would actually make the work easier.

Management had another reason for introducing training: It was contemplating discharging some of the worst offenders, but felt that it should give these men every opportunity to improve before it took such drastic action. Systematic training would head off union charges that the men had not been properly instructed.

The department head, in collaboration with the Industrial Engineering Department, prepared a training manual that outlined all the steps required in doing this particular job. One of the first-line supervisors was chosen to administer the training during the regular work routine of the department. He spent several hours with each employee, going over the procedures step by step in good J.I.T. fashion.

The results were discouraging. No improvements in productivity were forthcoming. The operators claimed that the trainer was a spy seeking evidence that they were malingering rather than trying to train them. Furthermore, "He knows less about the job than we do—we should be training him."

1. What mistakes, if any, were made in this training situation?

2. Describe completely how you would handle these problems, including the selection of the trainer.

Problem IV

The Bayworth Pharmaceutical Company has had a long-established training program for laboratory technicians. Women employees in lower-paying jobs who wish to become technicians are taken into a three-year training program. Under the direction of senior technicians, trainees rotate through all the jobs in the laboratory involving technicians. In addition, the company gives a series of supplementary courses in mathematics, introduction to organic chemistry, and methods of quantitative and qualitative analysis on a six-hour-per-week basis. (Half of this time is not compensated for, since the class meets after working hours.) Successful completion of the course program and a recommendation from the department supervisor entitle an employee to be promoted to laboratory technician, with a starting salary of $115 per week. The beginning trainee salary of $75 is increased by $10 at the end of each year.

Eight years ago, during the development of a new vaccine, huge government orders necessitated a rapid expansion of several of the company's laboratories. Lacking adequate manpower, the management of the laboratories sought a short-cut solution for this personnel problem. In consultation with lower levels of supervision, new job descriptions were developed reflecting a change in the division of labor. Rather than relying on fully trained, all-around technicians, management trained employees to do individual laboratory jobs, such as specimen analysis, preparation, and equipment testing. An alert employee could be trained in three months to do one of these jobs. The salary was fixed at $90 per week for these new jobs, which were titled "laboratory assistants."

In recent years a number of these assistants, who, through careful observation and informal trial have learned most of the other jobs in the laboratory, have been promoted to the job and salary of technician. Out of the original group of 18, in fact, nine have been so promoted.

At present the laboratory employs a total of 30 technicians. However, a sharp dip in the demand for this type of company product has necessitated a 30 per cent reduction in the number of technicians. (All the assistants who had not been promoted already have been transferred to other divisions.)

The 21 technicians who have completed the formal training program have signed a petition requesting that the laboratory adopt a policy of transferring first all employees who have not graduated from the training program. The petition argues that the training-program graduates have made financial and other sacrifices to attain their present position, and that by implication the company has guaranteed them a special status which is superior to that of any technician not so trained.

If this request were honored, several excellent technicians who came up through this informal program and have been on the job for more than five years would have to leave the laboratory, while other technicians who were hired less than a year ago would remain. Further, these women argue that such a policy would represent arbitrary discrimination against them, since they have been formally promoted to their present position by management. The immediate supervisors want to retain the long-service employees because of their knowledge and skill. Furthermore, the self-trained group includes several of the best employees.

1. Could this intergroup struggle have been foreseen?
2. What steps could have been taken to prevent this problem from occurring?
3. What effect may this dispute have on the future of the training program?
4. As a member of management, how would you evaluate the variables in this situation?
5. What policy decision can provide a reasonable solution to the present problem and a basis for future laboratory development?

Problem V

The AB Chemical Company expects to double its work force over the next two years and will need a substantial number of new crew chiefs, men who hold quasi-supervisory positions in gangs working on a technical distillation process. In order to give employees the technical background required to handle such a job, management decides to sponsor a series of after-hours classes in elementary chemistry and the technical processes connected with the work. These classes are to meet two nights a week for six months.

Management's problem is this: Should the course be open to all employees who wish to attend, or to just an invited few who are most likely to be appointed to the crew chiefs' job? Of course, more instructors may be required if the course is open to everyone. But the chief problem is that if an employee gives up two nights a week for six months, he will feel that the company is morally committed to giving him a promotion.

Yet, if management permits only a picked few to attend, it in effect will be barring all others from consideration for promotion.

1. What advice would you give to this company?
2. What will be the impact on morale if customer-demand fails to expand as predicted, and if even some of the specially picked men cannot be promoted?

Management development is one of the fastest-growing areas in personnel, for there is a growing realization that an effective management team is at least as important to the survival of the organization as any tangible item on the balance sheet. In this chapter and the next two we will consider the broad area of management development. This chapter will be concerned with some of the general problems of providing people with experience that will enable them to develop their fullest potentialities. The next two chapters will handle two specific areas: performance evaluation and management training.

Interest in management development is almost entirely a post-war phenomenon. Management awoke with a shock at the end of World War II to find that it had a serious shortage of trained executives in the middle and lower levels of management. During the depression few executives were hired; during the war almost no one was available. Consequently, by 1945, managerial ability was concentrated in the upper age brackets, among men close to retirement. The vast expansion of industry in the post-war period made it all the more critical for new executive material to be discovered—and in a hurry.

22

Management

Development

Even though the immediate post-war gap has been filled, interest in management development continues to grow. Why? In the first place, the number of managerial jobs is rising faster than the size of the work force generally. (From 1940 to 1954 the number of managerial jobs went up 67 per cent; the size of the total work force, only 35 per cent.)[1] Running a company—which now calls for dealing with unions and the government, and coordinating increasingly involved technical activities—is becoming a steadily more complicated job. This growth in the number of managers may foreshadow the completely automatized world in which everyone will be a supervisor.

In addition, there is a growing feeling that management is a *profession* for which special training is required. As Harold F. Smiddy, Vice President of General Electric, has said, "Perhaps the most provocative—and important—idea on which we are proceeding is that managing should be regarded as a distinct type of work, with its own disciplines, its own criteria for achievement; something which is both learnable and teachable." [2] Evidence of this emphasis is the growth of business schools and professional organizations, such as the American Management Association. Professionalism implies the need for special skills and for formal training and apprenticeship.

In part, this growing professionalism reflects the widening gap between the ownership and control of American corporations. More and more, control over corporate destinies is falling into the hands of hired or "professional" managers, whose reward, in addition to salary, resides in the sense of personal satisfaction that comes with having done a good job and with having one's achievements recognized by other managers. Getting ahead has come to mean rising within the "management profession," rather than going into business for one's self.

Thus management development as a program has received impetus both from the increased demand for managers and from their own growing sense of professionalism.

The Changing Emphasis: An Overview

Before looking at management development in detail, let us take a bird's eye look at the changing emphasis in this area. Like many other rapidly expanding specialties, management development has had its growing pains. Because of the critical shortage of manpower after World War II, the early emphasis was on crash programs to discover individuals (both inside and outside the company) who would be capable of moving quickly to top-management jobs. In the effort to ferret out such exceptional men, there arose

---

[1] Robert K. Stolz, "Is Executive Development Coming of Age?" *The Journal of Business*, Vol. 28, No. 1 (January 1955), p. 49.

[2] Quoted by Herbert Harris, "How Managers Are Made," *Nation's Business* (March 1956), p. 91.

a widespread use of tests [3] and evaluation forms designed to identify traits that might point to *future* ability rather than to *present* performance. The men thus singled out were given special training away from the job (often at universities) and were marked for rapid promotion.

As might be expected, this program led to a wave of resentment among those who had not been selected as a "crown prince," and a feeling that it was unfair to base promotions on vague character traits instead of on proved performance. Also, since the selection process tended to emphasize the safe, conformist, all-around man, there seemed to be a prejudice against the unusual individual who was able to get things done in spite of "character deficiencies." Consequently, observers began to suspect that by weeding out deviationists, management might also be weeding out the very men who would produce the original ideas of the future.

Changing Emphasis in Management Development
(*extremes are exaggerated*)

	Early Days of Management Development	More Recent Tendencies
Promotional planning	Move the picked few quickly from job to job in order to give them maximum experience.	More opportunity for everyone to move to a different job when he is ready; some planned movement; special "broadening" assignments to outstanding candidates.
Testing	Great emphasis.	Little emphasis.
Performance evaluation	Chiefly for use by top management.	Chiefly for use by man himself.
	A tool to compare one man with another.	A springboard for discussion on how a subordinate can do a better job.
	Emphasis on traits and potential.	Emphasis on behavior, on what a man can do to improve his performance on his present job.
	Objective, numerical evaluation.	Subjective; emphasis on getting subordinate's feelings.
Training	For a picked few.	For everyone.
	Primarily off-the-job, even outside the company.	Largely coaching, group discussion.
	Conducted by staff or outsiders.	Conducted by line management.
	Concerned with top management problems.	Concerned with problems at current level.

Partly for these reasons, emphasis in recent years has switched from the hunt for the ideal "organization man" to a more routine, continuing program of training designed to help *all* managers perform more adequately on their

[3] For a discussion of tests as a means of measuring supervisory ability, see pp. 450-451.

present job (after all, opportunities for promotion are limited).[4] Instead of forcing people to meet a prescribed pattern, the desire is to create conditions that will permit *self*-development.

Evaluation forms are being used as a tool to enable the supervisor to discuss with his subordinates how they can improve their performance, rather than as a means for selection. There have come other changes as well: personality traits (which cannot be changed easily) are receiving less emphasis than performance (which can); training is coming to be regarded as a regular line function rather than something outside the daily routine of management. The primary responsibility for training is being shifted away from staff to line management.

Planning for Management Development

In planning for management development, the company must predict its long-range managerial manpower needs and decide how to meet them; it must also schedule the shorter-range movements of individuals from one job to another. The values of careful planning are many:

> . . . It insures an orderly flow of people, trained and available to fill vacancies as they occur.
> . . . It helps forecast and spotlight areas where training or even outside recruiting is necessary.
> . . . It insures that everyone has a chance to be considered and that nobody gets lost in the shuffle.
> . . . It makes it possible to bring people up from the ranks rather than having to recruit from outside.

LONG-RANGE PLANNING

Ideally, management should try to predict the company's supervisory and executive needs for as far into the future as possible. "Of all economic resources, high-level manpower takes the longest time to develop, and thus it demands the most careful consideration in planning for the future. . . . For the most part, companies are preoccupied with their immediate requirements and with short-run development projects. In long-range manpower planning, most companies really don't know where they are or whither they are going." [5]

The first question to decide is whether the company will try to develop executives through promotion from within, or hire them as needed from

---

[4] From a study of records in one not untypical company it was found that not more than one-third of the supervisors were likely to be promoted once again during their supervisory career, and only one-tenth were likely to be promoted twice. Earl Brooks, "An Experimental Program for Executive Development," *ILR Research*, Vol. 1, No. 2 (March 1955), p. 11.

[5] Samuel E. Hill and Frederick Harbison, *Manpower and Innovation in American Industry* (Princeton, N.J.: Industrial Relations Section, 1959), p. 66.

among the men who have proved themselves with other companies. (This latter practice is called "pirating," and is becoming increasingly risky, difficult, and expensive.) The degree to which "job-hopping" is accepted varies a great deal from industry to industry. In retailing it is well accepted. In manufacturing generally, however, good men at the top positions are becoming increasingly reluctant to switch from one job to another, since a shift usually means that they must give up valuable fringe benefits and pension rights. Often the men who are most anxious to move to new jobs are those who have failed on their old ones; yet if a sudden need arises, these may be the only men on whom the company can draw. Promotion from within, on the other hand, raises morale, provides an incentive for junior executives to put forth their best effort, and eliminates the need for a long orientation period when a higher position is filled.

The chief advantage of bringing men in from outside is that they introduce a fresh, new approach to management problems. Of course, too many fresh approaches may disrupt the organization, but there are times when original contributions are needed, particularly when the organization has sunk into the doldrums or when quick adjustment must be made to new markets or products.

Most organizations fill the majority of their management needs through promotion from within. This means that plans must be made for 30 or 40 years into the future, for the newly hired college graduates of the 1960's may well provide the top management of the 1990's.

Clearly, long-range planning of this sort must be highly tentative. In the shorter-range development of individual managers, far more precise planning is possible.

SCHEDULING OF PROMOTIONS AND TRANSFERS

Many large companies keep careful track of the progress of each of their managers and tentatively schedule their future movements from job to job in order to insure that they will get optimum training and experience. Normally, policy in this area is the responsibility of a top-level management committee, while the administrative work is handled by the personnel director or a special coordinator of management development who reports directly to the president.

The key tools in scheduling programs of this sort are *executive inventories* and *replacement charts*. An executive inventory consists of a file card for each executive with such information as: age, length of service, education, positions held within the company and with other companies, results on psychological tests, hobbies, membership in outside organizations, and so forth. More important are his superiors' evaluation of his work since he first came with the company, a statement by his present boss on the type of experience he still needs, and an estimate on how far he may be expected to go in the future.

At times these data are placed on business machine cards. When a new job opens up, all management need do is to set the standards as to the type of man best qualified. The machine does the rest. There are those who claim that once the standards are properly set, only a minimum of human judgment is required.

Many companies like to look several jumps ahead. They are interested in more than just finding who is most qualified at the moment. Some try to schedule movements five or ten years in advance. This is where replacement charts are useful. The chart below is typical, though it somewhat exaggerates the range of possibilities among six men.

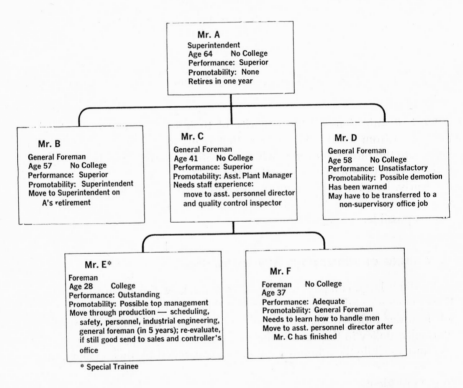

Mr. A
Superintendent
Age 64   No College
Performance: Superior
Promotability: None
Retires in one year

Mr. B
General Foreman
Age 57   No College
Performance: Superior
Promotability: Superintendent
Move to Superintendent on
    A's retirement

Mr. C
General Foreman
Age 41   No College
Performance: Superior
Promotability: Asst. Plant Manager
Needs staff experience:
    move to asst. personnel director
    and quality control inspector

Mr. D
General Foreman
Age 58   No College
Performance: Unsatisfactory
Promotability: Possible demotion
Has been warned
May have to be transferred to a
    non-supervisory office job

Mr. E*
Foreman
Age 28   College
Performance: Outstanding
Promotability: Possible top management
Move through production — scheduling,
    safety, personnel, industrial engineering,
    general foreman (in 5 years); re-evaluate,
    if still good send to sales and controller's
    office

* Special Trainee

Mr. F
Foreman   No College
Age 37
Performance: Adequate
Promotability: General Foreman
Needs to learn how to handle men
Move to asst. personnel director after
    Mr. C has finished

From individual file cards and replacement charts it is possible to plan many years in advance. For instance:

Mr. Q
Jan. 1960   Manager, Plant 1
June 1962   retires (to be replaced by Mr. R)

Mr. R
Jan. 1960   Superintendent, Plant 2 (to be replaced by Mr. S)

Jan. 1961   Plant Engineer, Plant 1 (to be replaced by Mr. T)
June 1961   Asst. Plant Manager, Plant 2 (position to be created—not be
             replaced)
June 1962   Manager, Plant 1

Mr. S
Jan. 1960   General Foreman, Plant 2 (to be replaced by Mr. U)
Jan. 1961   Superintendent, Plant 2

Note that Mr. R is to be moved successively through two jobs to give him
the experience necessary to take Q's job. The job as Assistant Plant Manager
is to be created especially for him so that he can act as an understudy to
Mr. Q. Also, note that Q's retirement involves not only R but also S, T, U,
and possibly a dozen other members of the organization.

Providing Experience

The purpose of all this planning is to insure that the right man is available with the right experience at the right time. Naturally there is no absolute
agreement on the best way of providing men with the experience they need.
For instance, how long should a man stay on a given job before he moves
on? How much variety of experience should he get? How much special
attention should be given to the unusual "comer"? Although answers to these
questions differ widely, we shall consider four typical kinds of program:
understudies, systematic rotation, "jet" trainees, and special "broadening"
assignments. Many companies use a combination of these programs.

UNDERSTUDIES

Before an executive can be moved to a higher position, a replacement
must be available to take his place. To insure that the upward movement of
personnel is not impaired, many companies are requiring each manager to
designate an understudy. Here is an extreme example:

> One company provides double desks for all executives, with a candidate
> for ultimate responsibility sitting opposite the present executive. The men
> in training act as assistants to the executive, make field studies for him,
> investigate special problems, and fill in on the job when the executive is
> away from his desk.[6]

The understudy program is the least ambitious form of development program and requires the least centralized control and use of replacement tables.
And yet, modest though it is, it raises many problems. Should there be a

---

[6] Glen U. Cleeton and Charles W. Mason, *Executive Ability* (Yellow Springs, Ohio:
The Antioch Press, 1946), p. 246.

single understudy or several? If there is only one, those who have not been chosen may give up all hope of getting ahead. If there are several, intense rivalry will spring up among them.

When should understudies be selected? Some companies require a new manager to select a successor-elect almost as soon as he moves to his desk,[7] on the grounds that early selection gives maximum opportunity for the understudy to gain experience and insures that someone is prepared to take over immediately in case of an emergency. On the other hand, the appointment of an understudy at too early a stage may impair the morale of other men who feel themselves qualified for the job. If the executive waits for a year or so before naming an understudy, he may choose an entirely different man, perhaps a slow-starter who can prove his merit only over a period of time.

Many of these problems are avoided when the supervisor makes no formal designation of an understudy until a few months before he leaves for his new job. Then he can give all his subordinates, including the slow-starter, an equal opportunity for training and experience. And if no one from within the department proves qualified, then someone may be brought in from outside.

SYSTEMATIC ROTATION

In many companies the rising executive regularly moves from one job and location to another once every two to five years. These movements are usually accompanied by promotions or salary increases. Normally, rotation is regarded as a sign of progress; to stay frozen in one job for too long a time means that there is no more chance to advance. Rarely is a man *forced* to move. But if he declines an opportunity for rotation, he is given to understand that his chances for advancement will be severely limited.

Companies that practice systematic rotation must maintain tightly centralized programs and make extensive use of replacement charts and schedules. The decision on who is to be moved, and where and when he is to be moved, must be made on a coordinated, company-wide basis.

Such programs are expensive. Besides the company's out-of-pocket expenses for administering the program and defraying the costs when managers move their residence from one location to another, there is a substantial loss in executive time when a man gives up an old job and sets about learning a new one. Why, then, are so many companies willing to undergo this expense?

1. A systematic rotation program that requires a manager to move from department to department and plant to plant develops, not specialists, but generalists—men who can take a broad, company-wide point of view, men whose chief ability is handling people and making decisions. Presumably, when managers with such experience reach top positions they will be able to

---

[7] Often the selection is made by the management development committee—as in the case of Mr. R—and the manager has relatively little to say about it.

make balanced decisions in full awareness of the ramifications of each decision on every department.[8]

2. The outsider who comes into a department often brings with him new ideas and fresh points of view. Since the new man has no vested interest in the old ways of doing things, he can make changes quickly and can engage in fruitful interaction with the old-timers in the department. In contrast, a man who has been in the department for many years has many personal ties and must always be careful not to step on his friends' toes.

3. Rotation makes it possible to compare one man against another. It tends to give everyone an equal chance. With a program of understudies, by contrast, no man can advance till his boss dies, retires, quits, or moves up, and, in departments where there are lots of good men, some talent is bound to be wasted. Rotation also protects a man from being frozen in a job merely because his department is expanding less rapidly than the rest. It also gives him a chance to make a good showing in the line of work for which he is best suited.

4. Rotation makes certain that several people are prepared to assume executive responsibility for every division of the company. For example, the Large Product Sales Division may have room for only five supervisors, but as many as fifteen executives may have worked there. If the large-product market were suddenly to improve, the needed executives could be moved into this department with the greatest of ease. Otherwise, it might be necessary to look for people outside the organization.

In spite of the obvious advantages of systematic rotation as a program of management development, it does give rise to certain problems:

1. Rotation often means that the manager must pull up stakes and move to another location. This is particularly hard on children, who must constantly readapt to new schools and new friends. After going through the experience several times of dropping old friends and being thrown among complete strangers, children learn not to make close friendships and tend to withdraw into themselves.

The parents have a hard time too. Beyond the time and emotional strain involved in packing, unpacking, and finding a new house, constant movement makes it difficult for them to sink their roots into the community and disrupts their ties with relatives and friends.[9] Particularly to the adult who has poured love and energy into creating a garden or fixing up a house, abandoning one's home is a painful experience.

---

[8] This holds true even on the foreman level. The findings of the General Electric study (see p. 125) showed that seven out of eight most efficient foremen had previous staff experience, while only one out of eight least efficient foremen had such experience. General Electric Company, Public and Employee Relations Research Service, *The Effective Manufacturing Foreman* (processed, 1957), p. 18.

[9] See Elsa Gidlow, "Promotion? No Thanks—Not if I Have to Move Again," *Sales Management*, Vol. 81, No. 3 (July 18, 1958), p. 35.

Sooner or later most people who are obliged to move around a good bit learn to adjust. They learn not to make close friends, not to become closely involved in community affairs, not to develop long-term ties of any sort. They learn to put company above family, community, or friends. Thus we have the phenomenon of the company man and the company wife, about whom so much has been written in recent years. If this rootless existence impairs the manager's performance or creates severe family tensions, the company for which he works is bound to suffer.

Many outstanding managers have simply refused to continue in the "rat race" (these are the heroes of many contemporary novels). Fully aware that to refuse a transfer may kill all chance of further advancement, they still insist on staying put. Clearly, executive manpower is not being used to maximum efficiency when managers are selected on the basis of their willingness to rotate rather than on their innate ability.

2. Just as the prospect of rotation discourages the executive from undertaking long-range projects at home, so it makes him reluctant to take a long-range approach to his job. If a man knows he will be transferred in two years' time, he will concentrate on short-range projects with a quick pay-off—immediate cost reduction, for instance, rather than personnel development. He knows that he will have none of the satisfaction of completing long-range projects and, when they are completed, the credit will go to his successor. Understandably, he is tempted to make changes that *look* good, since there rarely is time to test how well they will work out in practice.

Rotation penalizes the slow-starter. The man who takes a long time to adjust to the people he works with and to learn his way around may actually be the best man. But if he is constantly rotated, he never has enough time on a given job to prove his ability.

3. The rotation system is like a highly competitive game of musical chairs. Every time there is another round of promotions and transfers, some people are left behind. And the system, as practiced by most companies, puts a high premium on conformity. As long as you do *adequately,* you are retained. An *outstanding* job may help you somewhat, but a *mistake* will knock you completely out of the running. As a consequence, the smart rising young executive plays it safe; he avoids taking risks. He knows that he will rarely be on one job long enough to insure that long-run, risky decisions will pay off.

4. Rotation also has an undesirable effect on the department that is turned over to a new boss who is unfamiliar with its special problems. Since the purpose of rotation is training, the new supervisor is assigned to the job not because he is the best man for it (that person might be an underling with years of experience in the department), but because the job is the best for him (that is, it provides him with the most training).

As we noticed in our discussion of supervision, the good supervisor gets to know his subordinates as individuals, works through their informal organizations, and understands and respects their social norms. It may take a new supervisor months or years to learn both the technology and social geography of his department. All he knows at the outset are the formal rules of the organization. These he may enforce even when it is inappropriate.

If he is wise, he lets his subordinates train him for the job. His lack of knowledge may force him to delegate responsibility (yet there are some supervisors who insist on making decisions without proper knowledge). In the early months, in most instances, it is the subordinates who help the supervisor, rather than the supervisor who helps the subordinates. Eventually the new supervisor begins to institute a policy of his own. Often, however, department and supervisor have just become accustomed to each other's idiosyncracies when the supervisor is transferred, a new man comes in, and the process begins all over again.

If carried too far, the policy of regular rotation may throw the affected departments into almost constant turmoil. The employees, knowing that their boss won't be with them for long, never develop respect for him. They learn to resist his attempts to introduce change (which are often inept due to his lack of knowledge) and to develop strong group standards, which the supervisor of the moment finds almost impossible to modify. (Often the old-time working supervisor or an informal leader becomes the real head of the department.) As a long-service clerk in one office put it:

> "Bosses come and go. Each one has his pet peeves. We pretend to go along; but to tell you the truth we run things our own way."

5. An unintended result of rotation in some cases is the development of subtle class distinctions. The men who are moved at regular intervals develop friends all over the country; they tend to feel as a group and to identify with the company as a whole. Those who stay put develop defensive reactions and identify with their own department against the "carpetbaggers" from outside. This cleavage leads to misunderstanding and poor communications, with top management exerting pressure to get the local "stick-in-the-muds" to accept change and with local management strongly resisting every effort.

In an earlier chapter we pointed out that the supervisor is a man in the middle. His job is to represent his subordinates to his superiors and his superiors to his subordinates. He must try to maintain a balance, and if he favors anybody it should be the subordinate. The rotation system swings the balance sharply the other way. The man who is being rotated cannot afford to take the time and energy to develop relations downward; he must always look ahead to that next promotional shift.

6. The rotation system may easily become overcentralized and inflexible. The plant manager, for instance, may have little to say about who is moved into his plant, and may be forced to accept as an assistant someone he has never seen before. A supervisor who is promoted under these circumstances is less likely to show loyalty to his boss than he would if the boss had been personally responsible for the promotion.

Long-run replacement schedules often look better on paper than in practice. People quit or die; business recessions dictate cut-backs in operations; products fail to develop as expected; men turn "sour." In short, there are too many variables to make planning for very far in the future much more reliable than crystal-gazing.

In conclusion, rotation has both advantages and disadvantages. Some managers find it challenging and exciting. Others find it frustrating, both for themselves and their families. Some departments would benefit from being shaken up by outsiders, but others would suffer in morale and efficiency in the hands of a supervisor unfamiliar with the special human and technical problems of the situation.

In spite of its personal and financial costs, rotation provides useful training for the potential executive, particularly if the rotations are not too frequent. But management should rotate only those men who are genuinely anxious to move and should not discriminate against those who prefer to stay put. Furthermore, management should insure that the rotated executive does not disrupt the departments to which he is assigned.

"JET" PROGRAMS

Many companies conduct special training programs for recent college graduates. Trainees in these programs, which run for as long as two years, are often known as "jets" (junior executive trainees). The purpose of "jet" programs [10] is to provide the trainee with a general orientation to the company and its policies, and to provide the company with an opportunity to observe and evaluate the trainee intensively.

> General Electric spends roughly $5 million annually on an extensive training program, in which some 1,000 college graduates are given instruction by GE employees and opportunities for a variety of on-the-job experiences for periods from one and one-half years upwards. This program comprises a number of alternative curricula in the different aspects of the company's operations, and the trainee has the option to elect one or another "major" under the guidance of his supervisor much as he did in college.[11]

Typically, "jets" are rotated from department to department every few months, holding such jobs as that of salesman or junior foreman. Often on-the-job training is interspersed with formal classes, seminars, and discussion groups. Every month or two the trainees are carefully evaluated by their

---

[10] These programs go by various names: executive trainee program, cadet program, management development program, college trainee program, and so forth. Though there may be no confusion in the particular company, an outsider may confuse these programs with some broader aspect of management development.

[11] Reinhard Bendix, *Work and Authority in Industry* (New York: Wiley, 1956), pp. 319-320.

supervisor of the moment and by the over-all program coordinator. Trainees who completely fail to measure up to expectations are dropped; others are counseled on how to do a better job. At the end of the formal training period, each trainee is assigned to the department to which he seems best suited.

The advantages of such programs to both the company and the trainee are considerable. They provide the recent college graduate with an easy transition from the campus to the very different atmosphere of business. Further, they give him a breadth of experience and insight that he never would obtain were he to stay in a single department. Indeed the whole process is designed to help trainee and company pick the job for which the trainee is best qualified.

But these programs have disadvantages as well. The "jets" are not observed under natural conditions, and they are rarely in a department long enough to make a natural adjustment to it. Everyone knows that they are special individuals and treats them accordingly. Furthermore, "jet" programs tend to over-indoctrinate the potential supervisor with one point of view, usually the one that conformity and the ability to get along with people are all-important. Were all members of management indoctrinated with a single point of view, everyone would tackle problems in exactly the same way and there would be little encouragement for a man to take a new, different, or unconventional approach.

Also, the non-college men in an organization sometimes display intense antagonism toward these so-called "crown princes." [12] The fact that the company is hiring college men and training them specifically for management positions means that promotional opportunities for non-college men are reduced. As one foreman commented:

> "Look at that kid there. His dad had money enough to send him to college and so he is a big shot. Right now he's assistant foreman and he don't know one per cent of what the men he bosses know. Five years from now he'll be my boss and he still won't know anything. So I got to watch how I treat him. Look how he struts around. The men hate him."

Because of this antagonism, many companies avoid according special treatment to newly hired college men. And if they do conduct a special training program, they try to include a few non-college men who have come up from the ranks.

SPECIAL "BROADENING" ASSIGNMENTS

As we have seen, both job rotation and "jet" programs often have harmful effects on the departments to which the rising executive or trainee is attached. Further, while any rotation policy gives trainees broader ex-

---

[12] See "The Crown Princes of Business," *Fortune,* Vol. 48, No. 4 (October 1953), p. 151.

perience, this experience is all at a low level. Yet the types of skill required for executive success may be very different at various levels of the organization. At the lower levels, technical ability, a willingness to obey orders, and skill in dealing with people may be the chief requirements. At higher levels, the ability to innovate and to make bold, long-range decisions become more important.[13] The men who do outstanding jobs at lower and middle levels of management may be totally ineffective at top levels. On the other hand, the go-getter, the pattern-breaker, who might do brilliantly at the top might well seem very inadequate in a subordinate post.

Many observers of the industrial scene are concerned lest modern industry create too many "organization men," conformists who are mainly concerned with getting along and pleasing the boss, and not producing enough of the nonconformists who are needed at the top.[14] Sometimes outstanding men lose their spark as they work their way slowly upward; and since, at the lower levels, getting ahead depends on the recommendations of one's immediate boss, some men never have a chance to advance because the boss is too unimaginative to appreciate their abilities (or even feels threatened by them).

As a means of distinguishing the men who are outstandingly qualified for top-level positions, some companies are giving their promising junior executives special assignments which permit them to sample top-level responsibilities. The nature of these assignments varies greatly. Normally they are devised on a temporary or part-time basis—in addition to the executive's regular job. Some organizations have "junior boards of directors" or "management cabinets" [15] to which the senior board of directors may refer special problems (or the junior board may consider substantially the same agenda as the senior board). More frequently, trainees are assigned to capital budgeting, product development, or long-range planning committees where they work in the company of more senior executives. At times a trainee may be assigned to study a problem area, prepare recommendations, and present and defend them in person before a top-management committee.[16]

If such special assignments are to be successful as development tools, three requirements must be met:

1. The problems assigned must be genuinely "broadening"—that is, they must cut across departmental lines and involve long-range planning.

---

[13] See, for instance, Perrin Stryker, "The Rarest Man in Business," *Fortune,* Vol. 59, No. 5 (May 1959), p. 119. See also, Norman H. Martin, "Differential Decisions in the Management of an Industrial Plant," *Journal of Business,* Vol. 29, No. 4 (October 1956), pp. 249-260.

[14] See William H. Whyte, Jr., *The Organization Man* (New York: Simon and Schuster, 1956).

[15] For an early example that has stimulated much discussion, see Charles P. McCormick, *Multiple Management* (New York: Harpers, 1938).

[16] See Arjay Miller, "Reporting to Top Management at Ford," *California Management Review,* Vol. 1, No. 1 (Fall 1958), pp. 30-37.

2. The trainees must operate under the direct observation of top executives who are personally responsible for evaluating their performance.

3. The problems must be *tough*, challenging ones—tough enough so that the merely adequate answer appears unsatisfactory and so that the truly outstanding man can show his real merit.

Special assignments should be designed to give the rising junior executive top-level experience both in operating on his own and in serving as a committee member. "There must be evaluation of the results not only by the senior committee members but also by the juniors themselves. The juniors' evaluations must be evaluated. There must be a chance for juniors (anonymously?) to indicate those of their colleagues whom they judge to show superior intelligence, ability to accomplish, leadership, etc." [17]

A properly administered program of broadening assignments has many advantages: it frees the junior from overdependence on his boss and gives him "high visibility" where he can be observed and evaluated by a large number of top executives. It permits the junior to be judged on his ability to handle a top-level job, not just on his ability to cope with lower-level jobs. It minimizes the "crown-prince" problem, since the trainee performs his special assignments in the presence of higher management rather than in the presence of subordinates. It may bring a wealth of useful suggestions to the attention of top management, and it gives the junior invaluable experience.

These programs, however, are primarily designed to select and develop *top* managers. How about the average supervisor whose promotional opportunities are limited? Certainly special broadening assignments will be useful for him too. The average supervisor, however, has little opportunity to make major innovations or long-range decisions and is likely to function primarily as a specialist in one aspect of the organization rather than as a generalist. Yet organizational survival depends as directly on strong middle and lower management as it does on strong top management. Opportunities to grow should be provided for every man at every level. Even the man who will never be promoted can improve his performance on his present job.

Development as a Managerial Responsibility

How can opportunities for development be provided for everyone in the organization? In later chapters we shall discuss performance evaluation, evaluation interviews, coaching, and training in general. Yet formal training and development programs can play only a small part in the over-all

[17] Thomas L. Whisler, "Performance Appraisal and the Organization Man," *The Journal of Business*, Vol. 31, No. 1 (January 1958), p. 26.

development program. Every supervisor can learn a great deal on his own job if he is encouraged to do so by his superiors all the way up the line.

The basic question is this: What importance does management place on development? Does management ever reward supervisors for doing an outstanding job of training subordinates? Or do the chief rewards always go to the supervisor who keeps immediate costs low and gets production out? Does the reward system encourage the supervisor to think that developing subordinates is a waste of time? Often subordinates learn that their only reward for training a subordinate is to have him leave and replaced by someone with less experience.

> One unpublished study made within a gigantic corporation indicated that those who had reached the highest positions were not remembered by anyone in the company as having done anything significant in developing men, while those who had achieved the reputation of being wise and effective counselors invariably reached only modest levels.[18]

Professor Earl Brooks of Cornell University describes the problem as follows: [19]

> Every executive is like a juggler, juggling balls so fast that he cannot stop. Some of these balls are heavy balls and if he drops them he really hurts his toes. Other balls are light and it doesn't matter what happens to them. The supervisor learns that if he drops the ball on production or costs he quickly gets into trouble. But nobody really cares if he drops the ball on personnel development.

For a development program to be effective, every executive and every supervisor must assume the personal responsibility (1) for helping his immediate subordinates develop, and (2) for insisting that these subordinates in turn contribute to the development of those under them.

The most effective development occurs in an atmosphere where management permits self-development. "Is management willing to take a chance on its men, greeting an occasional failure as the price of taking risks?" [20] Does the supervisor feel free to make suggestions? Is he encouraged to contribute his ideas? How much responsibility does he have? Does he take part in making management decisions? Is there supervision by results rather than in detail? Does the supervisor feel that he has to cover up when he makes mistakes, or can he talk his problems over with his boss without fear of being blamed? It is hard for people to grow under close supervision, because they are afraid to try out new ways.

Further, as we have seen, the formal organization of the company itself affects the manner in which men behave. Flat organization and organization

---

[18] *Ibid.*, p. 22.
[19] Unpublished lecture, Moog Servocontrols, Nov. 22, 1959.
[20] Robert K. Stolz, "Getting Back to Fundamentals in Executive Development," *Personnel*, Vol. 30, No. 6 (May 1954), p. 456. This is an excellent article.

by product (instead of by function) makes it easier for a man to develop new ways of doing things and to be his own boss.[21]

"All this may be summed up in the statement that executives develop best in those organizations which are already well managed by recognized standards of good management."[22] A permissive atmosphere in the organization at large helps stimulate individual growth.

Conclusion

The strength of any organization depends largely on its management. If the organization is to remain strong, it must provide opportunities for the continuing development of competent replacements for those who die or retire.

Development is a matter of demand and supply. It is important to predict future needs for management manpower and to establish programs designed to supply competent men to fill vacancies as they occur. However, since it is impossible to look to the future with certainty, any development program must be flexible. Clearly it is desirable to have an orderly system that gives everyone an equal opportunity (dependent on real ability) for training, experience, and consideration for promotion. But an over-rigid rotation or promotional system can put the company into a strait jacket.

Further, special programs are not enough. Overemphasis on a few select "crown princes" may be harmful to the morale and efficiency of the whole organization. Development should not be confined to a select few, though it may be desirable to give the most promising candidates special opportunities (and challenges). The most effective development program is the one that involves every member of management, both as a trainer and a trainee. Management must give to the development of human assets the same priority it gives to the development of physical assets.

In the next two chapters we shall discuss two important developmental tools: performance evaluation and training.

Problem I

The Bemus Company was founded in the basement of its president, Andrew Bemus, about ten years ago. Mr. Bemus had developed a highly sensitive instrument which immediately found use both in defense and civilian production fields. As a consequence, the firm grew very rapidly. It had seven employees nine years ago, 200 employees five years ago, and over a thousand today.

As of today, most of the company's top management consists of Mr. Bemus'

---

[21] For a good discussion of this point, see Margaret L. Jones, "Executive Development Takes New Step," *Dun's Review and Modern Industry*, September 1953.

[22] Paul Pigors and Charles A. Myers, *Personnel Administration*, 3rd ed. (New York: McGraw-Hill, 1956), p. 118.

earliest associates, many of whom are under the age of 45. They are a highly self-confident group who have worked together closely over the years.

And yet trouble seems to lie ahead. Sharp competition from other companies has developed for the first time and profit margins have fallen. Labor costs are obviously too high and there is much confusion and divided responsibility in management. Most decisions are made by the top management group and there is little delegation of authority. Many of the more recently hired engineers complain that their ideas are given very little consideration by the inner clique—and that there is little or no chance for promotion since all the top jobs are handled by younger men. As a consequence, three of the more brilliant recent hires have resigned after spending only a short time with the company.

1. What sort of management development program does this company need?

2. Assuming that you were recently hired from the outside as personnel director, what steps would you take to win acceptance for this program?

In the typical large company every executive and supervisor is subject to a periodic evaluation of his performance. These evaluations are very important tools in management development. As with other aspects of management development, the primary purpose of *performance ratings* has shifted in recent years. Originally a device to guide management in selecting supervisors for promotions or salary increases, they are now also used as a training device to help all levels of management to improve their performance. In keeping with this new emphasis, the performance rating is communicated to subordinates in an *evaluation interview*. Properly conducted, these interviews serve as a vital coaching tool.

The armed forces pioneered the development of evaluation procedures as a means of making a systematic comparison of large numbers of officers. Suppose, for example, the army is faced with the problem of picking 1,000 men for promotion to 1st lieutenant from a group of 20,000 2nd lieutenants. Since no one individual knows all 20,000 men personally, some rating technique must be used to provide an objective basis of comparison. Each officer is rated by his superior

23

Performance
Evaluation

(or in some cases by committees) and those with the highest rating are considered first for promotion (though other factors may be taken into account).

In industry, an effective performance-rating program offers management many advantages:

> ... Better men are selected for promotion.
> ... Each man is considered for promotion or salary increase on the same basis as everyone else.
> ... There are fewer charges of favoritism.
> ... Subordinates are motivated to work harder in order to win a favorable rating.
> ... Departmental efficiency can be measured in situations where there are no obvious physical products or profit results.
> ... Long-range personnel planning is facilitated, since the promising younger man can be easily spotted and transfers can be more easily custom-tailored to meet the needs of individuals.
> ... Subordinates who need special training can be identified.
> ... Each supervisor is forced to sit down periodically and think through how each of his subordinates is developing and then (if an evaluation interview is required) to discuss their progress with them.

Performance evaluation is often conducted at the hourly-paid level as well as at the management level. (In the former case it is usually called "merit rating." See pp. 604-608.) Although we shall emphasize management performance rating in our discussion, most of what we say applies to merit rating as well.

Performance evaluation consists of two steps: the performance rating itself and the evaluation interview. We shall consider each in turn.

Performance Rating

Stripped to its essentials, performance rating is just a matter of filling out an appraisal form. Normally the form is completed by the immediate supervisor of the man who is being rated, and then the rating is checked by the supervisor's boss. Sometimes the rating is made by a committee consisting of the direct supervisor, the supervisor's boss, and one or two others who are in a position to judge the man who is being rated. Committee ratings have one great advantage: they bring several viewpoints to bear on the rating and offset the immediate supervisor's special bias. The committee meetings themselves, however, may be extremely time-consuming. In some companies the forms are filled out by the immediate supervisor in collaboration with the personnel director, who takes advantage of the rating session to help the supervisor think through ways of doing a better job of developing the subordinate in question.

The types of rating form used vary tremendously, depending on the philosophy behind the particular evaluation program. We shall look first at the conventional rating method and its limitations. Then we shall examine newer approaches to rating, some of which are designed to obtain highly objective evaluations, others of which are frankly subjective. Finally, we shall consider a fundamental question that underlies all forms of rating procedure: What should we try to rate—basic personality traits or behavior on the job? And we shall examine some of the procedures that have been designed to evaluate behavior.

CONVENTIONAL RATINGS

Illustrated on p. 530 is a conventional rating form used by many companies. This check-the-box type of form (often called "graphic rating" or "rating scale") is very simple to fill out. What is really important is the over-all quantitative score, which makes it possible to compare large numbers of managers against one another. The ratings on specific factors do serve a purpose, however, in helping to pin-point areas in which the subordinate needs further development.

In spite of its deceptive simplicity, graphic rating has severe limitations. Note, for example, some of the basic assumptions that lie behind it: One assumption is that each of the factors (cost control, judgment, etc.) is of *equal* importance and that this holds true on *all* jobs. Yet clearly on some jobs judgment is more important than effectiveness in dealing with people, and on other just the reverse is true. Another assumption is that all these qualities are "additive"—that, for instance, the fact that a candidate is strong on job knowledge will offset his lack of dependability.

Unwilling to accept these assumptions, some companies no longer require separate ratings on each factor; instead, they ask supervisors to give their men just one single rating on over-all ability, perhaps in numerical terms from one to a hundred or in descriptive terms from "unsatisfactory" to "outstanding." Yet unless some reference is made to ratings on particular factors, over-all ratings are of little help in deciding whether a *particular* man should be promoted to a *particular* position. In fact, his special combination of abilities might suit him for something entirely different. Certainly over-all ratings are of little value in determining what sort of training a man needs. Nor do they provide specific enough information to help a subordinate figure out how he can improve his performance.

Thus graphic ratings are not particularly useful in making accurate comparisons among large numbers of employees, and over-all ratings are too general to help management in filling job vacancies or in training.

HUMAN ERRORS IN RATING

In addition, both forms of quantitative rating, whether based on specific factors or over-all ability, are subject to certain human evaluative

	Unsatisfactory	Fair	Good	Very good	Exceptional	

Name _____ Position _____ Date rated _____

Date hired _____ On position since _____ Points _____

	Unsatisfactory	Fair	Good	Very good	Exceptional	

Job knowledge
Extent of theoretical knowledge and practical know-how as related to present job.   1   2   3   4   5   _____

Judgment
Ability to obtain and analyze facts and apply sound judgment.   1   2   3   4   5   _____

Organizing ability
Effectiveness in planning own work and that of subordinates.   1   2   3   4   5   _____

Attitude
Enthusiasm shown for job; loyalty to company and superiors; ability to accept criticism and changes in company policy.   1   2   3   4   5   _____

Dependability
Reliability in carrying out assignments conscientiously and with effectiveness.   1   2   3   4   5   _____

Creativity
Ability to apply imagination to job, to develop new plans, cut costs, etc.   1   2   3   4   5   _____

Dealing with people
Ability to get along with others; tact, diplomacy; ability to command and influence people   1   2   3   4   5   _____

Delegation
Ability to assign work to others and to coordinate others through distribution of workload and responsibility.   1   2   3   4   5   _____

Leadership
Ability to stimulate subordinates to perform their jobs effectively   1   2   3   4   5   _____

Personal efficiency
Speed and effectiveness in carrying out duties not assigned to subordinates.   1   2   3   4   5   _____

Total Points _____

Evaluated by: _____

Unsatisfactory: 10-16 points

Title: _____

Fair: 16-25 points
Good: 26-35 points

Approved by: _____

Very good: 35-44 points
Excellent: 45-50 points

Title: _____

Conventional rating form.

errors. (Incidentally, these same errors distort merit rating and job evaluation, to which we will return in later chapters.)

Clarity in standards   Unless all raters agree on what is meant by such terms as "good" or "excellent," their final ratings simply cannot be compared. To cite an extreme example, the rating scale in one hospital included Excellent, Very Good, Fair, Satisfactory, and Unsatisfactory. Several head nurses objected to using the term "satisfactory," on the ground that "no nurse is ever really satisfactory." To them "satisfactory" meant "better than excellent."

Excessive leniency or strictness   As every student knows, there is a big difference betwen hard and easy markers. Supervisors in industry often hesitate to give low ratings for fear of antagonizing their subordinates and making them less cooperative.[1] Furthermore, the supervisor may be afraid that low ratings will reflect on his own ability. There is always a chance that his boss will say, "If your subordinate is as bad as all this, why don't you do something about it?" Some executives regularly rate new employees very low, then gradually raise them—thus making the employee feel good and displaying to their superiors their excellence as trainers.

In many organizations there is a tendency for average ratings to rise over time. Thus during World War II practically every enlisted man got the highest rating. To get the next-to-highest rating was evidence of downright incompetence.[2]

The halo effect   There is a natural tendency for the rater to be influenced in rating one factor by the kind of rating he gives on another. In fact, the individual rater tends to give each man approximately the same rating on all factors. If a rater has a general feeling that a man is good, he will rate him high on all factors—and vice versa.[3]

Influence of a man's job   Performance rating is designed to evaluate how well a man does on a *particular* job. Although in theory it is vastly different from job evaluation (which rates the job, not the man), in practice there is

---

[1] One study showed that supervisors in a government department gave much higher ratings if they expected to have to show them to the men they had rated than if they expected the ratings to remain confidential. Fred Massarik, Irving R. Wechsler, and Robert Tannenbaum, "Evaluating Efficiency Rating Systems Through Experiment," *Personnel Administration,* Vol. 14, No. 1 (January 1951), pp. 42-47.

[2] Similarly in 1940 over half of all ground officers were rated superior or best—which meant that the system was useful only in eliminating the mediocre, not in selecting the outstanding. E. Donald Sisson, "Forced Choice—The New Army Rating," *Personnel Psychology,* Vol. 1, No. 3 (Autumn 1948), p. 366.

[3] The supervisor can reduce this halo effect by rating all his men on a single item before going on to the next—rather than rating one man at a time.

a common tendency to give a man on a higher-paid job a higher rating just because he is doing that job.

All these human errors in rating can be at least partially counteracted by insuring that the supervisors who do the rating are properly trained. Group discussion of the natural tendencies toward bias in rating seems to be more effective than straight lectures.[4] Another useful training technique is for the instructor to give the class a thumbnail sketch of the requirements of a given job and the behavior of an individual in it. Then each student rates the individual, the ratings are compared, and, through discussion of why different ratings are given, differences in interpretation and approach are ironed out.

Yet training of this sort is expensive and is not always effective in eliminating bias. As a consequence, many personnel researchers have tried to develop new rating procedures which are less affected by the rater's personal bias and which make it easier to compare objectively the performance of large numbers of employees.

OBJECTIVE RATING SCALES

Two of the best known of the newer forms of objective rating are *forced distribution* and *forced choice*.

Forced distribution [5] is familiar to many students as the old principle of "grading on the curve." The supervisor who uses this system of rating is expected to rank subordinates by class, instead of ascribing a set of rating points to each individual. In a typical system the top 10 per cent of the men are placed in the highest class, 20 per cent in the next, 40 per cent in the middle bracket, 20 per cent in the next-to-lowest, and 10 per cent in the very bottom class. Ordinarily, only one over-all rating of ability is given, rather than a series of ratings on separate factors.

This system obviously eliminates any danger that the supervisor will be over-lenient, or the possibility that the standards will be interpreted in different ways by different supervisors. Moreover, the system is easy to explain and administer. Yet this scheme has distinct drawbacks: In effect, it assumes that all groups have the same proportion of average, poor, and outstanding men. But this is not likely to be true, particularly where there are only a few men on a given job. If there are only five men in a given job classification, for example, all may be excellent, and yet the supervisor must

---

4 Jacob Levine and John Butler, "Lecture vs. Group Discussion in Changing Behavior," in Dorwin Cartwright and Alvin Zander, eds., *Group Dynamics* (Evanston, Ill.: Row, Peterson, 1953), pp. 280-286.

5 See Joseph Tiffin, "Merit Rating: Its Validity and Techniques," *Rating Employee and Supervisory Performance* (New York: American Management Association, 1950), pp. 17-19.

select one for the bottom category. (This is the very point that gives rise to student gripes against grading on the curve in small classes.) Ratings of this sort not only seem unfair, but encourage an unhealthy kind of competition, not just to do better, but to do better than the other man (or perhaps to make him look worse).

Forced choice, a radically different approach, was developed by a distinguished group of psychologists at the end of World War II for use in rating army officers. Its purpose is to eliminate as far as possible any human bias by setting up a system in which the rater is presented with four possible statements about a person, such as:

	Most	Least
Doesn't try to pull rank	____	____
Knows his men, their capabilities, and limitations	____	____
Low efficiency	____	____
Uses a steady monotone in his voice	____	____

The rater is expected to check two items, one of which is the *most* and the other the *least* characteristic of the person being rated. Two of these are apparently favorable and two apparently unfavorable. However, only one of the favorable items gives a plus credit; the other, if checked, gives no credit at all. Similarly, only one of the two negative items affects the final result. The zero-credit items (in this case, possibly, "Doesn't try to pull rank" and "Uses a steady monotone") are ones that have been shown by tests to have significantly less correlation with military efficiency than the two that give credit.[6] The important thing is that the rater doesn't know which items are the ones that count. His own prejudices and biases are minimized, since his only function is to give an objective description of the subordinate's performance by checking the blanks. If an electro-sensitive pencil is used, the rating itself can be made by IBM machine.

Following the war, the forced-choice technique was adopted by many industrial firms. It has the advantage of reducing such forms of bias as leniency and the halo effect; no training is required to prepare a supervisor to use it; and there is some evidence that it does a better job of pin-pointing the best men than do simpler forms of rating—that is, it correlates more highly with ratings by fellow employees and with objective factors such as productivity.

Though from many points of view forced choice seems clearly the best

---

[6] For a description of how these tests were constructed, see E. Donald Sisson, "Forced Choice—The New Army Rating," *Personnel Psychology,* Vol. 1, No. 3 (Autumn 1948), pp. 365-381. For more general descriptions of the forced-choice technique, see Marion W. Richardson, "Forced Choice Performance Reports," in M. Joseph Dooher and Vivienne Marquis, eds., *Rating Employee and Supervisory Performance* (New York: American Management Association, 1950), pp. 35-46; and Mathew Radom, "How to Select Employees," in Manufacturing Series, No. 208 (New York: American Management Association, 1953).

system of rating, its use has not spread widely after the initial postwar spurt. In the first place, the system is expensive to install, for the items must be custom-tailored to the demands of the particular job and company. (Suppose a set of four items contained these two favorable items: "Has a constant flow of new ideas" and "Shows careful judgment." A choice of the first might represent a good mark for an advertising executive but a bad mark for a banker.)

Forced choice is often resented by both raters and ratees. The implicit assumption behind the system is that supervisors cannot be trusted to rate fairly, an assumption that naturally prejudices them against its use. A department manager summarized the common attitude: "I try to reward my good men by giving them good ratings—but you just have to guess what those psychology boys [who set up the items] want. No one understands how it works. Some of the men call it promotion by Ouija Board." A final objection is that forced choice makes it difficult or impossible to use ratings for the purpose of counseling employees.

Some rating specialists have reacted to the criticism of "forced distribution" and "forced choice" by "fighting back with ... [schemes with] ... even more statistical horsepower." [7] Many observers, however, doubt that statistical approaches to rating are really fruitful. They feel that little is accomplished by any attempt to reduce the complex human personality to a numerical value, and that, in any case, this value is of little help to the supervisor when he faces the difficult task of training subordinates or deciding who should be promoted to fill a given vacancy. As a consequence, there is a general trend in American business today away from objective, quantitative ratings and toward more subjective, descriptive ratings.

SUBJECTIVE RATINGS

The simplest type of subjective rating is based on a form that asks such general questions as: "1. What is the supervisor's performance in his present duty? 2. To what extent does he give indication of future development?" The rater answers each of these questions with a brief essay. Other evaluation forms ask more specific questions, such as, "How does the supervisor get along with staff departments?"

Many rating forms of this type include both qualitative and quantitative questions. On one typical form the rater is required to check a box, as in rating scales, but is also expected to make additional comments. (In the example on p. 535, note that only one portion of the form is shown.)

---

[7] Thomas L. Whisler, "A Realistic Role for Merit Rating," *The Journal of Business,* Vol. 28, No. 1 (January 1955), pp. 25-36.

A somewhat more complicated form is on p. 536. Note that only a section of the form has been reproduced.

Cooperativeness with other departments	Always helps other departments without being asked	Helpful on most occasions	Gets along reasonably well	At times has difficulty with other departments; slow to offer help	Frequently has difficulty with other departments
	☐	☐	☐	☐	☐

Explain why you gave this rating: _____

_____

_____

Companies that use these more subjective types of rating are on the whole more concerned with applying the ratings to the coaching and evaluation of employees than to the selection of men for higher management positions.[8] For this reason, the tendency is to emphasize behavior rather than traits, and to tailor-make the evaluation form as a springboard for evaluation interviews, and thus help the subordinate develop himself.

Traits or Behavior?

In recent years there has been a notable shift of emphasis in what is evaluated—a shift from inherent personal traits to specific behavior. As we mentioned earlier, management development was originally introduced into many companies as a crash program designed to reveal executives who were promotable to top positions. Actual performance on the job was often considered secondary, in part because the emphasis was all on the individual's *potential* for development, and in part because many of the men rated had little or no experience in managerial positions. Consequently, there was no performance that could be rated.

---

[8] The U. S. Army's experience with rating officers for promotion is instructive. Until the end of World War II, the Army used a conventional point-system rating scale. Then, as we have mentioned, it experimented with forced choice until about 1950. From 1950 to 1958 a variety of forced distribution was used. Most recently the Army has switched to a more simplified form which for the first time is designed largely as an aid in counseling subordinates. As a high-ranking army officer has told us, "We have just about given up mechanical aids to help us in selecting who will be promoted. Frankly, I think this is all to the good since it makes the promotion board scan a man's complete record—as it should."

PERFORMANCE APPRAISAL OF MANAGEMENT PERSONNEL

NAME *Jones   Robert   C.*   ORGANIZATIONAL UNIT *Development*
　　　(Last)　　　(First)　　　(Initial)　　　　　　　　　　　　　　　　*Laboratory*

POSITION TITLE *Project Director* SALARY GRADE   *VI*   DATE HIRED *Jan. 23, 196—*

ON PRESENT POSITION SINCE *Oct. 15, 196—* DATE OF LAST APPRAISAL *March 15, 196—*
　　　　　　　　　　　　　　(Date)

INSTRUCTIONS

1 — Read carefully the name of the factor and its definition. Answer carefully the questions asked on the left side of the page. These questions generally require a "yes" or "no" answer but may be answered by "occasionally" or "frequently."

2 — When the definition of the factor is clearly understood and the questions have been answered, check the box opposite the statement which describes most typically the employee's performance.

3 — If words or phrases in the box you check do not apply, cross them out. If words or phrases opposite other boxes do apply, encircle them.

4 — Consider performance in each factor over the entire rating period. Do not be unduly influenced by recent events or incidents!

1 — POSITION KNOWLEDGE

This factor appraises the man's demonstrated understanding of basic principles, techniques, and practical and theoretical "know-how" as related to his present position.

First, answer these questions

1 — Is further instruction, training or experience necessary before he will be thoroughly familiar with his position as described? *yes*

2 — Does he know the relationship of his job to other functions in his department? — other departments and his division? — the Company *fairly well*

3 — Have your contacts with him indicated that he has had the desired knowledge of management policies and programs? *needs some improvement*

4 — Does he know the basic principles of his field and and apply them to his position in a practical manner? *not completely practical*

5 — Is he alert to trends and improvements in his field, and does he adjust his operation to apply them? *yes*

6 — Since the last appraisal, has he in any specific way added to the extent or diversity of his practical knowledge or experience for the job? *yes*

Second, check the appropriate box

☐ (1) Demonstrated a lack of understanding of basic principles. More extensive job knowledge necessary. Lacks appreciation of current developments.

☐ (2) Demonstrated fair understanding of basic principles and methods, but required coaching. Indicated definite weaknesses in some phases of work. Weak in appreciation of current developments and needs more experience.

☐ (3) Demonstrated good standard knowledge of all phases of the position. (Somewhat limited in experience) and application of new developments, but meets all requirements for satisfactory position performance.

☑ (4) Demonstrated above-standard knowledge of ~~both~~ theoretical ~~and practical~~ aspects of work. Good understanding of major developments in the field and their application.

☐ (5) Demonstrated exceptional mastery of all phases of the position. (Outstanding grasp of principles,) techniques and procedures. Good understanding of related functions.

In order of importance, state three performance characteristics which need improvement with respect to his present position.

1. *Emotional stability*
2. *Dealings with subordinates*
3. *cost control*

What might he do to improve his job performance?
Try harder to get along with other people. Don't blow his stack all the time. Be more practical.

Are there any factors in the health, personal life or other outside influences which may have affected his performance during this appraisal period?
Divorced wife last month

Comments
A very able scientist who finds it hard to get out of the clouds. His subordinates respect his ability though many are irritated by his moodiness. Possibly he may settle down when he solves his family problems.

Adapted from a form used by The Carborundum Co. Courtesy, The Carborundum Co.

As a result, the early emphasis in rating was on such factors as optimism, initiative, drive, imagination, and ability to learn. A typical form asked for a rating on "personality," which was defined as "the external mannerisms consciously or unconsciously adopted in meeting situations." There were five points on the scale:

1. radiant, confident, poised, courteous
2. pleasant, forceful
3. likable
4. ill at ease, not too forceful
5. negative, colorless

What has proved wrong with this emphasis on traits? In the first place, the ratings secured are of little use in helping an employee do a better job. For instance, it is hard for a man to make a real change in his "personality," though he might put up a false front and pretend to be "radiant, confident, cheerful, courteous."

More important, an emphasis on traits gives the advantage to the conformist, "the individual who has nothing wrong with him. More particularly, [the] emphasis on human relations favors the individual who always gets along with other people and never rubs anybody the wrong way." [9]

A large chemical company, for example, offers the following choices for the single trait, "cooperation":

1. Adapts self very well without sacrificing standards. Goes out of his way to promote common end.[10]
2. Willing and eager to please. Works in complete harmony with group. Adaptable and courteous.
3. Generally adapts self to persons and situations. Responsive to leadership and reasonably tactful.
4. Poor mixer. Tries to run with the ball. Occasionally indulges in obstructive argument.
5. Concedes nothing. Obstructive, antagonistic.

Note that by favoring the man who is "willing and eager to please" over the one who "tries to run with the ball," this company is in effect molding its own character.

As we mentioned in Chapter 1, middle management often does consist of "other-directed" individuals with a strong human-relations orientation. Yet those at the very top are more likely to be 100 per cent rugged individualists.

---

[9] Robert K. Stoltz, "Is Executive Development Coming of Age?" *The Journal of Business,* Vol. 28, No. 1 (January 1955), p. 50. It could be argued that this is not so much the fault of rating traits as the fact that the wrong traits are emphasized. A company could just as easily use trait-rating to pick nonconformists. See Stanley Stark, "Executive Personality and Psychological Testing," *Current Economic Comment,* Vol. 20, No. 2 (May 1958), pp. 15-32.

[10] Ernest Dale and Alice Smith, "Now Report Cards for Bosses," *New York Times Magazine* (March 31, 1958), p. 56.

How many of the great tycoons of industry have been "radiant, confident, poised, courteous"? "Charles E. Wilson guided the vast General Motors organization to oustanding success despite his admitted susceptibility to foot-in-mouth disease. Henry Ford, Sr., got along pretty well without too much sense of humor. And Abraham Lincoln would never have been given a passing mark if his contemporaries had thought to grade him." [11] As Stoltz puts it, "realistically speaking, most executives are curious combinations of strengths and weaknesses." [12]

After all, management is primarily interested in *results*.[13] As a consequence many companies have experimented in rating results directly.

RATING BY RESULTS

When supervisors are rated by results, rather than by some other person working with some sort of rating technique, the rewards go to the man who gets things done, rather than to the glad-hander who makes a good impression but who may be less effective on the job. There are two common methods of rating by results: by use of *critical incidents,* and by use of *performance standards.*

Critical incidents   The critical-incident technique of rating is also known as the "critical requirement system" and the "performance record program." [14] The first step is to draw up for each job a list of *critical job requirements.* For a foreman, for instance, these requirements might include "improving equipment," "getting along with staff," "meeting schedules," and so forth. Typical job requirements for a sales manager might be "developing new customers" and "avoiding losses."

Once the critical job requirements have been determined, the next step is to train supervisors to be on the lookout for *critical incidents* or examples of success or failure on the part of the subordinate in meeting the requirements. "An incident, to be worthy of recording, must be critical to job success or failure, must be factual rather than opinion or hearsay and must be out of the ordinary; either outstandingly good performance or outstandingly poor performance." [15] The supervisor lists the incidents as he observes them and

---

[11] *Ibid.,* p. 58.

[12] *Ibid.,* p. 51.

[13] However, management that emphasizes results should be cautious about promoting a man to a higher job purely on the basis of his performance in a lesser one. This is a valid criterion only to the extent that the requirements of the jobs are comparable, which is often not the case. See Stark, *op. cit.,* p. 25.

[14] This system has been adopted rather widely by the government. See John C. Flanagan, "A New Approach to Evaluating Personnel," *Personnel,* Vol. 26, No. 1 (July 1949), pp. 35-42; John C. Flanagan and Robert K. Burns, "The Employee Performance Record," *Harvard Business Review,* Vol. 33, No. 5 (September 1955), pp. 95-102.

[15] W. H. Gilman and E. P. Comer, "Selecting a Method of Performance Evaluation for Hourly Employees," *Supervision* (November 1957).

gradually builds up a record for each subordinate, with the "debits" on one side and the "credits" on the other:

Dealing with union

9-21-60 Failed to consult with steward before making transfer.	8-6-60 Persuaded steward to withdraw grievance in regard to employee discharged for excessive absenteeism.
11-7-60 Made transfer in violation of sect. 39(c) of contract.	12-3-60 Gave excellent answer to union grievance.

Normally, no attempt is made to balance the "debits" and the "credits." And yet the critical-incident method does provide the raw materials for the more conventional type of rating previously discussed.

The great advantage of this approach is that all ratings are based on objective evidence rather than on a subjective evaluation of traits. To insure objectivity, the supervisor is requested to record each incident immediately instead of trying to think back over, say, the last six months before making a rating. (Thus he is also improving his ability as an observer.)

On the other hand, care must be taken to insure that the supervisor's record-keeping does not degenerate into supervision in detail. He should emphasize *what* is accomplished, not *how* it is accomplished. Further, keeping a "little black book" in which all mistakes are recorded conflicts with the philosophy that supervision should not overemphasize blame-finding. When a supervisor records an unfavorable incident, he should be careful to tell the subordinate about it at the time and give him every chance to tell his side of the story.

Performance standards The use of performance standards as a rating device is not too different from the critical-incident approach. Here specific quantitative standards are established, such as "increases output per man by 10 per cent" or "cuts training time in half." [16] Once such goals are established, it is relatively easy for the supervisor to determine whether his subordinates are achieving them. This is supervision by results in its simplest form.

In Chapter 14, we saw that overreliance on statistical measures can at best give only a partial picture of supervisory behavior, and at worst can result in a serious distortion of this behavior. Even profits do not provide a sufficient standard of performance, for high profits in a given year may be obtained at the cost of ill will or poor maintenance.

A modification of the performance-standards approach rates supervisors in terms of their observed human relations rather than in terms of cost or

---

[16] See Edward C. Schleh, *Successful Executive Action* (Englewood Cliffs, N.J.: Prentice-Hall, 1955), p. 30; for a slightly different approach, see David W. Belcher, *Wage and Salary Administration* (Englewood Cliffs, N.J.: Prentice-Hall, 1955), p. 301. An excellent discussion is contained in Arch Patton, "How to Appraise Executive Performance," *Harvard Business Review*, Vol. 38, No. 1 (January 1960), pp. 63-70.

output. This scheme requires that definite standards of behavior be established, such as "should contact methods department at least twice per week," "should respond within two hours when control chart indicates overtime hours are climbing," "should reduce contacts with own subordinates to x amount." The supervisor is then observed and his observed behavior is compared against the standard. This approach takes into account the fact that productivity is always a product of many variables outside the individual's control. On the other hand, such a system is quite difficult to design, and once it is designed it seems to dictate in quite rigid detail not only what a supervisor should do but *how* he should do it.

Let us state once again that evaluation techniques based on actual behavior are designed, not so much to identify potential for higher positions, but rather to evaluate the manager's *present* performance and to guide him to do a better job. In what specific ways may such evaluations be used to help subordinates improve their performance?

The Evaluation Interview

Many companies now require each supervisor to sit down periodically with each of his subordinates to discuss his performance with him. The evaluation report is ordinarily used as a springboard for the discussion. Evaluation interviews serve two purposes: (1) They enable the evaluation to serve as a form of feedback, which helps the individual know his progress and where he stands in the eyes of his boss, and (2) they provide an opportunity for the supervisor to counsel the subordinate on how to improve his performance.

In some companies the supervisors are never told how they have been rated; ignorant of where they stand, their morale is seriously impaired. In most organizations, however, management feels that it is only fair to inform them of the results of ratings. As one junior executive commented, "Before this evaluation system was installed, the only time the boss would tell how you were doing was when you were really in trouble. If he'd say 'I'd like to talk to you about your future' that meant you were really going to get chewed out."

Yet too often supervisors recoil at the thought of having to tell another man how he stands or what he needs to do to improve himself, "They fool themselves into believing that the subordinate knows all this from day-to-day contacts on the job, and they are often shocked to learn that the boss 'never told me how I was doing.'" [17] Actually, the evaluation interview helps

---

[17] Paul Pigors and Charles A. Myers, *Personnel Administration*, 3rd ed. (New York: McGraw-Hill, 1956), p. 124.

minimize misunderstanding between supervisor and subordinate. Here is an illustration:

> A research engineer in a food-processing plant had worked for several years on various projects, and seemed to be working all the time. He seemed to be working on very important projects. Yet in three years no worthwhile project was finished and turned over to the sales department to improve the product line. Right along side of him, another research engineer contributed five major items to the line.
>
> When the research head reviewed these two individuals, he recognized the error. He sat down with the first research engineer and explained very carefully what was expected of him. In fact, he held back a raise because no real accomplishment had been made. In the next year this research engineer brought to a head three of the items on which he was working, and turned them over to the sales department.[18]

Evaluation interviews are not easy to conduct, and if they are poorly handled they may lead to hostility and greater misunderstanding. Consequently, many companies have spent a great deal of time and effort on training their supervisors to handle evaluation interviews, giving particular emphasis to skill in the use of non-directive techniques. To insure that no essential part of the interview is left out, supervisors are often encouraged to follow a standardized outline. For example: [19]

1. The supervisor tells the subordinate the purpose of the interview, and that it is designed to help him do a better job.

2. The supervisor then presents the evaluation, giving the strong points first and then the weak points. (There is no reason why the supervisor has to show the entire evaluation to the subordinate, nor, as we shall mention later, does he have to be 100 per cent frank about the subordinate's prospects.)

3. Next the supervisor asks for general comments on the evaluation. He anticipates that the subordinate may show some hostility to negative evaluations and allows him to blow off steam.

4. The supervisor then tries to encourage the subordinate to give his own picture of his progress, the problems he is meeting, what he can do to solve them, and how his supervisor can help him.

5. The interview ends with a discussion of what the subordinate can do by himself to overcome his weak points and what the supervisor can do to help. The supervisor tries to accept any criticism or aggression on the part

---

[18] Edward C. Schleh, *Successful Executive Action* (Englewood Cliffs, N.J.: Prentice-Hall, 1955), p. 27.

[19] See Bernard J. Corner, "The Communication of Merit Rating," *Personnel,* Vol. 30, No. 2 (September 1953), p. 88; Earl G. Planty and C. A. Efferson, "Counseling Executives after Merit Rating or Evaluation," *Personnel,* Vol. 27, No. 5 (March 1951), pp. 384-396; Norman R. F. Maier, *Psychology in Industry,* 2nd ed. (Boston: Houghton Mifflin, 1955), pp. 623-629; Benjamin Balinsky and Ruth Berger, *The Executive Interview* (New York: Harpers, 1959), Chapter 9.

of the subordinate without argument or contradiction. He helps the subordinate save face and does not expose his unjustified alibis. (Note: No matter how the interview is handled, more time will be spent on the bad points than on the good ones.)

Some supervisors start the interview by asking the subordinate, "Tell me, how do *you* think you are doing?" Then they show the subordinate the evaluation. This approach has the advantage of letting the subordinate tell his side of the story first; it is often easier for a man to criticize himself than to accept criticism from others. Were it not for the fact that the subordinate knows that he is about to receive an evaluation from his boss, this would be an excellent form of training. Under the circumstances, however, the subordinate may well feel uncomfortable while he is on the hot seat waiting for the "verdict."

DIFFICULTIES IN CONDUCTING EVALUATION INTERVIEWS

In recent years many companies have become discouraged with the type of evaluation program just described. The rating period often turns out to be a time of apprehension and discomfort for supervisors and subordinates alike. As a result, many supervisors just go through the motions of conducting interviews and some "forget" about them altogether. It is not uncommon for supervisors to hand subordinates their rating without comment, or to explain the rating in a rather embarrassed fashion without giving the subordinate a chance to comment or reply.

Why are supervisors generally so unenthusiastic about the evaluation program? Many have little skill in non-directive interviewing procedure; others feel that their primary function is "to get production out" and have very little interest in taking time from their "main job" to develop subordinates. (As one executive put it, "This is personnel's idea; personnel ought to carry the ball. I think it's a bunch of nonsense.")

Yet even supervisors who are sympathetic to the principles of supervisory development feel uncomfortable when they have to criticize subordinates. One supervisor commented, "I dread the time when I have to give ratings. Nobody appreciates them and I get into an endless series of arguments which make it just that much tougher to get the work out." This reluctance is particularly evident when the rating plan requires the supervisor to discuss the subordinate's personality traits. Douglas McGregor concludes:

> The conventional approach, unless handled with consummate skill and delicacy, constitutes something dangerously close to a violation of the integrity of the personality. Managers are uncomfortable when they are placed in the position of "playing God." The respect we hold for the inherent value of the individual leaves us distressed when we must take responsibility for judging the personal worth of a fellow man. Yet the conventional approach to appraisal forces us, not only to make such judgments and to

see them acted upon, but also to communicate them to those who have judged. No wonder we resist.[20]

Subordinates also tend to react to performance evaluation with defensiveness, suspicion, and hostility.[21] They hope that the boss will recognize their merits, but fear that he will criticize their faults unfairly. Since many are primarily concerned with defending themselves, they resist the boss' criticisms and suggestions. Subordinates in this state of mind are hardly in a mood to "learn" from the interview. In fact, the interview may seriously impair the supervisor-subordinate relationship by creating animosity and misunderstanding.

Another explanation for the widespread resistance to conventional forms of evaluation interviews lies in certain assumptions that lie behind them: (1) people want to be told where they stand, and (2) if they are told, they can change for the better. Neither assumption is universally valid. Let us look at two examples:

> A liberal-arts college decided to rate all faculty members from 1 (to be dropped) to 5 (deserves immediate promotion). The rating program was conducted by a joint faculty-student committee. A 65-year-old professor was given a 2 grade on the grounds that his teaching lacked luster and he was hard to understand. He was too old to change his ways and the college had not the slightest intention of dropping him a few years before his retirement. But the professor's grade for a lifetime of devoted service to his college was a D! The shock contributed to a heart attack shortly afterward. Some people don't really want to know where they stand, nor will the knowledge help them.

> The second case involved a laboratory division head who was brilliant technically, but suffered from shyness and insecurity in dealing with people. Would telling him of his failing improve his dealings with people? Of course not. Certainly it would not help him gain self-confidence. The only thing that might help him would be a form of psychotherapy much deeper than his superior could offer.

Obviously there is no simple answer to the question of whether an evaluation interview will be useful or what sort of interview should be used in a given situation. It depends directly on the personality of both the supervisor and the subordinate. Moreover, the supervisor should use the form of interview that he finds most comfortable. For instance, the supervisor who tries to use the non-directive interview with no understanding of the approach will simply give the subordinate the impression that he is two-faced.

---

[20] "An Uneasy Look at Performance Appraisal," *Harvard Business Review*, Vol. 35, No. 3 (May 1957), p. 90. See also Spencer J. Hayden, "Getting Better Results from Post-Appraisal Interviews," *Personnel*, Vol. 31, No. 6 (May 1955), p. 542.

[21] For an interesting study of such reactions, see Kenneth E. Richards, "A New Concept of Performance Appraisal," *The Journal of Business*, Vol. 32, No. 3 (July 1959), pp. 229-243.

In any event, the supervisor should recognize that the objectives of the interview vary from one person to another. For example:

1. Where the fault is difficult or impossible to correct, as in the two cases described above, there is no point in discussing it at all (unless the subordinate demands to know why he hasn't been promoted).

2. If a man has faults that are correctable, it may be better to let him bring them up himself when he sees fit. Since evaluation interviews are held periodically, there is no need for the supervisor to be disappointed if the subordinate doesn't give a perfect self-analysis during the first session. The important thing is that the subordinate make gradual progress in correcting his limitations where he can, and in accepting his limitations where he cannot overcome them.

3. In some cases an individual's performance may be so poor as to raise the possibility of his being discharged. Under such circumstances it is only fair that he be given warning, even though there is little chance of changing his behavior.

Still one fundamental objection remains: this sort of approach demands that the supervisor be a part-time psychiatrist. As the management development chief at Standard Oil of Ohio once asked: "Are we in the business of changing people or are we running a business? Are we interested in personalities or are we interested in on-the-job results?" [22]

NEW APPROACHES TO EVALUATION

Douglas McGregor has suggested an approach that may minimize some of the problems we have mentioned.[23] Instead of requiring the supervisor to rate his subordinates, each subordinate is requested to establish, for himself, short-range performance goals, ways in which he can improve his own efficiency and that of his department. Together, the supervisor and subordinate talk over what is required to meet these goals. At the end of six months they meet again to evaluate how the subordinate has done, to discuss how he could do better, and to set goals for the next six months. Note that this approach emphasizes the *future*, which can be changed, rather than the *past*, which cannot. It emphasizes specific behavior rather than character traits.

This type of evaluation is consistent with the non-directive approach, since the subordinate sets his own performance standards and evaluates himself. Of course, there is always the possibility that the subordinate may set his targets too low or rate himself too highly. However, "Most subordinates tend to underestimate their potentialities and achievements. Moreover, sub-

---

[22] O. A. Ohmann, "Executive Appraisal and Counseling," *Michigan Business Review,* Vol. 9, No. 6 (November 1957), p. 21.

[23] *Op. cit.,* pp. 89-94.

ordinates normally have an understandable wish to satisfy their bosses and quite willingly adjust their targets or appraisals if the superior thinks they are unrealistic." [24]

Standard Oil of Ohio uses an approach that is in some ways even more unconventional than that suggested by McGregor. This program calls for planning, appraisals, and counseling to be handled together. As in the more conventional approach, the first step is to set up a committee. But instead of rating the individual's personality traits, as in the past, the committee concentrates on helping him to plan for the problems he will face in the ensuing year. The subordinate's interviews with both the committee and his own boss are devoted to a discussion of the subordinate's goals in the coming year and the problems he may face in reaching them.

> Now we are looking at counseling in a much more impersonal way. We are defining the objectives the manager is expected to reach and directing his planning to their most effective accomplishment. . . . This procedure gives the subordinate an opportunity to make his own evaluation of the operating results. When he is discussing results he is actually appraising himself and probably gaining some insight on how he might improve his own attitudes, methods or behavior.[25]

If an evaluation interview of this sort is to succeed, not only the subordinate's performance but also the relationship between supervisor and subordinate should be reviewed. The supervisor should ask the subordinate what he, as supervisor, can do, refrain from doing, or do differently to help the subordinate do an even better job. This approach gives greater balance to the interview, since each party is evaluating the other and there is clear recognition that the subordinate's efficiency is greatly affected by what the supervisor does. Also, it gives the subordinate a chance to bring up problems and to air complaints that he might otherwise have kept to himself. (Except for the fact that it occurs at stated intervals rather than continuously, the Standard Oil approach is no different from what we called "training" and "handling of mistakes" in Chapter 7.)

When the evaluation interview is concerned primarily with explaining why management has failed to give a man a promotion or pay increase, the negative "judging" aspects predominate. For this reason some companies are trying to eliminate discussions of promotion and salary adjustments from the evaluation interview so that the interview can be used almost entirely as a training instrument. Here we have moved full circle from evaluation's original function as a selection device.

Some companies isolate any evaluation of a man's potential almost completely from an evaluation of performance on his present job. They use different forms for each purpose, with the form used for selection putting greater emphasis on traits. Two separate sets of evaluation interviews are

[24] *Ibid.*, p. 91.
[25] *Op. cit.*, p. 24.

held. This practice reduces the unsatisfactory compromise that often results when evaluation is used for a variety of purposes. Also it avoids "undue emphasis . . . on 'upwards-and-onward' possibilities to the neglect of improvement in present responsibilities." [26]

"Also-rans"

Regardless of what use is made of the evaluation interview, particular attention should be given to the "also-rans," the people who are passed over when promotions are made.[27] As soon as it becomes known that there is a vacancy in higher management, great hopes are kindled at the lower levels and many people will be frustrated when the final decision is announced. In some companies a man who has put in a bid for promotion and is then passed over is almost expected to look for another job.

When a man has been rejected, it is essential to explain to him *why* he was passed over. " 'Also-rans' are happier in their organization when they feel the race has been fairly run; when they have positive evidence of thought being given them; and when they know that some recognizable procedure—not favoritism—has been used." [28] In the long run, moreover, an explanation of the promotion makes it easier for subordinates to accept the *legitimacy* of the man who is moved up.

If the company has a regular program of evaluation interviews, of course, there will be less need for these elaborate explanations. The interviews will help each employee achieve a realistic attitude toward his prospects and give him a clear indication of how he stands. They tend to counteract over-optimism and provide "ladders of escape which will insure [subordinates'] being able to accept adverse decisions and still maintain a normal self-respect." [29] Indeed, if a man is told why he was not promoted and what he can do to overcome his faults, the very fact that he was passed over may motivate him to work harder, rather than impair his willingness to cooperate.

There is much that a company can do to reduce the feeling that a supervisor is a failure merely because he has stopped advancing.[30] If salary schedules make allowance for years of service on the job, for example, the supervisor who has been by-passed can still look forward to increased earnings. He can be given training courses to help him improve his performance

---

[26] Earl Brooks, "An Experimental Program for Executive Development," *ILR Research*, Vol. 1, No. 2 (March 1955), p. 12; see also Richards, *op. cit.*, p. 529.

[27] See Virgil K. Rowland, "They Also Ran . . . ," *Executive Selection, Development and Inventory*, Personnel Series, No. 171 (New York: American Management Association, 1957), pp. 47-50.

[28] *Ibid.*, p. 56.

[29] *Ibid.*, p. 55.

[30] For a good discussion, see W. R. G. Bender, "No Room at the Top," *Management Review*, Vol. 48, No. 7 (July 1959), pp. 9-14.

on his present job. He can be named to committees and assigned special company and community responsibilities. And his boss can show that he values the man's opinion by asking for his suggestions on matters of importance. Indeed, the more intimately a man participates in the organization, the less importance he attaches to the formal status of his job.

Conclusion

Performance evaluation serves two important functions in the management-development program: (1) it provides a systematic, objective means for selecting who should be promoted or receive salary increases, and (2) it provides a training tool to help supervisors improve their own performance and train their subordinates. Yet, as we have seen, these two objectives often conflict. It is largely because of this conflict that the whole field of performance evaluation has become so controversial and has given rise to so many clashing schools of thought.

In theory, selection and training can be combined into one attractive management-development package. Ratings can be used by higher management for selection purposes and also as a form of feedback, through the evaluation interview, to inform subordinates on where they stand and to suggest ways in which they can do better. Unfortunately, the information management receives from an evaluation program designed primarily to permit an objective comparison of a large group of employees is seldom useful in the coaching of individuals.

In our opinion it would be wise for management to separate the selection and training aspects of evaluation altogether. Normally, ratings should be made only when it is important to compare the abilities of a group of candidates for a given vacancy. Ratings should not be used for determining whether an individual manager deserves a salary increase or whether he deserves to be moved the next step up on the promotional ladder.

In fact, instead of preparing over-all ratings, it would seem preferable for management to use the rating form to construct a profile of each candidate's strengths and weaknesses in different areas. Management can then use such profiles as an aid in determining which candidate has the constellation of abilities best suited to the job in question. In other words, rating should be used not as a means of *judging a supervisor's past performance,* but only as a means of *determining his suitability for promotion to a given job.* Ratings for this purpose should not be confused with periodic performance evaluation interviews.

We have seen that in many organizations both supervisor and subordinate have come to dread the day when evaluation interviews must be held: the subordinate is afraid of being criticized unjustly and the supervisor is apprehensive about provoking the subordinate's antagonism. Evaluation interviews would be more useful if the supervisor did not have to pass judgment on the subordinate. The evaluation interview should be no more than a periodic informal discussion between supervisor and subordinate in which the subordinate airs his problems, the supervisor suggests ways of solving them, and both try to clear up points of misunderstanding.

Actually, the good supervisor recognizes that coaching of this sort should occur more frequently than once every six months; he holds the equivalent of an evaluation interview whenever he thinks a subordinate will profit from it, and he does not need to be prodded into conducting interviews at a special time. On the other hand, the poor supervisor will probably only go through the motions of a proper evaluation interview (which may do more harm than good) or perhaps ignore it altogether.

A company-wide policy requiring periodic evaluation interviews is most useful for the *average* supervisor, for it forces him to take time off from his duties, to think through how each of his subordinates has been progressing, and then to sit down with each man to talk over their long-range relationships. (Although a simple rating form sometimes helps a supervisor marshal his thoughts before beginning the interview, this form should not be used for any significant purpose by higher management.)

In the sense in which we are discussing it here, the evaluation interview is just one form of coaching; it is, however, an integral part of the training program that we shall discuss in the next chapter.

Problem I

Robert Jackson, age 25, has been with the advertising department, of which you are manager, for three years as a copy man. His job is to design advertisements for use in newspapers and magazines. He must work closely with the girls in the art department, with the members of the sales department, and with the Vice President, Sales and Promotion, who is in charge of the whole division.

Bob is an extremely enthusiastic worker with lots of good ideas. When you hired him you had great hopes that he would advance rapidly. He still can, but he has considerable trouble in dealing with people. He is too impatient with the girls in the art department, seems to fidget whenever he notices one of them taking a break, and is constantly pushing them to finish his work. In dealing with the people in the sales department, he makes it perfectly clear that his ideas are always best. During a recent conference, when the Vice President was thinking out loud, Bob shouted out his own answer, and cut the VP off. It was a good answer, and the VP didn't mind, but some of the other people thought Bob had behaved badly. You are quite concerned about the animosity he is creating in your department.

Company policy requires that each employee have an evaluation interview every six months. There are no performance-rating forms.

1. What should your strategy be in handling the evaluation interview with Jackson?

2. Role-play this interview. Jackson is quite sure that his ideas are good and will press for an immediate promotion.

Management training is one of management's most powerful tools in developing an effective organization and training is important at every level of the organization. For instance, the new foreman who has risen from the ranks has usually had very little formal training in the non-technical human-relations side of his job. As he rises higher in the management hierarchy, he must constantly adopt broader perspectives and learn new skills—the specialist must learn to be a generalist.

Although in many companies training is technically the responsibility of the personnel department or a special training department, still it should command the attention of everyone in management. Everyone who leads others is a trainer, whether he likes it or not.

The people who engage in management training range from the top executive studying Plato at an Ivy League college to the general foreman explaining to a new foreman how to fill in a time sheet. There are tremendous differences in the subject matter, materials, and teaching personnel used in these training programs. Some deal with the specific technology of a particular firm. Others

24

Management Training

take up technical areas, safety, job evaluation, or accounting. In recent years, too, there has been an increasing emphasis on subjects not directly related to the job, such as developing reading speed, creative thinking, or HOBSO ("How Our Business System Operates"—a standardized program in economics).

Since the most common form of training deals with the problems of "human relations" or "supervision," we shall concentrate on this area of training in our discussion. Remember, though, that many of the principles we shall present apply to other forms of training as well (for instance, training sales personnel on how to sell, or on how to handle customer relations).

Even human-relations training is too vast an area, however, for us to cover adequately in a single chapter. The best we can do is sample a few questions here and there: What are the goals of training? How do organizational problems make training more difficult? What principles should underlie a successful training program? What are the basic training techniques? Who should conduct the training? How can a company evaluate whether its program is worth the time and effort spent on it?

The Goals of Training

Before we can have a realistic understanding of the goals of training, we must first decide what can and what cannot be taught. A supervisor cannot be *taught* effective human relations. He cannot be *taught* to do the right thing at the right time. Indeed, as we have tried to make clear in other chapters, no single over-all answer exists that will cover every situation that may arise. The most that training can be expected to do (and only under the most favorable circumstances) is this:

1. It can help the individual become more sensitive to the human-relations environment in which he works. It can give him better questions to ask and thus make him a better observer of human behavior. It can improve his skills in diagnosing the motivations and needs of other people—why they behave as they do.

2. It can help the individual understand why he behaves as he does, how he reacts to given stimuli, and how his behavior affects others.

3. To a certain extent it can equip him with skills, such as interviewing techniques and conference leadership, that will help him handle the situations in which he is placed. However, these skills are of little or no value unless the trainee has gained the insights mentioned under (1) and (2) above.

In brief, the most that training in human relations can do is help the individual adjust to his environment. If the environment within the organization militates against effective human relations, however, no amount of training will induce changes in supervisory behavior on the job. Instead, trainees become frustrated when they are unable to apply what they have learned in class. For training to be effective, there must be an organizational climate that insures the freedom to experiment with new patterns of supervision and to learn through making mistakes. The thesis of this chapter, then, is simply this: *the effectiveness of training depends on the quality of the training itself and on the atmosphere that prevails in the over-all organization.*

Organizational Problems

The influence of the organization—in particular, the attitude of top management—is crucial to the success of a training program, for as long as management thinks of the training process as something apart from everyday activities on the job, the chances that training will affect behavior are slim indeed.

In many companies management regards training as of only marginal importance and consequently gives it only token support. Many managers feel that training is purely a staff function for which line has no responsibility. Yet attitudes of this sort are quickly discerned by the trainees themselves, who may begin to feel that training is a waste of time and resent being held as a captive audience in a training class.

Again, many training programs are instituted by top management merely because it is the fashionable thing to do. Little thought is given to the critical questions: What is the training intended to accomplish? In what ways should the trainees change their behavior? What can management do to help them make those changes?

Few rigorous attempts have been made to evaluate the effectiveness of training (later, we shall discover why such evaluation is so difficult). However, two studies stand out.[1] In each case, just before the supervisors entered training, their subordinates were asked questions on how well they thought the supervisors did their job. After the supervisors had finished their training, the subordinates were asked the same question again. The purpose, of course, was to discover whether the training had made any difference in behavior that was observable by the subordinates.

The results? Very disappointing. In one case, the subordinates reported that their bosses' behavior had changed for the better immediately after training was completed, but that within two years it had reverted to its pre-

---

[1] Edwin A. Fleishman, Edwin F. Harris, and Harold E. Burtt, *Leadership and Supervision in Industry: An Evaluation of a Supervisory Training Program* (Columbus: Bureau of Educational Research, The Ohio State University, Monograph No. 33, 1955); T. Hariton, *Conditions Influencing the Effects of Training Foremen in Human Relations Principles,* reported in Norman R. F. Maier, *Principles of Human Relations* (New York: Wiley, 1952), pp. 184-192.

training level. The second case involved two divisions of the Detroit Edison Company. One division showed a gain, the other a loss.

How can we explain these ambiguous results? The training programs themselves may have been at fault, but a better explanation is probably that what the trainees learned in class just wasn't useful on the job. Instead, it conflicted with the behavior expected of them by their bosses and even by their subordinates.

Confirmation of this hypothesis is shown in the surprisingly different reactions of the two divisions in Detroit Edison. In Division 1, where subordinates reported that the behavior of their supervisors improved after training, the foremen felt much more confident than did the foremen in Division 2 that what they learned in the course would help them get ahead. In Division 1 there was evidence that higher management was already practicing the principles taught in the course, while in Division 2 they were not. If training is to be worth while, trainees must feel free to apply what they learn and to change their behavior if they wish. When the organizational climate denies this freedom, subordinates are more likely to imitate their boss than to follow what they have learned in class.

Managers often talk as though it were only their subordinates' behavior that needed changing, not their own. They fail to recognize that their own behavior affects that of their subordinates, and that it is difficult to change one without changing the other.[2] No wonder many a student has told us after class, "I wish my boss would take this stuff. He is the one who needs it."

In some companies the philosophy of those who conduct the training programs is in direct conflict with the day-to-day practice of line management. Where higher management does not support the objectives of training *in practice,* supervisors feel uncertain about whether to follow the theory of the course or the example of their boss. As a result, they appear vacillating and inconsistent. For instance, subordinates might well become confused if their hard-as-nails supervisor started to listen to them before bawling them out. Naturally, subordinates, uncertain of whether their boss is going to be "tough" or practice "human relations," find this unpredictability highly frustrating. Under the circumstances, it may be a blessing that so many supervisors leave their training in the classroom and never let it interfere with their daily behavior.

Clearly, only limited results can be obtained by training lower management alone, particularly if the training is of the typical classroom variety. Possibly the best way to train a foreman is to train his general foreman first; but it is difficult to train the general foreman until the superintendent has been trained, or at least induced, to behave in a manner that permits those on lower levels to try out new techniques.

---

[2] For an excellent discussion of this point, see Mason Haire, "Some Issues of Industrial Training," *The Journal of Social Issues,* Vol. 4, No. 3 (Summer 1948), pp. 44-45.

Does this mean that the only way to start is with the Board of Directors? Perhaps. The Board of Directors of one of the nation's largest oil companies has established a Human Relations Committee, whose job, in effect, is to train top management. Top management then trains the next-lower level of management and so on down the line in carefully planned program until finally the general foreman trains the foreman.

As we shall see, there are very definite advantages in having every boss train the people he supervises. And yet there are supervisors, otherwise competent, who are just poor trainers. Training conducted by line personnel is not the complete solution to the problem.

More important than *who* conducts the training is the organizational atmosphere in which it occurs. (See our discussion on pp. 523-525.) Effective human-relations training (in the sense in which we are using the term) is almost impossible to achieve under autocratic management—it simply cannot be bootlegged into the organization.

Ineffective and Effective Training

INEFFECTIVE TRAINING

Prior to discussing effective training we shall first describe five typical forms of poorly conceived training programs. These forms are not meant to be mutually exclusive. In fact, any given program may include several or even all of them. As you read the next few pages, ask yourself: (1) Why does management offer such programs? And (2) What impact are they likely to have on trainees?

Gimmicks and froth   Training in some companies is on the level of the after-dinner speech and the booster talk. "It substitutes good intentions and wheezes for intelligent reflection about experience." [3] Instructors come armed with attention-getting jokes, cute parlor tricks, and gadgets. One highly paid consultant distributes a set of cards to his students with commandments such as "Smile" and "Use a Firm Handshake." Each student is expected to put one card in his pocket each day as a reminder.

Many instructors look upon human-relations training as a form of salesmanship. They think that the key to success lies in *putting over* their message; they regard their lectures as the equivalent of the inspirational sermon or the coach's last-minute spiel before sending the boys out onto the field. This attitude accounts for their vague generalities, their appeals to loyalty, and their use of presentations rather than group discussion.

As for content, programs of this sort often consist of folksy platitudes ("You can catch more flies with honey than you can with vinegar"), oversimplified

---

[3] Fritz Roethlisberger, "Training Supervisors in Human Relations," *Harvard Business Review*, Vol. 29, No. 5 (October 1951), p. 51.

psychology ("The single, most important thing a worker wants is recognition"), and a list of desirable traits ("A supervisor should be loyal, ambitious," etc.). Yet traits such as loyalty, decisiveness, judgment, and ability to think cannot be taught, at least not explicitly. Changes in basic attitude cannot be induced through force of logic, and certainly not through a preachy sort of exhortation.

Frequently the organization itself is responsible for the superficiality of the training. If top management accepts training on tolerance as a frill, the training staff tends to stick to safe, inspirational, shot-in-the-arm generalities which are "good for the men" but noncontroversial.

"Bringing the boys into line"   Sometimes top management really expects training to improve supervisory behavior. And yet no one makes any effort to find out why supervisors behave as they do; instead, training is regarded as a magic cure for whatever is wrong. Programs of this sort often fail because the trainer concentrates on selling management's point of view or on forcing a desired change, rather than on helping subordinates work out their own problems.

One of the authors was once asked by a personnel director to set up a training program for the following purpose:

> We know that front line supervision isn't giving us the loyalty and enthusiasm it should. We want them to feel part of the organization. We know that lots of times they get policy from our level which they only go through the motions of carrying out, or they tell their men, "That's what top management wants." We want them to understand that they are part of the team.

Note that the trainer was expected to build up enthusiasm and loyalty. There was no suggestion that top management had any responsibility for the existing situation or that perhaps top management itself should change.

Yet the supervisors who are brought into a training program of this sort know very well that its very existence is a kind of indirect criticism. And, being criticized with little opportunity to reply, they respond by taking the defensive, passing the buck, and making excuses.

Subordinates resist being forced into change, particularly if there is an implied assumption that what they are currently doing is wrong. Instead of the changing, the trainees may spend their time comparing what the company does with what it says. As one trainee told us, "When the Big Boss says promotions are made here on merit, who's kidding who? It's who you are related to that counts."

Abstract theory   A third form of ineffective training is devoted to abstract theories and rules of behavior, often dressed up in psychological garb. Yet supervisors tend to think in terms of their own problems rather than in terms of generalized theories. Indeed, if the training is to be effective, the *primary* *emphasis* should be on the trainees' own problems. Often the theories presented seem to the trainees as oversimplified or difficult to apply. As one supervisor put it, "It's all theory—bookstuff. It has nothing to do with supervision." Here is a dialogue between two foremen:

> Joe: What did you have in class today?
> Sam: The subject was how to treat the shop steward.
> Joe: How do you treat him?
> Sam: Be nice to him.
> Joe: Oh (he pauses). Well, we had time study. You won't mind that too much.[4]

Why was Joe so antagonistic? Not because he was opposed to being "nice" to stewards, but because he resented the oversimplification. If interviewed, Joe might say, "It isn't that simple. There are times when you are too busy to be nice. There are times when being nice means accepting insolence and showing weakness—when being nice means giving the union exactly what it wants. There are few problems that can be solved *just* by being nice."

There is evidence that when supervisors are asked how they handle subordinates, it is the poor ones who answer in terms of general principles like "treat everyone equal." The good supervisor usually gives specific examples from his own experience. The poor supervisor talks a good game; the good one practices it.

The charm school Many a training course preaches that the secret of supervisory success lies in dressing up one's personality, in "making friends and influencing people." Yet the formula "be nice—show interest in the other person" is too superficial to be of much help in industrial life. A veneer of "niceness" may actually do more harm than good, since most employees easily see through it. It is hard to act convincingly in a manner that is inconsistent with one's true personality.

The charm-school approach may actually lower employee morale. When a supervisor spreads a thin layer of "graciousness" over all his contacts, the employee inevitably becomes suspicious. He has no way of knowing whether he is doing the right thing or the wrong thing. He can never be sure just where he stands, because he is not sure whether his supervisor is "putting it on" or being sincere.

The pat program Some instructors follow a rigid outline which they refuse to vary to meet the particular needs of the trainee. Their communication is mainly one-way: *to* the group. To capture class interest, they use a host of audio-visual aids, such as movies, slides, and other gimmicks. They invite participation only for the purpose of extracting the "right answer." They are

---

[4] James R. Surface, "Resistance to Training," *Harvard Business Review*, Vol. 32, No. 2 (March 1954), p. 75.

careful to keep the class "in control," for if it wandered off the carefully prepared path, they would be lost.

A variation of this approach is the "canned" program prepared by an outside consultant or by top management, which instructors are required to follow without change.[5]

Naturally the tendency in programs of this sort is to give the trainees a set of oversimplified answers. For instance, handling a problem always involves four steps: (1) get the facts, (2) evaluate, (3) make the decision, (4) follow up. Rarely is it suggested that there may be a step between (2) and (3) called "consult with higher management" or "consult with the union."

Summary. These five forms of training are much alike. Their common failing is that they emphasize generalities and praiseworthy maxims but fail to help trainees to handle their daily problems. Any effective program of training must start from the felt needs of the trainees themselves. (Notice that we don't say "unconscious" needs, or needs recognized by the trainer or by higher management but not by the trainees.)

Conditions for Effective Training

All we have said so far has been negative. What are the *positive* conditions that are required to make a training program a success?

1. The people who are to take part in the program must *want* to change; they must be dissatisfied with their old way of doing things. In short, they must feel a need for training.[6] A wise personnel director once told us that he never starts a training program until the people to be trained (as well as their supervisors) are anxious for the program and sure of the problems they want to discuss. If men are forced into a training program against their will, they may well resent and sabotage it.

This is one reason why newly promoted men react better to training programs than do those who have been on the job a long time. The oldtimers feel that they know all the answers—after all, they have had lots of experience. But the new men are hunting desperately for help.

2. The program must be addressed to the trainees' own problems and must be realistically adapted to their own needs.[7] There is no point in discussing union grievance procedure with supervisors who never have any contact

---

[5] Some "canned" programs (for instance, those used by the Bell Telephone System; see p. 570) do permit the instructor considerable freedom and allow for class discussion.

[6] One authority suggests that it is sometimes useful to administer "shock treatment" to supervisors to make them aware of their inadequacies and to instill in them the "conviction of sin." John M. Pfiffner, *The Supervision of Personnel,* 2nd ed. (Englewood Cliffs, N.J.: Prentice-Hall, 1958), pp. 462-463.

[7] However, there is danger that a program may become *too* realistic and, through taking up immediate, short-run problems, become bogged down in detail.

with a union. One way to insure that a training program is built around problems as the trainees see them is to invite them to participate in setting up the program (or at least to survey their felt needs before launching the program).

3. Trainees must be encouraged to work through to their own conclusions. The only way they can understand a problem is to think it out for themselves. Real learning is "gut" learning. This is as true in human relations as it is in mathematics. Particularly in the area of emotional (as distinct from conceptual) learning, people learn *primarily* through experience, not through passive listening.

A trainee can memorize what the instructor thinks is right, but he can never make it his own—he will never really "internalize" it or believe in it. If there is to be a carry-over from the classroom to the shop or office, it is essential that the trainee *feel* through the problem, experiencing and overcoming its difficulties as he works toward a solution. We emphasize the word *feel* because many of the problems in this area are emotional, involving the ways in which people see and feel about the people and events that affect them deeply.

It is important for the trainees to accept their conclusions as purely their own, rather than suspect that a fast talker has tricked them into accepting ready-made solutions. Remember our previous quotation from Robert Burns: "He who is convinced against his will, remains of the same opinion still."

4. Human-relations training is usually more effective when it is conducted in groups, for most attitudes in this area are group-conditions. For instance, a foreman will be less likely to consult with his steward if his fellow foremen feel that this is being soft.

We have already discovered that group decisions are an effective means of changing attitudes (see Chapter 12). When group norms are involved, it is easier to change members of the group than it is to change individuals. When a group of supervisors with common problems decides to change together, no individual has the unsettling feeling of being a pioneer, of being different.

5. A training program should give trainees a chance to let off steam. As we have seen, human relations involves feelings and emotions and often leads to frustration. Typically, attitudes and behavior begin to change only when the trainees recognize that they all have problems in common that they have been unable to solve satisfactorily (for instance, an unreasonable steward or a tardy worker). It helps if they can work off their resentment a bit before moving on to the next step. The opportunity to share one another's burdens reduces their feeling of frustration and makes them more willing to consider new approaches.

But the new approaches themselves are anxiety-laden. People fear and resist new ways of doing things. Before they will accept change, trainees must have an opportunity to express their doubts. The skillful trainer detects these emotional undercurrents and brings them out into the open where they can be examined objectively. Otherwise, the trainees may express intellectual approval of proposed changes, but continue to harbor hidden doubts.

6. A training program is more effective if it makes allowance for the difficulty of giving up old ways of doing things. Understandably, people feel more secure with old patterns of behavior that have proved reasonably satisfactory in the past.[8] And they resent suggestions that their performance has been unsatisfactory. Similarly, they object to outsiders telling them what to do; they feel that their long experience makes them better qualified than any trainer.

One rewarding approach is to encourage trainees to consider new practices without attacking the old ways directly—that is, to ask them to consider a range of alternatives without committing themselves to any particular one. They should be encouraged to test the new ways to see for themselves whether they are an improvement. Only after they have tried out the new procedures on an experimental basis can they be expected to change their behavior permanently.

7. Training is more effective if it develops usable skills. Too often, training time is devoted to repeating meritorious platitudes such as "be loyal" or "be nice to stewards." For training to mean anything it must move from the intellectual level to the practical level of supplying skills that will be useful to the trainee on his own job.[9] Further, these must be skills that management will permit him to use within the organization.

Training Techniques

Now let us examine some of the more common training techniques. In view of the variety of training objectives and the great range of sophistication among trainers and trainees, no one form of training is uniformly superior to another. The most we can do is try to find the situations for which each form is most appropriate.

LECTURES

Lecturing, the traditional form of teaching, gives the trainer the greatest degree of control over the training situation. It enables him to present the material exactly as he wants to, with no danger that anyone will talk back.

But lecturing has obvious limitations as a training technique. As every student realizes, many lecturers are boring and some are entertaining with-

---

[8] This is another reason why recently promoted supervisors make better training material: they have fewer bad habits to discard.

[9] For an argument that management training should be theoretical, see Willard E. Bennett, "Master Plan for Management Development," *Harvard Business Review*, Vol. 34, No. 3 (May 1956), pp. 71-84.

out being instructive. The instructor who can keep his class constantly stimulated through the sheer force of his ideas—and who is powerful enough to effect a change in the behavior of those who listen to him—is rare indeed.

The most valuable use of lecturing is to present background facts (such as the provisions of a new union contract) or to enable the trainer to present his own point of view (when there is no real need for the trainees to develop their own). Because audience participation is limited, lectures are least valuable in changing attitudes and in developing skills. The most they can do in those areas is to pose problems that stimulate the trainees to think for themselves.

Movies have almost all the advantages of lectures and are usually more dramatic. They cannot, however, be readily adapted to the needs of each audience and, unless they are very general in their coverage, it may prove prohibitively expensive to make a special one for each type of program. Other types of audio-visual aid tend to reduce the spontaneity and flexibility of the program, but they are of obvious value to poorly qualified instructors. In fact, a well-designed "canned" program is better than an uninspired lecturer floundering on his own.

GUIDED CONFERENCES

In order to escape the limitations of straight lecturing, many companies have turned to the "guided-discussion" type of conference in their training programs. In a guided conference the instructor knows in advance what information or procedures he wants to bring out. The training sessions are similar to small, discussion-type university classes (except that there are no exams).

These conferences have certain limitations, however. Unless the discussion is directed to the felt needs of the participants, they may well feel that the whole session is useless. In a university class, the professor is assumed to be an expert. Not so in the plant. "Practically never do the trainers have more experience at being foremen than the trainees. The contrary is usually true, to the extent that very few trainers have ever been foremen. I think we can say that the world's foremost experts on the problems of being foreman are foremen." [10]

The conference leader should be careful not to cram things down people's throats, things that they may regurgitate in class but won't take back to work. Too often, training directors deserve such criticisms as these:

> They do not accomplish what they are supposed to do, that is, to help supervisors with the human aspects of their jobs. Many of them raise "loaded" questions, give facile answers that cannot be applied to concrete situations, and discuss unreal situations, situations that have never existed except in someone's imagination. In many of these the conference leader

---

[10] Surface, *op. cit.*, p. 301.

is armed with points the trainees are supposed to make. He is allowed so much time to draw these points out, and should the trainees fail to respond, he is instructed to draw them out himself. . . . What so often astonishes me is how docilely supervisors go through these verbal hoops and how readily, they learn the proper verbal response to please the instructor.[11]

A good conference leader is flexible enough to adjust his pace to that of the class. He encourages participation and, to a limited extent, permits diversions into side topics not on his original schedule. He tries to get everyone into the act, but he definitely is master of ceremonies. He has a specific goal to which he eventually hopes to lead the class. In short, he makes use of all the skills of conference leadership that we described in Chapter 11.

Yet there is a constant danger in a guided conference that the group will become overdependent on the leader. Expecting him to give *the* answer to their problems, the trainees are reluctant to go through the hard work of working out their own answers. The conference may easily degenerate into a session in which the leader asks questions and the trainees give pat answers.

In conclusion, guided conferences induce genuine learning when (1) the leader concentrates on asking questions rather than on providing answers, and (2) insures that his questions are relevant to the problems actually faced by the group.

SENSITIVITY TRAINING

Traditionally, the guided conference places primary emphasis on the needs of the organization. What has been called "sensitivity training," however, is more concerned with helping supervisors gain greater insight into themselves and into the manner in which others react to them. Instead of talking about abstract problems *outside* the group, discussion is centered on what is happening *within* the group itself. Sensitivity training helps each man understand how he *actually does* behave—an awareness that he must have before he can decide in theory how he *should* behave. To give an example:

At one early meeting, in a recent workshop, one executive got up from his chair and remarked to the stunned group: "I don't think this discussion is getting anywhere! I move that we appoint a committee to set up an agenda and report back their recommendations. Maybe this way we'll get something done. Are there any *serious* objections?" No one said anything. "All right, then, who would like to be part of this committee?" Four men raised their hands. The five left for an adjacent room.

During their absence, those remaining seemed infuriated. Their displeasure toward the five who had left was obvious. When someone asked why no one had objected, he was told there was no point "in getting killed by a steam roller."

---

[11] Roethlisberger, *op. cit.*, p. 47. One training director told us, "Training makes the students accomplished actors. They sound great in class, but don't change on the job."

The "secessionists" returned after a few minutes. When asked how they thought the group would respond to their recommendations, they felt sure there would be great interest in what they had to say. The trainer asked for a show of hands. The overwhelming majority was interested in neither the report nor its recommendations.

The rest of the session was spent in helping the five see what had happened. Much was said about authoritarian attitudes, "talking down," lack of respect for the integrity of the group, and aggressive, irritating mannerisms. A rude shock was followed by a slow awakening.[12]

In a well-conducted sensitivity-training program, the trainees in effect train one another, though the trainer helps by asking a few skillful questions which raise problems that the group may purposely (but perhaps unconsciously) have been ignoring. Learning takes place through analyzing one's own emotions, rather than through intellectual logic. There is no fixed agenda, and often no apparent limits are set on the content of the discussion. The group talks about what seems important to it at the moment.

Sensitivity training has been called the "laboratory" method of training, because, in effect, the group is experimenting on itself.[13] There is a close relationship between this form of training and group psychotherapy (and even psychoanalysis).

Whereas the lecture is the most rigidly controlled form of training, sensitivity training is the most loosely controlled form. Yet paradoxically the very fact that the trainer exercises such loose control demands that he be highly skillful. The few instances in which he intervenes in the discussion make the crucial difference between a rambling bull session and a genuine learning experience.

Since sensitivity training often touches on areas of high tension and deep frustration, the trainer must be able to recognize when a trainee is being subjected to more criticism than he can handle, and must take immediate steps to protect him. If the criticism grows too sharp, the victim may even suffer a mental breakdown. Certainly he will become so tense and defensive that he is no longer able to learn. Moreover, if the session becomes overly painful, the participants may turn their aggressiveness against the trainer, or may decide that the program is useless and abandon it altogether.

As might be expected, sensitivity training has aroused considerable controversy.[14] The critics of this technique charge that at worst it creates levels

[12] Robert Tannenbaum, Verne Kallejian, and Irving R. Weschler, "Training Managers for Leadership," *Personnel*, Vol. 30, No. 4 (January 1954), pp. 257-258. Reprinted by permission of the American Management Association.

[13] Much of the pioneering work in this area was done by the National Training Laboratory for Group Development (often called the Bethel group). More recently, the Human Relations Research Group, University of California, Los Angeles, has done important work in transferring the Bethel techniques to industrial settings. See National Training Laboratory in Group Development, *Explorations in Human Relations Training* (Washington: National Education Association, 1953).

[14] For example, William F. Whyte, *Leadership and Group Participation* (Ithaca: New York State School of Industrial and Labor Relations, Bull. No. 24, 1953), pp. 9-15, 17-26.

of tension higher than many people can handle, and that at best it is a highly frustrating series of unproductive conferences. In particular, it has been attacked as leading to enmity and bad feeling rather than to insight and improved behavior. Defenders of the technique respond that all true learning entails tension and frustration, and that only through an emotional experience can trainees evolve answers that really fit their needs.

There are many inexperienced leaders who act as if tension and frustration were ends in themselves. Unless the leader can help the group interpret the reasons for its tension and fit them into some meaningful framework, the whole program is a waste of time and even dangerous to the participants.

In conclusion, sensitivity training is a high-powered technique that should be used only by a leader of unusual skill and maturity.

PROBLEM-SOLVING CONFERENCE

Sensitivity-training conferences are primarily concerned with individual adjustment. Problem-solving conferences (often called staff conferences or self-development conferences) take up specific work problems suggested by the group. As material for discussion, the trainers and trainees need take only one or two of the daily incidents in a supervisor's life.

Problem-solving conferences differ from the guided conference in one important respect: the leader has no particular content objective. His function is twofold: (1) to help the group arrive at a practical solution to their problem, and (2) to help them "generalize" or devise principles from their solution that they can apply to similar problems in the future. By asking questions, the instructor gets the group to consider deeper problems and wider implications than they normally would.

> In one medium-sized plant an evening conference of supervisors was held every two weeks. One of the authors acted as consultant to a committee of top-management people who took turns running the conference sessions.
>
> At one session several supervisors spoke about the growing habit among employees of making coffee on the job. (Of 450 employees, 200 were in various laboratories, 150 in production, and 100 in the office.) The lab people had started the practice and now it was spreading to the production and office floors. The supervisors objected to the loss of time involved and the sloppy appearance of hot plates all over the plant. The question was: What should be done? Prohibit the practice altogether? Look the other way? Install coffee-vending machines? Have an official coffee break? Wheel coffee to each department?
>
> The first-line supervisors were not sure about top management's policy on this matter. Some were even hesitant to admit they tolerated the practice. Some felt the practice should be prohibited, yet felt this could be done only on a plant-wide basis. Many had in fact permitted coffee breaks as long as top management didn't notice.
>
> Out of the heated discussion came a growing realization that the prob-

lem could not be solved by setting up a uniform policy throughout the plant. Top management made it clear that they would consent to any decision made by the group. The final decision was to permit each supervisor to exercise his own discretion.

The discussion then turned to the principles the supervisors should apply in setting this policy. Should they consult with employees? How? What should be done to keep the privilege from being abused? At the end, the chairman got the trainees to summarize how the principles they had agreed on might be carried over to other problems, such as tardiness, quitting work early, gambling, and so forth.

In problem-solving conferences the chairman acts as a conference leader, but he may introduce spells of role-playing or ask the group to reflect on its own behavior and attitudes, as in sensitivity training. Since it is most important that the group set its own agenda, the chairman may spend most of the first meeting just getting suggestions from participants.

When the sessions are led by the group's supervisor, they are very similar to the weekly planning meetings that some supervisors hold with their subordinates, except that the emphasis is explicitly on training.

Some observers insist that problem-solving conferences are not properly a form of training. But if the chairman can get the group to make the all-important transfer of insight from the particular problem discussed to other problems of the same nature, it seems clear the problem-solving conference is one of the most effective training techniques available.

THE CASE METHOD

This technique, which has been popularized by the Harvard Business School,[15] is one of the commonest forms of training, particularly for higher executives. (Many of the cases that we present at the end of chapters are typical of the cases used in this method.) The case method is similar to the problem-solving conference, except that the case is presented by the leader instead of being suggested by the group. The fact that the trainees are not personally involved in the problem discussed permits them to take a more objective point of view.

The success of the case method depends directly on the ability of the instructor.[16] Under an unskilled instructor, the trainees tend to look upon the case as a puzzle that can be solved by finding the right answer. They make value judgments about each character and try to identify the "villain." Often, too, a poorly conducted discussion will degenerate into a rambling session from which the participants derive no learning. Or else the leader may

---

[15] See Kenneth R. Andrews, *The Case Method of Teaching Human Relations and Administration* (Cambridge: Harvard University Press, 1953).

[16] Our analysis is influenced by Fritz Roethlisberger, *Training for Human Relations* (Boston: Harvard University Graduate School of Business Administration, 1954).

master-mind them into accepting his own conclusions or even ram them down their throats.

A skillful instructor, on the other hand, emphasizes useful ways of thinking about human relations rather than ways of reaching specific conclusions.[17] He puts his stress on:

1. Increasing the trainee's power of observation, helping him to ask better questions and to look for a broader range of problems (for instance, not "Who is to blame?" but "Why did it happen?").

2. Encouraging the group to look for more and more implications in each solution, keeping them away from pat analyses and oversimplified solutions.

3. Helping the student to discard vague principles, such as "Be tactful" or "Apply the golden rule," and urging him to consider not only *what* to do but *how* to do it.

4. Encouraging the trainees to test their solutions against reality.

In the university classroom the case method introduces a note of realism that is absent from abstract, theoretical discussions. For management trainees in industry, however, cases are always less realistic than the actual problems that arise on the job. A well-chosen case may provoke *objective* discussion, but the lack of *emotional* involvement may make it difficult to effect any basic change in the behavior and attitudes of the trainees. After all, human-relations training is more concerned with developing skills and self-insight than with providing intellectually satisfying solutions. "Executives have been observed to analyze beautifully and verbally solve a case that focuses on 'understanding the other person' and five minutes later show little or no ability to use this knowledge in a hot argument with the man across the table.[18]

To obtain greater emotional involvement, the trainer may have to use some of the techniques of sensitivity training. For instance, he can focus attention on the conscious and semiconscious values and thought processes that prompted the trainees to arrive at a given solution.

INCIDENT PROCESS [19]

The incident process is an organized and somewhat dramatized way of handling the case method; it is of particular value to unskilled discussion leaders. The incident process involves five steps:

---

[17] For a description of how a case might be presented to a group of foremen, see A. Zaleznick, *Foreman Training in a Growing Enterprise* (Boston: Harvard University, Graduate School of Business Administration, 1951), pp. 227-30. Andrews, ed., *op. cit.*, gives several examples of the case method in the university class room.

[18] Chris Argyris, *Personality and Organization* (New York: Harpers, 1957), p. 221.

[19] This process was developed by Paul and Faith Pigors. See their *Incident Process: Case Studies in Management Development* (Washington, D.C.: The Bureau of National Affairs, 1955).

1. The trainees are given a short description of an incident, such as:

> N, on leaving work, passed by guard T without opening his lunch box. Thereupon T called N back and opened his box; inside there was a ball of twine. T reported the matter to N's foreman, who then discharged N.[20]

(Obviously there is more to the story, but this is a realistic start. We rarely have the full story when we start investigating a situation.)

2. The trainees now interview the discussion leader to get more facts (the discussion leader has been briefed on them beforehand). One trainee then summarizes the facts as they have been obtained.

3. The trainees next decide on what the central issues are.

4. Each trainee is asked to write a brief decision, which is discussed by the group.

5. Finally, the group discusses the broader meaning of the case in an effort to tie it in with similar situations or to suggest means of preventing such problems from arising in the future.

Typically the incident process is used in discussion of human-relations cases, but manufacturing, sales, or purchasing problems might also be used.

ROLE-PLAYING [21]

This technique calls for parts to be assigned to students who act them out as they would in real life.[22] It differs from ordinary drama in that the actors are given no lines to memorize; rather, they must improvise as they go along. (For examples of cases susceptible to role-playing, see pp. 260-262.)

Among the advantages of role-playing are:

1. It helps participants to appreciate other points of view, as, for example, when a foreman plays the role of a union steward.

2. It helps trainees to experience a situation emotionally.

3. It makes trainees somewhat tense and therefore more self-conscious and analytical of their behavior than they would be in real life.

---

[20] Adapted from Joseph Shister, *Selected Cases in Industrial Relations* (Buffalo: Department of Industrial Relations, University of Buffalo, 1953), p. 85.

[21] This technique was first popularized by J. L. Moreno, *Who Shall Survive* (New York: Beacon House, 1953), as a technique for inducing mentally ill patients to act out their emotional problems. It was adapted for industrial use by disciples of Kurt Lewin. See Alex Bavelas, "Role Playing and Management Training," *Societry*, Vol. 1, No. 2 (June 1947), pp. 183-91; Leland Bradford and Ronald Lippitt, "Role Playing in Supervisory Training," *Personnel*, Vol. 22, No. 3 (Nov. 1945), pp. 142-152. An outstanding guide to the use of role-playing in industry is Norman R. F. Maier, Allen R. Solem, and Ayesha A. Maier, *Supervisory and Executive Development: A Manual for Role Playing* (New York: Wiley, 1957).

[22] A variety of role-playing is the skit, in which a few participants present a situation to the class, which then discusses it as in the case method.

4. It permits trainees to show imagination and daring in devising solutions, since they are not playing for "keeps." No harm is done if they make a mistake.

Even the trainees who merely observe a role-playing session profit from observing the mistakes of others. Certainly this is a highly dramatic technique for arousing interest and stimulating class participation.[23]

Role-playing is far more fruitful when it is followed by class discussion. Before the session starts, the trainer may suggest crucial areas for the students to observe and then use these areas as a framework for the subsequent discussion.

COMPARING TECHNIQUES

As we have seen, it is impossible to say that one training technique is better than another, for the value of any given technique depends on many factors: (1) the instructor's personality and ability, (2) the trainees' maturity, background, and willingness to learn,[24] (3) the trainees' and the company's previous experience with human-relations training,[25] and (4) the trainees' opportunity to transfer to the job what they learn in class.

Here is a brief summary of the advantages of each technique:

Primary Purpose	Technique
Explaining facts and procedures; expounding general principles	Lectures, guided discussion
Developing analytical skills and the ability to ask oneself questions	Case method, incident process
Developing awareness of oneself and one's impact on others	Sensitivity training, role-playing
Carry-over from class to job	Problem-solving conference, (to a lesser extent) role-playing
Inducing change in behavior	Role-playing, sensitivity training, problem-solving conferences
Insuring good training with unskilled trainers	Lectures, incident process
Opportunity for emotional catharsis	Sensitivity training, case method, problem-solving conference

---

[23] For a discussion of how role-playing can be used to shock trainees into realizing the extent of their problems, see Leland Bradford and Paul Sheats, "Complacency Shock as a Requisite for Training," *Societry*, Vol. 2, No. 1 (April-August 1948), pp. 40-42.

[24] Recent college graduates take more easily to formal classroom instruction than older men with little formal education. Similarly, as we have pointed out, the man who is new on the job is more anxious to learn than is the old-timer who has developed patterns of behavior that give him reasonably satisfactory results.

[25] Incident process is a good way of breaking the ice in a new training program.

Who Does the Training?

In exploring the question of who does the actual training, we shall start with the form of training most remote from the trainee's day-to-day contacts: university executive development. Then we shall look in turn at training in company institutes, training by outsiders, training by line personnel, and, finally, training by staff personnel or the training department.

UNIVERSITY "EXECUTIVE DEVELOPMENT PROGRAMS" [26] *(Theoretical Training)*

On many campuses it is a fairly common sight to see middle-aged, balding men going back to school for advanced training. Specialized programs for members of middle and top management who live on campus are becoming increasingly prevalent in American colleges.

Most of these courses are centered around a discussion of broad management problems, and are often conducted by means of the case method. They are usually designed to create a broader perspective and a greater tolerance and sensitivity toward other points of view, although some schools offer instruction in specialized skills, such as accounting, rapid reading, public speaking, and creative thinking. A few companies, such as AT&T, send groups of top executives to "ivy league" colleges to study such subjects as art, literature, economics, and history. These companies believe that the intellectual discipline required to handle Plato or theoretical economics may well prove useful in handling the company's everyday problems as well.[27]

What advantages does the typical university executive development program have over the usual in-company training? In the first place, the executives are isolated from their jobs and their families, perhaps for the first time in years. This isolation gives them an opportunity to make a fresh evaluation of themselves and how they do their jobs. In a sense, the program is a secular equivalent of the religious retreat. Moreover, the executives learn fresh points of view from their association with counterparts in other companies. The authors' experience is that management trainees work considerably harder than the typical undergraduate and derive tremendous stimulation from dealing with difficult intellectual problems.

But university training is not a cure-all. Some companies have genuinely unique problems, and the patterns of behavior that the executive learns at

---

[26] See Kenneth Andrews, "Is Management Training Effective?" *Harvard Business Review*, Vol. 35, No. 1 (January 1957), pp. 85-94; Melvin Anshen, "Better Use of Executive Development Plans," *Harvard Business Review*, Vol. 33, No. 6 (November 1955), p. 67; Melvin Anshen, "Executive Development: In-Company v. University Programs," *Harvard Business Review*, Vol. 32, No. 5 (September 1954), p. 83.

[27] Frederick E. Pamp, Jr., "Liberal Arts as Training for Business," *Harvard Business Review*, Vol. 33, No. 3 (May 1955), pp. 42-50.

college may not be consistent with management policy. Consequently, the trainee may come home dissatisfied and upset because he knows that he will be unable to put into practice what he has learned.

Evidence suggests that university training is more valuable for men who have just been promoted or are about to be promoted, since these are the ones who feel and are most in need of an expanded viewpoint; confronted by a new job, they are anxious to develop new skills and willing to discard old points of view. This enthusiasm for learning is especially strong among staff specialists, such as accountants or salesmen, who are being promoted into line positions where they will be faced with an entirely new set of problems.

Since only a limited number of executives can be sent to university programs, management must exercise great care in selecting them. The man who is picked may feel that he is slated for rapid advancement and may alter his expectations and behavior accordingly; if he fails to get promoted soon after he returns, he is likely to feel cheated and demoralized. On the other hand, those who are not selected may consider their being passed over as almost a demotion.

> One company made its selection between two people with identical positions solely on the basis that one man had more free time at the moment. The other man, who was actually better qualified, decided that his opportunities for advancement in the company were limited and soon got a better job elsewhere.

University-run programs are not the only opportunities available to executives to develop a broader, fresher point of view through exchange of ideas with executives from other institutions, or to acquire special training away from the job. The American Management Association offers a number of seminars similar to the university development programs but shorter in length. Various clubs and conventions of foremen and managers also give executives a chance to make intercompany contacts and compare experiences. In addition, many concerns pay part of the expenses of employees who take special courses or go to night school. In few of these instances, however, is there the feeling of retreat that marks the longer, on-campus course in which the executive is isolated from his daily routine.

COMPANY-RUN INSTITUTES

A few large companies have set up their own management-training programs. Executives are chosen from throughout the company and sent to some isolated, attractive location for a training program of a week or more. These companies feel that they can provide the same benefits as university programs and also help develop loyalty to the company and an understanding of other departments. Certainly, if students are taken from all the branches of an organization like General Electric or AT&T, a very wide range of experience and viewpoint will be represented. And yet, though the jobs of these men differ greatly, they all work under the same management philosophy; as a consequence, there may be fewer novel approaches to problems than when the students came from many different companies.

OUTSIDERS

A good many companies hire outsiders, often at high fees, to run their training programs. These men are either members of consulting firms, college professors, or free-lancers with experience in training, and they vary greatly in their sophistication and ability. Some of them offer packaged courses (often a combination of inspirational platitudes and gimmicks) which they apply to every company regardless of its needs. Others try to develop special programs to meet the particular needs of each situation.

Why do companies hire outsiders? For the company without any other training program it may be the easiest solution; now it can have training without burdening top management with the chore. Further, there is the feeling that an outsider, particularly if he is from a university, will command more respect. "They've heard us before. You are a new face and a college professor. They'll listen to you."

Outsiders generally work under heavy handicaps, however, for they know very little about the company, its problems, or its policies. More important, even if supervisors listen to what the outsider has to say, they will continue to behave on the job in the way their boss wants them to behave.

But outsiders often make a real contribution in teaching content courses such as engineering or public speaking, as consultants in helping companies think through and set up their own training, and in programs where they confine themselves purely to the role of moderator or observer—as in sensitivity training or the case method. Even here, though, an insider with the requisite skills would probably do a better job than an outsider.

LINE PERSONNEL

Many types of training may be lumped together under the general category: line-run training. Every supervisor, for instance, trains by example, and individual coaching is an important form of training. Similarly, every time a supervisor talks to a group, he is in effect conducting an informal class. There is little point in making a sharp distinction between training and supervision, for each partakes of the other. Perhaps the best training program of all is the supervisory conference called to discuss current production problems.

There are many strong arguments for having line management conduct formal training programs as well as informal training:

1. Often the teacher learns more than his pupils. The very fact that a supervisor must teach may make him more conscious of his own human-relations practices. Indeed, he may carry over to the job the pattern of listening to others in class.

2. When the supervisor does his own training there is less chance that the subordinate will learn one form of behavior in class and another on the job. Since coaching, instruction, and order-giving are all coordinated, subordinates experience a consistent policy of supervision.

3. The classroom setting affords supervisors and subordinates an opportunity to talk over long-range problems that they may have been too busy to consider on the job.

In setting up a class, is it better to have students come from many departments or just from one? In favor of having all students come from the same department and meet under a common boss are these arguments: (1) they will talk about common problems, (2) they can get their bosses' approval of new ideas on the spot, and (3) it is more efficient to try to change the group as a whole, rather than to work separately with individuals.[28]

On the other hand, many companies prefer to hold "interdepartmental conferences" in which a few representatives from every department meet together with supervisors as instructors.[29] These conferences make it possible for the trainees to meet people from other departments, to become familiar with their problems, and to compare points of view.

Let us look for a moment at one carefully designed training program in which line management plays a very significant role—that of the Bell Telephone System.

> This program includes all levels of management from top executives to front-line supervisors in an integrated program run largely by line management itself.[30] The program format is based on the reactions of past students.
>
> At the top is a company institute at Asbury Park, New Jersey, which top executives attend for periods of up to four weeks.[31] Some outside speakers are called in, but the program is devoted mainly to case-method discussions.
>
> For lower levels of management Bell offers shorter courses on an inter-

---

[28] Floyd C. Mann, "Studying and Creating Change: A Means to Understanding Social Organization," *Research in Industrial Human Relations,* Conrad Arensberg and others, eds. (New York: Harpers, 1957), p. 163.

[29] Normally it is not wise to bring together in a class people from widely different levels of the organization. The differences in status are hard to forget and free discussion is difficult to obtain. For an analysis of these points, see "Designing the Training Group," *Adult Leadership,* Vol. 2, No. 2 (June 1953), pp. 12-22.

[30] "Bell's Training Program: Broadest of Them All," *Business Week,* August 10, 1957, p. 143; Melvin Anshen, "Executive Development: In-Company vs. University Programs," *Harvard Business Review,* Vol. 32, No. 5 (September 1954), pp. 86-90.

[31] Top-management people are also sent to university executive development programs or to the special humanities courses already discussed.

departmental basis in major cities throughout the country. Among the course titles are "Evaluating and Coaching People" (five days) and "Learning by Listening" (three days). These shorter programs often involve role-playing or case-method discussions. The cases are sometimes presented by means of a movie, but the ensuing discussions are led by a member of higher line management. These courses are "canned" in the sense that the cases, the sequence of discussion, and sometimes even the questions asked are planned in advance. But the basic technique is discussion, and many of the line instructors show considerable flexibility in modifying the "package."

The program is set up and monitored by a small group of experts, some from outside the Bell System. But the administration of the program and the actual classroom training is all handled by line supervisors on a rotating basis.

COACHING

Perhaps the most valuable form of training is coaching by one's superior right on the job.

> Leadership is not something that is learned by reading about it, by listening to somebody talk about it, or even by discussing it in a conference. Leadership is learned by *doing*, under the watchful eye of somebody who has learned the art and is willing to take the time to give constructive criticism.[32]

Like other forms of teaching, coaching is most effective when it encourages the trainee to learn by himself. What does this mean in terms of day-to-day activities?

1. The supervisor should provide for enough delegation of authority to enable the trainee to learn from his own mistakes.

2. The supervisor should set goals and standards of performance toward which the trainee can work.

3. The supervisor should require the trainee to be very explicit about the steps he takes in handling a problem, asking such questions as "How much authority did he delegate to subordinates? What standards did he set up? How did he communicate to those below?" [33]

4. The trainee should be given "special assignments which require [him] to develop new sources of information, work with other people, and thus move outside his job routine into a broader field of work." [34]

---

[32] J. W. Miller, "Foreman Selection and Development: Key to Efficient Operation," *Assuring Adequate Reserves of Key Personnel*, Personnel Series No. 169 (New York: American Management Association, 1956), p. 9.

[33] See Louis A. Allen, "Does Management Development Develop Managers?" *Personnel*, Vol. 34, No. 2 (September 1957), pp. 18-25.

[34] Stanley E. Seashore, "The Training of Leaders for Effective Human Relations," *Some Applications of Behavioral Research*, Rensis Likert and Samuel P. Hayes, Jr. (New York: UNESCO Publications Center, 1957), p. 21.

5. The supervisor should provide constructive criticism, encourage the trainee to talk through his problems, and help him discover for himself how and why he has made mistakes.

Above all, the supervisor must practice good human relations himself. Since his subordinates copy him, they learn his bad traits as well as his good.

Training through coaching is successful on a company-wide basis only if each level of management holds the next level responsible for training results —in other words, only if the supervisor's boss starts asking questions when the supervisor's subordinates are inadequately trained. Unfortunately many otherwise good executives are very poor at developing those under them. In some instances a supervisor's training ability can be improved through classroom instruction in training techniques or through coaching by his own boss. However, since there are many "hard-core" supervisors who do not respond to this sort of training, there will always be a place for the other forms of training we have discussed.

The Role of Staff Personnel in Management Training

What is the role of staff personnel in management training? Many companies assign staff men, usually from the personnel department, to serve as class instructors. Yet these men often suffer some of the same handicaps that hamper complete outsiders. In fact, the existence of rivalry between staff and line within the company may make their job even more difficult. Ideally, for all the reasons we have already mentioned, it would be better for line personnel to conduct these training programs themselves.

Why, then, is it so common for training to be considered primarily as a function of the personnel department? Many well-meaning executives believe that training is a peripheral activity that has nothing directly to do with line's primary job of production. They feel that training is a simple matter of teaching, and that teaching, like dentistry or surgery, is best left to specialists. Further, many highly competent executives fear that they will become tongue-tied in class. They would rather slough off the job to the experts and concentrate on what they regard as more essential activities. And it is true that many line supervisors are poorly qualified to act as teachers.

In any case, many personnel departments are more than anxious to assume the responsibility for management training. Every personnel director is interested in building up a record of accomplishments—and a successful training program is just that. It is usually easier for the personnel department itself to run classes than it is to go through all the work of patiently prodding reluctant line managers to set these courses up. Yet staff-run classes have many limitations, particularly if they are met with only grudging support from line.

What role *should* the personnel department play in management training? The answer depends on such factors as higher management's general philosophy of human relations and supervision, its understanding of the importance of training as a line function, and the ability of line personnel, both as supervisors and as trainers.

Ideally, the functions of staff should be:

1. To train the trainers—to equip them with skill in using such techniques as role-playing and conferences.

2. To act as coach or consultant to line supervisors who desire such help.

3. To provide teaching materials, such as cases or incidents.

4. To coordinate and arrange classes and to handle housekeeping details.

5. To provide some sort of feedback in an effort to evaluate the effectiveness of the program both for the trainers themselves and for higher management.

A training program based on such a clear-cut distinction between line and staff responsibilities cannot be introduced all at once, however. Normally, the personnel department must work long and patiently before line management is willing to accept the concept that training is a continuing line responsibility. During the transition period, before this concept is accepted, it may be necessary for the personnel department to accept a large measure of direct responsibility.

For instance, staff may institute a course with a line executive acting as co-instructor, and then gradually turn over to him more and more responsibility for leadership. Then, as an increasing number of supervisors develop experience, they begin to do the training on their own. As the program progresses, the training director may concentrate his efforts on educating the supervisors in the techniques of training.

The personnel department should also seek to involve higher management more and more directly in the training program. The training director may, for example, ask to interview members of higher management in an effort to identify specific areas in which training is needed and to pinpoint specific improvements that should be made. Even better, he can organize a top-management committee to review the abilities and deficiencies of subordinates (perhaps using individual evaluation data as a springboard) and to suggest ways of correcting deficiencies. These committee deliberations are themselves a valuable form of training for the participants. Indeed, the personnel director's job will be much easier if he can start his training program (however camouflaged) at the highest possible level.

Evaluating Training *(Sampling Testing)*

As we have seen, the field of management training is still in its infancy. Many of its proponents, flushed with enthusiasm, have made extravagant claims and have relied excessively on gadgets that promise wonderful results with a minimum of effort. But the time has come for sober second thoughts, for evaluation, and for research.

What do we mean by evaluating training? Management is beginning to ask the personnel department to prove its value, much as the engineering department demands proof of the value of one piece of equipment over another. (A training director once told us, "For me, evaluation is job insurance —to prove the value of training and to make sure our department is not eliminated in the next economy wave.") Yet convincing proof, objective and demonstrable, is difficult to obtain in the training field.[35]

One way of evaluating training is to ask the students themselves to evaluate the program and to make suggestions for improving it. The value of such "customer reactions" is doubtful, however, since the participants try to be polite and usually give a kind answer. Moreover, real learning is often painful and frustrating, and the shot-in-the-arm inspiration-peddler may win the popularity contest over the teacher who poses difficult questions and refuses to give pat answers.

A second evaluation technique is to measure the change in student attitudes that takes place during the course, perhaps by means of before-and-after tests. Unfortunately, a change in attitude expressed in class may not mean a change in behavior on the job.

A third but more difficult test is to measure change in on-the-job behavior. A series of questions may be administered before and after training to the trainees' supervisors and subordinates. Or else performance-evaluation forms before and after training may be used as an index to change.

To many members of management, the most crucial test is this: Does training reduce costs? Does it make supervisors more efficient? Obviously, training directors would be greatly relieved if it could only be *proved* that training cuts costs or raises production. Yet it is not enough to show that costs in a given department went down after its supervisors went through training, for many other factors might be responsible, such as better materials or longer production runs.

The ideal method of evaluating training is to take a number of groups doing the same work under identical conditions and then to train the supervisors in some of these groups and leave the other groups as controls. To our

---

[35] See W. R. Mahler and W. H. Monroe, *How Industry Determines the Need for and Effectiveness of Training,* Personnel Research Section, Report 929, Department of the Army, 1952.

knowledge there has been only one experiment that has measured the impact of training on costs.[36]

> In this experiment supervisors in two departments were trained in "democratic techniques" and those in two others were placed under close supervision (itself a form of training). After a year's experience, the departments placed under close supervision were found to have better cost records; however, their morale was lower and their turnover higher. The researchers predicted that in the long run the democratically trained supervisors would have better cost records because they did not waste human resources. Thus the results were inconclusive.

The truth is that we have no real proof that training of *any* sort is effective. We still cannot make an objective comparison between one form of training and another, or say with certainty who should be trained and how. Nor will we be able to do so until further research has been undertaken.

And yet the question of how to *measure* the effectiveness of executive training may, in fact, be less important than the question of deciding on *goals*. Instead of emphasizing methods, perhaps those who are responsible for evaluation should concern themselves with such hard-headed questions as, "What are we trying to accomplish? What kind of organization are we trying to build? In what ways do we want supervisors to change?" Until these questions are answered realistically, it is premature for management to try to refine its methods.

Conclusion

Little can be expected of training if management regards it as a peripheral staff function or a quick cure-all to basic problems.

1. Training is a means by which a superior can induce a subordinate to do a better job without having to supervise him in detail. The good supervisor provides an atmosphere in which subordinates can constantly learn new skills and develop their highest capabilities.

2. The most effective training comes from one's superior. Whether he intends to or not, the superior is always training his subordinate through the demands he makes, the behavior he rewards, and the behavior he punishes.

3. Classroom training is a useful supplement to on-the-job training if it is designed to improve the supervisor's ability to observe and think about human relations, rather than to provide him with pat answers. Classroom training helps the executive digest his experiences on the job and also enables him to learn faster on the job.

---

[36] Rensis Likert, "Measuring Organizational Performance," *Harvard Business Review,* Vol. 36, No. 2 (March 1958), pp. 41-50.

4. Unless classroom training is consistent with the behavior desired by superiors, it will lead to frustration, confusion, and wasted effort.

Problem I

(The following case is based on the experience of one of the authors and illustrates some of the problems involved in organizing successful management training. The story will be told in the first person.)

The AB Company had 15 plants scattered through the country. I was involved in only one plant, where I worked with Andy Jackson, the plant training director. After I had known him for a while he told me that the training program had started at a meeting of the 15 plant managers. Bud Alston had just been put in as company-wide training director.

> He sold the president on the idea there ought to be a development program in every plant; it was the modern, progressive thing. Bud is a great salesman. So the president brought him to the meeting and said, "We've been thinking about a supervisory development program and Bud will tell you about it." I doubt if any of the plant managers knew the slightest bit about training before Bud spoke and I doubt if they knew much more after. One man spoke against it. He said, "My foremen are pretty good as they are. I don't want anyone changing them." The rest were quiet.

So the program was initiated. Each plant manager was asked to pick a training director from among his men. That's how Andy got his job; before that he had been safety director. The program got off to a flying start; all the new training directors spent three weeks learning their job at a resort hotel.

> We really got the works, how to run movies, buzz sessions, role-playing, conference leadership, just about everything except how to handle management back home. There were outside speakers, a big banquet every week. We figured the company put out $1,000 on each of us—companies don't spend money like that unless they are serious. I went home in a blaze of enthusiasm.
> Only there were no brass bands to meet me. Now I was safety *and* training director. That was a blow. I figured someone else would take over safety. But I was going to get a training program somehow. The plant manager said he would back me up on anything. However, when I tried to get the foremen released for classes, the production superintendent said he needed them on the job. I took that to the plant manager; he felt maybe we ought to hold the classes after work on their own time. I asked for suggestions on what to cover. He said anything I said went; I was 100 per cent in charge.
> I waited till Bud Alston came in town. He sized things up quickly and soon it was settled that foremen would get overtime for coming to class. So I started my classes. We had sessions on first aid, safety, job evaluation, and conference leadership. But this wasn't going so well—not enough interest—so that's why we went to the University for help.

Of course, I didn't know all this background when Andy and John Lindstrom, the personnel director, called on me to ask if I would conduct an eight-week course for their foremen. I asked, "What do you want? What do your foremen need?" Lindstrom replied, "Well, we came to you because you are an expert. I understand you have done a good deal of this before. We'd like our foremen to get all the latest information on human relations. We're got a pretty old group, most of them have been with the company for 25 or 30 years and all they know is production."

We talked a while. I suggested that it might be desirable for me to work with the superintendents and general foremen to get their ideas on what should be done with the foremen. Even some of the general foremen might be trained as instructors so they could teach the foremen themselves.

"No," said Lindstrom, "our top management is just too busy and frankly I don't think one of them has the temperament to be a teacher. We want the best. That's why we picked you."

I agreed to take on a job that I felt was going to be a tough one. The first class was not too bad. I lectured on what workers want from their jobs. Lindstrom was there and so was the plant superintendent. My only trouble was the classroom. We were next to the machine shop and it was often hard to hear.

Next session the superintendent was absent (he never returned). I switched the subject and tried to get discussion on day-to-day problems of supervision. Lindstrom took part and it seemed that when the other men talked, they were looking to him for approval. After the session was over Lindstrom told me he thought it would be better if I lectured, since the men were really interested in hearing my ideas, not their own.

For the next few weeks I plunged into interview technique, starting out with a lecture on why it pays to listen. Soon I had the class broken down into pairs, each pair enacting an interview. The group seemed to do reasonably well, but I sensed a certain hostility toward me—and each session it got worse. Getting answers to questions was like pulling teeth, and when I got right ones, I had the feeling that the people didn't believe what they said.

On the sixth session Lindstrom was out of town. I decided to take advantage of his absence by bringing the problem out in the open. I said, "I have the feeling that a lot of you think this kind of approach, listening and all, might be fine for a professor, but just doesn't have any practical value, that it is a waste of time." I stopped and paused for a reply. Over a minute rolled by until somebody was brave enough to say, "You tell us we should listen to our employees' problems. But how are we going to get them to talk to us in the first place? They take their problems to their stewards."

I wrote his objection on the blackboard and waited for some more.

"Also, you say we should consult with the steward before we make any changes. I agree. But if we do that the personnel department will be on our neck for instigating grievances. Anyway the stewards get information from management before we do."

"Why do we have to listen politely to worker grievances when management won't listen to ours?"

Now it was my turn. "All right," I said. "Why do workers go to see the steward instead of you? What can you do to get them to see you?"

Everyone had an answer to that. I've rarely seen so enthusiastic a group. "They see the steward because management listens to them and not us. In fact the only way we foremen can get a needed improvement in the department or get a man a raise is to see the steward. . . ." And so on.

Things died down for a second. Then a hand popped up. "I have a question for you, Professor. The men in my department all stop work about fifteen minutes before quitting time and gather around the time clock. How can you get them to stay on the job?"

(A wonderful question for discussion, I thought, but I suspected it was loaded.) "What have you tried so far?" I asked.

"Well I tried asking them not to congregate, but they laughed at me. I gave one a warning slip, but management tore it up. Unless I get some backing, I can't do a thing. What do *you* think?" I ducked the question, and tried to explore some more positive approaches without much luck. The group was too interested in telling me their troubles. And I was worried what management would think when they found I was running a session like that.

It was probably fortunate that Lindstrom attended the rest of the sessions. I suggested it might be useful for him to spend a little time explaining the company's interpretation of the union contract. He felt not: the foremen were too close to the union as it was, and if he were to discuss company strategy it would soon leak back to the union.

A year later, Andy, the training director, and I were reminiscing. Andy had been sounding out the foremen on their reactions to the program, asking questions like, "How did you like it? Did you get anything from it?" His conclusions:

> Well, they enjoyed it. It was something very new. And they would like another course like it. But, if by "get anything from it" you mean a change in behavior—no, I'm afraid there is no change. They still think the only thing the company wants is production and that is what they try to get. I doubt if the course changed anyone at all. There was one fellow who was rather disappointed. He told me, "When the program started I thought there would be great changes. At last the company has found the foremen and we will be in on things. But I guess it doesn't mean anything at all."

1. What was wrong with this training program?
2. If you were Andy Jackson, the training director, and had to work under the conditions described here, what kind of program would you set up? How would you go about winning acceptance for it?

INCENTIVES

FOR EFFECTIVE PERFORMANCE

Having the right people in the right jobs at the right time is only one part of management's responsibility to develop and maintain personnel policies. Employees and managers alike—and the organization in which they work—are also vitally interested in the conditions of employment. These affect every working hour.

No one is surprised to find that employees expect payment for the services they render. The problem arises when the organization has to determine *how much* money each employee is to receive for the work he or she performs. Each firm must make a number of interrelated decisions concerning the relative magnitude of its wages and salaries (as compared with those in other organizations) and the relative rates for different jobs within the firm. Chapter 25, "Wage and Salary Administration," presents

criteria for both kinds of management decisions.

Employees receive income from the firm in exchange for work performed, but how much work constitutes a "fair day's work" or the effort that management can reasonably expect? "Work Measurement Techniques," described in Chapter 26, illustrate some of the methods that have been developed by the industrial engineers who have been struggling for many years to answer this question. Unfortunately, the unresolved problems in this area are still substantial. The techniques that have been developed do not provide precise, incontrovertible results. Nevertheless, the student of personnel should be familiar with the application of these techniques to the setting of work loads.

Moreover, time studies frequently serve as the basis for financial incentive plans covering production workers. Increasingly, management has turned to wage-payment systems that emphasize work accomplished rather than just the number of hours spent on company premises. But even incentive plans that seem to be logically defensible and psychologically sound may produce a wide variety of complex personnel problems. These problems are analyzed in Chapter 27, "Individual Incentive Systems."

The incentive programs discussed in Chapter 27 have been developed for individual employees. The shortcomings of these programs have motivated a search for other means of rewarding employee productivity, ingenuity, and group effort. A variety of techniques have been tried, and their relative advantages are summarized in Chapter 28, "Incentives for Group Participation."

Although unsafe work procedures and accidents are not a direct wage cost to the firm, they may have a substantial effect on both operating profits and productivity, not to mention their cost in human terms. "Safety," Chapter 29, reviews the areas in which effective managerial action can reduce or eliminate the hazards of work.

The cost of employee compensation is not limited exclusively to wages and salaries. Another source of employee remuneration—and one that is continuously increasing in importance—is discussed in Chapter 30, "Service and Benefit Programs." Popularly known as "fringe benefits," these programs are now an established component of nearly every organization's personnel program. Much more is involved in their administration than mere agreement to pay for vacations and insurance. In fact, some of the most perplexing questions in personnel arise in this area. Whether or not the benefit programs serve as an incentive for increasing productivity depends on how successfully management answers these questions.

Ask a man why he works and chances are he will say to earn a living. True, men and women want more from their job than just a wage or salary—yet this is a basic need. Even teachers and ministers, who may willingly accept less take-home pay for more on-the-job satisfaction, regard *relative* pay as highly important. A professor may be unconcerned about the fact that he earns less than a bricklayer, but still he may become enraged if Professor X across the hall, with six less publications than he, gets a salary increase while he does not. Alleged wages and salary inequities are among the most dangerous sources of friction and low morale in the organization.

Without a sound system of *wage administration,* wages are often determined on the basis of "personalized," arbitrary decisions without regard for the over-all wage structure. Wage administration is a *systematic procedure* for establishing a sound compensation structure. (For the sake of brevity, we will talk of "wage administration" rather than "wage and salary administration," since roughly the same problems are involved.) By reducing inequities between employees' earnings, a good wage-administration program raises

Wage and Salary Administration

individual morale and reduces intergroup friction. It also sets wages high enough to permit the company to recruit satisfactory employees (but not so high as to cause unnecessary expense), motivates people to work for promotions, reduces union and employee grievances, and enables management to exercise centralized control over the largest single item of cost: wages and salaries. But, as we shall see, some of these objectives are in conflict.

Aspects of Wage and Salary Administration

There are four closely related aspects of wage administration: wage and salary surveys, job evaluation, merit rating, and incentives. *Wage and salary surveys* are designed to determine the general wage and salary level in the community and industry, thus giving the company a base for setting its own rates. *Job evaluation* establishes the relationships between wages on various jobs within the company. Together, wage surveys and job evaluation set the "base" or minimum rates for each job.

Instead of setting one rate for each job, many companies establish a series of rates or *steps*. A new employee normally starts at the *base rate* for the job; then, as he gains proficiency and seniority, he advances through *merit rating* to higher steps. (Merit rating on one job should not be confused with *promotion* from one job to another.)

Companies with *incentive* plans pay the base rate only for a "normal" amount of production, as determined by time study. If a worker produces more than normal, he receives an extra incentive bonus. Similarly, salaried personnel may qualify for bonus earnings of one kind or another.

The personnel department is normally responsible for the administration of the wage and salary program. Indeed, larger personnel departments have special divisions that concentrate on this one function. Top management, however, has a continuing responsibility to review wage and salary policies, and every level of management may become involved in merit rating and in introducing a new job-evaluation program.

In this chapter we shall review the factors that must be taken into account in setting the over-all wage level through wage and salary surveys, then we shall look at job evaluation and merit rating, and finally we shall consider some of the special problems involved in salary administration for executives and engineers. (Incentives will be considered in Chapter 26.)

Determining the Over-all Wage and Salary Level

Determining the over-all wage and salary policy—whether to pay wages and salaries that are high, average, or below-average as compared with standards elsewhere—is one of management's most difficult decisions. What factors must management take into account in making this decision?

1. The company wage policy is related to its recruitment and selection policy, for high wages attract more job applicants and permit management to choose employees from a wider reservoir of talents. Moreover, they help maintain morale and make employees more reluctant to quit their jobs. And yet high wages in themselves do not guarantee motivation for high production (see Chapter 5).

2. If a company is anxious to gain a reputation in the community as a good employer and a good citizen—as are many public utilities—it may decide to pay high wages to insure good public relations. Small companies not in the public spotlight are not under compulsion to follow suit.

3. Unionized companies may be forced to pay high wages as a result of union pressure. Non-unionized companies may pay equally high wages to keep the union out. Yet if wages are too high, other employers may object that the company is "unstabilizing the market" and may exert subtle pressures to bring the company into line.

4. A company's profitability sets limits on its wage policy. The company that is losing money cannot afford to pay more than the minimum; the company that is known to be profitable is expected by the community and its employees to pay liberally.

5. Employment conditions in the area naturally affect wage policy. When there is a great deal of unemployment, a non-unionized company may be able to hire all the men it needs at little more than the minimum wage set by law.[1] When the labor market is tight, an employer may have to pay more than the going rate if he is to recruit qualified new employees.

Once the company has decided on its over-all wage policy, the next question it must answer is this: What are other companies paying on *comparable* jobs? This information is useful in determining whether the company is meeting community standards and also in bargaining with the union. The U.S. Bureau of Labor Statistics collects data for many jobs in large cities, and local chambers of commerce and employers' and trade associations often make available more detailed data. There are times, however, when a company is obliged to conduct a *wage survey* itself.

This is not an easy task. What are "comparable" jobs in other companies? It is simple enough to call another company and ask, "What are you paying your machine operators?" The other company answers $2.20 an hour; that makes you feel good, since you pay $2.30. But the other company failed to mention that their operators also earn incentive bonuses and do easier work than yours. To insure getting data that are really comparable, the survey should be made in person by means of oral interviews.

---

[1] As of 1960 the minimum wage set in interstate industry by the Fair Labor Standards Act was $1 an hour, though the Walsh-Healey Act required firms which sold to the government to set wages somewhat higher.

Rarely are two jobs performed in exactly the same way in different firms. Consideration must also be given to fringe benefits and continuity of employment. It is traditional, for instance, for maintenance men in factories to get lower pay than maintenance men who work for construction firms, because the latter are less assured of steady employment and receive fewer paid holidays, vacations, or other fringe benefits.

What companies should you use as the basis of your comparison—companies in the same community regardless of industry, or companies throughout the country in your industry? The management of nation-wide firms faces the problem of whether to pay uniform wages throughout all their plants or to adjust to the local wage patterns in each community. At times it is far from clear in what industry a firm should be classified. For instance, is a firm that makes rubber soles in the shoe industry or the rubber industry?

After the wage-survey figures have been gathered, great caution must be exercised in interpreting them, particularly if, as often happens, there is no central tendency or clear "going rate." The survey itself, however, does provide a series of bench-marks against which the company can compare its present wage and salary rates and decide whether adjustments are necessary to make them consistent with its over-all wage policy.

The company should keep its rates under constant review—if the workers are unionized, of course, management will have little chance to forget this need. New wage surveys should be made periodically to determine whether the company's rates are getting out of line. Wage rates undergo constant change—in recent years, in an almost steadily upward direction. Adjustments may also be dictated by changes in the cost of living or in company profitability or productivity.

Once the over-all wage level has been set, the company can turn to a consideration of individual rates. Here job evaluation is widely used.

Job Evaluation

WHAT IS JOB EVALUATION?

Strictly speaking, job evaluation is a method of determining the *relationship between* wage rates, not the rates themselves. In practice it is hard to consider these two questions separately. In theory, for instance, the completion of a job-evaluation program need not lead to any increase in the total wage bill: some people will get increases, others decreases. In practice, however, some increase in the wage bill is necessary if the program is to be accepted by the employees; normally no one gets his wage cut. Furthermore, if the rates that are finally set for any job are out of line with prevailing rates for that job in the community, the job-evaluation program may have to be adjusted.

Job evaluation is a systematic way of applying judgment, but it does not eliminate the need for exercising judgment. It is not an automatic process, for it is administered by people and is subject to all the human frailties.

In this section we will first present a very general picture of how a job-evaluation program is conducted. This background will make it easier for you to understand the problems involved in applying job evaluation to a particular situation. Our purpose is not to transform you into a job-evaluation expert, but simply to present some of the policy questions that job evaluation raises.

There are many methods of job evaluation, some of which are quite simple, but many of which are extremely complicated. In essence, however, all forms of job evaluation are designed to enable management to determine how much one job should pay relative to others. Most companies use one variation or another of the *point system* of job evaluation, though the *factor-comparison method* is also quite common.[2]

The Point System

The point system involves four steps, which we will first describe briefly and then discuss at some length:

Step 1: A manual or yardstick is drawn up (for an example, look at pp. 612-613), which provides a set of standards against which each job can be compared. Notice that the manual lists a number of *factors* on which each job is to be rated and then breaks each factor down into a number of *degrees*. Each degree is worth a certain number of *points*.

Step 2: The requirements of each job are described and listed in a standardized fashion in what is called a *job specification* (see p. 589 for an example).

Step 3: Each job—as described in the job specification—is rated, one factor at a time, in accordance with the manual. A point value is assigned to each factor. Then the points are added up.

Step 4: Each job is slotted into a *job classification* in accordance with its evaluated point total. A wage rate is then assigned to the job.

Step 1: SETTING UP THE MANUAL

It is very difficult to draw up a job-evaluation manual that is consistent and free from ambiguity, and that will give a fair evaluation of the relative

---

[2] The standard method of factor comparison is described in Eugene J. Benge, Samuel L. Burk, and Edward N. Hay, *Manual for Job Evaluation* (New York: Harpers, 1941). For variations, see Edward N. Hay, "Four Methods of Establishing Factor Scales in Factor Comparison Job Evaluation," *The AMA Handbook of Wage and Salary Administration* (New York: American Management Association, 1950).

worth of each job. Because of this difficulty many companies adopt standardized, ready-to-use plans prepared by such organizations as the National Metal Trades Association or the National Office Management Association. Yet other companies, particularly those that have jobs with unique characteristics, prefer to draft their own custom-made manual. In either case, management should be aware of some of the problems involved in preparing job-evaluation manuals. (For example, see pp. 612-613.)

Selecting factors   What are the factors or dimensions on which the jobs are to be evaluated? Each factor represents a certain characteristic of the job that management feels is worth compensating. Two of the best-known custom-made plans, those of the National Metal Trades Association and the National Electrical Manufacturers Associaton, use the following factors, with the weights indicated:

<table>
<tr><td align="center">**Skill (total 50%)**</td><td align="center">**Responsibility (total 20%)**</td></tr>
<tr><td>Education 14%</td><td>Equipment, process 5%</td></tr>
<tr><td>Experience 22%</td><td>Material or product 5%</td></tr>
<tr><td>Initiative and ingenuity 14%</td><td>Safety of others 5%</td></tr>
<tr><td></td><td>Work of others 5%</td></tr>
<tr><td align="center">**Effort (total 15%)**</td><td align="center">**Job Conditions (total 15%)**</td></tr>
<tr><td>Physical demand 10%</td><td>Working conditions 10%</td></tr>
<tr><td>Mental or visual 5%</td><td>Hazards 5%</td></tr>
</table>

Naturally, different factors are used evaluating supervisory jobs than in evaluating, say, production or clerical jobs. A job-evaluation manual for supervisory jobs might list such factors as public contacts, staff contacts, complexity of duties, responsibility for money, and number of employees supervised—factors that would be largely irrelevant on hourly-paid jobs.

Some plans have used as many as forty factors, but the trend has been to use considerably fewer. A plan with fewer factors is simpler and easier to understand, and statistical studies have shown that almost the same results are obtained when only two or three factors are used. There are two reasons:

> The first is the *halo effect* (see p. 531), the tendency of evaluators who rate a job high on one factor to rate it high on others, particularly if the factors are closely related.
>
> The second is that in practice some factors are more *effective* than others. An example may help clarify this concept of effectiveness: Suppose an examination has only two questions, each worth 50 points. The instructor grades each paper exactly 30 points for Question I, but disperses his grades on Question II from zero to 50. Since all students receive exactly the same grade on Question I, obviously Question II has the crucial "effectiveness" in determining differences between a high and low total grade on the over-all examination. Similarly in industry, the majority of jobs in a given situation may be pretty much alike, with differences concentrated on a few effective factors.

Thus increasing the number of factors may not result in a more "accurate" job evaluation. Still, it may be desirable to have a reasonably large number of factors to help "sell" the program to employees and to reduce complaints that important factors are not being considered.

Selecting degrees   Just as inches are the basic unit in determining length, so degrees are the basic unit in measuring the importance of any one factor in a given job. There is no set rule governing the number of degrees into which a factor should be broken down. If the scope of the jobs to be evaluated covers a wide range, from unskilled through highly skilled, there will be a large number of degrees. However, if there are too many degrees it may be hard to distinguish one from another.

It is helpful to define the degrees as closely as possible. "Lifts weights in excess of 50 lbs." is more specific than "Lifts heavy weights." But there is a danger in being *too* specific. For instance, physical effort is more than a matter of pure weight-lifting; constantly carrying a number of small bulky objects may be more tiring than infrequently lifting an easily grasped heavy object.

Assigning weights to factors and degrees   Next, point values must be assigned to each degree of each factor. The table below summarizes the point values that have been assigned by the manual on pp. 612-613.

Points assigned to factors

	Degrees						
Factors	1	2	3	4	5	6	7
Education	20	40	60	80	100	120	140
Training	20	40	60	80	100	120	140
Physical effort	25	50	75	100			
Dexterity	60	120	180	240			
Mental effort	20	40	60	80			
Responsibility	25	50	75	100			
Working conditions	20	40	60	80	100		
Safety	20	40	60	80	100		

At best, this process must be completely arbitrary. One must, for example, decide whether a requirement of "two years of college or equivalent" is worth more or less points than "hard work with constant physical strain."

The number of points may total 500 or 1000 or even more. The reason is purely psychological: It is easier to justify not putting a man into a higher rate range if he is 10 points off out of 1000 than if he is 1 point off of 100. Similarly, the lowest degree is never fixed at zero. Presumably to give a man a zero on any factor would be insulting. Note that since the relative standing of the jobs is the thing that counts, it makes no difference if point values are added or multiplied, provided each factor is treated in the same way.

Step 2: DRAWING UP JOB SPECIFICATIONS

Although many knotty problems of judgment are involved in drawing up the job-evaluation manual, in practice the really difficult disputes start when job evaluation moves from the general to the specific—that is, with the drawing up of job specifications.

Job titles   The first question is one that we discussed in an earlier context (pp. 477-478): What does a particular job consist of? How should one draw the boundaries around a specific job title? Particularly in the clerical and technical fields, this decision may not be easy to make. It may be that every secretary does work that is somewhat different from that of every other secretary. Should all secretarial work be classified under one job title? Or should there be a separate job title (and a separate pay rate) for each secretary's job? The Vice President for Sales is out of town a great deal, so his secretary must make many decisions for herself. Should this added responsibility give her more pay than the secretary to the Executive Vice President? Bob Jones is in charge of the Red Feather drive this year. Does this mean that he should receive higher pay? And so forth.

Similar problems arise on production jobs. For instance, material-handling may be considered as one job or several. In a company where the men insisted on higher pay for handling heavier material, management ended up with a separate job title for each material handled—over 100 job titles! Excessive elaboration of job titles may "deprive management of flexibility of assignment, restrict the workers' training and competence to the narrowest of fields, make seniority systems burdensome and impractical, and turn each job into a narrow caste to which a worker clings because outside it he is untrained and insecure." [3]

The common union insistence that a man should not work outside his classification has important ramifications here (see p. 476). Questions of status are also involved. A highly skilled maintenance man might object to the same job title as someone with no skill at all. A man who is proud of being "in charge of incoming vouchers" may be very unhappy to have his title changed to "Clerk II."

Job description   Next, each job must be described—that is, a list must be compiled of its duties and responsibilities (see figure on p. 614 for an example). Particularly in unionized plants the job description must be prepared with great care, since many union members refuse to work outside their job description.

---

[3] Clark Kerr and Lloyd H. Fisher, "Effect of Environment and Administration on Job Evaluation," in Paul Pigors and Charles A. Myers, eds., *Readings in Personnel Administration* (New York: McGraw-Hill, 1952), p. 390.

Code No. X 100

Total Points 281

Job Title ___Grinder - Rough (Castings)___

Department ___49 - Grinding___   Section ___Foundry___

Factor	Rating	Basis of Rating
1 General Knowledge	1 (5)	Requires the ability to understand English, understand and carry out specific oral instructions and recognize signs.
2 Experience	4 (48)	Requires 6 to 9 months experience to perform routine semi-skilled work of grinding fins, burrs, gates, etc., from a wide variety of Blanko attachments and castings using various sizes and types of grinding wheels on stand grinder and hand air grinder.
3 Judgement	3 (21)	Some judgement required on standardized rough grinding operations where variations in location of burrs, fins, gates, etc., on a wide variety of Blanko attachments and castings. Involves making decisions such as correct grinding wheel to use, distance between wheel and rest and type of rest best suited for job and maximum production.
4 Initiative & Ingenuity	2 (14)	Performs work of grinding gates, fins, burrs, etc., off castings, according to limited detailed instructions in following standard grinding methods but makes occasional changes in grinding rests and set-ups to grind castings in more efficient manner.
5 Manual Dexterity	4 (24)	Considerable manual skill and speed in the use of fingers, hands, and arms on repetitive operations of holding castings between rest and grinding wheel and manipulating part in most efficient manner and against wheel without use of grinding rest and burring of Blanko attachment where burrs are ground off by rapid touching of head and open end on side of wheel.
6 Accuracy	2 (16)	Moderate accuracy required in performance of rough grinding duties involving removal of fins, burrs, gates, etc., from a wide variety of castings where care must be taken to insure removal of the proper amount of metal.
7 Physical Activity	4 (28)	Sustained repetitive physical activity in manipulating Blanko attachments and castings between rest and wheel and burring of Blanko attachments and castings on wheel when rest is not used. Requires manual pressure for all types of grinding.
8 Strength	5 (25)	Requires the strength and physical activity to constantly handle castings weighing up to 5 lb and lift 30 to 50 lb

Total Points	281	
Date	1/2/60	

Source: L. C. Pigage and J. L. Tucker, *Job Evaluation* (Urbana, Illinois: Institute of Labor and Industrial Relations, University of Illinois, 1955), pp. 28-29. Reprinted by permission.

Management faces a dilemma here. If it includes only a few of a man's duties in a job description, he may well refuse to perform others. Yet every additional requirement in the description tends to inflate the number of points given to the job and therefore improves the union's case for getting more pay.

Job description cannot be performed in a vacuum, for it impinges on many areas of status and informal organization. An impressive job description builds up one's prestige. Purely as a matter of pride, everyone wants his job description to sound difficult. Companies that have tried to base their job descriptions on questionnaires filled out by the employees themselves have discovered that there is a strong tendency to puff up one's job beyond recognition.

Job specification   The next procedure is to formulate the job specification itself, which involves breaking the general job description down into specific categories, one for each factor. Here, for each job, one must decide such questions as how many years of schooling are required, how much noise is involved, and so forth. (An example of a job specification is illustrated on p. 589.) A careful job specification is useful in selection and training as well as in actual job evaluation.

Step 3: ASSIGNING POINTS

Now we come to the critical point: rating each job by assigning a certain number of degrees to each factor. The points are then computed and added together. The total is the *evaluated point score* for the given job (in the example on p. 589, 281 total points).

Though job specifications and the job-evaluation manual may make rating easier and more systematic, rating is still entirely a matter of judgment. As such, it is subject to all sorts of human bias, including:

The halo effect   (See our discussion, p. 531.)

Leniency   Often raters tend to be overly generous in handing out points. There is no harm in this provided they are equally generous with all jobs, since job evaluation is a matter of *relative* standing.

Consistency   Regardless of how carefully the manual has been written, there will be countless questions of interpretation. The problem is to achieve consistency in interpretation. Seemingly irrational decisions which are consistent with each other may be better than more rational decisions that are inconsistent.

> One plan assigned 100 points for constant noise and 80 points for intermittent noise. One machine on which many of the employees worked made a great deal of noise 300 times a minute, but this job was classified

as having intermittent noise. When a new job was established in this shop, the union insisted that it should be evaluated as being subject to "constant noise." Management objected on the ground that this noise had been rated as intermittent for years, that if 20 points were added to this new job for constant noise, then 20 points should be added to all other jobs in the shop and that doing this would amount to giving a general wage increase to 30 per cent of the employees. The company argued that the union should wait until the contract expired to demand a change.

Eventually the matter went to arbitration. Though the arbitrator agreed that the noise sounded pretty constant to him, he still ruled for the company. He pointed out that the purpose of job evaluation was to establish *relative* wage rates, and that to give this one job an additional 20 points would disturb the traditional relationship between jobs.

Step 4: DETERMINING THE WAGE RATE

From this point on, evaluation schemes vary a great deal. We will describe one common variety.

Once the point scores for each job have been calculated, they are plotted on a graph with point scores on one axis and present wage rates on the other. Notice that on p. 592 the utility assemblyman is evaluated at 300 points and now makes $2.05 an hour.

Next a trend line is drawn through the data, either freehand or in accordance with some mathematical formula. Jobs that lie above the trend line presumably are overpaid; those that lie below are underpaid. In the example given, the assembler is overpaid by 5 cents an hour, the tool and die man is underpaid by 10 cents.

If the trend line has been properly drawn, the cost of bringing the underpaid jobs *up* to the trend line is just balanced by the savings achieved by bringing those that are overpaid *down* to the line. If the rates are adjusted in this way, roughly half the employees will get wage increases and half will get wage cuts. However, such widespread wage cuts will make it extremely difficult to win acceptance of the plan (since the man who is about to get a cut will normally react much more violently than the man who is about to get a raise). Management can adopt two approaches to make the change more palatable:

1. "Sweeteners"   Management may decide to offer a "sweetener"—that is, a wage adjustment that will make the plan more acceptable. For example, it may draw the trend line 10 cents above the present mid-point, causing fewer workers to suffer wage cuts. The utility assembler, for instance, would get a 5-cent raise instead of a 5-cent cut, while the tool and die man would get a 15-cent raise. This sweetener is sometimes called an "adjustment for inequities." Note that it costs the company as much as an across-the-board wage increase. (Normally the size of the "sweetener" is determined by reference to collective bargaining or wage surveys.)

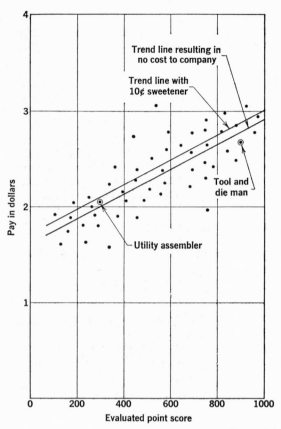

Determining the wage rate.

2. "Red-circle rates" Management may also guarantee the men who are now overpaid that as long as they *personally* are on this job the rate will not be cut. However, anyone who takes their place will receive only the rate set by job evaluation. This is traditionally called "red-circling" the job. Often, too, where there is a general wage increase, the men on red-circle jobs get no increase, or only a partial increase, until the evaluated rate catches up with the red-circle rate.

Job classifications Actually, instead of separate wage rates for each job, it is common under job evaluation to bracket jobs with roughly similar point totals into *job classifications* (sometimes called labor grades), each of which will receive the same rate of pay (see chart on p. 593).

Since moving from one job classification to another constitutes a promotion, management should give careful thought to the number of job classifications it establishes (see pp. 473-474). If there are too few classifications, it will be hard to promote employees and give them the feeling that they are moving ahead. On the other hand, if there are too many grades, every time

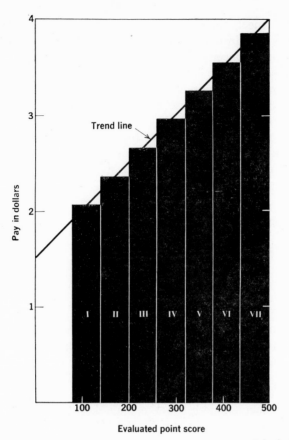

Job classification chart.

a man changes his work slightly, he may move into a different classification with a different rate of pay. Too many changes create expense and confusion.

Policy Problems

There is far more to job evaluation than merely going through the mechanical procedures that we have just described. True, by following these procedures management can tentatively slot each job into a classification and for each classification it can set a wage or salary rate. However, job evaluation cannot provide scientifically determined or objectively fair rates. As we have seen, it is a highly subjective process and there is much room for judgment and human error.

But it is not enough to strive for complete, laboratory-like objectivity. The crucial question is not whether management has followed the job-evaluation procedures with scrupulous care, but whether the resulting wage and salary structure meets the objectives of sound wage administration that we discussed on p. 581. In particular, does the structure provide rates that (1) seem fair to those concerned and (2) will attract and retain enough competent employees to do the job?

In short, an effective program of job evaluation should be concerned with employee values on the one hand and with going market rates on the other. These criteria are sometimes called "internal" and "external" standards. A technically sound job-evaluation plan that ignores either of these standards is bound to lead to tremendous friction and to fail in achieving its objectives. To complicate matters even further, these standards themselves are often in conflict.

INTERNAL STANDARDS

Who gets compared   Usually there are separate job-evaluation programs for production, technical, supervisory, and clerical personnel. Perhaps from a theoretical point of view it would be fairer to compare jobs in all these categories against each other, but the practical difficulties would be enormous. The less jobs have in common, the more difficult it is to compare them.

The job requirements of nurse, sales engineer, and riveter, for example, have so little in common that it would be almost impossible to get agreement on which factors are the relevant ones to compare. How is one to compare the skill or responsibility required by these very different jobs? Fortunately, there is little need to do so. People tend to compare their jobs only with those "close by" them. A clerical worker is unlikely to compare her wage with that paid for any specific production job (though she may feel that all production workers earn too much). Consequently, it is possible to establish separate programs for each group and to exercise a separate set of criteria for each program.

It has even been suggested that there should be separate job-evaluation programs for automated and non-automated jobs.[4] On automated jobs, responsibility is the most important factor; on non-automated jobs, skills are most important. A program that gives equal weight to both factors might not be fair to either kind of job.

Rates should seem fair   In Chapter 3 we discussed the determinants of status and suggested that a major cause of employee discontent is the *status inconsistency* that develops when various measures of status, such as job title and size of office, get out of line. Two of the major determinants of status are the nature of a man's work and the size of his paycheck. Great dissatisfaction arises when the *people concerned* decide that these determinants are out of

---

[4] John R. Bright, "Does Automation Raise Skill Requirements?" *Harvard Business Review*, Vol. 36, No. 4 (July 1958), p. 98.

line. The individual is unhappy if he thinks his pay is too little, relative to what others get for the same work. The others are unhappy if they think his pay is too high, relative to theirs. One purpose of job evaluation, therefore, is to realign the status ladder so as to reduce the perceived inconsistencies between pay and job requirements.

Employees in most situations have a pretty good idea of what various jobs are worth. In part this is a matter of tradition. Job A has always paid more than Job B. Yet the "accepted" wage structure varies widely from one situation to another.

> A number of specific examples come to mind: (1) In one company all the major maintenance crafts are in the same labor grade and rate range. The evaluated result follows the previous custom of equal payment. In a neighboring plant these same craft skills carry historical differentials. In each instance they are accepted as correct. (2) Within one industry several different skilled jobs are at the top of the pay ladder in different companies. Where Job A is at the top it appears to be regarded as the most skilled by management and employees alike. The same holds true where Job B is most highly paid.[5]

For this reason job evaluation may be most readily accepted—and most acutely needed—in new plants where there are no traditional rates and in old plants where technological change has thrown all the old job responsibilities and wage relationships into a state of flux.

In any case, care must be taken not to disturb established status hierarchies. If employees are generally satisfied with current pay relationships, why upset the applecart to achieve the theoretical equity afforded by job evaluation? If Job A has always paid more than Job B, in the eyes of the employees Job A is a better job. An "A" man has always had a tendency to look down on a "B" man. Now suppose job evaluation leads to higher pay for Job B than for Job A. The pay on Job A has not been cut, but status is a relative thing and Job A now has lower status than Job B. The "A" men consider themselves demoted; they are frustrated, lose interest in their work, and may even quit or take a militant anti-management position in the union.

Job evaluation can also unwittingly upset promotional sequences. Let us assume that Jobs A and B are in the same "seniority district"—that is, when there is a vacancy in either job, men from the entire "district" may bid for it. Naturally if Job A originally paid more than Job B, the senior men would tend to move to Job A and turn down Job B. Moving to Job A would be considered a promotion. Now job evaluation reverses this relationship: Job B becomes the better job. The men who had previously chosen Job A over Job B are understandably bitter. Then senior men on Job A will be getting

[5] E. Robert Livernash, "Wage Administration and Production Standards," Arthur Kornhauser, Robert Dubin, and Arthur Ross, eds., *Industrial Conflict* (New York: McGraw-Hill, 1954), p. 336.

less than the junior men on Job B. Of course, management may permit the senior men on Job A to "bump" the junior men from Job B, but the bumping period will be one of confusion and expense to management and of great ill-feeling on the part of employees.

Another problem arises in evaluating hard, dirty jobs. According to worker logic, clean jobs are better than dirty ones. A new man should start at the bottom, at the hardest, dirtiest, least desirable job. Then, as he acquires seniority, he should move up to better, easier, higher-paying jobs. But this is contradictory to the logic of job evaluation, which says that more points should be given for hard work and dirty conditions. Yet people will resist being "promoted" into a higher-paying job that has lower status. In practice, this problem is solved by giving very low point values to the factors of physical effort and job conditions [6]—or by socially separating the two kinds of job so that there will be little invidious comparison. At times management disregards the logic of job evaluation almost completely; dirty jobs are paid more than clean jobs. But the dirty job is a starting job through which all employees must move. As a man gets promoted, he moves by the ordinary process of seniority from a dirty, low-paid, low-status job to a cleaner, higher-paid, higher-status job.

Similar problems arise when job evaluation fails to take into account such job characteristics as opportunities for overtime or promotion. For instance, Job X pays 2 cents more an hour than Job Y, but Job Y is generally considered a better job because it presents greater opportunities for overtime. If evaluation raises Job X's differential to, say, 15 cents an hour, the men who had previously picked Y over X will feel cheated. On the other hand, if Y's hourly pay is increased still further, others may say that this is unfair, since Y's weekly pay may now exceed that of Z, a job that everyone agrees is more demanding than Y.

Similarly, a man who has a so-called dead-end job, on which there is little opportunity for promotion, feels that he should be somehow recompensed for this disadvantage. So does the man whose job has been automatized. Perhaps his work requires less skill and effort than before, but his output has vastly increased and he feels that some of the benefits should go to him. Yet strict job evaluation would say that since less skill and effort are required, the wage for the job should be cut.

Under strict job evaluation, too, it makes no difference whether the work is performed by a man, a woman, or a member of a minority group. Morally this is just. Yet both management and union should recognize that many workers feel that so-called "women's" jobs, or jobs that are typically performed by minority groups, should pay less. We do not suggest that concessions should be made to undemocratic prejudices, but that both union and

---

[6] And yet several authorities have argued that too little emphasis is given to physical effort. Barkin, *op. cit.*; Kerr and Fisher, *op. cit.*

management should be aware that there will be resistance to change if an attempt is made to eliminate or ignore this discrimination.

Thus there are many factors that wage administration must take into account other than the abstract requirements of the job as determined by job evaluation. It should be emphasized again that the objective is to obtain wage standards which *seem fair* to the people involved. The outsider should not substitute his frame of reference for that of the people involved (except possibly on moral grounds to prevent sex or ethnic discrimination).

EXTERNAL FACTORS

It is not enough for wage administration to achieve internal consistency, however, for employees and their unions compare their wages with those paid on comparable jobs in other companies. If wages lag behind those paid for similar work elsewhere, some employees may quit, the rest may grow dissatisfied, and it will be harder to hire new men. External comparisons are more likely to be made in some situations than in others.

1. Skilled maintenance men and unskilled common laborers are more likely to make such comparisons than are workers who hold jobs in the middle range of the spectrum. Maintenance jobs are pretty much alike throughout the community; the carpenter, for instance, knows what he can earn elsewhere. To a lesser extent the same is true of unskilled laborers' jobs, the starting jobs at which new employees are hired.

There is less market pressure on semi-skilled jobs. These are not hiring jobs; instead, one must have considerable seniority to earn them. A semi-skilled employee may become dissatisfied with low pay but he is less willing to quit because he will lose his seniority, pension rights, and so forth. In any case, most semi-skilled jobs are relatively specialized; there are fewer comparable jobs, so fewer comparisons are made.

2. Comparisons are more likely to be made in times of full employment when a new worker can choose among employers and when older employees can transfer to jobs elsewhere. We repeat, however, that few workers make systematic comparisons before accepting a job (see p. 434), and most employees are reluctant to quit a job on which they are reasonably happy just to make higher pay elsewhere.

3. Workers are less likely to make comparisons if the plant is geographically isolated or if the type of work is so highly specialized that there are few comparable jobs.

Thus the pressure to meet comparable rates is higher in times of full employment and in certain job ranges. Many companies use wage surveys in order to keep their wages from getting inadvertently out of line, either in terms of over-all wage levels or of specific jobs.

RECONCILING INTERNAL AND EXTERNAL STANDARDS

What should a company do when internal and external standards conflict, when the rates set by job evaluation are lower than those set by the market? High-wage companies need not worry too much about this problem, since most of their evaluated rates are well above those of the market. However, the lower the company's average pay, the more likely there is to be conflict between market rates and those established purely through job evaluation.

Job evaluation frequently favors different groups from those favored by the market. "The jobs which tend to rate high as compared with the market are those of janitor, nurse, and typist; while craft rates are comparatively low. Weaker groups are better served by an evaluation plan than by the market; the former places the emphasis not on force but on equity. Ideally, for a system of factors to accurately reflect the market, it should give heavy weight to those considerations to which the market most responds: skill, job conditions and bargaining power." [7]

Some sort of adjustment is required when the market rate on a specific job is higher than the evaluated rate. Many companies pay an "out-of-line" rate. Other companies engage in trial-and-error adjustments to make their job-evaluation scheme conform more closely to market forces. For instance, if some rates are well above the market and others below, the job-evaluation manual may be giving the wrong weights to the various factors, and these weights should be corrected. "If working conditions were given the major weight and skill a minor weight, there would be no correlation with the realities of the market place." [8] In some job-evaluation plans, "balancing points" are added to the point totals produced by ordinary job evaluation in an effort to make the results accord more closely with prevailing rates.

The greater the difference between evaluated rates and market rates, and the lower the company's average pay, the more point-juggling and factor-balancing will be required to devise an acceptable wage structure. Finally, there comes a point where job evaluation simply isn't worth the trouble. A really low-wage employer in a highly competitive industry, for instance, will have little use for job evaluation. He will just pay the lowest rate he can to recruit or retain employees for each job.

Many companies follow market rates exclusively for skilled jobs and use job evaluation only for semi-skilled jobs on which it is difficult to make comparisons with other companies. Or a company may pay prevailing rates on jobs where such rates exist, and then use job evaluation to interpolate other job rates between those set by the market.

---

[7] Kerr and Fisher, op. cit., p. 392.

[8] Edward Robert Livernash, "Wage Administration and Production Standards," Arthur Kornhauser, Robert Dubin, and Arthur Ross, eds., Industrial Conflict (New York: McGraw-Hill, 1954), p. 336.

Thus if job evaluation is flexible enough, there need be little conflict between the rates it establishes and the external standards set by the market.
But this very flexibility may lead to dissatisfaction with internal standards.
According to job evaluation, Jobs Q and R are equally difficult, and for years
they have been paid the same rate. Then a tremendous demand arises in the
community for workers to do Job R. So on the principle or adjusting to market
rates, R's pay is raised while Q's remains the same. The man on Q protests,
"My job is as hard as his. Why shouldn't I get an increase too?" Wage
administration must constantly face dilemmas of this sort. Whether satisfactory adjustments can be made, however, depends at least as much on how
the plan is administered as on the rates that are set.

Administration [9]

Any system of job evaluation is doomed to failure unless it is accepted
as fair by all parties concerned. Introducing a job-evaluation plan involves
all the problems discussed in Chapter 12. Employees fear that job evaluation
will upset the old structure of social relations; supervisors fear that it will
deprive them of their traditional prerogative to set the wages of those who
work for them; the union fears that it will reduce the scope of collective
bargaining. All may well look on job evaluation as an impersonal, impossible-
to-understand system which threatens their old established ways of doing
things.

One way of reducing these fears is to make the plan easier to understand;
indeed, there is a strong trend toward greater and greater simplicity. Another
is to involve the maximum number of people in administering the plan. In
general, the larger the number of people who take part, the more likely the
plan is to be accepted—though there is always danger that if too many people
are involved in the early stages so much time will be spent in discussion that
the plan will never be put into effect at all.

In a non-unionized organization the job-evaluation program is usually
administered by a committee representing a broad range of departments and
levels of management, possibly with rotating membership to broaden participation as much as possible. The line supervisors involved are consulted at
every stage, and their approval is required before a job specification is made
final. Moreover, the individual workers are consulted when the job specifications are drawn up.

Usually the personnel department acts as general coordinator for the
program, though a few companies assign this task to the industrial engineering department. (It can be argued that job evaluation is more properly the
personnel department's function, since above all the program demands flexi-

---

[9] For an excellent discussion, see Kerr and Fisher, *op. cit.*

bility and skill in dealing with people.) Sometimes the personnel department writes the job specifications; sometimes this is done by the committee itself. In almost every case the final rating is performed by the committee. After the new rates are tentively decided upon, the committee must give ample opportunity for objections to be heard and must be willing to make changes where necessary.

One of the problems of administration is deciding on the proper degree of centralization: Should job evaluation be conducted on an office-wide, a plant-wide, or a company-wide basis? To what extent should the individual supervisor be permitted to make exceptions in special cases (e.g., to grant a salary increase to avoid losing an exceptionally good man)? Too much centralization severely limits the freedom of the individual supervisor or plant manager; too little makes it possible for an individual supervisor to be exceptionally liberal, thus adding unnecessary expense and raising the danger that others will feel discriminated against. The trend is toward allowing supervisors to make exceptions, but only with the approval of the personnel department.

Once a plan has been set up, constant "maintenance" is needed to keep inequities from arising. Changes may occur either in wage rates elsewhere or in the job requirements of particular jobs. New jobs are created and must be evaluated. Suppose, after a plan has been put into effect, that one group is still very much upset over the wage rate it has received. Neither wage rates elsewhere nor job requirements within the company have changed. Should the job-evaluation committees give this group another hearing and perhaps yield to their pressure? Many authorities suggest that the committee should be quite willing to make adjustments *before* the plan is finally adopted, but that it should strongly resist pressure for change *after* the plan has been adopted. If the committee does not stand fast, every discontented group in the plant will continue to make trouble and unrest will persist indefinitely.[10]

Some companies make use of outside consultants in installing job-evaluation programs. The consultants may actually do the whole task, from writing the job description through rating the jobs and setting the rates. The more reputable consultants, however, recognize that if the plan is to win acceptance, those who will be affected by it must participate in making the evaluation; consequently, they insist on confining their activities to training and trouble-shooting. Job evaluation is a responsibility that management cannot easily delegate to an outsider.

THE ROLE OF THE UNION

Union attitudes toward job evaluation vary greatly, more in response to the over-all quality of union-management relations than to union policy toward job evaluation as such. Union objections center around the charge that

---

[10] For an example, see *ibid.,* p. 390.

job evaluation is a management tool used to restrict or eliminate collective bargaining. By its very nature, some union leaders argue, job evaluation prevents a realistic consideration of market forces or bargaining strength, and makes it impossible to work out adjustments suited to individual needs. It is "just hocus-pocus which prevents workers from understanding the pay system under which they work ... a cumbersome calculus in which nothing seems to add up." [11]

Nevertheless job evaluation is often introduced in the first place in response to the union's insistence that something be done to eliminate wage inequities. Union proponents of job evaluation argue that "the basic concepts of job evaluation were used by trade unionists long before these ideas were formalized into a systematic body of thought. ... As soon as negotiators recognized that a tool and die worker warranted a different scale than a broom sweeper, then job evaluation had been introduced into collective bargaining. Like Molière's famous character, many trade unionists may be surprised to find that they have been talking prose all their life." [12] Job evaluation, they would argue, is merely a systematic framework for negotiation.

In practice, the role of the union varies from outright opposition to complete participation. The UAW, for instance, is firmly opposed to evaluation. As a consequence, some automobile manufacturers engage in informal evaluation for their own purposes, but make no use of it in negotiations.

In contrast, some of the unions that believe in complete participation appoint specially trained international representatives to assist in the process. Local unions often select members, who are then trained by management, to sit on joint union-management evaluation committees. These committee members participate equally with management in writing job descriptions, rating jobs, and setting rates. In some cases the members may take an active part only in rating jobs and setting rates, though they have the right to protest and review job descriptions.

A different approach is for the company to conduct the entire evaluation, but to secure union approval at every stage, or to guarantee the union the right to object only to the end-product.

One reason for the union's reluctance to take an active part in the evaluation procedure is its realization that job evaluation is a dirty job. Many of the questions that arise concern disputes between union members over who should have higher status. Regardless of how impartial the union officers try to be, some members will accuse them of favoritism. Rather than make them-

---

[11] Boris Shiskin, "Job Evaluation: What It Is and How It Works," *American Federationist* (July, August, September, 1947), as cited in Edward N. Hay, "The Attitude of the American Federation of Labor on Job Evaluation," *Personnel Journal*, Vol. 26, No. 5 (November 1947), pp. 168-169.

[12] William Gomberg, "A Collective Bargaining Approach to Job Evaluation," *Labor and Nation* (November 1946).

selves the butt of complaints, many officers would prefer to let management take the responsibility and reserve for themselves the freedom to criticize from the sideline. For this same reason, management is often glad to pass the buck to the union, if it will accept it.

Regardless of the union's role, disputes over rates play a large part in union politics.

> To take a typical example, a public utility union included, among other members, DC and AC operators. At one time the president was a DC operator who, through his activities on the evaluation committee, was able to get for his group an extra 5 cents an hour, on the ground that their job required extra physical effort. Resentment against this apparent favoritism helped contribute to his defeat at the next election. The AC group, which gained power, was able to win a 5-cent advantage for itself on the grounds that its equipment, being more modern, required more responsibility. In retaliation, the DC group tried to lead the local into an affiliation with a new international union.

Job evaluation is more difficult to administer if the company is obliged to deal with several unions, for each will be concerned with how it makes out relative to the others, and each will be reluctant to make concessions in its relative position. For that matter, job evaluation is also difficult to administer if there are internal disputes within one union.

Management has good reason to encourage the union to take an active role in job evaluation and not just to force it to accept partial responsibility for the final result. To repeat the theme of this chapter, one of the primary objectives of job evaluation is to devise a wage structure that workers regard as fair. And the union is in an ideal position to sample and present worker opinions. A personnel director once told us that the first time he regretted not having a union in his office was when he started a job-evaluation program there. He selected a committee of employees as a sounding board, but he felt that they were far less willing to express their true opinons than an equivalent union committee would have been. For this reason many of the inequities felt by the employees at large were never expressed.

Whether job evaluation is desirable depends directly on the state of union-management relations. Certainly a joint committee will turn into a battleground if a cold war is in progress between the parties. In any case, it is almost impossible to devise a successful plan in the face of strong union opposition. On the other hand, if management is flexible in its attitude toward job evaluation and if the union is favorable to it, there may be very little distinction between bargained and evaluated rates.

There seems to be some evidence that acceptance will be easier to achieve if the parties first agree on the amount of the wage increase or "sweetener" to be provided before they proceed to establish relative job ranks. Once boundaries have been set to the amount to be distributed, consensus comes more readily than when the sky is the limit.

When Should Management Engage in Job Evaluation?

Job evaluation has been adopted in many companies just because it is the "proper" thing to do. Those responsible for its administration are often more concerned with developing a technically perfect product than in measuring its impact on people or in finding out whether it is accomplishing what it is designed to do. As two observers have commented:

> The tendency is to ... plug loopholes, to ferret out imprecision and make it precise, to define jobs more and more exactly ... to substitute means for ends, to forget that the objective is simply the acceptable determination of wages for a group of employees and to lavish more and more care on the production of a systematic end result which will be logical, polished, and final.[13]

And yet management should be aware that job evaluation is always expensive to administer and to keep up to date, and that it almost invariably leads to headaches for management and to friction with workers and unions. By altering relative wage rates, job evaluation disrupts established social and psychological relationships and opens a Pandora's box of troubles. Once management starts handing out wage increases, everybody expects something—and most people are likely to be at least partially disappointed. Even though management institutes evaluation in response to the union's demands for fairer wage rates, friction with the union over the administration of the program is almost inevitable.

As a consequence, many personnel directors feel that job evaluation, like appendectomies, should be avoided unless they are really necessary. So long as problems are not too serious, job evaluation may be postponed by patching things up here and there or by pragmatic negotiations with the union. The real question is whether evaluation will improve matters enough to be worth the trouble—or whether it will actually make matters worse. Job evaluation may be desirable if wage rates are far out of line with what employees feel are fair, or if the union is constantly complaining of inequities. But if the employees and the union are not too unhappy with the existing wage structure, it would seem foolish to create unnecessary friction.

We shall conclude this section with a list of some of the circumstances under which job evaluation has the best chance of success:

1. When it does not cause undue disruption of either traditional wage patterns or established promotional ladders.

2. When the company's over-all wage level is relatively high, so that not too many adjustments or exceptions must be made to meet market

---

[13] Kerr and Fisher, *op. cit.*, p. 394.

pressures, *or* when the company is so isolated from other firms (either in terms of geography or job requirements) that comparisons with wages elsewhere are difficult to make.

3. When relations with the union are generally good, when the union accepts an active role in administering the program, and when there is little internal conflict within the union.

4. When there is broad participation in administering the program throughout all levels of management.

5. When the company is willing to pay a "sweetener" to encourage acceptance.

Merit Rating

Merit rating is used by many companies to determine which employees should receive *merit increases* that will lift their wages or salaries above the minimum rate set by job evaluation. These companies hope to reward outstanding performance and provide motivation for all employees to work harder.[14]

Instead of a single wage or salary rate for each job, companies that practice merit rating normally have a *rate range*. For instance, the rate range of Job Class III might be from $2.20 to $2.60 (see chart below). Typically, each range is divided into a series of intervals or *steps* (the steps are $.10 apart in the chart). A new employee starts at the bottom step and is subject to periodic *merit reviews*, usually conducted by his supervisor. These reviews determine whether the employee should receive a raise that will carry him up one or more steps. They are made at regular intervals, possibly every four, six, or twelve months. In conducting the review, the supervisor often makes use of a *merit-rating form* (see p. 606), which provides a convenient means of summarizing the employee's weaknesses and strong points. After the review has been completed, the supervisor ordinarily sits down with the employee to communicate the results in a *merit-rating interview*.

Merit rating gives rise to several special problems, each of which we will discuss in turn.

RATE RANGES

Rate ranges normally overlap—that is, the highest step in one job classification may pay more than the lowest step in the next job classification. In the following chart, for example, the top step of Job Class III pays $.20

---

[14] Merit rating is useful in deciding who will be promoted from one job to another as well as in deciding who will get raises (see Chapter 23).

more than the lowest step of Job Class IV. What happens if an employee is at the top step of one job classification—must he take a cut in pay in order to move into a higher job classification? Normally he does not; he carries his old rate of pay with him and starts from the equivalent step in his new classification.

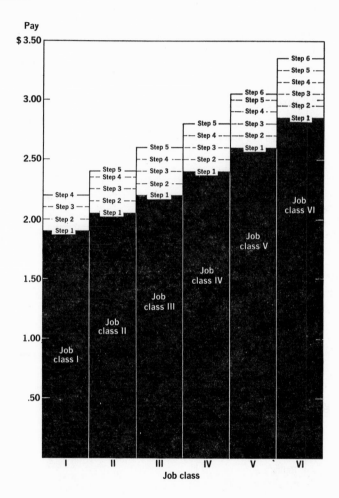

Not uncommonly, the rate ranges for higher job classifications are wider than those for lower job classifications. In our example, Job Class I has a range of only $.30 while Job Class VI has a range of $.50. Wider ranges are customary on higher-paid jobs to provide employees with more opportunity to display unusual skills on more difficult work. Also, as jobs become more difficult and important, it is more worthwhile to give employees a substantial financial incentive to contribute outstanding work.

MERIT REVIEWS AND MERIT INTERVIEWS

Merit rating of hourly-paid and lower-ranking salaried employees involves many of the problems of performance rating that we discussed in Chapter 23. There are numerous types of rating form, though the check-the-box type illustrated below is the most typical. As in performance rating, there are numerous sources of bias, such as the halo effect and over-leniency, which serve to reduce the effectiveness of the rating process.

```
NAME  Howard Bowman      JOB  Tool crib attendant
DATE  7/16/60      FOREMAN  David Thatcher
If on job less than six months state time        —

Supervision Required                    4
Job Knowledge                           2
Attitude, Conduct, Cooperation          4
Safety                                  3
Housekeeping                            2
Absenteeism and Tardiness               4
Adaptability                            2
Judgment                                1
Quantity                                4
Quality                                 2
        Total                          28
Remarks:  An able employee who shows a
          tendency to be lazy. He knows
          his job well but is frequently
          late to work and uncooperative
          with other employees.

Reviewed by Board   [✓]    Rating Code: 1. Top
Rating              [3]                 2. Above average
                                        3. Average
                                        4. Below average
                                        5. Unsatisfactory
```

In theory, the merit-rating interview gives the supervisor a chance to discuss each subordinate's problems with him and to coach him to do a better job. In practice, supervisors show little sympathy for the interview process and tend to conduct their interviews in a mechanical and insensitive manner; it is possible, of course, to improve their proficiency through careful training.

UNION ATTITUDES TOWARD MERIT REVIEWS

Unions in general oppose merit rating, insisting that it opens the door to rivalry and bad feeling between employees and to favoritism on the part of supervisors. They would prefer that all employees receive the same rate, and feel that if there is to be a rate range employees should move up from step to step purely by seniority.[15] (Of course, unions prefer a formalized system of merit rating over giving the employer complete freedom to set wage rates as he wishes.)

When merit-rating systems are established in unionized plants, the union tends to pressure management into giving each employee an increase every time a rating period comes around. If an employee is skipped over, the union files a grievance and requires management to explain why he did not receive an increase. Understandably, grievances of this sort often lead to recriminations and bad feelings between supervisor and subordinates. Yet where management yields to such pressures, wage increases from one step to another become completely automatic and depend exclusively on seniority rather than performance. Sometimes a compromise is worked out whereby employees automatically move up one step each review period until they reach the "mid-step" halfway between the top and bottom of the range. Pay increases above the mid-step are given purely at the discretion of management.

WHEN SHOULD MERIT RATING BE USED?

In theory, merit rating should relax the rigidity of job evaluation (which emphasizes the job, not the man who performs it) and should provide recognition for performance. It should also raise both productivity and morale, since employees who do a good job are rewarded. In practice, however, employees often come to expect that raises will be given automatically, instead of as a reward for good work. Indeed, for an employee to be denied an increase is sometimes regarded as a form of discipline, and is sharply resented unless it is clearly justified. Moreover, a poorly administered merit-rating program may lead to constant tension and ill feeling between supervisors and subordinates (and between management and union).

In general, merit rating should not be introduced unless the employees themselves accept the principal that there may be a legitimate difference in compensation among employees who hold the same job title. If employees think such distinctions are unfair, they are bound to resist any attempt to create them. Such distinctions are most likely to be accepted by highly

---

[15] Unions of professional engineers, who are of course an exceptional group, are generally in favor of salary increases on the basis of merit rather than seniority.

skilled workers and by white-collar workers. On highly skilled production jobs there is a significant difference between outstanding performance and merely adequate performance, while white-collar workers are particularly anxious to advance in their work.

Finally, merit rating should not be attempted unless subordinates have confidence that the rating will be fair. Ratings do more harm than good if employees assume that there is any arbitrariness or favoritism in the way they are made. Thus a company would be wise to forgo merit rating unless its supervisory practices are generally sound and it enjoys good union-management relations.

Salary Administration for Executives

Salary administration for executives involves most of the problems that apply to clerical and production employees, but it also involves certain peculiar problems of its own. In evaluating executive performance, many companies use a modified version of the standard job-evaluation procedure—that is, they go through the normal steps of job description, point rating, and establishing salary grades and salary ranges. And yet executive jobs are particularly hard to describe. They are more complex than lower-level jobs, and many of them are unique. For instance, the manager of Plant A, which concentrates on experimental work, has a different set of responsibilities from those of the manager of Plant B, which specializes in routine, mass-production work. Yet both executives have the same title: "Plant Manager."

> Job descriptions for managers not only are more important than for clerical or hourly workers; they are also more difficult to prepare, because the supervisor is given "areas of responsibility" rather than specific work assignments, and the procedures he follows in accomplishing these objectives are not officially proscribed.[16]

Obviously most of the factors used to evaluate subordinates' jobs (such as skill or working conditions) are not appropriate to an evaluation of executive responsibility. Executive jobs, after all, require a great deal of decision-making, planning, and supervision of others. Yet these special executive skills are often difficult to define, measure, or reduce to the "degrees" that are required by most forms of job evaluation.

Moreover, since there is usually a great difference between the efficiency

---

[16] Robert E. Sibson, "Plan for Management Salary Administration," *Harvard Business Review*, Vol. 34, No. 6 (November 1956), p. 104. For a job-description plan designed primarily for executives, see John K. Hemphill, "Job Descriptions of Executives," *Harvard Business Review*, Vol. 37, No. 5 (September 1959), pp. 55-67.

with which two men perform the same job at the executive level, executive jobs are usually assigned salary ranges (for instance, $12,000 to $16,000) rather than a specific salary ($14,500). "The width of salary grades—the within-grade progression or percentage by which the salary of the man classified at the top of the grade exceeds that of the men at the bottom of the grade—should depend theoretically on the extent to which the performance of the individual job holder can determine the value of the job. In other words, how much can man-worth affect job worth?"[17]

The progress of each executive, from the bottom of his salary grade to the top, should be determined by periodic salary reviews, perhaps every six months or every year. This is the equivalent of merit rating at lower levels. In such a salary review, how large a salary increase an executive receives is largely determined on the basis of an evaluation by his direct superior (see Chapter 23). It is because individual differences are so significant at the executive level that performance evaluation is more important than job evaluation. The two programs must be closely coordinated, however, to prevent inequities from arising (for instance, to prevent executives of equal merit from being paid more in Division A, which has a generous division manager, than they are in Division B, whose manager is more cost-conscious). Many companies permit a certain amount of flexibility in their evaluation system to provide for individual bargaining—that is, to make it possible to grant a special raise to keep a good man who has had a better offer from another company.

As one goes higher up in the management hierarchy, one finds that base salaries are supplemented more and more heavily with extra compensation in the form of bonuses (often based on the profitability or effectiveness of the executive's own department or of the company as a whole), in the form of fringe benefits, such as stock options or company-paid membership in the country-club. "The amount of this extra compensation typically averages from 10% to 15% of the base compensation for middle management, and as much as 100% or more at the top."[18]

The details of the executive salary program are often kept secret—either by design, or because of poor communications. Understandably, top management fears that all sorts of rivalry and bad feeling will develop if each executive knows what his colleagues are getting, and it is probably wise not to make specific salary figures public. But there is less justification for keeping an executive from knowing how he himself stands. At times, for example, an executive who receives $17,500 a year has no idea whether

---

[17] Sibson, *op. cit.*, p. 112. Since the individual is so much more important than the job at these levels, it has been suggested that job evaluation should never be applied to top management.
[18] *Ibid.*, p. 103.

he is already at the top of his salary grade, or whether he can reasonably expect to receive several thousand dollars more in annual salary increases without having to go to a higher-ranking job. Typically, executives are completely in the dark about what is expected of them on the job or the manner in which they are being judged and rewarded. Uncertainty of this sort leads to the suspicion that advances are distributed in an arbitrary manner, purely on the basis of favoritism. Nothing is more harmful to the executive's morale than the feeling that he is being "cheated" on his salary.

Salary Administration for Engineers and Scientists

The application of standard job-evaluation techniques is even more difficult with engineers and scientists than it is with executives. In professional work there is even ambiguity about when an employee has moved from one job to another, for job definitions here are quite elastic. An engineer, for example, may be required to work on a more difficult assignment for several months before the change in his job status is officially recognized by a formal promotion. And the distinction between an engineer doing "more responsible" work and an engineer doing "less responsible" work is often vague. The jobs of both may change over time as new projects come in and old ones are completed.

As a consequence, the emphasis in salary administration for engineers is usually on the individual worth of the particular engineer rather on the job he is doing at the present. Yet engineering supervisors often claim that it is hard to measure individual professional ability. Since engineers normally work on projects that have never been attempted before, it is difficult to predict in advance how long a given project should take. Two engineers may be assigned to what seem to be equally time-consuming projects. Yet Engineer A finishes long before Engineer B. Is this because Engineer A is better? Or because his solution is slipshod? Or because the two projects were not really of equal difficulty?

Engineering supervisors also tend to exaggerate the difficulty of making judgments on the quality and quantity of professional output.[19] In any case, the trend is toward setting engineering and scientific salary rates largely on the basis of a man's education and seniority. Thus two engineers,

---

[19] It has been suggested that "standard times" be established for engineering research projects, and that incentive bonuses be given to those who take less than standard time to complete their project. James L. Wyatt, "Are Creative People 'Different'? Developing Incentives in Scientists and Engineers," *The Management Review,* Vol. 48, No. 7 (July 1959), pp. 20-24, 82-85. We see enormous difficulties in such an undertaking.

both with a master's degree and ten years' experience, will get roughly the same salary unless one is clearly outstanding. Many national scientific and engineering societies publish statistics on the salaries received by men with various degrees and various years of experience following graduation. Depending on the company's over-all wage policy (pp. 582-584), it can decide to base its salaries on the median, above the median, or below the median shown by these "career lines." Unfortunately, the rigid use of career lines as the sole basis of setting salaries leaves little opportunity to reward individual excellence.

In recent years the starting salary for newly graduated engineers has tended to rise faster than the salary paid to more experienced men. In some firms engineers with five or ten years' experience are paid little more than recent graduates. Consequently, many engineers feel that the only way to get a salary increase is to take a job with another company. The discontent provoked by inept salary administration has even led some engineers to form their own unions.

Managements in many companies have tried either (1) to apply to engineers and scientists the same rules and procedures of salary administration that are used with other types of employees, or (2) to make mechanical use of career lines. Both approaches are too rigid. Difficult at it may be, management should try to develop a salary-administration program which meets the unique needs of engineers and scientists.

Conclusion

Monetary reward is the primary motivation for most employees, and yet many are more concerned about how their earnings compare *relatively* to the earnings of other employees than they are about their absolute take-home pay. Without a sound wage and salary administration program, it is almost impossible for management to recruit or maintain a work force motivated to strive for the company's long-range objectives.

Wage administration is a particularly delicate activity, since it deals with one of our most sensitive areas, our pocketbook. And, since it results in the comparison of one man with another, it cannot help but lead to emotionally fraught rivalries and resentments. The struggle for a salary increase often shows human behavior at its very worst.

There are some managers who feel that the way to avoid all these problems is to retreat to the Olympian heights of "scientific objectivity." But, as we have seen, such aloofness requires that they ignore many of the most troublesome economic and human relationships in our society.

At best, wage and salary administration can only channelize conflict and provide for a systematic review of difficult problems.

Problem I

The following is a simplified example of a *poorly designed* job-evaluation manual. Read it carefully and try to find the bugs, the areas of inconsistency, and the areas of ambiguity.

Job-Evaluation Manual

Degrees	Points

Education

1.	None required.	20
2.	Ability to speak English.	40
3.	Four years school or equivalent.	60
4.	Grade school or equivalent.	80
5.	Graduate of high school or equivalent.	100
6.	Two years college or equivalent.	120
7.	College degree or equivalent.	140

Training required

1.	Less than one week.	20
2.	One week to four weeks.	40
3.	Four weeks to six months.	60
4.	Six months to a year.	80
5.	A year to two years.	100
6.	Two years to four years.	120
7.	More than four years.	140

Physical Effort

1.	No significant amount required.	25
2.	Frequent handling of lightweight material. Must lift or handle objects of less than five pounds.	50
3.	Repetitive or sustained physical effort. Usually handling light or average weight material or occasionally working with heavyweight material. Lifting not over 30 pounds.	75
4.	Hard work with constant physical strain or immediate severe strain. Lifting over 75 pounds required.	100

Dexterity

1.	None required.	60
2.	Low degree of dexterity required.	120
3.	Considerable skill and craftsmanship required.	180
4.	Very high order of skill.	240

Job-Evaluation Manual (cont.)

Degrees	Points

Mental effort

1.	Flow of work is intermittent. No pressure of work. Attention required only at intervals.	20
2.	Operation requires frequent but not continuous attention. Inspection work where flaw is easily detected.	40
3.	Close attention is required at all times. Eye-hand coordination needed.	60
4.	High degree of concentration. Very close, exacting use of eyes.	80

Responsibility

1.	Little possibility for mistakes.	25
2.	Small losses might occur but mistakes are easily caught. Errors might go up to $15 a week.	50
3.	Substantial loss possible before errors are discovered. Worker must exert care. Losses might be very great but normally shall not exceed $50 a week.	75
4.	Responsible for an important operation. Errors could cause substantial damage to equipment or material.	100

Working conditions

1.	Works regularly under desirable working conditions.	20
2.	Works regularly under poorer than average working conditions; illumination and ventilation are considered only adequate (as in enclosed vault or work-room space).	40
3.	Works under conditions which entail some sacrifice of personal comfort. Subject to heat, noise, dirt, and cold.	60
4.	Works under difficult conditions such as high, though not continuous noise, heat, cold (such as work in refrigerator), and so forth.	80
5.	Works under highly hazardous or difficult conditions, such as continual high noise, constant movement from refrigerator or hot room, constant dust.	100

Safety

1.	Almost no hazards.	20
2.	Some chance of personal injury such as scratches and bruises.	40
3.	May be subject to moderately serious injury if proper precautions are not taken.	60
4.	Exposure to health hazard which might result in incapacitation if proper precautions are not observed. Minor accidents are common.	80
5.	Must be constantly on guard against serious accidents which often occur in spite of precautions.	100

Problem II

Using the above job-evaluation manual and the following job decription, evaluate the job of a press and liner operator. Notice that this job description is also inadequate. Observe the areas of ambiguity that develop as you try to apply the manual.

Job Description of Press and Liner Operator

This girl works in a can-making factory. She stamps out ends for the cans on a machine which makes 200 ends a minute.

The girl works in front of the machine. Sheets of metal are put into the rear by men. Circular ends are punched out by a metal punch which resembles a cookie-cutter. These ends pass through several complicated operations and drop onto a rack.

The girls take piles of ends and put them in crates. Each pile includes about 40 ends and weighs about 3 lbs. A good deal of dexterity is required, otherwise the ends will slither all over the floor. Lift-truck operators take filled crates to storage until needed.

The girls also watch the machine closely, stop it when something goes wrong and make minor repairs. Major repairs are made by mechanics.

Usually the girls can tell if something is going wrong by changes in the noise. The punch makes a very loud staccato sound.

When ends are coming through poorly, each one can be inspected separately. Otherwise a girl can talk to the girl next to her. Girls must stand all day except for short rest periods.

Girls can and do cut their fingers on ends, although they are encouraged to wear gloves. Also, if they don't shut the machine down when making repairs (they are instructed to do so), they can seriously injure their fingers.

If they fail to pay attention to their work, a lot of bad ends can go past them. These must be re-inspected by inspectors and discarded. Such inattention rarely lasts more than 20 minutes. Ends are worth perhaps 1/4 cent.

About three weeks are required to train a girl. There are no education requirements other than the ability to speak English. However, the company believes that girls with low intelligence are not aware when the machine is operating improperly.

Problem III

The foundry has always been regarded as one of the worst places to work in the Pushem Manufacturing Co. The work is hot, dirty, and heavy. Brawn rather than brains is considered the chief requirement to get the job done.

Yet according to the job evaluation plan, "physical ability" and "working conditions" are weighted relatively lower than "responsibility," "training," and "skill." As a consequence, most of the foundry jobs are rated at the bottom of the wage scale.

In recent years it has become increasingly difficult to get foundry help. Management has had to take men who could not get jobs elsewhere—thus further lowering the already low social status of the foundry in the eyes of the other men in the plant. The whole matter has now reached a crisis. There are now 17 vacancies in the foundry and it is impossible to hire new men at the evaluated rate.

1. How should this problem be handled? Should management completely revise its job-evaluation program? Should it make foundry jobs an exception to job evaluation?

2. How should management deal with the reactions of other workers if it decides to increase foundry wages but not other wages?

Problem IV

The following problem shows the contrasting attitudes of a union president and a personnel director on what the wage rate should be on a newly automated job. (The negotiations between these two men are suitable for role-playing.)

Role for Union President

The company has just introduced some new punch presses which are dramatically more efficient than the old ones. Each operator now handles four presses instead of one. Production per machine has gone up 30 per cent, while the number of employees in the department has been cut from 24 to 6.

With the new equipment, the operator no longer has to feed stock into the machine and remove it by hand. All this is now done automatically. All the operator need do is take the stock from "skids" and insert it into the "feed mechanism." This takes him about five minutes per press and needs to be done only once an hour. The remaining 40 minutes of every hour he must watch for breakdowns. If the press stops, or if it produces defective parts, he is instructed to turn off the power and call the set-up man.

The operator is now responsible for much more expensive equipment than he was formerly, and, of course, his output is enormously higher. A very substantial increase over the old rate of $2 an hour is in order.

Role for Personnel Director

The union's facts are correct as far as they go, but they tell only half the story. The old job presented a constant hazard to the employees' fingers and the new job is much safer. During the 40 minutes in which the employee is watching, he need be only "semi-alert." The presses rarely break down and the operator can easily spot defective work without moving from the stool that has now been provided for him.

Although "responsibility for equipment," as a factor in job evaluation, has increased substantially, it has been more than offset by the decreased physical effort and danger involved in the work. In fact, since the operator is now largely a machine-tender, his job ought to be cut 15 cents an hour. A new employee can be broken in on the job in less than an hour; formerly, it took several weeks for an employee to develop the rhythm he needed to feed and remove parts quickly enough to meet production standards.

Problem V

The Bayside National Bank has just decided to open a branch in Cotter's Bay, an exclusive resort located about 15 miles from Travis, a large city. There is no bank there at present.

Bayside is anxious to determine the appropriate wage for the clerical staff it expects to hire. Clerks in the bank's offices in Travis receive a starting wage of $40 a week, but through promotions they can work up to $65. As a matter of company policy, these wage rates have been set at the mid-point of the range for other banks in Travis.

A survey of the local businesses at Cotter's Bay, primarily realty and insurance offices and offices for local stores, indicates that the "going rate" for qualified clerical personnel is $60-75 a week. The higher rates in Cotter's Bay may be attributed in part to the substantially higher cost of living in this resort town, the limited number of young women seeking employment, and the fact that there are no other banks in Cotter's Bay. Banks in Travis have traditionally paid lower wages than other businesses, on the grounds that banks offer better working conditions and higher prestige.

1. What should the Bayside Bank establish as its hiring rate for clerical personnel? What factors should be considered in making the decision?

2. Could the bank justify to its Travis employees the fact that it was paying higher wages in Cotter's Bay?

The purpose of time study is to help management establish standards for the amount of work an employee should turn out within a given period. These standards have many uses: they help the supervisor allocate work fairly and judge whether a man is performing satisfactorily; they help management predict the labor requirements and the probable costs of new products and techniques; and, most important, they serve as the basis for piece-work and incentive plans (see Chapter 27).

The supervisor or personnel administrator rarely conduct time studies themselves—normally this responsibility is assigned to industrial engineers. In this chapter we will briefly outline some of the time-study techniques and phraseology for the benefit of the non-engineer.[1] Our chief emphasis, however, will be on the difficulties that time study sometimes creates for supervisors and personnel administrators.

[1] For a general description of this area, see Phil Carroll, *Time Study for Cost Control* (New York: McGraw-Hill, 1943). An excellent pamphlet is L. C. Pigage and J. L. Tucker, *Motion and Time Study*, Bulletin 24 (Urbana: Institute of Labor and Industrial Relations, University of Illinois, 1954). The authors are indebted to Paul E. Sultan, *Productivity and Wage Problems, Theories and Policies*, mimeographed, 1954.

Work Measurement

Techniques

ORIGINS

Time study is a relatively new technique. It first achieved popularity as a superior means of determining the "standard output" on which the piece rates used in incentive plans could be based.[2]

Early forms of incentives were not based on time study at all, however. A typical approach was that of the Halsey Gain Sharing Plan, which was first presented to the American Society of Mechanical Engineers in 1891.[3] Under this plan, management in effect offered to share with workers any savings in labor costs brought about through increased production. Suppose a 50 per cent gain-sharing plan were put into effect in a plant where a group of workers had been producing 100 pieces an hour at $1.00 an hour. Now, if they could produce 150 pieces in an hour (that is, if they could do an hour and a half's work in one hour), they would get half the time savings, or $.25, as bonus.

Although such plans were once common, they have been largely abandoned for plans based on time study in which the worker enjoys a 100 per cent reward from increased production. For instance, if he increases production by 10 per cent, his earnings go up 10 per cent too. There have been a number of reasons for this shift:

1. Workers—and later, unions—insisted that any less than a proportional 100 per cent reward was a form of stealing. Indeed, during World War II one union demanded a 110 per cent bonus for extra work, on the grounds that the extra work was more than proportionally hard.

2. Since bonuses were based on the existing rate of production, employees who had been taking life easy enjoyed very large increases in earnings, while those who had been working hard right along made very little more. Moreover, some groups decided to peg their production low while waiting for piece rates to be set.

3. In theory, the piece rates set up under gain-sharing plans were not to be altered when management introduced new and better ways of production. Rather, the workers would continue to share in the increased savings in labor costs. But this created serious inequities, for employees who benefited from technological improvements received higher wages than those who did not. In actual practice, management found it difficult to resist the temptation to cut rates.

---

[2] Time study was an important part of the Taylor System and the Scientific Management movement. Taylor first used it at the Midvale Steel Company in the 1890's. See Frederick W. Taylor, *The Principles of Scientific Management* (New York: Harpers, 1911). This book is a "must" for all serious students of industrial relations.

[3] Among other gain-sharing plans which were once quite popular are the Rowan, Barth Variable Savings, Taylor, Merrick, Gantt, and Emerson Plans. For a description of the whole family, see David Belcher, *Wage and Salary Administration* (Englewood Cliffs, N.J.: Prentice-Hall, 1955), pp. 332-346.

For all these and other reasons most present-day incentive systems are based on standards developed through time study.[4]

Time study makes it possible to determine the *normal* time required to do a particular job. But industrial engineers insist that before time study can be undertaken the *one best way* must be determined through *motion study*.

Motion Study

Considered broadly, motion study (often called "work simplification") encompasses the entire field of industrial engineering—namely, the determination of the most efficient method of production. It is related to plant design and materials-handling as well as to operator techniques. Here, however, we shall look at only those techniques of motion study that affect individual workers.[5]

Essentially, motion study involves: (1) analyzing how the job is currently being done, (2) questioning whether steps can be eliminated or combined, and (3) setting up a quicker, easier way of doing the job. In Taylor's words, the objective is to "eliminate all false movements, slow movements, and useless movements ... collect into one series the quickest and best movements."[6] To help in the systematic framing of questions, the industrial engineer makes use of flow and process charts, operations charts, and micromotion charts.

Flow charts plot the progress of a product through the plant from raw material to finished product. *Process charts* analyze the steps taken, using special symbols to highlight the various steps, such as:

Operation	◯	Transportation	○
Inspection	☐	Temporary storage	▽
Permanent storage	▽		

Through the use of these charts the industrial engineer can raise such questions as: Can the parts be made more accessible to the worker? Can conveyors be used? Are certain steps duplicated?

---

[4] One study of over 200 plants disclosed that only 16 per cent of all employees who did incentive work were still paid under a gain-sharing plan that gave them less than 100 per cent reward; in these plants only 6 per cent of time standards were still set by historical data. "The Truth About Wage Incentives and Work Measurement Today," *Factory*, Vol. 117, No. 4 (April 1959), p. 77.

[5] Ralph M. Barnes, *Motion and Time Study*, 2nd ed. (New York: Wiley, 1940), is an extremely useful introduction to this field.

[6] Taylor, *op. cit.*, pp. 117-118.

OPERATION CHART

Present METHOD

Page 1 of 1

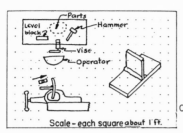

Scale - each square about 1 ft.

Operation Straighten Welded "T" Bracket

Operation No. 25 _____ Dept. 13

Parts Weld "T" Bracket _____ Part No. 1040

Machine Bench _____ Mach. No. None

Specif. No. None _____ Draw. No. None

Operator & No. U. Doit _____ Fixt. No. None

Charted by Jon Doe _____ Date Any time.

Left hand				Right hand
Reach for part	○	▽		Wait for left hand
Grasp part	◯			
Carry to vise	○	○		Reach for vise handle
Position in vise	◯	◯		Grasp handle
Hold for tightening vise	▽	◯		Tighten vise
Release part	◯	◯		Release handle
		○		Reach for hammer
		◯		Grasp hammer
Idle	▽	○		Carry hammer to vise
		◯		Hit part to straighten
		○		Carry hammer aside
		◯		Release hammer
Reach for part	○	○		Reach for vise handle
Grasp part	◯	◯		Grasp vice handle
Hold part	▽	◯		Open vise
Remove part from vise	◯	◯		Release vise handle
Carry part to level block	○			
Sight part for straightness	◯	▽		Idle
Aside part	○			
Release part	◯			

SUMMARY

	L.H.		R.H.
	7	Operations	9
	5	Movements	5
	3	Holds & delays	2

LCP-52-Form 3

OPERATION CHART

Suggested METHOD

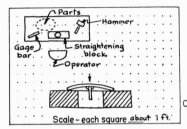

Gage bar. Straightening block. Operator. Parts. Hammer.

Scale - each square about 1 ft.

Page 1 of 1

Operation Straighten Welded "T" Bracket

Operation No. 25 ___ Dept. 13

Parts Weld "T" Bracket ___ Part No. 1040

Machine Bench ___ Mach. No. None

Specif. No. None ___ Draw. No. None

Operator & No. U. Doit ___ Fixt. No. S101

Charted by Jon Doe ___ Date Any time

Left hand			Right hand
Reach for part			Reach for hammer
Grasp part			Grasp hammer
Carry part to block			Carry hammer to block
Position part in hole in block			Wait
Release part			Strike part
Reach for gage bar			Aside hammer
Grasp gage bar			Release hammer
Carry gage bar to part			Reach for part
Gage part for straightness			Grasp part
Aside gage bar			Aside part
Release gage bar			Release part

SUMMARY

COMPARISON

L.H.		R.H.	Original Method		Suggested Method
6	Operations	5	16	Operations	11
5	Movements	5	10	Movements	10
—	Holds & Delays	1	5	Holds & Delays	1

LCP-52-Form 3

Operation charts.

According to the present method the operator must reach for the part and place it in the vise with his left hand. He then uses his right hand to hit it with a hammer. Both hands are required to take it out of the vise and finally the left hand alone is used to test it for straightness on the leveling block. Neither hand is used continuously. The suggested system uses two new pieces of equipment: a straightening board, which is much more convenient than the vise for fitting the bracket, and a gage bar to take the place of the leveling block. These two new pieces of equipment make it possible for both hands to be used simultaneously, thus saving 5 operations and 4 holds and delays. Source: L. C. Pigage and J. L. Tucker, *Motion and Time Study* (Urban, Illinois: Institute of Labor and Industrial Relations, University of Illinois, 1954), pp. 20-21. Reprinted by permission.

Operations charts plot the manner in which a given operator performs his task, usually by indicating separately what he does with each hand (see pp. 620-621). Here too the purpose is to question existing procedures and to suggest easier ways of performing the task. What motions can be eliminated? Can "gross," simple movements be substituted for "fine," more complicated movements which require greater dexterity? Can the sequence of operations be rearranged so that both hands will be kept busy where before one was idle? Can symmetrical, rhythmic, or circular motions be substituted for straight-line, jerky, or uncoordinated motions?

Micromotion charts (sometimes called simo charts) are the product of the fertile imaginations of the Gilbreth husband-and-wife team (some may remember them as the subjects of *Cheaper by the Dozen*). Far more precise than operations charts, micromotion charts are based on motion pictures which provide a slow-motion analysis of each motion. The Gilbreths broke down all body motions into seventeen basic motions or therbligs (Gilbreth spelled backwards), each with its own symbol. Some of these are:

Micromotion studies eliminate the need for a stop watch (which is used in other forms of time study) since the speed of an operation can be computed from the number of frames of film required to picture it. Further, micromotion charts help minimize debates over the accuracy of a study. Still the system is not very commonly used, largely because of the cost of preparing the films and making the extremely fine analyses required.

LIMITATIONS OF "ONE BEST WAY"

The industrial engineer uses all these motion-study techniques in an effort to determine the *one best way* for a worker to do a particular job. Behind this effort, of course, lies the assumption that there actually is one best way. What are the limitations of this assumption?

First, it tends to force everybody to work in the same way; it seems to ignore the fact that people are different. The best method for a right-hander, for instance, might be different from that for a "leftie." Moreover, it disregards the fact that over a long period of time varying one's work method may be less fatiguing than constantly doing the same thing.

Motion study often pays little attention to the sequence in which motions are taken or to the value of pauses. Carried to its logical extreme, this insistence on the "one best way" would eliminate the windup from the baseball pitch. The tendency in motion study is to consider each motion separately, rather than to determine whether it contributes to *over-all* efficiency. Considered by itself, the windup is clearly an unnecessary motion.

More important, behind this assumption lurks an implication that the seasoned worker's years of experience on the job are useless and that an engineer with a few hours' observation can find the one best method. To be sure, the engineer with his trained and questioning mind can spot mistakes that the worker on the job has always overlooked. Yet it is not safe to ignore the worker's experience altogether.

Further, even if the method that the engineer finally devises is clearly better than the existing method, there may be trouble in getting workers to accept it. Certainly if they are skeptical of the engineer's method and enthusiastic about their own, chances are they will turn out higher production by sticking with the less efficient method.

> One of the authors was observing a worker in a shop. As the foreman approached, the worker quickly hid a small brace and began to work in an obviously less efficient way. When asked why he did so, he answered, "When the foreman's around I do it his way. My way is better but I took my idea to engineering and they said the stop watch said their idea was quicker. But I know I make more money on piece work my way."

The point is not that the worker's method was more efficient—perhaps it wasn't—but that the worker *thought* it was better and refused to accept anyone else's.

A final criticism is that to the extent that work is reduced to one fixed routine, it may well become dull and boring. Acting on the principles of motion study, a group of British engineers are supposed to have submitted the following report after attending a symphony.[7]

> For considerable periods the four oboe players had nothing to do. The number should be reduced and the work spread more evenly over the whole of the concert, thus eliminating peaks of activity.
>
> All the twelve violins were playing identical notes; this seems unnecessary duplication. The staff of this section should be drastically cut. If a larger volume of sound is required, it should be obtained by electronic apparatus.
>
> Much effort was absorbed in the playing of demi-semi-quavers; this seems to be unnecessary refinement. It is recommended that all notes should be rounded up to the nearest semi-quaver. If this were done it would be possible to use trainees and lower-grade operatives more extensively.
>
> There seems to be too much repetition of some musical passages. Scores should be drastically pruned. No useful purpose is served by repeating on the horns a passage which has already been handled by the strings. It is estimated that if all redundant passages were eliminated the whole concert time of two hours could be reduced to twenty minutes and there would be no need for intermission.

---

[7] *Council Compass,* Vol. 13, No. 3 (July 1957), p. 16.

The above "report" was printed in an engineering journal, an indication that engineers themselves are aware of the limitations of too simplified an approach to motion study. In fact, industrial engineers today are increasingly taking into account the factors that we have discussed, such as individual differences and the need to introduce variety into work. In cooperation with industrial psychologists, they are making more and more use of carefully controlled psychological and physiological experimentation. Indeed, the field of human engineering (which is concerned with designing such apparatus as aircraft control panels) is simply an extension of motion study. Many industrial engineers have become aware of the problems and limitations of their staff role, and are spending more time advising managers and workers on ways of working out their own solutions—rather than dictating to them the "one best way."

In spite of these encouraging signs, there are still many industrial engineers who insist that the "one best method" approach is *the* only scientific and proper way to determine how men should do their job. The unyielding insistence of these men often intensifies the human-relations frictions that grow up when time-study and incentive systems are introduced.

Once the proper way of doing a job has been determined by motion study, it is possible to begin time study.

Time-study Procedure

Time study is a procedure for determining the *standard time* required to do a job. Usually it consists of four steps:

1. Selecting the employee and describing the job.
2. Determining the *observed* time.
3. Applying a correction factor.
4. Introducing *allowances* for fatigue, personal time, and contingencies.

SELECTING THE EMPLOYEE AND DESCRIBING THE JOB

A typical union contract includes the following provision:

> The time standards shall be based on the time required by a qualified normal employee working at a normal pace under normal conditions, using the proper method with normal material at normal machine speeds.

Notice how often the word "normal" is used: What are the normal machine speed, normal material, and normal conditions? Usually these are prescribed by the industrial engineer and all the details are listed on the time-study form. It is essential that these details be listed accurately, for if, some months later, a worker feels that the sheet of metal on which he is now working is thicker than that which was used when the original time study was made, he can always claim higher piece-rate earnings than originally allowed.

What is the "proper method"? That is the one best way, of course, which we have already mentioned.

What is meant by "normal" worker, "normal" work pace? Behind these questions lies a major area of contention between management and union. In most cases the industrial engineer makes no effort to find a "normal" employee. Instead he times a more or less typical employee, and, then, if the man seems to be working at a pace which is slower or faster than "normal," the engineer applies certain corrections to bring the employee's observed speed in line with what it would be if the employee were working at a normal pace.

TIMING THE JOB

Once the worker has been selected and the job conditions thoroughly described, the engineer is almost ready to start timing. But first he must break the job down into *elements,* each of which will usually be timed separately. An element is a clearly distinguishable motion, such as "place piece in jig." It should have a definite starting and stopping point, and it should last long enough (at least 3 seconds) to make accurate timing possible.[8] The engineer is interested not only in the total time for the entire *cycle,* but also in the time for each element. Close examination of "elemental" times enable him to determine exactly in what parts of the job there are needless operator, machine, or materials delays.

The engineer usually works with a stop watch,[9] and a form on which to record the time measured for each element. There are two methods of timing, both of which have their adherents. With the *snap-back* method the stop watch is snapped back at the end of each element, and the time for that element is recorded. In the *continuous* method the watch is never stopped until the study is completed; however, the time is recorded at the end of each element. When the study is finished, the elapsed time for each element is determined by subtracting each reading from the previous value. The chief advantage of the snap-back method is that it enables the skilled observer to tell at once when a worker is spending an unusual amount of time on any element and makes it possible for him to search out the cause at once. A

---

[8] Short elements are difficult to measure. One study found that a group of experienced time-study men, observing an operation taking .10 minutes (6 seconds), made a mean observation of .09674 minutes (off 3.5 per cent) while their standard deviation was .0107. This means that a majority of observations were at least 15 per cent off. William Gomberg, *A Trade Union Analysis of Time Study,* 2nd ed. (Englewood Cliffs, N.J.: Prentice-Hall, 1955), pp. 73-76.

[9] The "marstochron," an electric timing device, is more accurate, yet more cumbersome than the stop watch.

majority of authorities seem to favor the continuous method, on the grounds that it is more accurate and provides a record of everything that happens.[10]

How long should the study cover? Practice varies, but it is usual to time enough job cycles to insure that an adequate sample is obtained. Unless the whole operation is unusually long, at least ten or twenty cycles are ordinarily observed.[11]

Once the timing has been completed and the necessary calculations made, the observer is left with a number of readings for each element. If he has observed 20 cycles, he will have 20 readings for each element. Doubtless these readings will vary. The usual practice is to throw out all "abnormal" values—those that are too high or too low. But it is not easy to determine which readings are *too* high or *too* low. Naturally the union will want to throw out the low values, and management will challenge the high ones. One compromise is to throw out only those values for which the observer has indicated either that part of the element was omitted (too low) or that extraneous motions were introduced (too high).

Next the time-study man selects some sort of "average." There are four sorts of "average" in use: the mean, the median, the mode, and "good time" (in the strict sense, the last is not an average at all). Let us assume that the observations on a given element, listed in order of magnitude, came to: 10, 10, 11, 11, 11, 12, 12, 12, 12, 13, 13, 13, 14, 14, 15, 16, 17, 18, 22. Here the mode, or the *most frequent* time, would be 12, and the median, or the *half-way* point, 13. If the 22 were struck out as being abnormal, the mean, or garden-variety *average*, would be 13. Probably the most common average used is the mode. Occasionally the study will be based on *good time*, which is flexibly defined as the fastest time that an operator can maintain with some consistency. In our example this would probably be 11.

APPLYING A CORRECTION FACTOR

The next step is to apply a correction factor to adjust for the fact that the worker observed may be working at a pace slower or faster than "normal." Correction factors are applied in two ways, through effort-rating and through leveling.

---

[10] See Gomberg, *op. cit.*, pp. 76-85.

[11] The typical procedure at this point has been attacked as statistically unsound. It has been argued that the time-study man rarely gets a statistically adequate sample, nor is he sure that his readings are representative or that his data show what statisticians call "stability." See Gomberg, *op. cit.*, and Adam Abruzzi, *Work, Workers and Measurement* (New York: Columbia University Press, 1956). To these criticisms the time-study man may answer that he "collects data to familiarize himself more intimately with the job and to perceive the distortions, abnormalities and variations. . . . These are to help him reach a sound *personal* evaluation of the proper time value. The results cannot and are not designed to be checked by statistical criteria." Solomon Barkin, "Diversity in Time Study Practice," *Industrial and Labor Relations Review*, Vol. 7, No. 4 (July 1954), p. 452.

Effort rating is the simplest approach.[12] The time-study man merely estimates at what percentage of normal the operator is working. (He can make an effort rating for the job as a whole or separately for each element.) If he estimates that the operator is working at only 90 per cent of normal pace, then the observed time is obviously too long. The normal time can be obtained by multiplying the observed time by .90.

NOTES	CYCLE	ELEMENTS 1	2	3	4	5	6	7	8	9	10	11	12	13	14
A FUMBLE	1	7	14	31 *A*	14	23	35								
	2	6	15	21	16	22	36								
B WIPED NOSE	3	7	13	21	22	21	39 *B*								
	4	8	14	23	17	23	36								
Z MISSED READING	5	6	15	21	15	22	Z								
	6	7	13	20	16	21	36								
	7	9	15	19	16	22	35								
	8														
	9														
	10														
	11														
	12														
OBSERVED TIME		.07	.15	.21	.16	.22	.36								
RATING		.75	.75	.75	.75	.75	.80								
CORRECTED TIME		.05	.11	.16	.12	.17	.29								

ALLOWANCES

PERSONAL   *5 %*   TOTAL CORRECTED TIME ___ *.90*

FATIGUE   *5 %*   ALLOWANCES AT *20* % ___ *.18*

CONTINGENCIES *10 %*   ALLOWED TIME   *1.08*

           20 %

In this time study, the average used is the mode and elements have been timed in accordance with the snap-back method. The number of readings is illustrative only. There are not enough values shown here to determine a standard time for a job.

Effort rating assumes that the observer has in the back of his head some standard of what constitutes normal pace. Taylor and his followers felt that normal pace could be determined objectively and *scientifically*, but today it is pretty generally conceded to be purely a matter of judgment. What one man considers normal performance, another may consider soldiering.

---

[12] Ralph Presgrave, *The Dynamics of Time Study* (Toronto: University of Toronto Press, 1940), pp. 76-107.

How is the standard to be determined? Basically this is the age-old question of what constitutes a "fair day's work," the subject of frequent union-management negotiation. Sometimes the parties can agree on standards for a few bench-mark jobs. The 1946 contract between United States Steel and the Steelworkers Union defined a "fair day's work" as "that amount of work that can be produced by a qualified employee when working at a normal pace. . . . A normal pace is equivalent to a man walking without load, on smooth, level ground at a rate of three miles per hour." [13] Or, another example:

Shoveling sand

> *Material:* River sand, moisture 5.5% approx.; weight per cu. ft. 100-110 pounds.
>
> *Equipment:* Materials handling box (steel); effective height above floor 32"; shovel, no. 2 furnace.
>
> *Working conditions:* under roof; smooth concrete floor; all other conditions normal.
>
> *Production rate:* for shoveling sand from pile to box, average weight sand on shovel 15 lbs.; 12.5 shovelsful per minute.[14]

Such mutually agreed-upon standards provide bench-marks against which the time-study man can compare the normal pace for other jobs. For instance, when rating a man shoveling gravel, the time-study man may ask himself, "How fast does he seem to be working compared with a man shoveling sand 12.5 shovelsful per minute?" (The student should note that this is a most difficult comparison to make!)

Non-union plants (and many unionized plants as well) normally follow bench-mark standards set by leading industrial engineers. One such standard calls for typing 50 words a minute or dealing a deck of cards in 30 seconds [15] (but one engineer insists that only 27 seconds are required [16]).

Often movies are taken showing employees working at standard pace.

> The Society for Advancement of Management used essentially this approach. Films were prepared for 24 operations at five different work paces. These 120 separate performances were viewed by 1,800 engineers in over 200 industrial companies, and the resulting 150,000 ratings constitute the basis of the final standards.[17]

---

[13] Cited in Daniel Bell, "Work in the Life of an American," *Manpower in the United States,* William Haber and others, eds. (New York: Harpers, 1954), p. 10.

[14] *Ibid.*

[15] Presgrave, *op. cit.,* pp. 140-153.

[16] Frederick W. Shumard, *A Primer of Time Study* (New York: McGraw-Hill, 1940), pp. 64-73.

[17] Belcher, *op. cit.,* p. 353, citing V. A. Flynn, "A Word on the Rating Films," *Advanced Management,* Vol. 18, No. 4 (April 1953), p. 29.

Films of this sort may be prepared jointly by union and management,[18] although more often they are prepared by management engineers alone. When run at the speed that has been negotiated as "normal," they provide criteria by which to judge the pace of men on new jobs. Such films are also used in training time-study men to judge "normal" pace.

In spite of its seeming simplicity, effort rating has been attacked as being arbitrary and imprecise. Why?

1. Time-study men rarely claim to be more than 95 per cent accurate; yet if the time-study man makes a 5 or 10 per cent error in computing the proper time for a job, the worker's piece-work earnings may be affected by as much as $.20 to $.30 an hour. Long strikes have occurred over wage disputes involving smaller amounts than this.

2. In following the effort-rating approach, the time-study man assumes that by observing a worker he can tell how hard he is working. For instance, he assumes that by knowing what the normal pace is for shoveling sand he can also judge the normal pace for shoveling gravel.[19] Yet a pace that is normal for one job may be very hard to maintain on another.

3. At best, all the time-study man can do is be *consistent*—that is, he can compare one man against the standard and say whether this man is working faster or slower than the standard, and by how much. But since all the bench-mark standards are matters of controversy and judgment, one can never really tell whether the time-study man is *accurate*. For example, there are experimental studies which show that trained time-study men are likely to rate a given worker as slower than does a man without training.[20] (In other words, a time-study man may be more pro-management in his ratings than the man in the street.) But who is to say that the time-study man is more or less accurate in his judgment of what is "normal pace" or a "fair day's work" than an untrained individual?

Consistency is a very important objective in itself, however. If standards are inconsistent, a man on a "loose" standard can do his day's work (or make "base-rate" pay) with less effort than can a man who is on a "tight" standard. In fact, one of the greatest causes for dissatisfaction over incentives is the fact that some rates are "tighter" than others. If all rates are equally tight or equally loose, everyone may be getting paid too much or too little but there are no perceived inequalities between rates.

4. Unfortunately there is considerable evidence that time-study men often do not achieve a high level of consistency. The real test of consistency is whether or not several time-study men, each timing and rating a different

---

[18] For example, Sec. 58 (a) 5, Agreement between the Carborundum Co. and Local 12058, United Chemical Workers, CIO, dated Sept. 18, 1950.

[19] Taylor himself recognized this problem and made careful studies to determine optimum shovel sizes and work paces for various types of material. Time-study men today are not always this careful.

[20] See Abruzzi, *op. cit.*, Chapter 4.

worker (all of whom are doing the *same* job) will arrive at the same conclusions on the proper time to allow. A number of experimental studies have been made of this question, each using experienced time-study men as subjects. These studies conclude: [21]

(a) Two time-study men may differ in their ratings of the same job by as much as 2 to 1. Differences of 25 per cent to 50 per cent are common.

(b) Time-study men tend to underestimate differences in performance. For instance, if the same movie is run at 1000 frames per minute and then at 500, the time-study man will recognize that the new speed is slower, but not by 50 per cent—perhaps only by 35 per cent.

5. Perhaps one of the biggest drawbacks of effort rating was expressed to us by a time-study man:

> Unless you have had a great deal of experience, you are always deceived by the man who has been on the job for a long time. His efforts are so smooth that he looks like he is doing very little work—while a new man might look totally exhausted putting out the same amount.

To alleviate this last problem, *leveling* was developed.

Leveling Leveling is another means of applying corrections to raw observed data to compensate for the fact that the worker observed may be working faster or slower than "normal" pace.[22] Leveling takes into account not only effort, but also skill, consistency, and conditions. When a time-study man levels a worker's performance on a job, he rates it by each one of these factors (see table on p. 631), adds the indicated percentages together, and then multiplies the observed raw time by this sum to get the correction required. For instance, if a worker is working at "excellent skill," he is working faster than the "normal" worker and his observed time is too fast. To get a "normal" time, a correction must be added. Similarly, if a worker shows "poor consistency," his time is too slow and a correction must be subtracted. Let us assume that the observed time for a job is .60 minutes and the worker is rated as working at superskill (+15%), good effort (+5%), with fair conditions (−3%), and fair consistency (−2%). The sum of these corrections is +15%. This means that 15% of .60 minutes, or .09 minutes, must be added to the .60 minutes to give a "corrected time" of .69 minutes.

This system is even more arbitrary than effort rating, and it has most of effort rating's disadvantages. How is one to determine, for instance, whether a person's skill is excellent or only good? (Films are available to train time-study men in making this determination, but who is to say that the standards

---

[21] For a discussion of these studies, see Abruzzi, *op. cit.*, Chapters 3 and 4. Roughly the same criticisms were made much earlier by Robert F. Hoxie, *Scientific Management and Labor* (New York: Appleton, 1916).

[22] This system was developed by S. M. Lowry, H. B. Maynard, and G. J. Stegemerten. See their *Time and Motion Study*, 3rd ed. (New York: McGraw-Hill, 1940), Chapters 16-19.

Leveling Factors *

Skill			Effort		
+15%	Superskill		+13%	Excessive	
+13%			+12%		
+11%	Excellent		+10%	Excellent	
+ 8%			+ 8%		
+ 6%	Good		+ 5%	Good	
+ 3%			+ 2%		
0%	Average		0%	Average	
− 5%	Fair		− 4%	Fair	
−10%			− 8%		
−16%	Poor		−12%	Poor	
−22%			−17%		

Conditions †		Consistency	
+ 6%	Ideal	+ 4%	Perfect
+ 4%	Excellent	+ 3%	Excellent
+ 2%	Good	+ 1%	Good
0%	Average	0%	Average
− 3%	Fair	− 2%	Fair
− 7%	Poor	− 4%	Poor

* Adapted from Lowry, Maynard, and Stegemerten, *op. cit.*, p. 233.

† The question of working conditions has given rise to a great deal of controversy. The union often complains that although working conditions on the shop floor are poor, management insists on making the time study under ideal work-flow and material conditions.

set in the film are accurate?) Further, why should the minimum rating for skill be −22%—why not −27% or −33%? [23]

Standard data Because of the obvious disadvantages of traditional forms of time study, industrial engineers are turning increasingly to so-called standard data (sometimes known as synthetic data).[24] The use of standard data completely eliminates the need for timing each individual job. How?

[23] Lowry, Maynard, and Stegemerten recommend the discharge of workers with skills below poor. *Ibid.*, p. 209. They defend their system by saying their data are consistent with numerous studies showing the normal range of human abilities in various fields. For critical analysis, see Gomberg, *op. cit.*, Chapter 13; Abruzzi, *op. cit.*, Chapter 3.

[24] One study of 302 plants disclosed that 30 per cent of all plant standards were set by standard data, as contrasted to 49 per cent by time study, and 21 per cent by other methods. "The Truth About Wage Incentives and Work Measurement Today," *Factory*, Vol. 117, No. 4 (April 1959), p. 77.

First, the one best method for each job is determined, as discussed above, and waste motions are eliminated. Then the basic motions for each hand are carefully listed. Once this is done, reference is made to the "standard times" which have been developed by engineering firms for each basic motion.[25] In the example circled in the table on p. 633, moving a ten-pound part from skill to machine is allowed .08 minutes. The standard times allowed for each motion are merely added together to get the equivalent of "corrected time."

The advantages of this technique are many. By side-stepping time study and the rating problem, it eliminates endless union-management wrangles (that is, if the union accepts the standard data and, what is more unlikely, if its members accept its results). A worker can no longer fool the time-study man by pretending to work fast, nor does the time-study man (now better called an industrial engineer) have to worry about being outsmarted. Nor is there any problem of consistency. Standard data make the whole rate-setting process quicker, cheaper, more mechanical, and less subject to personal discretion.

But if the standard-data method is so advantageous, why isn't it used universally? There are many objections to it.[26]

The method assumes that the time for each motion can be determined independently of how it fits into the overall sequence—in other words, that the time required to perform one motion in an operation is independent of the time required to perform another. But this would be true only if each movement started at rest and ended at rest. Numerous studies have disproved this assumption of *independence*. In fact, the over-all time for an operation can rarely be determined by adding up the independently determined times of the parts. An efficient worker develops a rhythm in his work, and his speed in any one part of the job depends in part on what he has just done and what he intends to do next.[27] (Some standard-data systems distinguish between the time required to lift an object when the hand starts from rest and when it is already in motion. Few go further than this and most do not go that far.)

Moreover, although it is probably true that most motions can be broken down into a fairly small number of categories, no motion will fit any category

---

[25] Some systems provide times for fairly lengthy motions of the size of elements, while others break the job down into finer parts roughly the size of therbligs. One author even provides times for "nerve reactions—eye to brain—or reverse—.0003" minutes and "eye focus—get image clear—.0020 to .0040" minutes. Walter G. Holmes, *Applied Time and Motion Study* (New York: Ronald, 1938), p. 244, cited in Gomberg, *op. cit.*, p. 225.

[26] See Abruzzi, *op. cit.*, Chapters 13-15; Gomberg, *op. cit.*, Chapter 15.

[27] The speed at which a baseball player can run from home plate to first base depends on (a) whether he has just bunted or driven a line drive, and (b) whether he intends to stop at first or go on to second. It might also depend on whether he is first man up and still slightly tired from running in from center field at the end of the previous inning.

DRILL PRESS

1. HANDLING ELEMENTS	WEIGHT IN PART ONLY						UNIT TIME	U/C	EXT. TIME
	0-.5	.5-5	5-15	15-30	30-40	40 UP			
A. PARTS FROM SKID TO MACHINE	.010	.050	.080	.100	.120	.140			
REPLACE TO SKID									
B. PLACE IN JIG – REMOVE	.036	.040	.050	.060	.080	.120			
C. PLACE & REMOVE JIG SECTION	.032	.035	.044	.055	.075	.110			

2. JIGGING ELEMENTS	WEIGHT OF PART AND FIXTURE								
	0-10	10-40	40-50	50-60	60-70	70 UP			
A. BLOW CLEAR OF CHIPS	.040	.060	.080	.100	.120	.120			
B. WIPE BEARING POINTS @	.030	.030	.030	.030	.030	.030			
C. CLOSE AND OPEN LEAF	.033	.033	.048	.052	.060	.060			
D. ¼ TURN SCREW	.040	.040	.040	.040	.040	.040			
E. SCREW, NUT, KNOB, JACK BY HAND	.065	.080	.090	.090	.090	.090			
F. SOCKET HEAD SCREW	.081	.081	.081	.081	.081	.081			
G. CAM LOCK OR QUICK CLAMP	.036	.036	.036	.036	.036	.036			
H. NUT OR BOLT BY O. E. WRENCH	.123	.123	.130	.150	.162	.162			
I. FIXTURE CLAMP – UNFASTENED	.047	.057	.070	.080	.090	.098			
J. PLACE AND REMOVE PIN	.070	.108	.108	.108	.108	.108			
K. HOLD CLAMP OR "C" WASHER	.047	.047	.049	.052	.052	.052			
L. PREPOSITION JIG BEFORE ATC	–	.012	.020	.030	.038	.046			
M. JIG ON AND OFF ANGLE PLATE	.030	.030	.040	.060	.080	.100			
N. INDEX JIG OR PART PER INDEX	.004	.029	.035	.044	.060	.076			
O.									

* FOR TAPPING ON 707 ALLOW DOUBLE ATC AND WD *

3. MOVEMENT ELEMENTS	SMALL	MEDIUM	LARGE	LARGE SINGLE SPINDLE	NATCO 701 707*	NATCO 735 737			
A. ADVANCE & WITHDRAW TOOL	.025	.033	.043	.054	.022	.170			
B. INDEX JIG ON TRUNNIONS	.045	.056	.070	.083	.056	.090			
C. MOVE JIG ON ROLLER TABLE	–	–	.059	.059	–	.080			

4. HANDLE TOOLS AND BUSHINGS		MAGIC CHUCK			WIZARD CHUCK	SINGLE SPINDLE			
	SIZE TOOL	#1 SMALL	#2 MED.	#2 LARGE	LARGE	LARGE			
A. CHUCK TOOL		.030	.040	.055	.055	.065			
B. UNCHUCK TOOL		.020	.030	.045	.045	.050			
C. PLACE BUSHING IN JIG		.030	.040	.055	.055	.065			
D. REMOVE BUSHING FROM JIG		.030	.040	.055	.055	.057			
E. CHUCK TOOL AND PLACE BUSHING		.040	.052	.075	.075	.095			
F. UNCHUCK TOOL – REMOVE BUSHING		.030	.042	.056	.056	.058			
G. MOVE BUSHING TO ADJACENT HOLE		.040	.050	.065	.065	.065			
H. REPLACE TOOL OR BUSHING ONLY		.040	.052	.075	.075	.095			

5. GAGE PART (+ BY # BETWEEN GAGINGS)

A. MICROMETERS	.150	D. PLUG		.210	G. FLUSH PIN		.120
B. DEPTH MICS.	.180	E. SNAP		.060	H. TEMPLATE		.190
C. RING GAGE	.210	F. THREAD		.350	I. SCALE		.080

6. MISCELLANEOUS ELEMENTS

A. RAP WITH MALLET – FIRST RAP		.030	ADDED RAPS @		.008
B. BRUSH OIL ON TOOL – FIRST TOOL		.044	ADDED TOOLS @		.006
C. START AND STOP MACHINE	.048		D. CHANGE SPEED		.030
E. MOVE SKID OF PARTS (+ BY # PCS. ON SKID)					1.500
F. PLACE SKID RING (+ BY # PCS. RETAINED BY RING)					.300
G. BLOW OUT BLIND HOLE	.080		ADDITIONAL HOLES @		.010

TOTAL HANDLING TIME

Typical standard data table.

perfectly. And some motions are unique (for example, those of Gypsy Rose Lee)—to force them into a category would be highly arbitrary.

Any firm that uses a standard-data system accepts the prescribed times as the normal pace for the basic motions. But there are various standard-data systems, each with its own set of synthetic data. This means that for the same set of motions there may well be several sets of times—and why not, since there is no generally accepted definition of what constitutes normal pace? Unions are even more suspicious of standard-data schemes than they are of regular time-study systems. As one international representative expressed it:

> MTM [28] is management's idea of the right time. We have ours and we settle the matter by collective bargaining. The trouble is that some managements think that MTM is the answer and won't bargain at all. Naturally we can't accept that. MTM is an effort to take something which is really a matter for joint judgment out of collective bargaining and tries to give management the right to give the final answer.

In spite of these criticisms, standard-data systems do provide a rough check on the times obtained through direct observation. And when such a system is applied to a number of roughly similar jobs, such as using a drill press in a standardized fashion, it may result in considerably greater consistency between standards. One union, the International Ladies Garment Workers', has developed its own standard data for use in setting piece-rates for dresses. As the union's Director of Management Engineering once said, "The secret of its success is that it is viewed as a completely pragmatic method. It introduces a greater degree of consistency into the settlement of piece-rates than would be available without it." [29]

> The authors once studied a forge shop in which union and management had agreed on standard time values for each element of the operation. These times were posted on the shop wall to enable workers to compute their own time for each job.

ALLOWANCES

Once the time for a particular job has been determined, either by corrected time study or on the basis of standard data, the time-study man adds a certain percentage *allowance* to this time to account for what the worker may lose during the day for personal time, fatigue, or unexpected contingencies.

Normally, the *personal* allowance is set arbitrarily at 5 per cent. The purpose of this allowance is to permit the worker to attend to his personal affairs, such as going to the washroom or to the drinking fountain.

The *fatigue* allowance is designed to compensate for the worker's increasing tiredness as he does his job. Fatigue allowances are often set uniformly for all jobs; it is obvious, however, that some jobs are more tiring than others, and larger allowances are sometimes made for heavier jobs.

---

[28] Method-Time Measurement, a form of standard data.
[29] Gomberg, *op cit.*, p. 217.

Attempts have been made to measure fatigue scientifically on different jobs, but these have not been fruitful.[30] As we have seen, fatigue is partly a psychological factor that is influenced by the worker's home life, his relations with his fellow workers and his foreman, and his attitudes toward his job. Theoretically it might be possible for a worker to claim a higher fatigue allowance because he has a poor foreman. In practice, no such nonsense is allowed.

Allowance for contingency is a general catch-all category that may include setup time, delay for materials, delay for minor breakdowns, time for oiling, and other stoppages beyond the operator's control. Sometimes an arbitrary allowance is made to cover all such contingencies. More often, a contingency allowance is computed on the basis of a rough time study made over a period of several days.

DOWNTIME

Downtime refers to the pay a worker receives when he is unable to earn his regular incentive pay. Downtime may be incurred as a result of a major breakdown in machinery (minor breakdowns are included under contingencies), or because a worker is performing a "daywork job"—for instance, training a new employee, doing a special assignment on which no incentive standard has been developed, or handling a union grievance (where the company pays for this). Whenever management sets up an incentive system, it must answer two questions in deciding downtime policy: (1) When is downtime to be paid? (2) How much is to be paid for downtime?

Some contracts provide that downtime be paid for all delays of over ten minutes (sometimes 12, 15, or 20 minutes). A provision of this sort, however, encourages a worker who has already undergone an eight-minute delay to make it last two minutes more. Consequently, many contracts now provide that no downtime will be paid for the first ten minutes (or whatever figure is used) of each downtime period.

Naturally there is some question about whether a given delay will be included under downtime (and paid separately each time it occurs) or under contingencies (and paid on an incentive basis). Take oiling a machine as an example. If this delay is covered by downtime, the worker may be excessively slow in oiling. But if it is included under contingencies, the worker will be

---

[30] See A. T. Welford, "The Psychologist's Problem in Measuring Fatigue," *Symposium on Fatigue*, W. F. Floyd and A. T. Welford, eds. (London: Lewis, 1953), pp. 183-191; Lucien A. Brouha, "Fatigue—Measuring and Reducing It," *Eighth Annual Time Study and Methods Conference Proceedings* (New York: Society for the Advancement of Management, 1953), pp. 57-66.

motivated to spend as little time as possible on oiling and may do permanent damage to his equipment.

Custom and unions contracts vary a great deal on how much a worker should be paid when he is on downtime. Often he is paid the base rate, as set by job evaluation. At other times he is paid the "average earnings" which he normally receives while on piece-work. Sometimes downtime is paid at a stated percentage, say 110 per cent of the base rate (often this is called the "scale").[31]

Under certain circumstances "average earnings" may be abused. In one factory it was discovered that workers were spending as little as 10 per cent of their time on incentive work and the rest of the time on special activities which paid downtime. Since their rate of speed on incentive work determined their earnings for the rest of the year, naturally there was strong motivation to work exceptionally hard then and to take things easy the rest of the year. On the other hand—as might be expected—workers greatly resent being put on downtime if all they receive is the base rate.

Conclusion

Time study represents an attempt by management to introduce objectivity into the process of determining how hard a man should work or, if he is on piece-work, how much he should earn. And yet, though the intentions of management in introducing time study are often the best, time study is highly controversial and unpopular among both unionized and non-unionized workers. Why should this be?

Probably the chief reason for its unpopularity is that management often disregards the fact *though time study is a systematic method of exercising judgment, it does not do away with the need for judgment.* Results reached by time study are neither "scientific" nor beyond dispute. Indeed, many subjective decisions must still be made: in the choice of work methods (since there is probably no *one* best method), in the timing and averaging of observed times, in the making of corrections through leveling or effort rating, and in the determining of allowances.

At the same time, we must not rush to the conclusion that time-study techniques are useless. Used intelligently, they can narrow areas of ambiguity and provide the evidence on which unions and managements can make intelligent decisions. But both parties must still exercise judgment and discretion.

---

[31] One study of 245 plants disclosed that 47 per cent paid the base rate for trial work on new products, 34 per cent paid average earnings, and 19 per cent paid according to some other plan, often the "scale." "The Truth About Wage Incentives and Work Measurement Today," *Factory, op cit.,* p. 81.

Problem I

Using the following time-study data (timed in hundredths of a minute), calculate the time that should be allowed on this job by means of the effort-rating approach.

Cycle	Element			
	1	2	3	4
1	17	22	26	29
2	17	22	27	34
3	16	21	28	39
4	18	21	29	29
5	19	20	30	36
6	25	22	31	31
7	17	23	29	33

Allowances

fatigue 5%
personal 5%
contingencies 10%

The employee was estimated to be working at 130% of normal speed through all cycles. To compute the first element, use the mode; for the second, "good time"; for the third, the median; and for the fourth, the mean. (In practice, of course, but one system would be used.)

(For answer, see bottom of p. 678.)

Now that we have explored the role of time and motion study in setting work standards, let us look at the incentive plans that make use of these standards. The basic principle underlying these plans is very simple: Employees will be more productive if their income is tied to the amount of work they turn out rather than just to the amount of time they spend on the job.

The use of incentives as part of wage or salary systems is consistent with the theories of employee motivation and supervision that we presented in Chapters 5 and 6. Incentive systems provide a built-in reward that should encourage greater effort.

Most incentive systems are based on piece-work —that is, individuals or groups are paid on the basis of the number of units they produce. Such plans are most common in mass-production industries, where the conditions essential to incentive systems are most likely to prevail:

1. Standardized work and working conditions with relatively continuous processing.
2. Measurable units of output assignable to individuals or small groups.
3. Quantity of output proportional to employee effort and attention.

Individual Incentive Systems

Where these conditions are not present—for example, on a constant-paced assembly line—piece-work plans are less useful.

There are other "payment by result" plans that do not make use of time and motion study standards or their equivalents. These plans call for salesmen's commissions, or for efficiency bonuses paid to supervisors and non-production workers. Although this chapter will concentrate on piece-work plans in mass-production industry, some mention will be made of these other incentive systems.

In the sections that follow, we shall try to explain this paradox: Incentive wage-payment systems have many obvious advantages that should make them a very useful management technique, yet their application often generates serious problems of administration that vitiate their effectiveness.

Why Use Incentives? *To bring workers together*

BUILT-IN MOTIVATION

Ideally, incentive plans are superimposed upon a carefully constructed wage structure determined by job evaluation. The time-study engineer usually attempts to set the production standard at a level that will permit the average employee who applies himself to the job to make additional earnings of from 20 to 25 per cent above the evaluated base rate. It is this possibility of making additional earnings that provides the impetus for an employee to work harder under an incentive system. Most other employee benefits are granted almost automatically to the worker who performs at a minimum level of effectiveness; some are proportional to length of service, but few are related to accomplishment. Incentive plans, however, establish a direct relationship between performance and reward. (In the preceding chapter we considered some of the problems involved in determining these standards.) Most plans provide that for production below this level, the employee will still be guaranteed his evaluated rate—based on the type of work he is doing; the supervisor, of course, is expected to take action if a worker's production falls too far below this standard.

ADDED JOB INTEREST

The possibility of making extra money, of racing the clock, of pitting one's abilities against "normal" performance—all add an extra dash of interest to jobs that are inherently monotonous and tedious. This opportunity to set goals, and the chance to improve one's "score," provide the employee with a sense of accomplishment.[1]

---

[1] The importance of this type of job satisfaction was discussed in Chapters 1 and 2.

"When I am going hell bent for election on a good piece-work job, the evening passes very swiftly and I do not realize that I am tired until it is all over. On these daywork jobs I get so bored I could stand in the aisle and yell. . . ." [2]

LESS WORKER-MANAGEMENT CONFLICT

Incentive plans provide the sense of common interest between workers and management. They emphasize the fact that both will benefit from higher production and from improvements in supporting services, such as scheduling and quality of materials. The supervisor has less need to push for higher output, and the employees feel that they can vary their pace to suit their moods without antagonizing the supervisor. In a very real sense, these plans increase the opportunity to apply what we have called "general supervision."

INCREASED CONTROL OVER LABOR COSTS

Incentive plans also help the firm to control its labor costs. By insuring that employees will be paid on the basis of production, rather than on the number of hours they work, piece-rate systems enable the firm to predict its labor costs in advance. Particularly in highly competitive industries like textiles and clothing, this ability to look ahead is highly important. Piece rates also make it possible for management to develop more accurate cost-accounting estimates in establishing budgets and in preparing bids on new contracts.

This is a rosy picture we have painted. Surely it would seem that incentive systems should eliminate many of the sources of industrial conflict and employee-relations problems—after all, they encourage delegation of responsibility, increase worker motivation, and strengthen management's control. Unfortunately, the results have proved disappointing, for incentive plans have been the source of serious friction between labor and management. In fact, many observers attribute the rapid growth of unions in certain companies directly to the existence of incentive payment systems. How can we explain this paradox? Why should a program that is theoretically sound prove so deficient in practice?

Impact of Incentives

To understand why incentive plans tend to generate conflict, we must first assess the impact of these wage-payment systems on employees. In this

---

[2] William F. Whyte, *et al.*, *Money and Motivation* (New York: Harpers, 1955), p. 32.

section, which is based on recent empirical research, we will identify how employees react to incentives.

THE WORK GROUP IMPOSES A CEILING

It is unrealistic for management to assume that individual employees will respond to the opportunity for additional earnings by producing as much as they can. The members of certain inexperienced work groups may react that way, but most employees are quick to learn that such behavior is *dangerous*. Why do they feel it is dangerous?

Employees fear that if they begin to pull down earnings that are "too high" under a particular piece rate, management, particularly the time-study department, will decide that the rate is too generous. As we saw in the preceding chapter, time study is not an exact science. When employees begin to earn incentive premiums of 30 or 40 per cent above the base rate on the job, chances are that management will begin to question its time-study findings.

Management usually promises it will not "cut rates" except when changes are made in working conditions or in the methods by which the job is done. Employees, however, believe that management will always be able to find an excuse to restudy a job on which incentive earnings are obviously very high.

Further, many workers fear that if they increase their production markedly they will work themselves out of a job—that is, that management won't be able to sell the increased output.

Moreover, incentive plans may threaten the status hierarchy within the group, since older workers—who customarily have the highest status—may be unable to match the pace of their younger colleagues and thus find that their relative earnings have declined. Naturally, to protect their social position the older workers put pressure on the younger ones to "take things easy."

In response to all these factors, the work group begins to establish norms as to what is the proper or safe level of output (often these norms are called "boggies"). Just as the college student who hands in a very long term paper or an "A" exam is derided as a "curve-buster," so the employee who overproduces is belittled as a "rate-buster." New employees are indoctrinated into the group's standard almost as soon as they enter the department:

> This was my first job. The foreman told me I was on piece work and to make just as much as I could. I was scared and anxious to make a good impression so I tried pretty hard.
>
> About an hour had passed when several guys told me "Take it easy, guy—don't knock yourself out." I thought they were showing kindness, so I thanked them and kept plugging ahead.
>
> Then an older man came to me and said, "Let me give you a piece of advice. The most we ever make on that piece is sixty an hour, and a new

man doesn't make that much. If you want to make any friends here, I'd watch your count pretty closely."

"How come?" I asked.

"Because if we put out more than that, they'll cut our rates. We will have to work that much harder for the same amount of money."

As a result of these pressures, a relatively "straight-line" production curve is established for each employee and for the group as a whole. There will be certain variations from this curve because of factors beyond the workers' control, of course; but in general everyone will try to maintain and report approximately the same "safe" output. If the group inadvertently over-produces, this excess is concealed and reported on a day when the group falls short of its normal production.

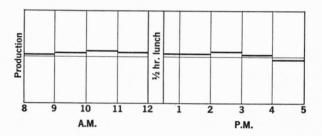

Typical production curve as affected by restriction of output. This is almost a straight line, with some variations introduced to keep it from looking too suspicious. (Curve is based on an assumption that employee production is measured hourly.)

In most work groups there are usually a few nonconformists or "rate-busters." These men, who do not rely on group acceptance as a source of job satisfaction, ignore the group's norms and produce at a level substantially above the agreed-on ceiling.[3] They trade their social acceptability in return for higher income. The friction that develops between rate-busters and the other group members may explode into severe supervisory problems. Efforts of the group to get the rate-buster to conform may show themselves in the sabotage of equipment as well as in ostracism—neither of which is conducive to harmonious working relationships.

The forces that keep the straight-line output curve from exceeding some upper limit also serve to keep it from falling *below* some predetermined reasonable level. And in this respect the group's efforts to control output actually work to management's advantage. Individual workers are reluctant to be considered excessively lazy or unskillful; therefore the ability to "make out" —to earn a reasonable incentive bonus—becomes a mark of prestige. Further-

---

[3] Melville Dalton, "The Industrial Rate Buster: A Characterization," *Applied Anthropology* (Winter 1948).

more, very low output would attract the attention of engineers and supervisors, who might eventually make undesirable changes in methods or standards. To protect its members from such a danger, the group establishes a *floor* as well as a ceiling for the output curve.

GETTING A BETTER RATE

Employees under an incentive plan do not restrict themselves to manipulating the output level, however. They also struggle with management and the time-study department to obtain more desirable or "looser" rates. They know that the time-study engineer cannot evaluate precisely how many pieces per day or per hour each worker should be able to complete; they know that he must resort to certain subjective judgments (what we called "leveling" in the preceding chapter). Consequently they suspect that management will try to make them work harder than they should to obtain a reasonable bonus, or even that management will establish such "tight" rates that it will be impossible to make satisfactory earnings.

TIMING A NEW JOB

This distrust shows itself most dramatically when the time-study engineer appears in the shop to study a job that requires a new rate. What happens is aptly described in the following verbatim account:

(Starkey is advising Tennessee, a relatively inexperienced worker, in the ways of dealing with time-study men.)

"If you expect to get any kind of a price, you got to outwit that. . . . You got to use your noodle while you're working, and think your work out ahead as you go along! You got to add in movements you know you ain't going to make when you're running the job! Remember, if you don't . . . them, they're going to . . . you! . . . Every movement counts!

". . . You were running that job too damn fast before they timed you on it! I was watching you yesterday. If you don't run a job slow before you get timed, you won't get a good price. They'll look at the record of what you do before they come around and compare it with the timing speed. Those time-study men are sharp! . . ."

(Later Starkey describes Ray Ward, one of the "heroes" of the department.)

"Ray knew his drills," said Starkey. "He'd burn up a drill every four or five pieces when they were timing him, and say the speed was too high for the tough stuff he was running. Tough stuff, nuts! They'd lower the speed and feed to where he wasn't burning up the drills, then afterwards he'd speed up and cut through that tough stuff like cheese."

"What I want to know," said Tennessee, "is how in hell could Ward burn up the drills like that? You can't just burn up a drill when you feel like it."

"It's in the way you grind the drill," said Starkey. "Ray used to grind his own drills, and he'd touch them up before they timed him. The wrong kind of a grind will burn up a drill at a lower speed than the drill can take if it's ground right for the job." [4]

Many other studies make it clear that this case is neither unusual nor unique. It has been said that ". . . no time-study man living is clever enough to best a moderately clever mechanic and discover the true time." [5]

A recent study of management's problems in administering incentive programs gives additional examples of the deceptions engaged in by employees during time-study checks:

> [The employee] had succeeded in obtaining a standard of 120 coils per hour for a job on which the workers could easily produce 300 coils per hour. He did this by distorting the tension on the steel. When the time-study men requested that the mill be speeded up, the uneven tension on the steel would cause a breakdown.
>
> [Other deceptions involved] oiling belts on machines to decrease friction and thus to reduce actual machine speeds; saving up defective materials to be used during time studies; using slow drive gears; and surrepetitiously cutting yarn to increase down time. [6]

ARGUMENTS OVER ALLOWANCES

Aside from the tricks of the trade designed to mislead the time-study man, there are many points on which legitimate differences of opinion may exist. In the preceding chapter, for example, we noted that allowances for contingencies often need to be made in setting rates. Both sides may disagree over the frequency and importance of equipment failures, material shortages, or imperfections that delay and hamper the employee in his production. Obviously the employees want to insure that the allowances are ample; management wants to insure that they are kept within reasonable limits.

Time-study engineers come to see the employees as tricksters who feign difficulties when jobs are being timed, are dishonest about their ability to do the job within the time allotted, and are always pressuring for looser standards, whether legitimate or not. Time-study engineers may even over-compensate for the expected bluffs and shenanigans of employees. If they are tricked into setting too "loose" a rate, they will be subject to serious embarrassment. Their ability as industrial engineers is called into question when employee earnings on a newly timed job soar to astronomical levels. Expecting the worst, they take extra pains when first setting a rate to make sure it is reasonably tight. Employees recognize this tendency and try to make sure that they don't have to accept the rate the company first establishes for a new job.

---

[4] Whyte, *et al., op. cit.,* pp. 15-17.

[5] H. Dennison, "What Can Employers Do About It?" in Stanley Mathewson, *Restriction of Output Among Unorganized Workers* (New York: Viking, 1931), p. 188.

[6] William B. Wolf, *Wage Incentives as a Managerial Tool* (New York: Columbia University Press, 1957), p. 26.

THE NEGOTIATION PROCESS

Thus the introduction of new jobs often marks the outbreak of an extended cold war between employees and management. Employees may have learned by experience that if they object vigorously to the rates set by management's industrial engineering department, and if they fail repeatedly to meet the standard output set by the time-study engineer, eventually they may be able to win a slight loosening of the rates. Management recognizes that by giving in to such pressures it may only encourage further slowdowns, grievances, and similar protests. It also recognizes, however, that if the workers are able to bottleneck output, a small concession will be cheaper than a prolonged struggle.

Frequently when workers and company disagree on a rate, a "trial period" is set up during which both sides have a chance to see how the rate works out before it is made official. This expedient, of course, simply just shifts the battleground. During this period employees still have everything to gain by attempting to "prove" that the rate is too "tight," and management, particularly the first-line supervisors, is saddled with the unpleasant job of cajoling, persuading, and pleading with employees to give the standards a "fair try." So the cold war rages until the employees are convinced that they can do no better and management is satisfied that it has won something approximating a reasonable standard. The ultimate result is a "negotiated" rate that may or may not accurately reflect the time-study data prepared for the job.

A recent best-selling novel contains a colorful description of this cold war.

> The setting of rates and the reaction by the operators is a routine you have to go over again and again, forever and ever apparently, as long as there shall be garment rates, and broken needles. You study carefully and set the rate, say 49½ cents a dozen for hemming. You post the rate and then the operator has a fit. She says she "can't make nothing on that rate." She says she's been here on the line for 23 years and no young squirt time-study man is going to push her around. You tell her there's a lot of factors involved (what would we do without those involved factors?), and that management wants to meet the operators half way and continue to enjoy mutual confidence for the highest production, Sleep Tite quality, and high earnings based on output and ability. The operator says she "can't buy no groceries on mutual confidence" and is going to go to work at the Packing Plant unless something is done about the rate. The other girls in the unit glare at management and exchange significant looks and talk so much about it all day that production goes off 12 dozen. You promise to analyze the situation and make an "eight-hour study" to check for any factors that might have been overlooked (or involved).
>
> Next time, the time-study man takes an all-day study and finds that he forgot to allow one-half minute per hour for "grasp scissors with left hand, clip estimated two threads per dozen, return and release scissors to position on machine table," and this raises the rate .0015 per dozen.

You announce this raise to the operator and she invokes the Sherman Anti-Trust Law and the Emancipation Proclamation and says she is being crucified.

Then there is a formal protest by the union president. You hold a meeting in his private office. "Mutual confidence" is mentioned.

The operator says she can't eat mutual confidence and that she can't make even 75 cents an hour on that rate, and she has been here on the line 23 years.

You agree to raise the rate from 49½ cents per dozen to 50¼ cents. Two weeks later the operator is running away with the rate and making $1.33 an hour, within 17 cents of the machinist, who is the best machinist in the area and knows more about a Singer machine than the Singer people.[7]

AFTER THE RATE IS SET

While they are being observed by the time-study man, employees try to prove that they have to work very slowly indeed. Then, after the rate has been set, they do just the opposite. They try to find short cuts: ways of running the machine faster, using special jigs or fixtures, leaving out some of the required operations. To avoid punishment for using unapproved short cuts, and to avoid retiming of the job, all these tricks must be kept secret.

Thus employees may earn large incentive bonuses but productivity may not increase proportionately. Sometimes management is deceived into thinking its rates are "in line" because the incentive earnings do not appear abnormally high. Of course, as we have seen, this in part merely reflects the adroitness of the work group in establishing output ceilings. "Loose rates" are hidden by carefully controlled output restriction, and the benefits from these rates are taken in the form of increased leisure on the job rather than increased earnings.

LIVING WITH THE RATE

Even after the battle seems to be over and the employees begin to work under an established rate, management's problems are still not solved. By pressuring job-setters, maintenance men, tool-room personnel, and even supervisors to "adjust" the time records and to report incorrectly the time when an employee began a particular job or the time when a breakdown occurs, employees can inflate the amount of time their machines were idle due to factors "beyond" their control, and can understate the time they were actually able to devote to their job. Thus employees can earn more money without working harder.[8]

On some jobs, employees are also able to take advantage of the "product

---

[7] Richard Bissell, *7½ Cents* (Boston: Little, Brown, 1953), pp. 132-134.

[8] Donald Roy, "Work Satisfaction and Social Rewards in Quota Achievements," *American Soc. Review,* Vol. XVIII, No. 5 (October 1953).

mix." When they have a number of tasks to do, each with its own time-study rate, they can build up their incentive earnings by working hard on the jobs with looser rates, and coast on the jobs with tighter rates, producing just enough to avoid trouble. This device, of course, upsets the production schedule.[9]

In their efforts to earn high bonuses, employees may pressure management for higher-quality materials, more assistance in handling materials and tools, and better maintenance. They are also likely to neglect work that does not help them increase their earnings—for example, keeping their work area clean, oiling the equipment, and caring for tools. As a result, management is confronted with higher overhead costs that detract from the direct improvements in output provided by the incentive plan. Frequently, too, these plans provide that employees will receive "average earnings" during delays that are beyond their control. This provision, in turn, motivates employees on occasion to seek delays and to fail to take adequate care of their own equipment. Moreover, this excessive emphasis on quality may induce employees to pay only perfunctory attention to quality. As a result inspection costs rise significantly.

In administering incentive plans it is assumed that job changes which make the employee's work easier or faster will be reflected in changes in the incentive rate for the job—that is, as improvements are made in the process, new rates will be established calling for higher production. In practice, however, management is often reluctant to begin the long tedious struggle over rate-setting, and therefore does not insist that a new rate be set every time a change is made in the job. And in fact management may never learn of the change, since employees have good reason to hide short cuts and improvements that they themselves discover in running the job. (After all, they reason, why should we be required to put out more work for the same pay just because we have shown some imagination.) At times, the foreman may know of the change, but—as we shall see later—he has little desire to cause dissension by reporting it.

Thus these minor job changes have a cumulative effect, causing piece rates to loosen more and more. The result is unjustifiably high earnings in relation to employee effort, and failure of the company to benefit from the investments it makes in improved technology, scheduling, and supervision.[10] Actually these "creeping rates" may nullify most of management's potential gains from the incentive plan.

To make matters worse, when one group succeeds in gradually loosen-

[9] Donald Roy, "Efficiency and 'The Fix,'" *American Journal of Sociology,* Vol. LX, No. 3 (November 1954).

[10] Robert H. Roy, "Do Wage Incentives Reduce Costs?" *Industrial Labor Relations Review,* Vol. 5, No. 2 (January 1952), pp. 195-209. For an excellent discussion of these problems, see Herbert R. Northrup, "The Other Side of Incentives," *Personnel,* Vol. 36, No. 1 (January-February 1959), pp. 32-41.

ing its rate, others then demand the same improvements, particularly when there is a union that is supposed to provide equal benefits for all:

> Taking advantage of the continuous technological changes that characterize the industry, the local unions seize opportunities to press home a wage gain for a particular job. A few such changes in incentive earnings, flowing out of changes in technology and job content, lead to inequities in relationships between jobs and this affords additional negotiating opportunities for the union.[11]

Thus a slight concession made by management in order to avoid serious disagreement may mushroom over time into substantially higher labor costs. And once this process has been initiated, it is almost impossible to reverse. A work group that has grown accustomed to relatively lucrative piece rates is understandably reluctant to accept a cut-back, even though the company's market position becomes unfavorable.

At best, rate-setting is a tedious process and work groups resist retiming even more strongly than they resist the original time study. Moreover, employees fear that management may resort to engineering changes on the job just as an excuse to "get another crack" at a piece rate that has proved too loose.

Management may in fact have to take advantage of this device. Most incentive plans guarantee that a rate, once established, will not be changed arbitrarily but only when the job changes. Where earnings are excessive, management may seek to find technological changes in order to have the opportunity to retime the job.

COERCIVE INTERGROUP COMPARISONS

Because incentive plans may affect relative earnings, potentially they can upset long-established status relationships between groups. Certain groups do work that has traditionally been considered as relatively low-paying and undesirable. Under a loose incentive rate, these groups may begin to earn substantially more than do workers on higher-status jobs. Almost invariably, intergroup bickering and dissatisfaction will arise, leading eventually to pressures on management to re-establish the traditional relationship between rates.

The following case suggests the intense feelings that may arise when differences in the relative "looseness" of incentive rates upset traditional differentials:

> Management was anxious to secure high output in a department that had recently secured an important government contract and set a very

---

[11] N. Goldfinger and E. M. Kassalow, "Trade Union Behavior in Wage Bargaining," in George W. Taylor and Frank C. Pierson, *New Concepts in Wage Determination* (New York: McGraw-Hill, 1957), p. 78.

loose rate. Although this department contained some of the lowest-rated jobs in the plant, the new incentive plan permitted earnings that far exceeded those of other departments. Long-service employees were outraged that young men who had been in the plant for less than a year were earning substantially more than they. One worker, a former union officer, summed up their sentiments:

"Can you imagine how I feel walking into a bar and getting my check cashed next to some youngster who has only been in the plant a few months? He maybe gets thirty dollars more than I do and I've been around here for 15 years."

The implication is clear: Management cannot really live by the maxim, "We never cut a rate." When, for whatever reason, one group of workers begins to earn bonuses so large that their relative position in the earnings hierarchy is altered, the unstabilizing affect on other groups may force management to take action—sometimes a contrived engineering change that will justify retiming. In any case, reducing a rate is a painful process for all concerned. The lesson it teaches employees with high earnings is to exercise greater restraint—that is, greater control over output—next time.

Each group working under incentives is sensitive to changes in the incentive earnings of other groups, since these changes upset the status hierarchy of the plant. Further, management will be more likely to give them a "tight rate" after some other group has "run away" with a "loose rate." Management, therefore, can expect to find these work groups pressuring one another to hold back output and demanding like concessions when a slightly easier rate does turn up.

Other groups in the plant are often affected by incentive systems, even though they themselves do not share in them. Workers who transport materials, for example, or who do maintenance or tool-room work, may be pressured into increasing their efforts to help incentive workers earn a greater bonus. These so-called "indirect employees" work harder and harder, plant production increases, and yet their earnings remain unchanged. In fact, their relative position in the earnings hierarchy may deteriorate. Understandably, these workers demand special wage concessions to restore them to their former position.

IMPACT ON THE UNION

The local union is often torn by differences of opinion over the value of incentives. Some groups, particularly younger employees, welcome incentive rates. Older and less fortunately situated employees, particularly "day workers," may fight for higher hourly rates that will counterbalance the incentive earnings of other employees. The fact that certain groups are making higher earnings than others may actually embarrass the union, particularly in deciding whether or not to accept management's efforts to "retime" the very lucrative jobs. The over-all result is political instability for the union leader, who must choose whether to concentrate the union's bargaining strength on defending the "lucky" groups or on fighting for those less fortunately situated.

Controlling Incentive Problems

Since, as we have noted, incentive systems have a high potential in motivating employees, it is worth asking how management can overcome the problems we have described. If they are not overcome, employee effort that might otherwise be devoted to increased productivity will be directed primarily to obtaining looser rates or to beating the rate once it is established. In addition, intergroup conflicts will dissipate cooperation and damage over-all morale.

As practice diverges more and more widely from theory, management's first reaction may be disillusionment with the incentive plan. Before installing the plan, management may have heard glowing accounts of how production would go up by 30 or 50 per cent and how costs would come down commensurately. The results may be far less salubrious.

The problems of day-to-day administration create unexpected costs. Handling complaints and grievances consume costly time and energy. Worker reactions sometimes take the form of slow-downs or even strikes, as well as costly subterfuges to win looser rates and to beat existing ones. The industrial engineering techniques themselves, which are necessary to keep the incentive plan up-to-date as changes are made in methods and equipment, require significant expenditures. Even the costs of figuring payrolls go up under the incentive system. Only when management is realistic about the complexity of incentive problems can it begin to make improvements.

IMPROVING THE SUPERVISOR-EMPLOYEE RELATIONSHIP

One of the most rewarding starting points in meeting incentive problems is the supervisor-employee relationship. Research suggests that employees are more likely to respond positively to incentives if they believe that their supervisor has some influence over the rate-setting process.[12] We have seen that the effective supervisor must be willing and able to *represent* his subordinates, to respond to suggestions from them, and to bring their problems to the attention of higher management. (See Chapter 15.) Where the supervisor has no voice in the incentive system and no specialized knowledge of how it works, or where he feels that the whole process is "out of his hands," it is highly unlikely that the system will function successfully. Thus

---

[12] See Donald Pelz, "Influence: A Key to Effective Leadership in the First Line Supervisor," *Personnel*, Vol. 29 (1952), pp. 209-217.

the successful administration of an incentive plan requires the active and intelligent participation of the first-line supervisor.

Unfortunately, however, the supervisor is often left out of the rate-setting and administrative processes. Because of the technical complexities of the plan, management ordinarily engages industrial engineers as special staff personnel to handle the whole plan. Also, fearing that concessions in one department will cause the mushrooming effect that we have already described, management often deprives the supervisor of the right to suggest that rates be raised, lest he succumb too readily to employee pressure.

Actually, the foreman has a strong incentive to support his work group in its struggle with management. Loose rates leave employees happy and eliminate the "cold war" type of grievances, slowdowns, and the like. Employees working under loose rates have energy left over to pitch in during an emergency when the supervisor needs their help. In addition, his own production record is likely to look better when employees have easy rates and always make a 20 or 30 per cent bonus.

Basically, the supervisor wants to minimize trouble with employees and at the same time satisfy his obligations to upper management. When the incentive rates are "loose," the plan works smoothly and there is no need for him to prod his subordinates into high productivity. When the rates are tight, however, he may be in trouble. When employees complain they can't "make out" with the rates that time study has imposed, the supervisor feels caught in the middle. Lacking adequate knowledge of the techniques of time and motion study, he feels incapable of making a qualified judgment on who is right. He is caught between the pressures of employees to "loosen" the rate and the pressures of management to get the employees to produce and stop malingering. Particularly when incentive earnings upset the traditional earnings differentials in his department, he is subjected to a great deal of pressure from those who have lost out.

Frequently the supervisor is tempted to respond to an employee question about his standard by saying, "Look, I don't understand it either; those engineers in time study work these things out, not me. If you're dissatisfied, they're the ones to argue with; I can't help you."

But this attitude undermines the whole system. Once the employees realize that their supervisor is isolated from the rate-setting process, they fear that they will be taken advantage of. The supervisor soon communicates his disrespect for or lack of understanding of the system to his subordinates, and they, in turn, are encouraged to help themselves by resorting to trickery and trumped-up records. The supervisor must be trained in the administration of the incentive plan and made to feel that it is part of his job. His skills in handling rate grievances must be cultivated. When employees find that he is informed and willing to "go to bat" for them when they are right, and unwilling to collude with them when they are wrong, the whole tenor of the system is likely to improve.

IMPROVING THE SUPERVISOR-TIME STUDY RELATIONSHIP

Before this improvement can be achieved, however, the relationship between time-study personnel and the supervisor must be put on a sound basis. This is one of the staff-line relationships that we described in Chapter 18, and as such it is well stocked with problems. There is the natural antipathy between the production man, who is likely to have been promoted through the ranks, toward the smart specialist who may be a relative newcomer to the organization. This antipathy is aggravated by the fact that time study is often a source of difficulty to the supervisor.

As we noted above, the supervisor's lot is much happier when the standards are relatively "loose." Production is unlikely to go along without interruption, employee morale is consistently high, and the department has little trouble meeting production quotas. The supervisor may be tempted to help employees disguise their restriction of output and even to take the initiative in discouraging "rate-busters."

To the time-study man, such supervisory attitudes are anathema, for he knows that even slight concessions on rates quickly grow to major proportions as other groups demand the same "loose" rates. Intraplant pay distortions spring up when easy rates make it possible for some employees to make disproportionately high earnings, and the time-study men are embarrassed when evidence suggests that they have been unable to set good tight rates. As a result they feel that the supervisor is too weak, too willing to concede to employee and union pressure, and unsympathetic toward the need for "scientifically correct" standards and frequent retiming.

The following hypothetical dialogue between a supervisor and a time-study man illustrates their different points of view:

A Time-study Man and a Supervisor
Discuss a New Standard

Supervisor: "It looks to me as if that rate is pretty tight and we are going to get a lot of gripes from the operators."

Time-study Man: (To himself) "How does he know; he hasn't even looked over the study—in fact, he probably doesn't even understand time study; he just wants to avoid any personal troubles with the men."

(To Supervisor) "Well, I've done a careful job, and I think it is a good standard."

Supervisor: (To himself) "Here is another one of those know-it-all kids who thinks he has learned in a couple of days what it took me 15 years to learn. There's no use trying to reason with them."

(To Time-study Man) "I've already heard a number of complaints from the men that they can never make out under this new standard. I wonder whether there might not be some factor that was overlooked in the study."

Time-study Man:	(To himself) "Just as I thought, he doesn't have the ability to get his people to accept the new standard; they are so used to only doing half a job that tightening up seems unfair." (To Supervisor) "If they would only give it a chance and really try it out, I know they could make it, but they prefer to gripe rather than work."
Supervisor:	(To himself) "There is not much use even talking to him; he doesn't care about what happens *after* he sets the rate. In fact, he probably gets a pat on the back from his boss for the amount he increases the standard on the job; the greater the increase the more likely he is to get a raise himself. I'm left holding the bag as far as dealing with the men is concerned and with the new quality problems that are going to come up when they try to beat it and with more tooling breakdowns and costs which those guys never figure on." (To Time-study Man) "O.K. We'll see what happens but I can tell you right now we are in for trouble on this."
Time-study Man:	(To himself) "Sure, if that's the way the supervisor feels about the standard already, what can you expect from the men? We'll have trouble from them." (To Supervisor) "If they'll only give it a fair trial I know it's going to work out."
Supervisor:	(To himself) "They think they can never make a mistake! Everything was fine here until he came in." (To Time-study Man) "We'll see. . . ."

The solution of such conflicts of interest demands both organizational change and training. William F. Whyte, generalizing from a study of the Inland Steel Container Company, has described the type of reorganization that will eliminate many of the problems we have described:

> No longer was he [the time-study man] to be a free-wheeling, apparently autonomous agent who carried the threat of change with him wherever he went in the plant. Instead, management decided that he should not enter a department for purposes of making a study unless he had written approval by one of two production management officials. Furthermore, he had to present this clearance to the foreman in whose department he was to work, and the foreman then took the initiative in bringing in the union steward so that the three of them could discuss the work that was to be done. Then, before the work was started, the foreman and steward would accompany the time-study man to the worker or workers whose jobs were to be studied so that the next steps could be explained to them.[13]

Notice that this approach shifts the time-study man into a truer staff position. The next step is for management to provide the kind of training in industrial engineering techniques that will enable the supervisor to deal intelligently with the problems raised by time and motion study.

Effective handling of incentive problems at lower levels also requires the

---

[13] Whyte, *et al., op. cit.*, p. 229.

use of simple formulas for converting production into earnings. Many companies develop unnecessarily complex formulas that neither supervisors nor employees understand; neither can calculate the effect of a particular day's production or a particular breakdown on earnings. A simple though necessary step in improving receptivity to incentives is the use of simple, direct plans that do not give the impression of deception on the part of management.

IMPROVING THE UNION-MANAGEMENT RELATIONSHIP

It would be highly unrealistic to assume that the administration of an incentive plan can be removed from the arena of union-management bargaining. Just because the rate-setting process is dependent on the quasi-scientific time-study procedures described in the previous chapter, management often assumes that "bargaining" over rates should not and cannot take place. But, as we have seen, time study involves many subjective questions of judgment, and the rate-setting process involves sensitive differentials in the earnings of both individuals and groups, as well as the determination of how much effort is to be required for how much income. These are problems that are central to the interests of all employees and their unions.[14]

The best guarantee of success in administering an incentive plan is a smoothly functioning grievance procedure for handling systematically and expeditiously the problems that arise. Where union and management have established a healthy, harmonious relationship, the problems illustrated in this chapter, though they may not be eliminated altogether, can be worked out with a minimum of disturbance. Where hostility and distrust prevail, the incentive plan will almost inevitably break down.

AUXILIARY INCENTIVE PLANS

Recognizing that other people in the organization are affected and in turn affect the incentive workers, management frequently attempts to develop financial incentive plans that will motivate them. In addition to the immediate supervisors themselves, hourly employees who transport materials, maintain equipment, make and distribute tools, and do inspection work are in a position to influence the pace and efficiency with which incentive employees work.

These so-called non-productive, auxiliary workers, who "service" the production workers, are not on incentive. And, as might be expected, these non-productive workers resent this "discrimination." They complain with justice that their efforts are essential to the incentive employees' earnings, and whenever the incentive employees work harder, they must work harder, too—without compensation. Naturally this situation tends to lower their morale.

---

[14] William Gomberg, "Union Interest in Engineering Techniques," *Harvard Business Review*, Vol. 24. No. 3 (Spring 1946), pp. 356-365.

Many managements have recognized the justice of this complaint and have attempted to devise forms of work standards and incentive plans which can be applied to these neglected groups. Unfortunately, this is not easy. True, industrial engineers are convinced that they can develop incentives for any type of job.[15] But management must be careful to keep the measurement procedures from becoming so complicated and costly as to vitiate any possible savings from improved productivity. Further, as we have seen, complex plans that involve intricate weightings and a host of variables are difficult to explain and justify to employees. When they can't understand the formulas used, it is unlikely that they will either accept the programs as fair or be motivated to increase their efforts on the job.

Because of all these difficulties, many companies have simply tried to provide extra compensation for auxiliary employees in proportion to the piece-work earnings of the incentive workers, on the assumption that their work increases roughly in the same ratio as the size of the bonus earnings. Thus supervisors get a monthly bonus that is tied to the bonus earned by their subordinates, and other indirect workers get a supplement based on the incentive earnings or the total production of the employees they service. In the case of a tool-room worker, the formula might be based on total plant production; the bonus of material-handlers might be based on the production of the department or departments they service.

The theory behind this practice is sound enough, but management must realize that the increase in work load of the auxiliary workers may not always be in proportion to the extra incentive earnings of the production workers. Clearly, workers whose efforts have not increased should not be rewarded with bonuses. In fact, technological change has made many of these jobs easier and simpler through the years. And where such changes have not been introduced, additional employees may have been hired to handle the additional work.

Moreover, the manager must be careful not to encourage undesirable practices by providing auxiliary bonuses. An inspector who is paid a bonus in proportion to the incentive earnings of the group as a whole may decide to be less diligent in looking for rejects. Extra precautions need to be taken to check his work (and this means extra costs). A supervisor, similarly, who is rewarded in proportion to the incentive earnings of his subordinates may be motivated to agitate for looser rates for his men and to be careless in administering the plan. For example, he may deduct short breakdowns from the employee's time on the job, or give him special allowances for faulty materials, contrary to the formula governing the incentive plan. The supervisor may also become careless about other cost elements in his department, such

---

[15] Because these procedures are relatively complicated, they are not reported in this text. For a brief summary, see David Belcher, *Wage and Salary Administration* (Englewood Cliffs, N.J.: Prentice-Hall, 1956), pp. 380-384.

as the costs of good housekeeping, low scrap waste, good safety practices, and the development of new ideas on methods, layout, and equipment.

In a survey of current practice, Belcher finds that management is moving toward more well-rounded pay plans for supervisors—giving some credit for the production performance of subordinates but also attempting to evaluate and direct attention to the other activities of the supervisor (such as simplifying jobs, reducing waste, improving housekeeping, and handling employee-relations problems effectively) and giving credit and economic rewards for these activities.[16] Belcher's caution is appropriate for all incentive plans:

> The supervisors' base pay must be correct *before the plan is installed.* . . . The incentive plan cannot be a substitute for a deserved pay increase nor a device to offset pay inequities within the supervisory group. . . .[17]

Conclusion

It is not unusual for management to regard financial incentive plans as a cure-all. Faced with weak and ineffective supervision, difficulties and delays in work flow, low morale, and unsatisfactory output levels, management decides that all these problems can be solved by incentives.

Actually, an incentive plan neither eliminates nor reduces the need for good supervision; it requires alert, skilled supervisors who can facilitate the rate-setting process and handle the difficulties inherent in any plan. Worker confidence and good relationships with employees and union are essential if the plan is not to become bogged down in constant bickering. Each management must weigh the costs involved and decide for itself whether or not incentives will produce a net gain. Careful administration and vigilance may produce a gain, but the gain does not come automatically. Just installing incentives does not guarantee lower costs.

Management, in instituting an incentive plan, must be willing to pay the price of administering it. It must be willing to struggle with grievances, and to correct inequities and imbalances in the wage structure resulting from differences in the relative "tightness" or "looseness" of incentive rates in various parts of the organization. It must also avoid the temptation to establish a looser rate when critical production is at stake. Concessions made during good times will cause trouble when profit levels decline. But with good administration, it is reasonable to expect that productivity will be improved under an incentive plan:

> It is also true, of course, that although wage incentive payment plans and related techniques do not release all the worker's productivity ca-

---

[16] *Ibid.*, pp. 392-395.
[17] *Ibid.*, p. 393. (Italics are ours.)

pacity, they do by and large liberate a greater share of it than comes from time work systems.[18]

Also, certain healthful pressures may be generated in the work group itself by incentive plans. Employees under incentives become concerned over unnecessary work delays or material shortages, equipment problems, and scheduling. They urge management to expedite the flow of work because they now have a stake in the effectiveness of the organization. Thus any incentive plan depends upon a well-engineered work flow: materials coming in and leaving as scheduled, equipment and tools in good condition, and working conditions maintained at prearranged levels.

In short, incentive systems cannot compensate for managerial ineptness. Rather, they demand managerial excellence. They are wasteful when they are used to bring production levels *up to* reasonable standards; they should be used only to compensate employees for performance *above* reasonable standards. Then they are a genuinely useful managerial tool.

Problem I

The Office Manager for your company's executive offices has called you in to discuss his labor-cost problems. He is seeking help from the personnel department in halting the steady rise in office costs and what he feels is a trend toward lower individual productivity. Specifically, he wants to know whether the experience of companies with incentive plans in manufacturing operations would have any applicability in his office environment. He thinks he may want to develop a type of "production standard" for the more routine jobs: IBM card-punch operator, stenographer, file clerk, mimeograph-machine operator, collator, and similar positions.

1. In discussing this matter with him, what knowledge about the operation of incentive plans would you use in framing questions and making comments?

2. What criteria would you apply in deciding whether or not formal incentive plans would be useful in the office?

3. How would you decide whether any or all of these jobs were suitable for such plans?

4. What problems would you envision in administering an incentive plan in such an office?

Problem II

A group of production employees is refusing to work any faster than "base rate" in protest against the elimination of a soft-drink machine near their work area. Top management is pressuring supervision "to do something" quickly, for scheduling throughout the plant is being affected by the decreased output here. Direct supervision is reluctant to succumb to employee pressure, both because of the bad precedent that would be set and because the machine itself was a nui-

---

[18] Gomberg, *op. cit.*, p. 365.

sance—cups, bottle caps, and bottles were strewn about the area, and the dispenser encouraged loitering. Disciplinary measures are being considered against the ringleaders for organizing a "slowdown." Some members of management are urging caution, claiming, as the men themselves do, that the employees do not have to work at an *incentive pace*. The company provides the opportunity for workers to earn a bonus if they wish to work more intensively than a *daywork pace*, but this decision is up to the employees. Other members of management take the opposite point of view—in accepting work on a job with an incentive rate attached, the worker obligates himself to try for such additional earnings, and this is a concerted effort to hold back production.

1. Comment on the merits of the divergent opinions within management on the employees' obligation to seek incentive earnings.

2. Discuss what management's approach should be to the workers' protest action. (There is no union in the organization.)

Problem III

Machine-shop employees are constantly wrangling among themselves and with their supervisor over work assignments. Several senior employees have filed grievances claiming that their foreman is discriminating against them. Here is a typical case:

> Waljack claims that his incentive earnings were cut 40 per cent the previous week because the supervisor assigned him several jobs that had very "tight" rates. During the same period most of the other employees, nearly all of whom had less seniority than Waljack, received highly desirable jobs with "looser" rates. Waljack further claims that the supervisor did all this on purpose to punish him, because he dislikes him.
>
> When the superintendent reviewed this particular grievance he was told by the departmental foreman that it was not serious. "This is just another effort by the older men to get all the good jobs and leave the dregs for the younger employees. What they want me to do is to spend hours analyzing every job that comes into the department and figure out just how much bonus the operator is going to get on it. Then I am supposed to plan out the work so that the senior workers get only the high-paying ones and when they finish one good one, I will have another choice job to give them. This way I would spend my whole day working out earnings schedules rather than planning the most efficient way to schedule production in my department."

The superintendent also spoke to the union chief steward about the problem. The steward said that the union felt that the company's incentive system provided an easy means for the foreman to reward his friends and punish those whom he didn't like (and who might be vigorous union supporters). The union wanted management to come up with a proposal to take this power away from their foremen.

The superintendent learned that the department itself was divided on this issue. Some of the men were afraid that the union would set up a system whereby the good work was distributed according to length of service, which would mean that the newer employees might take a real wage cut. At the same time they were not happy about the supervisor holding these assignments over their heads "as a club."

The personnel department cautioned that any management decision here might have far-reaching implications. The supervisor's right to make work assignments was a crucial element in management's ability to run the plant efficiently. The union would be in a good position to limit this vital prerogative if it got a foot in the door in a case like this one.

1. As the superintendent, how would you evaluate the case? Assuming that Waljack had some grounds for making his complaint, how would you deal with it in such a way as to avoid other problems?

2. Can the right to make work assignments be separated from other aspects of incentive-plan administration?

Problem IV

The union is demanding an extra 10-cent hourly wage increase for all hourly employees on jobs without incentive plans, because "their relative earnings have suffered as a result of the bonus earnings of the pieceworkers." The company is aware that there has been a great deal of grumbling about the fact that lesser-skilled production workers are beginning to get pay checks almost equal to those of skilled maintenance workers. However, management can also argue that these increased earnings are a result of increased effort on the part of the production workers. Furthermore, the maintenance workers have vigorously opposed suggestions that their jobs be time-studied for the purpose of establishing an incentive plan.

1. How important is this complaint, and what should the company do about it?

2. Why have the maintenance workers resisted switching to an incentive plan?

3. What are the potential effects of a special 10-cent increase for non-incentive workers?

4. One proposal is that the company strengthen its merit-rating program. This would permit supervisors to reward extra effort on the part of employees doing non-routine work. The extra earnings might approximate the extra income they would get if they were doing routinized work that had time standards. What do you think of this proposal?

Problem V

In a recent audit of incentive earnings in the company, the general manager of manufacturing was shocked to discover that employees in the smelter have never earned more than a 5 per cent bonus and frequently earn no bonus at all. In reviewing the situation with departmental management, he learned the following:

a. The employees claim that the rates are too "tight" and that it is impossible to get into the bonus bracket.

b. They also claim that the quality of the material is so variable that it really isn't worth the effort to try for a bonus. "On a day when you work hard something goes wrong in the process and your earnings are no higher than if you hadn't tried so hard."

c. For the past two years the department has averaged about six hours a week overtime (paid as nine hours of work). The additional earnings resulting from this overtime work approximate the extra compensation that would be available if normal bonuses were being earned in the department.

1. Given these "leads," what further information would you need to evaluate this situation? With whom would you talk and what would your objective be?

2. What alternative "solutions" could be developed, assuming that any one of the above factors (or all three) turned out to be factual and relevant?

3. How would you "apply" each of these solutions? How would you handle the union, departmental supervision, and industrial engineering in order to preserve incentives in this department?

4. Why should fact (c) be of any significance here?

5. How would your evaluation be affected if you learned subsequently that one small group of employees in the department with a reputation for unusual unity and cohesiveness consistently earned a 15 to 20 per cent bonus? These men have worked together for a number of years while most of the other parts of the department have been staffed by relative newcomers, many of whom do not seem very friendly with one another.

Problem VI

The Superior Floor Covering Company has an incentive program for its salesmen. Incentive earnings are based on the amount of sales in relation to an assigned quota. The quota is computed each year by management, taking into account the number and type of customers in each salesman's territory and the previous year's sales records for the company and for its competitors. In the administration of this incentive program, the following problems have arisen. Suggest the type of analysis you would undertake to provide data that might lead to a solution and the alternative plans you would consider in eliminating these difficulties. Note also the parallels between the problems here and those involving blue-collar, manufacturing incentive plans.

1. Some of the best salesmen now have too many accounts in the areas assigned to them. From the company's point of view it would be advantageous to reduce the size of the districts covered by each of these men and to add several new salesmen who could give more thorough coverage. However, the outstanding salesmen resent this proposal, claiming that it would penalize them for their success. Furthermore, they argue that while their sales records are high now, some of their good accounts may go to competitors and then they will be worse off than other salesmen who have not had their districts "trimmed."

2. The top-earning salesmen also complain that their base quotas increase each year, reflecting their previous success. This, too, they feel is discrimination for success.

3. Management believes that the company is not acquiring as many new accounts as it should. So-called "missionary work," trying to induce a store that has not previously purchased Superior products to become a customer, takes more time and energy than selling old customers. Also, the results of this missionary work may not show up for several years. The present incentive plan gives no credit for this type of work. Should extra allowances be given for new accounts? How will this affect the over-all sales effort of the company?

4. When business is booming within a salesman's territory, he may receive high bonus earnings even without great effort on his part. When there is a great deal of unemployment in his territory or when competition decides to lower prices to penetrate this new market, his bonus earnings may decline even though his sales efforts are at a maximum. How can these factors be taken into account so that the incentive plan will motivate and reward effort rather than reflect fortuitous circumstances?

In this chapter we shall discuss some of the approaches that have been devised to provide somewhat broader employee motivation than is furnished by individual incentive plans. These approaches serve a dual purpose: (1) to increase productivity and (2) to improve morale by giving employees a feeling of participation in and identification with their company.

As we discussed in the last chapter, individual incentive plans often do not provide adequate motivation. Even when they are successful in inducing employees to work harder, their value as an incentive is reduced by output restriction, conflicts over rate-setting, and intergroup conflict. Nor are high wages, fringe benefits, and good working conditions in themselves a complete answer to the problem of motivation. These inducements may be effective aids in recruiting and retaining good employees, but they provide little help in motivating them to work harder.

We will make a critical examination of five techniques that are being used by management to provide greater motivation: (1) group piecework, (2) profit-sharing, (3) suggestion systems,

28

Incentives for Group
Participation

(4) employee-management and union-management consultative commit-tees, and (5) the Scanlon Plan. Let us look at each in turn.

Group Piece-work

In group piece-work, each member of the group receives a bonus based on the output of the group as a whole. Notice that this plan differs from indi-vidual piece-work, in which each employee receives a bonus based on his individual output. The "group" may include the entire plant or company. More frequently it consists of a single department or the men who work on a single process or product. In these smaller groups, output standards are usually set by time study, just as they are in individual piece-work.

Group piece-work is particularly useful when the job assignments of mem-bers of the group are so interrelated that it is difficult to measure the contri-bution of any single employee to total production. For example, where eight girls work together on a small assembly line packaging pharmaceuticals, the speed of any one employee is governed by what the others are doing. Group piece-work makes it possible to reward workers who provide essential serv-ices to production workers, yet who under individual piece-work are usually paid only the regular day rates. Since all the members of the group share in the same bonus, conflict is reduced between workers on "tight" rates and workers on "loose" rates. Moreover, in theory at least, since everyone's earn-ings are dependent on everyone's efforts, the group may put pressure on the laggard individual to work harder.

Group piece-work encourages cooperation among employees, whereas in-dividual piece-work militates against cooperation. Rather than struggling with one another over choice work locations, materials, and job assignments—the sources of much friction under individual piece-work—the employees work out their own allocation problems, knowing that everyone will share in the final result. For example, waitresses who pool tips are often eager to help each other out of jams.

On the other hand, group piece-work shares many of the disadvantages of individual-incentive plans. The workers still fear that if they produce too much management will cut the rates. Many of the intergroup differences that we discussed in the previous chapter remain. Also, since each individual may feel that his own efforts have very little effect on the over-all output of the group, he may experience less motivation to work harder than he would under individual piece-work.

Group piece-work systems that include the entire company or plant are less common than those that include only a single department. These broader systems are usually based not on time study but on some general measure of production, such as pounds produced or value of goods produced. For example, it was proposed in one union-management negotiation session in the automobile industry that the company put aside $10 for every car produced and that the whole fund be divided among all the employees. Company-wide systems often call for less than 100 per cent gain-sharing—that is, a 10 per cent increase in production results in a less than 10 per cent increase in earnings.

Company-wide plans naturally eliminate the intergroup incentive problems and fights over time study that we discussed in the previous chapter. Most important, they make employees less fearful of the introduction of new equipment, since all gains in productivity are usually shared by all employees (in contrast to individual piece-work, where the gains can be taken away through a new time study).

In smaller plants, company-wide piece-work systems may provide some incentive for the average employee to work harder. However, in larger plants where hundreds or even thousands of employees share in the bonus, the employee may feel there is little relationship between his own effort and the ultimate reward, and consequently may feel little motivation to increase production. Moreover, the union may oppose the scheme unless the amount of the bonus and the method of computing it are determined through collective bargaining.

Profit-sharing

In profit-sharing plans, the employees receive a bonus that is normally based on some percentage (often 10 per cent to 30 per cent) of the company's profits beyond some fixed minimum.[1] For example, employees might receive 25 per cent of all profits in excess of 6 per cent on the company's net worth. In some corporations (for instance, Eastman Kodak) the amount of bonus is dependent on the size of the dividend paid to stockholders.

In some profit-sharing plans the bonus is paid directly to the employees, usually at the end of each year. In other plans the bonus is deposited in a welfare or pension fund. These are often called *deferred* plans, because payment of the benefits is "deferred" until the employee retires or makes use of the welfare fund. With such deferred plans, the company hopes to obtain the advantages of both profit-sharing and fringe-benefit programs.

Profit-sharing has had a long history, but for various reasons it has not been very widely adopted in this country. One of the best-known plans is that of the Lincoln Electric Company, which in some years pays a bonus that doubles employees' pay. Sears Roebuck, Procter and Gamble, and Eastman Kodak also have profit-sharing plans of one type or another. Profit-sharing

---

[1] For a general discussion of profit-sharing plans, see Bryce M. Stewart and Walter J. Couper, *Profit Sharing and Stock Ownership for Wage Earners and Executives,* Industrial Relations Monograph 10 (New York: Industrial Relations Counselors, Inc., 1945).

plans, however, are more common in smaller companies, particularly those in which the workers are not unionized.

The advocates of profit-sharing claim many advantages for it as a means of strengthening the sense of involvement that employees feel toward the company: it makes them feel like partners in the enterprise, it motivates them to work harder, cut waste, push sales, and so forth. And, under the deferred plans, profit-sharing makes it possible for the company to provide pensions and fringe benefits without increasing fixed costs, for the company makes contributions only in profitable years.[2]

Yet profit-sharing has severe limitations, which may explain its failure to be more widely adopted. For one thing, it provides even less relationship between individual effort and ultimate reward than do group piece-work plans. After all, the employee knows that profits depend on a great many factors other than his individual performance: for example, the state of the market, sales efficiency, technological development, and so forth. Moreover, the fact that the bonus is paid only once a year means that there is a long delay between effort and reward, and this delay tends to impair the worker's feeling that he is working toward a goal. To complicate matters even further, many workers find it hard to understand how profits are computed, and, particularly where labor-management relations are bad, they may suspect that a good deal of sleight of hand is involved in the calculations.[3]

What actually happens is that employees tend to regard profit-sharing as just another fringe benefit ("added gravy"). Naturally they are happy to get a bonus once a year, but they recognize little concrete relationship between how hard they work and how much they get. Further, once they begin to count on their profit-sharing bonus to maintain their standard of living, they may become extremely resentful in years when no bonus is paid. Under deferred profit-sharing plans, pensions and welfare benefits are put on a rather insecure basis, for they depend not on how long an employee has been with the company but on whether the company has made a profit during that time. Still, in companies that can afford no other form of pension plan, even this is probably better than nothing.

Although profit-sharing has been extremely successful in some companies, many have tried it for a few years and then abandoned it. Its success seems to depend to a large extent on the company's over-all personnel policy and on the state of union-management relations. Although, particularly in smaller companies, it may provide motivation for employees to work harder, its chief

---

[2] Many companies provide a form of profit-sharing for their top management through the device of stock options. Provided the price of the company stock goes up, these options can be exercised in such a way as to provide what are technically capital gains and thus subject to a much lower income tax.

[3] The president of one company with a profit-sharing plan once told us, "I don't think my profit figures are any of my employees' business. I give them a bonus each year which is fair. They trust me." But do they? And do they really feel that they are *involved* in a profit-sharing plan?

merit would seem to be in raising morale, in keeping the union out (if this is indeed a merit), and perhaps in reducing pressure for wage increases.

Suggestion Systems

Suggestion systems are quite common in American industry. Their purpose is twofold:

1. To give management the benefit of employee suggestions on how to improve company efficiency. The average worker may have countless ideas on how to cut waste, eliminate unnecessary motions, prevent safety hazards, and so forth. Unless there is some systematic way of bringing these ideas to management's attention, a reservoir of ingenuity and experience may be overlooked.

2. To raise employee morale through giving them a chance to express their ideas on how the job should be done, to display their creative talents, and to take pride in seeing their ideas accepted—in other words, to reduce the employee's feeling that "as far the company is concerned I'm just a machine. Nobody wants my ideas."

In the typical suggestion system the worker writes his idea out on a special form and drops the form into a special box. All suggestions go directly to the suggestion director or to a suggestion committee. The practicability of each suggestion is then explored and evaluated, usually in consultation with the supervisors who might be affected. If the suggestion is accepted, the employee receives a reward, often 10 to 25 per cent of the savings produced by the suggestion during the first year. For suggestions whose savings cannot be measured, token awards are paid of from $3 to $25. If the suggestion is rejected, most companies insist that the employee be given a detailed explanation of why it was turned down, along with encouragement to make more suggestions in the future. It is customary to promote suggestion plans by means of active publicity programs, posters, articles in plant newspapers, award presentations, and so forth.

A reasonably successful plan may elicit 25 to 50 suggestions from every hundred employees each year, 25 to 35 per cent of which will be acceptable. Frequently, however, results are a good bit less impressive than that. One explanation for poor employee response to a given suggestion plan may be that it is ineptly administered, with inadequate publicity or explanation of how the program is run. Moreover, delay in evaluating suggestions may give employees the impression that their ideas are not being given serious consideration. If the suggestion needs considerable time to be evaluated, progress reports should be isssued to the employee to let him know that his idea has not been forgotten.

Since a majority of suggestions are normally rejected, the way in which suggestions are turned down is of crucial significance to the success of the plan. One authority recommends that "the turndown letter should be delivered to the employee in person by the investigator and/or the employee's immediate supervisor, so that the matter can be discussed and further questions answered." [4]

Even with good administration, suggestion plans often have only limited success. Employees may feel that the rewards are too meager, particularly when they amount to only 10 per cent of the first year's savings. This means that management keeps the remaining 90 per cent the first year and 100 per cent of the savings in future years. Of course, even when awards are small on a percentage basis, it is not unusual for an employee to earn several thousand dollars for an unusually good suggestion.

Employees may fear that their suggestions will backfire—that in effect they may be suggesting themselves out of a job. The man who makes a labor-saving suggestion is not likely to be very popular with his fellow employees, even though no one loses his job right away. The reward for the suggestion goes to the individual, but the suggestion may affect the entire group—sometimes with unpleasant results. Understandably, a group attitude may develop that discourages employees from making suggestions.

The very fact that suggestions are submitted and rewarded on an individual basis may generate serious resentment within the group. On the worker level especially, many of the best ideas grow out of long-term group discussions. If one man turns in an idea as his own suggestion, the rest may accuse him of larceny. In a sense, the suggestion system discourages teamwork in working out ideas and encourages individual workers to keep their ideas to themselves.

In addition, all suggestions must be submitted in writing, even though the average worker can do a much better job explaining himself orally, particularly if he can demonstrate his idea and answer questions directly.

In most instances the suggestion system by-passes the foreman. Yet many suggestions point up areas where the foreman has fallen down on the job or suggest ideas that the foreman should have thought of by himself. Understandably, employees fear that the foreman may retaliate if his failures are exposed, and as a consequence hesitate to make suggestions at all. Some companies try to get around this problem by giving the foreman credit for all suggestions made in his department, by having his employees submit their suggestions directly to him instead of to the suggestion committee, and by involving the foreman in evaluating suggestions and handing out rewards.

Suggestion systems sometimes arouse union opposition because, as a form of upward communication, they usurp what the union regards as one of its

---

[4] Herman W. Seinwerth, "Suggestion Plans—Their Value to the Personnel Relations Program," Paul Pigors and Charles A. Myers, eds., *Readings in Personnel Administration* (New York: McGraw-Hill, 1952), p. 460.

rightful functions. Consequently, many companies permit union representatives to sit in on the suggestion committee, in an effort to win union cooperation in implementing the plan and to alleviate workers' fears that their ideas are not being fairly evaluated.

In general, the success of the suggestion system depends largely on the quality of the over-all personnel and labor-relations atmosphere. If the union suspects management's every move, and if supervisors discourage subordinates from doing things on their own—then employees will keep new ideas to themselves.

To sum up: a well-run suggestion system may yield a never-ending stream of ideas which cut costs and increase the employees' feeling of accomplishment and participation. Yet many plans are poorly administered. Even when well administered, they often by-pass both foreman and union, and place primary emphasis on the individual, though most problems involve the entire group.

Consultative Committees

In an attempt to avoid the suggestion system's exclusive emphasis on individual workers, many companies have tried to elicit broader group participation by setting up consultative committees. The purpose of these committees is to improve two-way communication with lower levels of the organization. They give lower-ranking supervisors or employees a chance to express their points of view directly to top management, thus by-passing intermediate levels.[5] For example, the first-line supervisors may elect representatives to meet weekly or monthly with the general manager to present and discuss current problems, ask about the rumors, pose questions, and ventilate gripes.

Management may institute similar committees for consultations with hourly-paid employees or their union. Joint worker-management or union-management consultative committees are active in many areas such as solving production problems, cutting waste, reducing accidents, planning recreational programs, and soliciting for the Community Chest.[6]

Union-management committees normally work in three areas:

1. *Collective bargaining*. Consultative committees have proved extremely useful in facilitating collective bargaining on such matters as job evaluation,

---

[5] For a description of how one company makes use of consultative committees that blanket the entire organization, see Elliott Jaques, *The Changing Culture of the Plant* (New York: Dryden, 1952).

[6] Numerous consultative committees were established during World War II under the prompting of the War Production Board. See Dorothea de Schweinitz, *Labor and Management in Common Experience* (Cambridge, Mass.: Harvard University Press, 1949). For the postwar experience, see Ernest Dale, *Greater Productivity through Labor-Management Cooperation,* Research Report No. 14, New York: American Management Association, 1949.

incentive rates, and job transfers. These committees permit the orderly, systematic consideration of problems that would otherwise be handled piecemeal through the grievance procedure.

2. *Fringe benefits.* Often joint committees assist in athletic programs, handling welfare funds (derived from the profit from coffee machines), and so forth. These are areas in which the company has no special interest so long as workers are satisfied, and is glad to let the union share responsibility.

3. *Production problems.* In some industries consultative committees have been established to explore persistent production problems, such as scrap, productivity, and safety. Committees of this sort are common only in companies that enjoy good labor-management relations, however, since production decisions are traditionally conceded to be management prerogatives.

In unionized companies, consultative committees give the union leadership an opportunity to make a positive contribution toward running the company rather than merely sitting on the sidelines and filing grievances. Often they provide management with a valuable source of information on worker and union problems, and provide union officials with a better understanding of management's problems. Thus, they have a potential ability to improve the general tenor of labor-management relations.

Sometimes non-unionized companies set up consultative committees composed of representatives who are elected directly by the workers or appointed by the foremen. Here caution must be exercised to insure that these committees do not violate the provisions of the National Labor Relations Act, which prohibits employers from assisting in the formation of employee organizations that may have union-like functions.

When consultative committees, either union-management or worker-management, work effectively, they improve the quality of both upward and downward communication within the company. They give the workers a chance to by-pass middle management and bring their suggestions, problems, and gripes directly to the men who actually make the decisions. Management may use these committees as a sounding board by releasing information on sales trends, safety problems, and so forth, in the hope that it will be passed along to workers at lower levels.

In short, consultative committees provide many of the same advantages that are derived from face-to-face conferences between subordinates and their immediate supervisor (see Chapter 8)—such advantages as lowered resistance to change, greater feeling of autonomy, better understanding of why orders are issued, and more effective implementation of instructions.

Nevertheless, joint committees labor under several disadvantages which sometimes limit their effectiveness:

1. Committee members may not communicate effectively with the workers back in the shop. Indeed, as they learn more and more about management's point of view, they may become more and more removed from the other workers. They may become extremely aware of production or safety problems, but they may fail to pass their enthusiasm on to the rest of the shop. Production committees, for example, are rarely successful unless the committee members energetically canvass their constituents for ideas.

2. Consultative committees run the risk of impairing the morale and status of the middle managers whom they by-pass.

3. The success of these committees depends pretty much on the over-all quality of labor-management relations. If committee meetings are looked upon primarily as battlefields in a continuous war between union and management, then little will be accomplished.

4. Finally, consultation in itself does not provide a specific incentive for individual employees to participate. True, employees do gain personal satisfaction from influencing company policy and seeing their ideas adopted, but in our society we require a more specific goal toward which we can work, most often in the form of an economic reward. Thus the consultative committees that have proved most fruitful have been those with some highly specific incentive for cooperation: to win the war, to save the company from going out of business,[7] to earn more pay, or to remove accident hazards.

The following case illustrates some of the factors that contribute to the success or failure of a consultation plan.[8]

> During World War II employees of the Toronto plant of Lever Brothers were working 48 hours a week. The union proposed that if management would cut the work-week to 40 hours with no loss of earnings, they would work harder, accept manpower cuts, and point out enough inefficiency so that as much would be produced in 40 hours as had previously been produced in 48. With misgivings, management agreed to accept the union proposal on a trial basis.
>
> A joint committee was established consisting of the plant manager, his assistant, and three top union officers. This committee met regularly to consider methods of cutting costs in each department in turn. But before each meeting the superintendent asked the departmental foreman for his suggestions while the steward canvassed the union members for their ideas. No suggestion was put into effect until everyone was consulted.
>
> Eventually sufficient savings were realized and the hours were reduced. The union then asked management if their members could earn the right to sickness and accident pay through the same methods. Management refused to extend the procedure. The joint committee died and some time later the union officers were defeated.

---

[7] One of the earliest plans involved the attempts of the Amalgamated Clothing Workers to help financially embarrassed clothing firms to stay in business. See Sumner H. Slichter, *Union Policies and Industrial Management* (Washington, D.C.: The Brookings Institution, 1941).

[8] Adapted from William F. Whyte and others, *Money and Motivation* (New York: Harpers, 1955), Chapter 13. The case was originally written up by William R. Dymond

Why did this plan succeed at first and then fail later on? Labor relations had been generally good prior to the plan's introduction. Individual workers, and lower and middle management, were all given a chance to make suggestions. There was a definite goal to work toward. However, once the goal was reached the system fell apart.

But why were the officers defeated? While the parties were working together to cut costs and to make it possible to reduce hours, there was a tremendous increase in communications among all levels. Then management's refusal to set a new goal eliminated the primary incentive for the workers or union officers to present new suggestions. Upward communication declined. However, the officers were accustomed to a high level of activity and now undertook to initiate a whole series of new projects for the members, such as a new seniority system and a change in union affiliation. The members previously had accepted pressure because they themselves could initiate suggestions and they hoped for shorter hours in return. Now that the pressure was only one way, downward, the members rebelled and rejected their officers.

The moral of this story is that if consultative committees are to be successful in solving production problems there must be participation throughout all levels of the organization as well as a definite incentive or goal to unite everyone's efforts. On the other hand, such complete participation is not required if the committee's efforts are restricted to handling collective-bargaining problems or fringe areas. Probably this explains why consultative committees have been most useful in solving specific, limited problems. They do not, in themselves, provide motivation for higher production or a general sense of participation.

The Scanlon Plan   (the whole group is involved)

The Scanlon Plan is one of the most promising approaches yet suggested to securing widespread employee participation and obtaining industrial peace and higher productivity as well.[9] Although the plan is still not widely accepted, we shall discuss it in some detail because it seems to avoid many of the problems raised by other plans. The plan consists of two basic parts: (1) a wage formula or incentive, and (2) a new form of suggestion system.

[9] The late Joseph Scanlon, author of this plan, rose from an ordinary worker in a steel plant to be a top officer of the United Steelworkers of America and later a Lecturer at the Massachusetts Institute of Technology. For fuller discussion of the plan see Russell W. Davenport, "Enterprise for Everyone," *Fortune,* Vol. 41, No. 1 (January, 1950), pp. 55-59; William F. Whyte and others, "The Scanlon Plan," *Money and Motivation* (New York: Harpers, 1955), Chapter 14; Frederick G. Lesieur, ed., *The Scanlon Plan: A Frontier in Labor-Management Cooperation* (New York and Cambridge: Wiley and The Technology Press, 1958); George Strauss and Leonard R. Sayles, "The Scanlon Plan: Some Organizational Problems," *Human Organization,* Vol. 16, No. 3 (Fall 1957), pp. 15-22.

The *wage formula* is designed to distribute the gains of increased productivity proportionally among all employees involved. Although each formula is tailor-made to the needs of the particular company, typically wages are tied to the sales value of goods produced, so that, for example, for every 1 per cent increase in productivity there is a 1 per cent increase in wages and salaries. In contrast to usual incentive plans, bonuses are paid to the clerical force, salesmen, supervisors, and sometimes even to top management.

Notice that this is really a form of group piece-work covering the entire plant. As we have seen, a bonus of this sort is valuable not only as an incentive to productivity, but also as a form of feedback or yardstick by which the plan's success can be measured by the participants themselves.

The mechanics of the *suggestion system* are simple: In each department a union *production committeeman* is elected or appointed by union officers. The production committeeman and the foreman constitute a departmental *production committee*, which meets periodically to discuss suggestions from individual employees and to formulate general plans for the improvement of productivity. Rejected suggestions or suggestions that affect the plant as a whole are referred to a plant-wide *screening committee*, which includes top management as well as the union leadership.

This suggestion system may be likened to an enlarged version of the typical union-management grievance procedure. The written suggestion is in many ways similar to the written grievance, the production committeeman corresponds roughly to the steward, and the meetings of the screening committee are somewhat equivalent to third-stage negotiations between management and the union grievance committee. However, the suggestions relate to every phase of production, not just to complaints about contract violation—and the purpose is to improve company efficiency, not just to protect individual rights.

Note how the Scanlon Plan differs from the typical suggestion system: Instead of individual rewards for accepted suggestions, the group gains as a whole through a higher bonus whenever productivity is increased. The union takes an active part instead of worrying whether suggestions will result in a speedup. Individuals cooperate with each other in developing suggestions instead of keeping their ideas to themselves. Further, under a suggestion system management normally waits passively for workers to submit suggestions; frequently under the Scanlon Plan management itself suggests problems for mutual discussion.

Before the Scanlon Plan was put into operation in a particular printing plant, management had tried to introduce a conveyor system. The plans had been developed exclusively by the engineers, without consulting the employees. The system immediately ran into trouble and the employees showed little interest in making it work.

After the Scanlon Plan was accepted management decided to try another conveyor system, but to introduce it in a different manner. Employees were shown a small scale model of the proposed layout and encouraged to make criticisms and suggestions for improvements. On the basis of these comments the joint production committee made modifications to eliminate "bugs" that the engineers had not foreseen. The new system was enthusiastically accepted by the employees.[10]

Both the quantity and quality of suggestions seem to be higher under the Scanlon Plan. An annual rate of one suggestion for every three workers is considered quite satisfactory under the usual suggestion system.[11] Under the Scanlon Plan the rate may be more than doubled.[12] More important, with the usual system, normally only one suggestion out of four can be used.[13] With the Scanlon Plan the acceptance rate has risen to 80 per cent.[14]

As a means of increasing productivity, the Scanlon Plan has met with varied success. Gains of over 40 per cent are not uncommon, however. For example, take the experience of the LaPointe Machine Tool Company over a period of 58 months. Here the monthly bonus ranged from 0 to 52.1 per cent, with no bonus at all during 16 months and bonuses in excess of 20 per cent during another 20 months.[15]

In summary, there are gains for everybody under a successful Scanlon Plan: (1) more and better suggestions, (2) higher productivity and profits, (3) decreased resistance to change, (4) better union-management relations, (5) greater cooperation among work groups and between individuals and their supervisors, and (6) increased motivation to work. Because of these advantages, use of the plan has spread rapidly in recent years.

And yet the Scanlon Plan, promising though it seems, is not a cure-all for all industrial ills.[16]

1. If the plan is to be successful, management must be willing to make substantial changes in its attitudes. Traditional company prerogatives must be forgotten. Foremen, superintendents, and even the company president must learn to consult with subordinates and be willing to listen to sharp criticism. Many managers find this adjustment too hard to make, and the

---

[10] Adopted from George Shultz, "Worker Participation in Production Problems," *Personnel*, Vol. 28, No. 3 (November 1951), pp. 201-211.

[11] Paul Pigors and Charles A. Myers, *Personnel Administration*, 3rd ed. (New York: McGraw-Hill, 1956), p. 370.

[12] George Shultz and Robert P. Crisera, "The LaPointe Machine Tool Company and the United Steelworkers of America," *Causes of Industrial Peace Under Collective Bargaining, Case Study No. 10* (Washington, D.C.: National Planning Association, 1952), pp. 58-59.

[13] Herman W. Seinwerth, "Suggestion Plans—Their Value to the Personnel Relations Program," in *Getting and Using Employees' Ideas*, Production Series, No. 165 (New York: American Management Association, 1946).

[14] Shultz and Crisera, *op. cit.*, p. 58.

[15] *Ibid.*, p. 55.

[16] The section that follows is adapted from Strauss and Sayles, *The Scanlon Plan: Some Organizational Problems*.

thin-skinned individual or the confirmed autocrat must either be restrained or else removed from positions of authority.

In companies that already practice general supervision and enjoy a good system of upward and downward communication, the transition of the Scanlon Plan may be relatively easy. Others may find that the plan requires adjustments that they are unwilling to make.

2. The Scanlon Plan presents the union with a real dilemma. In fact, the plan is bound to fail unless the union officers give up the militant view that the "member is always right." But there is also a danger that the officers may become too concerned with jacking up production. If they refuse to handle individual grievances and concentrate too much on pushing their members to work harder, the members may become resentful, give the plan only passive support, and even reject their officers at the next election. Indeed, as the officers become more and more closely identified with management's point of view, they tend to become alienated from the average member. This dilemma may be resolved if the officers are careful to explain new developments to the rank-and-file and to listen carefully to their reactions.

3. As we have seen, one of the disadvantages of traditional incentive plans is that they engender ill-feeling among groups—both where technology makes one group's earnings dependent on the production of another group, or where groups suspect each other of having "loose" rates. The Scanlon Plan presumably eliminates this problem by establishing plant-wide incentives. But a plant-wide incentive means that each individual's earnings are dependent on the effort of the entire plant. Harder work by any one individual will bring him only negligibly higher monetary return. Hopefully, self-satisfaction, the desire for praise from fellow workers, and interest in the group as a whole will be sufficient to elicit high productivity. But for this to happen there must be a high degree of cohesion and employee identification with the plant as a whole.

How likely is this to occur? The answer depends on a number of factors, including the size, homogeneity, and history of the work group. One thing is certain: There are bound to be some rivalries among groups, and constant skill in human relations is required by all parties to prevent these rivalries from reaching serious proportions. All the evidence is that loyalty to the face-to-face group is greater than to the plant as a whole. It is too much to expect the traditional differences between the office and the shop and among various departments to cease the moment the plan is introduced.

In fact, the plan may actually generate greater interdepartmental antagonism. No longer is it possible to unite against a common enemy—management. Now it is easy to pass the blame for poor production along to another group—for Department X to say, "Why should we work so hard when Department Y has fallen so far behind?" The larger the plant, the greater are the possibilities for dissension, and the more difficult it becomes to maintain support for plant-wide production goals.

4. The Scanlon Plan has been successful both in very depressed companies, where the employees have cooperated to save their jobs, and in prosperous companies, where the employees realized that there were big bonuses to be won. The plan may well be less successful in industries where the market conditions make it difficult to sell increased output and where greater productivity may in fact mean fewer jobs (in economic terms, where demand is inelastic). Nor do we know what happens when a successful plan goes through a long period of poor earnings (some have weathered short periods).

In short, the Scanlon Plan seems to be most successful where both union and management are able to make substantial changes in their patterns of behavior, where good internal communications exist within and between both groups, and probably only in smaller organizations.

Conclusion

We have looked at five different plans designed to raise employee morale, develop teamwork, and promote a sense of identification with the entire organization. All these plans imply a more sophisticated approach to motivation than do the philosophies of authoritarianism, paternalism, bargaining, or competition (see Chapter 5). All seek to provide on-the-job satisfaction for doing a better job.

And notice, too, that all seek to reach these goals through changing human relationships. Group piece-work and profit-sharing aim for greater cooperation among individuals. Suggestion systems and consultative committees seek to improve communications between individual employees and higher management. The Scanlon Plan seeks to attain both objectives.

Each of these plans has been adopted by management as a panacea for a whole range of industrial-relations ills. Yet none of them will work well except in an atmosphere of good labor-management relations and sound supervisory, organizational, and personnel practices. In our opinion, the *basic relationships* among the members of the organization must be sound before any one of these plans can be put to effective use.

Problem I

It all started when Harry Beard phoned and asked me to "come out to the plant and give us a little advice on our suggestion system." I readily agreed, though I told him I was dubious about what I could do in a single visit. However, before hanging up I asked him how he was involved and what was the problem. He said, "My job is chiefly trouble-shooting and right now I'm up to my ears on a new product line we're installing—almost completely automatic. But the Plant Manager wants me to do something about suggestions. We have a plan but it isn't working.

We get a fair number of piddling ideas on safety and housekeeping—but almost nothing which saves us any money. We have a new plant here and there must be lots of ideas around—lots of things need improvement and the workers must see them—but we have the worst record in the company—and you know how the Head Office watches these things."

I arrived at the plant at noon. Harry had invited me for lunch and I had visions of the nearby Country Club. Instead we went to the plant cafeteria with the Plant Manager, the Industrial Engineer, and the Personnel Man. Table talk was dull and the food worse. I decided to let them broach the subject at hand. I did notice that everyone deferred to the Manager's ideas—even on sports. Then to the conference room—attractive but noisy. Plant Manager opened up, "Harry brought you here because he said you had some ideas on suggestion systems."

"He wants his answer wrapped up 1-2-3 in cellophane," I thought, and countered, "Well, first I'd like to get a little idea of your problem."

The Plant Manager did most of the talking, though the others broke in at times to underscore his words. There was plenty of opportunity for suggestions, he felt, but no good ones were forthcoming. With a plant of 2,000 employees, last year they had 750 suggestions, but of these only 300 were acceptable—and of these on 230 the savings were unmeasurable, so only the minimum $3 reward was given. Total awards last year came to $1,510. The largest: $55.

I asked what determined the size of the award. "We pay 10 per cent of the first year's savings." He must have seen my inward shudder, for he asked, "Is that low?"

"Not very," I added tactfully. "Awards seem to vary from 10 to 25 per cent. Have you thought of raising it?"

"We can't. It's set by corporation policy. For a while we paid $5 as the minimum reward, but then we heard the company policy was $3. Of course it made us seem rather cheap to cut it down."

My questioning then turned to the mechanics of the program. "Suggestions are made on this form," he said as he handed it to me. "You see, the suggestor's name goes on a special tab which the Suggestion Director tears off, so that no one but he knows who made the suggestion. That way we eliminate favoritism."

"Are you the Suggestion Director?" I asked the industrial engineer.

"Oh, no," said the Plant Manager. "We have a full-time man. I've never met him, but I gather he does a pretty good job. Possibly you might like to meet him—you might give him a few pointers." I nodded. He continued, "To get back to our system. The Suggestion Director refers each suggestion to the man in whose area of responsibility it lies—to the foreman, the maintenance department, and so forth. They investigate the suggestion. If they think it is good, they pass their recommendation back to the Suggestion Director, along with their estimate of likely savings. The suggestion committee takes up the accepted suggestions and decides how much the award should be."

"Has the union shown any interest?" I asked—hopeful that this question might lead to pay dirt.

"Oh, yes, the union president sits in on every meeting," he said.

Just then the Personnel Director interrupted: "I never got a chance to tell you that at the last meeting the International Representative showed up. The union wanted to have three men sit in on meetings in the future. I told the Representative that he could attend this meeting, but in the future we'd let only one man in. After all, it's purely a company committee."

"That's right," said the Manager. "We can't let the union run away with this."

"Do you have any idea how the union feels about this?" I asked. I knew the answer, but hoped to stimulate them to do a little thinking.

There was a slight pause, then the Industrial Engineer answered, "They take the position that these suggestions shouldn't force anybody out of a job. I think they're scared that just that will happen. Frankly, I think maybe the union is sabotaging it."

"Do you think there is any justification for their fears?" I asked, trying not to sound argumentative.

"I suppose there is," he replied. "Seventy per cent of our costs are in labor. You can't save anything in material. We're in a highly competitive industry and we're going to have to save on labor costs."

There was a pause. I said nothing, hoping for further discussion. There being none, I asked, perhaps a little gruffly, "Well, where do you think the weak points of the program are?"

They paused. Then the Plant Manager spoke up, "I've been wondering whether our form (on which the suggestions are made) is adequate. I wish you would look it over."

This set me back. I tried another tack. "How do the foremen feel about it? Is there any chance they think these suggestions threaten them—point out things they should have noticed themselves?"

"Not that I've heard," said the Industrial Engineer. "After all, good suggestions would improve the efficiency of their department—and they will do better on their EIP."

"What's that?" I asked.

"EIP—that's our Efficiency Improvement Plan. Every member of management is rated monthly on a number of factors such as cost control, production, scrap, and so forth."

"Are foremen rewarded under EIP for the number of suggestions made in their department?" I asked. The Industrial Engineer shook his head.

There was some more discussion, along the same vein. Finally, the Plant Manager said, "Well, I have another meeting. Harry will take you around the plant, answer any questions, and I will be anxious to hear your recommendations."

After he left, Harry gave me the "Grand Tour." It was a beautiful plant—most of the operations involved assembling—almost all routine—a great deal of finger work.

Finally Harry pointed: "There's the Suggestion Director's office." He was in a glass cubicle, right off the main assembly line, with two other men, both industrial engineers.

Bill Dongle obviously had been waiting for us. He seemed a little nervous as he shook my hand. Harry was fairly tactful: "Bill, as you know, we've been talking a bit about suggestions among other things and we were sure he (the consultant) wanted to get the real picture from you."

"That's right, I do. I gather your program sounds pretty much like the normal— that is, you're having the normal number of headaches."

Bill looked a little relieved. I felt sorry for him as he started telling his problems. Among others they were:

"I don't get much cooperation from the foremen. They don't seem to talk it up among their men. When I do refer suggestions to them, they always seem to be negative. Lots of times they turn down ideas which I think are pretty good—in fact, sometimes they put them in later on—and do I catch hell from the men. Also they take so long to make a report. Sometimes it is six months till a man gets an acknowledgment that we have accepted his ideas—he may even see it being put into effect, but the procedure is, we don't tell a man his suggestion is accepted until the award committee figures out how much it is worth. Sometimes, of course, if the suggestion is not written up too well, I call the man in to talk about it—and that lets him know we're thinking about it. You know—maybe I should talk to every man who has a suggestion—that lets him know we're interested. It would be better than our usual short note saying that we have accepted it or rejected it."

"Harry, what do you think?" I asked.

Harry said, "It might be a good idea, but I don't know about taking all the men off their jobs."

"Maybe I could see them on the job," Bill volunteered. It was agreed he might do this—though Harry wondered whether Bill's presence might make the other workers think that the man who made the suggestion was a "company man."

I then asked, "I gather you feel that foremen turn down some good ideas. I wonder if anything can be done about this?"

(We discussed this for a while, but you can figure out for yourself what Harry and Bill decided.)

Near the end of the discussion Bill said, "What we've got to do is get the foremen to show more interest."

I asked, "To what extent does supervision indicate to the foremen that they are backing the suggestion plans?"

"Well," said Harry, "it's mentioned all the time in the company magazine and the plant newspaper."

To myself I asked, "Who writes these newspapers? Staff."

To them I asked, "Do you know of any situation where a foreman has been praised by his superior for getting good suggestions or questioned when he got none?"

Both shook their heads, but perhaps the import of my question slipped by them.

Later Bill returned to the original theme. "All the suggestions we get are trifles. Perhaps if we could get a few good ideas and give some really big awards, it would get the ball rolling. You know we have scrap and safety contests between departments. The record of all the departments are posted monthly as well as their improvement over previous months. Perhaps we could do this with suggestions."

We discussed this for a while. Then I had a bright idea. I asked to go over some typical suggestions. We took two from the file that seemed more complicated than most.

The first involved a change in the carrier that held the product as it passed through the assembly line. I noticed the company had spent $800 to make the change, but the suggestion was classed as "housekeeping—no measurable savings," and got the minimum $3.

"Why put it in," I asked, "if there are no savings?"

"Well," Bill said, "before we made the change there was always the chance that a piece might fall off. This would cause a great deal of damage—but you just can't estimate the chance of its falling off or how great would be the damage."

Another accepted suggestion involved a minor change in an operation. Harry said, "It did make the job easier to do and a little faster. But since the union wouldn't let us retime the job, there were no savings. So we paid just $3."

The phone rang and I had a short pause to collect my thoughts. I had a lot of questions to answer—and quick:

Why were so few suggestions made?

I hadn't talked to any workers, but what did they *probably* feel about the whole scheme?

How did the union officers feel?

How did the foremen feel?

Assuming I were plant manager (nice to daydream), what would I do to solve the problem?

Ah, I'm just a consultant and there are definite limits to the ideas they are willing to accept—no point in suggesting things they won't carry out. But what has my brief experience with this company taught me about the way they handle problems? How good is the union-management relationship, for instance? Why was the Suggestion Director so tense?

Are there any suggestions I could make that would be *likely to be accepted* and that would also change the attitude of the workers, of the union, of the foremen?

The Plant Manager wanted ideas on how to improve the application blank. What does this indicate?

Above all, what next? How should I go about putting my ideas across? Should I make a written report? Should I give my ideas to the Suggestion Director, to Harry, or to the Plant Manager? Or do I need to do further research? If so, what questions should I seek to answer?

More fundamentally, I wondered whether the whole situation might have some implications for staff-line relations.

How's my interview technique? What am I trying to accomplish? Should I have followed some of these points more deeply?

(Answer to problem on p. 637: 1.56 minutes.)

Accident prevention is an area in which American industry has just cause for pride. Since 1926 our industrial injury frequency rate has dropped from 24.2 to 10.9, a truly remarkable victory that deserves to be ranked with the development of Salk vaccine and the "miracle drugs." [1] And yet there is still much to do. In a single year as many as two million people may be the victims of disabling work injuries, and the total monetary cost of these injuries has been estimated as high as four or five billion dollars.

Workmen's Compensation

Widespread interest in safety dates back roughly to 1910, with the passage of workmen's

[1] United States Bureau of Labor Statistics *Handbook of Labor Statistics,* Bulletin 1016 (1950), p. 179; *Monthly Labor Review,* Vol. 83, No. 1 (January 1960), p. 843. The term "injury frequency rate" refers to the number of lost-time accidents per million man-hours worked. Thus, if a company with a thousand workers on a forty-hour week had one lost-time accident per week, it would have a frequency rate of 25. Notice that minor accidents which do not involve loss of time are not included in computing this ratio.

29

Safety

compensation laws in many states. Prior to that time the tendency in industry was to look upon manpower as expendable and to weep a minimum of tears when an employee was injured or killed. (There were pioneering companies strongly motivated by humanitarian impulses, but these unfortunately were in the minority.) This attitude was the target of social reformers who contended that management should be assessed at least part of the cost of the medical expenses and lost wages incurred by those who were injured in its service. Only then, argued the reformers, would industry take steps to reduce the appalling number of cripples, widows, and orphans being created each year.

Prior to the passage of workmen's compensation laws, a man injured at work could sue his company for damages, but this was not an easy task. In the first place he had to hire a lawyer and sue through the courts, an expensive and time-consuming process. Even then, the company could avoid incurring liability in a number of ways: through the *fellow servant doctrine,* if it could prove that another worker was responsible; through the *contributory negligence doctrine,* if it could prove that the worker himself was at least partly to blame; and through the *assumed risk doctrine,* if it could show that the work was inherently dangerous and the worker knew this when he took the job.

Now, instead of going to the courts, all a worker need do is file a claim with the compensation board. Although the board's proceedings are often time-consuming and technical, they are far less so than the usual legal proceedings. A lawyer is not necessary, although sometimes desirable. More important, management is directly responsible for all accidents *arising out of and in the course* of a worker's employment. A few examples may indicate what this phrase means. Management may be responsible if: [2]

> Two workers engage in rough-house in the company cafeteria at lunch hour and one knocks out another's tooth.
>
> After work is over, an employee stubs his toe in the company parking lot.
>
> A painter with a heart condition gets a heart attack and falls off a ladder.
>
> A salesman in the field away from home is injured in an auto accident while driving to a movie at 10 P.M., after his sales calls.
>
> A 50-year-old maintenance man works 72 hours without a break and two days later dies of a heart attack.
>
> A man gets a slight bruise. Six months later cancer develops on the site and evidence indicates it was caused by the bruise.

In most states if an employee is injured under circumstances such as the above he receives free medical expenses plus a proportion of the income he loses for all the weeks he cannot work. In New York, for instance, he would

---

[2] The laws vary considerably from state to state. Under the circumstances listed, however, the company would be liable in many states.

get two-thirds of his previous weekly pay—but no more than $50. Since average weekly earnings in New York in 1960 were over $90, the vast majority of injured workers receive the maximum, $50. There are many who consider this compensation inadequate, particularly if a man and his family must live on it for the rest of his life. In addition to this basic compensation, if a worker suffers so called "scheduled injuries" to specified portions of the body he receives additional payments for a specified number of weeks. Among the typical payments in New York are these:

Loss of arm	312 weeks	*Loss of eye*	160 weeks
Loss of leg	288 weeks	*Loss of 4th finger*	15 weeks

In most states, industrial diseases (for example, silicosis, which is common in mines) are also covered.

Most employers take out insurance to meet these risks, either through a state insurance fund, or through private companies. In a few states the employer can choose between the state fund or private carriers. In any case, the company's insurance rate depends on its "experience." By keeping its accidents low a company can reduce its costs substantially; a poor safety record can be enormously expensive.

Naturally the desire to keep insurance costs down affords a powerful incentive for companies to reduce accidents. However, the direct cost of insurance is not the only cost the company must pay. It must also cover the cost of loss of production caused by the accident, the cost of training a new man to take the injured one's place, the cost of dislocations created by the sudden loss of a skilled man, and so forth. In addition, it is often difficult to find people to work in dangerous departments. Some authorities estimate that for every dollar of direct compensation cost there are four dollars of indirect cost, plus, in the case of a serious accident, intangible costs in loss of morale and community reputation.

For these reasons almost every large company carries on an elaborate safety program with a full-time safety staff. Even small concerns find it worth while to have some sort of safety activity. However, these programs differ widely in techniques and in effectiveness.

Alternate Approaches to the Safety Problem

Students and practitioners in the field of safety have approached the problem from a number of points of view. At the extremes have been: (1) the engineering approach, which assumes that accidents can be avoided by constructing a "safe" plant, free from potential hazards, and (2) the selection approach, which assumes that accidents can be avoided by refusing to hire workers whose personality characteristics or physical make-up would suggest that they are "accident-prone." The first approach emphasizes physical environment, the second emphasizes individual personality. Although both have considerable validity, there has been a growing realization that both are oversimplifications of the problem, and that a major cause of accidents is the *relationship* of the individual to his environment—or, to put it in simpler terms, poor working habits.

In an effort to eliminate poor working habits, management's first reaction has been to work through a staff safety department whose function is to make and police safety regulations, to analyze accident causes, and to conduct a safety-education program. Increasingly, however, companies are beginning to see that this too is a rather limited approach, and are coming to regard safety as a line responsibility that should be handled by the supervisor in each department—with the help of the staff safety department.

There are, then, four main approaches to safety: (1) engineering, (2) selection, (3) staff, and (4) line. Let us examine each of them in turn.

The Engineering Approach: The Physical Environment

Because of differences in technology and physical environment, some industries are more hazardous than others. As the following table indicates, logging is thirty times as dangerous as communications. Furthermore, within an industry some jobs are more likely to lead to accidents. Thus a clerk in a lumber mill may well be safer than a buzz-saw operator.

Injury Frequency Rates in Representative Industries *

All manufacturing	10.9
Aircraft	2.9
Communications	1.79
Explosives	2.4
Logging	63.8
Mining, coal	34.12
Railroads	15.03
Blast furnace and steel mills	3.7
Woolen and worsted textile	16.2

* Sources: Communications, railroads, and mining figures from *Accident Facts* (Chicago: National Safety Council, 1956); other figures from *Monthly Labor Review*, Vol. 83, No. 1 (January 1960), pp. 111-112.

Each of these accident rates is a function of (1) how inherently dangerous the industry is, and (2) what management has done to eliminate accident causes. For instance, the low rate in communications is in part due to the Bell System's strenuous safety program. The explosives industry is the safest of all manufacturing industries precisely because safety is so clearly of overriding importance. Worsted textile's relatively poor showing may reflect the less progressive personnel policies and impoverished state of many textile mills.

Indeed there is evidence that accident rates are lowest in very small and very large companies. In small companies work interest is high and the employer can supervise his employees directly. Very large companies conduct extensive safety programs that middle-sized companies cannot afford.

The engineering approach concentrates on reducing these technological hazards by redesigning machinery, equipment, and working procedures. To date, this approach has been extremely fruitful. Indeed a very large part of the credit for the substantial reduction in accidents over the last 30 years must go to safety engineers for introducing safeguards ranging from Geiger counters in radioactive work, additional "props" in mines, mirrors positioned at sharp corners, to rounded corners on office desks.[3]

Certain human-relations problems arise in gaining acceptance of safer work methods, for even if the new way is no harder than the old, it is different. It breaks established ways of doing things, and, where piece-work is involved, learning the new way may even result in loss of income. All the problems of resistance to change discussed in Chapter 12 are involved.

> One company installed a device consisting of a steel-cored cable to pull workers' hands out of the way when they got too close to the press. No notice of the change was given either to the union or the workers. When the president of the union heard of the new device he objected strongly to the workers being "chained" to their machines. The men refused to work with it.[4]

These workers may have felt that this device, though safer, was just one step along the road to transforming workers into machines. Had they been consulted in advance about whether they were willing to try the device, probably much less resistance would have arisen.

> In another plant, the safety man had great difficulty persuading young girls to wear safety nets on their heads. "They're too ugly," the girls complained. When he provided more stylishly designed net-caps and gave each girl her choice of color, the problem disappeared. The same thing happened with safety shoes once the men were allowed to choose from among different models.

Safety devices are also resented if they require extra motions or cut down incentive earnings. The safety man must consider normal human motions and, if possible, design a technique that makes the work easier or at least does not require special effort. For instance, on some processes the standard procedure is (1) position piece in machine, (2) put up guard, (3) operate machine, (4) take down guard, and (5) remove piece. Here the worker is strongly tempted to save two steps by operating without a guard. A fixed guard would eliminate this problem.

---

[3] Credit also must be given to improvements in lighting, ventilation, and better heating, all of which tend to reduce the accident rate.

[4] Almost identical versions of this case appear in Paul Pigors and Charles A. Myers, *Personnel Administration* (New York: McGraw-Hill, 1958), pp. 464-475, and in Michael J. Jucius, *Personnel Management* (Homewood, Ill.: Irwin, 1955), pp. 705-707.

Employees often make a game of trying to avoid the use of safety devices—they regard evasion as a chance to show their independence. The workers in one plant told gleefully of the heroic figure who had deceived management for years by wearing goggles with the glass taken out. Sabotage of this sort is particularly prevalent if the worker can make higher earnings by dodging time-consuming safety measures.

> Many injuries are caused when workers position material under a press and leave their fingers there too long. Some companies have installed controls which require that the worker push a button with each hand some distance from the press before the press will operate. Since this takes time and effort, and results in loss of incentive earnings, however, workers devise a way of pushing the two buttons at the same time with a stick.

Even when workers show no particular resistance to safety devices, they sometimes forget to use them. For this reason engineers try to design equipment that simply cannot be operated if safety measures are ignored. In general, it seems wiser not just to add attachments to the machine to make it safer, but to redesign it from the beginning.

The human factor is not simple to analyze. Safety measures that reduce part of a hazard, for example, may actually increase the number of accidents, since they encourage workers to become less careful.

> In electrical installation work, it was found that accidents occurred because inspectors sometimes pressed high tension bars with their flashlights. Exchanging the fiber-barreled flashlights with metal ones overcame this source of accident. Since the metal ones obviously were conductors, the men adjusted to this properly and avoided making contacts with their flashlights. The fiber-barreled flashlights were not conductors for low voltage, but conductors for high voltage, and the men did not adjust themselves to the limited degree to which these fiber cases were safe.[5]

Similarly, three-lane highways have proved more dangerous than two-lane highways, since they encourage people to take risks.

Safety engineers have been quick to recognize that exclusive emphasis on mechanical safety measures has reached a point of diminishing returns. They have achieved such great success in devising safer equipment and devices that today the vast majority of accidents are caused by human rather than mechanical failure. Machinery has in many cases been made almost as safe as technology will permit.

The causes of accidents may be divided into *unsafe conditions* (that is, technology and physical environment) and *unsafe acts*. Progress has been so rapid in eliminating unsafe conditions that it has been estimated that 88

---

[5] Norman R. F. Maier, *Psychology in Industry*, 2nd ed. (Boston: Houghton Mifflin, 1955), p. 508.

per cent of all accidents are now caused by unsafe acts—that is, in most cases it is the worker who is unsafe, not the machine.[6]

The Selection Approach: Accident-Proneness

When we study a group of workers who are all doing the same job and are all subject to the same physical environment, we usually discover that a few workers have substantially more accidents than the rest. In the following table, which gives the distribution of accidents among 648 employees of a British shell factory,[7] notice that less than 10 per cent of the women had over half the accidents.

Number of accidents	Number of women
0	448
1	132
2	42
3	21
4	3
5	2
Total	648

Other evidence of the same phenomenon lies in the fact that those who have more than the average number of accidents in any one given period of time are likely to have more than the average number later on.[8] We all know people who are always stumbling and dropping things. Regardless of whether they are driving a car, pouring milk, or counting change, they make mistakes.

Evidence of this sort has led researchers to try to identify the physical and psychological characteristics that make an individual likely to have accidents—that is, that make him "accident-prone." Tests have been devised, for example, to measure a worker's manual dexterity, rhythm, reaction time, and short-distance vision.

One interesting study has been made of the relationship between *perceptual* and *motor* speed. Perceptual speed was measured by testing the individual's ability to sort out items that had slightly different shapes; motor speed was measured by testing his ability to place pins in wooden trays. The study revealed that workers whose perceptual speed was greater than their motor speed were found to be less likely to have accidents. Here we have objective support for the old adage that it pays to look before you leap.[9]

---

[6] H. W. Heinrich, "The Accident Cause Ratio—88:10:2," *The American Society of Safety Engineers Journal,* Vol. 73 (May 1956), p. 18.

[7] Cited in Maier, *op. cit.,* p. 520.

[8] Alexander Mintz and Milton L. Blum, "A Re-examination of the Accident Proneness Concept," *Journal of Applied Psychology,* Vol. 33, No. 3 (June 1949), pp. 195-211.

[9] Charles A. Drake, "Accident-proneness: A Hypothesis," *Character and Personality,* Vol. 8, No. 4 (June 1940), pp. 335-341.

Psychological factors also seem to have a strong relationship to accident-proneness.[10] Just as many illnesses (such as ulcers and high blood pressure) spring in part from psychological causes, so there are individuals whose high accident rate seems related to psychological disturbances. Either they are so concerned with their own problems that they forget to take proper safeguards, or else it seems almost as if they unconsciously want to be injured in order to punish themselves or avoid a difficult situation. Workers who are unusually impulsive or have aggressions to work off on the job may have more accidents. One authority generalizes that accident-prone people are "an impulsive, irresponsible group. In general they are abnormally interested in satisfying pleasures of the moment. They dislike planning for the future and profit rarely from past experience. They are people of action, rather than planning." [11]

Evidence suggests that accident-prone workers have a generally poor adjustment to work: they make a higher number of short trips to the dispensary,[12] they have a higher number of unexcused absences,[13] and they are less efficient on the job.[14]

Accidents may also be related to temporary emotional stress.

> An example is the case of a mechanic with a long record of freedom from accidental injury. Unexpectedly, within the space of six months, this man developed what appeared to be an accident habit, with four major and six minor injuries to himself and considerable damage to company equipment. It took very little investigation to discover a problem involving feelings of guilt concerning an extra-marital affair, which started before his first injury.[15]

One author estimates that workers are worried, apprehensive, or in some other " 'low' emotional condition" only about 20 per cent of the time, yet half their accidents occur during that time.[16]

Many accidents occur on no-attention jobs when something unexpected happens that interrupts the worker's usual rhythm. Instead of smoothly adapting to the interruption, accident-prone individuals "manifest a sort of disorder in their defense reaction mechanism. They panic easily and feel this inner shock as a 'moment of terror.' " [17]

---

[10] Much of the pioneering work in this area was done by the late Flanders Dunbar. See her *Psychosomatic Diagnosis* (New York: Harpers, 1943).

[11] Alan McLean, "Accidents and the 'Human Factor,' " *The Personnel Journal*, Vol. 34, No. 9 (February 1956), pp. 424-443.

[12] Maier, *op. cit.*

[13] J. M. M. Hill and E. L. Trist, "A Consideration of Industrial Accidents as a Means of Withdrawal from the Work Situation," *Human Relations*, Vol. 4, No. 4 (1953), pp. 357-380. It is interesting that the Caspar Milquetoast type who asked for permission before being absent had a better safety record than those who were never absent at all.

[14] Georges Friedmann, *Industrial Society* (Glencoe, Ill.: Free Press, 1955), p. 114.

[15] McLean, *op. cit.*

[16] Rexford B. Hershey, "Emotional Factors in Accidents," *The Personnel Journal*, Vol 15, No. 2 (June 1936), p. 60.

[17] Friedmann, *op. cit.*, p. 114, citing *Journal de Psychologie* (1937), pp. 290-294.

How can a worker who is psychologically accident-prone be spotted before he is hired? This is a difficult problem. To date, personality tests have not proved particularly useful.[18] Tests that measure the degree of an individual's emotional reaction (in terms of glandular changes) to unexpected occurrences and tremor, however, do show some relationship to accidents, particularly if the individual is tested under stress.[19]

Perhaps the interviewer's assessment of the applicant's over-all emotional stability is as valuable a test as any: Does he seem like the kind of person who will fly off the handle when subjected to stress? Does he seem likely to be so distracted by personal problems that he will pay little attention to his work? The supervisor who watches a new worker during the probationary period should ask himself similar questions while deciding whether or not to keep the man. Does the worker become excited under tension? Does he talk more? Is he less rational? Or does he become quiet and withdrawn? All these are danger signals.

Authorities disagree on whether or not it is possible to screen out accident-prone individuals. One author states that preventing "accident proneness is largely a by-product of proper selection and placement, professionally planned and carried out." [20] Others are less willing to commit themselves. One concludes that

> . . . the time honored approach of the psychologist and the psychiatrist which emphasizes identification of subtle personality conditions which predispose to accidents by some employees seems to be a less promising approach than that which emphasizes study of the total psychological climate in which the typical employee works. If proneness (or liability) to accidents exists such tendency may be a group psychological phenomenon as well as an individual psychological phenomenon.[21]

It is probably safe to say that in American industry, with the exception of the transportation industry (truck and bus drivers, and airplane pilots), little apparent effort is being made to identify the accident-prone at the hiring stage. There seems to be considerable doubt among operating personnel about the accuracy of any of the tests so far developed in discriminating between safe and accident-prone workers. Furthermore, particularly during periods of expanding employment, the personnel department has little opportunity to pick and choose among otherwise qualified applicants. (See our discussion on pp. 449-450.)

---

[18] F. J. Harris, "Can Personality Tests Identify Accident-Prone Employees?" *Personnel Psychology*, Vol. 3, No. 4 (Winter 1950), pp. 455-459.

[19] E. Farmer and E. G. Chambers, *A Study of Personality Qualities in Accident Proneness and Proficiency*, Industrial Fatigue Research Board, Report No. 55 (1929).

[20] Alfred J. Cardall, "Psychological Factors in Accident Prevention," *The Personnel Journal*, Vol. 26, No. 8 (February 1948), p. 290.

[21] William A. Kerr, "Accident Proneness in Factory Departments," *Journal of Applied Psychology*, Vol. 34, No. 3 (June 1950), p. 167.

It seems clear that work conditions and individual accident-proneness are only two of the many determinants of accidents. Accidents are partly the fault of individuals, partly the fault of technology, and partly the fault of such factors as group attitudes and improper supervision. Management has begun to realize that neither industrial engineering departments nor employment departments can alone or in conjunction stop accidents completely, and the emphasis has shifted toward the establishment of separate safety departments.

The Staff Approach: The Safety Department

The safety director is a staff man who usually reports to the personnel director or the industrial engineer, although in some organizations he is directly responsible to the plant manager. His functions normally include the general promotion of safety education (through posters and safety campaigns, for example), analyzing the causes of accidents, preparing accident statistics and records, purchasing safety equipment, and so forth.

But these activities are only incidental to the safety director's main responsibility for devising and administering a plant-wide safety program. He is usually given a grant of power that reads somewhat like this: "To inspect the plant for unsafe conditions, to promote sound safety practices, to make safety rules, and to report, when necessary, violations to the plant manager." Powers as broad as these, of course, may well lead to conflict with line supervisors.

> The safety man sees a grinder working without the required goggles. Should he speak to the grinder, the foreman, or the plant manager? Whatever he does will make someone feel as though he has been by-passed.

> The safety man decides that the drop-hammer mechanism is unsafe. He feels that the worker should be required to push a button every time he wants the hammer to operate. This would be safer but would cut production. To whom should he speak first? How should he handle the expected opposition?

Problems such as these are almost inevitable once a staff man assumes responsibility for making and enforcing rules (see Chapter 18). How are the line supervisors likely to respond to such an extension of staff activities?

1. If the safety director pre-empts too much authority, the supervisors may decide that safety is the safety man's responsibility and forget about it altogether.

2. The supervisors may sabotage or ignore safety regulations that they have had no part in making. Often they feel (sometimes with justice) that a particular rule should not apply to their particular situation.

3. The supervisors and the safety director may just pass the buck back and forth. Whenever an accident occurs, each may put the blame on the other. If production costs rise too high, supervisors can always say that the safety man is at fault (this is particularly true where the safety man has the authority to order new equipment).

4. In most cases, accidents are caused by a worker doing his job in a dangerous fashion. Yet if the safety director instructs a man on how to do his job, he is usurping one of the supervisor's primary responsibilities. Sometimes the supervisor tells the worker what he *should* do and the safety director tells him what he *should not* do. This too can often lead to conflict.

5. Both the supervisors and the workers may begin to resent the safety man's efforts to implement his program. One safety man complained:

> "I feel like a cop. Everybody suspects me. When I come around everybody covers up, especially the men. All I am trying to do is help them. Yet I never get cooperation from anyone. I got to fight every inch of the way."

No wonder safety men often retreat from their efforts to enforce safety rules and try to achieve the same results through "educational" activities. As long as the safety director sticks to posters, propaganda, and contests, he is unlikely to get into anyone's hair.

PUBLICITY

Such publicity devises as posters, slogans, and contests form the backbone of many safety programs. Most posters and jingles are punchy and amusing. But, apart from giving workers a slight chuckle, how much can these devices be expected to accomplish? For an answer to this question we must turn to psychologists who have studied how attitudes and behavior can be changed.

In general, psychologists agree that posters and jingles are reasonably effective in making consumers think of a particular brand when buying commercial products such as cigarettes—or even in creating new needs for such appliances as color TV. But these devices seem to be less effective in changing basic attitudes. "Dogmatic methods are not satisfactory for conveying emotionally-powerful ideas which are inherent in personal, physical safety." [22]

Workers soon come to regard posters as part of the scenery. They glance at them from time to time, but are unlikely to remember the tricky safety message at the crucial moment when they are in a hurry and about to take a risk. Most safety posters in effect say "Work safely." Yet no one gets injured on purpose. Like exhortations not to sin, constant repetition of the dire consequences of taking risks seems to have little effect.

---

[22] McLean, *op. cit.*, p. 344.

Many organizations insist that all employees attend periodic safety meetings, often run by the safety department. These meetings are quite valuable if they provide for group discussion of problems that are actually faced by the employees. Ordinarily, however, the participants simply sit and listen to canned programs couched in fairly unsophisticated terms. A head nurse told of the experience in her hospital:

> "We are supposed to attend a safety meeting once a month. You can always predict what will happen: one month they show you how to use a fire extinguisher, another month they tell you not to leave mops where people can trip over them and to make sure that the floors aren't waxed too heavily. Every six months they show us a movie—the same one—I know it by heart. I got better things to do; I have patients to take care of."

Many safety directors sponsor contests between departments in the hope that they can make a dramatic reduction in the accident rate by means of group pressure and competitive spirit. They post elaborate charts to mark the contestants' standings, and present small prizes such as pens or cigarette lighters to all the workers in the winning department. Observations suggest, however, that the safety director is usually far more enthusiastic about the contest than are any of the so-called contestants. The success of a contest usually depends on the degree to which the supervisors and the men themselves are involved and participate in the planning. Normally the contestants are not asked whether they want to engage in a contest, and the prizes are rarely large enough to provide much motivation.

In some cases, such contests do have an impact on the supervisor, but in a negative manner: if his department does too badly, he may get into trouble with higher management. This brings us to the question of what use should be made of accident records and statistics?

RECORDS AND ANALYSIS

Normally whenever an accident occurs the supervisor is required to fill out a form including such information as the time, place, and cause of the accident, the extent of the injury, and a statement of what can be done to prevent such accidents in the future. Some of these forms are so complicated that the supervisor feels they have been designed as punishment for permitting an accident to occur.

Records of this sort serve several purposes: (1) they are useful if litigation arises involving workman's compensation, (2) they serve a control function, since, like cost and turnover figures, they indicate to higher management areas of supervisory inefficiency, and (3) they help management diagnose the causes of accidents, and thus provide a springboard for corrective measures.

It is the responsibility of the safety department to review, classify, and tabulate these reports. In fact, the safety program sometimes degenerates into a "whodunit" as the safety director tries to assign each accident to its proper category. Often it is extremely difficult to fix responsibility for a given accident. For instance, because the maintenance department has failed to keep a machine in proper order, oil drips out on the floor; the janitor fails to sweep it up; and a worker from another department runs through the department, slips, and hurts himself. Which department should be assigned the blame? The maintenance department, the department in which the fall occurs, or the department whose man is hurt?

Some safety men insist that the best way to prevent accidents is to conduct elaborate, continuing research into their causes. Actually, however, it seems less important for the safety department to know *why* accidents occur than for the foremen and workers to do something to eliminate them.

Carefully recorded statistics do provide higher management with a useful control in putting pressure on lower levels of supervision. And they serve as valuable case materials in safety-committee meetings which may lead to corrective action by supervisors.

THE STAFF ROLE: AN EVALUATION

A young man was appointed as the first personnel director of a small company that had a particularly bad safety record. One of his first official acts was to cancel the company's contract with an agency that supplied safety posters. Why did he take such an unorthodox act? His answer was very revealing: "I wanted everyone to know that just because we had safety posters didn't mean that we had a safety campaign."

There is a regrettable tendency in the safety field, as in other areas of personnel administration, to rely on gadgets to provide easy solutions to hard problems. The process is a familiar one. Management recognizes that accidents are a serious expense. "Something must be done about it!" Line management is too busy, so an expert is hired, a specialist who can handle the problem for them. This done, line management breathes a sigh of relief: "That problem is solved."

The safety man realizes that he can achieve results only by eliciting the cooperation of the supervisors and workers. Yet to them safety is *his* job, not theirs—they are too busy. So in frustration he resorts to "gadgets," easy answers, measures that require little cooperation from line management. Perhaps he concentrates on posters, snappy slogans, elaborate statistical analyses of accidents and accident causes, safety contests between departments. Or, if he feels courageous enough to take a more direct approach, he insists that foolproof gadgets be placed on machines, since it is clearly impossible to change worker attitudes. Or else he devises elaborate tests to eliminate the accident-prone at the gate before they are hired.

But a safety program of this sort is sometimes worse than none at all, for it lulls management into assuming that all its problems have been solved. As long as safety is primarily a staff function, the foreman will not give it high priority. Too often the safety man receives only lip service from a management that is much more interested in its "primary responsibility" of production. A safety program can be made effective only if the line supervisors and the workers are determined to make it work. A safety director by himself cannot make a plant safe.

The safety man does have a vital function to perform, however: He must be an adviser and counselor, an expert on both human relations and engineering, a man who helps but does not supplant the foreman. For instance, if during his rounds the safety man observes a worker who is operating unsafely, he should neither instruct the worker (except in emergency) nor report it to top management. Instead, he should discuss the matter with the foreman. Together they should try to figure out why the worker is motivated to take risks and how he can be motivated to avoid them. Even more important, the safety man should help coordinate line management's safety activities—activities in which the union and individual workers also participate. Let us look at these activities for a moment.

The Line Approach:
Safety as a Supervisory Responsibility

The following story illustrates the advantages to be gained when safety is made a line responsibility.

> In 1949 the Thatcher plant of a nation-wide company had an injury frequency rate of 21. Two years later its rate was 5, the lowest in the company.
>
> Even in 1949 the Thatcher plant had been conducting an active safety program in accordance with the directives issued by the national office. Safety posters were prominently displayed on every bulletin board. Over the main entrance to the plant was a sign that read: "——— days since the last accident." Every month information was posted on all the bulletin boards comparing the accident rate by departments. Safety guards had been placed on all machines. Mirrors had been installed at every sharp turn in the hallways and on the stairways.
>
> And yet the plant was cursed with an abnormally high number of accidents, most of them caused by unsafe acts, not unsafe conditions. A lift truck careening around a corner scooped up an unwary worker. Girls cut their fingers on sharp edges because they failed to wear the gloves provided them. A mechanic positioned his ladder carelessly and fell off it while inspecting some high machinery. Two 18-year-old boys were rough-housing in the locker room; one stumbled over a bench and broke a rib. And so forth.

At last top management notified the plant manager that his job depended on his reducing the accident rate immediately. He was instructed to appoint a full-time safety director. The new safety director intensified the plant's publicity program and carried on constant safety checks through the plant in an effort to discover unsafe conditions and unsafe work habits.

More important, he began to enlist employee participation by working through the union. In consultation with the union, a plant-wide safety committee was established consisting of the safety director, personnel director, and several general foremen, together with one representative selected by the union from each department. The union committeemen were limited to a one-year term, in order to give as many workers as possible a chance to participate in the program.

Before each monthly meeting, the committee made a plant-wide safety inspection, with the assistance of the foreman and the union steward in each department. As the members went through the plant, they noted such hazards as slippery floors, mushroomed hammers, and improper guards. At the meeting, these hazards were discussed, along with suggestions submitted by rank-and-file workers. After the committee members had agreed on what should be done in each case, they relayed instructions to the proper supervisor, who was required to report at the next meeting on whether or not he had carried them out. The committee also analyzed all the accidents that had occurred during the preceding month.

The union took a direct interest both in checking up on management and in keeping its own members in line. The safety committeemen wore a special button and were authorized to stop unsafe acts committed by union members. At the meetings, committeemen often reported on how "I stopped Bill Smith from running across the hall. I told him, he'd be sure to kill himself." Or "There was a new man just in who didn't know how to lift things properly. I showed him how to do it."

Line management was quick to recognize that the plant manager meant business with the new program. In addition to preparing the usual written reports on accidents, each foreman now had to give the plant manager a personal report. As one foreman said: "I never want to go through an experience like *that* again. I never felt so small in all my life. I know one thing, there will be no more accidents in my department."

Gradually, the foremen began to realize that preventing accidents was just as important as keeping up production. They became extremely receptive to suggestions from the safety committee. (On occasion, too, they tried to evade assuming responsibility for accidents. As one foreman said: "See that man. He's doing me a great favor. He strained his arm yesterday but I asked him to come in and just pretend to work. I don't want to have any accidents on my record.")

The net result of this many-pronged program was an outstanding improvement in safety performance.

This case highlights the fact that safety is essentially a line problem, though staff can help. There is little difference in the managerial problems involved in cutting accidents and raising production. Both involve questions of motivation, enforcement of standards, and working through groups.

GROUP FACTORS

There are, as we have seen, accident-prone individuals. But safety is to a considerable extent a function of group attitudes. In a gang of teen-agers it may be smart to take risks; in a group of mature businessmen irresponsibility is frowned on. To miners as a group, safety is of tremendous importance. (In one gypsum plant the "prop" man, who installed wooden props to hold up the roof, was found to enjoy high social status even though his job required little skill.[23]) United States corporations operating plants in certain Latin-American countries have found that accident rates are difficult to reduce there because of the widespread feeling that using a safety device is inconsistent with being a red-blooded man.

Clearly, the establishment of proper group attitudes is one of the most important requirements of an effective safety program. This is particularly true when the safety rules make the workers' jobs harder or more unpleasant, or are regarded as an unjustified restriction on freedom. Hairnets are unattractive; goggles and safety belts are uncomfortable; pushing a safety button often requires an extra motion.

If management can get the group to participate in the safety program, safe work habits may become accepted as a group norm that will be enforced by the group just as rigorously as any production "bogey." The group itself may punish the man who takes chances or fails to use proper equipment. In many plants no-smoking rules are consistently ignored in spite of constant attempts to enforce them. Not so in oil refineries. Here the legitimacy of the rule is well accepted. One employee reported that "regardless of who you are in the plant, if you see someone smoking you can stop him. I know. The first day I was there I absentmindedly reached for a butt and was practically lynched. The boys have special fun catching visitors, especially big shots." Here we have a group-enforced pattern of behavior—a group standard.

Group meetings provide a unique opportunity to ferret out possible accident hazards and to elicit suggestions that would not have occurred to line supervision or the safety department. After all, the men on the spot know more about their jobs than anyone else. Furthermore, most safety rules are easy to ignore and difficult to enforce. Rules are much easier to enforce if those who must obey them also have a voice in drawing them up.

THE UNION

In contrast to wage determination and discipline, safety is an area in which the interests of labor and management are identical. Everyone gains by keeping accidents at a minimum, and no safety program can be

---

[23] Alvin Gouldner, *Patterns of Industrial Bureaucracy* (Glencoe, Ill.: Free Press, 1954), p. 12.

conducted effectively without joint effort. Ironically, however, unions and management often use the question of safety as a pawn in the struggle for power.[24]

Many members of management take the position that the union has no right to be consulted on matters of safety. As one personnel director explained, "Safety is so important in our industry that we cannot share responsibility. We have worker safety committees in each department, but we keep these sharply separate from the union."[25] Unions frequently resist management's efforts to install safety equipment or to enforce safety rules. On the other hand, many wild-cat and legally called strikes have been caused by management's insistence that men work under conditions they regard as unsafe.

There are a few encouraging signs of cooperation in safety matters, however. Joint union-management safety committees, like the one in the Thatcher plant, are becoming increasingly common. In fact, they are perhaps the most successful of the various sorts of joint union-management committee that have been tried.

For these committees to be genuinely successful, the rank-and-file members must feel they are playing a real part in the safety program. Rules negotiated with top union officials alone are less likely to be accepted than rules to which a large number of individual employees have contributed. Too many joint safety committees consist only of top local officers who may have less knowledge of conditions in a given department than does management. Yet if union cooperation is to be obtained, the top officers should participate in setting up the committee and in selecting its members.

SUPERVISION

To a large extent the attitude of the rank-and-file workers toward safety is a reflection of the attitude of their immediate supervisor. A worker in a railway freight yard once told the following story:

> There's a company rule that you aren't supposed to cut between cars. If the safety man sees you he will give you three days off. But the supervisor doesn't care. In fact, when you have to get the numbers of some cars, that's the only way to get it. If you don't get the numbers, he'll give you time off. And he is more likely to catch you than the safety man.

---

[24] Actually, union-management cooperation in safety may serve as a starting point for cooperation in other fields. As Herbert Hoover put it years ago, "Good-will and cooperation with respect to safety—which is a noncontroversial subject as between employer and employee—lead to good-will and cooperation in other more delicate problems of shop management, such as hours of work and wages." Quoted in Friedmann, *op. cit.*, p. 118.

[25] The union president told us: "These committees are a waste of time. Management pays no attention to what they bring up. If it was a union committee, we could force management to clean things up. They really are more interested in production than safety here. As for us, it's safety first."

In safety, as in other areas of supervision, the attitudes of the foremen in turn reflect the attitudes of higher management. To the foreman operating under the pressure typical of modern industry, maximum production and maximum safety are simply incompatible. One can be achieved only at the expense of the other. (Perhaps this is a short-sighted point of view, but it is sometimes difficult for the foreman to take any other.) If management really wants "Safety First," it must clearly indicate that it is willing to pay the possible cost in terms of lower production. It must get tough with supervisors who permit unsafe practices to continue. It must show that it consults the safety records in deciding who should get promoted. If management talks loud about safety but permits a dangerous condition to persist for "just another few days" so that no production will be lost, it must expect only lip service from everyone down the line.

Companies that have the best safety records customarily use accident reports as one of the control statistics by which supervisory efficiency is judged. As we discovered in Chapter 14, however, overemphasis on such records may induce supervisors to bend all their efforts toward *looking* good. They may fall into the habit of buck-passing, and may even try to persuade injured workers to report to work in order to avoid being charged with a "lost-time accident."

What, specifically, can the supervisor do to promote safety?

1. He can train new employees. The foreman should do more than merely exhort the new employee to work safely. He should point out to him the possible causes of accidents and should help him develop work habits and motions that will keep him out of danger.

> "Such actions as assuming a posture which allows a man to lose his balance if a wrench slips, holding a finger in line with the cutting edge so a finger injury occurs if there is a moment's inattention or if an error is made . . . and holding the face so close to a grinding wheel that particles of steel may injure the face, are examples of behavior elements which should be eliminated from the work pattern." [26]

2. He can make it clear that, though he wants high production, he won't insist on workers working so fast that they run risks. [27]

3. He can listen to and consult with employees. Often the foreman gets

---

[26] Maier, *op. cit.*, p. 513.

[27] There is some evidence that the accident rate is higher when the job pace is too fast for workers to maintain. (Friedmann, *op. cit.*, p. 117.) A conflicting study made at the Camden RCA works, however, showed that departments on incentive had approximately the same accident rate as those on day work, even though other factors (such as monotonous work, low job prestige) would lead one to expect accidents to be higher. As an explanation of this unexpected finding, the author suggests that incentive systems "appear to make [the worker] more alert to make a reasonable production goal and this alertness apparently makes him safer in his operations." (Kerr, *op. cit.*, p. 170.)

his best safety ideas by keeping his ears open and making it clear that he is interested in suggestions.

4. He can engage in constructive discipline. He can tactfully point out to employees when they are working unsafely, and he can be firm in imposing punishment when lesser measures fail.

5. Finally, he can make a habit of checking on unsafe conditions and unsafe behavior as part of his daily routine. In some General Motors plants each foreman is expected to speak to at least two of his employees each day about safety.[28] The foreman should be on the lookout for employees who seem emotionally upset; if necessary, he should either counsel them or transfer them to a safer job. In some companies, supervisors are required to make a daily "morale check" of all employees engaged in dangerous work.

Conclusion

There is no one sure-fire approach to safety. The engineering approach has paid off remarkably well, but it seems to be rapidly reaching the limits of its effectiveness. The most safely engineered car in the world is a murderous weapon in the hands of an unsafe driver—and the same is true of industrial equipment.

There is less unanimity about the selection approach to safety. Debate still continues about the value of interviews and tests in eliminating accident-prone workers. Certainly such screening cannot eliminate the carelessness and accidents that spring from temporary emotional disturbances. Further, evidence suggests that risk-taking is largely a group phenomenon. In a situation where there is heavy pressure for production or where fellow employees encourage one another to take chances, almost everyone begins to take the hazardous short cuts that lead to injury.

So long as management regarded accident prevention as a problem that could be solved exclusively through an engineering approach, or exclusively through a selection approach, there was some justification in considering safety as a separate, special program. Safety engineers could be expected to install safe equipment; proper psychological tests could be expected to eliminate the accident-prone. But once management realized that safety was intimately related to *the way people work*, it became clear that only line supervision could handle the problem.

Safety demands the support of every level of management. Workers must participate as well as supervisors, for workers often spot danger areas and devise effective solutions. But when they fail to perceive safety as something

---

[28] One company credits this technique with a reduction in the accident frequency rate from 33.43 in 1950 to 8.34 in 1953. Bureau of National Affairs, Personnel Policy Forum, *Company Safety Program*, Survey No. 29 (February 1953), p. 17.

vital to their welfare, they will resist the most carefully devised safety program. Safety must be considered as a responsibility for the whole organization; any attempt to departmentalize it inevitably leads to confusion and inefficiency.

Problem I

Personnel Director: "We've got to constantly watch our production people [on safety]. Our safety man must go over all orders for tools. A lot of our departments have high explosion dangers and we've got to use spark-proof hammers. But a spark-proof hammer costs three times as much and only lasts a third as long, so the foremen are always trying to get steel ones."

Question: "If the safety man objects to what the foremen want to buy, who has the final say?"

Personnel Director: "The safety man all the time. We want to build up a good record."

1. Discuss the impact of this point of view on line-staff relations.
2. What would be a better approach?

Problem II

The following quotations are taken from various safety manuals. Comment on each in turn.

"Every worker should be given a safety handbook and made to familiarize himself with it."

"In order to keep workers on the alert, those in charge of safety education should make use of posters prominently displayed and frequently changed."

"The competitive spirit does wonders. Build up competition between departments."

"The key to effective safety is to build up interests. Always have something new, a new gimmick, a new gadget, a new way to rouse a chuckle."

Problem III

You are Vice President in charge of Industrial Relations for a large company with many plants scattered throughout the nation. In going over your monthly report from the Jonesville plant, you notice a significant increase in the accident rate. You had planned to go to Jonesville some time this month in any case, and you now resolve to look into the problem.

1. What are the possible explanations for this increase in accidents?
2. Bearing in mind that you are a staff man, describe in a step-by-step fashion how you plan to deal with this problem.

Fringe benefits—insurance, holidays, pensions. overtime pay, and other benefits—now make up a significant part of employee remuneration.[1] Perhaps 20 to 30 per cent of a firm's labor costs may go to cover these items, and it is likely that the proportion will continue to increase. In this chapter we will examine the reasons for the growth of fringe benefits and the special problems involved in administering them.

What Are Fringe Benefits?

There is no rigid, all-inclusive definition of fringe benefits, but the following list suggests some of the items that are commonly included under this term:

Paid vacations, paid holidays, and Christmas bonuses.
Paid rest periods, lunch periods, wash-up time, and the like.

---

[1] The term "fringe benefit" became popular during the 1940's as a means of referring to the whole bevy of employee benefits provided by the employer in addition to traditional direct-wage payments.

30

Service and Benefit
Programs

Overtime pay for hours worked beyond the "regular" work period. The Fair Labor Standards Act requires a 50 per cent premium to be paid for all hours worked in excess of 40 per week for firms engaged in interstate commerce. Many companies also pay overtime for work on holidays, weekends, and beyond eight hours in a single day.

Hospitalization and *medical benefits.*

Sickness and accident benefits for the continuance of part or all of an employee's regular wage or salary while he is ill.

Old Age and Survivors' Insurance Benefits (popularly called Social Security). These are paid directly by the federal government, but to finance them the company must pay (as of 1960) a 3 per cent tax on the first $4,800 of each employee's annual earnings. The employee must pay another 3 per cent.

Pension plans to supplement federal benefits.

Thrift and saving plans by which the company supplements any savings put aside by employees (within specified limits). Sometimes the supplement is in the form of savings bonds or company stock.

Unemployment benefits paid by state governments but financed by taxes on the employer's payroll.

Supplemental unemployment benefits (sometimes misnamed "Guaranteed Annual Wage Plans") to supplement unemployment benefits paid by the state.

Workmen's Compensation to pay for medical and hospital bills and provide partial payment for lost earnings while an employee is disabled due to an industrial accident or illness.

Severance pay given to employees whose jobs are permanently eliminated.

Recreation programs, including company-financed social, athletic, and recreational clubs.

Subsidies to reduce employee expenses for cafeteria food, work clothing, and tools.

Discounts on company products, company securities, and so forth.

Tuition rebates for education and special training.

Medical, legal, and personal counseling.

Notice that some of these items, such as company contributions to the Federal Old Age and Survivors' Insurance program, state unemployment insurance funds, and Workmen's Compensation, are required by law. Many companies, however, supplement these benefits with programs of their own.

Omitted from the above list are certain items that might properly be considered as fringe benefits: Isolated company locations, for example, often require that the company carry a major share of the cost of housing, community schooling, and recreation programs, and so forth. In many firms, sales personnel and executives consider liberal expense allowances and trips to exotic resorts (for conventions or customer good will) as fringe benefits.[2]

---

[2] The Internal Revenue Service may rule to the contrary, of course.

MAGNITUDE OF PROGRAMS

When management is considering the addition of another employee, it is unrealistic to take into account only his wage or salary, for fringe benefits will probably be a continuing liability.

The following table, compiled by the editors of the *Harvard Business Review*,[3] shows the relative importance of the various types of benefit program.

Type of Benefit Program	Cost (cents/hour)
Premiums for time worked (overtime, etc.)	7.86
Pay for time not worked (holidays, vacations, sick pay, etc.)	14.44 *
Employee benefits (insurance, work clothing, pension plans, etc.)	17.60 †
Employee recreation activities	.26

* About 50 per cent of this figure consists of vacation payment costs.
† About 40 per cent of this figure consists of pension plan costs.

Notice that the lion's share of company fringe costs are devoted to (1) employee benefit plans, such as insurance and pensions, and (2) vacation and holiday pay and other payments for time not worked.

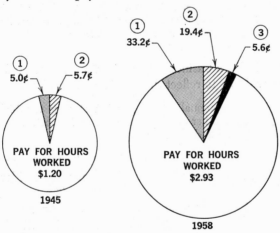

① Pensions, insurance, supplemental unemployment benefits, and social security
② Vacation pay and misc. adjustments
③ Pay for holidays not worked

Total employment cost per man hour for wage employees in the iron and steel industry. (Source: American Iron and Steel Institute.)

The steel industry has calculated that its "fringe costs" increased tenfold in the 20 years from 1940 to 1960. Their data, incorporated in the chart above and the one on p. 702, show the magnitude of this increase as compared to the slower rate of increase in direct wage payments.

[3] A. M. Fisher and J. F. Chapman, "Big Costs of Little Fringes," *Harvard Business Review*, Vol. 32, No. 5 (September-October 1954), pp. 38-39. Data are for 1952.

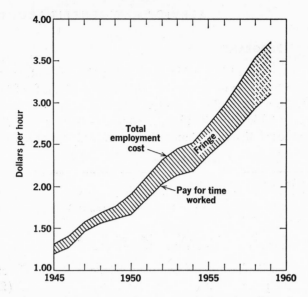

Difference between average pay for time worked and total employment costs per man hour in the iron and steel industry. First National City Bank Monthly Letter, *Business and Economic Conditions,* January 1960, p. 4. (Source: American Iron and Steel Institute; 1959 estimated from data for first six months.)

Somewhat cynically, a business economist once commented on the failure of wage rates or salaries to reflect the real income level of the employee:

> In this world the annual rate of pay is a statistic to which employers add more and more other employment costs and from which the Government subtracts more and more taxes.[4]

The cost of benefit programs conducted by United States firms in overseas plants are still higher. In Latin America, for example, confidential estimates by management consulting firms give the figure as 145 per cent of direct labor costs. In Western Europe, the figures are somewhere between those for the United States and Latin America. Professor Emile Benoit of the Graduate School of Business at Columbia University has provided us with these data:

Percentage Added to Average Hourly Wage Rates by Social Charges Paid by a U.S. Manufacturer in Europe—April, 1957

Additional direct cost to employer, added to wages, including unemployment insurance, sickness benefits, old age and invalidity pensions, workmen's (injury) compensation, paid holidays, family allowances, etc. Does not include amounts paid out of general tax revenues (which are relatively heavier in U.K.).

	Holland	Belgium	France	Italy	W. Germany	U.K.
Direct Social Charges	28%	29%	43.8%	52.4%	29.4%	12%

---

[4] First National City Bank Monthly Letter, *Business and Economic Conditions,* January 1960, pp. 4-5.

Why Fringe Benefits Have Expanded

Why has the amount of money devoted to these programs risen so rap-idly in recent years? In theory at least, all these benefits could be purchased by employees from increased direct wages. Why then has management chosen to provide them in addition to wages? The answer to this question requires us to look outside the firm.

EMPLOYEE DEMANDS

Paradoxically, as our country has become richer and more self-assured, the desire to eliminate risk and increase personal security has grown stronger.[5] And the prevalence of fringe benefits reflects a strong urge on the part of employees to eliminate insecurity from every conceivable source. This urge was certainly intensified by the passage of the Social Security Act of 1938.

Besides more security, employees are also demanding more leisure, and leisure has become a significant component of our high standard of living.[6] Food, clothing, and shelter are no longer enough; leisure time has an impor-tance of its own. Employees want paid holidays and paid vacations so that they will have both the time and the money to pursue recreation. (Of course, some demands for increased leisure are really efforts to spread work by re-quiring the firm to hire or retain more employees to fill in for those on vaca-tion or on working shorter hours.)

The widespread employee desire for "psychological" assistance in paying for savings and insurance is another environmental factor working on man-agement. Many employees find it more convenient to have their contributions for health and welfare benefits deducted from their paychecks than to pay them by themselves. If this money never appears in their paychecks and is never available for them to spend, the whole process becomes less painful. Thus many of these programs provide *forced savings* without demanding hab-its of thrift. For example, under the General Electric Saving Plan an employee may elect to have up to 6 per cent of his earnings deducted from his pay-check and deposited in a company savings account. (The company matches half of this amount, provided the employee leaves his savings in for at least three years.[7]

---

[5] For an interesting analysis of the almost universal American desire to eliminate risk and insecurity, see John K. Galbraith, *The Affluent Society* (Boston: Houghton Mifflin, 1958), Chapter 8. See also our discussion in Chapter 1.

[6] *Fortune* magazine takes issue with this point, arguing that, given the opportunity, employees would prefer higher income to leisure, citing as evidence the increasing number of workers who hold two jobs and the struggles among employees themselves for the privilege of working overtime. (*Fortune*, November 1959, p. 137.)

[7] In addition, the employee enjoys the interest and dividends paid on these sums. All the employee's contributions are invested in U.S. savings bonds, and he may elect to have the company's contribution invested either in savings bonds or in company stock.

Employees have other compelling reasons for favoring benefit programs. Many of these benefits, like paid vacations and holidays, give hourly workers increased status in the organization and in the community, placing them on a level closer to that of salaried employees. Other benefits, like premiums for certain types of overtime and irregularly scheduled work hours and call-in pay, serve as a control mechanism on the employer and discourage him from taking advantage of workers. Americans have also become more health-conscious and are increasingly anxious to enjoy preventative and remedial treatment through health-insurance programs. The privileges and benefits provided by these programs cannot be won by individual employees; they must be procured on a company-wide basis.

UNION DEMANDS

The special conditions prevailing during and just after World War II also help explain the expansion of company-paid benefits. During the war, when union-management negotiations became deadlocked, both the union and management learned that the offer of or the demand for some special concession like an extra holiday with pay or pay for jury duty would resolve the stalemate. Over a period of time, these concessions increased in number and importance far beyond the expectations of the original negotiators. By the end of World War II, unions had shifted their position dramatically: instead of opposing company welfare programs as paternalistic, they had come to insist on them as the worker's proper due.

Unions also became increasingly skillful in parlaying a fringe benefit offered by one company in lieu of greater wages into similar grants elsewhere. Non-union firms found they had to follow suit if they were to attract labor during this prolonged period of shortage. A great impetus was given to these efforts by a Supreme Court ruling in 1949 that pensions were a bargainable issue. Previously, there had been some doubt that a union could require management to negotiate over pensions. The efforts of the War Labor Board to control inflationary forces by rigidly limiting direct-wage increases also helped turn the attention of both unions and companies to the possibility of providing alternate rewards for labor. To avoid disputes and to provide equity, the WLB provided several rulings on what fringe-benefit settlements it considered appropriate, and in the process it evaluated practices of several of the more progressive firms. This continuing investigation also helped spread the acceptance of fringe benefits. Once granted, these special provisions became firmly rooted among the normal conditions of employment.

Company Attitudes Toward Fringe Benefits

Management as a group has tried to check the expanding role of government by providing private security programs for employees either as a supplement to or as a substitute for the type of public social-security programs established by other countries of the world.

There are very real pressures on management to grant fringe benefits comparable to other firms in the industry or the community, and many such health and welfare plans merely reflect a "follow-the-leader" pattern of adoption. In some instances, both government tax policy and the principle of spreading risk over a large group make it more economical for companies to pay health and welfare benefit costs than for employees to pay them out of their earnings, which are taxable. Many fringe benefits are either not taxed (because they are paid for directly by the employer) or else the tax payment is deferred until a much later period, when the individual's liability may be less (e.g., after retirement).

Our explanations for the growing popularity of fringe benefits have taken us outside the firm to a consideration of broad, cultural trends in the community at large. But are there any reasons why management itself might want to channel off funds that would otherwise go into direct compensation? Many reasons of this sort have been advanced.

MORALE IMPROVEMENT

Employees seek security as well as leisure, and deprivations in either area may lead to paralyzing unrest that reflects itself in decreased effectiveness. Clearly, then, it is to management's advantage to maintain a sound health and welfare program. Furthermore, employees do make coercive comparisons between organizations, and even though the direct wages paid by Company A may be a good bit higher than those paid by Company B— enough higher, in fact, for employees to pay for their own private annuities —Company A employees may still be resentful that they do not have a company-paid pension program like the one offered by Company B.

There is no question that employees have come to expect service and security programs from their employer, and they evaluate their company in terms of its willingness and ability to provide a whole range of vacation-insurance-benefit programs.[8]

Many companies establish recreation programs for a more immediate reason. They view company-sponsored bowling teams, resort facilities, and social clubs as a means of bringing together various levels of the organization in an informal, pleasant environment. When supervisors share common team membership with their subordinates, it is hoped that human relations will improve.

But many observers are critical of this approach. Free time, they argue, should give employees an opportunity to express a diversity of interests—

---

[8] The attractiveness of these programs to prospective employees is evidenced by the fact that help-wanted ads tend increasingly to list fringe benefits along with, or even instead of, salary.

going to the theater, attending a ball game, sitting at home and reading, or tending the garden. Especially when conformity is required on the job, free time should enable individuals to strike out on their own, unencumbered by company influence. The American tradition of pluralism—with its emphasis on varied groups competing for the interests and affiliations of citizens—is endangered when companies, or unions for that matter, try to exercise control over the leisure-time activities of individual workers.[9]

Organized recreational activities are based on the assumption that most employees have the same interests and motivations. Sometimes company-sponsored activities take on a note of compulsion, even though management intends them to be voluntary.[10] Many employees resent being forced to attend after-hours social events conducted by the company.

Further, some programs go so far in their effort to provide employees with security and welfare benefits that they smother the individual. By providing lavish health, recreational, and educational benefits, the firm may foster a sense of overdependence among some employees and a destructive resentment against excessive paternalism among others. Company programs also may weaken the community's efforts to stimulate citizen participation in its own programs.

Sooner or later, each company must decide how much is "enough" and how much is "too much." It must decide where the line should be drawn between services and programs that ought to be provided by the family, the community, and church and political organizations, and services that ought to be provided by the firm. The simple criterion of "satisfying employee needs" is not adequate. Human wants are multitudinous, and dissatisfaction that will affect job performance may come from many sources beyond the reach of management. Few companies would want to involve themselves in marital or religious problems, for example.

Services designed to build employee morale may backfire with disastrous effect, as some companies that operate plants overseas or in company towns have discovered. Service programs that provide housing, food, schools, and the like often develop into rich sources of worker grievances. When is it "fair" for the company to raise house rentals or the price of food in the company restaurant? How often should hash be served? Even when the company funnels substantial amounts of money into such programs, they persist as sources of discontent and petty grousing. Understandably, many firms are eager to cede responsibility for them to the employees themselves in order to save time, energy, and morale.

---

[9] An elegant statement of this point of view is provided by Dr. Clark Kerr, President of the University of California, in his article "What Became of the Independent Spirit?" in *Fortune*, Vol. 48, No. 1 (July 1953), pp. 110-111, 134-136.

[10] See Conrad Arensberg, "Work and the Changing American Scene," in *Research in Industrial Human Relations*, C. Arensberg, *et al.*, eds. (New York: Harpers, 1957), pp. 57-68.

EMPLOYEE REHABILITATION

A somewhat narrower objective of many service and benefit programs is to help employees meet personal problems that may affect their job performance. Adequate insurance programs, for example, will alleviate fears about being able to meet high medical expenses.

Many companies also provide a limited amount of health, legal, and personal counseling in an effort to help employees with minor problems. In effect, the company serves as a detection station, and genuinely troubled employees are urged to get professional help. It is thus hoped that lingering unattended-to personal problems will be avoided and employees will maintain a healthier personal outlook. Medical, legal, and social-work groups in the community at large are not enthusiastic about company programs that threaten to usurp their functions, however, and enlightened companies are careful not to invade professional preserves.

Our own attitude is that services of this type should be kept at a minimum except in situations where employees cannot procure them for themselves. In isolated locations, for example, where the work involves unusual health or legal hazards, in-company service programs may be almost obligatory. It seems regrettable, however, to discourage employees from taking responsibility for their own affairs. They are not dependent children, and they need not be protected from *every* hazard. Some employees who fail to take care of themselves may turn out to be inefficient workers, but the cost of assuming full responsibility for their welfare may prove far in excess of the benefits enjoyed either by them or by the company.

BENEFITS AS A REWARD FOR SERVICE

Many fringe benefits are weighted to favor the senior employee. The length of vacations and the amount of pension benefits, for example, increase with length of service. In fact, some plans specify that employees will lose all their pension and savings credits if they leave the company before reaching retirement age. These programs, it is felt, reward long service and discourage turnover, and are a necessary concomitant to sound policies of management development and promotion from within.

Yet fringe benefits too heavily weighted in favor of long-service employees have certain drawbacks: they may discourage employees from leaving who ought to leave, and they may make it difficult for the company to discharge unsatisfactory employees who have accumulated rights to substantial benefits. Moreover, they tend to make the methods of measuring seniority bones of contention within the organization.

Management can escape these disadvantages by easing the rigid relationship between length of service and benefits received. For example, it can extend to employees the privilege of taking with them company contributions to the pension plan if they decide to leave for another job. This practice, which is called "vesting," provides for employee equity in pension contributions *before* retirement age. Vesting privileges increase company pension costs substantially, perhaps as much as 40 per cent over the cost of non-vested pension plans. The reason for this is quite simple: many employees normally leave the firm before retirement and their pension costs are returned to the company.

In some industries there is a great deal of employee mobility—for example, in construction, clothing manufacture, and entertainment. Here the unions have negotiated industry-wide pension agreements which provide that an employee will retain all his pension credits as he moves from employer to employer within a given industry. Most pension plans, however, provide that an employee will receive benefits only if he stays on with the company to the age of retirement.[11]

Vesting is used at executive levels as well as at lower levels in the hierarchy:

> [Some executives] see liberal vesting as a way of easing out executives who don't make the grade. The president of a billion dollar oil company which has adopted liberal vesting puts it in these terms: Take a 50-year old vice-president who has been with the company 20 years but isn't pulling his weight in his new post. If the company fired him, the officer wouldn't get a dime's pension; few other companies would take him on because he represents too large a pension cost.
>
> But with liberal vesting, the officer could retire right now on a tidy pension or go into the job market and tell prospective employers that his retirement was already taken care of.[12]

Unfortunately, however, rewards based on length of service sometimes displace more important incentives. Fringe benefits that are bestowed equally upon all employees, regardless of merit (e.g., company-paid hospitalization), or are given in proportion to length of service (e.g., vacations), fail to reflect the difference between the good and the mediocre employee. And the dramatic growth in the value of savings-pension funds may even encourage employees to look forward to retirement benefits as their major compensation.[13] Programs of this sort clearly do little to motivate superior performance.

---

[11] Of course, many plans do make provision for early retirement for health reasons after a minimum number of years of service.

[12] "Most vesting schedules provide for gradual acquisition of a 100% status—say, 25% after five years' service, 50% after 10. . . . ," *Business Week*, "Those Startling Private Pension Plans" (January 31, 1959), pp. 102-103.

[13] A recent newspaper account reported that a truck driver with 44 years of service with Sears Roebuck retired with accrued profit sharing-pension benefits of $289,000 (including contributions of $5,928 from his own wages).

FACILITATING TRANSITION PERIODS

Management may also use benefit programs as a device for easing the employee's transition from one status to another.[14] For example, an unavoidable shift from regular employment to unemployment may be softened by means of severance pay plans, supplementary unemployment benefits, and loan programs. Similarly, a pension plan will safeguard the welfare of employees who are obliged to retire at some specified age (typically between 65 and 70).

Another forced transition for employees—one that is likely to be a traumatic experience for them—occurs when a company announces the permanent closing of one of its plants. In fact, some companies procrastinate in making this decision, even though it is ultimately unavoidable, because of the dire effect it will have on the community and on its own reputation. Severance-pay plans that provide for lump-sum payments to permanently discharged employees help to reduce this shock considerably.

Many companies absorb the cost of retraining employees in an effort to encourage them to improve their abilities on their present job or to prepare themselves for a shift to a more responsible post. Finally, management can facilitate the movement of employees to a new plant by paying the costs of moving and re-establishing their homes.

In the process of facilitating the accommodation of employees to change, these benefit programs also simplify many managements decisions. For example, pension plans specifying compulsory retirement at a given age have these advantages:

1. Management does not have to make the difficult and controversial decision as to when each employee is no longer able to work effectively or as to when his health would be endangered by continued employment.

2. The approximate costs for retirement benefits can be estimated and budgeted in advance for the total organization.

3. Promotion steps are opened up automatically, as senior employees retire, thus providing "new blood" for the organization and an incentive for younger employees.

Recently, however, there has been growing criticism of mandatory retirement. Not everyone grows old at the same rate, and chronological age may be a poor measure of vigor and effectiveness. A man who is forced to retire at an age when he is still active and vigorous undergoes a severe shock, and may find it impossible to compensate for the loss of the social and egoistic satisfactions that come from regular work. Moreover, the economic costs of premature retirement are high, both for the company and for the economy. The

---

[14] This philosophy contrasts sharply with the earlier attitude that people should prepare themselves for any and all contingencies by exercising thrift and frugality.

valuable skills of a highly experienced employee are lost, and the long-range costs of his pension are proportionately higher. If a man is able and willing to work beyond the normal retirement age, it would seem unwise to cut off his employment arbitrarily.

It seems likely that the practice of mandatory retirement will be significantly modified in the years ahead. For example, an employee may be permitted to retire at 65 with full benefits, but may be permitted to stay on to 70 if he passes an annual physical examination. Or he may be required to take a longer vacation each year after he reaches a certain age.

AVOIDING INDIVIDUAL DISCRIMINATION

Prior to the widespread adoption of the various plans we have been discussing, a good many benefits were provided voluntarily by charitably disposed companies. Conscientious owners and managers lent money to long-service employees who found themselves in economic straits as a result of illness, injury, or layoff. And many firms extended pension benefits and regular holidays as a matter of company largess. But, since employees had no established rights to these benefits, they were susceptible to gross discrimination. The regularized company policies and contractual obligations of recent years have served to eliminate the possibility of such discrimination.

Unfortunately, however, even formal, contractual programs give rise to charges of inequity, for not everyone benefits equally from them. Some employees are far more interested in present income than in future benefits, and they feel that they are being penalized by the growing emphasis on pension and savings programs. In addition, differences in age, health, length of service, size of family, and sex have a significant effect on the amount of benefit individual workers derive from such programs. For example, the introduction of supplemental unemployment benefits which cost about 5 cents per employee hour has caused dissension among many senior employees. Why? Because it is the less-senior employees who are most likely to become unemployed and thus derive benefit from these programs.

Conflicting claims also arise among various groups whenever a company installs a medical or insurance program. If wives and children are to be insured, for example, money will go to them that might otherwise have been devoted to higher benefits for older workers.

IMPROVING PUBLIC RELATIONS

Generous fringe benefits help create a more favorable "image" of the company in the eyes of the public, thus making it easier for management to recruit high-caliber employees and to maintain amicable relationships with the entire community. Like fair wages and salaries, adequate health and welfare programs impress the community with the value of the firm, particularly as these programs become more widely identified with what constitutes a "good company." [15]

Problems of Administration

Fringe benefits give rise to many complex administrative problems. Here we can suggest only a few of the types of problem that administrators of benefit programs must face.

EMPLOYEE PARTICIPATION

Where possible, employees should participate in these programs. The management of recreation programs, in particular, should be taken over by employees *on their own time*. If they show themselves unwilling to spend the necessary time and effort to put a program across, this should be a clear sign that the program has not elicited enough interest to warrant its continuance.

The fact that employees have accepted responsibility spares the company many time-consuming and embarrassing decisions. Should Bill Jones be replaced by Sam Smith as first baseman on the company ball team? Should the bowling uniforms be financed by the welfare fund, or should this fund be reserved for activities that benefit all employees? Similarly, an employee-managed credit union saves the company from having to make difficult decisions in extending and collecting emergency loans.

Finally, most people are far more appreciative of what they have done for themselves than of what has been done for them. Employee control tempers the resentment against paternalism that is directed toward many fringe-benefit activities.

EMPLOYEE FINANCING

Should employees make any contribution to the expense of the firm's benefit programs? If they do not share in the costs, they tend to forget how expensive the programs are. Free programs are often "taken for granted," and, since the employees carry none of the financial burden, their demands become more and more unrealistic. As we have already suggested, employees should be made to realize that the money going into these plans is an alternative to higher wages and salaries. Having employees share the costs also

---

[15] Increasingly, unions are competing with management in developing benefit programs that will attract employee and community interest. Union-sponsored hospitals and clinics which provide health services at substantial reductions, or at no cost at all, to union members, and even subsidized vacation resorts, are becoming common.

makes it possible to adjust assessments to the benefits received—this elimi-nates some of the discriminatory features of benefit plans.

On the other hand, most unions and employees are strongly opposed to "contributory" programs. Of course, we have already mentioned the tax advantage—company contributions are usually not taxable as income to the employee (except after pensions are received as income). Moreover, since many employees feel that they have earned the benefits that are granted, they cannot understand why they should pay part of the cost any more than they pay part of their own wages.[16]

In attempts to dramatize to employees the expense of fringe benefits, management can present costs as:

> Cents per hour per employee.
> Percentage of total annual payroll.
> Cost per employee per year.
> Annual cost of benefits for all employees.

Many companies also issue an annual report to each employee summarizing the total amount contributed in his name to various benefit funds, as well as the current status of his pension accumulation, insurance protection, vacation allowance, and so on. Some of these reports seek to highlight how much of the company's total expenditure for each employee never appears on his paycheck. Others are designed to provide a simple accounting of the employee's current status in the programs and to summarize the company's contributions. For example, Eastman Kodak sends its employees a form that includes such items as these:

1. Your group life insurance coverage for this year.
2. Your monthly contribution for life insurance.
3. Your total annuity up to this date.
4. The amount of annuity accredited to you this year.
5. The length of vacation to which you are eligible this year.
6. The percentage of your normal pay, payable for sickness allowance as of this date.
7. The number of weeks of sickness allowance for which you are eligible as of this date.

Of course, in all these efforts the hope is that employee demands will be moderated by the realization that benefit programs are an *alternative* to higher wages and salaries. It is unlikely, however, that techniques of this sort will diminish employee pressure for increased contributions to these programs. As we noted in Chapter 1, more generous fringe benefits may simply be regarded as a substitute for other forms of advancement.

---

[16] These sentiments are strengthened by the union practice of announcing welfare gains at the same time as, or in place of, wage gains: "We got 5 cents in direct wage improvement and another 5 cents to be applied to our insurance and pension plan." Any added benefit is usually described as being worth x cents per hour.

ELIGIBILITY

Which employees are eligible for fringe benefits? The answer to this question has a profound effect on the cost of the programs. The more liberal the eligibility rules, the higher the cost. For example, companies usually try to restrict pay for a particular holiday to employees who were in attendance both before and after the holiday. Otherwise employees might be tempted to convert the holiday into a vacation by taking several days off. Similarly, sickness benefits must be carefully controlled in order to keep employees from taking advantage of them. Some companies do not pay for the first day or even the first week of illness. Others require that the company nurse visit the employee's home to make sure that he is not malingering.

Attempts by employees to discover loopholes in benefit plans also contribute substantially to their cost. The company may find itself paying out benefits that are not deserved, and it may also have to spend extra money for "control" purposes—that is, checking holiday-pay records, administering sick pay, and so on. Conflicts over eligibility sometimes lead to bad feelings, complaints, and union grievances—all of which are threats to morale.

How would you decide such cases as these:

1. Jones claims holiday pay for the Fourth of July, even though he failed to report for work on the third. His reason: his car broke down.
2. Smith claims sickness pay, although when the nurse dropped in to see him he was not at home. His explanation: sick as he was, he had to take his wife to visit her invalid mother.

Checking up in order to test the validity of such excuses is an extremely unpleasant and time-consuming task.

Claims for overtime allowances are also a source of trouble. There are hundreds of claims that cannot be predicted in the formal agreement setting forth the conditions under which such premiums should be paid. For example, Brown is asked to come in an hour early to do some work before the start of his regular shift, but he is permitted to leave an hour early at the close of the day. Is he entitled to "overtime"?

In almost every other type of company benefit program the answer to the question: "Who is eligible to receive these benefits?" will have a major impact on its cost.

Special Financial Problems

Management must recognize that when it introduces a benefit plan it commits some part of the firm's future economic resources. Even where there is no legal obligation to do so, employees often feel that management has made a moral commitment to continue the program indefinitely. Before entering into a program, then, management should make a thorough, realistic evaluation of its cost, both short-term and long-term.

DIFFICULTY OF COMPUTING COSTS

It is extremely difficult for management to make accurate cost predictions for fringe-benefit programs. Before deciding to grant a 5-cent per hour wage increase, management can estimate quite accurately the resulting additional labor costs it will incur. But this is not true when it is contemplating benefit programs. For example:

1. The cost of a pension plan is directly influenced by the rate of turnover. If a great many employees leave the company before they are eligible for their pensions, and if the plan does not provide for vesting, the costs will be relatively low. But if most employees stay with the company until pension benefits become due, the costs will be relatively high.

2. Similarly, the cost of sick-pay benefits depends on the incidence of illness; the cost of severance pay on the number of employees dropped from the employment rolls.

3. Many states review the turnover record of a given company in determining how much the company should be assessed for the unemployment insurance fund. Employers with low turnover pay relatively less than employers with high turnover.

4. Many pension plans used to, and some still do, provide for a certain monthly payment at retirement *less* any social security payments to which the retired worker is entitled. Consequently, as federal law governing social security payments was progressively liberalized, employer contributions to company pension funds were progressively reduced.

5. Changing interest rates in the economy affect the premiums that companies have to pay for privately financed insurance programs.

6. Each company may choose from among many alternative means of financing the more expensive types of benefit programs. Pensions, for example, may be financed on a pay-as-you-go basis, which means that the company incurs a direct cost only as each employee retires and begins to receive pension payments. Other companies "fund" their plans—that is, they make regular payments to a pension account during the working life of each employee (typically, a certain percentage of his income or so many cents per hour). These funds are administered either by the company or jointly by the company and the union. Still other companies engage a bank or an insurance company to serve as trustee of the fund or to sell policies (annuities) with regular premiums, as a means of accumulating the reserves from which payments to retired employees will eventually be made.

These alternative means of financing involve very different costs, produce very different tax benefits, and have very different effects on the capital and liquidity of the organization. Understandably, the difficult decisions that must be made in instituting a coherent benefit program are commonly entrusted to experts. We cannot deal with these complex questions here, but they are adequately covered in more specialized publications.[17]

Management has made some effort to stabilize its financial position vis-à-vis benefit programs by specifying fixed costs at the outset, particularly in plans negotiated with a union. Rather than guaranteeing to provide certain health and welfare benefits, for example, management promises to contribute 5 cents an hour to a health and welfare fund. The sum thus accumulated is invested at going market rates, and the income is used to defray the cost of the benefits.

CREEPING COSTS

One reason for the difficulty in making accurate predictions of the cost of benefit programs is their tendency to grow more and more expensive over time. Pressures from employees who observe "fringe" rewards in other companies, plus the post-World War II inflation, have led to a rapid increase in the cost of pension and insurance plans. Moreover, many unions are striving for pension benefits that will provide employees with 70 per cent of their pre-retirement income—a much higher percentage than earlier plans provided. Vacation allowances are often liberalized over time, as are provisions for rest periods, recreational activity, and so forth. Furthermore the cost of many benefits goes up automatically as wages and salaries rise. For instance, overtime payments and vacation benefits calculated on the basis of the employee's regular salary increase in direct proportion to increases in his salary level. One company estimates that each 1-cent hourly wage increase brings with it a 0.3-cent increase in fringe benefits.[18]

A 1960 survey concludes that fringe-benefit costs increased 12 per cent during 1959 while direct payroll costs were going up only 8 per cent.[19]

---

[17] See, for example: Jay V. Strong, *Employee Benefit Plans* (Washington, D.C.: Bureau of National Affairs, 1951); "Pension Plans and their Administration," *Studies in Personnel Policy No. 149,* National Industrial Conference Board; Robert Tilove, "Employee Benefit Plans," in *A Decade of Industrial Relations Research,* N. Chamberlain, *et al.,* eds. (New York: Harpers, 1958), pp. 146-173 (Tilove's footnotes at the end of this article provide an excellent current bibliography of materials in this field); "Computing the Cost of Fringe Benefits," *Studies in Personnel Policy No. 128,* National Industrial Conference Board.

[18] National Industrial Conference Board, "Preparing for Collective Bargaining," *Studies in Personnel Policy No. 172,* p. 105. This study is also an excellent summary of the financial details of various benefit programs, and the problems that arise in negotiating these plans with unions.

[19] *The New York Times,* January 11, 1960, p. 89. These figures do not include the full range of fringe benefits cited at the beginning of the chapter; they include only company contributions to: unemployment insurance; old age, survivors', and disability insurance; private pension and welfare plans; and compensation for injuries. In 1959, these items accounted for 6.8 per cent of the total compensation costs of American companies.

Need for Constant Review

If management is to insure that its benefit programs are working out in practice as originally planned, it must subject them to constant review.

A company introduces ten-minute rest periods to reduce worker fatigue. Checks must be made to determine whether these rest periods are being maintained at 10 minutes or are being gradually lengthened, and whether the time chosen is most appropriate for combating fatigue. (In one company, employees were able to convince their supervisor that they should take their rest period as an end-of-the-day wash-up break; here the break no longer served its original purpose.)

A company broadens its health program to include psychotherapy. After the new program has been put into effect, the company should review its records to determine how many employees are using the program and whether it seems to be worth the expense as compared to other benefits that might be obtained at the same cost.

A company that provides extensive out-patient services may decide to alter its insurance plan in order to discourage the use of expensive hospital facilities and encourage the use of clinics.

The trend toward vacations involving long-distance travel may make it desirable for the company to shut down its summer camp, since it is being used by only a small proportion of the work force.

ANALYZING UNDERLYING INCENTIVES PRODUCED BY FRINGE BENEFITS

We have already noted that fringe benefits may shift the balance of incentives away from concern with present performance toward an exaggerated interest in tenure and even in retirement. And there are other "built-in" incentives which management may not at first be aware of, but which may have a major impact on the true cost of the program. Slight adjustments in the way the program is administered will often modify the strength of these incentives.

In reviewing its experience with benefit programs, management may discover that they are actually working against other company objectives. For example, the provision of fully paid sick leaves may encourage employees to take time off even when they are not ill. This practice impairs production, saddles supervision with the continuing problem of finding temporary replacements, and creates a double cost: sick pay plus lost time. Consequently, management may decide to experiment with ways of changing the direction of this built-in incentive. Some companies, for example, have found that by permitting employees to convert, at predetermined intervals, a certain portion of their sick leave into additional holiday pay, over-all costs are reduced and unnecessary absenteeism is discouraged.

Companies in the glass industry have experimented with a scheme whereby individual employee accounts are set up to cover supplementary unemployment benefits. Any money that is not needed for this purpose may be used by the employee to improve his pension payments or even to augment his savings. This arrangement provides employees with an incentive to help management in its efforts to stabilize employment and to perform more effectively in a competitive market.

The 1959-60 steel industry negotiations introduced another innovation. As we have seen, the costs of company welfare plans are highly uncertain, since they depend on the incidence of illness, accidents, and so forth. Under the agreement worked out between the steel companies and the Steelworkers' Union, increases in certain welfare benefits beyond a specified cents-an-hour amount will be paid to employees as an alternative to raises in hourly wages stemming from increases in the cost of living.

Sometimes a relatively small group of employees receive much more than their proper share of a benefit plan, to the disadvantage of others. For example, readily available compensation benefits for injuries may actually induce a few workers to injure themselves or to fake accidents. The company should make clear to the entire work force just how the costs of these unnecessary benefits penalize more honest employees. Hopefully, group pressure will be exerted on the offending employees, and management will be supported in its attempts to discourage malingering through disciplinary action.

In short, management should try to impress employees with the true cost of benefit programs, and should get them to understand that the elimination of unnecessary or frivolous expenditures will make more money available for other benefits.

Relationship to the Over-all Personnel Program

Benefit programs are an integral part of the over-all personnel program; they cannot be considered in isolation. As an example, let us look at some of the programs that have been developed to deal with the problem of alcoholism in industry.[20]

Some companies take the position that alcoholism is strictly a private matter, at least until it becomes chronic. When it does become chronic, even a long-service, loyal employee must be discharged, because his problem now affects his job performance.

As an alternative to this highly "laissez-faire" approach, other companies now treat alcoholics as *both* a medical *and* a disciplinary problem.

---

[20] Our discussion here has benefited from the work of Harrison Trice, particularly his informative study, *The Problem Drinker on the Job,* Bulletin No. 40 (Ithaca, N.Y.: New York State School of Industrial and Labor Relations, 1959).

1. They train supervisors to detect incipient cases and to report them to the personnel department.

2. They require the supervisor to discuss the problem with the offending employee, pointing out that his unsatisfactory performance and excessive absenteeism will lead to penalties and eventually to discharge. They have trained counselors or members of the medical staff to encourage the employee to undertake appropriate treatment, making it clear that the company is willing to help but that it is also the responsibility of the employee to help himself.

3. They help the employee arrange for treatment either from trained personnel within the organization (usually medical personnel with special training in problems of alcoholism) or in the community (clinics, groups like A.A., and so forth).

4. They involve the union as an ally in detecting alcoholics and in rehabilitating them. Stewards are sometimes able to convince the employee that he will lose his job unless he gets his problem under control. Early involvement of the union may help forestall grievances later on.

5. They establish clear policies specifying who is responsible for counseling alcoholics and what benefit programs (such as health insurance and leave of absence) are available to afflicted employees.

We have used alcoholism simply as an example of the close relationship that exists between any specific area of employee services and the entire range of company service and personnel programs. Notice that this one example has impinged on a whole range of policies and activities: discipline, supervisory training, union-management relations, the role of staff groups like the employee-relations and medical departments, and the availability of company insurance and leave of absence. Many policy decisions need to be made concerning who is going to take initiative and responsibility for conducting all the various parts of any service program. In addition, it should be clear that these programs very quickly require significant company expenditures, not only for executive time consumed in their administration, but for record-keeping, special facilities, and so forth.

Conclusion

Managers wise in the ways of personnel relations will undertake a variety of programs to insure that the working environment is conducive to superior job performance. Working conditions, quality of supervision, selection, training, and promotion programs—all are designed to develop a quality of human relationships within the organization that will motivate workers and provide need satisfaction.

But why should management want to do more than simply provide adequate wages and salaries in return for satisfactory job performance? Isn't management's primary role to produce goods or services for some body of consumers? True, employees must be recruited and encouraged to stay with the firm. But isn't it enough just to pay them a fair day's wage for a fair day's work? In this chapter we have tried to present the answers to questions of this sort.

And yet a sound, realistic personnel program cannot be based on the simple prescription: we shall satisfy our employees. Human wants and problems are multitudinous and diverse. The family, the community, and social, religious, and political organizations provide services and assistance that no company could or would want to provide. Child-rearing, religious, and legal problems, for example, are in general outside the province of the firm. Management must realize, however, that there is no sharp dividing line between the job and home, for domestic fears about illness and security have a direct impact on the employee's ability to work effectively.

But management must draw the line somewhere. At what point should it say, "This is an employee problem that we will have nothing to do with?" This is a question that every organization must answer for itself.

Few observers doubt that employee benefit and service programs will continue to grow in importance. A minority says, "I would ask business to revert to the view that labor is a factor of production . . . to buy the labor power of the worker and to leave his psyche alone." [21] Whether or not this attitude seems realistic to you will depend on your attitude toward the whole area of personnel administration. In any case, it seems clear that the problems of administering employee benefit and service programs are among the most difficult personnel problems confronting management.

Problem I

The ABC Company decides that it will cooperate with a community-wide program to "hire the handicapped." The company agrees to seek out jobs that can be done by workers with eye-and-limb handicaps and to try to recruit suitable candidates from the community.

1. What jobs should be selected? Who decides? According to what criteria?
2. How should pay rates be determined for these jobs? Who decides? According to what criteria?
3. Who makes the hiring decisions? According to what criteria?
4. What additional safety and insurance provisions will be required?
5. What impact will the program have on present employees? On their seniority? On their promotional opportunities?
6. What role, if any, should the union have in implementing the program?

---

[21] Clark Kerr, *op. cit.*

Problem II

The Wilton Plastic Company is located in a community of 20,000 and employs 500 people. The only golf club in the community is about to go bankrupt and can be purchased at a "sacrifice price."

   1. What criteria should the company use in deciding whether to buy the club for its employees?

Problem III

Your plant is located in a medium-size midwestern city. It employs 800 workers. You have recently received a petition signed by 200 employees requesting that an annual Catholic holiday be observed as a company-wide paid holiday. At the present time you have six paid holidays. You have only a modest allowance for fringe benefits. Two smaller companies in the area observe this day as a paid holiday, but other large firms in the community do not recognize it as such. About 70 per cent of your employees are Catholics, and half of them have children in parochial schools that give the day off.

   1. Should the company grant this request?
   2. What additional information would you want before making a decision?
   3. What criteria would you use in making the decision?
   4. If you granted the day as a holiday, would you be willing to give compensating time off for workers who do not celebrate it? (Christmas is a paid holiday, although 10 per cent of the employees are of Jewish origin.)
   5. If the union had made a formal request on this issue during negotiations, would your decision be any different?
   6. What difference would it make if this were a branch of a multi-unit company, with other plants in communities in which there were few Catholics?

Problem IV

The Faraday Insurance Company undertook a blood-bank program in response to what seemed to be an important employee need. When a company employee or a member of his family was ill and required a transfusion, one or more other employees who had voluntarily signed up would be called by the company personnel office to report to one of the local hospitals. Recently, the Personnel Department has noted that the costs of this program are greater than originally anticipated. Often a great many telephone calls have to be made before a donor can be located. This task requires almost the full-time services of one clerk. Moreover, some donors do not return to work until the next day, even though the transfusion has been given in the morning, and overtime replacements have to be brought in.

   1. How would you weigh the cost of this program against the benefits it provides?
   2. Is there any way of cutting costs without nullifying the advantages of the program and without damaging the company's reputation?

MANAGEMENT'S RESPONSIBILITIES

It may seem strange to elevate a single chapter to the level of a "part" of our book. But it seemed appropriate to us to "step back" from the pressures of day-to-day personnel problems to ask some broader questions. Although it would be presumptuous of us to refer to this last chapter as a philosophical treatment of "management's responsibilities in dealing with people," we have at least tried to suggest some of the long-range implications of these responsibilities. At some point the administrator has to ask himself what *values* he will observe in making human-relations decisions. How should he weigh "human" against "profit" considerations? Should he even try to weigh them? These are not easy questions to answer, although many critics of business, and many businessmen themselves, are quick to criticize contemporary trends in the personnel and human-relations field. Many of these criticisms are reviewed here.

nlike such specialties as engineering or finance, personnel administration involves the management of *human beings*. The engineer, for instance, need never give a thought to the impact his maintenance program will have on the "personality" of his equipment. The accountant busies himself with tractable, obedient figures. But the manager must keep himself constantly alert to the impact of personnel administration on the employee as an individual and as a citizen. And he must understand the subtle relationships that prevail between corporate efficiency and employee satisfaction.

Historical Perspective

For hundreds of years, managers have been aware of their special obligations to employees. The early New England textile manufacturer, for example, often provided elaborate opportunities for his "charges" (typically young girls) to worship and to gain an education. Some owners, of course, were flagrantly paternalistic—eager to extend benefits in order to receive praise for their

31

Management's Responsibilities in Dealing with People

generosity. But even the worst of the "robber barons" might provide housing facilities, grant Christmas gifts, and distribute other forms of largess to those who worked for him. By the 1920's many companies had institutionalized these obligations by establishing a special department—the personnel department—to deal with the legitimate needs of their employees. ("Legitimate" needs, as we have seen, were defined in many different ways.)

The personnel department was sometimes regarded as a buffer between management and workers, as the workers' "representative" who could be counted on to intervene on their behalf. Although management often encouraged this attitude simply to keep the union out, there was also a sincere feeling that every organization needed a "conscience," someone who could speak for employees and who would be responsible for their welfare. Many managers genuinely believed that their decisions should be guided by concern for human beings as well as by a desire for profit maximization. In making layoffs, companies often gave special consideration to men with families or with long service, even though they might be less efficient than the men actually dismissed.

Cynics argued that these humanitarian policies were only a reflection of management's deep-seated opposition to unions, or evidence of a selfish desire to raise morale in order to boost productivity. Clearly, however, some managers went beyond dollars-and-cents considerations and were genuinely altruistic. Unfortunately, their gestures of good will and their efforts to be just were haphazard and erratic. John Jones, whose needs happened to come to the attention of top management, received excellent treatment; Gus Smith, who was not quite so lucky, lost his job, even though his claim for consideration was as valid as Jones'. Some personnel directors proved effective spokesmen for employees; others had neither the interest nor the ability to do so.

In more recent years the rule of law has been substituted for individual decision-making. The rights of employees have come to be guaranteed either by union contracts or by explicit management policies, and specific rules now protect employees from discrimination in such areas as wages, promotions, and discipline.

Satisfaction vs. Profitability

And yet the rules, contract clauses, and precedents still do not furnish a ready answer to one critically important question: What are the legitimate needs of employees, and when is it justifiable to put those needs aside in favor of the profit needs of the company? Unfortunately, most personnel problems still cannot be resolved simply by reading the company manual or the union contract. And the most important problems of all have a dismaying tendency to crop up between the rules, in the uncharted territory where there are no clear precedents, no obvious "right" or "wrong" answers.

Since problems of this sort have little meaning in the abstract, let us look at a hypothetical case that will illustrate their very real complexity.

THE DUFFY CASE

Bill Duffy is the head of a clerical department in a large brokerage office. Most of the work is relatively routine though of considerable importance to the company. Duffy's department has always been known for its high morale and for its ability to maintain work schedules.

Duffy started with the company right after finishing high school. Although he is just celebrating his 55th birthday, he has already accumulated about 35 years of seniority. In many ways, he seems much older than his years. He lacks stamina and his thinking processes are slower than those of many of his older colleagues.

Over the past year, the responsibilities of managing the department have been pretty much taken over by the assistant department head, Joe Jenkins. When a difficult problem comes up, the clerks now turn to Joe for an answer. People outside the department also consult Joe when they need advice or help on some special project. Duffy continues to sign forms that need the signature of the department head, and he is consulted as a matter of form on all major policy questions. But Jenkins has become the real head of the department.

At a recent meeting, Bill Duffy's case came before the top management of the firm. A couple of the men present thought that the company should encourage Duffy to accept early retirement, although they recognized that this would be a serious psychological and financial blow to him. His retirement benefits would be less than half of what they would be if he continued to work until he reached 65. It might be possible to demote him to a less responsible position, but there were no jobs open that would fit his capacities. After reconsidering the matter, management decided to retain Duffy in his present position, feeling that too "harsh" an approach to the problem would prompt substantial dissatisfaction in the organization. Some questions were raised about Jenkins, but the group decided to postpone consideration of this problem until there was clear evidence that he was dissatisfied with the situation.

What questions have gone unanswered in this case, particularly in the relationship between individual needs and organizational goals? What decision would good personnel policy have suggested? What criteria should have been used in reaching that decision?

Equity considerations and individual satisfaction

1. How much does the company "owe" an employee who has given 35 years of loyal service? What obligation does it have to him?

2. Can this obligation be met in financial terms? What is the relationship between Duffy's dissatisfaction, on the one hand, with being only a "figure head" and his satisfaction, on the other hand, with maintaining his salary and title?

3. Should management adopt a more liberal policy toward early retirement for long-service employees who become "disabled"?

4. Is it fair to Jenkins, whose salary is approximately 30 per cent lower than Duffy's, to let him assume the responsibilities of a managerial job without granting him the prestige and economic rewards that normally go with it?

Organization and profit considerations

1. What effect would Duffy's forced retirement have on the morale and performance of other long-service employees? Would it be more harmful than their realization that inefficiency and ineptness are protected by the fiction of having a formal department head and a real one? What impact will management's decision have on employees' attitudes toward opportunities for promotion?

2. What would be the long-run costs of establishing more liberal early-retirement benefits? How would these costs compare with the apparent savings offered by the present policy?

3. What is the effect on department efficiency of having two managers? Can Duffy's salary be justified in terms of the contribution he is making?

4. Will management's decision have any effect on the company's ability to recruit highly motivated young men?

These are only a few of the highly complex questions raised by this case. Note that some of them are related to the short-run or immediate repercussions of the decision and others to its long-run implications. All, however, involve certain intangibles, conjectures, and risks. Management is constantly obliged to weigh individual welfare against company efficiency.

In short, this case, like a host of similar cases, raises two fundamental problems: (1) How much importance should management ascribe to efficiency as against human satisfaction, and where does one draw the line? And (2), assuming that management can resolve this first problem, what are the best ways of achieving maximum efficiency and maximum human satisfaction?

In the process of trying to solve these problems, management must take into account all the factors that we have discussed in the preceding chapters. What at first glance appears to be a single personnel problem is normally intertwined with a whole host of other personnel problems. This case, for example, is tied in with the company's promotion policy as well as with its policies on fringe benefits (pensions and severance pay). Also involved are job evaluation, recruitment, organizational structure, individual needs and motivations, and the attitudes of the work group.

The manager must constantly seek to resolve the diverse and conflicting claims of individuals and groups both in the short run and in the long run. And yet, since he cannot ascribe exact weights to each factor, or predict the future with any real accuracy, he must rely heavily on intuition, personal judgment, and probability.

Nor do employee needs and company needs fit into neat, separate compartments. There is no simple answer to what course of action is "equitable" or what decisions will improve "efficiency," for the two objectives are intimately associated. There are very few decisions that affect employee satisfaction which do not also have a direct bearing on work efficiency.

The Contemporary Scene:
How Much Human Relations?

In recent years management has undoubtedly begun to show greater concern for the welfare of its employees. True, strong unions, government regulations, and labor shortages have contributed heavily to this shift in attitude, but enlightened executives are sincere in their acceptance of human relationships as a vital part of managerial responsibility. In fact, the human-relations movement has profoundly altered the qualities that have traditionally been associated with the successful business leader. No longer is he judged solely on his drive, ambition, decisiveness, or ability to make money. Now he is also expected to develop cooperative, satisfying relationships within the organization.

Both the economic position and the psychological position of subordinates have improved tremendously over the last generation. The emphasis on human relations has tended to take the bite out of authority and the harshness out of arbitrary rules; it has promoted compassion and dignity at the work place. There is less likelihood of arbitrary discharge, less discrimination in handing out rewards. Work loads are easier and supervision is fairer. At least in larger companies, employees have ample opportunity to protest inequities through union or company grievance procedures. No one would pretend that we have achieved Utopia, but tremendous progress has been made.

Recently, however, the human-relations approach to management has been subjected to a sustained and unexpectedly strong attack from observers who stress efficiency and productivity above all other management objectives. These criticisms, which have come from many sources, reduce themselves to the following charges:

1. The human-relations approach tends to complicate what are essentially very simple problems. All that is required in dealing with people is honest common sense and the application of the golden rule.

2. The human-relations approach leads management to interfere in the personal life of employees, to take over community functions, and to encroach on areas that are outside the province of the business organization.

3. The human-relations approach is immoral, since it manipulates people and dupes them into accepting changes that really are against their best interests.

4. By overemphasizing people at the expense of productivity, the human-relations approach may prove disastrous to the organization.

Let us look briefly at each of these charges. Since they are so commonly leveled, the student of personnel administration—whether in the university or the business firm—must expect to run across them in one form or another.

DOES THE HUMAN-RELATIONS APPROACH COMPLICATE SIMPLE PROBLEMS?

Recently in a talk before a group of businessmen, we tried to explain how complicated human relations really are; we emphasized all the factors that the manager should take into account before he makes a decision involving people. We felt reasonably proud of our presentation, but our complacency was shattered during the discussion period by the following comment from the floor: "Professor, doesn't everything you say boil down to the golden rule? I've had forty years' experience in industry and I've found that the important thing is to be honest and sincere with people. Show an interest in them and you'll never have any human-relations problems."

But are sincerity and good will enough? We think not. Remember the Duffy case.

The findings of modern psychology suggest that applying the golden rule is just too simple an approach, mainly because it assumes that everyone has identical needs. It encourages the superior to treat his employees as if they had the same desire to compete and get ahead as he has. But many people have very different motivations: they prefer group solidarity to individual achievement.

We do not believe that most personnel problems can be dealt with simply, even by men of good will. In the Duffy case, for example, a great deal of insight into the total organizational situation would be required before management could make a truly ethical decision. Is it more ethical to transfer an older employee to a lower-paying job, or to terminate his employment and give him early-retirement benefits?

Unless management is aware of the impact of each decision on the individual and on the group, it cannot know whether it is acting to the advantage or to the detriment of the members of the organization. It is not enough to ask, "How would I want to be treated in a similar situation?" This projection of oneself into the position of the other person may lead to unwise and highly unjust actions. Individuals differ one from the other, and the supervisor who seeks to act ethically in his relationships with subordinates must be willing to look at life through their eyes as well as through his own. Accurate knowledge about the human relations within the organization is as important as the desire to behave ethically.

Many disastrous mistakes are made with the best of intentions. A kindhearted supervisor decides not to penalize an employee who has family troubles even though he is persistently late and fails to meet production standards. The situation grows worse and worse until finally the employee is discharged. Were the supervisor's intentions good? Of course they were. But they led him to injure both the individual and the organization. No businessman really lets concern for others control everything he does. Were he completely motivated by charity and altruism, he would never try to take business away from a competitor and he would never discipline a subordinate. What the ethically motivated businessman *does* believe is that he should take into account the welfare of others *along with* other factors.

DOES THE HUMAN-RELATIONS APPROACH INVOLVE MANIPULATION?

Personnel administrators are often charged with trying to manipulate their employees.

> In many cases human relations has been used or is intended to be used, to manipulate, to adjust people to what the boss thinks is reality, to make them conform to a pattern that seems logical from the top down, to make them accept unquestioningly what we tell them.[1]

> The . . . evil of the "human relations" fad is its repeated violation of the dignity of the individual. It becomes a technique for manipulating people. There are certain areas that should be free of the boss's review and his standards of performance. Today, we stick our noses into other people's business, analyzing their motives and judging their lives. We should be able to take a man at face value and not always fret about what he really means. Too many of us are trying to be little tin Freuds . . . consciously trying to be a gentleman. If it doesn't come from the heart, it is phony.[2]

It is claimed that such techniques as non-directive interviewing and group decision-making are designed to get employees to do things they don't want to do, or at least that they don't realize they are doing. A familiar example is the supervisor who pretends to be interested in his subordinates

---

[1] Peter F. Drucker, "Human Relations: How Far Do We Have to Go?" *Management Record* (March, 1959).

[2] Malcolm P. McNair, "Too Much 'Human Relations'?" *Look* (October 28, 1958).

and to consult with them, but only in order to disguise his essentially authoritarian approach.

Fortunately, most employees are quick to spot insincerity. Gimmicks and deceit are soon exposed, as some companies have learned to their sorrow. The only group that is duped is management itself, which has underestimated the intelligence of its employees.

We see little danger that brainwashing, mass persuasion, or subliminal suggestion will win much acceptance in personnel administration. The power of suggestion may be quite effective in persuading a customer to buy one brand of cigarettes rather than another—but this is because cigarette brands are not very different and because most customers have no vested interest in which brand they smoke. Brainwashing may change basic attitudes in prisoner-of-war camps where the individual is isolated from alternative sources of information. In the typical work situation, however, personnel decisions are of immediate importance to the people involved; employees do have a vested interest in what happens to them on the job. Further, few companies can isolate their employees from other points of view. Whatever the company or the individual supervisor says and does, it is discussed and criticized by employees on the job, by the union, and by other groups in the community. Management's pronouncements can always be checked against the viewpoints of others. Clearly, the employee is not likely to succumb to propaganda; indeed his suspicion is often so great that it is hard for management to get the truth across to him (see Chapter 9), let alone falsehood.

Some critics argue that the supervisor is resorting to manipulation whenever he tries to minimize conflict and gain acceptance for a point of view or for some change. But is there anything objectionable about efforts to weigh alternative courses of action and to select the one that avoids personnel problems? Is it not, rather, highly desirable for management to enlarge its perspective to include rational solutions to its human-relations problems? In short, are not human relations deserving of as much careful attention as engineering and finance?

HOW GREAT ARE THE SOCIAL OBLIGATIONS OF BUSINESS?

With the rapid advance in the size and influence of American industry there has arisen a vigorous debate over its proper responsibilities toward the community as a whole and toward employees and consumers. Rather than repeat all the arguments that have been proffered, we shall concentrate on one issue: Apart from long-run profit maximization and scrupulous observance of the law, what social obligations does management have toward its employees?

There are many who feel that business must concern itself with value questions as well as with economic questions. Because of its size and influence alone, business cannot practically or morally take the position that it has no social responsibility for its actions. Economic and social problems are inextricably interwoven. All business decisions have social consequences, and if management does not take its social obligations seriously government will inevitably impose further restrictions on management's prerogatives. Many of the laws now on the books reflect public outrage over the abuses committed by unrestrained businessmen.

On the other hand, many sincere businessmen feel that business should not pose as the guardian of the general welfare. They, too, argue on practical and moral grounds.

First, they claim that management cannot mediate among the competing claims of stockholders, employees, suppliers, and the community. The businessman owes his first responsibility to the owners of the business, which means that he must devote primary attention to profits and efficiency. When he takes other interests into account, he abdicates that responsibility. In fact, only by concentrating on profits and efficiency can he bestow the greatest benefits on the community as a whole. These observers argue that only then will he make economic use of the company's personnel and material resources, with maximum production and minimum costs.

Second, these critics insist, excessive concern over the individual usually leads to paternalism, with all its attendant evils. Attempts to plumb the employee's personal feelings and attitudes thrust the company into areas that are properly the province of the individual, the family, and the community. (The union adds that only an organization which is directly responsible to workers—that is, the union itself—can protect the individual's welfare consistently and vigorously.)

DOES THE HUMAN-RELATIONS APPROACH
IMPAIR MANAGERIAL EFFICIENCY?

"Management has been sold a bill of goods by human relations. In the process of coddling people it has lost sight of its major objective—getting work accomplished profitably. Management's job is to get the work done and to let employees worry about themselves."

This is the considered view of many critics of the human-relations movement in management.[3]

To assess the validity of this charge, we must place the problem in historical perspective. Only a short time ago business was being accused of neglecting personnel problems. Now it is being accused of ignoring business objectives in its attempts to "coddle" people. Why this remarkable shift?

---

[3] Many criticisms of this sort have appeared in the *Harvard Business Review*; for instance, Malcolm McNair, "Thinking Ahead: What Price Human Relations?" Vol. 35, No. 2 (March-April 1957), pp. 15-39; Robert N. McMurray, "The Case for Benevolent Autocracy," Vol. 36, No. 1 (January-February 1958), pp. 82-90.

Many companies discovered only recently that they had any personnel problems at all. Years ago, when businesses were smaller, most managers (who were also the owners) knew their employees personally and were able to handle problems informally. Turnover was not particularly worrisome, for good replacements were readily available. Unions were weak. Perhaps most important, there was no professional concern with the job of management— certainly not with personnel administration. Businessmen busied themselves with buying and selling in the marketplace and gave little thought to organizational problems. No manager considered himself inept or ineffective simply because he had high turnover or labor strife—this was the fault of weak foremen or troublemakers in the work force.

Today, businesses are large and impersonal. Trained employees are harder to replace, and alert unions are ready to transmute management's mistakes into costly grievances. It is generally accepted that all levels of management have a continuing responsibility for solving human-relations problems—that these are not just transitory phenomena or the result of bad luck.

In the course of this rapid transformation of the executive into a professional, and this rapid acceptance of personnel administration as a management responsibility, it is not surprising that many mistakes have been made. Naive managers seeking quick and easy solutions have been victimized by charlatans. Companies have purchased expensive suggestion systems, engaged zealous speakers, prepared expensive give-away brochures, and have footed the bill for whole kits of supervisory gimmicks in the mistaken belief that there were simple, quasi-mechanical techniques for solving employee-relations problems. Rather than trying to understand the functioning of organizations, the nature of groups, and the importance of individual differences, some companies have gone overboard in embracing such cure-alls as "participative management" or "public speaking for everyone." There has been a regrettable follow-the-leader acceptance of anything called "human relations."

Some managers have simplified human relations to the point of absurdity. They insist that good management is just a matter of liking people and inducing them to like you. "Getting to know your people" is the sure guarantee of success, perhaps tempered by this warning: "Don't get pushy about production; it annoys people."

The principle of two-way communication has been particularly abused. Some authorities seem to assume that all trouble within the organization is purely and simply the result of "misunderstanding." Jones misinterprets Brown's motives and Brown fails to realize that Jones is operating within a different frame of reference. The moment the communication dam is broken, understanding will flood through the organization.

Given this simple definition of the management problem, one might well ask why improvement has been so long in forthcoming. A ready answer is that the human being is recalcitrant, hard to change. Some ardent "human-relationists" throw the whole problem right onto the psychiatrist's couch. There has been a mushrooming of quasi-therapeutic cures for insensitive, uncommunicative people: role-playing, group therapy of one kind or another, sensitivity training, non-directive counseling. Apparently the hope is to change the manager's personality, to make him show more "consideration," to induce him to be less autocratic.

What is wrong with this approach? At least three things, in our opinion:

1. True, some problems are created and others are magnified by poor communications. But many problems cannot be solved by better understanding alone. They can be solved only by carefully wrought changes in technology, work procedure, organizational structure, or personnel policies.

2. True, counseling and training may improve communications and may even help people develop skills—and that is all to the good. But changing personality is an expensive, arduous job, with a poor prognosis.

3. Human relations is not an end in itself. The purpose of business is not to make people happy (though some have argued otherwise) but to achieve its over-all goals of productivity and profitability. And the purpose of *human relations* is to help management elicit the cooperation of people in working toward those goals.

Although we decry the uncritical acceptance of human relations as a magic cure, we feel that it is a mistake to go to the opposite extreme. The manager cannot be concerned about getting work done without also being concerned about people. Even in the fully automated factory or office, important jobs must still be done by human beings. Their willingness to coordinate their efforts with those of other people and with the system and equipment developed by engineers is an essential component of a successful organization.

In his efforts to conquer disease, man has resorted to charms, incantations, and witch doctors. But no one would suggest that just because he put his faith in gimmicks and myths in the past he would be better off today to ignore the problems of illness and concentrate on "living." [4]

The manager cannot ignore the human-relations problems of his organization and concentrate exclusively on getting the work out. Getting the work out depends on getting cooperation out of people. The future will see increasing, not decreasing, attention paid to the human-relations problems of the organization.

---

[4] Faddism, of course, has not been limited to the personnel field. A review of popular trends in medical care confirms the observation that even fields closer to the natural sciences have their transitory styles and fashions. See H. S. Weichsel, "Fashions in Medicine," *Harper's Magazine* (November 1959), pp. 69-75.

Conclusion

We hope the reader has not been discouraged by our survey of the human problems inherent in the organization. As most managers have learned, there are no perfect, final solutions to these problems. Every area we have explored is rich in challenges to the decision-making skill of the executive.

Only when we place these problems in the larger context of American life does their full significance become apparent. The individual human being, and his opportunities for development and satisfaction, have a high value in our culture. We expect our institutions to provide him with a chance to express and satisfy his needs and to fulfill his capabilities. The evolution of private organizations that are consistent with and complementary to our democratic political institutions is a high achievement in itself. Throughout the ages, man has struggled to achieve individual freedom without jeopardizing the safety and welfare of others, and to engage in productive work that will satisfy the economic and physical needs of himself and society. Not unexpectedly, severe conflicts arise between the needs of the individual and the needs of the groups and organizations that make up society. As the administrator makes choices between organizational efficiency and the satisfaction of individual needs, he is acting as a mediator in this inevitable, and, we believe, socially useful, divergence of interests.

Name Index

A

Abruzzi, Adam, 626n, 629n, 630n, 631n, 632n
Adams, Leonard, 430n
Allen, Louis, 571n
Allport, Gordon, 499n
Andrews, Kenneth R., 563n, 564n, 567n
Anshen, Melvin, 567n, 570n
Arbuckle, Douglas, 219n
Arensberg, Conrad, 44n, 570n, 706n
Argyl, Michael, 125n, 140n, 154n
Argyris, Chris, 46n, 107n, 173n, 296n, 333n, 346n, 438n, 564n
Atkinsen, 10n

B

Back, Kurt, 61n
Bakke, E. Wight, 30n, 101n
Baldamus, W., 22n
Baldwin, George B., 53n
Bales, R. F., 239, 246n, 247n, 253n, 255n, 257
Balinsky, Benjamin, 541n
Bamforth, K. W., 383n
Barbash, Jack, 101n
Barkin, Solomon, 596n, 626n
Barnes, Ralph M., 619n
Bavelas, Alex, 74n, 203, 368n, 565n

Beane, Kenneth D., 242n, 243n
Beem, H. P., 344n
Belcher, David W., 539n, 618n, 628n, 655n
Bell, Daniel, 32, 41, 430n, 628n
Bellows, Roger M., 324n
Bender, W. R. G., 547n
Bendix, Reinhard, 10n, 12n, 14n, 310n, 359n, 520n
Benge, Eugene J., 585n
Bennett, Willard E., 558n
Benney, Mark, 227n
Benoit, Emile, 702
Berger, Ruth, 541n
Berry, Paul, 170n, 254n
Bion, W. R., 245n
Bissell, Richard, 646n
Blau, Peter M., 51n, 130n, 165n, 332n
Block, Clifford H., 170n, 254n
Bloomberg, Warner, Jr., 44n
Blum, Fred H., 19n, 486n
Blum, Milton L., 685n
Bradford, Leland, 240n, 565n, 566n
Brayfield, Arthur H., 114n
Bright, James R., 54n, 594n
Brills, A. G., 43n
Brooks, Earl, 512n, 524, 546n
Brouha, Lucien A., 635n
Brown, Clarence W., 440n, 503
Bugelski, Richard, 498n
Burk, Samuel L., 585n
Burling, Temple, 17n, 27n, 57n, 65n, 133n, 137n, 182n, 356n, 500n
Burns, Robert K., 538n
Burtt, Harold E., 551n
Butler, John, 532n

Subject Index

A

Ability:
    as criterion for promotion, 463, 464
    measurement of, 463, 464
Accident-prevention (*see* Safety)
Accident-proneness, 685-688:
    physical factors in, 685
    psychological factors in, 686, 687
Accidents, causes of, 684, 685
AFL-CIO, 91
Alcoholism, 717, 718
Allowances, factor in time study, 634, 635
Amalgamated Clothing Workers Union, 265
American Federation of Labor, 82
American Management Association, 510
American Telephone and Telegraph Company, 569
Application blank, as selection technique, 440
Arbitration, 95, 299
Arbitrator, role in disciplinary grievances, 299
Attention requirements of job, as factor in job satisfaction, 40, 41
Attitude surveys, as means of upward communication, 323-325
Authority:
    delegation of, 126-131
    exercised by supervisor, 148-160
    as method of motivating people to work, 106-111

Automation:
    effect on job satisfaction, 52-54
    effect on promotion policies, 460, 461
    effect on transfer problem, 477, 478
Auto workers union, 47, 91, 601

B

Bargaining, as method for reducing resistance to change, 276, 277
Bell Telephone System, 570, 571
Benefit programs (*see* Fringe benefits)
Boredom, as psychological reaction to mass-production work, 33-35
"Brainstorming," 254
"Bumping," 480
Business, social obligations of, 730, 731
Business agent, 89
Bypassing, effect on communications, 309

C

Case method in management training, 563-564
Centralization, in organization structure, 388-390
Chairman, role in meetings, 243-257

742

N

O

P